First Edition

triumphlearning™

New York Coach

Mastering the High School Standards

Algebra I

New York Coach, Mastering the High School Standards, Algebra I, First Edition T203NY ISBN-13: 978-1-62362-255-8
Contributing Writers: Leslie Aiuvalasit and Colleen O'Donnell Oppenzato **Cover Design:** Q2A/Bill Smith **Cover Illustration:** Jim Crosley

Triumph Learning® 136 Madison Avenue, 7th Floor, New York, NY 10016

Printed in the United States of America. 10 9 8 7 6 5 4 3 2 1

Contents

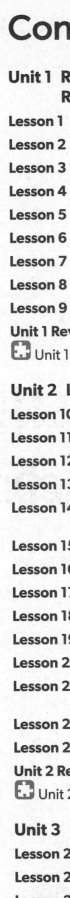

New York State Common Core Learning Standards for Mathematics

		Page	Standards
Unit 1	**Relationships between Quantities and Reasoning with Equations**	4	
Lesson 1	Units and Dimensional Analysis	6	N.Q.1, N.Q.2
Lesson 2	Accuracy	12	N.Q.3
Lesson 3	Interpreting Expressions	18	A.SSE.1a, A.SSE.1b
Lesson 4	Working with Properties	24	A.REI.1
Lesson 5	Writing Equations in One Variable	30	A.CED.1, A.CED.3, A.REI.1, A.REI.3
Lesson 6	Writing Inequalities in One Variable	38	A.CED.1, A.CED.3, A.REI.1, A.REI.3
Lesson 7	Writing Equivalent Equations (Problem Solving)	44	A.CED.4, A.REI.1, A.REI.3
Lesson 8	Writing Linear Equations in Two Variables	50	A.CED.2, A.CED.3
Lesson 9	Writing Exponential Equations in Two Variables	56	A.CED.2
Unit 1 Review		62	
	Unit 1 Performance Task	66	
Unit 2	**Linear and Exponential Relationships**	68	
Lesson 10	Rational Exponents	70	N.RN.1, N.RN.2
Lesson 11	Functions	76	F.IF.1, F.IF.2
Lesson 12	Key Features of Functions	82	F.IF.4, F.IF.5, F.IF.9
Lesson 13	Average Rate of Change	92	F.IF.6, F.IF.9, F.LE.1a, F.LE.1b, F.LE.1c
Lesson 14	Graphing Functions	100	A.REI.10, F.IF.5, F.IF.7a, F.IF.7e, F.IF.9, F.LE.3
Lesson 15	Solving Systems of Linear Equations (Problem Solving)	108	A.REI.5, A. REI.6
Lesson 16	Using Functions to Solve Equations (Problem Solving)	116	A.REI.11
Lesson 17	Graphing Inequalities (Problem Solving)	124	A.REI.12
Lesson 18	Translating Functions	134	F.BF.3, F.LE.2
Lesson 19	Reflecting Functions	144	F.BF.3, F.LE.2
Lesson 20	Stretching and Shrinking Functions	150	F.BF.3, F.LE.2
Lesson 21	Functions in Context (Problem Solving)	160	F.BF.1a, F.BF.1b, F.LE.1b, F.LE.1c, F.LE.2, F.LE.5
Lesson 22	Arithmetic Sequences (Problem Solving)	166	F.IF.3, F.BF.1a, F.BF.2, F.LE.1b, F.LE.2
Lesson 23	Geometric Sequences (Problem Solving)	172	F.IF.3, F.BF.1a, F.BF.2, F.LE.1c, F.LE.2
Unit 2 Review		178	
	Unit 2 Performance Task	182	
Unit 3	**Descriptive Statistics**	184	
Lesson 24	Displaying and Analyzing Data	186	S.ID.1, S.ID.3
Lesson 25	Investigating Measures of Center	194	S.ID.2, S.ID.3
Lesson 26	Investigating Spread	202	S.ID.2, S.ID.3

New York State Common Core Learning Standards for Mathematics

		Page	Standards
Lesson 27	Constructing and Analyzing Box Plots	208	S.ID.1, S.ID.2, S.ID.3
Lesson 28	Constructing and Analyzing Two-Way Frequency Tables	216	S.ID.5
Lesson 29	Constructing and Analyzing Scatter Plots	224	S.ID.6a, S.ID.6b, S.ID.6c, S.ID.7
Lesson 30	Best Fit and Correlation	230	S.ID.6a, S.ID.6c, S.ID.8, S.ID.9
Unit 3 Review		238	
	Unit 3 Performance Task	242	
Unit 4 Expressions and Equations		244	
Lesson 31	Polynomials	246	A.APR.1
Lesson 32	Interpreting Complex Expressions	252	A.SSE.1a, A.SSE.1b
Lesson 33	Writing Equivalent Polynomial and Exponential Equations	258	A.SSE.2, A.SSE.3a, A.SSE.3b, A.SSE.3c, A.CED.4
Lesson 34	Writing and Graphing Quadratic Equations and Inequalities	268	A.CED.1, A.CED.2
Lesson 35	Solving Quadratic Equations	278	A.CED.1, A.REI.4a, A.REI.4b
Lesson 36	Solving Linear-Quadratic Systems	286	A.REI.7
Unit 4 Review		292	
	Unit 4 Performance Task	296	
Unit 5 Quadratic Functions and Modeling		298	
Lesson 37	Rational and Irrational Numbers	300	N.RN.3
Lesson 38	Key Features of Quadratic Functions	306	F.IF.4, F.IF.5, F.IF.7a, F.IF.8a
Lesson 39	Transforming Quadratic Functions	316	F.BF.3
Lesson 40	Absolute Value, Step, and Piecewise Functions	326	F.IF.7b
Lesson 41	Inverse Functions	332	F.IF.7b, F.BF.4a
Lesson 42	Comparing Functions	338	F.IF.6, F.IF.8b, F.IF.9, F.LE.3
Lesson 43	Modeling with Functions	346	F.BF.1a, F.BF.1b
Unit 5 Review		352	
	Unit 5 Performance Task	356	
Glossary		358	
Formula Sheet		365	
Math Tools		367	

Grade 8

Algebra I

Geometry & Algebra II

The Number System

Know that there are numbers that are not rational, and approximate them by rational numbers.

Expressions & Equations

Understand connections between proportional relationships, lines, and linear equations.

Analyze and solve linear equations and pairs of simultaneous linear equations.

Functions

Define, evaluate, and compare functions.

Use functions to model relationships between quantities.

Number and Quantity

Quantities

Reason quantitatively and use units to solve problems.

Algebra

Seeing Structure in Expressions

Interpret the structure of expressions.

Creating Equations

Create equations that describe numbers or relationships.

Reasoning with Equations and Inequalities

Understand solving equations as a process of reasoning and explain the reasoning.

Solve equations and inequalities in one variable.

Geometry

Geometric Measurement and Dimension

Explain volume formulas and use them to solve problems.

Number and Quantity

The Complex Number System

Use complex numbers in polynomial identities and equations.

Algebra

Seeing Structure in Expressions

Interpret the structure of expressions.

Arithmetic with Polynomials and Rational Expressions

Understand the relationship between zeros and factors of polynomials.

Creating Equations

Create equations that describe numbers or relationships.

Reasoning with Equations and Inequalities

Understand solving equations as a process of reasoning and explain the reasoning.

Functions

Interpreting Functions

Analyze functions using different representations.

Unit 1

Relationships between Quantities and Reasoning with Equations

Lesson 1 Units and Dimensional Analysis 6

Lesson 2 Accuracy 12

Lesson 3 Interpreting Expressions 18

Lesson 4 Working with Properties 24

Lesson 5 Writing Equations in One Variable 30

Lesson 6 Writing Inequalities in One Variable 38

Lesson 7 Writing Equivalent Equations 44

Lesson 8 Writing Linear Equations in Two Variables 50

Lesson 9 Writing Exponential Equations in Two Variables 56

Unit 1 Review 62

Unit 1 Performance Task 66

Units and Dimensional Analysis

UNDERSTAND When solving a problem, it is important to correctly identify the units being considered or measured. This may require converting a quantity given in one unit to a different unit. To do so, use **conversion factors**, such as 12 inches per foot or 0.001 meter per millimeter, to write a multiplication expression. Be sure to set up the conversion factors correctly so the result is stated in the appropriate units.

Paying attention to the units can help ensure that you perform the conversion correctly. Remember that 1,000 meters = 1 kilometer. Convert 8 meters to kilometers.

Try $\frac{1{,}000 \text{ m}}{1 \text{ km}}$: $\quad \frac{8 \text{ m}}{1} \times \frac{1{,}000 \text{ m}}{1 \text{ km}} = 8{,}000 \frac{\text{m}^2}{\text{km}}$

The units in the result, $\frac{\text{m}^2}{\text{km}}$, are not the appropriate units.

Try $\frac{1 \text{ km}}{1{,}000 \text{ m}}$: $\quad \frac{8 \cancel{\text{m}}}{1} \times \frac{1 \text{ km}}{1{,}000 \cancel{\text{m}}} = 0.008 \text{ km}$

The meter units cancel. The result is in kilometers, the correct unit.

You can convert units within a system of measurement or between different systems of measurement. Though it may require several steps, any unit of measure can be converted to another unit that measures the same property (length, volume, speed, and so on).

UNDERSTAND Examining the units as you perform calculations is a form of **dimensional analysis**. Dimensional analysis can aid in writing equations by determining how certain quantities can be combined. For example, to add or subtract two quantities, they must be expressed in the same units.

$7 \text{ cm} + 1 \text{ in.} \neq 8 \text{ cm or } 8 \text{ in.} \qquad 7 \text{ cm} + 2.54 \text{ cm} = 9.54 \text{ cm}$

When multiplying or dividing quantities, units can combine or cancel out. Using dimensional analysis will ensure that you combine quantities by using operations that result in an answer that makes sense. This is especially helpful with rates of change.

Suppose you eat 3 apples per week. How long will it take you to eat a bag of 12 apples? The answer will be in some unit of time. Can you solve by multiplying the quantities?

$$\frac{3 \text{ apples}}{1 \text{ week}} \times 12 \text{ apples} = \frac{36 \text{ apples}^2}{\text{week}}$$

This answer above is not given in a unit of time, so try dividing the quantities.

$$\frac{3 \text{ apples}}{1 \text{ week}} \div 12 \text{ apples} = \frac{3 \cancel{\text{apples}}}{1 \text{ week}} \times \frac{1}{12 \cancel{\text{apples}}} = \frac{0.25}{\text{week}}$$

This is not a unit of time either. Try swapping the terms.

$$12 \text{ apples} \div \frac{3 \text{ apples}}{1 \text{ week}} = 12 \cancel{\text{apples}} \times \frac{1 \text{ week}}{3 \cancel{\text{apples}}} = 4 \text{ weeks}$$

A week is a unit of time, so this calculation makes sense.

Connect

A police officer saw a car travel 1,800 feet in 30 seconds. The speed limit on that road is 55 miles per hour (mph). Was the car speeding?

1 Determine the units given and the units desired.

The car traveled 1,800 feet in 30 seconds, so the speed can be found in feet per second. To compare this rate to the speed limit, we need to convert it to miles per hour.

2 Find the necessary conversion factors.

The distance conversion is from feet to miles. There are 5,280 feet in a mile.

The time conversion is from seconds to hours. There are 60 seconds in a minute and 60 minutes in an hour.

3 Write a dimensional analysis expression.

Remember that the result should be in miles per hour. It may help you to first set up an expression using only the units, so you can see how the units will cancel.

$$\frac{\cancel{\text{ft}}}{\cancel{\text{s}}} \times \frac{\cancel{\text{s}}}{\cancel{\text{min}}} \times \frac{\cancel{\text{min}}}{\text{h}} \times \frac{\text{mi}}{\cancel{\text{ft}}} = \frac{\text{mi}}{\text{h}}$$

Now write the expression with numbers.

$$\frac{1{,}800\text{ ft}}{30\text{ s}} \times \frac{60\text{ s}}{1\text{ min}} \times \frac{60\text{ min}}{1\text{ h}} \times \frac{1\text{ mi}}{5{,}280\text{ ft}}$$

4 Evaluate the expression. Determine whether the car was driving faster than the speed limit.

$$\frac{1{,}800\,\cancel{\text{ft}}}{30\,\cancel{\text{s}}} \times \frac{60\,\cancel{\text{s}}}{1\,\cancel{\text{min}}} \times \frac{60\,\cancel{\text{min}}}{1\text{ h}} \times \frac{1\text{ mi}}{5{,}280\,\cancel{\text{ft}}} \approx 41\frac{\text{mi}}{\text{h}}$$

▶ The car was traveling at about 41 mph, which is slower than the speed limit of 55 mph. No, it was not speeding.

TRY

A car burns 0.85 gallon of gas per hour when idling. Express this rate in quarts per minute. Round your answer to three decimal places.

EXAMPLE A Dina took part in a diving competition. She dove 5 times, and her scores were 8.8 points, 9.0 points, 8.6 points, 9.5 points, and 9.2 points. If she calculates her score on an average dive, in what units should the answer be given?

1 Plan the calculation.

To find the average score, add up the individual scores. Then divide by the total number of dives.

2 Analyze the units.

All five scores have the same units: points. Adding them together produces a sum with the same units: points. Dividing that quantity by 5 dives will produce a quantity in points per dive.

▶ The average score should be given in points per dive.

EXAMPLE B A hospital's records indicate that, on average, 23% of babies born there are delivered by cesarean section. A total of 217 babies were born at the hospital last year, and a total of 220 were born this year.

What should be the expected number of babies born by cesarean section over both years?

1 Identify the quantities in the problem.

The numbers 217 and 220 stand for the numbers of babies born in the given years, so they can be written as 217 babies and 220 babies.

The number 23% expresses the number of babies born by cesarean section out of all of the babies born. Remember that % stands for $\frac{1}{100}$. This quantity can be written as $\frac{\text{23 cesarean births}}{\text{100 babies}}$.

The question asks for a number of cesarean births.

2 Write expressions that give the answer in the desired units.

The quantities 217 babies and 220 babies have the same units, so they can be added together to find the number of babies born over both years.

$$217 \text{ babies} + 220 \text{ babies} = 437 \text{ babies}$$

Now set up a multiplication expression to find the number of cesarean births.

$$437 \text{ babies} \times \frac{\text{23 cesarean births}}{\text{100 babies}} \approx$$
101 cesarean births

▶ About 101 babies were expected to be born by cesarean section over that time.

Can you think of a situation in which a quantity could be given in pounds of vegetables per day?

Choosing the correct units is important for displaying data in charts and graphs.

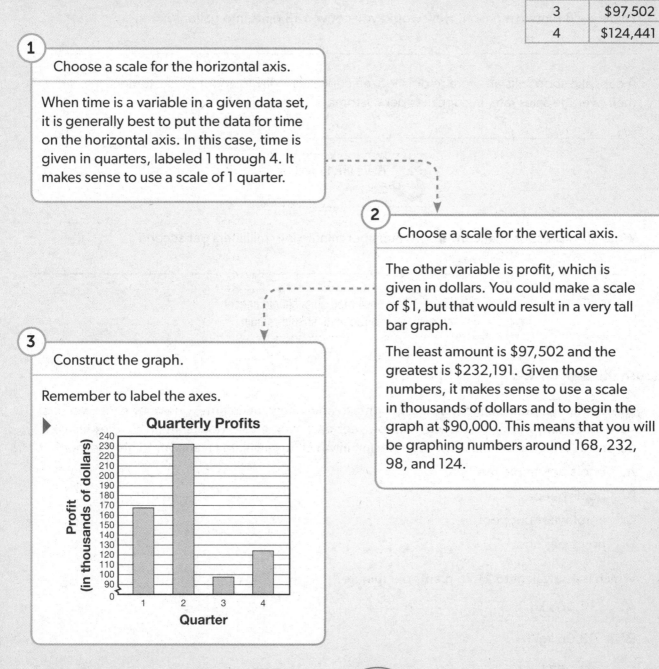

EXAMPLE C The table on the right shows the quarterly profits for a company over a 1-year period.

Quarter	Profit
1	$167,581
2	$232,191
3	$97,502
4	$124,441

Make a bar graph to display the data in the table.

1 Choose a scale for the horizontal axis.

When time is a variable in a given data set, it is generally best to put the data for time on the horizontal axis. In this case, time is given in quarters, labeled 1 through 4. It makes sense to use a scale of 1 quarter.

2 Choose a scale for the vertical axis.

The other variable is profit, which is given in dollars. You could make a scale of $1, but that would result in a very tall bar graph.

The least amount is $97,502 and the greatest is $232,191. Given those numbers, it makes sense to use a scale in thousands of dollars and to begin the graph at $90,000. This means that you will be graphing numbers around 168, 232, 98, and 124.

3 Construct the graph.

Remember to label the axes.

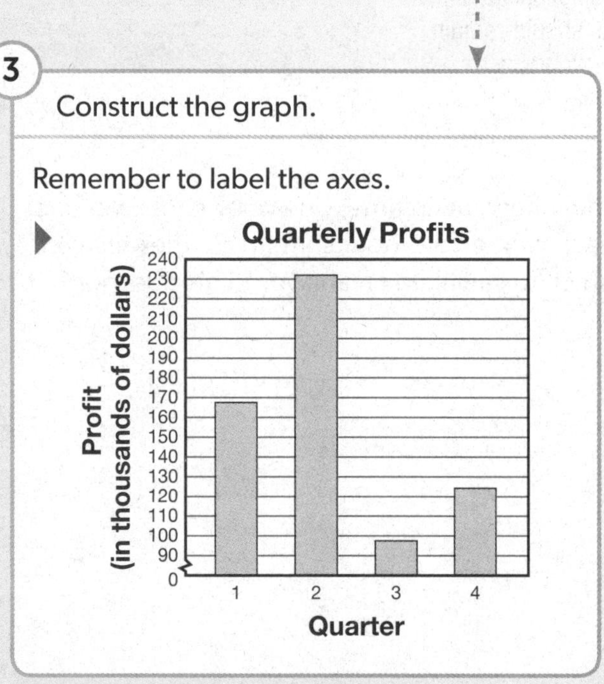

DISCUSS

Why might using a scale of hundreds of thousands of dollars make the graph misleading?

Practice

Write an expression for each conversion.

1. There are 1,000 grams in a kilogram. How would you convert 600 kilograms into grams?

____

2. There are 8 pints in a gallon. How would you convert 13 pints into gallons?

____

3. A cupcake shop sells an average of 14 dozen cupcakes a day to about 50 customers. What is their average sales rate, in cupcakes per customer?

____

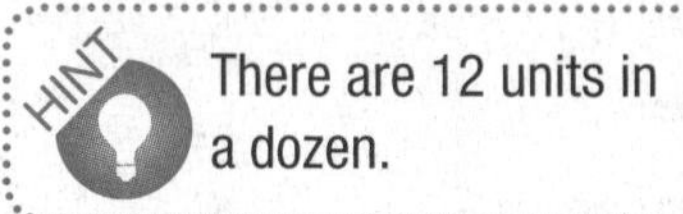
HINT
There are 12 units in a dozen.

4. Write an expression that converts 50 liters per minute into milliliters per second.

____

REMEMBER The unwanted units should cancel out and only the desired units should remain.

Choose the best answer.

5. The owner of a pool cleaning business wants to know how much time, on average, his workers spend cleaning a pool. Last week, 7 employees each worked a 6-hour shift. In all, they cleaned 42 pools. Which is the most appropriate unit in which to calculate an answer to his question?

A. pools per employee

B. pools per day

C. employees per pool

D. hours per pool

6. Which is equivalent to 21.76 grams per minute?

A. 1.306 kg/h

B. 13.06 kg/h

C. 36.267 kg/h

D. 362.67 kg/h

Solve.

7. While traveling in England, Sonia noticed that the price of gas was 1.4 pounds (£) per liter. She wondered how that compares to the price of gas in Atlanta, where she lives. On that day, the exchange rate was £1 = $1.56. Set up and evaluate a conversion expression to find the equivalent price in dollars per gallon. Use the conversion factor 1 L = 0.26 gal.

____

8. Ravi has started a business importing handwoven and embroidered linen from India. His Indian supplier charges him 460 rupees per meter for the fabric. He wants to make a profit of $4 per yard. How much must Ravi charge per yard for the imported fabric? Use the following information:
1 dollar = 57.3 rupees
1 meter = 1.09 yards

____

Use the table shown below for questions 9 and 10.

The following data show the population in a small town starting with the year 1980.

Year	1980	1985	1990	1995	2000	2005	2010
Population	2,782	3,219	3,788	4,490	5,176	6,490	6,151

9. To graph the data in a line graph, what units would you use for the horizontal axis? How would you label the axis? What scale would you use? _______________

____

10. To graph the data in a line graph, what units and scale would you use for the vertical axis?

____

11. EXPLAIN The graph on the right shows the recorded heights of a tomato plant grown in a laboratory.

How can you interpret the origin of the graph?

____

____

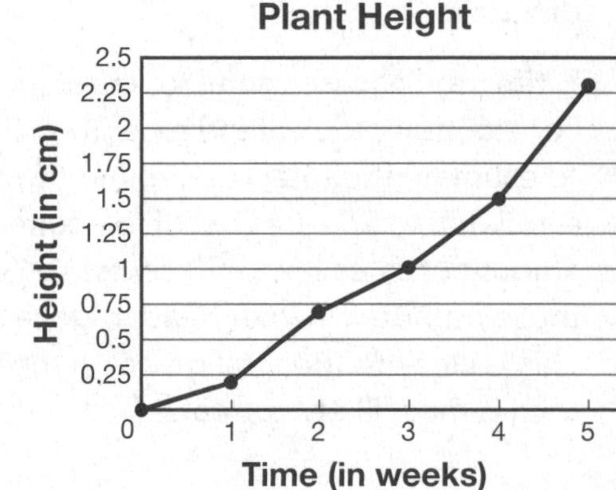

Accuracy

UNDERSTAND In arithmetic, the solution to an equation or the value of an expression is exact. The value of $1 + 1$ is exactly 2. However, in the real world, answers to problems are rarely exact. Measurements are often inexact because it is not possible to take an exact measurement. Sometimes human error causes inaccuracy. Other times, a value must be rounded.

For example, you may have used 3.14 in place of π. 3.14 is not the exact value of π, but the exact value of π cannot be written out and used to calculate because its decimal never ends.

The **accuracy** of an **approximation** or an **estimate** is how close it is to the actual value. An approximation or an estimate is always less accurate than an exact answer.

UNDERSTAND An approximation is a quantity used to represent a true measurement when the exact value cannot be determined or used.

Suppose you wanted to measure the width of your notebook. Using your ruler, you would likely find that it is about 21.5 centimeters wide. But is it exactly 21.5? Is it closer to 21.4? Might it be 21.400001 centimeters? If your ruler only has markings for millimeters, you could not use it to determine the width of your notebook to the nearest thousandth of a centimeter. So, instead, you use the approximation 21.5 centimeters to represent the true width, whatever it may be.

UNDERSTAND Estimation is different from approximation, because an estimate is made inexact on purpose in order to make calculations easier or to generalize about a population.

The population of a large city is generally given as an estimate in thousands of people, because it is a large number that changes continuously. It is impossible to know the exact population of a city at any given moment. For example, if a census shows that Atlanta's population is 419,978 people and Vidalia's is 34,837, we can choose to round these to 420,000 and 35,000. Then we can say that Atlanta has about 12 times the population of Vidalia.

Estimation can be useful for checking a result. For example, look at the receipt on the right. To estimate the total cost, round the cost of the sandwich to \$5, the cost of the coffee to \$1, and the amount of sales tax to 50 cents. You can easily add those numbers in your head to get a sum of \$6.50. This is close to the total given on the receipt, so that total is most likely correct.

Dan's Diner	
sandwich	\$4.95
coffee	\$0.88
sales tax	\$0.48
	\$6.31

Connect

For each scenario given below, determine if the answer is exact, approximated, or estimated.

A. Cheryl has confirmed 143 guests for her party. She thinks that each guest will eat about half a pound of brisket, so she decides to order $0.5 \text{ lb} \times 150 = 75 \text{ lbs}$.

B. John received 4 identical boxes of a bestselling book at his bookstore. The first box contained 12 copies of the book, so he figured that the shipment included a total of 48 books.

C. Imani made a flag in the shape of an isosceles right triangle. She wants to put trim along the edges of the flag, so she measures each side with a ruler. She finds that each leg measures 10 inches and the hypotenuse measures 14.1 inches.

1 Examine scenario A.

In order to decide how much brisket to order, Cheryl has rounded the number of guests up to 150 to make it a more round number. Also, her determination that each guest will eat 0.5 pound of brisket is an estimate, since different people will eat different amounts. This is an example of estimation.

2 Examine scenario B.

The number of books in the box, 12, is an exact number. John will not find a fraction of a book in one of the boxes. The number of identical boxes, 4, is also exact. Therefore, their product is an exact answer.

3 Examine scenario C.

Even if the legs were exactly 10 inches in length, by using the Pythagorean theorem, you can see that the hypotenuse would be $\sqrt{200}$, or $10\sqrt{2}$ inches. Because 2 is not a perfect square, the number $10\sqrt{2}$ is irrational. Imani's ruler cannot possibly measure this exact value. Therefore, 14.1 inches is an approximation.

DISCUSS

In what other situations would the answer be in the form of an estimate? an approximation? an exact answer?

EXAMPLE A The diagram shows a cell phone with rulers set along its base and height.

Determine the area of the phone's screen. Discuss the accuracy of your answer.

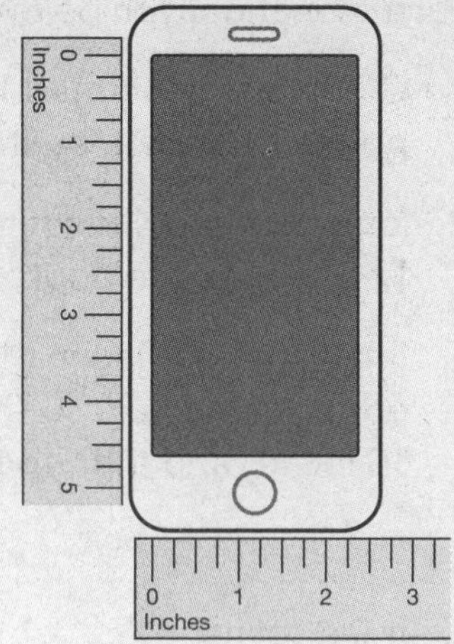

1 Determine the length and width of the screen.

The length of the screen falls between the $4\frac{1}{2}$-inch mark and the $4\frac{3}{4}$-inch mark on the ruler. Use $4\frac{3}{4}$ inches for the length.

The width of the screen falls between the $2\frac{1}{4}$-inch mark and the $2\frac{1}{2}$-inch mark on the ruler. Use $2\frac{1}{2}$ inches for the length.

2 Find the area.

To find the area, multiply the length and width.

$$4\frac{3}{4}\text{ in.} \cdot 2\frac{1}{2}\text{ in.} = 11\frac{7}{8}\text{ in.}^2$$

▶ The area of the screen is about $11\frac{7}{8}$ square inches.

3 Discuss the accuracy of your answer.

Both of the measurements taken with the ruler are approximations, because it was not possible to take exact measurements. Each measurement is approximated to the nearest quarter inch. The area that was calculated cannot be exact, because the measurements were not exact. Thus, the area calculated is also an approximation.

TRY

In the example above, both the length and width were rounded up to the nearest quarter inch. Try rounding each measurement down to the nearest quarter inch, and then calculate the area using those numbers. What is the difference between the calculated areas?

EXAMPLE B The table below gives the population from the latest census for three nearby counties.

County	Population
Jackson	324,109
Juniper	129,297
Pinewood	502,864

Find both an exact answer and an estimate for the total population of the region that consists of all three counties, and compare the results.

1 Find an exact answer.

Add the exact numbers to find an exact answer.

$$\begin{array}{r} 324{,}109 \\ 129{,}297 \\ +\ 502{,}864 \\ \hline 956{,}270 \end{array}$$

2 Estimate the answer.

Round each number to the nearest thousand, and then add the rounded numbers to find an estimate.

$$\begin{array}{rcr} 324{,}109 & \rightarrow & 324{,}000 \\ 129{,}297 & \rightarrow & 129{,}000 \\ +\ 502{,}864 & \rightarrow & +\ 503{,}000 \\ \hline & & 956{,}000 \end{array}$$

3 Compare the results.

The difference between the exact answer and the estimate is 270. Since the original numbers are in hundreds of thousands, a difference of several hundred is relatively small. In fact, if the exact answer were rounded to the nearest thousand, the result would be the same as the estimated answer.

DISCUSS

Suppose that you were in charge of collecting emergency supplies for Juniper County. When estimating the county population, would you round up or down?

Practice

For each situation, determine whether the situation involves an *exact answer*, an *approximation*, or an *estimate*.

1. A wedding planner needs to determine how many appetizers to order for between 200 and 220 guests.

   ____

2. A recipe that calls for 2 eggs is being doubled.

   ____

3. A square with a side 12 feet long has a diagonal of 16.97 feet.

   ____

4. An elevator has a capacity of 1,500 pounds. When 7 adults stepped onto the elevator, one of the passengers figured that the average weight of each adult is 150 pounds, for a total of 1,050 pounds.

   ____

5. Alicia looked at the thermometer and determined that the temperature is 14°C.

   ____

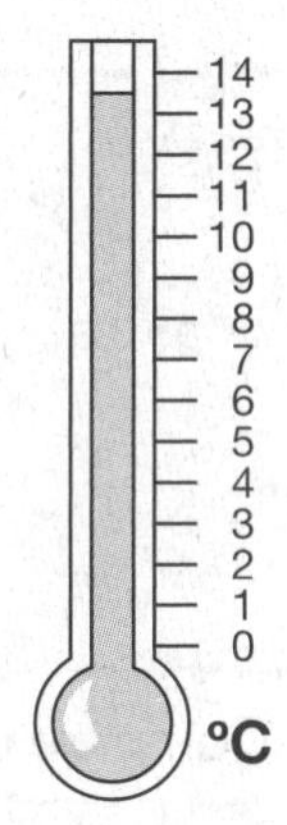

Choose the best answer.

6. Which of the following represents an exact quantity?
   A. The weather forecast for today calls for a high temperature of 81°.
   B. The rise of a hill is about 15°.
   C. A cat had a litter of 6 kittens.
   D. The maximum capacity of a bridge is 20,000 pounds.

7. For which of the following situations is an exact answer most needed?
   A. the maximum number of passengers on an airplane
   B. the number of spectators at a baseball game
   C. the number of blueberries in a batch of blueberry pancakes
   D. the number of people in a town

Solve each problem.

8. The picture on the right shows a bag of apples on a scale.

If the apples cost $1.79 per pound, what will the cost be for the full bag? Discuss the accuracy of your answer.

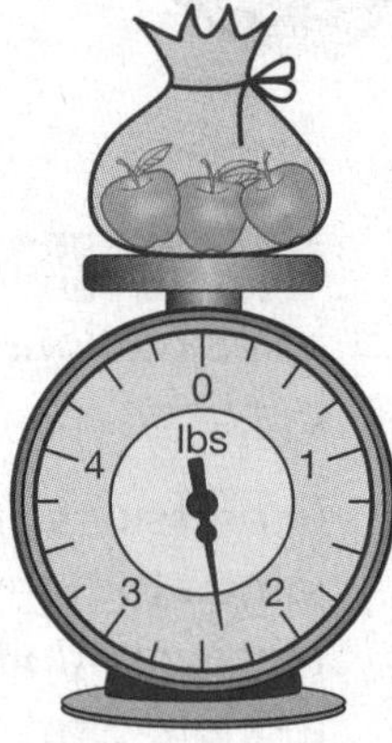

9. A doctor has prescribed a medicine to be given in a dosage of 0.01 mL per pound of weight of the patient. What is the dosage for a 124-pound patient? Discuss the accuracy of your answer.

10. Estimate a 15% tip on a dinner bill of $39.51.

11. COMPARE The table below shows the monthly rainfall, in inches, in Macon over a period of 6 months.

Jan.	Feb.	March	Apr.	May	June
3.20	2.52	1.84	1.03	2.11	3.04

Find the average monthly rainfall. ____________

Round each number to the nearest tenth of an inch and find the average. ____________

Round each number to the nearest inch and find the average. ____________

How do the three different averages compare? What can you conclude about rounding, place value, and accuracy?

12. CREATE Think of a situation in which an estimate is more useful than an exact answer.

LESSON 3

Interpreting Expressions

UNDERSTAND Mathematical expressions and equations can be used to model relationships and situations in the real world. Those models can be used to understand relationships between quantities and even to make predictions about them.

Expressions are made up of **terms**, which are composed of **constants** and/or **variables** joined together by mathematical operations such as multiplication and division. A constant that is multiplied by a variable is the **coefficient** of that variable. An expression may contain a single term or may be a string of terms joined together by operations such as addition and subtraction. When a mathematical expression represents a real-world situation, each part represents a different quantity or aspect of the situation.

Constants are numbers that do not change. For example, in the expression $x - 1998$, the constant 1998 is always subtracted from the variable, x. If Ian was born on January 1, 1998, his age can be given by the expression $x - 1998$, where x is the current year. The year in which Ian was born, 1998, never changes; it is a constant.

A variable is a letter or symbol that stands for a number and can take on different values. In an equation with two variables, there is often a **dependent variable** (or output value) and an **independent variable** (or input value). Ian's age, y, can be found by using the equation $y = x - 1998$. Ian's age and the current year change periodically, so they are represented by variables. Ian's age, y, depends on the current year, x, so y is the dependent variable and x is the independent variable.

UNDERSTAND The coefficient of a variable often represents a rate. A rate tells how one quantity changes in relation to another quantity.

Suppose that a babysitter charges a $10 fee for each job plus $8.50 per hour of babysitting. The expression $8.50h + 10$ gives the total charge for a job that lasts h hours. The variable, h hours, can take on different values according to how many hours the job lasts. The coefficient, 8.50 dollars/hour, represents the rate, or the amount billed for each hour. The constant, 10 dollars, is the flat fee that is charged for every job, regardless of how many hours it lasts.

The rate 8.50 dollars/hour relates how the charge in dollars changes as the number of hours increases. Notice that when the rate is multiplied by the variable, the units *hour* and *hours* cancel, giving a quantity in dollars.

$$\frac{8.50 \text{ dollars}}{\cancel{\text{hour}}} \times h\,\cancel{\text{hours}} = 8.50h \text{ dollars}$$

The constant 8.50 is the babysitter's rate, the variable h is the number of hours, and the term $8.50h$ is the cost, in dollars, for a given length of babysitting time.

Connect

Jorge has five male turtles and two breeding pairs of rabbits. The total number of animals that Jorge has m months after purchasing the rabbits can be approximated by using the expression $4 \cdot 2^m + 5$. What does each part of the expression mean in the situation?

1 Identify and examine the variable.

The variable in the expression is m, which represents the time, in months, since Jorge bought his rabbits. In this expression, the variable is an exponent. It means that for every month that passes, the term 2^m has another factor of 2; in other words, it doubles.

2 Examine the constant 2.

In the expression 2^m, the number 2 represents the repeated factor in the related multiplication (the number that is multiplied by itself m times). For every increase in m, the term is multiplied by 2. You can think of 2 as the rate of change in this situation.

3 Examine the constant 4.

A constant multiplied by an exponential expression represents an initial population. In this situation, 4 represents the number of rabbits Jorge started with.

4 Interpret the expression $4 \cdot 2^m$ in real terms.

We have found that, for every increase of 1 in the variable m, the term $4 \cdot 2^m$ is doubled. In the given situation, this means that the number of rabbits doubles each month.

5 Identify and examine the constant term.

The constant term in the expression is 5. It is added to the exponential term, and it is not affected by the value of the variable m. In the given situation, it represents Jorge's 5 turtles. Because all of the turtles are male, they will not reproduce, so their number will not increase from month to month.

TRY

A botanist places a single plant cell into a petri dish. The number of cells in the petri dish after h hours can be modeled by the expression 5^h. What does the number 5 in the expression mean in this situation?

EXAMPLE A Takashi is driving to his grandmother's house. He is driving at a constant speed and will not make any stops along the way. Takashi's distance in miles from his grandmother's house h hours after leaving can be described by the equation $d = 125 - 55h$. What does each part of the equation mean in the situation?

1 Identify and interpret the variables.

This equation contains two variables, d and h. The independent variable is h, and the dependent variable is d.

The problem statement identifies h as the number of hours Takashi has been driving.

The overall equation describes his distance, in miles, from his grandmother's house, so both sides of the equation must represent this quantity. So, both the variable d and the expression $125 - 55h$ must represent Takashi's distance from his grandmother's house.

2 Identify and interpret the coefficient.

The coefficient of h is 55. In a linear equation, a coefficient often represents a rate of change. In this case, 55 represents Takashi's constant speed. Since the distance d is given in miles and the time h is given in hours, the unit for the speed will be in miles per hour. The coefficient indicates that Takashi is driving 55 miles per hour.

3 Identify and interpret the constant term.

The constant term in the equation is 125. When Takashi begins driving, $h = 0$. When $h = 0$, $d = 125$, so 125 must be Takashi's initial distance, in miles, from his grandmother's house when he begins driving.

TRY

Emmett and his friends played a game that they invented. In the game, a team is awarded a certain number of points for each goal scored. A team loses points any time a team member commits a foul. The equation $p = 3g - 5f$ describes a team's score. What does each part of the equation represent?

EXAMPLE B Jenny pulled the stopper out of a full sink. The amount of water, in gallons, remaining in the sink for each minute that followed can be modeled by the expression $17 - 5m$. Interpret the parts of this expression.

1

Interpret the parts of the second term in the expression.

The second term consists of a variable, m, and a coefficient, -5. The variable m represents the number of minutes since the stopper was pulled.

The amount of water in the sink is changing. The variable m represents the amount of time passed, so the coefficient of m is the rate at which the water is changing. The coefficient -5 tells you that the amount of water is decreasing (because the rate is negative) at a rate of 5 gallons per minute.

2

Examine the effect of combining the two parts of the second term.

The term $-5m$ consists of a rate, $-5\frac{\text{gal}}{\text{min}}$, and an unknown amount of time, m minutes. Dimensional analysis helps you see how multiplying the coefficient and variable creates a value with different units.

$$\frac{\text{gal}}{\cancel{\text{min}}} \cdot \cancel{\text{min}} = \text{gal}$$

So, the product of a rate, $-5\frac{\text{gal}}{\text{min}}$, and a number of minutes, m, yields a new quantity, an amount of water in gallons. This is the amount of water that has drained from the sink.

3

Interpret the first term in the expression.

Before the stopper is pulled, $m = 0$ and the value of the expression is 17.

$$17 - 5(0) = 17 - 0 = 17$$

So, the constant 17 represents how much water was in the sink before the stopper was pulled.

How much water will be in the sink after 4 minutes? Does this expression apply to that time?

Practice

Complete each sentence.

1. In the expression $7x - 9$, the variable is ________.

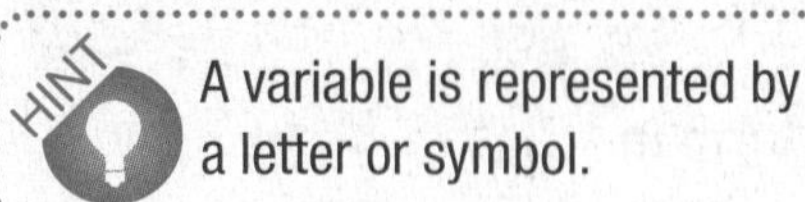

HINT
A variable is represented by a letter or symbol.

2. In the expression $3^y + 12$, the constant term is ________.

3. In the expression $90 + 5z$, the coefficient is ________.

4. In the equation $t = 0.7n - 1.3$, the dependent variable is ________.

Use the information below for questions 5–8. Choose the best answer.

A plumber charges a flat fee for each job, plus an hourly rate for the number of hours the job takes to complete. The total cost of the job, in dollars, can be modeled by the equation $y = 50 + 65x$.

5. What does the independent variable in the expression represent in this situation?

A. the number of jobs, y

B. the number of hours to complete the job, x

C. the cost per hour, \$65

D. the total cost for the job, y

6. What does the coefficient in the expression represent in this situation?

A. the number of hours to complete the job, x

B. the cost per hour, \$65

C. the flat fee, \$65

D. the flat fee, \$50

7. What does the constant term in the expression represent in this situation?

A. the number of jobs, x

B. the cost per hour, \$65

C. the cost per hour, \$50

D. the flat fee, \$50

8. What does the dependent variable in the expression represent in this situation?

A. the number of jobs, y

B. the number of hours to complete the job, x

C. the total cost for the job, y

D. the flat fee, \$65

Interpret the numbers and variables in the following questions.

9. A colony of bacteria doubles in number every hour. The expression $250 \cdot 2^h$ gives the number of bacteria after h hours. What does the constant 250 in the expression represent?

____

10. Bryn is riding his bicycle at a constant speed from school to the library. His distance from the library in kilometers x hours after leaving school can be modeled by the equation $y = 20 - 12x$. What do x, y, 20, and 12 each represent in the equation? Be sure to specify units.

____

____

____

11. INTERPRET The formula for the volume of a rectangular prism is $V = lwh$, where l is the length, w is the width, and h is the height of the prism.

If you write the formula as $V = (lw)h$, what new entity does the product lw represent?

____

In $V = (lw)h$, are the first term, lw, and the second term, h, dependent on each other? (Hint: Would changing the height of a prism change either its width or its length?)

____

12. EXPLAIN Ginny has 2 quarters. For every week that Ginny does all of her chores, her mother will increase the amount of money Ginny has exponentially. The equation $y = 0.5 \cdot 3^w$ describes the amount of money that Ginny has after w weeks of doing all of her chores. What does the term 3^w tell you about the situation?

____

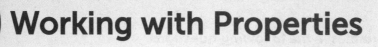

Working with Properties

UNDERSTAND Whenever you simplify or evaluate an expression, you use properties of real numbers. You probably use these properties without even realizing it. They are what justify many of the steps you take when working with expressions and equations.

Some important properties of real numbers are listed in the table below.

Associative property of addition	$(a + b) + c = a + (b + c)$
Commutative property of addition	$a + b = b + a$
Additive identity property	The number 0 is the **additive identity** for the set of real numbers. $a + 0 = 0 + a = a$
Additive inverse property	For every a, there exists an **additive inverse**, $-a$, so that $a + (-a) = (-a) + a = 0$.
Associative property of multiplication	$(a \times b) \times c = a \times (b \times c)$
Commutative property of multiplication	$a \times b = b \times a$
Multiplicative identity property	The number 1 is the **multiplicative identity** for the set of real numbers. $a \times 1 = 1 \times a = a$
Multiplicative inverse property	For every $a \neq 0$, there exists a **multiplicative inverse**, $\frac{1}{a}$, so that $a \times \frac{1}{a} = \frac{1}{a} \times a = 1$.
Distributive property of multiplication over addition and subtraction	$a \times (b + c) = a \times b + a \times c$ $a \times (b - c) = a \times b - a \times c$

Note that the multiplicative inverse of a number is also called its **reciprocal**.

UNDERSTAND Properties are also useful for manipulating equations in order to find solutions.

The properties of equality listed below can be used to isolate variables and find their values.

Reflexive property of equality	$a = a$
Symmetric property of equality	If $a = b$, then $b = a$.
Transitive property of equality	If $a = b$ and $b = c$, then $a = c$.
Addition property of equality	If $a = b$, then $a + c = b + c$.
Subtraction property of equality	If $a = b$, then $a - c = b - c$.
Multiplication property of equality	If $a = b$, then $a \times c = b \times c$.
Division property of equality	If $a = b$ and $c \neq 0$, then $a \div c = b \div c$.
Substitution property of equality	If $a = b$, then b may be substituted for a in any expression containing a.

Connect

Felix wrote the steps shown below while solving the equation $\frac{1}{2}(4 + x) = -3$.

$$\frac{1}{2}(4 + x) = -3$$

Step 1: $2 + \frac{1}{2}x = -3$

Step 2: $\frac{1}{2}x + 2 = -3$

Step 3: $\frac{1}{2}x = -5$

Step 4: $x = -10$

Use properties of real numbers and properties of equality to justify each step in Felix's solution.

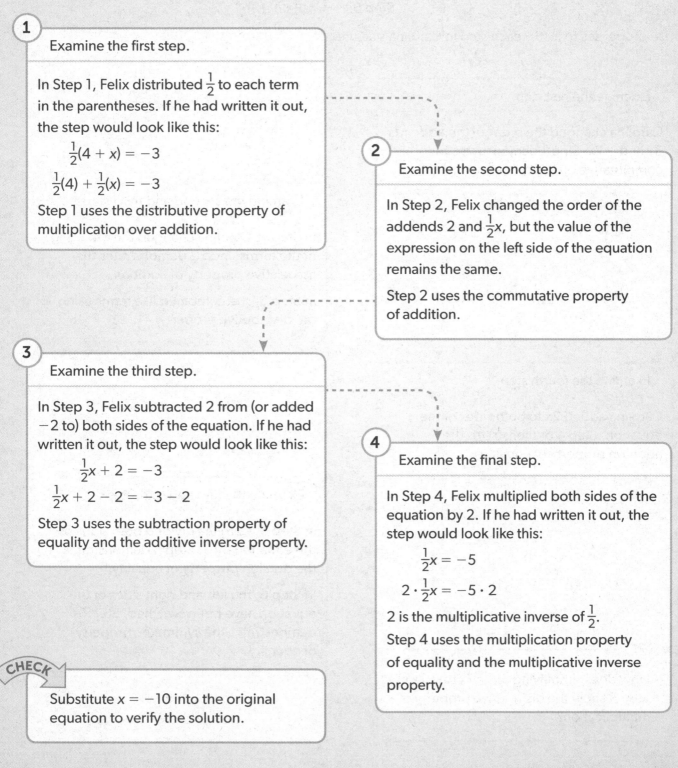

1 Examine the first step.

In Step 1, Felix distributed $\frac{1}{2}$ to each term in the parentheses. If he had written it out, the step would look like this:

$$\frac{1}{2}(4 + x) = -3$$
$$\frac{1}{2}(4) + \frac{1}{2}(x) = -3$$

Step 1 uses the distributive property of multiplication over addition.

2 Examine the second step.

In Step 2, Felix changed the order of the addends 2 and $\frac{1}{2}x$, but the value of the expression on the left side of the equation remains the same.

Step 2 uses the commutative property of addition.

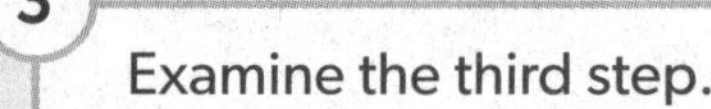

3 Examine the third step.

In Step 3, Felix subtracted 2 from (or added -2 to) both sides of the equation. If he had written it out, the step would look like this:

$$\frac{1}{2}x + 2 = -3$$
$$\frac{1}{2}x + 2 - 2 = -3 - 2$$

Step 3 uses the subtraction property of equality and the additive inverse property.

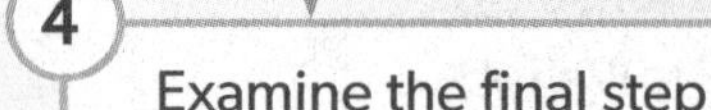

4 Examine the final step.

In Step 4, Felix multiplied both sides of the equation by 2. If he had written it out, the step would look like this:

$$\frac{1}{2}x = -5$$
$$2 \cdot \frac{1}{2}x = -5 \cdot 2$$

2 is the multiplicative inverse of $\frac{1}{2}$.

Step 4 uses the multiplication property of equality and the multiplicative inverse property.

CHECK

Substitute $x = -10$ into the original equation to verify the solution.

EXAMPLE A Carolina was given the equation $36 = 5x + (3y - 7x)$ and was asked to write it in slope-intercept form. The steps Carolina took are shown below.

$36 = 5x + (3y - 7x)$

Step 1: $36 = 5x + (-7x + 3y)$

Step 2: $36 = [5x + (-7x)] + 3y$

Step 3: $36 = -2x + 3y$

Step 4: $2x + 36 = 3y$

Step 5: $\frac{2}{3}x + 12 = y$

Step 6: $y = \frac{2}{3}x + 12$

Use properties to justify each step in Carolina's solution.

1 Examine the first step.

Carolina changed the order of the addends $3y$ and $-7x$. Step 1 demonstrates the commutative property of addition.

2 Examine the second and third steps.

In Step 2, Carolina changed the grouping of the terms. Step 2 demonstrates the associative property of addition.

In Step 3, she combined like terms using the distributive property.

3 Examine the fourth step.

Carolina added $2x$ to both sides of the equation. Step 4 demonstrates the addition property of equality.

4 Examine the fifth and sixth steps.

In Step 5, Carolina divided both sides of the equation by 3. Step 5 demonstrates the division property of equality.

In Step 6, the left and right sides of the equation have been switched. Step 6 demonstrates the symmetric property of equality.

DISCUSS

How does simplifying $5x - 7x$ to $-2x$ in Step 3 show the distributive property of multiplication?

EXAMPLE B Hakeem was given the equations $3x + 5y = 12$ and $y = 2 - x$. He used the following steps to find the x-value of the coordinate pair that satisfies both equations.

$3x + 5y = 12$

Step 1: $3x + 5(2 - x) = 12$

Step 2: $3x + 10 - 5x = 12$

Step 3: $-2x + 10 = 12$

Step 4: $-2x = 2$

Step 5: $x = -1$

Use properties to justify each step in Hakeem's solution.

1 Examine the first step.

The second equation tells us that $y = 2 - x$. In Step 1, Hakeem substituted the expression $2 - x$ for y in the first equation. This results in an equivalent equation. Step 1 shows the substitution property of equality.

2 Examine the second and third steps.

In Step 2, Hakeem distributed 5 over each term within the parentheses. In Step 3, he combined like terms. Both steps required the distributive property.

3 Examine the fourth step.

In Step 4, Hakeem subtracted 10 from (or added -10 to) both sides of the equation. Step 4 shows the subtraction property of equality and the additive inverse property.

4 Examine the fifth step.

Hakeem divided both sides of the equation by -2. Step 5 shows the division property of equality.

TRY

To find the y-value, Hakeem took the following steps.

$y = 2 - x$

Step 1: $y = 2 - (-1)$

Step 2: $y = 3$

Which property justifies Step 1?

Practice

Identify the property of real numbers that is demonstrated by the equation.

1. $12 + 0 = 12$ ______

2. $9 + d = d + 9$ ______

3. $7(2 - p) = 14 - 7p$ ______

4. $6p = 1 \cdot 6p$ ______

Identify the property of equality that is demonstrated.

5. $13q^7 = 13q^7$ ______

6. If $z = 12$ and $12 = 3 \cdot 4$, then $z = 3 \cdot 4$. ______

7. If $12t = 5s$, then $5s = 12t$. ______

8. If $n = 0.25p$ and $3p + 2n = 14$, then $3.5p = 14$. ______

Use the following information for questions 9 and 10. Choose the best answer.

Sarah used the steps shown below to solve the equation $\frac{3}{4} \cdot 7a \cdot \frac{4}{3} = 49$.

$\frac{3}{4} \cdot 7a \cdot \frac{4}{3} = 49$

Step 1: $\frac{3}{4} \cdot \frac{4}{3} \cdot 7a = 49$

Step 2: $1 \cdot 7a = 49$

Step 3: $7a = 49$

Step 4: $a = 7$

9. Which step can be justified by the commutative property of multiplication?

A. Step 1
B. Step 2
C. Step 3
D. Step 4

10. Which step can be justified by the multiplicative identity property?

A. Step 1

B. Step 2
C. Step 3
D. Step 4

Use properties to justify each step taken to solve the equations.

11. $8 + 7x - 8 = 49$

$8 - 8 + 7x = 49$ comutative

$0 + 7x = 49$ Additive inverse property.

$7x = 49$ ~~zero property~~ adative idengaty

$x = 7$ ~~distributive~~ division property

12. $\frac{1}{4}(x - 20) = -2$

$\frac{1}{4}x - 5 = -2$ destributive property

$\frac{1}{4}x = 3$ addition property of equality

$x = 12$ ~~adative inverse~~ ~~devision~~ multiplicative

Solve for *x* in questions 13 and 14. Use properties to justify the steps you use.

13. $x + 6 = 8$

−6 −6

x = 2   ~~negative~~

Property: subtraction of equality

14. $y = -5$

$x = y$

x = −5

Property: ~~equality~~ substitution

15. RESTATE The associative property of multiplication states that $(a \times b) \times c = a \times (b \times c)$. How would you express this property in words?

it regroups the numbers or letters. it doesn't change the order.

16. EXPLAIN Alexa solved the equation $5x = 4$ in the two ways shown below.

Method 1	**Method 2**
$5x = 4$	$5x = 4$
$5x \div 5 = 4 \div 5$	$\frac{1}{5} \cdot 5x = 4 \cdot \frac{1}{5}$
$x = \frac{4}{5}$	$x = \frac{4}{5}$

Use properties to justify the steps in each of Alexa's solution methods. What do Alexa's methods tell you about the relationship between the properties she used?

in method one she solves algabriacly. in method two she does the adative inverse and finds the answer. It works both ways.

Writing Equations in One Variable

Writing Linear Equations

UNDERSTAND In **linear equations**, variables are raised only to the first power.

The equation $12x - 7 = -5$ is linear because the variable, x, is raised to the first power. The equation $x^2 + 5y = 32$ is not linear because the variable, x, is raised to the second power.

The equation $y = \frac{2}{x}$ is also not linear. Remember that $\frac{2}{x}$ can be rewritten as $2(x^{-1})$. Since x is raised to a power other than 1, the equation is not linear.

UNDERSTAND The solution to a linear equation in one variable is the value that, when substituted into the equation for the variable, results in a true number statement, such as $1 = 1$. Linear equations in one variable usually have one solution, but some have no solution and others have an infinite number of solutions.

To solve a linear equation, isolate the variable. Manipulate the equation by using properties of numbers and properties of equality to get the variable by itself on one side. Some general steps for solving a linear equation in one variable are listed below.

- Add or subtract to get all variable terms on one side of the equation and all constant terms on the other side. The addition and subtraction properties of equality state that adding or subtracting the same number to both sides of an equation creates an equivalent equation.
- If possible, simplify each side by combining like terms. The distributive property justifies combining terms that have the same variables.
- Multiply or divide to remove the coefficient from the variable term. The multiplication and division properties of equality state that multiplying or dividing both sides of an equation by the same non-zero number creates an equivalent equation.

To check the solution to a linear equation, apply the substitution property of equality by substituting the solution for x in the original equation and then evaluating. If the result is a true number statement—if the numbers on both sides of the equal sign match—then your solution is correct.

UNDERSTAND Many real-world situations can be modeled by using linear equations. Linear equations can often be used to model situations that involve a constant rate. For example, a plane flying at a constant speed of 600 mph covers a distance of $600x$ miles in x hours. The time it takes to fly 2,000 miles can be found by solving the linear equation $600x = 2{,}000$.

In a real-world situation, the possible values of a variable can sometimes be limited. In some cases—such as measurements of time or length—a variable can only take on positive values. Similarly, when finding the maximum number of people that can ride an elevator, for example, the solution must be a whole number since you cannot have a fraction of a person.

Connect

The sum of two consecutive even numbers is 110. What are the two numbers?

1 Examine the information given in the problem.

There are two unknown numbers in the problem, and their sum is 110.

The two numbers are described as consecutive even numbers. This means that the greater number is 2 more than the lesser number.

The numbers must be integers because only integers can be even or odd.

2 Define a variable and write an expression for each number.

Let n be the lesser of the two numbers.

The greater number would then have the value of the expression $n + 2$.

3 Write a linear equation to describe the situation.

The sum of the numbers is 110.

So, $n + (n + 2) = 110$.

4 Solve the equation for the variable.

$n + (n + 2) = 110$	Remove the parentheses (associative property of addition).
$n + n + 2 = 110$	Combine like terms (distributive property).
$2n + 2 = 110$	Subtract 2 from both sides (subtraction property of equality).
$2n + 2 - 2 = 110 - 2$	Simplify (additive inverse property).
$2n = 108$	Divide both sides by 2 (division property of equality).
$\frac{2n}{2} = \frac{108}{2}$	Simplify (multiplicative inverse property).
$n = 54$	

5 Find the value of each number.

The value of n is 54, and n represents the lesser number.

The greater number is represented by $n + 2$. Use the substitution property of equality to find the greater number.

$54 + 2 = 56$.

▶ The two numbers are 54 and 56.

DISCUSS

Interpret the solution for the problem shown above. Is the solution reasonable?

Writing Exponential Equations

UNDERSTAND In an **exponential equation**, the variable is the exponent of a constant, which is called the **base**.

$6^s = 216$ is an exponential equation because the variable, s, is the exponent of a constant base, 6.

$212 = t^4$ is not an exponential equation because the variable, t, is the base of the expression and the exponent, 4, is a constant.

UNDERSTAND The solution to an exponential equation in one variable is the value that, when substituted into the equation for the variable, results in a true statement.

The same properties of numbers and properties of equality used to isolate the variable in a linear equation can be applied to solve nonlinear equations as well. For simple exponential equations, you can sometimes find the solution by using your knowledge of the powers of the base. Consider the equation $4 \cdot 2^{2x} + 1 = 17$. To solve, begin by isolating the term containing the variable, which is the exponential term.

$4 \cdot 2^{2x} + 1 = 17$ Subtract 1 from both sides (subtraction property of equality).

$4 \cdot 2^{2x} = 16$ Divide both sides by 4 (division property of equality).

$2^{2x} = 4$

Thinking through the powers of 2, we know that $2^2 = 4$. Use the substitution property of equality to replace 4 with 2^2.

$2^{2x} = 4$ Substitute 2^2 for 4.

$2^{2x} = 2^2$

Since $2^{2x} = 2^2$, then $2x = 2$. Solve this resulting linear equation for x.

$2x = 2$ Divide both sides by 2 (division property of equality).

$x = 1$

UNDERSTAND Exponential equations can be used to model situations in which a rate changes in a uniform way. Suppose that a business currently has 5 employees and the number of employees at the business doubles every year. The number of years it will take before the company has 80 employees can be found by solving the equation $5 \cdot 2^x = 80$.

Just as in a linear equation, the values of a variable in an exponential equation can sometimes be limited. For real-world situations, it is always important to remember what a variable stands for and to set appropriate limits. When counting objects, you cannot have negative numbers. Sometimes fractional values are appropriate—such as measurements of length or weight—and sometimes only whole number values will work—such as numbers of cats or dogs.

Connect

Tina raised the number 3 to a power and then added 19 to the result. She obtained the sum 100. To what power did she raise 3?

1 Examine the information given.

A number is raised to an unknown power. This means that the exponent will be represented by a variable in an equation. An equation with a variable for an exponent is an exponential equation.

2 Define a variable and write an expression for the exponential term.

The number 3 is raised to an unknown power. If x represents that unknown power, the exponential expression is 3^x.

3 Write an exponential equation for the situation.

After raising 3 to the unknown power, 19 is added to the result. This addition sums to 100.

$3^x + 19 = 100$

4 Solve the equation.

$3^x + 19 = 100$	Subtract 19 from both sides of the equation (subtraction property of equality).
$3^x + 19 - 19 = 100 - 19$	Simplify (additive inverse property).
$3^x = 81$	

Think through the powers of 3:

$3^1 = 3, 3^2 = 9, 3^3 = 27, 3^4 = 81$

Since $3^4 = 81$ and $3^x = 3^4$, $x = 4$ by the substitution property of equality.

▶ The unknown number is 4.

Substitute $x = 4$ into the equation you wrote and verify the solution.

EXAMPLE A A parking garage charges a \$2.50 base fee plus an hourly rate for each hour. The sign to the right gives the prices for up to 3 hours of parking.

Write and solve a linear equation to find the hourly parking rate.

Parking Rates	
1 hour	\$ 8.00
2 hours	\$13.50
3 hours	\$19.00

1 Examine the given information.

There is a base fee, which is a constant. The garage also charges an unknown hourly fee, which is multiplied by the number of hours spent in the garage.

2 Define a variable and write a linear equation to describe the situation.

Let r be the hourly parking rate.

The base fee is \$2.50. The number of hours is the coefficient of the unknown fee. If a customer parks for 3 hours, the total charge is \$19.00.

$$3r + 2.5 = 19$$

3 Solve the equation for r.

$3r + 2.5 = 19$	Subtract 2.5 from both sides of the equation (subtraction property of equality).
$3r + 2.5 - 2.5 = 19 - 2.5$	Simplify (additive inverse property).
$3r = 16.5$	Divide both sides of the equation by 3 (division property of equality).
$r = 5.5$	

4 Interpret the solution.

The variable r represents the parking rate in dollars per hour. The solution is $r = 5.5$.

▶ The parking rate at the garage is \$5.50 per hour.

The cost to park in this garage can be represented by the expression $5.5h + 2.5$, where h = number of hours. What restrictions are placed on the variable h?

EXAMPLE B The number of bacteria in a petri dish doubles each hour. At the start of an experiment, there were 300 bacteria in the dish. When the scientist checked again, there were 4,800 bacteria. How much time had passed?

1 Examine the given information.

The number of bacteria doubles each hour, so as the hour increases by 1, the number of bacteria is multiplied by 2. This situation can be modeled with an exponential equation with a base of 2. The original number of bacteria, 300, is multiplied by the number 2 raised to an unknown power. That product, after an unknown number of hours, equals 4,800.

2 Define a variable and write an exponential equation to model the situation.

Let h be the number of hours that have passed since the experiment began. After an unknown number of hours, h, there are 4,800 bacteria.

$$300 \cdot 2^h = 4{,}800$$

3 Solve the equation for h.

$300 \cdot 2^h = 4{,}800$ Divide both sides by 300 (division property of equality).

$\frac{300 \cdot 2^h}{300} = \frac{4{,}800}{300}$ Simplify (multiplicative inverse property).

$2^h = 16$

Think through the powers of 2:
$2^1 = 2, 2^2 = 4, 2^3 = 8, 2^4 = 16$

Since $2^4 = 16$, $2^h = 2^4$ by the substitution property of equality. So, $h = 4$.

4 Interpret the solution.

The variable h represents the number of hours. The solution is $h = 4$.

▶ Four hours had passed since the experiment began.

Substitute $h = 4$ into the equation you wrote and verify the solution. Then, reread the problem and make sure that the answer makes sense in the problem.

Practice

Write a linear equation or an exponential equation for each situation. Use x as the variable.

1. The sum of 3 consecutive integers is 72. ______________

> **REMEMBER** Consecutive numbers follow each other in counting order, like 11 and 12.

2. A rectangle's length is 3 feet longer than its width. Its perimeter is 62 feet.

____

3. The number of fruit flies in a population doubles every day. Everett collected 6 fruit flies for an experiment. After a certain number of days, the colony had grown to 48 fruit flies.

____

Solve each linear equation or exponential equation. Identify the property of real numbers or property of equality that allowed you to carry out each step.

4. $2y + 20 = 2 - y$ — Property

$3y + 20 = 2$ — Addition property of equality

______________ ______________

______________ ______________

5. $\frac{1}{2}(z + 2) = 4$ — Property

______________ ______________

______________ ______________

______________ ______________

6. $\frac{1}{2}(2^x) + 4 = 20$ — Property

______________ ______________

______________ ______________

______________ ______________

____

Solve.

7. The drama club ran a lemonade stand to raise money for its new production. The club made a profit of \$2 on each glass of lemonade sold and also collected \$67 in donations. At the end of the day, the club had raised a total of \$171. The club president calculated that 18.5 glasses of lemonade were sold. Is this reasonable?

____

8. A triangle has sides with lengths that are consecutive odd integers. The perimeter of the triangle is 141 centimeters. Sketch the triangle and label the lengths of the sides, using the variable a. Then find the lengths of the sides.

The lengths of the sides are _____ cm, _____ cm, and _____ cm.

9. Genevieve's grade for her history class will be the average of her midterm exam, final exam, and final paper. She received a 91 on her midterm and an 86 on her paper.

What grade must she get on her final exam to receive a grade of 90 for the class? ________

10. Raul raised 4 to a power, multiplied the result by 5, and then added 1. The result was 321.

To what power did Raul raise 4? _______

11. **WRITE MATH** Elisa raised the number 2 to the power of twice a number n. She then added 9. The result was 13. Explain how you can find the value of n.

____

____

____

12. **EXPLAIN** The number of cells in a sample doubles every minute. A doctor started with a sample of 25 cells and predicted that, after 5 minutes, he would have 32 cells. Is his prediction reasonable? Explain.

____

____

LESSON 6

Writing Inequalities in One Variable

UNDERSTAND The properties of real numbers apply to expressions in both equations and inequalities, and the properties of equality have corresponding properties of inequality. For example, according to the addition property of inequality, if $a > b$, then $a + c > b + c$. This means that inequalities can be solved by using many of the same steps you would use to solve equations.

The multiplication and division properties of inequality are slightly more complicated than their equality property counterparts. When multiplying or dividing by a negative number, you must reverse the inequality sign.

UNDERSTAND The solution to an inequality is not a single number but a range of numbers. One way to represent the solution is on a number line. The solution set $x \geq -4$ is graphed below.

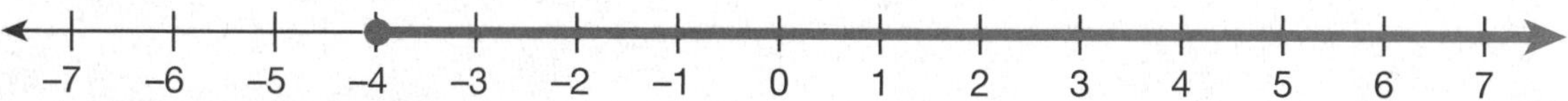

When graphing a solution set on a number line, write the inequality so that the variable is on the left side of the inequality symbol and then follow these rules:

- When the inequality symbol is $<$ or $>$, place an open (empty) dot on the endpoint to show that it is not part of the solution.
- When the symbol is $\leq$ or $\geq$, place a closed (filled-in) dot on the endpoint to show that the number is part of the solution.
- When the symbol is $<$ or $\leq$, shade to the left of the dot.
- When the symbol is $>$ or $\geq$, shade to the right of the dot.

UNDERSTAND In some cases, you will need more than one inequality or a **compound inequality** to describe a situation. For example, a real-world situation may be represented by $x \geq -3$ and $x < 2$. Some compound inequalities, such as the one just described, can also be written in the form $-3 \leq x < 2$.

If you graph both parts of a compound inequality on the same number line, the solution is the portion of the graphs that overlap.

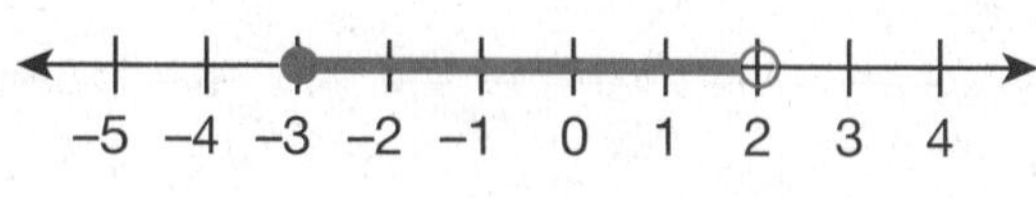

The solution sets for two inequalities sometimes do not overlap at all. When $x \leq 0$ and $x \geq 5$ are graphed on the same number line, there is no overlap. No value of x makes both inequalities true. This compound inequality has no solution.

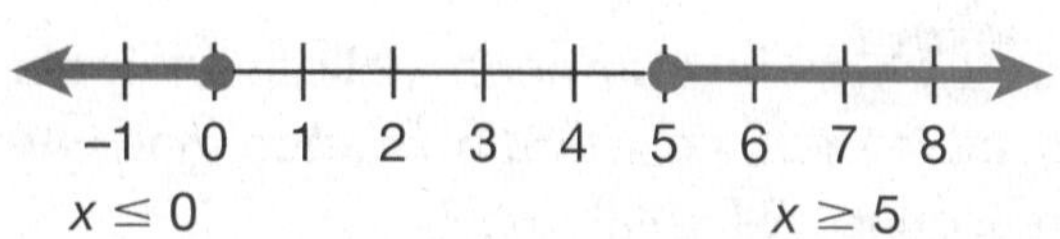

Connect

Ecologists studying a colony of rabbits in the wild found that the colony doubles in population every quarter of a year. At first count, the ecologists found 10 rabbits. After how many quarters will there be more than 80 rabbits? How long is this in years?

1 Examine the given information.

The rabbit population doubles from one quarter to the next, so the situation is modeled by using an exponential expression with a base of 2. The problem asks when the population will be more than 80 rabbits. Model the situation as an inequality with the greater than symbol, $>$.

2 Write the exponential inequality.

Let q be the number of quarters since the ecologists first counted the rabbits.

At first count, the colony had 10 rabbits. The number of rabbits doubles, or increases by a factor of 2, each quarter. The number of quarters, q, determines how many times to multiply by the factor. We want to know when the number of rabbits will be greater than 80.

$$10 \cdot 2^q > 80$$

3 Solve the inequality for q.

$10 \cdot 2^q = 80$	Divide both sides by 10 (division property of equality).
$2^q = 8$	Substitute 2^3 for 8 (substitution property of equality).
$2^q = 2^3$	Since the bases are the same, the exponents must be equal.
$q = 3$	The solution to the inequality is either $q > 3$ or $q < 3$.

4 Determine the solution.

Choose a number less than 3 and a number greater than 3. Use the substitution property of inequality to determine the solution set.

Try $q = 0$.	Try $q = 5$.
$10 \cdot 2^q \overset{?}{>} 80$	$10 \cdot 2^q \overset{?}{>} 80$
$10 \cdot 2^0 \overset{?}{>} 80$	$10 \cdot 2^5 \overset{?}{>} 80$
$10 \cdot 1 \overset{?}{>} 80$	$10 \cdot 32 \overset{?}{>} 80$
$10 \not> 80$	$320 > 80$ ✓

5 Interpret the result.

▶ The population of rabbits will be greater than 80 after more than 3 quarters, which is $\frac{3}{4}$ of a year, or 9 months.

TRY

Graph the solution $q > 3$ on a number line.

EXAMPLE A Jonah subscribed to a new service that streams music over the Internet. The service costs \$2.95 per month, but Jonah's rate is reduced by 15 cents for each new subscriber that he signs up. If there is no limit to the discount, how many users must Jonah recruit in order for him to stream music for free?

1 Examine the given information.

Jonah's monthly payment, if he recruits no subscribers, is \$2.95. His goal is to stream music for free, or to reduce his payment to \$0. For each new subscriber that he signs up, his monthly payment is reduced by 15 cents, so the rate of change is −0.15 dollars per person.

2 Write the linear inequality.

Let x be the number of people that Jonah recruits.

The rate of the discount, −0.15 dollars per person, must be multiplied by the number of people, x, to find the dollar amount of the discount. This amount is subtracted from the base cost, \$2.95. This discounted cost must be less than or equal to \$0.

$$2.95 - 0.15x \leq 0$$

3 Solve the inequality for x. Interpret the solution.

$2.95 - 0.15x \leq 0$ — Subtract 2.95 from each side (subtraction property of inequality).

$-0.15x \leq -2.95$ — Divide both sides by −0.15. Reverse the inequality symbol (division property of inequality).

$x \geq 19.\overline{6}$

▶ Jonah would need to recruit at least 20 people for the service to be free.

Since the calculations yielded $x \geq 19.\overline{6}$, why was the answer at least 20? What are the possible values of x in this situation? What are the possible amounts that Jonah might pay in a given month?

EXAMPLE B Olivia is going to the mall, where she plans to buy a coffee for \$3 and some scented soaps for \$4 each. She has a gift certificate for \$11 that she wants to use, but she can spend no more than \$35 in total, including the gift certificate. Write and solve a pair of inequalities to find the number of soaps that Olivia can buy. Then graph the solution on a number line.

1 Write two inequalities to model the problem.

Let s be the number of soaps that Olivia buys.

Since soap costs \$4 per bar, the total cost of the soaps is $4s$. She will also buy a coffee for \$3. The total amount that Olivia will spend is $4s + 3$.

She will spend at least \$11: $4s + 3 \geq 11$

She will spend no more than \$35: $4s + 3 \leq 35$

2 Solve the inequalities.

Use the subtraction property of inequality and the division property of inequality to solve the inequalities.

$4s + 3 \geq 11$	$4s + 3 \leq 35$
$4s \geq 8$	$4s \leq 32$
$s \geq 2$	$s \leq 8$

▶ $2 \leq s \leq 8$

3 Graph the solution set.

First, graph each inequality on its own number line.

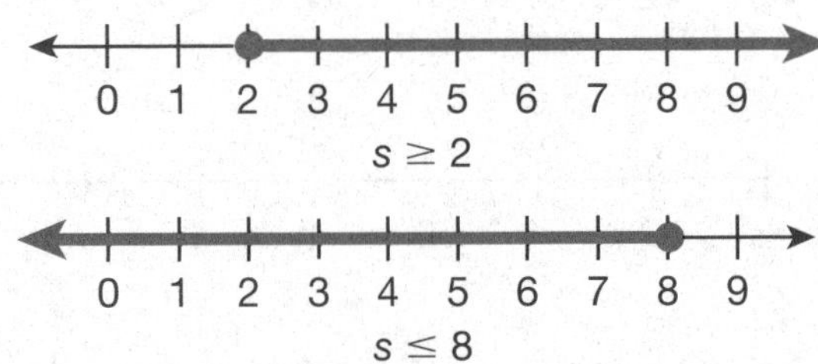

Find the part of the number line where the graphs overlap. Consider the context of the problem. Olivia cannot buy a partial bar of soap, so only integer solutions make sense. Graph the integers in the region of overlap to show the solution set.

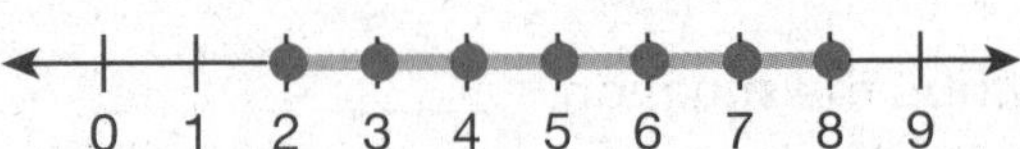

Can Olivia buy only 1 soap? Can she buy 10 soaps?

Practice

Solve each inequality.

1. $9x - 7 < 65$ __________

2. $-2a + 13 \leq 23$ __________

3. $2 \cdot 3^n > 54$ __________

4. $7b - 19 \geq 2b + 1$ __________

5. $1 - 5y > y - 3$ __________

6. $\frac{1}{2}(4^d) + 2 \leq 130$ __________

> **REMEMBER** When dividing or multiplying both sides of an inequality by a negative number, reverse the inequality sign.

The steps for solving the given inequality are shown below. Fill in a property to justify each step.

7. $-4(y - \frac{1}{2}) > -2$ Property

$-4y + 2 > -2$ __________

$-4y > -4$ __________

$y < 1$ __________

Graph the solution to each inequality.

8. $12c + 7 > 10c + 1$

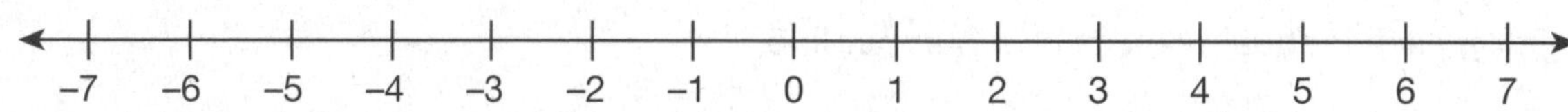

9. $19 - 3t \geq 34$

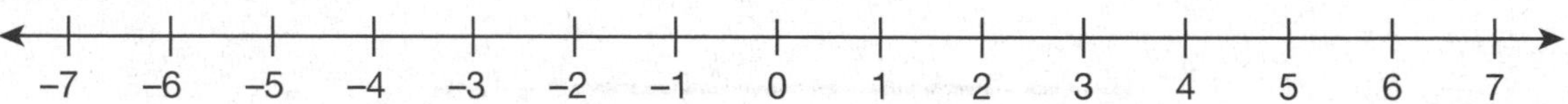

10. $3 \cdot 2^n + 1 < 25$

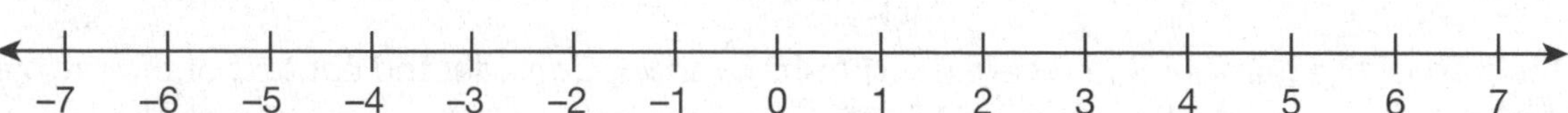

11. The sum of 2 consecutive integers is greater than 73.

Write an inequality to describe the situation. __________

Find the smallest two integers that fit this description. __________

Find the set of solutions that solve both inequalities.

12. $4x < 15 - x$

$x + 17 > 2x + 14$

____

13. $6y - 9 > 2y + 19$

$10 - y > 7$

____

14. $s + 1 \geq -19 - s$

$4s - 7 \geq 6s + 1$

____

Find the solutions that solve both inequalities. Then, if possible, graph the solution set.

15. $2x - 1 > -5 - 2x$

$3x + 5 < 13 - x$

____

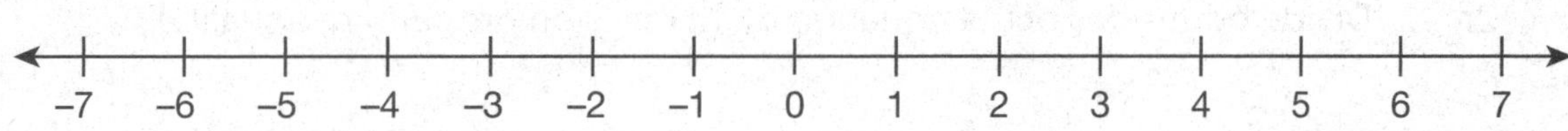

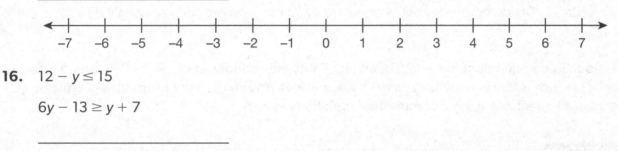

16. $12 - y \leq 15$

$6y - 13 \geq y + 7$

____

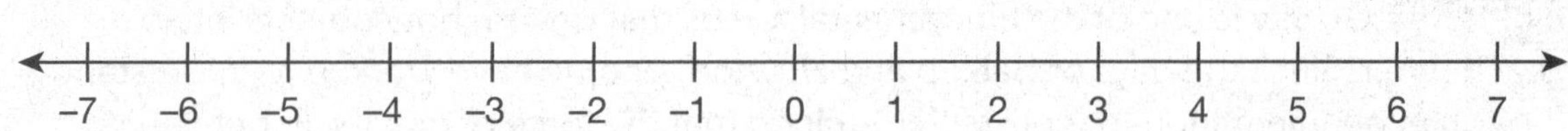

Solve.

17. A petri dish contained 50 bacteria at 8:00 A.M. The number of bacteria triples each hour.

After what time will there be at least 1,350 bacteria in the petri dish? ______________

18. APPLY José's math grade is the mean of his three exams. His grades on the first two exams were 82 and 93. What grade must he earn on his third exam to have an average of at least 90 for the class? Express your answer as a compound inequality. Keep in mind any constraints on the variable.

____

19. RELATE The symmetric property of equality states that if $a = b$ then $b = a$. Can you think of a similar property of inequality related to the inequality $a < b$?

____

LESSON 7 Writing Equivalent Equations

UNDERSTAND An equation describes the relationship between different quantities. Those quantities may be represented by constants or by variables. You can use properties of equality to rewrite an equation in order to see that relationship from a different perspective. When you transform an equation by using properties of equality, the resulting equation is equivalent to the original equation.

The formula $i = 12f$ gives the number of inches, i, equivalent to f feet. But suppose that you wanted to know the number of feet in 156 inches. You can use the division property of equality find a formula for the number of feet given i inches.

$i = 12f$ Divide both sides of the equation by 12 (division property of equality).

$f = \frac{i}{12}$

This equation is equivalent to $i = 12f$, but it highlights the quantity length in feet. Plugging in a number of inches for i immediately yields a value in feet. You can use the properties of equality to highlight quantities in more complicated equations as well.

UNDERSTAND Gravity is one of the fundamental forces that govern how objects interact with each other. Since the days of Galileo and Newton, people have worked to understand it. Through experimentation, scientists determined that the force of gravity, F, between two objects depends on their masses, m_1 and m_2, and r, the distance between them. The formula to calculate the force of gravity is:

$$F = \frac{(6.67 \times 10^{-11})m_1m_2}{r^2}$$

Astronomers searching the universe to discover new planets have used this relationship to learn about the objects that they find in space. By studying the orbit of a planet around its star, they can determine the force of gravity between the planet and the star. The relationship between mass and gravity then allows them to calculate the planet's mass.

You can rearrange the formula for the force of gravity to be a formula for the mass of one of the objects.

$F = \frac{(6.67 \times 10^{-11})m_1m_2}{r^2}$ Multiply by r^2 (multiplication property of equality).

$Fr^2 = (6.67 \times 10^{-11})m_1m_2$ Divide by $(6.67 \times 10^{-11})m_2$ (division property of equality).

$m_1 = \frac{Fr^2}{(6.67 \times 10^{-11})m_2}$

This equation is equivalent to the force equation, but highlights the mass m_1. If you know the mass of the star (m_2), the distance between the planet and the star (r), and the force of gravity between them (F), then this equation yields the mass of the newly discovered planet.

Connect

The formula below converts a temperature from degrees Celsius, C, to degrees Fahrenheit, F.

$$F = \frac{9}{5}C + 32$$

Write an equivalent formula to convert a temperature from degrees Fahrenheit to degrees Celsius.

1 Examine the problem.

The given formula represents degrees Fahrenheit, F, in terms of degrees Celsius, C. The problem asks you to find the reverse relationship: degrees Celsius, C, in terms of degrees Fahrenheit, F. To find this formula, you need to isolate the variable C on one side of the equation.

2 Write an equivalent formula.

When rewriting equations or formulas, it is often easiest to apply the order of operations in reverse. To isolate the variable C, start by undoing the addition (through subtraction) and then move on to undo the multiplication (by dividing).

$F = \frac{9}{5}C + 32$

$F - 32 = \frac{9}{5}C$ Subtraction property of equality

$\frac{5}{9}(F - 32) = C$ Division property of equality

$C = \frac{5}{9}(F - 32)$ Symmetric property of equality

Because the formula was transformed by using properties of equality, it is equivalent to the original equation.

▶ To convert degrees Fahrenheit to degrees Celsius, use the formula $C = \frac{5}{9}(F - 32)$.

3 Use the substitution property of equality to check your answer.

Use the given formula to convert 35°C to degrees Fahrenheit.

$F = \frac{9}{5}C + 32$

$F = \frac{9}{5}(35) + 32$

$F = 95$

Now, use the formula that you found for Celsius to convert 95°F.

$C = \frac{5}{9}(F - 32)$

$C = \frac{5}{9}(95 - 32)$

$C = 35$

Since the result is the same temperature we started with, 35°C, the formula appears correct.

TRY

The Ideal Gas Law states that $PV = 8.31nT$, where P = pressure, V = volume, T = temperature, and n = the amount of gas. Rewrite the equation to determine a formula for n.

EXAMPLE Juanita works as a salesperson at an electronics store. She earns a base salary of \$400 each week plus a 10% commission on her total sales. Her weekly pay is described by the equation $p = 400 + 0.1s$, where p is her total weekly pay and s is her total weekly sales. Juanita did not keep track of her sales last week, but her pay was \$1,380. Rewrite the given equation to find s. Then find her total sales.

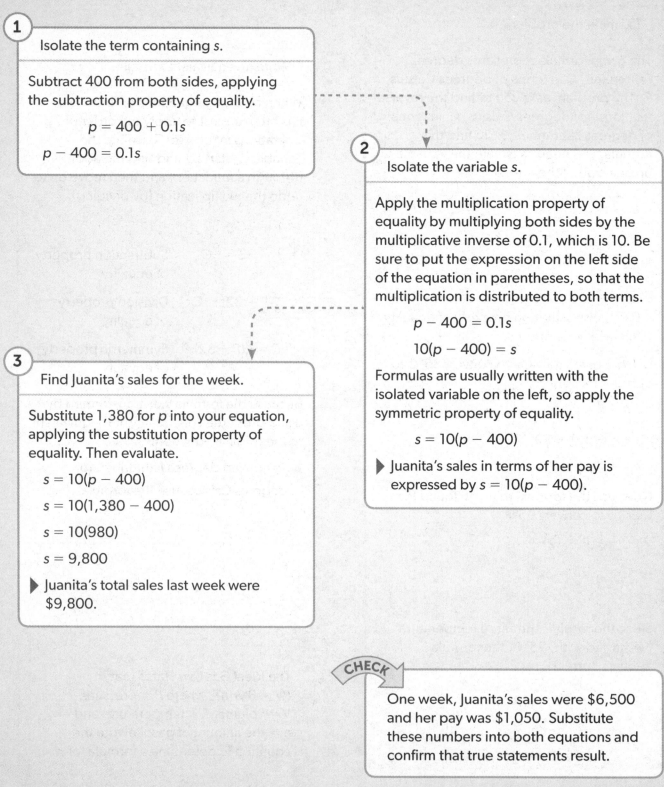

1 Isolate the term containing s.

Subtract 400 from both sides, applying the subtraction property of equality.

$$p = 400 + 0.1s$$

$$p - 400 = 0.1s$$

2 Isolate the variable s.

Apply the multiplication property of equality by multiplying both sides by the multiplicative inverse of 0.1, which is 10. Be sure to put the expression on the left side of the equation in parentheses, so that the multiplication is distributed to both terms.

$$p - 400 = 0.1s$$

$$10(p - 400) = s$$

Formulas are usually written with the isolated variable on the left, so apply the symmetric property of equality.

$$s = 10(p - 400)$$

▶ Juanita's sales in terms of her pay is expressed by $s = 10(p - 400)$.

3 Find Juanita's sales for the week.

Substitute 1,380 for p into your equation, applying the substitution property of equality. Then evaluate.

$$s = 10(p - 400)$$

$$s = 10(1{,}380 - 400)$$

$$s = 10(980)$$

$$s = 9{,}800$$

▶ Juanita's total sales last week were \$9,800.

One week, Juanita's sales were \$6,500 and her pay was \$1,050. Substitute these numbers into both equations and confirm that true statements result.

 Problem Solving

READ

In the distance formula $d = rt$, d is distance traveled, r is rate of speed, and t is time spent traveling. How could you find t if you knew d and r?

James will travel 250 miles from Savannah to Atlanta. If he drives at an average speed of 50 miles per hour (mph), how much time will he spend driving?

PLAN

We are given a distance, d, and a rate of speed, r. The unknown quantity is _______, t.

Rewrite the given formula to isolate t.

SOLVE

Rewrite $d = rt$ to express t in terms of the other variables.

$d = rt$

$\frac{d}{r} = t$ _____________ property of equality

$t = \frac{d}{r}$ _____________ property of equality

Let $d = 250$ and $r = 50$.

$t = \frac{d}{r}$

$t =$ _____________ _____________ property of equality

$t =$ _____________

It will take _______ hours of driving at 50 mph for James to travel from Savannah to Atlanta.

CHECK

Substitute $d =$ _______, $r =$ _______, and $t =$ _______ into the distance formula. Verify that a true statement results.

$d = rt$

_______ $\stackrel{?}{=}$ (50)(5)

_______ = 250 ✓

▶ The solution, _______ hours, is correct.

Practice

Rewrite each equation to isolate the indicated variable.

1. $12ab = c$ for a ________

2. $y = 9x + 2$ for x ________

3. $df = g - 10$ for d ________

REMEMBER Apply the reverse of the order of operations to isolate a variable.

Write the desired equivalent equation, and identify properties used to do so. Then solve.

4. Ohm's law of electricity states that $V = IR$, where V = voltage, I = current, and R = resistance.

Rewrite the equation for R. ________

If $V = 9$ volts and $I = 0.5$ amps, what is the value of R? ____ ohms

Rewrite the equation for I. ________

Which property of equality allows you to isolate R and I? ________

If $V = 110$ volts and $R = 2200$ ohms, what is the value of I? ____ amps

5. At a baseball game, hot dogs cost \$2.25 and sodas cost \$1.75. The total cost, t, for h hot dogs and s sodas can be described by the equation $t = 2.25h + 1.75s$.

Rewrite the equation to find s. ________

Which properties of equality allows you to isolate s? ________

If Costas spent \$18.25 and bought 5 hot dogs, how many sodas did he buy? ________

Isolate the indicated variable in each equation. Give a property to justify each step.

6. $\frac{1}{3}s - 8 = t$ for s — Property

________ ________

________ ________

________ ________

7. $z = 9x + 14xy$ for x — Property

________ ________

________ ________

________ ________

Choose the best answer.

8. Which of the following is equivalent to the equation $4r + 7s = q$?

   A. $r = 4q - 28s$

   B. $r = \frac{q - 7s}{4}$

   C. $s = 7q + 28r$

   D. $s = \frac{q + 4r}{7}$

9. Which of the following is **not** equivalent to the equation $a - 3b = 5c + 9$

   A. $a = 3b + 5c + 9$

   B. $b = \frac{1}{3}(a - 5c - 9)$

   C. $a - 3b - 5c = 9$

   D. $c = \frac{a - 3b + 9}{5}$

Solve.

10. The weight, in newtons, of an object in a particular location is equal to its mass, in kilograms, times the gravitational constant in that location. As a formula, this is written $w = mg$, where w = weight, m = mass, and g = the gravitational constant.

    An astronaut has a mass of 80 kilograms on Earth. On Earth's surface, the gravitational constant is $g = 10$ newtons per kilogram. What is the astronaut's weight on Earth? _____ newtons

    Rewrite the equation to isolate g. ____________________

    On the surface of the moon, the astronaut's weight is 128 newtons. What is the moon's gravitational constant? _______ newtons per kilogram

11. DEMONSTRATE Solve the equation $\frac{1}{4}p - 5n = 12$ for n. Then choose values for p and n and show that the two equations are equivalent. ____________________

12. APPLY A hairdresser charges $25 for a man's haircut, $35 for a woman's haircut, and $15 for a child's haircut. Her total income, t, can be described by the following equation, where m = the number of men's haircuts, w = the number of women's haircuts, and c = the number of children's haircuts.

    $t = 25m + 35w + 15c$

    Last week, the hairdresser's total income was $385. Her customers included 8 women and 2 children. If she wants to find how many customers were men, for which variable should she solve the equation? Solve the equation for that variable and find the number of men who got haircuts.

    ____

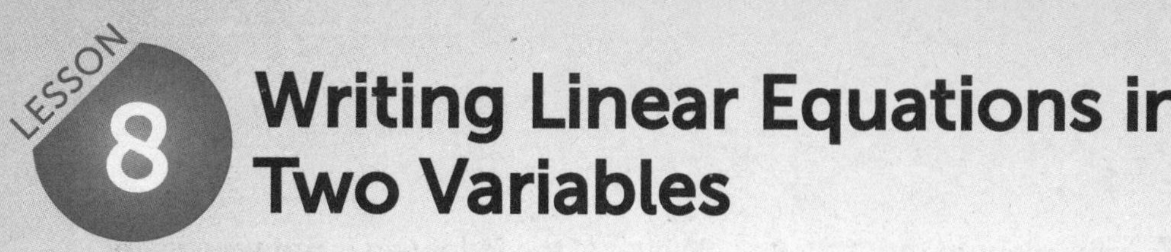

LESSON 8 Writing Linear Equations in Two Variables

UNDERSTAND Sometimes, the relationship between two quantities (such as distance and time) can be modeled by a **linear equation**. In such an equation, each quantity is represented by a different variable. Linear equations in two variables have many of the same characteristics as linear equations with one variable.

Consider the simple situation of filling a pool with water. Suppose that water pours into the pool at a rate of 50 gallons per hour. The equation below describes the relationship between the total number of gallons of water in the pool (y) and the number of hours (x) since filling began.

$$y = 50x$$

This equation relates two variables, y and x, and it is linear because both variables are to the first power.

UNDERSTAND A linear equation in two variables can be written in **slope-intercept form**, $y = mx + b$, where:

- y and x are variables
- m is the **slope** of the equation's graph, or its rate of change
- b is the ***y*-intercept**, or the y-coordinate where the graph intersects the y-axis

In the situation described above, the equation $y = 50x$ is in slope-intercept form. The graph of the equation will have a slope (m) of 50, the coefficient of x. Rewriting the equation as $y = 50x + 0$ shows that the graph has a y-intercept at (0, 0).

UNDERSTAND A linear equation in two variables can be graphed on a coordinate plane. Each axis of the plane represents one variable. The graph of a linear equation in two variables will be a straight line.

To graph an equation in slope-intercept form, first plot a point at the y-intercept, $(0, b)$. Then use the slope to find a second point. Finish by drawing a line through the two points.

To graph $y = 50x$, first plot a point at (0, 0). Using the slope of 50, or $\frac{50}{1}$, move 50 units up and 1 unit to the right to plot a second point at (1, 50). The line drawn through these points is the graph of the equation.

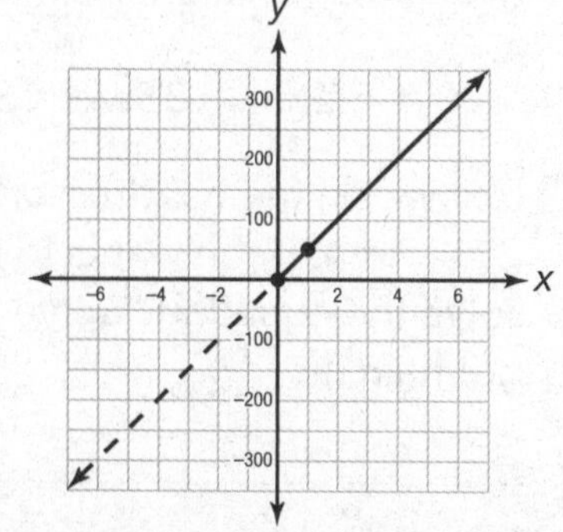

Connect

A botanist transplanted a plant that was 3 centimeters (cm) tall into an experimental soil. He then took measurements once a week and found an average growth rate of 0.5 cm per week. Write a linear equation in two variables to describe the height of the plant over time. Then graph the equation.

1 Examine the given information.

The two variables are the time since the plant was transplanted and the height of the plant. Time is the independent variable, and the height of the plant is the dependent variable, since the height of the plant depends on how much time has passed.

The plant grows an average of 0.5 cm each week. This is the rate of change, or slope.

At the start, when time equals 0, the plant is 3 cm tall. This is the *y*-intercept.

2 Define variables and write an equation.

Since time is the independent variable, let *x* be the number of weeks since the experiment began.

For the dependent variable, let *y* be the height of the plant in centimeters.

Write a linear equation with a slope of 0.5, or $\frac{1}{2}$, and a *y*-intercept of 3.

▶ $y = \frac{1}{2}x + 3$

3 Graph the equation.

Plot a point at the *y*-intercept, (0, 3).

Then, using the slope of $\frac{1}{2}$, move two units to the right and one unit up to plot a second point at (2, 4). Draw a line through the points.

▶

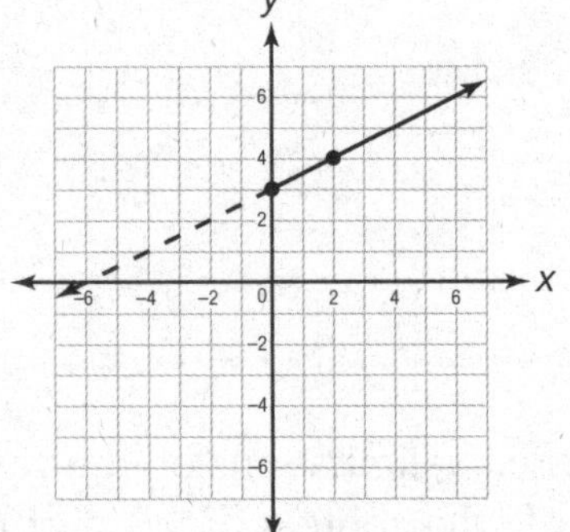

DISCUSS

The points (−4, 1) and (1,000, 503) are on the graph of the equation. Are these solutions to the problem?

EXAMPLE A Tommy has 200 fliers to hand out. He hands out an average of 15 fliers each hour. Write and graph an equation to model the situation.

1 Examine the given information.

The two variables are the time since Tommy started handing out fliers and the number of fliers remaining. Time is the independent variable, and the number of fliers is the dependent variable, since the number of fliers remaining depends on how much time has passed.

Tommy starts with 200 fliers, so this is the *y*-intercept.

He hands out 15 per hour, which is the rate of change. But the number of fliers remaining is decreasing, so the slope should be negative. The slope is −15.

2 Define variables and write an equation.

Let x be the amount of time that has passed in hours. Let y be the number of fliers that Tommy has. Write an equation in slope-intercept form with slope $m = -15$ and y-intercept $b = 200$.

▶ $y = -15x + 200$

3 Graph the equation.

Plot a point at the *y*-intercept, (0, 200). Then, use the slope of −15 to plot a second point. From (0, 200), move 1 unit to the right and 15 units down, and plot a point at (1, 185). Draw a line through the two points.

▶

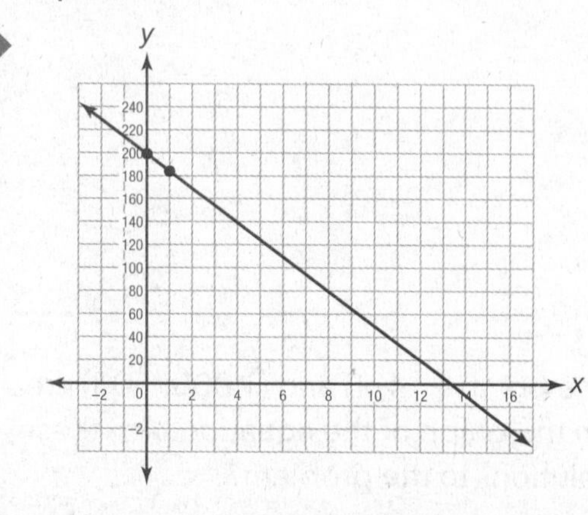

DISCUSS

What are the limitations on the variables x and y in the context of this problem?

EXAMPLE B A Web site sells MP3 downloads of music albums for $10 and Blu-ray discs of movies for $30. Fiona wants to buy some albums and some movies. She plans to spend a total of $150. Write and graph an equation to represent the situation.

1 Review the given information.

The variables in this situation are the number of albums to be bought and the number of movies to be bought. There is no clear dependent or independent variable, so you can assign the variables either way.

2 Define the variables and write an equation.

Let x be the number of albums to be bought, and let y be the number of movies to be bought.

The amount to be spent on albums is $10x$.
The amount to be spent on movies is $30y$.
The total to be spent must equal 150.

▶ $10x + 30y = 150$

Notice that this equation is not in slope-intercept form.

3 Find two points on the line.

Choose a value to substitute for x in order to find a point on the line. Let's choose 0.

$$10(0) + 30y = 150$$
$$30y = 150$$
$$y = 5$$

The point (0, 5) lies on the line.

You can also choose a number to substitute for y in order to find a point. Again, let's choose 0.

$$10x + 30(0) = 150$$
$$10x = 150$$
$$x = 15$$

The point (15, 0) lies on the line.

4 Graph the line.

Plot the points (0, 5) and (15, 0) and connect them with a line.

▶

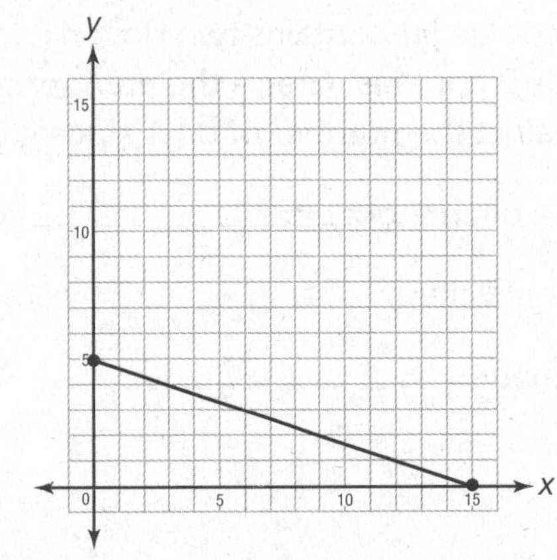

DISCUSS

What are the limitations on the variables x and y in the context of this problem?

Practice

Write an equation to describe each situation.

1. A number y is 6 less than twice a number x. ________

2. Dorothy's age, d, is 1 more than half of Matthew's age, m. ________

3. The number of boys, b, in the class is 3 times the number of girls, g, in the class. ________

Choose the best answer.

4. A beekeeper pays $30 to rent a booth at a farmers' market. She charges $5 for each jar of honey. The graph shows this situation, which is modeled by the equation $y = 5x - 30$. Which of the following is true?

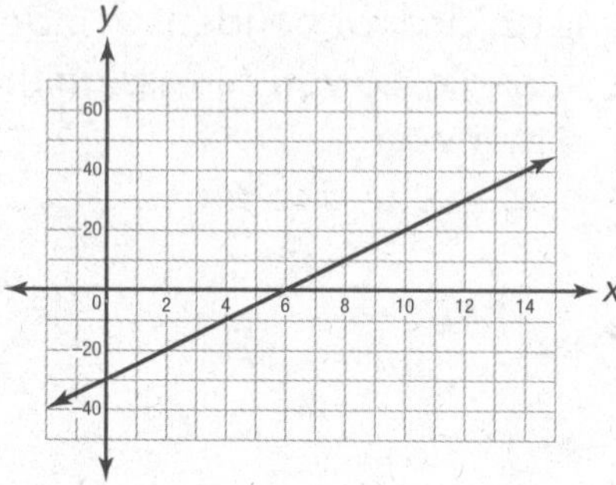

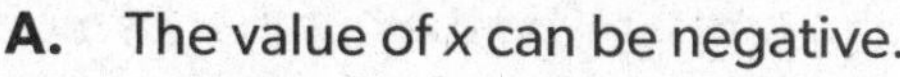

A. The value of x can be negative.

B. The value of y can be negative.

C. The value of x can be fractional.

D. The value of y cannot be zero.

Identify the rate of change and initial value for each situation. Write and graph an equation for the situation, providing labels for the axes of the graph.

5. A baker sells cupcakes at a local festival. He pays $50 to rent a booth, and he charges $2.50 for each cupcake. Graph his profit or loss, in dollars, against the number of cupcakes he sells.

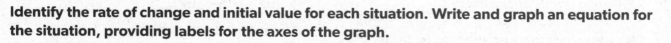

rate of change: $________ per cupcake

initial value: ________ dollars

equation: ________

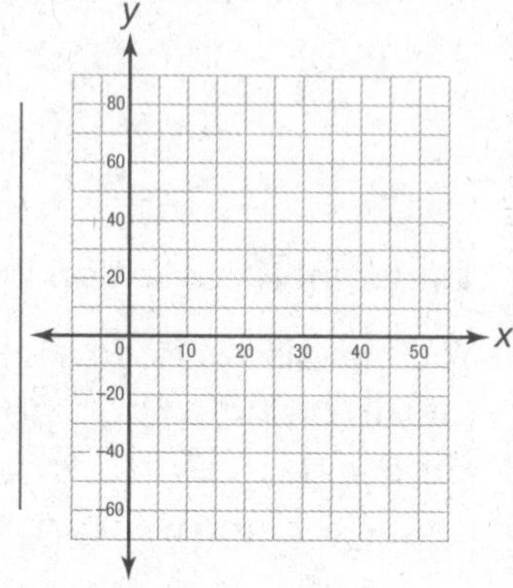

6. A cookie jar contains two dozen cookies. Every day, Nikki eats 2 cookies. Graph the number of cookies in the jar against the number of days since it was filled.

rate of change: ________ cookies per day

initial value: ________ cookies

equation: ________

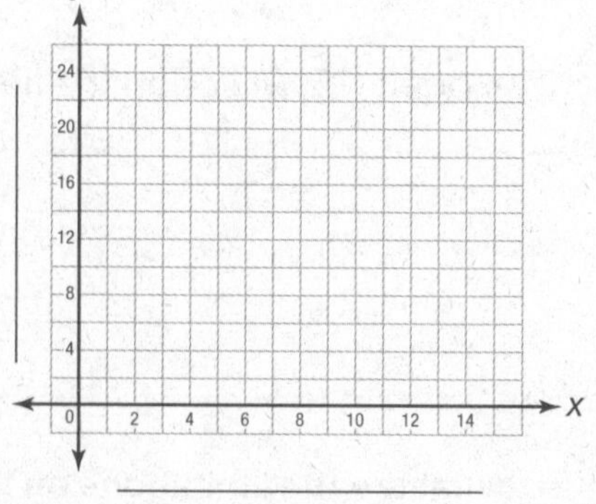

Solve.

7. **COMPARE** Ling's bank account has a balance of \$55. Every week, she will add \$20 to it. Bei Bei's bank account has a balance of \$120. Every week, she will withdraw \$10 from it. Write and graph an equation to describe how each girl's bank account will change. Compare the equations and their graphs.

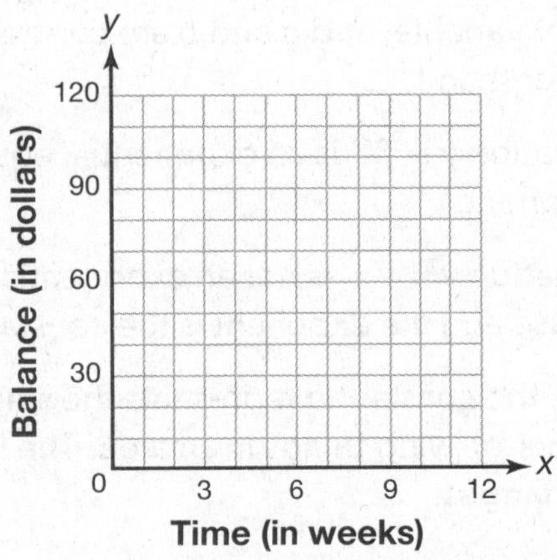

8. **DESCRIBE** A puppy weighed 5 ounces (oz) at birth and gained 3 oz each week for the first 10 weeks. The equation that describes the puppy's weight after x weeks is $y = 3x + 5$, as graphed below.

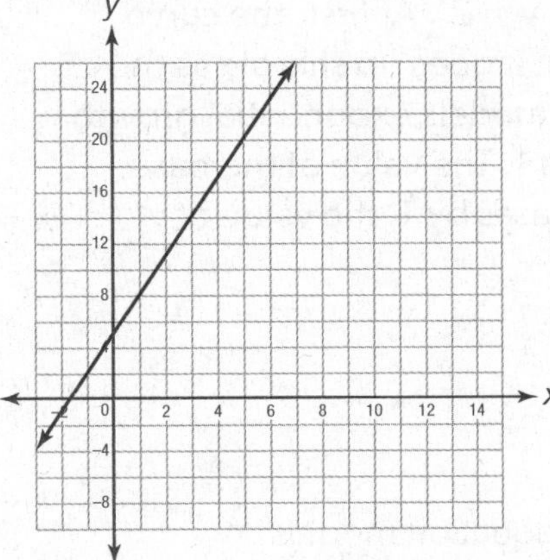

Describe the limitations of the variable x in this situation. Which points on the graph are **not** solutions for the given situation?

Writing Exponential Equations in Two Variables

UNDERSTAND An **exponential equation** is an equation in which the independent variable is an exponent. In the exponential equation $y = a \cdot b^x$, y is the dependent variable, x is the independent variable, and a and b are constants. The **base**, b, can be any positive real number other than 1.

The equation $y = 3^{2x}$ is an exponential equation because the variable, x, is in the exponent.

The equation $y = 7x^3$ is not an exponential equation because the variable, x, is the base and the exponent is the constant number 3.

In $y = a \cdot b^x$, the constant a represents the starting value of a quantity being measured, such as the number of living things in an area. The base b shows how that quantity changes as the variable x changes.

UNDERSTAND The graph of an exponential equation is not a straight line. It is a curve that is either always increasing or always decreasing.

For the equation $y = a \cdot b^x$, when the base $b > 1$ and $a > 0$, the equation models **exponential growth**. The graph on the right shows the equation $y = 2^x$. At first, the curve rises slowly above the x-axis, but it goes up sharply as the x-values increase. The equation models exponential growth because the base is greater than 1. The value of the base, 2, means that every time x increases by 1, the value of y doubles, or is multiplied by 2.

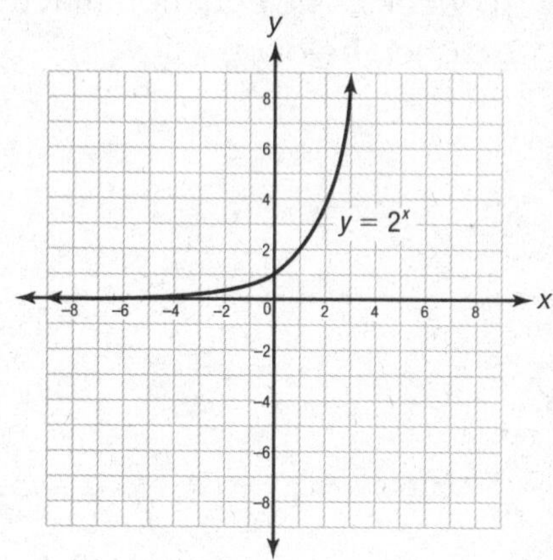

When $a > 0$ and $0 < b < 1$, the equation models **exponential decay**. The graph on the right shows the equation $y = \left(\frac{1}{3}\right)^x$. At first, the curve goes down sharply and then gets closer and closer to zero as the x-values increase. The equation models exponential decay because the base, $\frac{1}{3}$, is less than 1. The base tells us that every time x increases by 1, the value of y is multiplied by $\frac{1}{3}$.

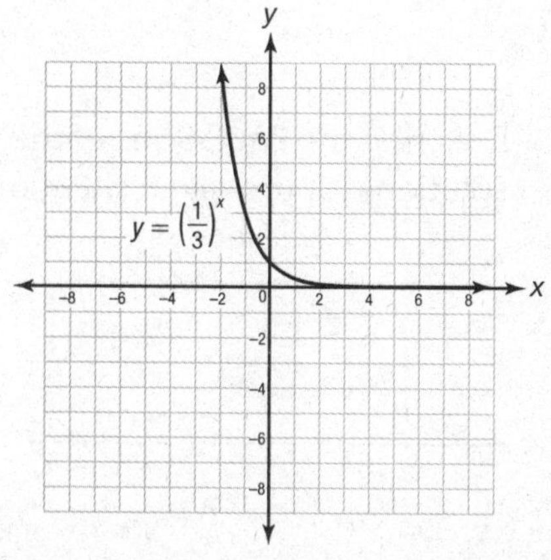

Connect

A colony of bacteria starts out with 150 cells and triples in population every hour. Write an equation that models the number of cells, y, after x hours. Then, graph the equation.

1 Determine the values of a and b.

The initial population of bacteria is 150, so $a = 150$. Every hour, the population is tripling, which is the same as being multiplied by 3. This means that the base, b, is 3.

2 Write the equation by substituting for a and b in $y = a \cdot b^x$.

▶ The equation that gives the number of bacteria cells, y, after x hours is $y = 150 \cdot 3^x$.

3 Use the equation to make a table of values.

x	$y = 150 \cdot 3^x$	y
0	$y = 150 \cdot 3^0 = 150 \cdot 1 = 150$	150
1	$y = 150 \cdot 3^1 = 150 \cdot 3 = 450$	450
2	$y = 150 \cdot 3^2 = 150 \cdot 9 = 1{,}350$	1,350

4 Graph the equation.

Plot the points from the table and connect them with a smooth curve.

▶

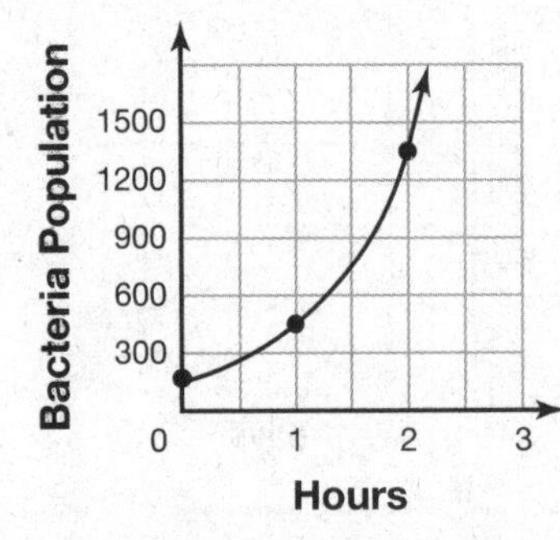

DISCUSS

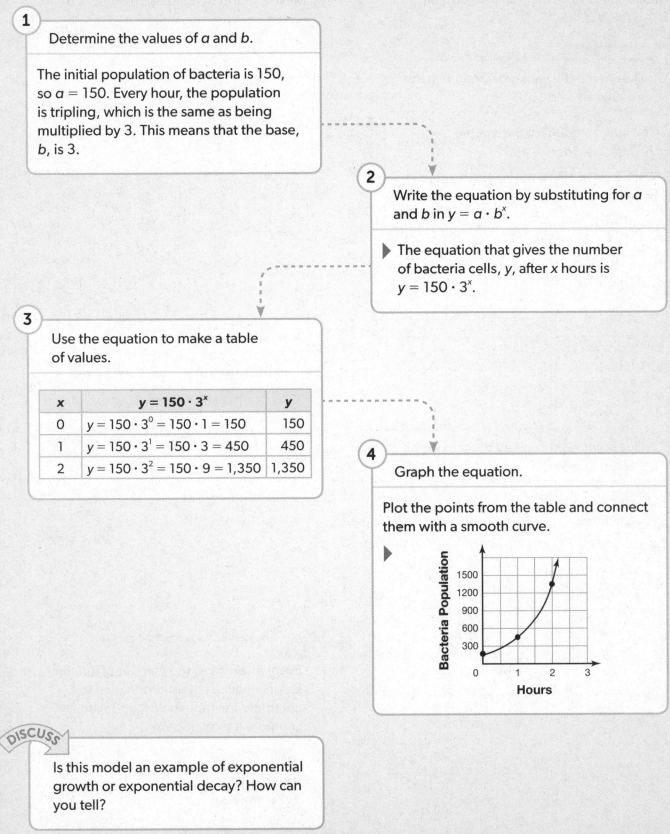

Is this model an example of exponential growth or exponential decay? How can you tell?

EXAMPLE A The half-life of a substance is the time it takes for half of that substance to break down or decay. The half-life of fermium-253 is 3 days. Write an equation for the amount remaining from a sample of 700 grams of fermium-253 after x days. Make a graph that models the decay of fermium-253.

1 Determine the values of a and b in the equation $y = a \cdot b^x$.

The initial amount of the sample is 700 grams. So, $a = 700$.

After 3 days, there will be half as much fermium, or 350 grams.

$$350 = 700 \cdot b^3$$

$$\frac{1}{2} = b^3$$

$$\sqrt[3]{\frac{1}{2}} = b$$

$$0.79 \approx b$$

2 Write the equation.

▶ $y = 700 \cdot (0.79)^x$

3 Plot points and connect them to graph the equation.

Use the equation to find the value of y at several times.

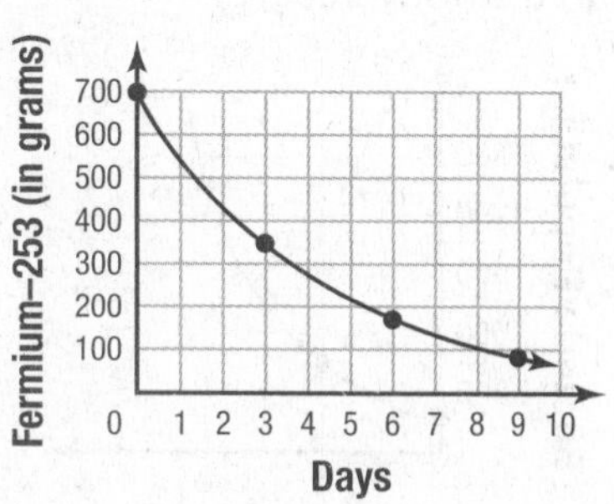

CHECK

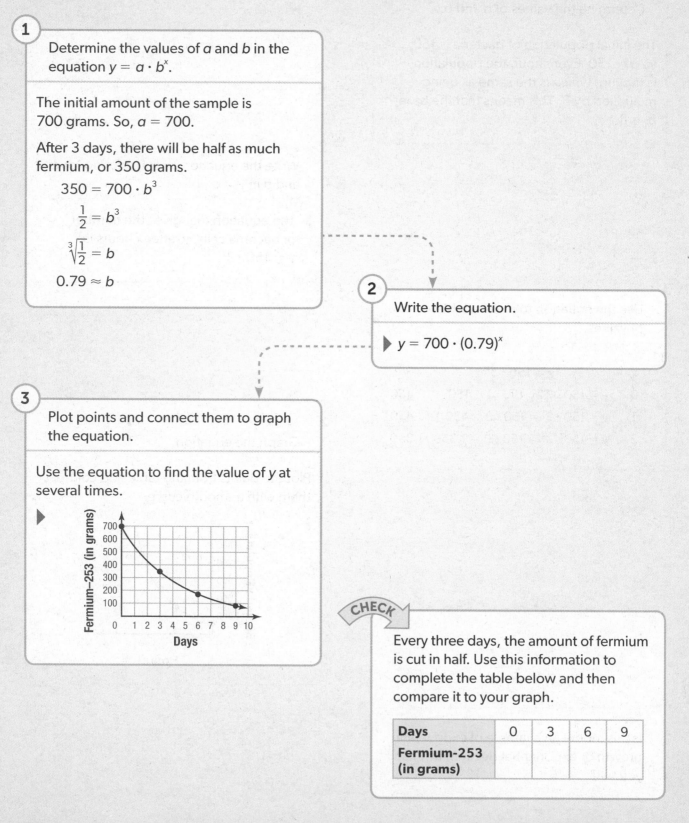

Every three days, the amount of fermium is cut in half. Use this information to complete the table below and then compare it to your graph.

Days	0	3	6	9
Fermium-253 (in grams)				

EXAMPLE B Compound interest is calculated by using the exponential function $A = P\left(1 + \frac{r}{n}\right)^{nt}$, where A is the accumulated amount after t years, P is the principal (the amount invested), r is the annual interest rate expressed as a decimal, and n is the number of times that the interest is compounded per year. Write an equation to find the amount that is accumulated when \$500 is invested in an account with a 3% annual interest rate, compounded monthly. Make a graph that shows how the account grows over time.

1 Identify the values of P, r, and n.

The principal, P, is the original amount that is invested, \$500. So, $P = 500$.

The annual interest rate is 3%. Expressed as a decimal, $r = 0.03$.

The interest for this account is compounded monthly, and there are 12 months in a year. So, $n = 12$.

2 Substitute the values of P, r, and n into the compound interest equation and simplify.

$$A = P\left(1 + \frac{r}{n}\right)^{nt}$$

$$A = 500\left(1 + \frac{0.03}{12}\right)^{12t}$$

▶ $A = 500(1.0025)^{12t}$

3 Plot points and connect them to graph the equation.

▶

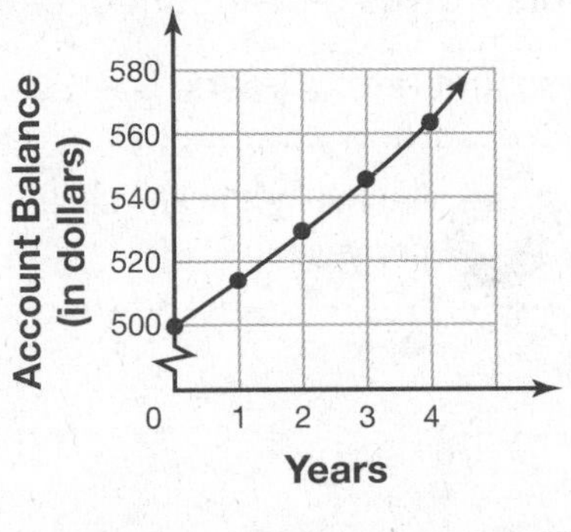

DISCUSS

How could you determine how much money would be in the account after 18 months?

Practice

Determine whether each equation is an exponential equation.

1. $y = 6 \cdot \left(\frac{1}{8}\right)^x$ ______
2. $y = \pi^x$ ______
3. $y = -12 \cdot x^{10}$ ______

Graph the following exponential equations.

4. $y = \frac{1}{6} \cdot 3^x$

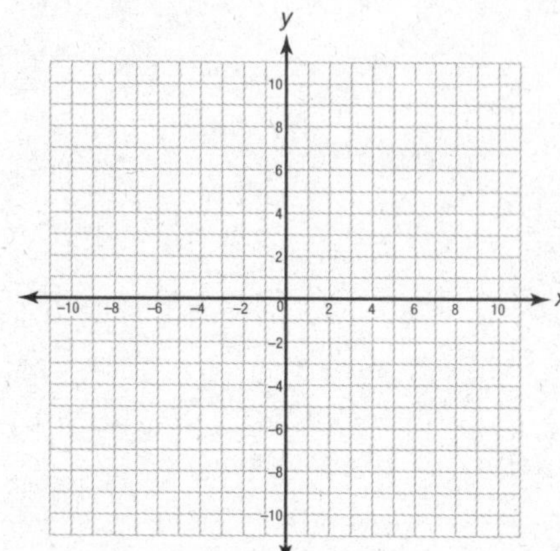

5. $y = 6 \cdot \left(\frac{1}{4}\right)^x$

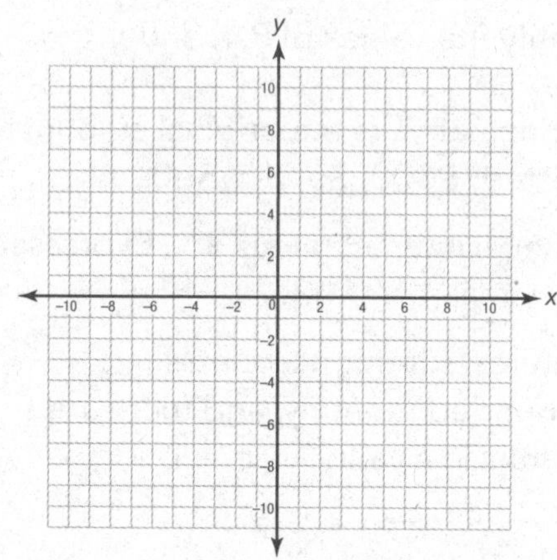

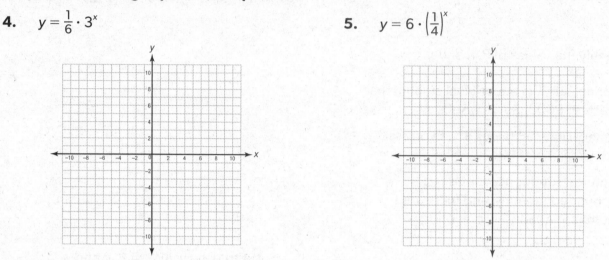

Find the base, *b*, for the exponential equation of the form $y = a \cdot b^x$ that describes each situation.

6. A colony of fruit flies doubles in population every day. The variable *y* gives the number of fruit flies after *x* days. $b =$ ______

7. Enrollment at a preschool has dropped by 4.5% each year. The variable *y* gives the number of students at the school after *x* years. $b =$ ______

The base is equal to $1 - r$, where *r* is the percent decrease expressed as a decimal.

8. A savings account earns 3% annual interest, compounded annually. The variable *y* gives the amount of money in the account after *x* years. $b =$ ______

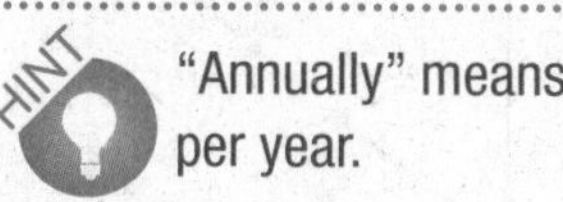

"Annually" means once per year.

Write an equation for each situation.

9. Sanjay bought a car for $18,500. According to his insurance company, the value of the car depreciates 5% each year. What will the value of the car be *x* years after Sanjay purchased it?

______

10. A colony of bacteria doubles in population every 24 hours. If there were 20 bacteria initially, how many bacteria will there be after *x* days?

______

Graph the relationship in each situation.

11. Membership in the Parents' Association at an elementary school has increased each year for the past 5 years by an average of 6%. This year, there were 211 members. Make a graph to represent the number of people in the Parents' Association over the next 10 years, assuming this trend continues.

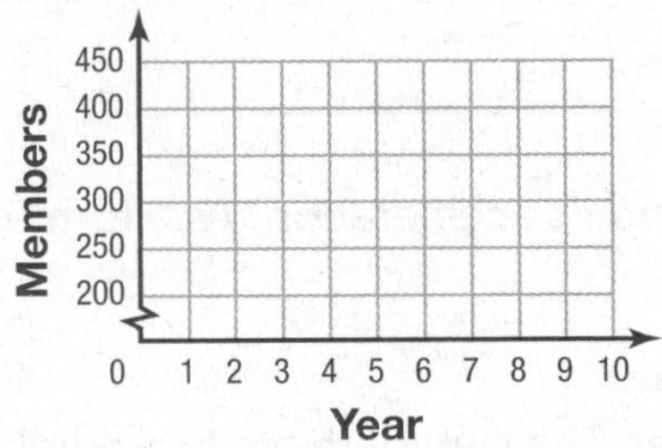

12. A scientist has a sample of 1,500 grams of flerovium-289, a radioisotope with a half-life of 30 seconds. Graph the amount of flerovium-289 in the sample over the next 3 minutes.

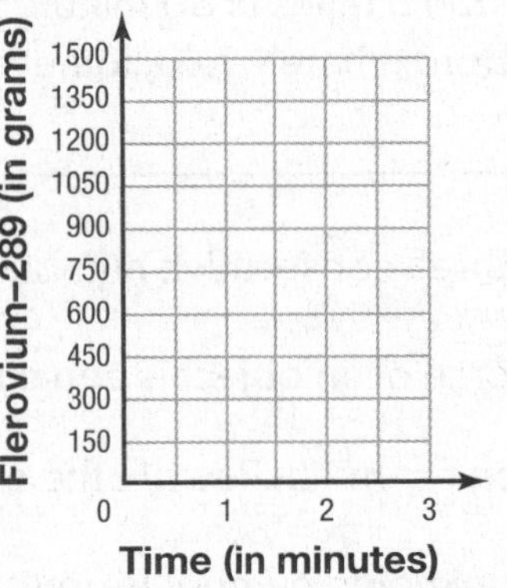

Solve.

13. PREDICT When a coffee shop opened at 6 A.M., there were 4 customers. At 7 A.M. there were 6 customers, and at 8 A.M. there were 9 customers. The number of customers continues to increase exponentially. Graph the number of customers in the coffee shop from 6 A.M. to noon. When will there be more than 30 customers in the coffee shop?

____

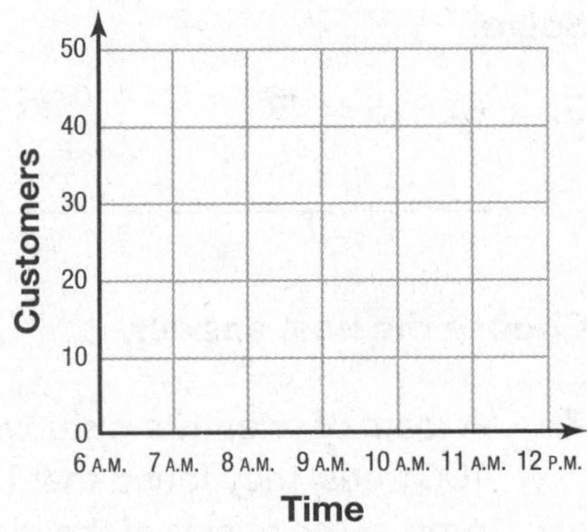

14. COMPARE Javier plans to invest $2,000 in a certificate of deposit, or CD, for a period of 10 years. His bank offers two types of CDs. The Super Saver has an annual interest rate of 4% compounded quarterly. The Thrifty Thriver has an annual interest rate of 4.5% compounded annually. Graph the amount of money that would be in each account for the next 10 years. Which option will give Javier more for his investment?

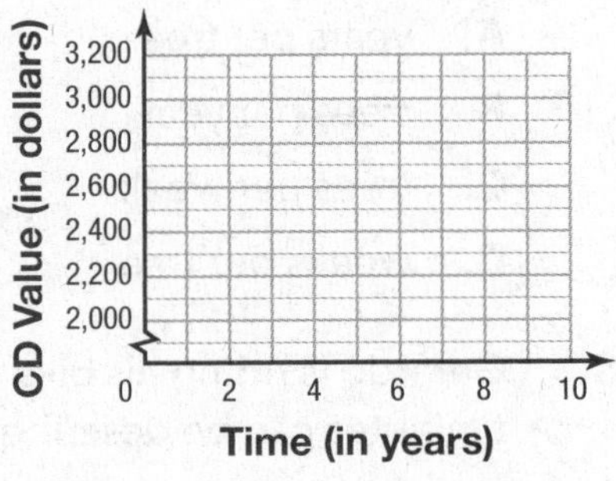

____

UNIT 1

Review

Solve each problem.

1. To qualify for a race, a runner must be able to run at a pace of at least 15 kilometers per hour. Noah ran 5 miles in 30 minutes. Does he qualify for the race? Explain your answer. (Note: There are approximately 1.6 kilometers in a mile.)

____

2. Find three consecutive numbers whose sum is 156. ____________

3. The force of an object is equal to the product of its mass and its acceleration. As a formula, this is written $f = m \cdot a$. Rewrite the equation by solving for m. ____________

4. One unknown number is double another unknown number. The sum of these two numbers is less than 58. Find the largest two integers that fit this description. ____________

Solve.

5. $6x + 5 = 47$

____

6. $2y + 29 = 8 - 5y$

____

Choose the best answer.

7. A team of scientists is studying the effects of a plant disease on a forest. In a population of 100 trees, they found that 12 of the trees contracted the disease in one month. They need to predict the effects of the disease over the next decade. Which of the following units should the answer be given in?

A. years per tree
B. trees per year
C. trees per week
D. weeks per tree

8. Gerardo is riding his bike to the movie theater. His distance in miles from the theater after t minutes can be described by the equation $9 - 0.2t$. Which of the following is true?

A. Gerardo is riding his bike at a rate of 0.2 mile per hour.
B. Gerardo is riding his bike at a rate of 9 miles per minute.
C. When he started, Gerardo was 0.2 mile from the theater.
D. When he started, Gerardo was 9 miles from the theater.

Interpret the parts of the given expression.

9. A population of wild hares doubles in size each month. The number of hares after m months can be described by the expression $22 \cdot 2^m$. Interpret the meaning of the constant 22.

____

10. Jean is opening a bank account with money that she got for her birthday. She will deposit money into the account each month. Her bank balance can be described by the expression $250 + 35m$. Explain what the quantities 250, 35, and m represent in the expression. Then explain what the quantity $35m$ represents.

____

____

____

Identify constraints on the variable.

11. A carpenter charges \$120 per job plus \$60 for each hour or portion of an hour. His fee for a job lasting h hours can be described by the equation $f = 120 + 60h$. What are the constraints on the variable h?

____

____

Choose the best answer.

12. The film club needs at least \$450 to hold a film screening. They have \$225, and they are selling used DVDs at a profit of \$5 each to raise the rest. Which of the following inequalities can be used to find the minimum number of DVDs they must sell to put on the screening?

A. $5d + 225 \geq 450$

B. $5d + 450 \geq 225$

C. $225d + 5 < 450$

D. $5d + 225 < 450$

13. Gina is adding a lace border to a circular pillow. The radius of the pillow is 8 inches, and she needs to decide how much lace to buy. Which length should she buy?

A. 16π inches

B. 50.265 inches

C. 51 inches

D. 100 inches

Write an equation to model the situation.

14. The number of bacteria in a sample quadruples every 24 hours. There were 20 bacteria in the sample initially. Write an equation to find b, the number of bacteria in the sample after d days.

____

Write and graph an equation to model the situation.

15. Padma works as a babysitter. She charges a \$10 fee to cover her transportation costs plus \$13 per hour to watch one child. Write an equation that gives her total pay, y, for a job lasting x hours.

____

Graph your equation on the coordinate grid on the right. Be sure to label the axes.

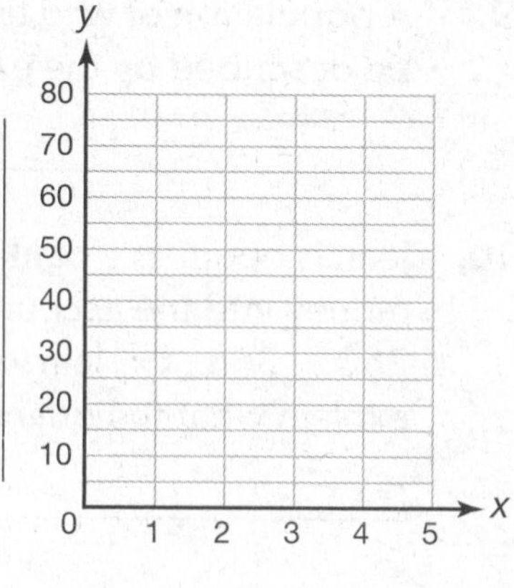

The following problems show solutions to linear equations. Justify each step with a property of equality or a property of real numbers.

16. $8x - 1 = 5x - 13$

$3x - 1 = -13$ Subtraction property of equality

$3x = -12$ _______________

$x = -4$ _______________

17. $-30 = 3(6 - 2x) - 18$

$-30 = 18 - 6x - 18$ _______________

$-30 = 18 - 18 - 6x$ _______________

$-30 = 0 - 6x$ Additive inverse property

$-30 = -6x$ _______________

$5 = x$ Division property of equality

$x = 5$ _______________

Describe the constraints on the variable in the equation.

18. As a grocery packer, Jason makes \$8 per hour. He also gets occasional tips from customers. After working a shift of h hours, Jason's pay, P, is described by the inequality $P \geq 8h$. What are the constraints of the variable P?

____

Solve.

19. Atsuo works as a salesman. He makes \$550 per week plus a commission of 10% on anything he sells. His pay each week, P, can be described by the equation $P = 550 + 0.1S$, where S is the total amount of his sales. He wants to figure out how much he needs to sell in order to make \$1,000 next week. Rewrite the equation to isolate S. Then, find the amount of sales he needs.

____

Solve the inequality and graph the solution.

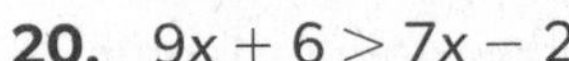

20. $9x + 6 > 7x - 2$

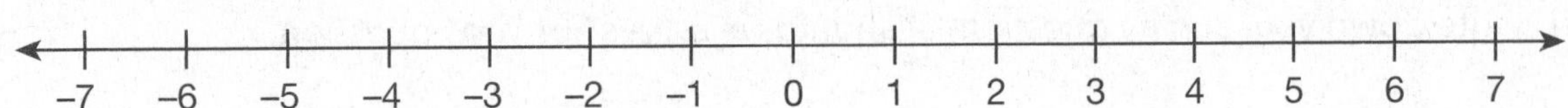

Answer the following questions.

21. PLAN Mrs. Chu owns a used car dealership. For the past 2 years, she has kept track of the number of cars sold during each quarter. She needs to create a bar graph for the following information.

Quarter	1	2	3	4	5	6	7	8
Number of Cars Sold	131	112	87	95	109	145	102	97

What variable should go on each axis? What scale should she use?

____

____

22. APPLY A kitten was born weighing 90 grams and gained 10 grams each day during the first week.

Define variables and write an equation to describe the kitten's weight over time.

____

____

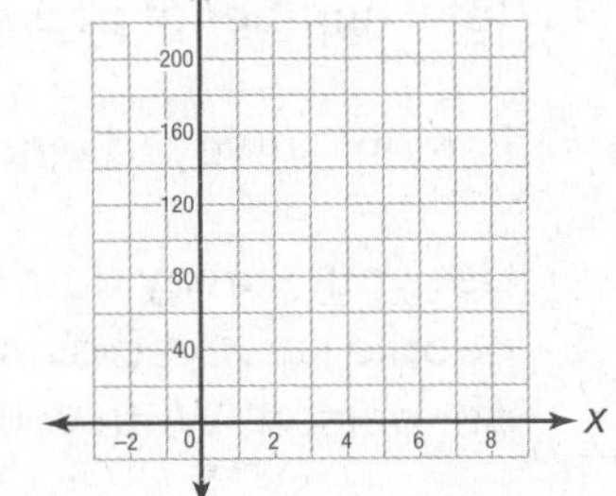

Graph your equation on the coordinate grid.
Do all of the points on your graph apply to the situation? Explain.

____

____

____

GATHER DATA AND MAKE PREDICTIONS

For this activity, you will work in teams and survey your classmates, and then use the data to make predictions about all of the students in the school.

Use the tally chart below and survey every student in your class or in your group about something in their lives. For example, you can ask if they own a cat or dog, if they have a brother or a sister, or if they have ever been to a particular place or eaten at a certain restaurant. First, write down your survey question—it should be a "yes" or "no" question.

____

Now, conduct your survey and fill in the tally chart below.

Yes	No

Review your results and make some calculations.

Total who answered "Yes": __________

Total who answered "No": __________

Total number of people surveyed: __________

Percent surveyed who answered "Yes" __________

Use your survey data to write a statistic, and present the statistic as a rate. For example, if 23% of people surveyed own a dog, then there are 23 dog owners per 100 people, or 0.23 dog owners per person. Write your statistic.

____

What is the total number of students enrolled in your school? __________

Use this information, along with your statistic, to make a prediction about the students in your school.

____

Finally, use your data to write and graph an equation. The equation should allow you to predict something about a group of any number of students, such as how many students in a class of 20 would have a dog. Be sure to choose a scale that makes sense for each axis and give your graph a title.

Equation: ______________________________

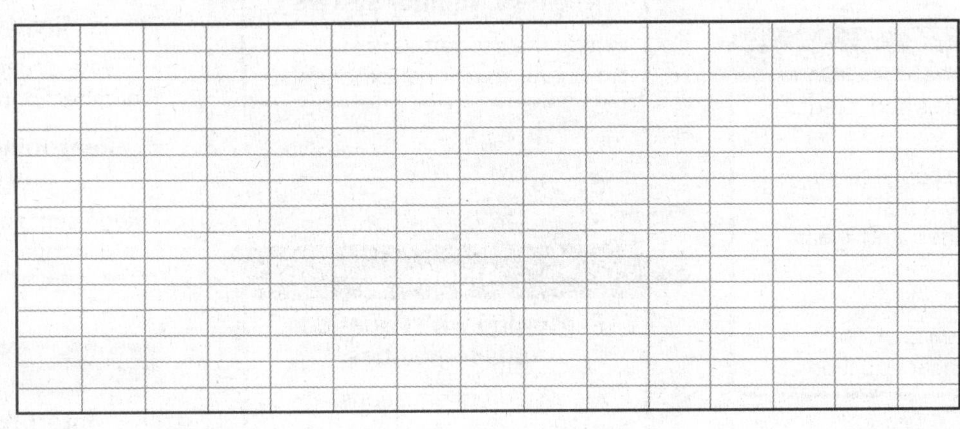

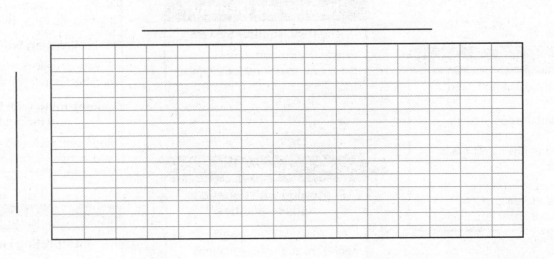

Describe the constraints on the variables in your equation and on the points on your graph.

____

____

____

Grade 8

The Number System

Know that there are numbers that are not rational, and approximate them by rational numbers.

Expressions & Equations

Work with radicals and integer exponents.

Understand the connections between proportional relationships, lines, and linear equations.

Analyze and solve linear equations and pairs of simultaneous linear equations.

Functions

Define, evaluate, and compare functions.

Use functions to model relationships between quantities.

Algebra I

Number and Quantity

The Real Number System

Extend the properties of exponents to rational exponents.

Algebra

Reasoning with Equations and Inequalities

Solve systems of equations.

Represent and solve equations and inequalities graphically.

Functions

Interpreting Functions

Understand the concept of a function and use function notation.

Interpret functions that arise in applications in terms of the context.

Analyze functions using different representations.

Building Functions

Build a function that models the relationship between two quantities.

Build new functions from existing functions.

Linear, Quadratic, and Exponential Models

Construct and compare linear, quadratic, and exponential models and solve problems.

Interpret expressions for functions in terms of the situation they model.

Geometry & Algebra II

Algebra

Seeing Structure in Expressions

Write expressions in equivalent forms to solve problems.

Creating Equations

Create equations that describe numbers or relationships.

Reasoning with Equations and Inequalities

Represent and solve equations and inequalities graphically.

Functions

Interpreting Functions

Interpret functions that arise in applications in terms of the context.

Building Functions

Build a function that models the relationship between two quantities.

Build new functions from existing functions.

Geometry

Congruence

Experiment with transformations in the plane.

Understand congruence in terms of rigid motions.

Similarity, Right Triangles, and Trigonometry

Understand similarity in terms of similarity transformations.

Expressing Geometric Properties with Equations

Use coordinates to prove simple geometric theorems algebraically.

Unit 2
Linear and Exponential Relationships

Lesson 10 Rational Exponents 70
Lesson 11 Functions 76
Lesson 12 Key Features of Functions 82
Lesson 13 Average Rate of Change 92
Lesson 14 Graphing Functions 100
Lesson 15 Solving Systems of Linear Equations 108
Lesson 16 Using Functions to Solve Equations 116
Lesson 17 Graphing Inequalities 124
Lesson 18 Translating Functions 134
Lesson 19 Reflecting Functions 144
Lesson 20 Stretching and Shrinking Functions 150
Lesson 21 Functions in Context 160
Lesson 22 Arithmetic Sequences 166
Lesson 23 Geometric Sequences 172
Unit 2 Review 178
Unit 2 Performance Task 182

Rational Exponents

UNDERSTAND An exponential expression includes a **base** raised to an **exponent**, or **power**. The properties of exponents can help you simplify many exponential expressions and solve equations involving exponents. Some of those properties are listed below.

Product of powers:	$a^n \cdot a^m = a^{n+m}$
Power of a product:	$(ab)^m = a^m b^m$
Power of a power:	$(a^n)^m = a^{n \cdot m}$
Power of zero:	$a^0 = 1$ for all $a \neq 0$
Quotient of powers:	$\frac{a^m}{a^n} = a^{m-n}$ for all $a \neq 0$
Power of a quotient:	$\left(\frac{a}{b}\right)^m = \frac{a^m}{b^m}$ for all $b \neq 0$
Negative powers:	$a^{-n} = \frac{1}{a^n}$ and $\frac{1}{a^{-n}} = a^n$ for all $a \neq 0$

An exponential expression can be evaluated for any **rational exponent**. Until now, you have worked primarily with integer powers, but sometimes you may need to simplify or evaluate an exponential expression for other powers. The properties of exponents can help you rewrite expressions with fractional exponents in a more familiar form.

You know that $2 \cdot \frac{1}{2} = 1$, $3^1 = 3$, and $\sqrt{9} = 3$. By applying the substitution property of equality and the power of a power property, you can find an equivalent form of a fractional exponent.

$3^1 = 3$	Substitute $2 \cdot \frac{1}{2}$ for 1.
$3^{2 \cdot \frac{1}{2}} = 3$	Apply the power of a power property.
$(3^2)^{\frac{1}{2}} = 3$	Evaluate inside the parentheses. Substitute $\sqrt{9}$ for 3.
$9^{\frac{1}{2}} = \sqrt{9}$	

Raising a number to the power $\frac{1}{2}$ is equivalent to taking its square root.

In general, an exponential expression with a fractional exponent involves a **root**. In converting between the exponential and **radical** forms, the base becomes the **radicand**, the denominator of the fraction becomes the **index** of the root, and the numerator of the fraction becomes an integer exponent for the expression.

A base a with exponent $\frac{1}{n}$ is the same as the nth root of the number a.

$a^{\frac{1}{n}} = \sqrt[n]{a}$ $\qquad$ $11^{\frac{1}{3}} = \sqrt[3]{11}$

A base a with exponent $\frac{m}{n}$ is the same as the nth root of the number a raised to the mth power.

$a^{\frac{m}{n}} = (\sqrt[n]{a})^m = \sqrt[n]{a^m}$ $\qquad$ $11^{\frac{5}{2}} = (\sqrt{11})^5 = \sqrt{11^5}$

Connect

Simplify the expression $\frac{\sqrt{x} \cdot \sqrt[3]{x}}{\sqrt[6]{x^5}} + x^{\frac{3}{2}}$.

1 Rewrite each radical expression using exponents.

In the expression $\sqrt{x}$, the unwritten index is 2, so $\sqrt{x} = x^{\frac{1}{2}}$.

In the expression $\sqrt[3]{x}$, the index is 3, so $\sqrt[3]{x} = x^{\frac{1}{3}}$.

In the expression $\sqrt[6]{x^5}$, the index is 6 and the exponent is 5, so $\sqrt[6]{x^5} = x^{\frac{5}{6}}$.

Now, rewrite the expression with no radicals.

$$\frac{\sqrt{x} \cdot \sqrt[3]{x}}{\sqrt[6]{x^5}} + x^{\frac{3}{2}} = \frac{x^{\frac{1}{2}} \cdot x^{\frac{1}{3}}}{x^{\frac{5}{6}}} + x^{\frac{3}{2}}$$

2 Simplify the numerator of the fraction.

Use the product of powers property to multiply the terms.

$x^{\frac{1}{2}} \cdot x^{\frac{1}{3}}$

$x^{\frac{1}{2} + \frac{1}{3}}$

$x^{\frac{3}{6} + \frac{2}{6}}$

$x^{\frac{5}{6}}$

Now, rewrite the expression.

$$\frac{x^{\frac{1}{2}} \cdot x^{\frac{1}{3}}}{x^{\frac{5}{6}}} + x^{\frac{3}{2}} = \frac{x^{\frac{5}{6}}}{x^{\frac{5}{6}}} + x^{\frac{3}{2}}$$

3 Simplify the fraction.

Notice that the numerator and denominator of the fraction are identical. Any fraction with the same numerator and denominator is equal to 1.

$$\frac{x^{\frac{5}{6}}}{x^{\frac{5}{6}}} + x^{\frac{3}{2}} = 1 + x^{\frac{3}{2}}$$

4 Rewrite the exponential expression as a radical.

To rewrite the expression $x^{\frac{3}{2}}$ as a radical, the base, x, will be the radicand, the numerator of the fraction, 3, will be an exponent, and the denominator, 2, will be the index of the radical.

▶ $1 + x^{\frac{3}{2}} = 1 + (\sqrt{x})^3$

Since the expression has a rational exponent that is an improper fraction, it can be written in another way.

$$x^{\frac{3}{2}} = x^{1 + \frac{1}{2}} = (x^1)(x^{\frac{1}{2}}) = x\sqrt{x}$$

▶ $1 + x^{\frac{3}{2}} = 1 + x\sqrt{x}$

TRY

Simplify.

$(5^{\frac{1}{c}})^d \cdot \frac{1}{5^{-\frac{d}{c}}}$

EXAMPLE A Use a table to graph the equation $y = 4^x$. Then, use the graph to confirm values of y for fractional values of x.

1 Make a table of values.

x	$y = 4^x$	y
-1	$y = 4^{-1} = \frac{1}{4}$	$\frac{1}{4}$
0	$y = 4^0 = 1$	1
1	$y = 4^1 = 4$	4
2	$y = 4^2 = 16$	16

2 Graph the equation using the values from the table.

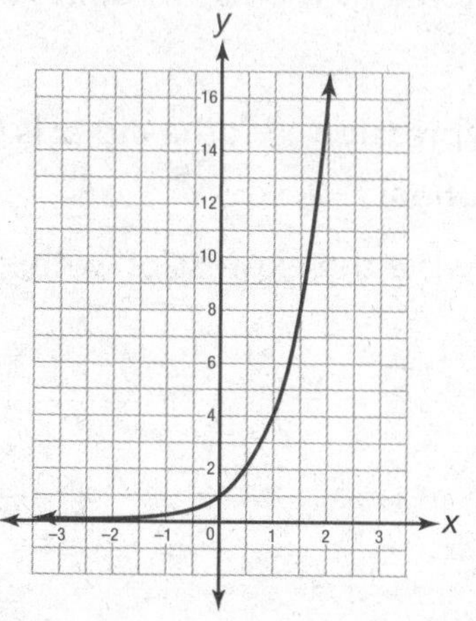

3 Make a table of values with fractional values of x.

x	$y = 4^x$	y
$\frac{1}{4}$	$y = 4^{\frac{1}{4}} = (2^2)^{\frac{1}{4}} = 2^{\frac{2}{4}} = \sqrt{2} \approx 1.414$	1.414
$\frac{1}{3}$	$y = 4^{\frac{1}{3}} = \sqrt[3]{4} \approx 1.587$	1.587
$\frac{1}{2}$	$y = 4^{\frac{1}{2}} = \sqrt{4} = 2$	2
$\frac{3}{2}$	$y = 4^{\frac{3}{2}} = (\sqrt{4})^3 = 2^3 = 8$	8

4 Compare the values in the table to the graph.

According to the equation, when $x = \frac{1}{4}$ and $x = \frac{1}{3}$, y is close to $1\frac{1}{2}$. The graph passes near $1\frac{1}{2}$ for these values of x.

When $x = \frac{1}{2}$, $y = 2$. The graph has a y-value of 2 halfway between the x-values of 0 and 1.

When $x = \frac{3}{2}$, $y = 8$. The graph has a y-value of 8 halfway between the x-values of 1 and 2.

▶ The values of the equation for fractional values of x match the graph above.

DISCUSS

Graph the equation on your graphing calculator and use the TRACE or TABLE function to confirm your answers. Are your calculations for $x = \frac{1}{4}$ and $x = \frac{1}{3}$ more or less accurate than those on the calculator?

EXAMPLE B Solve the equation $3^{\frac{x}{2}} = 9\sqrt{3}$ for x.

1 Write all terms as exponential expressions with the same base.

The left side of the equation has a base of 3, so rewrite the expression $9\sqrt{3}$ as an exponential expression with a base of 3.

$9\sqrt{3}$	Substitute 3^2 for 9.
$3^2 \cdot \sqrt{3}$	Rewrite the radical as an exponential expression.
$3^2 \cdot 3^{\frac{1}{2}}$	Use the product of powers property.
$3^{2+\frac{1}{2}}$	Find a common denominator and add.
$3^{\frac{5}{2}}$	

2 Solve the equation.

Substitute the expression you found above for the right side of the equation.

$3^{\frac{x}{2}} = 9\sqrt{3}$	Substitute $3^{\frac{5}{2}}$ for $9\sqrt{3}$.
$3^{\frac{x}{2}} = 3^{\frac{5}{2}}$	Since the bases are equal, set the exponents equal to each other.
$\frac{x}{2} = \frac{5}{2}$	Multiply both sides of the equation by 2.
$x = 5$	

▶ The solution to the equation is $x = 5$.

TRY

Solve the equation $64^y = 16$ for y.

Practice

Rewrite each radical expression as an exponential expression with a rational exponent.

1. $\sqrt{6^7}$ __________

2. $\sqrt[4]{2^3}$ __________

3. $\sqrt[5]{x^2}$ __________

REMEMBER The index of the radical becomes the denominator of the fractional exponent.

Rewrite each exponential expression as a radical expression.

4. $5^{\frac{2}{3}}$ __________

5. $12^{\frac{n}{2}}$ __________

6. $y^{\frac{4}{5}}$ __________

Simplify each expression by using the properties of exponents.

7. $(16^{\frac{1}{4}}) \cdot (16^{\frac{5}{4}})$ __________

8. $\dfrac{27^2}{27^{\frac{2}{3}}}$ __________

9. $(z^{\frac{1}{4}})^2$ __________

REMEMBER To multiply exponential expressions with the same base, add the exponents.

Choose the best answer.

10. Which is equivalent to $x^{\frac{5}{3}}$?

A. $x\sqrt[3]{x^2}$

B. $x^2(\sqrt[3]{x})$

C. $\sqrt[5]{x^3}$

D. $x\sqrt[5]{x^2}$

11. Which is equivalent to $\sqrt[6]{27n^{12}}$?

A. $3n^2$

B. $n\sqrt{3}$

C. $n^2\sqrt{3}$

D. $\sqrt{3n^3}$

Simplify each expression.

12. $(x^{\frac{1}{3}})(x^{\frac{4}{6}}) + (y^{\frac{1}{6}})^3$

13. $\left(\frac{a}{\sqrt[3]{a}}\right)^3$

14. $\left(\frac{b^{\frac{5}{2}}}{\sqrt{b}}\right) - (4b^4)^{\frac{1}{2}}$

15. $7(\sqrt[5]{32c^{15}})$

Solve each equation.

16. $2^y = \sqrt{8}$

17. $3\sqrt{3} = 3^{2x}$

18. $125^{\frac{a}{3}} = 5$

19. TRANSFORM Write the expression $\sqrt{32}$ in three different but equivalent ways.

20. ORDER Write each expression as a power of 2 with a rational exponent.

$16^{\frac{1}{3}}$: __________

$2\sqrt{2}$: __________

$\sqrt[8]{4}$: __________

$\frac{1}{2}$: __________

Using the exponents, order the terms from least to greatest.

Functions

UNDERSTAND A **relation** is a set of ordered pairs of the form (x, y). The equation $y = x + 4$ describes a relation. It relates the value of y to the value of x. A relation can be represented as an equation, a graph, a table, a mapping diagram, or a list of ordered pairs.

A **function** is a special kind of relation in which each **input**, the first value in the ordered pair, is mapped to one and only one **output**, the second value in the ordered pair.

This relation is not a function:
(**1**, 6), (**3**, 8), (**3**, 9)
The input 3 is assigned to two different outputs.

This relation is a function:
(**1**, 6), (**3**, 8), (**5**, 10)
Each input is assigned to only one output.

The set of all possible inputs for a function is called the function's **domain**. The set of all possible outputs for a function is called its **range**. The domain and range are sets that consist of values called **elements**. Look at the function shown in the mapping diagram. The domain for that function is the numbers $-4, -3, -2, -1$, and 0, or the set $\{-4, -3, -2, -1, 0\}$. The range is $\{-5, -4, -3, 2\}$.

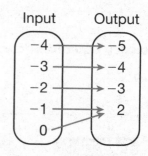

Input		Output
−4	→	−5
−3	→	−4
−2	→	−3
−1	→	2
0	→	2

A function can be written as an equation using function notation. In the equation $f(x) = 2^x + 1$, the notation $f(x)$ is read as "f of x." It takes the place of y and stands for the output of the function for the input x. So, when $x = 2$, $f(x)$ becomes $f(2)$, and $f(2) = 2^2 + 1 = 5$. This means that the function f includes the ordered pair (2, 5).

This same function can be represented by a graph. By replacing $f(x)$ with y, the equation can be graphed on the xy-coordinate plane. The set of all the points on that graph is the function.

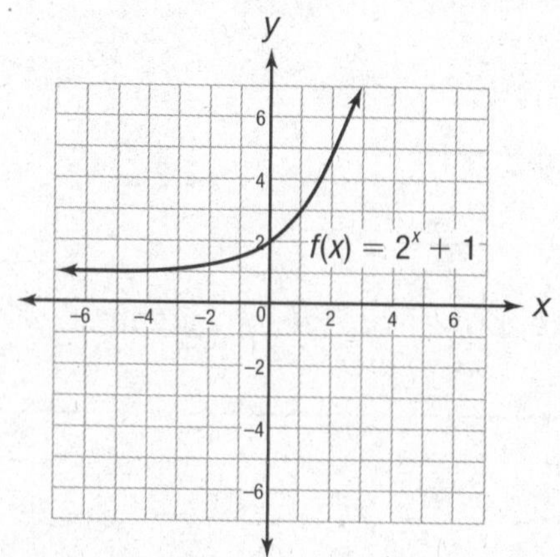

Most often, a function is named by the letter f and has input x, but a function can be named by almost any letter or symbol. For example, a function might be named $g(x)$ or $a(x)$. A function in another situation might be named $h(t)$, so that the variable representing the input is t.

Connect

Does this graph represent a function?

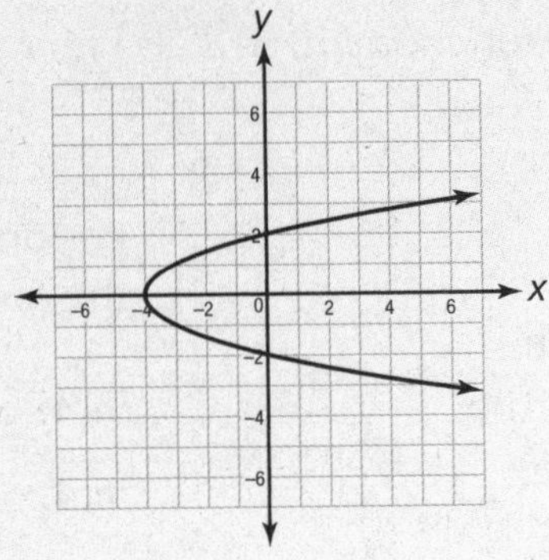

1 Perform the **vertical line test** by drawing a vertical line through the graph at $x = 5$.

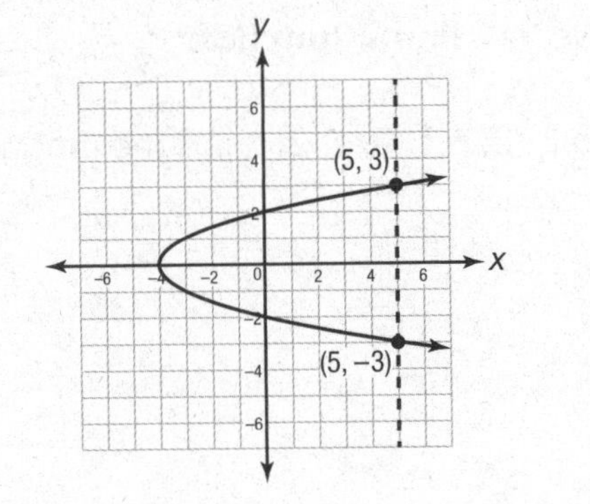

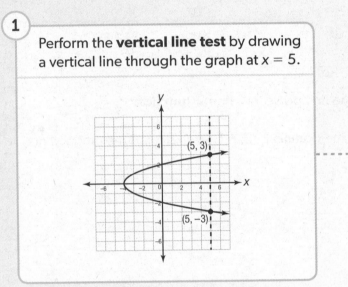

2 Determine if the graph represents a function.

If any vertical line drawn through a graph passes through more than one point, the graph does not represent a function. The vertical line passes through two points: (5, 3) and (5, −3). This means that the input value of 5 maps to two different outputs, 3 and −3, so the graph does not show a function.

▶ The graph does not pass the vertical line test. It does not represent a function.

Does this table represent a function?

x	−2	−1	0	1	2	3
$f(x)$	$-2\frac{3}{4}$	$-2\frac{1}{2}$	−2	$-2\frac{1}{2}$	$-2\frac{3}{4}$	−3

Look at the input values in the table.

No input, or x-value, appears in the table more than once, so each input corresponds to only one output.

▶ This means that the table represents a function.

Construct a mapping diagram by using the elements in the table. How can a mapping diagram help you determine if the relation is a function?

A function in which the input variable is an exponent is an **exponential function.**

EXAMPLE A Evaluate the exponential function $h(t) = 3^t + 1$ for $t = 4$.

1

Substitute 4 for *t* in the equation.

Evaluating a function means finding the output for a given input. In this case, the input is 4, so find the value of $h(4)$.

$h(t) = 3^t + 1$

$h(4) = 3^4 + 1$

2

Perform the calculations to find the output.

$h(4) = 3^4 + 1$

$h(4) = 81 + 1$

▶ $h(4) = 82$

A function in which the input variable is raised to the first power is a **linear function.**

EXAMPLE B The linear function $g(x) = 3x + 4$ has the domain $\{-2, -1, 0, 1, 2\}$. Find the range of $g(x)$.

1

Create a table of values to find all the elements in the range.

In order to find the elements of the range, evaluate the function for each value in the domain.

x	$g(x) = 3x + 4$	$g(x)$
−2	$g(-2) = 3(-2) + 4 = -2$	−2
−1	$g(-1) = 3(-1) + 4 = 1$	1
0	$g(0) = 3(0) + 4 = 4$	4
1	$g(1) = 3(1) + 4 = 7$	7
2	$g(2) = 3(2) + 4 = 10$	10

2

Collect the values of $g(x)$ into a set.

The values of $g(x)$ are −2, 1, 4, 7, and 10.

▶ The range of $g(x)$ is $\{-2, 1, 4, 7, 10\}$.

TRY

The function $P(t) = 10 \cdot 2^t$ can be used to represent the population of bacteria in a Petri dish after *t* hours. What are the values of $P(0)$ and $P(4)$? What do these values represent?

EXAMPLE C Look at the table. What values of a would make $f(x)$ a function? What values of a would indicate that $f(x)$ is **not** a function?

x	$f(x)$
−1	−1.5
3	6
a	14
6	17

1 Review the definition of a function.

Recall that a function is a relation in which every input, or x-value, maps to only one output, or $f(x)$-value.

So, if the table represents a function, no x-value can map to more than one $f(x)$-value.

2 Find possible values for a.

If $a = -1$, 3, or 6, an x-value would map to more than one $f(x)$-value. For example, if $a = -1$, the x-value −1 would map to both −1.5 and 14. This means that the relation would no longer be a function.

For any real number values of a other than −1, 3, and 6, every x-value would map to only one $f(x)$-value.

▶ The relation $f(x)$ is not a function when a is equal to −1, 3, or 6. The relation is a function when the value of a is any real number except −1, 3, and 6.

EXAMPLE D Find the value of the function $g(x) = 5x^{\frac{1}{3}}$ when $x = 8$.

1 Substitute the value of x into the function.

$g(x) = 5x^{\frac{1}{3}}$

$g(8) = 5 \cdot 8^{\frac{1}{3}}$

2 Evaluate the function.

Rewrite the rational exponent as a root. Since the denominator is 3, that will be the index of the radicand.

$g(8) = 5 \cdot 8^{\frac{1}{3}}$ Rewrite the exponent as a radical.

$g(8) = 5 \cdot \sqrt[3]{8}$

$g(8) = 5 \cdot 2$

▶ $g(8) = 10$.

TRY

Write two ordered pairs, each with the same y-coordinate. Could these two ordered pairs belong to the same function?

Practice

Determine whether each relation is a function.

1. 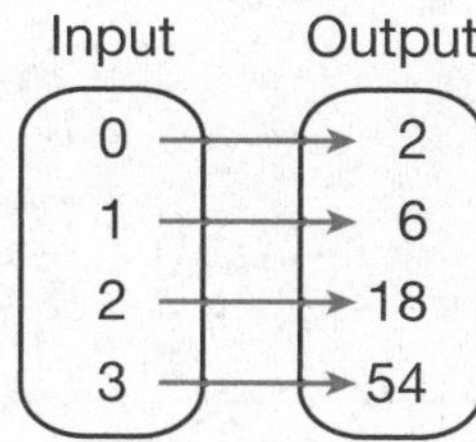

2. 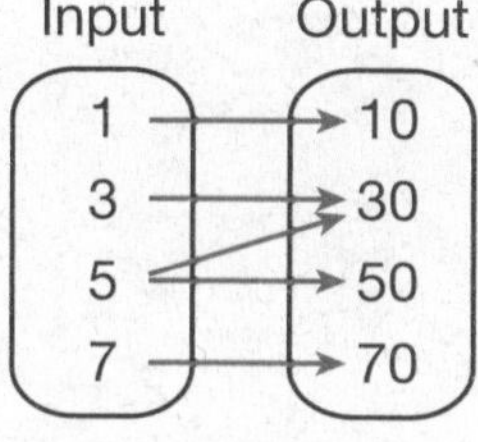

3. 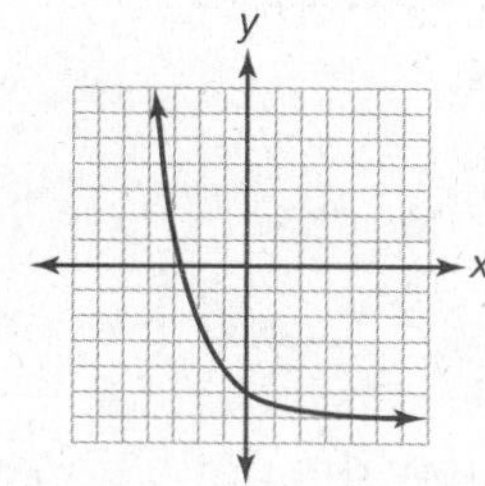

REMEMBER In a function, each input maps to only one output.

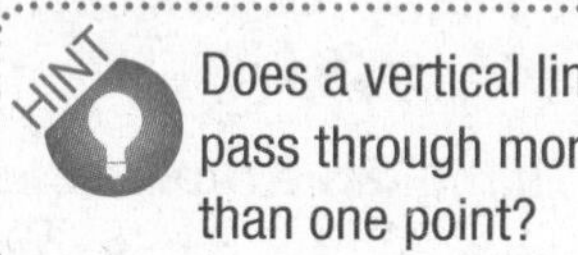

Does a vertical line pass through more than one point?

Evaluate the function for the given value of x.

4. $f(x) = 10x^{\frac{2}{3}}$ for $x = 27$

5. $g(x) = \frac{x^{\frac{1}{4}}}{9}$ for $x = 81$

Write *true* or *false* for each statement. If false, rewrite the statement so it is true.

6. The range of a function is the set of all of its inputs.

7. To graph the function $f(x) = x + 2$, you can draw the graph of $y = x + 2$ because the graph of f is the graph of the equation $y = f(x)$.

Choose the best answer.

8. Which value could **not** be substituted for a if the table represents a function?

x	$g(x)$
−3	24
a	4
1	4
2	−1

A. 1
B. 0
C. −1
D. −3

9. The function $f(x) = 2x^{\frac{2}{3}}$ has the domain {0, 1, 4, 9}. Which of the following is the range of the function?

A. {2, 2, 16, 54}
B. {0, 2, 16, 54}
C. {0, 2, 8, 162}
D. {2, 2, 16, 27}

Evaluate the functions for the inputs given. Show your work in the tables.

10.

x	$d(x) = \frac{x}{2} - 1$	$d(x)$
−4	$d(-4) =$	
−2	$d(-2) =$	
0	$d(0) =$	
2	$d(2) =$	
4	$d(4) =$	

11.

x	$f(x) = 10^x + 5$	$f(x)$
0	$f(0) =$	
1	$f(1) =$	
2	$f(2) =$	
3	$f(3) =$	
4	$f(4) =$	

Solve.

12. A ball dropped onto a hard floor from a height of 16 inches bounces back up to $\frac{1}{2}$ its previous height on each successive bounce. The function $h(b) = 16 \cdot \left(\frac{1}{2}\right)^b$ can be used to represent this situation. To what height, in inches, will the ball rise on its third bounce? (Hint: Evaluate $h(b) = 16 \cdot \left(\frac{1}{2}\right)^b$ for $b = 3$.) Show your work.

____

____

13. EVALUATE The total charge for a babysitting job that lasts t hours can be represented by the function $c(t) = 2 + 9t$. Evaluate this function for the domain {1, 2, 3}. Show your work and briefly explain what each pair of values means in this problem situation.

____

____

14. JUSTIFY If you switch the domain and range of a function, will the relation that results sometimes be a function? Will it always be a function? Give examples to justify your answer.

____

____

Key Features of Functions

Intercepts and End Behavior

UNDERSTAND The graphs and tables of functions contain various key features. These key features are often important for understanding functions and using them to solve problems.

The **x-intercept** of a function is the point $(a, 0)$ at which the graph intersects the x-axis. The **y-intercept** is the point $(0, b)$ at which the graph intersects the y-axis. In the graph of $f(x) = 3^x - 3$ shown, the x-intercept is $(1, 0)$ and the y-intercept is $(0, -2)$.

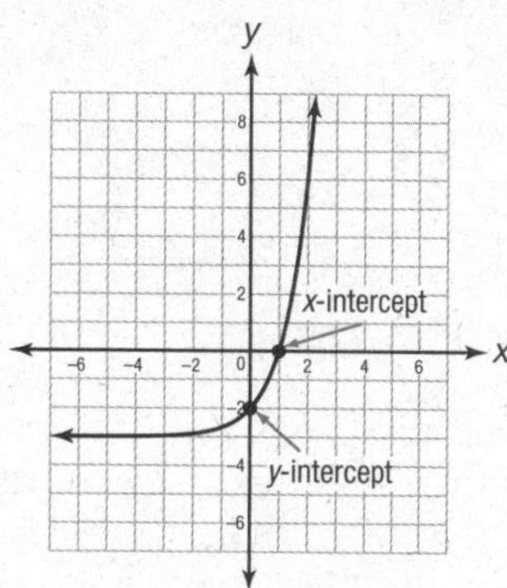

x	f(x)	
-2	$-2\frac{8}{9}$	
-1	$-2\frac{2}{3}$	
0	-2	← y-intercept
1	0	← x-intercept
2	6	

You can locate the x-intercept in a table by finding the row whose y-value is 0. The y-intercept is in the row whose x-value is 0.

Functions can also be described in terms of their **end behavior**. In the graph of $f(x) = 3^x - 3$, look at the arrows on each end of the graph. The arrow on the right end of the curve shows that as x increases, y also continuously increases. Since the value of y is continuously increasing, this function has no **maximum** value. The arrow on the left end of the curve shows that as x decreases (becomes more negative), y approaches but never reaches -3. This line that the graph approaches but never touches is called the **asymptote** of the function. Since the graph asymptotically approaches the line $y = -3$ but never intersects it, the function has no **minimum** value.

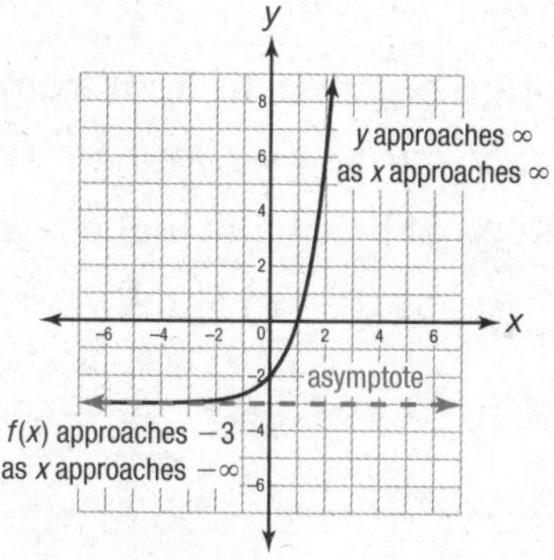

If enough values are listed in a table, you can estimate end behavior based on the values of $f(x)$. Starting from the top of the second column and moving down, notice that the value of $f(x)$ gets larger and larger. Starting from the bottom of the column and moving up, notice that $f(x)$ gets smaller (more negative) but never passes -3.

x	f(x)
-3	$-2\frac{26}{27}$
-2	$-2\frac{8}{9}$
-1	$-2\frac{2}{3}$
0	-2
1	0
2	6
3	24

↓ $f(x)$ increases without bound

↑ $f(x)$ decreases toward -3

Connect

The function $f(x) = \left(\frac{1}{2}\right)^x + 2$ is graphed below.

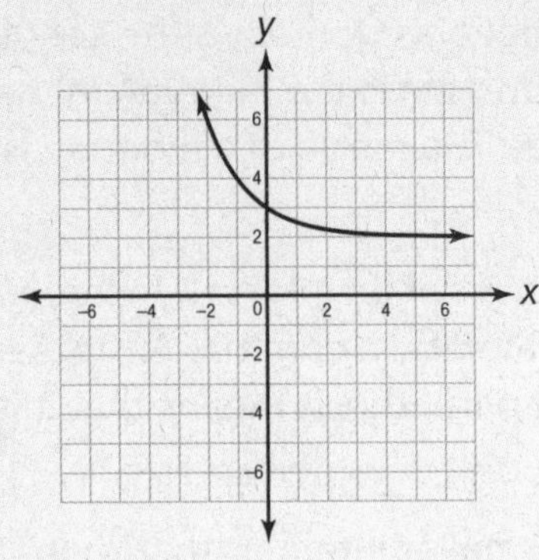

Identify the function's intercepts and describe its end behavior.

1 Find the x- and y-intercepts of the function.

Where does the graph intersect the x-axis?

The graph never intersects the x-axis, so the function does not have an x-intercept.

Where does the graph intersect the y-axis?

The graph intersects the y-axis at (0, 3). The function's y-intercept is (0, 3).

2 Describe the end behavior of the function.

What happens to the graph as x-values approach $-\infty$?

As x-values approach $-\infty$, y-values increase toward ∞.

What happens to the graph as x-values approach ∞?

As x-values approach ∞, y-values decrease toward 2.

This means that the function has an asymptote of $y = 2$.

TRY

Does the function have a minimum and a maximum? If so, what are they? If not, why not?

Intervals of Functions

UNDERSTAND Remember that a function's domain is the set of all possible inputs. For a function such as $f(x) = 3^x - 3$, the domain is the interval on the x-axis on which the function is defined, in which the graph exists. The range of a function is the interval on the y-axis containing all possible outputs.

Interval notation can be used to represent an interval. In interval notation, the end values of an interval are listed as a pair separated by a comma. A bracket beside a value means that it is included in the interval, while a parenthesis means that it is not. For example, the domain $[0, 5)$ is equivalent to $0 \leq x < 5$.

The domain can be broken up into smaller intervals that share a certain characteristic. For example, it can be useful to divide the domain into sections in which the value of $f(x)$ is positive and sections where it is negative.

Look again at a graph of the function $f(x) = 3^x - 3$. Determine the intervals where y is positive and where y is negative. The value of y is negative when $x < 1$. The value of y is positive when $x > 1$. Using interval notation, y is negative on the interval $(-\infty, 1)$ and positive on the interval $(1, \infty)$.

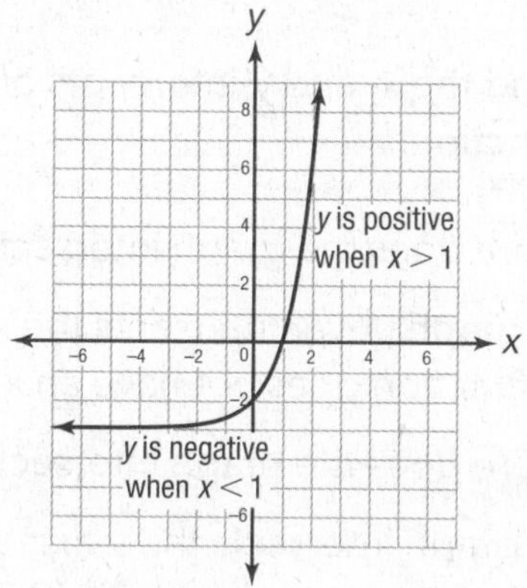

The domain can also be divided into sections where the value of $f(x)$ is increasing from left to right and where it is decreasing from left to right.

Look at the graph. From left to right, the graph is always curving upward. The value of y is always increasing as the value of x increases. This is true across the entire domain, from negative infinity $(-\infty)$ to positive infinity (∞). The function is always increasing. In other words, the interval of increase is $(-\infty, \infty)$.

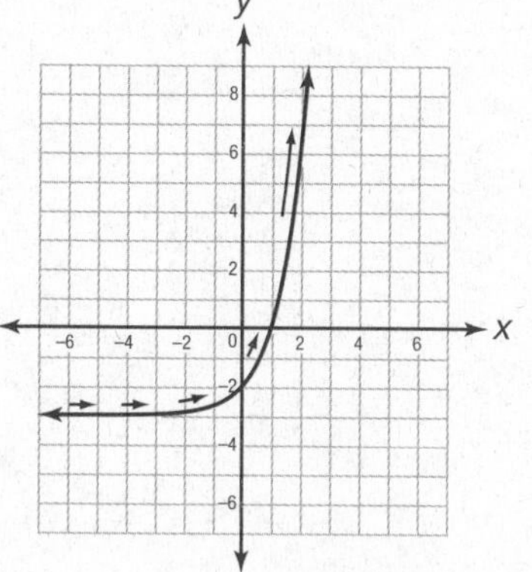

Usually, these intervals can also be determined from tables by looking at the values in the $f(x)$ column.

Connect

The graph below represents an exponential function f. The table below represents a linear function g.

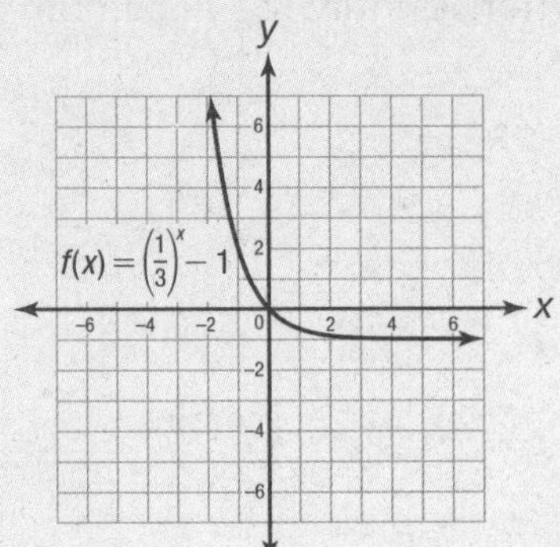

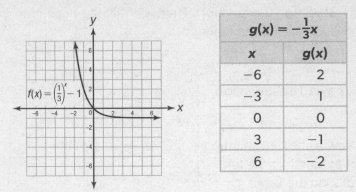

$g(x) = -\frac{1}{3}x$	
x	$g(x)$
−6	2
−3	1
0	0
3	−1
6	−2

Compare and contrast functions f and g by using these key features: domain; range; intervals of increase and decrease; and positive and negative intervals.

1 Identify the domain and range.

The end behavior of the graph of f shows that it extends indefinitely both left and right. Thus, its domain is all real numbers, or the interval $(-\infty, \infty)$.

Since f has an asymptote of $y = -1$, its range is $y > -1$, or the interval $(-1, \infty)$.

The table for function g does not list all values of x or $g(x)$, but it also does not give evidence of any boundaries (such as an asymptote). Since g is a linear function, without other information, you may assume that the domain and range are all real numbers.

2 Compare the intervals of increase and decrease.

The graph of f continuously curves downward. So, f is always decreasing.

The table for function g shows that as x-values increase, $g(x)$-values decrease, so g is also a decreasing function.

Both functions are decreasing across their entire domains. The interval of decrease is $(-\infty, \infty)$ for both functions.

3 Compare positive intervals and negative intervals for the functions.

The graph of f intercepts the x-axis at (0, 0). The third row of values in the table shows that g also has an x-intercept of (0, 0). The functions are always decreasing.

Functions f and g are both positive when $x < 0$, on the interval $(-\infty, 0)$, and negative when $x > 0$, on the interval $(0, \infty)$.

CHECK

Graph function g on the same grid as f. Compare and contrast the two graphs to check the answers on this page.

EXAMPLE A The domain of a linear function is $\{-1 \leq x \leq 2\}$. The function has an x-intercept at (1, 0) and a y-intercept at (0, −3). Graph the function. Then identify the maximum, minimum, range, and intervals of increase and decrease for the function.

1 Graph the function, paying attention to the restricted domain.

Plot the intercepts. Draw a line through the intercepts, but do not extend it to the left of −1 or to the right of 2 on the x-axis.

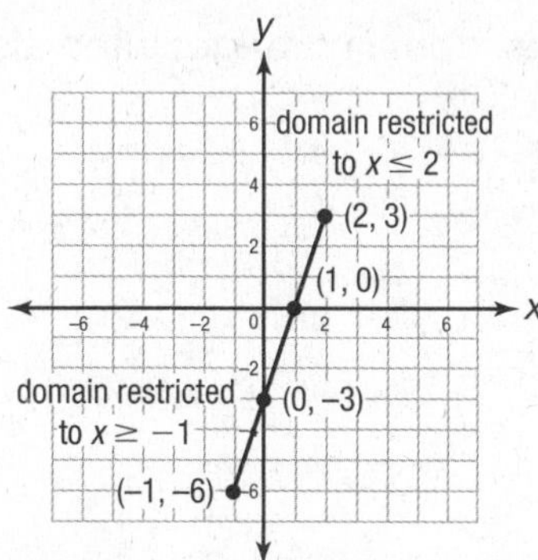

2 Describe the function's minimum, maximum, and range.

When the domain is restricted to $\{-1 \leq x \leq 2\}$, the lowest point on the graph is at (−1, −6). Thus, the minimum y-value is −6.

The highest point on the graph is at (2, 3). Thus, the maximum y-value is 3.

The range is all values of y greater than or equal to the minimum, −6, and less than or equal to the maximum, 3. This can be represented as $\{-6 \leq y \leq 3\}$.

3 Identify intervals of increase or decrease.

The line segment slants up from left to right, so the function is always increasing.

The value of y increases across the entire domain. The function increases on the interval $\{-1 \leq x \leq 2\}$.

TRY

Identify intervals where the linear function graphed above is positive and where it is negative.

EXAMPLE B A piano is being lowered from an apartment that is 18 feet above the sidewalk. The piano descends at a constant rate. The piano's elevation over time is represented by the linear function graphed below. Identify and interpret the key features of the graph.

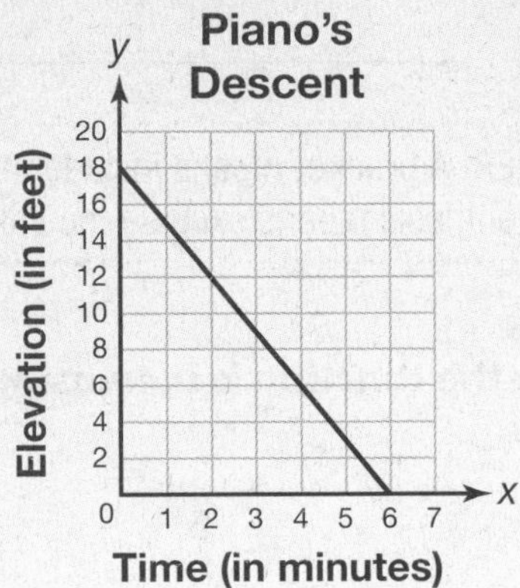

1 Identify and interpret the domain.

The graph is shown to exist on the domain [0, 6]. This domain contains the minutes over which the piano is being lowered.

2 Identify and interpret intervals of increase and decrease.

The function is decreasing for the entire domain. This means that the piano's elevation is always decreasing.

The function has no interval of increase. This makes sense because the piano is always being lowered and never being raised.

3 Identify and interpret the intercepts.

The *y*-intercept, (0, 18), represents the piano's initial elevation of 18 feet.

The *x*-intercept, (6, 0), shows that it takes 6 minutes for the piano to reach the sidewalk, at an elevation of 0 feet.

TRY

What is the range for this function? What does it represent in the problem?

Practice

Rewrite each domain in interval notation.

1. $\{5 < x < 100\}$ ______

2. $\{x \geq 0\}$ ______

3. {all real numbers} ______

REMEMBER A bracket means include the value, and a parenthesis means exclude the value.

For each graph, determine whether the function is increasing or decreasing. Identify the interval of increase or decrease.

4.

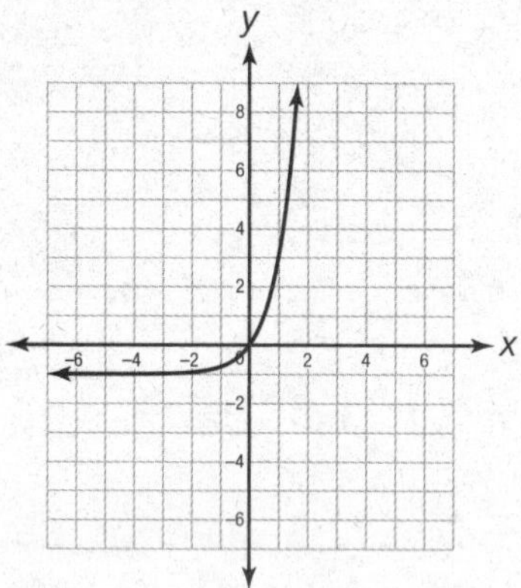

______

______

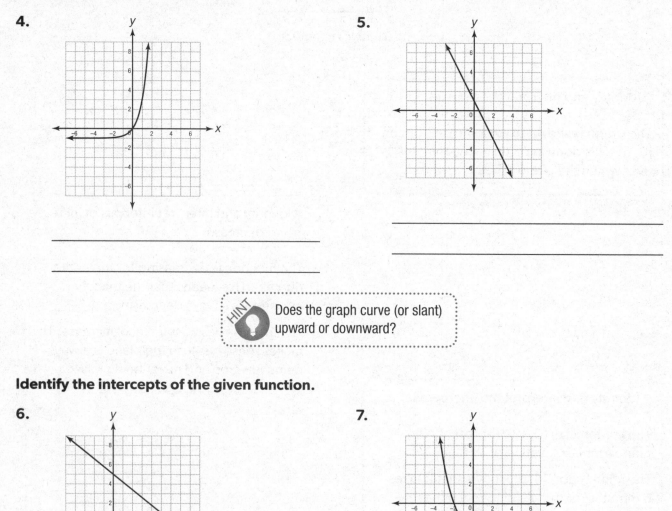

5.

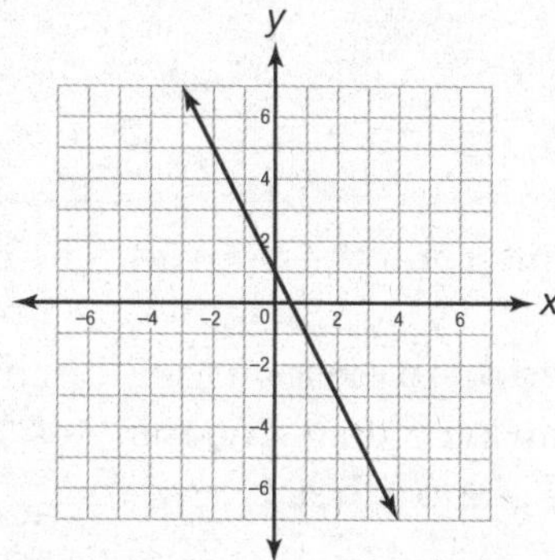

______

______

HINT Does the graph curve (or slant) upward or downward?

Identify the intercepts of the given function.

6.

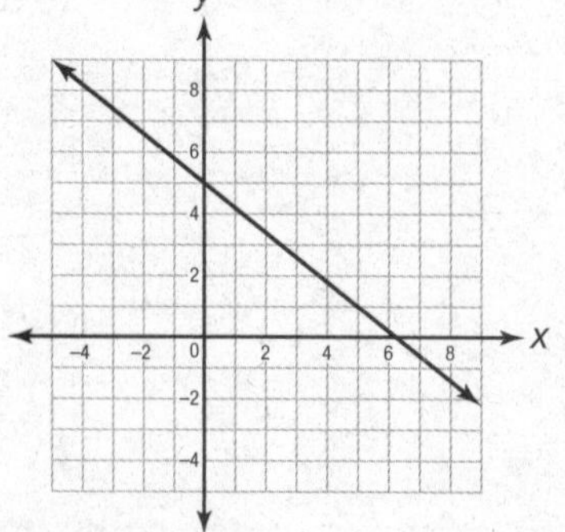

x-intercept: ______

y-intercept: ______

7.

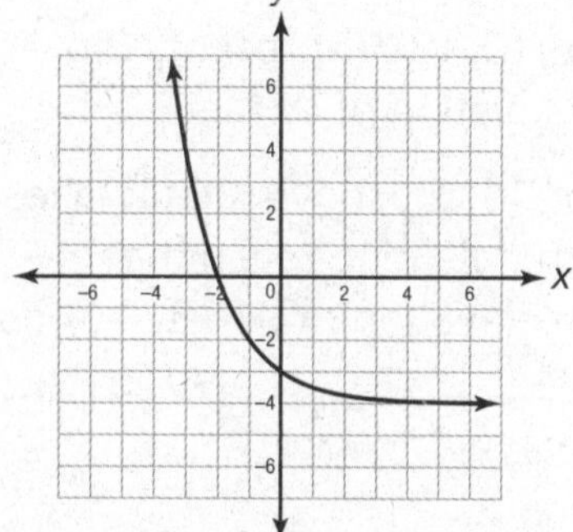

x-intercept: ______

y-intercept: ______

Identify the intercepts of the given function.

8.

x	-24	-12	0	12	24
$f(x)$	-8	-6	-4	-2	0

x-intercept: ______________

y-intercept: ______________

9.

x	-2	-1	0	1	2
$g(x)$	-9.99	-9.9	-9	0	90

x-intercept: ______________

y-intercept: ______________

Fill in each blank with an appropriate word or words.

10. A point at which a graph crosses the y-axis is a(n) ______________.

11. A function's ______________ is a line that the graph of the function approaches but never intersects.

12. The ______________ of a function describes how its $f(x)$-values change as x approaches positive infinity or negative infinity.

13. The greatest y-value on the graph of a function is the function's ______________.

Choose the best answer.

14. Which statement about this function is **not** true?

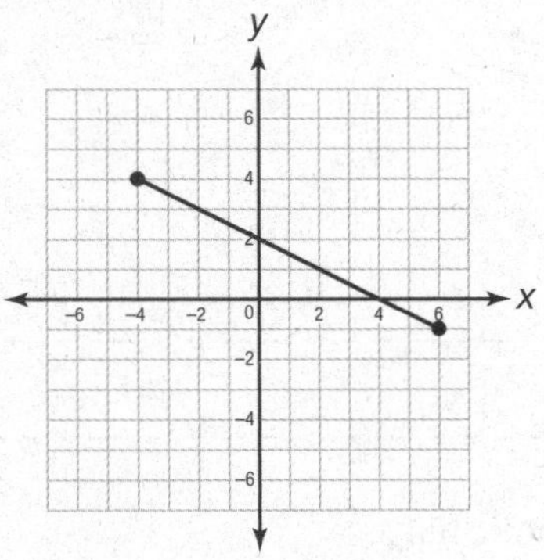

A. Its domain is $\{-4 \leq x \leq 6\}$.

B. Its range is $\{-1 \leq y \leq 4\}$.

C. It has a y-intercept at (0, 2).

D. It has a maximum of 6.

15. The table below shows some ordered pairs for an exponential function.

x	$f(x)$
-1	$-\frac{5}{6}$
0	0
1	5
2	35
3	215

Which statement about this function is **not** true?

A. Its x-intercept is the same as its y-intercept.

B. It is positive on the interval $(0, \infty)$.

C. It is increasing on the interval $(-\infty, \infty)$.

D. As x approaches $-\infty$, $f(x)$ approaches ∞.

Describe the end behavior of each function.

16.

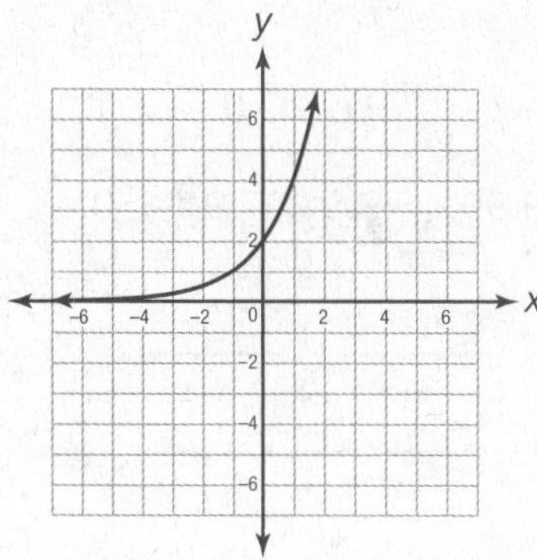

17.

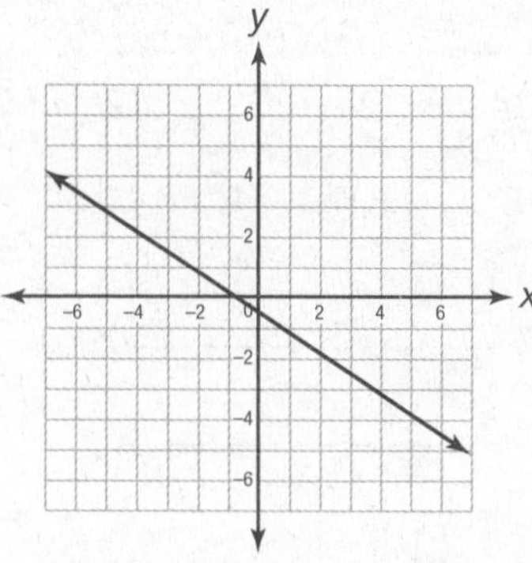

Use the graph and table below for questions 18–20. The graph represents exponential function *f*. The table represents some ordered pairs for linear function *g*.

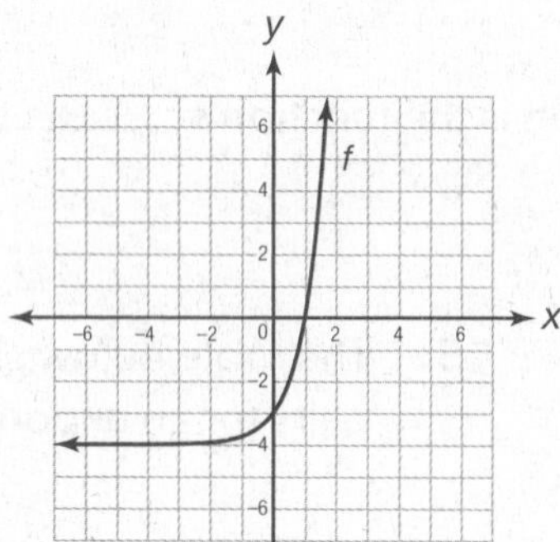

x	$g(x)$
−1	−8
0	−4
1	0
2	4
3	8

18. Compare and contrast the intercepts of the functions.

19. Compare the increasing and decreasing intervals of the functions.

20. Compare the intervals on which the functions are positive and those on which they are negative.

For each graph, describe the intervals where the function is positive and where it is negative.

21.

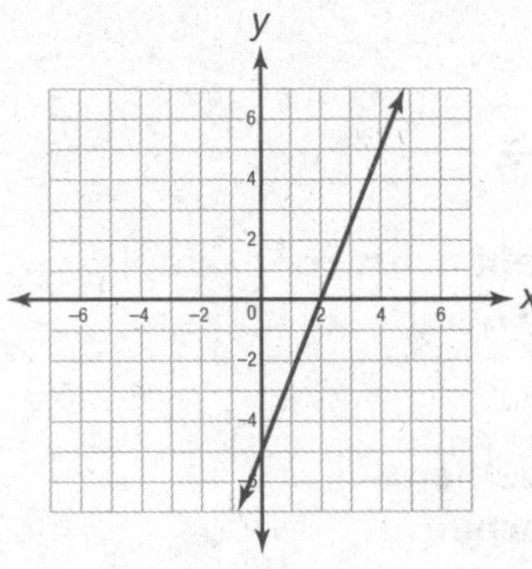

____

____

22.

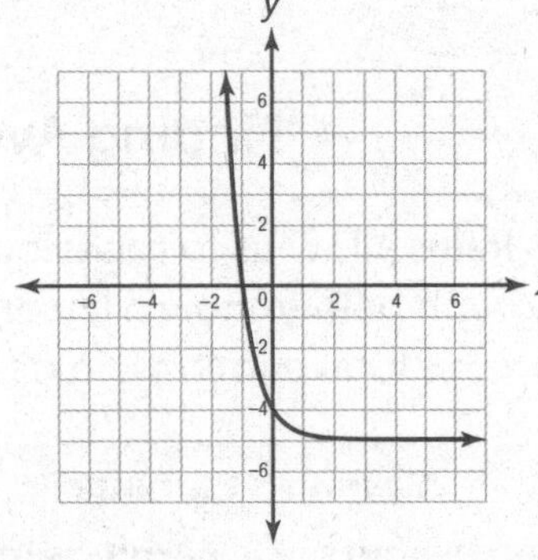

____

____

Solve.

23. INTERPRET A cylinder contains 20 milliliters of water. The water begins to leak out as represented by the linear function graphed on the right. Identify the intercepts and interpret what they mean in this situation.

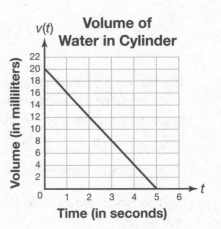

Volume of Water in Cylinder

$v(t)$

Volume (in milliliters)

Time (in seconds)

____

____

____

24. CREATE The cost of a taxi ride includes a \$3 fee plus \$2 for each mile traveled. So, a 1-mile ride costs \$5 and a 2-mile ride costs \$7. Create a graph to represent this linear function. Identify the domain for your graph and explain why you chose it.

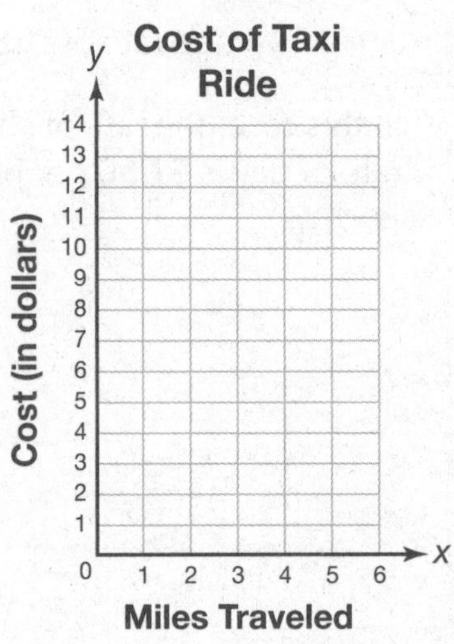

____

____

LESSON 13

Average Rate of Change

Finding Average Rate of Change

UNDERSTAND Rates allow us to relate quantities measured in different units. For example, the table and graph below show a linear function that compares the number of hours a cashier works to his total earnings, in dollars.

Cashier's Earnings	
Time in hours, x	**Earnings in \$, y**
0	0
2	15
4	30

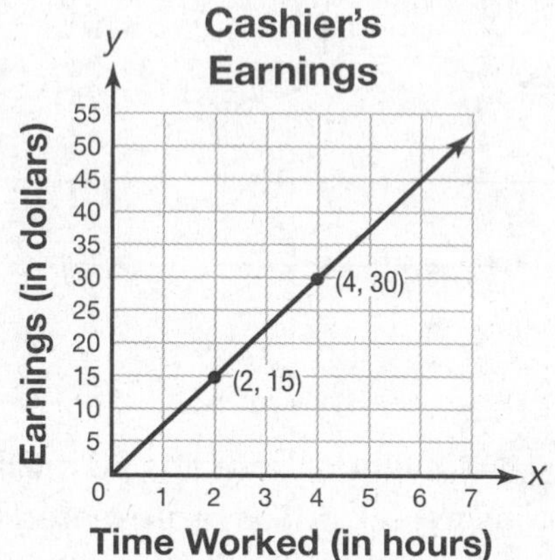

The cashier's earnings change, depending on the number of hours he works. His pay rate is an example of a **rate of change**. A rate of change shows how one quantity changes relative to another quantity. To calculate the average rate of change between two ordered pairs (x_1, y_1) and (x_2, y_2), use this formula:

$$\text{average rate of change} = \frac{\text{change in } y}{\text{change in } x} = \frac{y_2 - y_1}{x_2 - x_1}$$

For the function describing the cashier's earnings, choose two ordered pairs, such as (2, 15) and (4, 30).

$$\text{average rate of change} = \frac{30 - 15}{4 - 2} = \frac{15}{2} = 7.50$$

In this case, the rate of change compares dollars earned to hours worked. So, the cashier's rate of pay is \$7.50 per hour.

Connect

A basketball championship begins with 64 teams. Every time a team wins a game, it goes on to the next round. Once a team loses a game, it is eliminated from competition and does not play any more games. The number of teams in each round of the championship is a function of the round. That function is represented on the graph to the right. Compare the rate of change between rounds 1 and 2 to the rate of change between rounds 2 and 3.

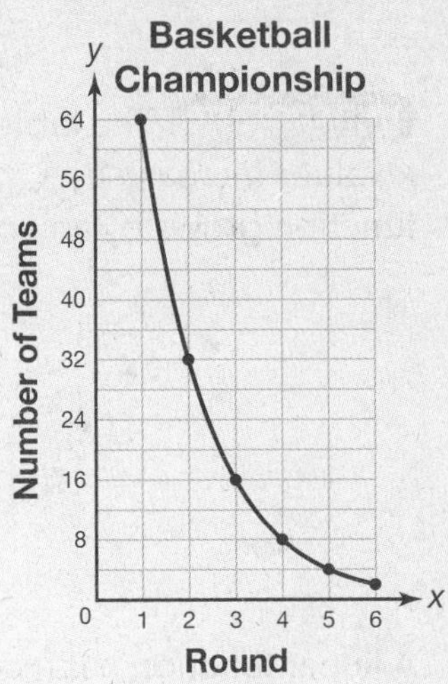

1 Calculate the average rate of change between rounds 1 and 2.

Find the rate of change from (1, 64) to (2, 32).

$\frac{32 - 64}{2 - 1} = \frac{-32}{1} = -32$ teams per round

Between rounds 1 and 2, the number of teams decreases at a rate of 32 teams per round.

2 Calculate the average rate of change between rounds 2 and 3.

Find the rate of change from (2, 32) to (3, 16).

$\frac{16 - 32}{3 - 2} = \frac{-16}{1} = -16$ teams per round

Between rounds 2 and 3, the number of teams decreases at a rate of 16 teams per round.

3 Compare the rates of change.

▶ The rate of change between rounds 1 and 2 is different than it is between rounds 2 and 3. The rate between rounds 2 and 3 is half what it was between rounds 1 and 2.

TRY

Choose a pair of points on the graph below and find the average rate of change between them. Compare your result with those of other students. Did they use the same two points?

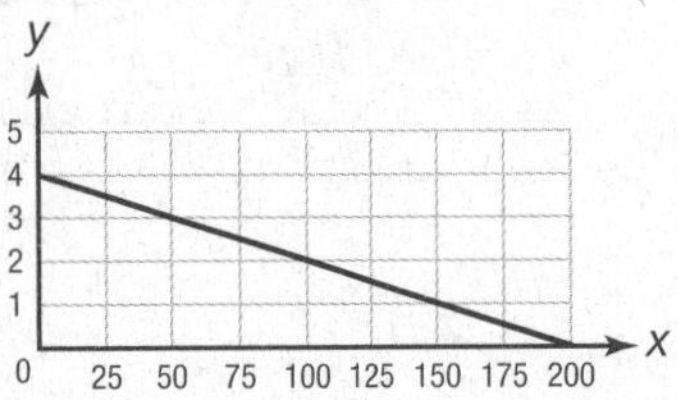

Comparing Average Rates of Change

UNDERSTAND The table below represents the linear function $f(x) = 2x + 1$. Notice that as x-values increase by 1, $f(x)$-values increase by a constant amount, 2. In other words, the function grows by an equal amount, 2, in each unit interval.

x	0	1	2	3	4	5
f(x)	1	3	5	7	9	11

(+1 between successive x-values; +2 between successive $f(x)$-values)

A linear function has a constant rate of change. Its average rate of change is the same no matter what interval you are observing. The constant rate of change of a linear function is its **slope**.

An exponential function has a graph that is a curve. An exponential growth function is always increasing, while an exponential decay function is always decreasing. The table below represents an exponential growth function.

x	0	1	2	3	4	5
f(x)	1	2	4	8	16	32

(+1 between successive x-values; ×2 between successive $f(x)$-values)

Notice that as each x-value increases by 1, each $f(x)$-value is multiplied by 2. The value of the function, $f(x)$, does not grow by constant amounts over equal intervals, so it does not have a constant rate of change. However, $f(x)$ does grow by the same factor over equal intervals. This function increases by a factor of 2, or doubles, over each unit interval.

The value of an exponential function grows by equal factors over equal intervals. If the factor by which the function changes is greater than 1, then the function represents exponential growth. If the factor is less than 1, then the function represents exponential decay.

The average rates of change for an exponential function grow by the same factor as the values of the function. For the table above, the average rate of change doubled over each unit interval.

x	0	1	2	3	4	5
f(x)	1	2	4	8	16	32

(+1 between successive x-values; +1, +2, +4, +8, +16 between successive $f(x)$-values; ×2 between successive changes)

Connect

Find and describe the average rate of change for four consecutive pairs of values in the table. What type of function is this?

x	−3	−2	−1	0	1
f(x)	64	16	4	1	$\frac{1}{4}$

1 Determine the average rate of change for consecutive pairs of values $(x, f(x))$.

Be sure that the intervals are the same between each pair of points. The difference between each pair of x-values in the table is 1 unit, so the intervals are the same.

between $(-3, 64)$ and $(-2, 16)$:

$$\frac{16 - 64}{-2 - (-3)} = \frac{-48}{1} = -48$$

between $(-2, 16)$ and $(-1, 4)$:

$$\frac{4 - 16}{-1 - (-2)} = \frac{-12}{1} = -12$$

between $(-1, 4)$ and $(0, 1)$:

$$\frac{1 - 4}{0 - (-1)} = \frac{-3}{1} = -3$$

between $(0, 1)$ and $\left(1, \frac{1}{4}\right)$:

$$\frac{\frac{1}{4} - 1}{1 - 0} = \frac{-\frac{3}{4}}{1} = -\frac{3}{4}$$

2 Compare the average rates of change in order to classify the function.

The average rates of change for the first four consecutive pairs of points are: $-48, -12, -3, -\frac{3}{4}$.

These rates are different. The rate of change is not constant, so this is not a linear function.

The value of $f(x)$ decreases by a common factor over each interval.

between $(-3, 64)$ and $(-2, 16)$:

$$\frac{16}{64} = \frac{1}{4}$$

between $(-2, 16)$ and $(-1, 4)$:

$$\frac{4}{16} = \frac{1}{4}$$

between $(-1, 4)$ and $(0, 1)$:

$$\frac{1}{4} = \frac{1}{4}$$

between $(0, 1)$ and $\left(1, \frac{1}{4}\right)$:

$$\frac{\frac{1}{4}}{1} = \frac{1}{4}$$

▶ Since the values of $f(x)$ change by an equal factor over equal intervals and that factor is $\frac{1}{4}$, this is an example of an exponential decay function.

DISCUSS

Why is it important to keep the intervals between each pair of values $(x, f(x))$ the same when comparing average rates of change?

EXAMPLE A Determine the average rate of change between several consecutive pairs of points for the function $f(x) = -3x + 2$. Describe how the function is changing and classify it.

1 Create a table of ordered pairs for the function.

x	$f(x) = -3x + 2$	$f(x)$
-2	$f(-2) = -3(-2) + 2 = 6 + 2 = 8$	8
-1	$f(-1) = -3(-1) + 2 = 3 + 2 = 5$	5
0	$f(0) = -3(0) + 2 = 0 + 2 = 2$	2
1	$f(1) = -3(1) + 2 = -3 + 2 = -1$	-1
2	$f(2) = -3(2) + 2 = -6 + 2 = -4$	-4

2 Determine the average rate of change for four consecutive pairs of values $(x, f(x))$.

Be sure that the intervals are the same between each pair of points.

between $(-2, 8)$ and $(-1, 5)$:

$$\frac{5 - 8}{-1 - (-2)} = \frac{-3}{1} = -3$$

between $(-1, 5)$ and $(0, 2)$:

$$\frac{2 - 5}{0 - (-1)} = \frac{-3}{1} = -3$$

between $(0, 2)$ and $(1, -1)$:

$$\frac{-1 - 2}{1 - 0} = \frac{-3}{1} = -3$$

between $(1, -1)$ and $(2, -4)$:

$$\frac{-4 - (-1)}{2 - 1} = \frac{-3}{1} = -3$$

3 Compare the average rates of change.

The average rates of change are all the same, -3.

Since the rate of change is constant, $f(x) = -3x + 2$ must be a linear function.

▶ The rate of change, or slope, is -3 for all pairs of values. The function is linear.

Does the equation $y = -3x + 5$ provide any clues about what the rate of change for the linear function is? Explain.

EXAMPLE B Compare the rates of change for $f(x) = 10^x$ and function g, which is represented in the table.

x	$g(x)$
-1	$\frac{1}{8}$
0	1
1	8
2	64
3	512

1 Create a table of values for f.

x	$f(x) = 10^x$	$f(x)$
-1	$f(-1) = 10^{-1} = \frac{1}{10}$	$\frac{1}{10}$
0	$f(0) = 10^0 = 1$	1
1	$f(1) = 10^1 = 10$	10
2	$f(2) = 10^2 = 100$	100
3	$f(3) = 10^3 = 1{,}000$	1,000

2 Find the average rate of change for three consecutive intervals for function f.

between (0, 1) and (1, 10): $\frac{10-1}{1-0} = \frac{9}{1} = 9$

between (1, 10) and (2, 100):

$\frac{100-10}{2-1} = \frac{90}{1} = 90$

between (2, 100) and (3, 1,000):

$\frac{1{,}000-100}{3-2} = \frac{900}{1} = 900$

The rate of change of the function f is not constant. Each average rate of change is 10 times the previous rate of change.

3 Find the average rate of change for three consecutive points for function g.

between (0, 1) and (1, 8): $\frac{8-1}{1-0} = \frac{7}{1} = 7$

between (1, 8) and (2, 64):

$\frac{64-8}{2-1} = \frac{56}{1} = 56$

between (2, 64) and (3, 512):

$\frac{512-64}{3-2} = \frac{448}{1} = 448$

The rate of change of the function g is not constant. Each average rate of change is 8 times the previous average rate of change.

▶ The average rates of change for function f are growing more rapidly than the average rates of change for function g.

By what factor are the values of function $f(x)$ growing? Does the equation $f(x) = 10^x$ help you determine that factor? How could you write an explicit expression for $g(x)$?

Practice

Fill in the blanks by writing an operation sign and a number to show how the $f(x)$-values are changing in each unit interval. Then classify each function as *linear* or *exponential*.

1.

	+1	+1	+1	+1	+1	

x	−1	0	1	2	3	4
$f(x)$	$\frac{1}{6}$	1	6	36	216	1,296

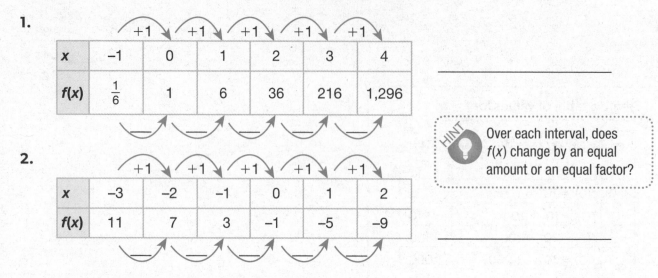

___ ___ ___ ___ ___

____

2.

	+1	+1	+1	+1	+1	

x	−3	−2	−1	0	1	2
$f(x)$	11	7	3	−1	−5	−9

___ ___ ___ ___ ___

____

HINT: Over each interval, does $f(x)$ change by an equal amount or an equal factor?

Fill in the blanks with an appropriate word or phrase.

3. The average ______________________ between two ordered pairs (x, y) is the ratio $\frac{\text{change in } y}{\text{change in } x}$.

4. In a linear function, the rate of change is also known as the ______________.

5. The average rate of change for a ________________ function is constant.

6. The average rate of change for an exponential function grows by equal ________________ per unit interval.

Use the graph for questions 7–10.

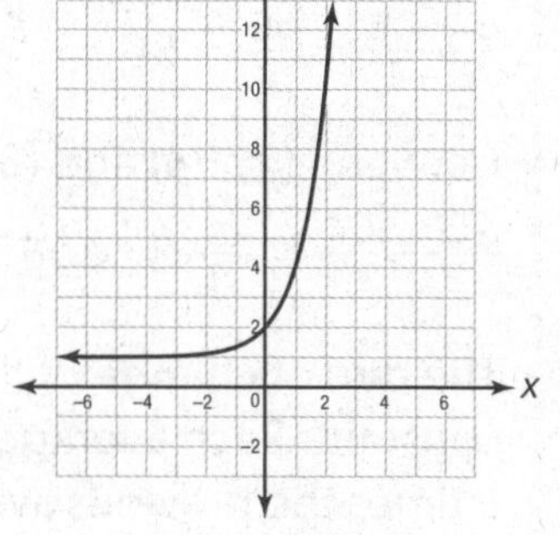

7. Determine the average rate of change between $\left(-1, \frac{4}{3}\right)$ and $(0, 2)$.

____

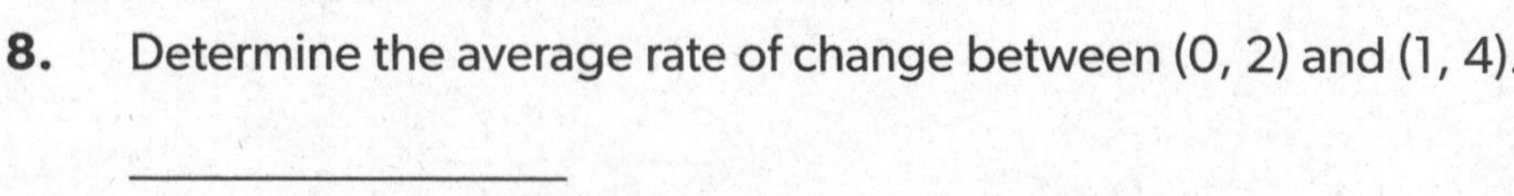

8. Determine the average rate of change between $(0, 2)$ and $(1, 4)$.

____

9. Determine the average rate of change between $(1, 4)$ and $(2, 10)$.

____

10. Write a sentence or two comparing the average rates of change you found. (If they vary, describe how they vary.)

____

____

Use the information about function $f(x)$, given as a table below, and function $g(x) = 5^x$ for questions 11–14.

11. Using the table on the right, find the average rate of change for three unit intervals for function f.

x	$f(x)$
−1	$\frac{1}{4}$
0	1
1	4
2	16

____

____

____

12. Complete the table to find four consecutive ordered pairs for the function $g(x) = 5^x$.

x	$g(x) = 5^x$	$g(x)$
−1	$g(-1) =$	
0	$g(0) =$	
1	$g(1) =$	
2	$g(2) =$	

13. Find the average rate of change for three unit intervals for function g.

____

____

____

14. Compare the changes in the values of functions f and g.

____

____

____

15. INTERPRET The graph shows how the total amount that a landscaper charges for a job changes depending on the number of hours she works. Identify the slope of the graph. Then interpret what this slope represents in this problem situation.

____

____

____

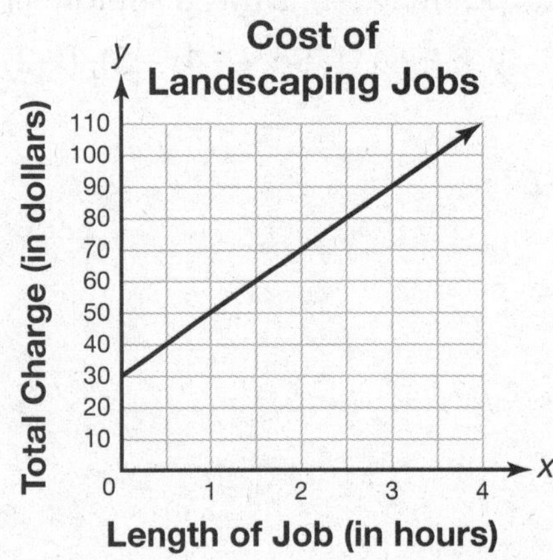

LESSON 14 Graphing Functions

Graphing Linear Functions

UNDERSTAND The various representations of a function give different details about the function. An equation in function notation explains the rule for generating an output from any given input. A table can list many, but usually not all, input/output pairs for the function. A graph is a visual representation of all the input/output pairs of the function.

The graph of a function is the graph of $y = f(x)$, so y takes on the value of the output. If you choose any point (x, y) on the graph of a function, the y-coordinate is the output of the function when the x-coordinate is the input. Every point on the graph is a solution to the equation $y = f(x)$.

To understand the most about a function, it is often helpful to translate from one form to another. By examining the equation of the function, you can often identify key features that will help you construct the graph of the function.

Examine the linear function represented symbolically as $f(x) = \frac{3}{2}x + 1$. Its graph on the xy-coordinate plane is $y = f(x)$ or $y = \frac{3}{2}x + 1$. The equation is in **slope-intercept form**, $y = mx + b$, where m represents the slope and b represents the y-intercept. For $y = \frac{3}{2}x + 1$, the slope or rate of change, m, is $\frac{3}{2}$, and the y-intercept, b, is 1.

This is enough information to graph the function. The y-intercept of a linear equation $y = mx + b$ is at $(0, b)$. For $y = \frac{3}{2}x + 1$, the y-intercept is at $(0, 1)$. Plotting this point starts your graph. Now you can use the slope to find another point on the graph. The slope is a rate of change that tells how to move from one point on the graph to another. It is the ratio $\frac{\text{change in } y}{\text{change in } x}$. Place your finger at the y-intercept and count 3 units up and 2 units to the right to find another point, $(2, 4)$. Draw a straight line through those points. Every point on the line is a solution for $y = \frac{3}{2}x + 1$. So, $(-4, -5)$, $(-2, -2)$, $(0, 1)$, and $(2, 4)$ are all solutions.

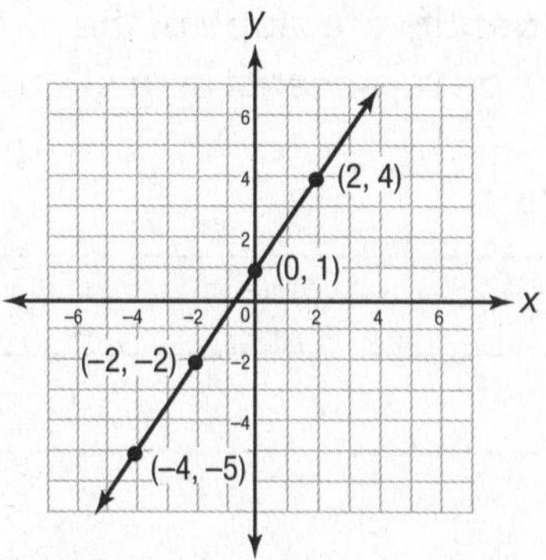

Sometimes, a linear equation will not be in slope-intercept form. In that case, you may need to put it in that form yourself before graphing it.

Connect

Graph the linear equation $6x + 3y = 12$ on a coordinate plane. Identify at least three ordered pairs that are solutions for the equation.

1 Rewrite the equation in slope-intercept form and identify the *y*-intercept and the slope.

$6x + 3y = 12$	Subtract $6x$ from both sides.
$3y = -6x + 12$	Divide both sides by 3.
$y = -2x + 4$	

2 Plot the *y*-intercept and use the slope to find a second point on the line.

After plotting (0, 4), count down 2 units and 1 unit to the right. Plot a point there at (1, 2).

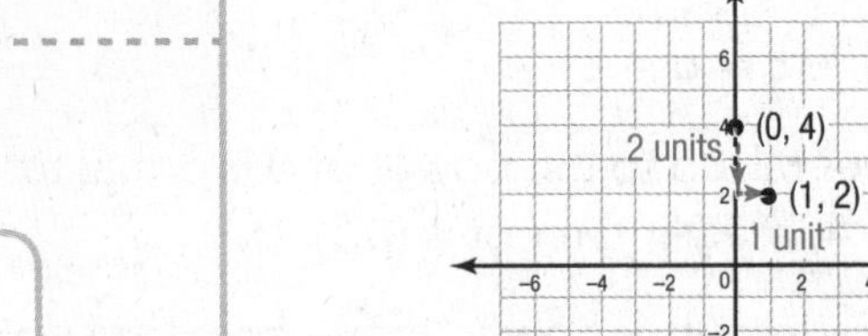

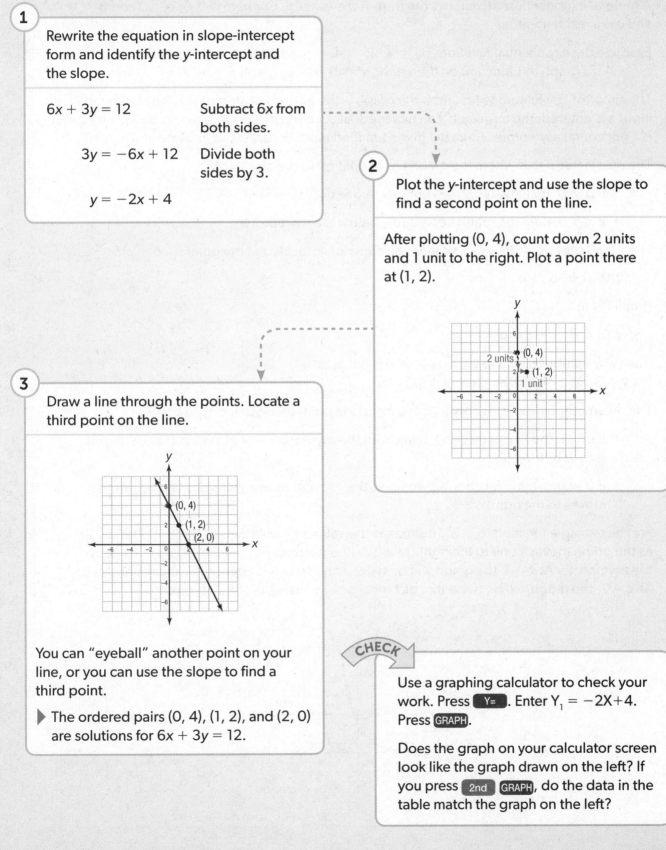

3 Draw a line through the points. Locate a third point on the line.

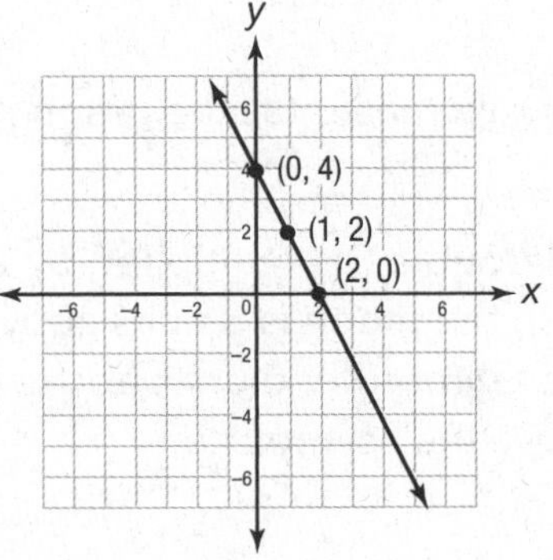

You can "eyeball" another point on your line, or you can use the slope to find a third point.

▶ The ordered pairs (0, 4), (1, 2), and (2, 0) are solutions for $6x + 3y = 12$.

CHECK

Use a graphing calculator to check your work. Press Y=. Enter $Y_1 = -2X+4$. Press GRAPH.

Does the graph on your calculator screen look like the graph drawn on the left? If you press 2nd GRAPH, do the data in the table match the graph on the left?

Graphing Exponential Functions

UNDERSTAND You can also use key features to help you graph an exponential function. A general exponential function has the form $f(x) = a \cdot b^x + c$, where $a \neq 0$, $b > 0$ and $b \neq 1$, and c is a real number.

Examine the exponential function $f(x) = 3 \cdot 2^x - 4$. In this function, $a = 3$, $b = 2$, and $c = -4$. To graph this function on the *xy*-coordinate plane, graph $y = 3 \cdot 2^x - 4$.

The simplest key feature to find from the graph is the horizontal asymptote. No matter what input x is entered, the term $a \cdot b^x$ can never equal 0, so $f(x)$ can never equal c. So the line $y = c$ is a horizontal asymptote. Thus, the given function has a horizontal asymptote at $y = -4$.

The parameter a tells where the graph lies in relation to the asymptote.

- If $a > 0$, then the graph lies entirely above the asymptote.
- If $a < 0$, then the graph lies entirely below the asymptote.

The *y*-intercept, $(0, f(0))$, of an exponential function is located at the point $(0, a + c)$.

$$f(0) = a \cdot b^0 + c$$

simplifies to

$$f(0) = a \cdot 1 + c = a + c$$

since any number raised to the power of 0 is equal to 1.
For $y = 3 \cdot 2^x - 4$, the *y*-intercept is $(0, -1)$.

The parameter b describes how to move from one point to another on the graph.

- If $b > 1$, the function curves away from the asymptote as x increases (as the graph moves to the right).
- If $0 < b < 1$, the function approaches the asymptote as x increases (as the graph moves to the right).

For the example function, $b = 2$. This means the value of y will double (be multiplied by 2) as the graph moves 1 unit to the right. At $x = 0$ (the *y*-intercept), the graph is 3 units above the asymptote. At $x = 1$, the graph will be twice as far from the asymptote, 6 units above it. At $x = 2$, the graph will be twice that distance, or 12 units, above the asymptote.

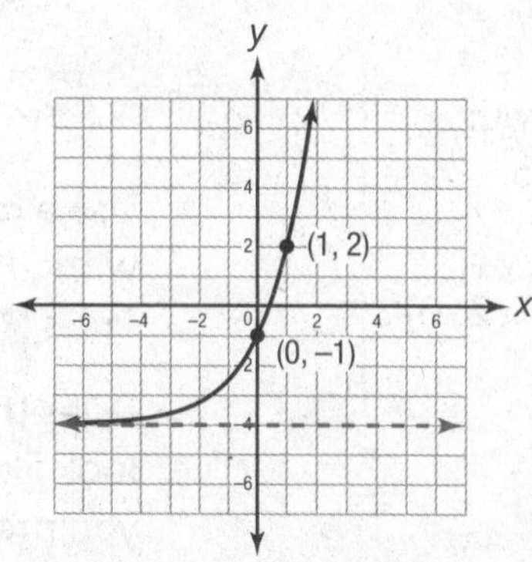

Connect

Use what you know about key features to graph $f(x) = 3\left(\frac{1}{2}\right)^x$.

1 Identify the parameters.

An exponential function has the form $f(x) = a \cdot b^x + c$.

In $y = 3\left(\frac{1}{2}\right)^x$, $a = 3$, $b = \frac{1}{2}$, and $c = 0$.

2 Identify the asymptote.

The asymptote is the line $y = c$, in this case, $y = 0$, or the x-axis.

3 Identify the y-intercept.

Any number raised to the power of 0 equals 1.

So, when $x = 0$, $y = 3\left(\frac{1}{2}\right)^0 = 3(1) = 3$.

The y-intercept will be at (0, 3).

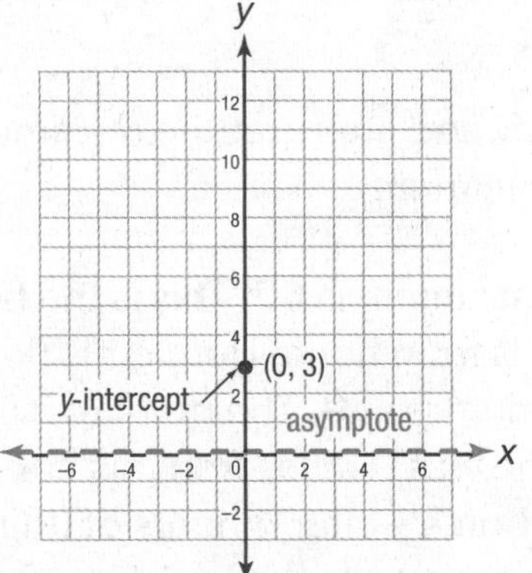

4 Use b as a factor to find additional points on the graph.

Since $b = \frac{1}{2}$, moving along the x-axis 1 unit means dropping half the distance to the asymptote. Since the y-intercept is 3 units above the asymptote, the graph will be 1.5 units above the asymptote at $x = 1$ and 0.75 unit above it at $x = 2$.

Since $0 < b < 1$, connect these points with a smooth curve that approaches the asymptote.

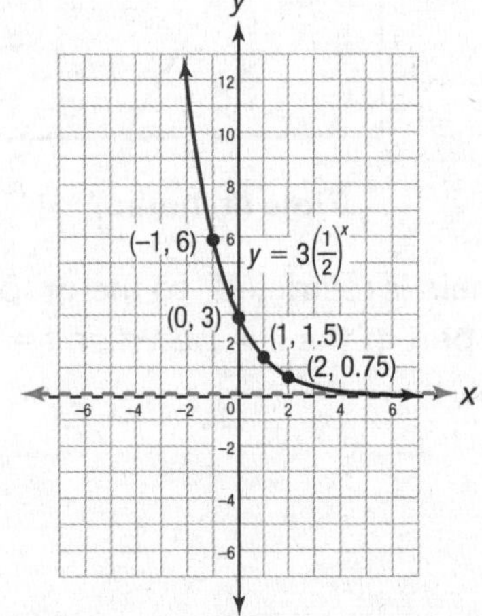

DISCUSS

How could you use the value of b to find points to the left of the y-intercept?

EXAMPLE A Sean is at his grandmother's house, which is 60 miles from his home. He starts riding home at time $t = 0$. His distance from his home, $d(t)$, after t hours can be modeled by the function $d(t) = 60 - 15t$. Graph the function for the domain $0 \leq t \leq 4$. Explain why the domain must be restricted in that way and what the maximum and minimum values mean in this situation.

1 Identify the type of function.

Is the function linear or exponential? The equation $d(t) = 60 - 15t$ has a variable, t, raised to the power of 1. So, the function is linear.

2 Identify the slope and y-intercept from the equation.

The graph of the function is the graph of the equation $d(t) = 60 - 15t$, or $d(t) = -15t + 60$, for all values of t between 0 and 4, inclusive. The slope, m, of the line is -15, and its y-intercept, $(0, b)$, is $(0, 60)$.

3 Graph the function, choosing an appropriate scale and label for each axis.

Plot the y-intercept. According to the slope, another point is 15 units down and 1 unit to the right, at (1, 45). Draw a line through those points.

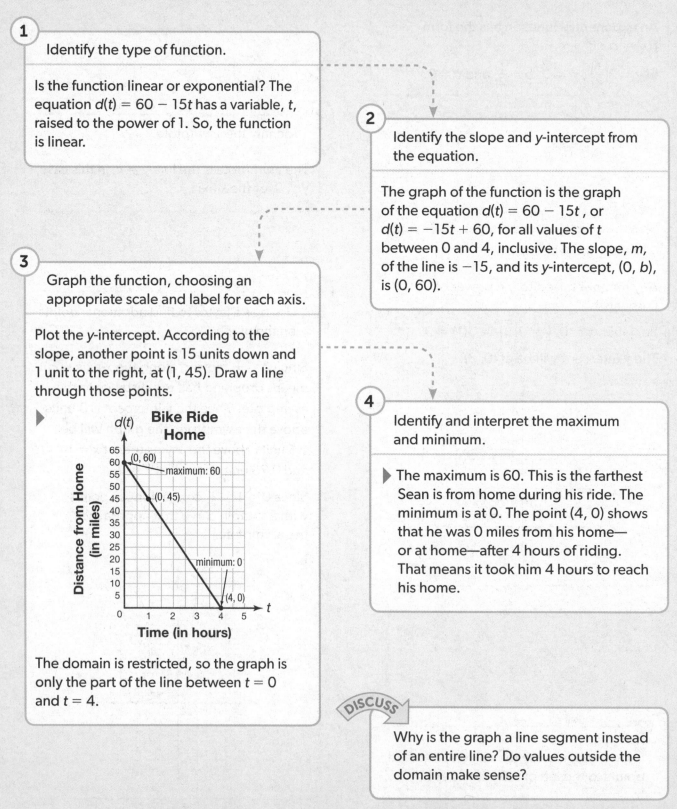

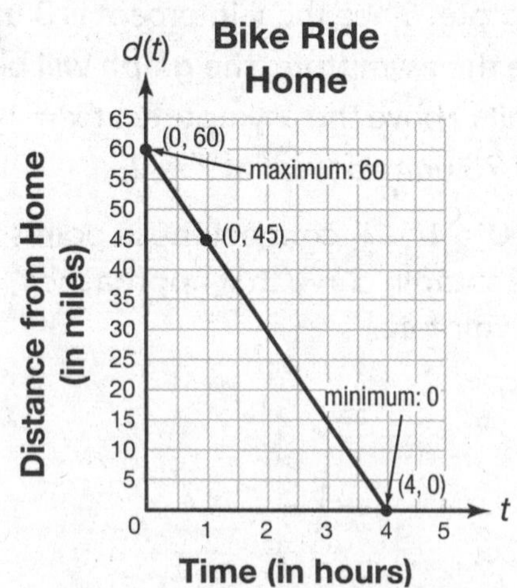

The domain is restricted, so the graph is only the part of the line between $t = 0$ and $t = 4$.

4 Identify and interpret the maximum and minimum.

The maximum is 60. This is the farthest Sean is from home during his ride. The minimum is at 0. The point (4, 0) shows that he was 0 miles from his home—or at home—after 4 hours of riding. That means it took him 4 hours to reach his home.

DISCUSS

Why is the graph a line segment instead of an entire line? Do values outside the domain make sense?

EXAMPLE B The equation $f(x) = 3x + 1$ represents a linear function f. The table of values on the right represents an exponential function g.

Graph functions f and g on the same coordinate plane. Then compare their properties.

x	$g(x)$
-1	$\frac{1}{3}$
0	1
1	3
2	9
3	27

1 Graph the functions.

To plot $f(x) = 3x + 1$, notice that it is in slope-intercept form. So, plot the y-intercept at (0, 1) and then count 3 units up and 1 unit to the right. Draw a straight line through the points.

To graph function g, plot and connect the coordinate pairs from the table.

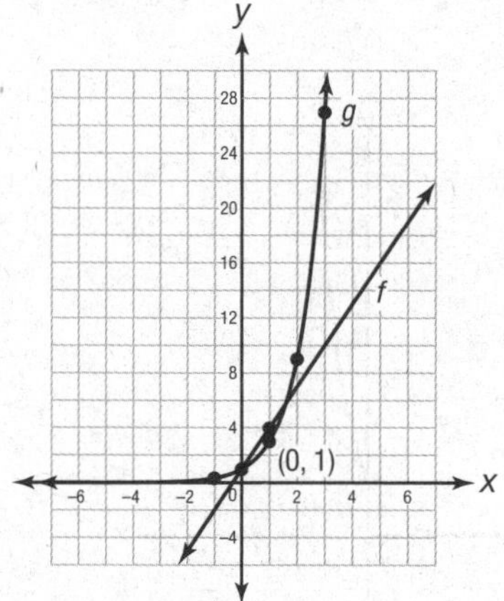

2 Use the graphs to compare the functions.

- Both functions have the same domain: the set of all real numbers.

  Function f has a range that includes all real numbers. Function g approaches but never touches the x-axis (the line $y = 0$), so its range is $y > 0$.

  Both functions have the same y-intercept at (0, 1).

  Both are increasing functions. However, shortly after $x = 1$, the graph of function g starts to increase at a much more rapid rate than the graph of function f, which continues to increase at a constant rate. Notice that around $x = 1.5$, the graph of function g overtakes the graph of function f.

DISCUSS

Will an exponential function always overtake a linear function? Explain and give or sketch an example.

Practice

Circle the ordered pairs that are solutions for the graphed function.

1.

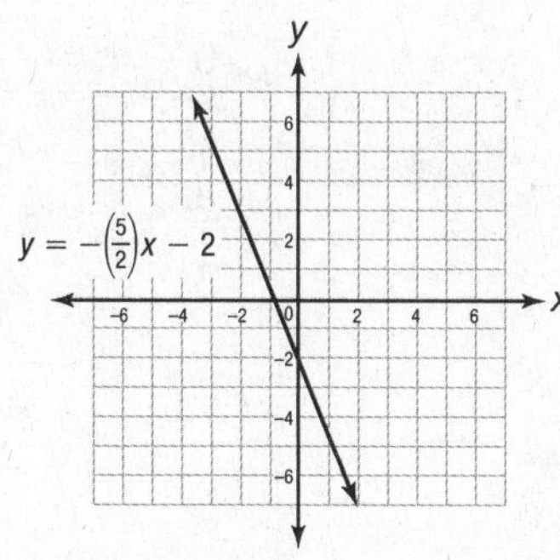

(−2, 3)

(0, −2)

(1, −3)

2.

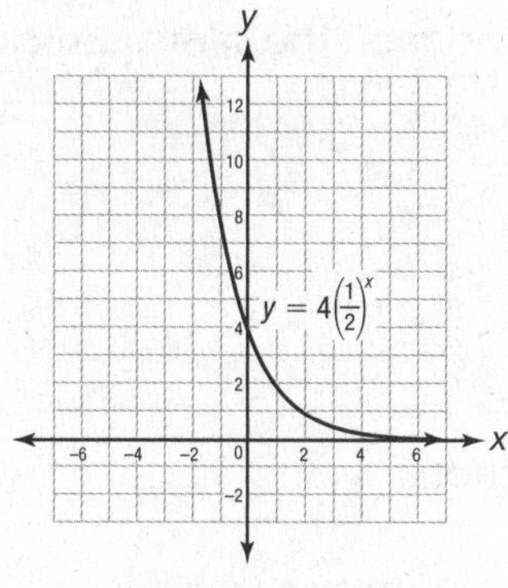

(1, 2)

(2, 1)

(4, 0)

REMEMBER Each point on the graph is a solution for the equation.

Choose the best answer.

3. Which graph represents the function $f(x) = 2(3^x)$?

A.

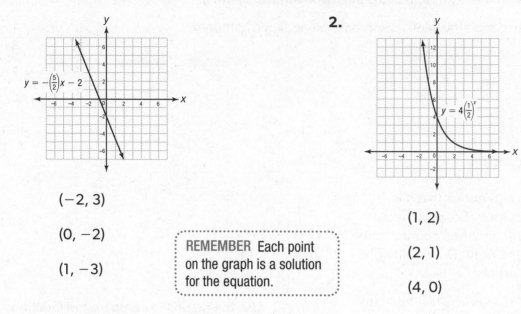

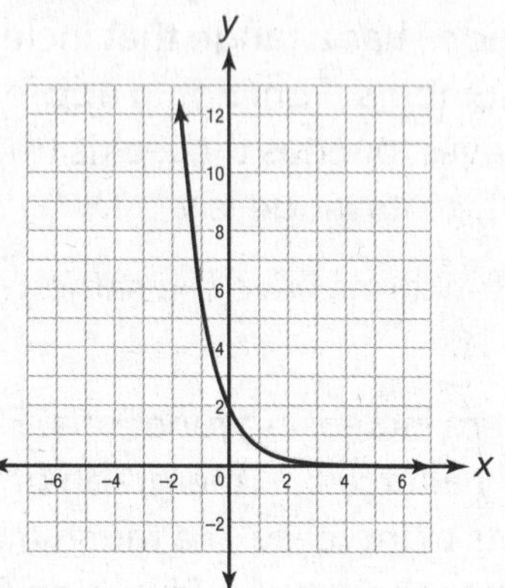

C.

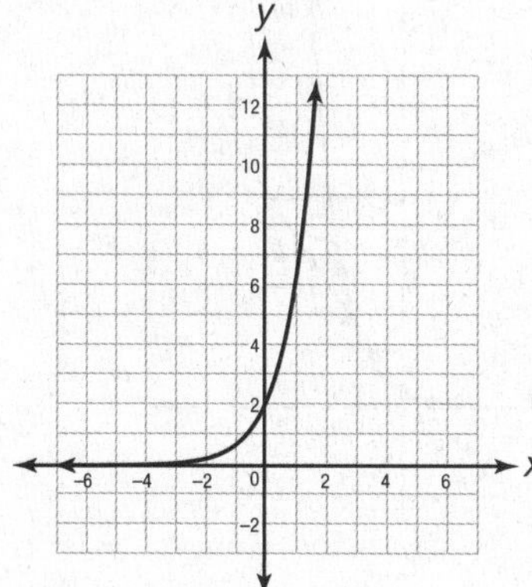

B.

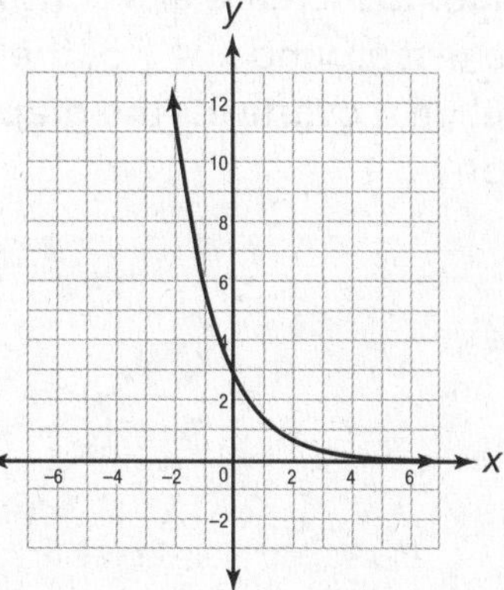

D.

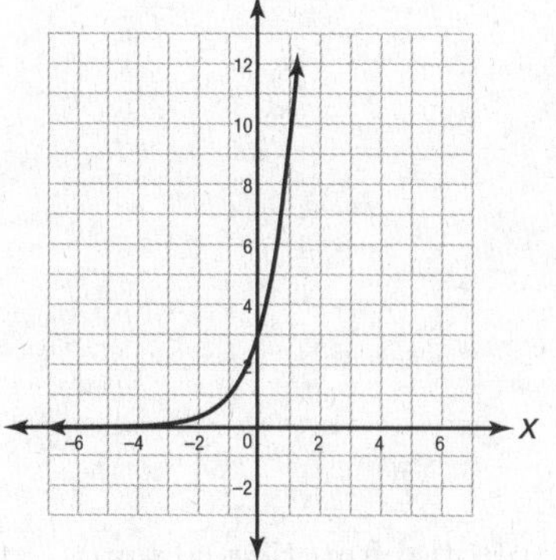

Graph each function.

4. $f(x) = -3x + 5$

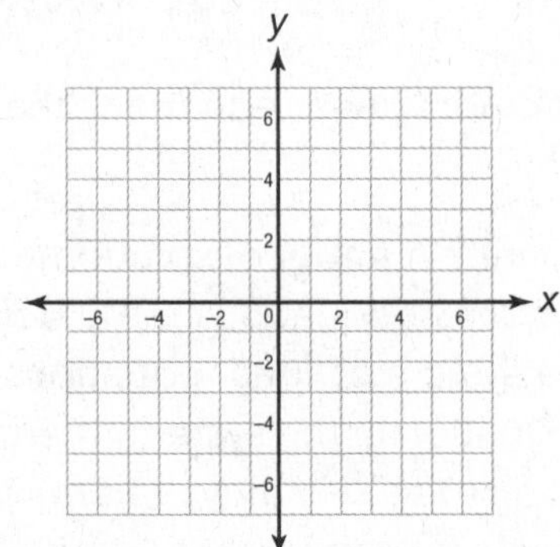

5. $f(x) = 4\left(\frac{1}{3}\right)^x$

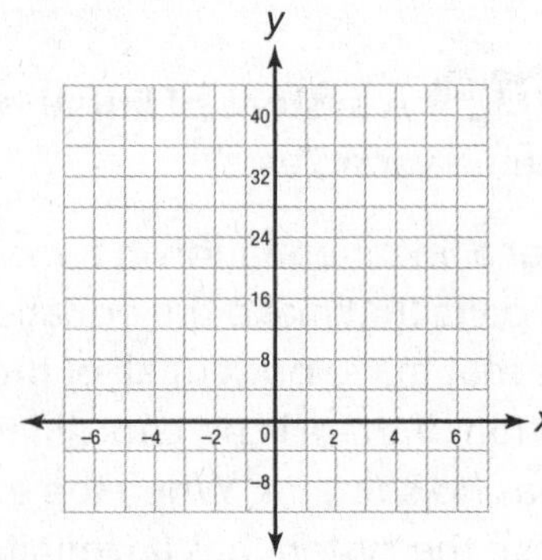

6. COMPARE The graph of $f(x) = 2\left(\frac{1}{5}\right)^x$ is shown on the coordinate plane. Graph $g(x) = 2(5^x)$ on the same coordinate plane. Then compare the end behavior of the two functions.

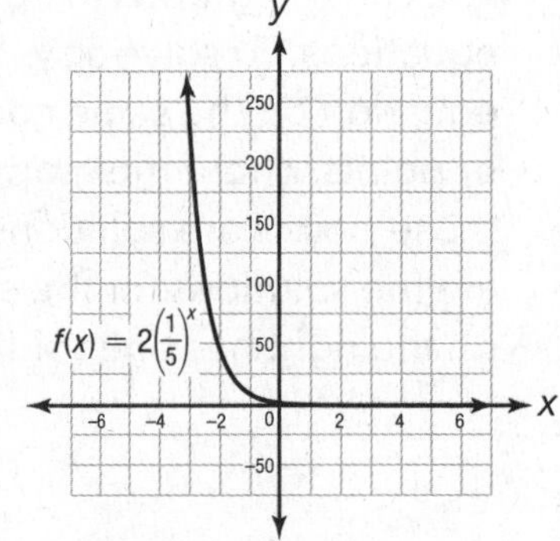

____

____

____

7. EXPLAIN A hurricane is located off the coast when scientists begin tracking its distance from land. Its distance from land, $d(t)$, after t hours can be modeled by the function $d(t) = 120 - 20t$. Graph the function for the domain $0 \leq t \leq 6$. Identify the maximum and minimum values. Explain what each represents in this situation.

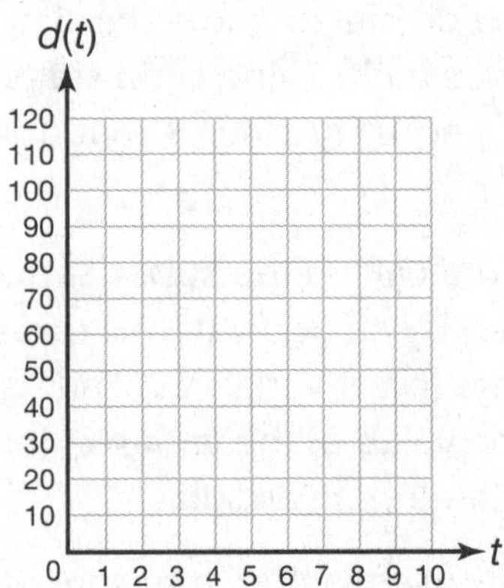

____

____

____

LESSON

15 Solving Systems of Linear Equations

UNDERSTAND A **system of linear equations** consists of two or more linear equations that use the same variables.

Recall that a linear equation in two variables generally has an infinite number of solutions: all of the (x, y) pairs that make the equation true. The solution to a system of equations is the point or points that make both or all of the equations true. Typically, a system of linear equations has one solution. If there is no coordinate pair that satisfies every equation in the system, then the system has no solution. When the equations have the same graph (because they are equivalent equations), the system has an infinite number of solutions: every (x, y) pair on that graph.

You can use graphs to approximate the solution to a system of equations. To solve a system of equations graphically, graph each equation on the same coordinate plane. The solution is the point or points where the graphs of the equations intersect. Because those points are solutions to every equation in the system, they are the solutions for the system. The system shown on the graph on the right has one solution: (3, 2).

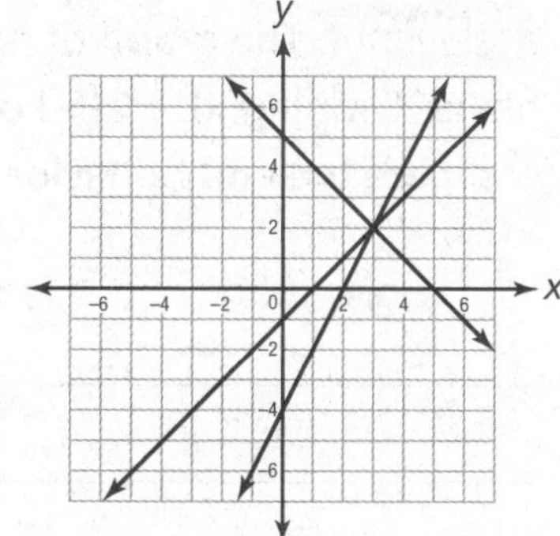

UNDERSTAND One way to solve a system of equations algebraically is to use the **elimination method**. In this method, equations are added and subtracted in order to eliminate all but one variable. This results in an equation in one variable, which can be solved. The value for that variable is then used to solve for the other variables.

Knowing the properties of equality is crucial to understanding how the elimination method works. For example, one step involves multiplying both sides of an equation by a constant factor. The multiplication property of equality assures that doing that will not change the solution of that equation.

Another way to solve a system algebraically is the **substitution method**. In this method, a variable in one equation is replaced by an equivalent expression from another equation. This results in a new equation that has fewer variables. This can be repeated until only one variable remains in the equation. The value of the variable can be found from that equation and then used to find the values of the other variables.

The substitution method is especially useful when a system of equations includes an equation with an isolated variable, such as $y = 3x + 7$. If the system does not include an equation in this form, you can take the necessary steps to isolate a variable in one of the system's equations.

Connect

Solve the system of equations by graphing.

$$\begin{cases} y = 2x - 6 \\ x - 2y = 6 \end{cases}$$

1 Write the equations in slope-intercept form.

The first equation is already in slope-intercept form.

Isolate y in the second equation.

$$x - 2y = 6$$
$$-2y = -x + 6$$
$$y = \frac{1}{2}x - 3$$

2 Graph the first equation.

Plot a point at the y-intercept, $(0, -6)$. Then use the slope, 2, to plot a second point at $(1, -4)$. Draw a line to connect the points.

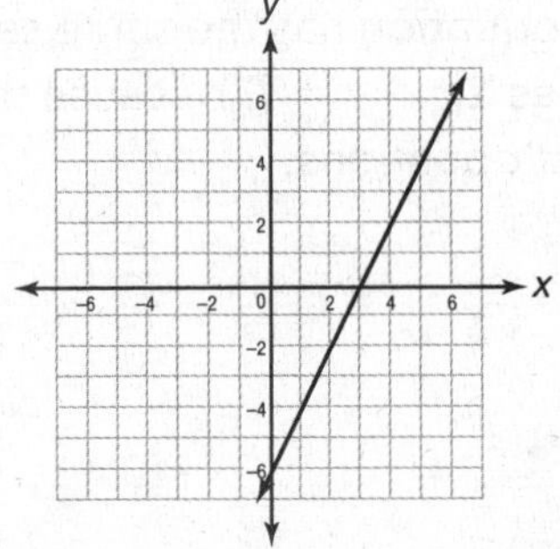

3 Graph the second equation.

Plot a point at the y-intercept, $(0, -3)$. Then use the slope, $\frac{1}{2}$, to plot a second point at $(2, -2)$. Draw a line to connect the points.

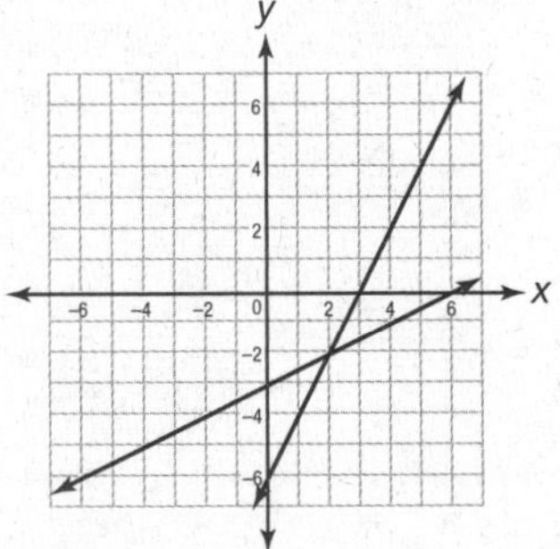

4 Find the solution.

To find the solution to the system, find the point where the lines intersect.

▶ The point of intersection appears to be $(2, -2)$.

CHECK

Substitute $x = 2$ and $y = -2$ into both equations in the system and confirm that true statements result.

EXAMPLE A Solve the system by using the elimination method.

$$\begin{cases} -3x - 2y = -10 \\ 2x + y = 7 \end{cases}$$

1 Choose which variable to eliminate.

Look at the coefficients of the y-terms. The y-term in the first equation has a coefficient of -2, and the y-term in the second equation has a coefficient of 1.

Use the multiplication property of equality to multiply both sides of the second equation by 2.

$$2(2x + y) = 2(7)$$
$$4x + 2y = 14$$

This new equation has the same set of solutions as $2x + y = 7$, because they are equivalent equations.

2 Combine equations to eliminate one variable.

The addition property of equality allows you to add equivalent values to both sides of an equation. Add the new equation to the first equation from the original system to eliminate y.

$$\begin{array}{r} -3x - 2y = -10 \\ +\ 4x + 2y = \ \ 14 \\ \hline x + 0 = \ \ \ 4 \\ x = \ \ \ 4 \end{array}$$

3 Use the value of x to solve for y.

The substitution property of equality allows you to substitute 4 for x in the original second equation in order to solve for y.

$2x + y = 7$

$2(4) + y = 7$ Substitute $x = 4$ into the equation.

$8 + y = 7$ Simplify.

$y = -1$ Subtract 8 from both sides of the equation.

▶ The solution to the system is the ordered pair $(4, -1)$.

CHECK

Substitute the x- and y-values of $(4, -1)$ into both equations in the system and verify that the solution is correct.

EXAMPLE B A system of equations and its graph are shown.

$$\begin{cases} x + 2y = 3 \\ x + y = 2 \end{cases}$$

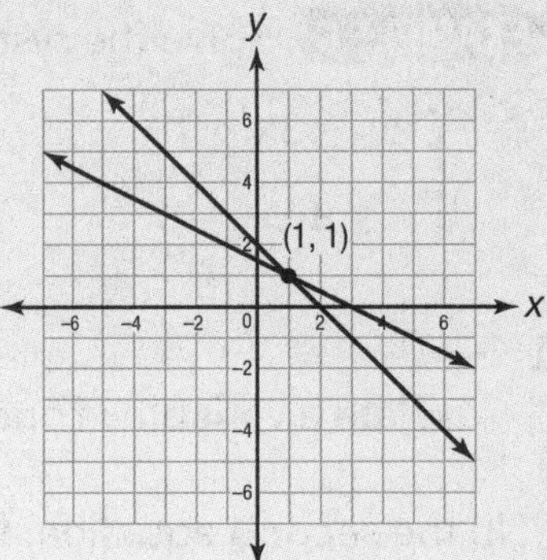

Use elimination to find the solution to the system. Show that the elimination method produces a new and simpler system of equations with the same solution as the original system.

1 Replace the first equation in the system.

Multiply both sides of the second equation by -1, and then add the result to the first equation.

$$\begin{array}{r} x + 2y = 3 \\ + \; -x - y = -2 \\ \hline y = 1 \end{array}$$

Replace the first equation with this equation to produce a new system.

$$\begin{cases} y = 1 \\ x + y = 2 \end{cases}$$

2 Replace the second equation in the new system.

Multiply both sides of the new first equation by -1, and then add the result to the second equation.

$$\begin{array}{r} x + y = 2 \\ + -y = -1 \\ \hline x = 1 \end{array}$$

Replace the second equation with this equation to produce a new system.

$$\begin{cases} y = 1 \\ x = 1 \end{cases}$$

3 Graph this new system.

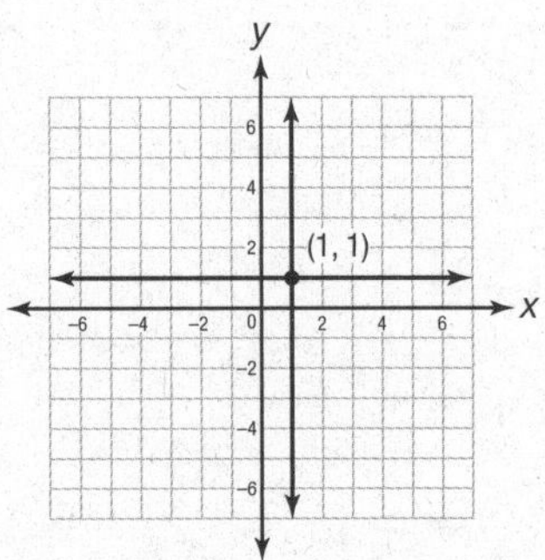

The systems have the same solution, (1, 1).

▶ Combining one equation in a system with a multiple of another equation yields a different system of equations with the same solution as the original system.

Compare the original system of equations to the final system of equations. In which system is the answer more obvious?

EXAMPLE C Solve the system by using the substitution method.

$$\begin{cases} 2y - 3x = 19 \\ x + 4y = -4 \end{cases}$$

1 Isolate a variable in one equation.

In the second equation, the coefficient of x is 1. So, the easiest course of action is to solve the second equation for x. Subtract $4y$ from both sides of the equation.

$$x + 4y = -4$$
$$x = -4 - 4y$$

2 Perform the substitution and solve for the other variable.

The substitution property of equality allows you to replace x with the expression $-4 - 4y$ in the first equation from the system. Doing so allows you to solve for y.

$$2y - 3x = 19$$
$$2y - 3(-4 - 4y) = 19$$
$$2y + 12 + 12y = 19$$
$$14y + 12 = 19$$
$$14y = 7$$
$$y = \frac{1}{2}$$

3 Use the value of one variable to solve for the other variable.

Apply the substitution property of equality again. Substitute $\frac{1}{2}$ for y in one of the equations and solve for x.

$$x + 4y = -4$$
$$x + 4\left(\frac{1}{2}\right) = -4$$
$$x + 2 = -4$$
$$x = -6$$

▶ The solution to the system is $\left(-6, \frac{1}{2}\right)$.

TRY

Solve the system by substitution.

$$\begin{cases} 4x - 3y = -1 \\ 3x + y = 9 \end{cases}$$

Problem Solving

READ

Bonnie has a jewelry-making business. She rents a studio space for $400 per month, and each necklace she makes costs her $15 in materials. She sells the necklaces for $55 each. How many necklaces must she sell in a month to make twice as much money as she spends? How much will she spend and how much will she make?

PLAN

Write and solve a system of equations.

Let n be the number of necklaces that Bonnie makes and sells in a month.
Let m be the amount of money Bonnie spends on the business that month.

Write an equation to represent the amount Bonnie spends for the month if she makes n necklaces at her studio.

$m =$ ________ + ________

Write another equation showing that the amount she makes by selling n necklaces is twice as much as she spends.

$2m =$ ________

SOLVE

Solve the system by using substitution.
The first equation has m isolated on the left side. So, substitute the expression on the right side for m in the second equation.

$2m =$ ________

2(____________________) = ______________

Now, solve the resulting equation for n.

$n =$ ________

Now, substitute the value of n into either of the original equations to find the value of m.

$m =$ ______________

$2m =$ ______________

CHECK

Substitute the values of n and m into the original equations.

Do the substitutions result in true equations? ________

▶ If Bonnie makes _____ necklaces, she will spend $______ and she will make $______.

Practice

Determine if the given ordered pair is a solution to the given system.

1. $\begin{cases} 3x + 7y = 12 \\ 6x - y = -4 \end{cases}$

(−3, 3)

____

2. $\begin{cases} 2x - 7 = -y \\ -5x + 13 = y \end{cases}$

(2, 3)

____

3. $\begin{cases} \frac{1}{2}x + \frac{2}{3}y = -2 \\ -\frac{3}{4}x - 2y = 9 \end{cases}$

(4, −6)

____

Choose the best answer.

4. A system of three equations is shown on the graph below.

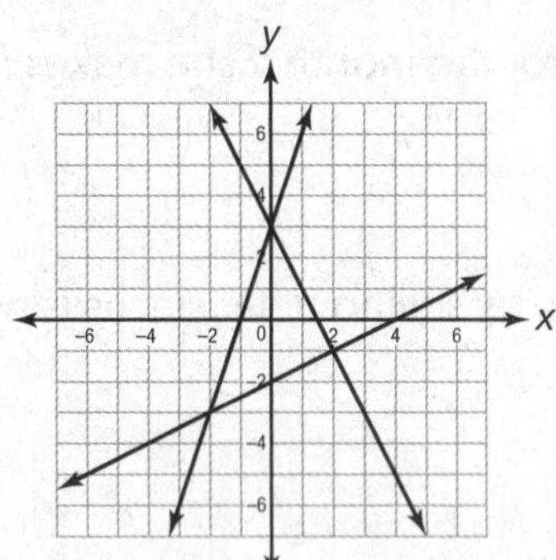

What is the solution to the system?

A. (2, −1)

B. (−2, −3)

C. (0, 3)

D. The system has no solution.

5. A baker rents space in a commercial kitchen for \$210 per week. For each pie he bakes, he spends \$4 on materials. He charges \$7.50 per pie. The graph below shows the baker's costs and revenues for a week in which he sells p pies.

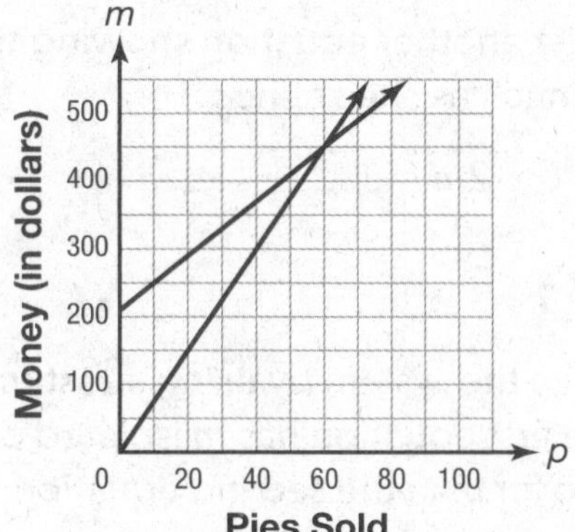

How many pies must he sell in a week in order to break even?

A. 20

B. 40

C. 60

D. He will never break even.

Solve each system of equations by using the method suggested.

6. $\begin{cases} 3x - 5y = 13 \\ 2x - y = -3 \end{cases}$

elimination

____

7. $\begin{cases} y - 2x = 5 \\ -2y + 7x = -4 \end{cases}$

substitution

____

Solve.

8. Sanjit has a collection of quarters and dimes worth $3.70. He has a total of 19 coins. How many quarters and how many dimes does Sanjit have?

____

9. Sonya opened a savings account with $200 and deposits $10 each week. Brad opened a savings account with $140 and contributes $40 each week. After how many weeks will Brad's account balance be twice as much as Sonya's? What will the balance be in each account then?

____

Solve each system of equations by graphing on the coordinate grid.

10. $\begin{cases} y = -x - 4 \\ y = 2x + 5 \end{cases}$

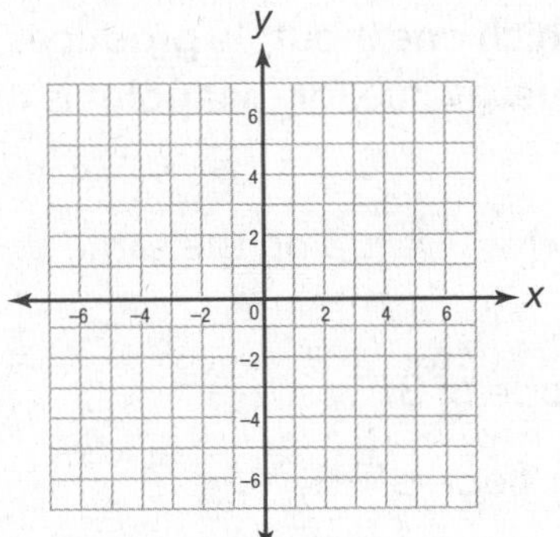

Solution: __________

11. $\begin{cases} 2x - y = 4 \\ \frac{1}{2}x + 10 = 3y \end{cases}$

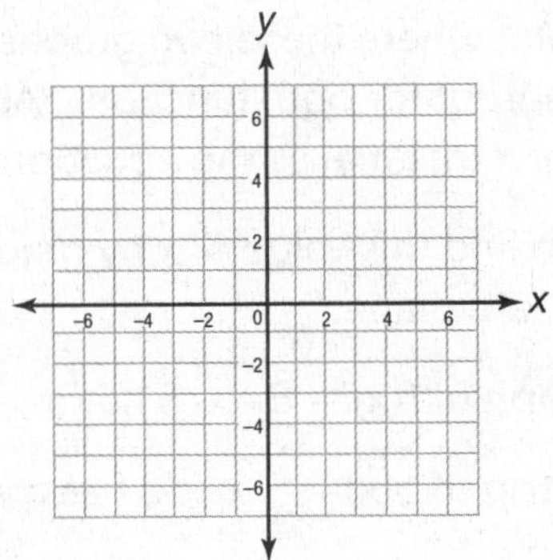

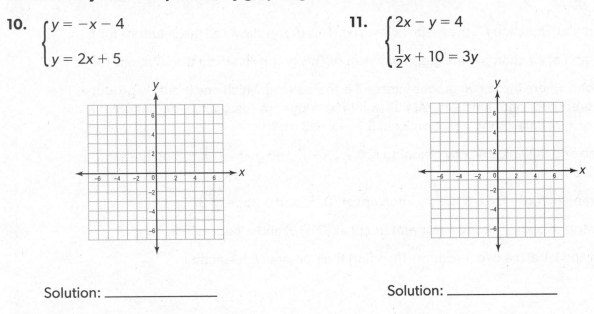

Solution: __________

Answer the questions below.

12. **EXPLAIN** How many solutions does the following system of equations have? How do you know?

$$\begin{cases} 2x + 6y = 18 \\ 3x + 9y = 27 \end{cases}$$

____

____

____

LESSON 16 Using Functions to Solve Equations

UNDERSTAND Solving a one-variable equation means finding the value of the variable that makes the equation true. So, solving $3x + 5 = -x - 3$ means finding a value of x that makes the left side of the equation equal to the right side.

You can treat each side of the equation as a separate function and let the two functions form a system, like this:

$$\begin{cases} f(x) = 3x + 5 \\ g(x) = -x - 3 \end{cases}$$

The graph of function f is the graph of $y = f(x)$. This graph shows all the solutions for f.

The graph of function g is the graph of $y = g(x)$. This graph shows all the solutions for g.

The point where these two graphs intersect is the point at which one input, x, produces the same output for both functions. At this point $f(x) = g(x)$, so the x-value for that point is the value of x that makes the equation $3x + 5 = -x - 3$ true.

You can find this value of x by graphing $f(x) = 3x + 5$ and $g(x) = -x - 3$ on the same coordinate plane.

The graph of $f(x) = 3x + 5$ has a y-intercept at (0, 5) and a slope of 3.

The graph of $g(x) = -x - 3$ has a y-intercept at (0, −3) and a slope of −1.

Graph and label the two functions. Then find their point of intersection.

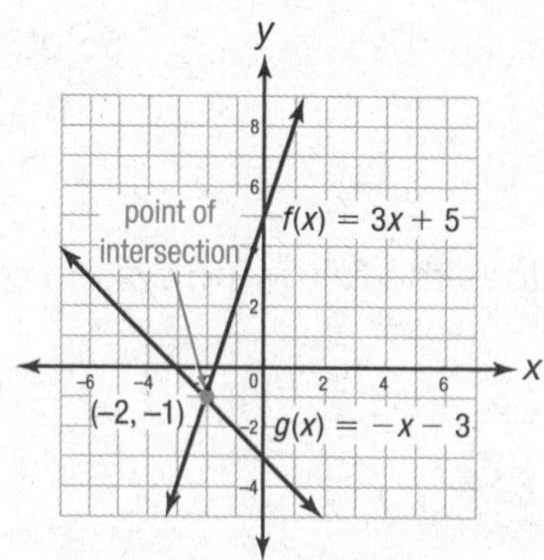

The graphs of f and g intersect at (−2, −1). The x-value of that ordered pair is −2, so the solution of $3x + 5 = -x - 3$ is $x = -2$.

Connect

Solve the following equation for x by making a system of functions and graphing.

$4x + 1 = 2x + 3$.

1 Treat the expression on each side of the equation as a function.

Let $f(x) = 4x + 1$.

Let $g(x) = 2x + 3$.

2 Graph each function in the system on the same coordinate plane.

The graph of f is the graph of $y = f(x)$, or $y = 4x + 1$. This graph is a line with a y-intercept at (0, 1) and a slope of 4.

The graph of g is the graph of $y = g(x)$, or $y = 2x + 3$. This graph is a line with a y-intercept at (0, 3) and a slope of 2.

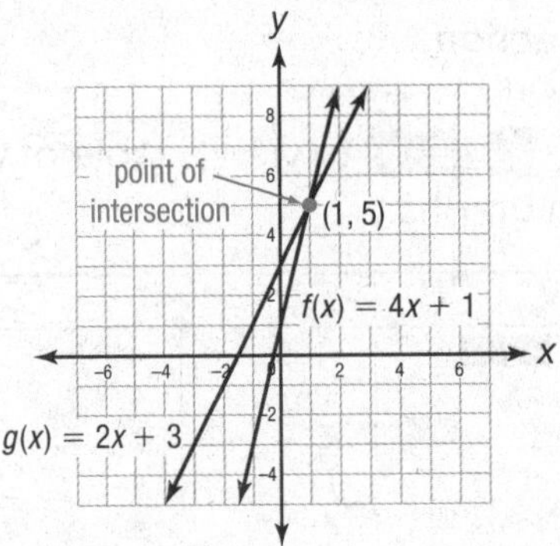

3 Find the x-coordinates of any points of intersection.

The graphs intersect at (1, 5).

The x-coordinate of that ordered pair is 1.

▶ The solution is $x = 1$.

CHECK

Solve $4x + 1 = 2x + 3$ algebraically and compare the solution to the one found above.

EXAMPLE Use a graphing calculator to solve for x: $2^{x-1} = 4$.

1

Treat the expression on each side of the equation as a function and form a system.

Let $f(x) = 2^{x-1}$.

Let $g(x) = 4$.

2

Graph the functions by using your graphing calculator and then find the point of intersection.

Press Y=.

For Y_1 enter 2^(X – 1).

For Y_2 enter 4.

Press GRAPH.

Your screen should show the following:

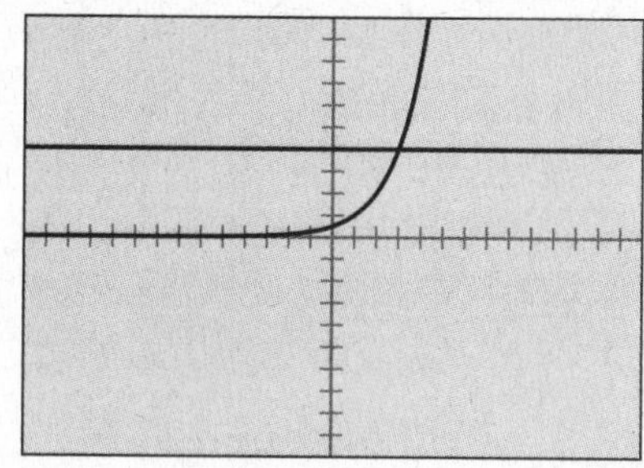

The point of intersection appears to be at $x = 3$.

3

Look at tables of values on your calculator to verify the point of intersection.

Press 2nd GRAPH to view a table of values for both graphs.

X	Y_1	Y_2
–2	.125	4
–1	.25	4
0	.5	4
1	1	4
2	2	4
3	4	4
4	8	4
X= –2		

The tables show that when X is 3, Y_1 is equal to Y_2 (both are equal to 4).

▶ The solution is $x = 3$.

CHECK

Using pencil and paper (not a calculator), complete the tables of values below for these functions. Show all work. Use the tables to check that $x = 3$ is the solution for $2^{x-1} = 4$.

x	$f(x) = 2^{x-1}$	$g(x) = 4$
0		
1		
2		
3		
4		

Problem Solving

READ

Cara and Cami are twins. They came up with a math puzzle. Cara says she is $(-2x + 3)$ years old, and Cami says she is $(-\frac{5}{2}x + 1)$ years old. What is the value of x? What are their ages?

PLAN

Since Cara and Cami are twins, you can set their ages equal and solve for x.

$$-2x + 3 = -\frac{5}{2}x + 1$$

Then evaluate one of the expressions ($-2x + 3$ or $-\frac{5}{2}x + 1$) to determine their ___________.

SOLVE

Use graphing to solve for x.

Let $f(x) =$ _______________.

Let $g(x) =$ _______________.

Graph each function on the coordinate plane to the right.

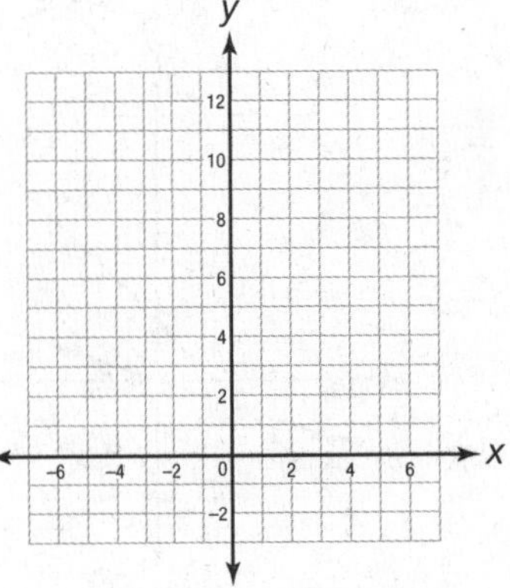

The point of intersection is (______, ______).

So, $x =$ ______. The y-coordinate, ______, represents the twins' ___________.

CHECK

Substitute that value of x into the original problem to verify that the two ages are the same and that the ages are the ones you found.

$$-2x + 3 = -\frac{5}{2}x + 1$$

$$-2(\_\_\_) + 3 \stackrel{?}{=} -\frac{5}{2}(\_\_\_\_) + 1$$

$$\_\_\_\_ + 3 \stackrel{?}{=} \_\_\_\_ + 1$$

____

Is this value of x the solution to the equation? _______________

▶ The value of x is ______. Each girl is ______ years old.

Practice

Write a system of two functions, *f* and *g*, that could be graphed in order to solve the given equation.

1. $7x + 11 = 8x - 1$

$\begin{cases} \_\_\_\_\_\_\_\_\_\_ \\ \_\_\_\_\_\_\_\_\_\_ \end{cases}$

2. $\frac{2}{3}x + 12 = -2x - 4$

$\begin{cases} \_\_\_\_\_\_\_\_\_\_ \\ \_\_\_\_\_\_\_\_\_\_ \end{cases}$

3. $3^t = 27$

$\begin{cases} \_\_\_\_\_\_\_\_\_\_ \\ \_\_\_\_\_\_\_\_\_\_ \end{cases}$

Assign each side to a function.

Solve each equation by using the given graph.

4. $x + 2 = \frac{1}{3}x$

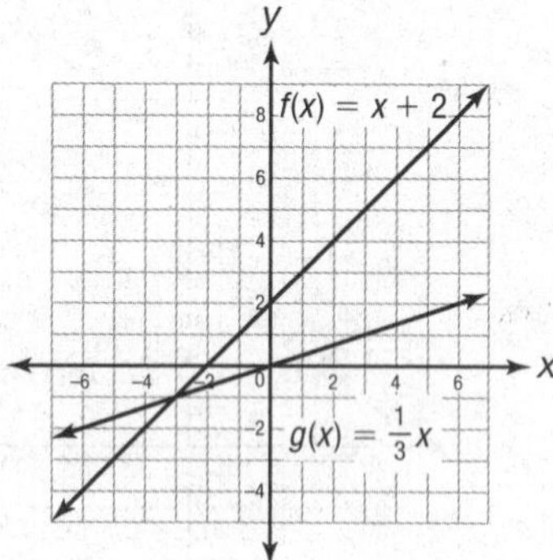

$x =$ ________

5. $-\frac{3}{2}x - 5 = -5x + 2$

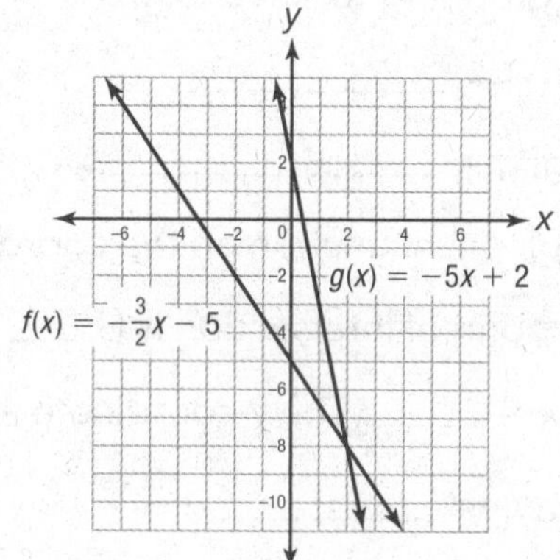

$x =$ ________

REMEMBER Look for the point of intersection.

6. $-x + 9 = \frac{3}{5}x + 1$

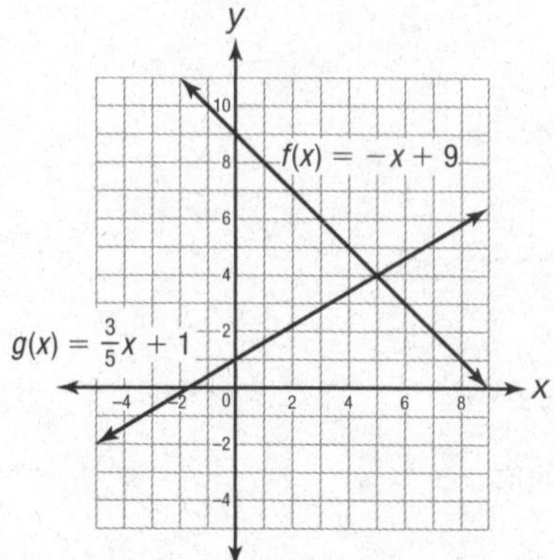

$x =$ ________

7. $\left(\frac{1}{2}\right)^x - 5 = -3$

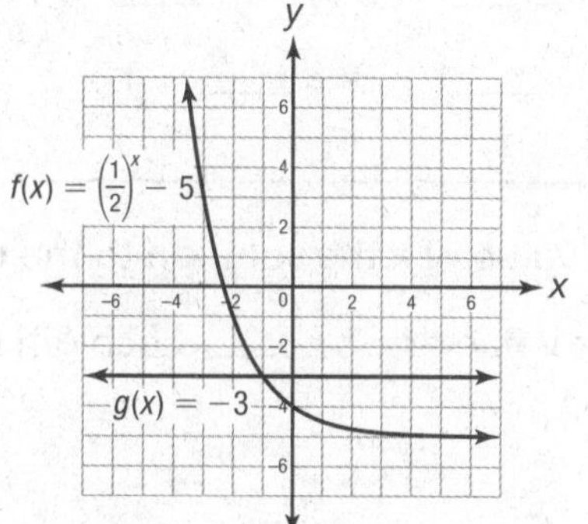

$x =$ ________

Solve each equation for x by using the given table.

8. $5^{x-2} = 25$

x	$f(x) = 5^{x-2}$	$g(x) = 25$
2	1	25
3	5	25
4	25	25
5	125	25
6	625	25

x = ______

9. $\frac{1}{2}x + 1 = \frac{3}{2}x - \frac{1}{2}$

x	$f(x) = \frac{1}{2}x + 1$	$g(x) = \frac{3}{2}x - \frac{1}{2}$
0	1	$-\frac{1}{2}$
$\frac{1}{2}$	$\frac{5}{4}$	$\frac{1}{4}$
1	$\frac{3}{2}$	1
$\frac{3}{2}$	$\frac{7}{4}$	$\frac{7}{4}$
2	2	$\frac{5}{2}$

x = ______

Complete the tables to solve each equation for x. Show your work.

10. $\left(\frac{1}{3}\right)^x = 3^x$

x	$f(x) = \left(\frac{1}{3}\right)^x$	$g(x) = 3^x$
−2	f(−2) =	g(−2) =
−1	f(−1) =	g(−1) =
0	f(0) =	g(0) =
1	f(1) =	g(1) =
2	f(2) =	g(2) =

x = ______

11. $-x + 5 = 2x - 1$

x	f(x) = ______________	g(x) = ______________
−2	f(−2) =	g(−2) =
−1	f(−1) =	g(−1) =
0	f(0) =	g(0) =
1	f(1) =	g(1) =
2	f(2) =	g(2) =

x = ______

Define a system of two functions and graph them on the coordinate plane to solve for *x*.

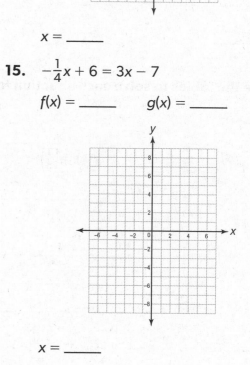

12. $x - 3 = -2x + 6$

$f(x) =$ _____ $g(x) =$ _____

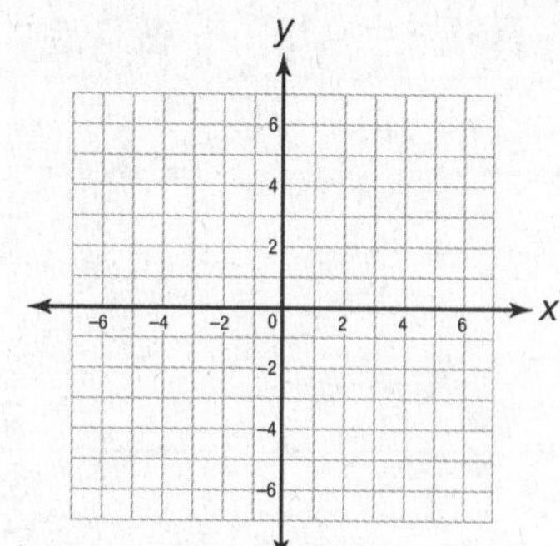

$x =$ _____

13. $-x + 2 = -3x - 4$

$f(x) =$ _____ $g(x) =$ _____

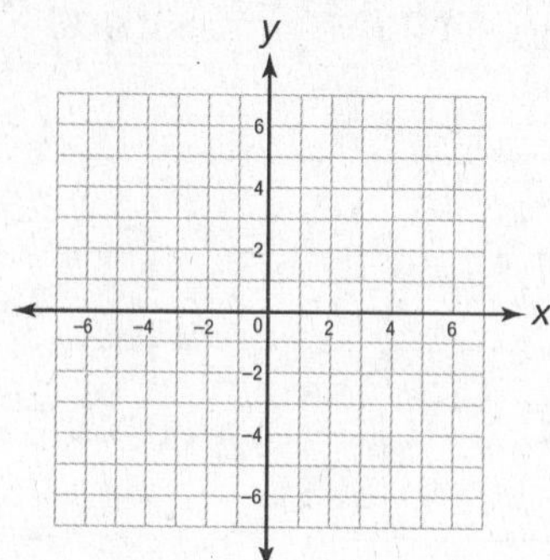

$x =$ _____

14. $4x + 5 = 0.5x - 2$

$f(x) =$ _____ $g(x) =$ _____

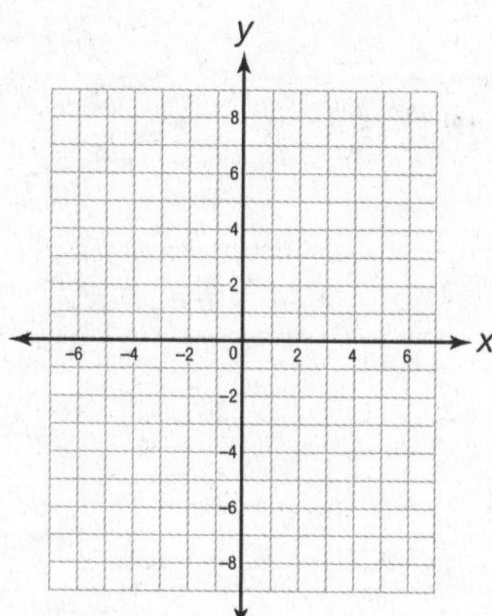

$x =$ _____

15. $-\frac{1}{4}x + 6 = 3x - 7$

$f(x) =$ _____ $g(x) =$ _____

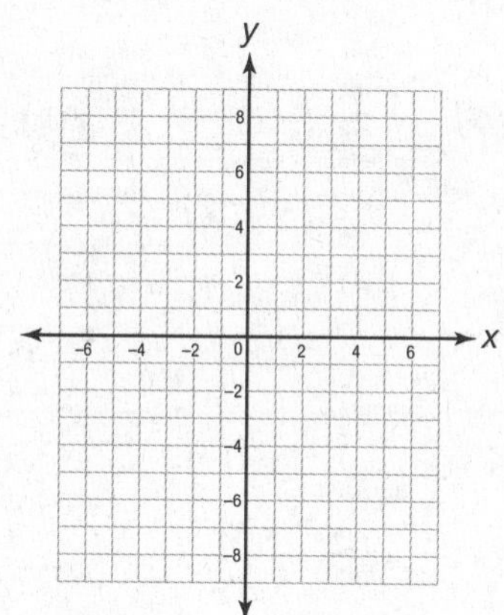

$x =$ _____

16. $2^{x+2} = 8$

$f(x) =$ _____ $g(x) =$ _____

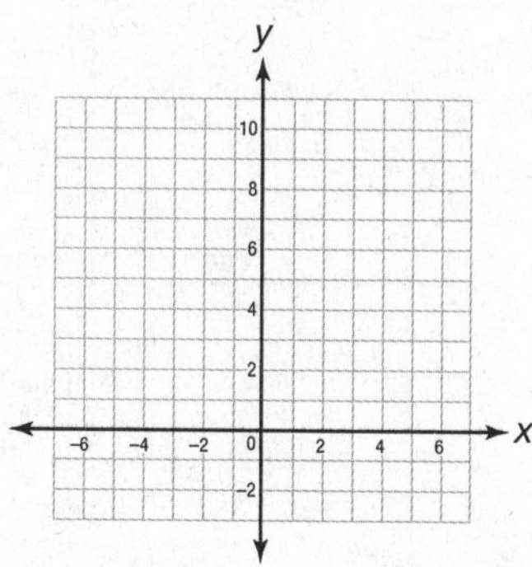

$x =$ _____

17. $\left(\frac{1}{2}\right)^x - 3 = 2^x - 3$

$f(x) =$ _____ $g(x) =$ _____

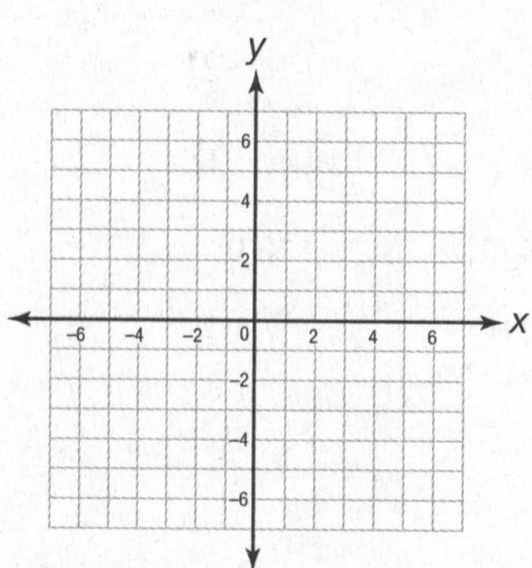

$x =$ _____

Choose the best answer. Use your graphing calculator to help you.

18. Lucia correctly used a graphing calculator to solve an equation for x. Her screen is shown to the right. The solution was $x = 2$.

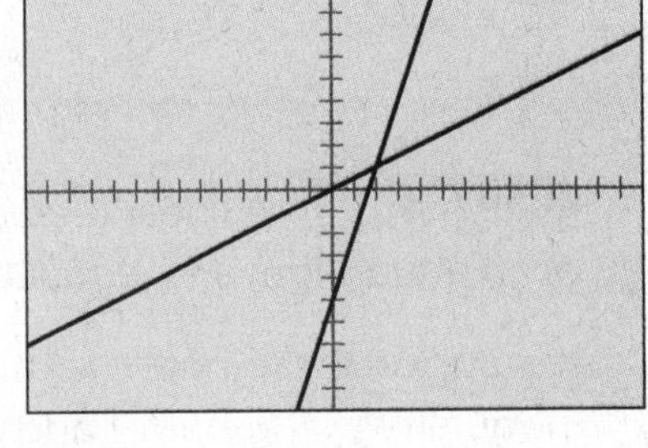

Which could be the equation she solved?

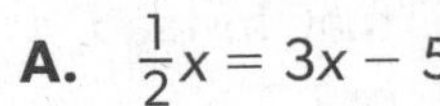

A. $\frac{1}{2}x = 3x - 5$

B. $\frac{1}{2}x = -3x - 5$

C. $\frac{1}{2}x - 5 = 3x$

D. $\frac{1}{2}x - 5 = -3x$

19. Adler correctly used a graphing calculator to solve an equation for x. His screen is shown to the right. The solution was $x = -1$.

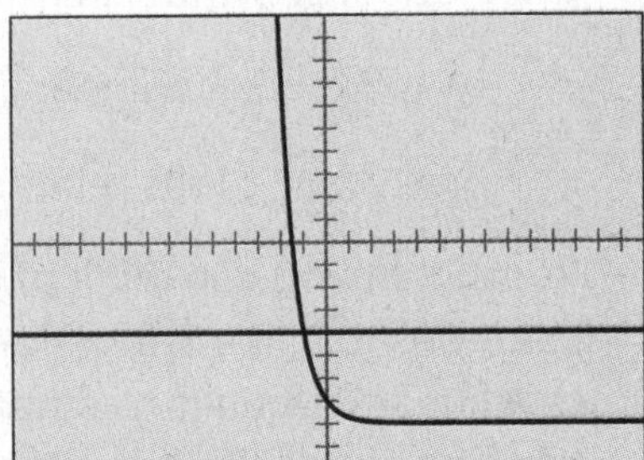

Which could be the equation he solved?

A. $\left(\frac{1}{4}\right)^x - 8 = -7$

B. $\left(\frac{1}{4}\right)^x - 8 = -4$

C. $\left(\frac{1}{4}\right)^x + 8 = 4$

D. $\left(\frac{1}{4}\right)^x + 8 = 8$

20. SHOW Ling decided to sell cupcakes at the county fair. Her ingredients cost her about 25 cents per cupcake. Renting a booth costs $30 per day. She sells each cupcake for $1. Ling's expenses can be modeled by the function $c(x) = 0.25x + 30.00$. Her income can be modeled by the function $p(x) = 1.00x$. How many cupcakes must she sell to break even?

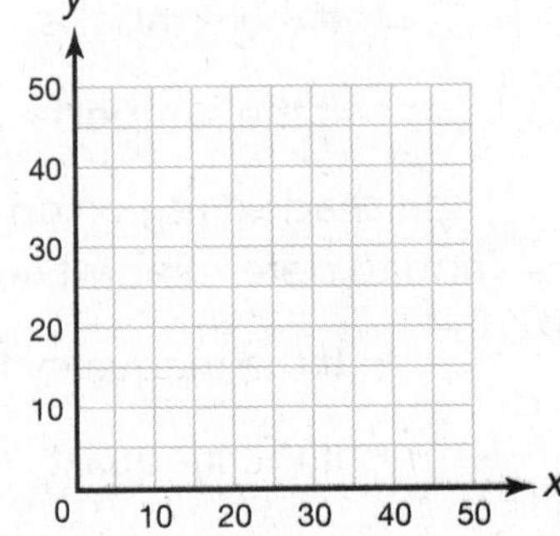

____

21. JUSTIFY Is there a value of x that makes $2^x = -2$ true? Rewrite the equation as a system of two functions and graph the system. Use your graph to justify your answer.

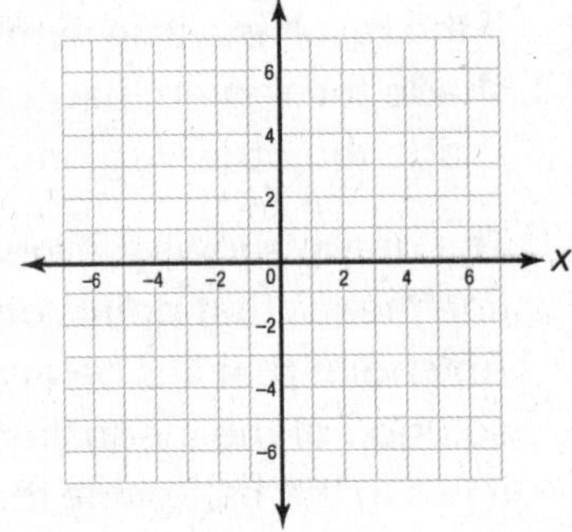

____

____

____

LESSON 17 Graphing Inequalities

Graphing an Inequality

UNDERSTAND A linear inequality is similar to a linear equation. The difference is that, instead of an equal sign, an inequality contains one of four inequality symbols: $<$, $>$, $\leq$, or $\geq$.

It is important to note that a linear inequality is not a function. For example, for the linear inequality $y > x$, both 1 and 5 are possible values for y when $x = 0$. Since there are multiple outputs (y-values) for one input (x-value), the linear inequality $y > x$ is not a function.

You can, however, use the concept of a function to help you solve inequalities. If you replace the inequality symbol in a linear inequality with an equal sign, you get a related equation.

$y > 3x + 2$ is a linear inequality.

$y = 3x + 2$ is its related linear equation.

Recall that you can think of $y = 3x + 2$ as $y = f(x)$ with $f(x) = 3x + 2$. Remember also that the solutions to a linear function can be graphed as a line on the coordinate plane. The solution to a linear inequality is a **half-plane**, the portion of the coordinate plane that lies on one side of a line called the boundary. The boundary is the graph of the related linear equation for the inequality. All of the points in the half-plane are solutions to the inequality.

To graph a linear inequality in the coordinate plane, graph its related equation in order to find the boundary line.

- If the symbol is $<$ or $>$, draw a dashed line. Points on the boundary line are not solutions.
- If the symbol is $\leq$ or $\geq$, draw a solid line. Points on the boundary line are solutions.

Then shade a region on one side of the boundary line. Put the inequality in slope-intercept form to determine where to shade.

- If the inequality has the form $y < mx + b$ or $y \leq mx + b$, shade below the line.
- If the inequality has the form $y > mx + b$ or $y \geq mx + b$, shade above the line.

You can also find the correct region to shade by choosing a test point and substituting its x- and y-values into the inequality. If the result is a true number sentence, such as $2 > 0$, then shade the region that contains the test point. Otherwise, shade the other region.

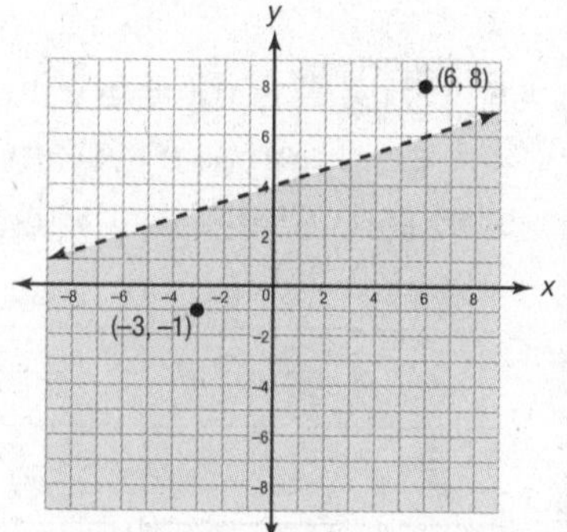

The graph shows the inequality $y < \frac{1}{3}x + 4$. The dashed boundary line means that points on the line are not solutions of the inequality. Any point that lies below the line, in the shaded half-plane, is a solution of the inequality. The point $(-3, -1)$ is a solution because it lies in the half-plane that shows all solutions to the inequality. The point (6, 8) is not a solution because it does not lie in the half-plane.

Connect

Graph the inequality $y \geq 2x - 5$.

1 Find the line for the related equation.

To write the related equation, replace the inequality symbol $\geq$ with an equal sign. The related equation is $y = 2x - 5$. The line $y = 2x - 5$ passes through the points $(0, -5)$ and $(1, -3)$.

2 Determine whether the line is solid or dashed.

The inequality symbol is $\geq$. So, the line is solid. Points both on the line and in one half-plane are solutions of the inequality.

3 Determine which half-plane to shade.

The inequality is already in slope-intercept form. The inequality symbol is $\geq$. So, shade the half-plane above the line.

4 Graph the inequality on a coordinate plane.

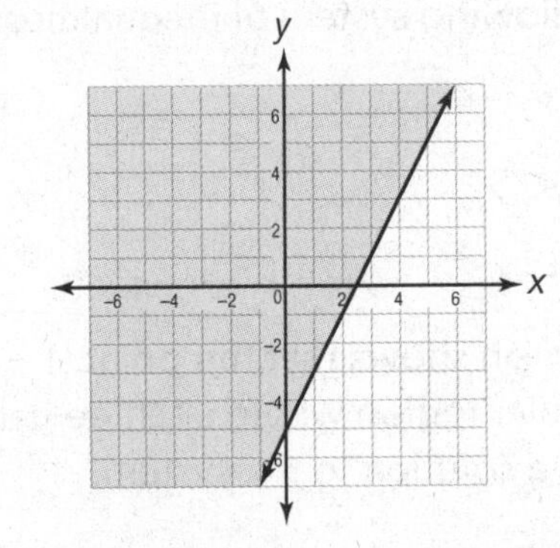

CHECK

The point $(-1, 1)$ is in the half-plane. Substitute these values of x and y into the inequality to confirm that this coordinate pair is a solution.

Graphing a System

UNDERSTAND The solution to a system of linear inequalities is also a portion of the coordinate plane. It consists of the points that are solutions for every inequality in the system. This is the part of the coordinate plane where all of the shaded regions overlap.

In a system of two inequalities, the solution to the system is the intersection of the two half-planes that are solutions to the individual inequalities. All the points that lie in that intersection are solutions for both inequalities.

The graph on the upper right shows the solutions to the following system of inequalities:

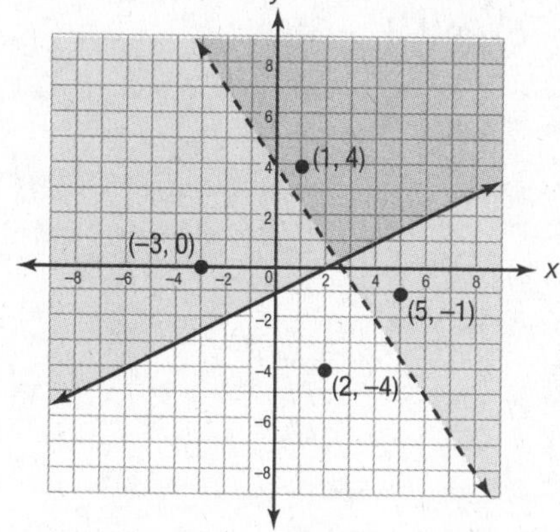

$$\begin{cases} y \geq \frac{1}{2}x - 1 \\ y > -\frac{3}{2}x + 4 \end{cases}$$

The point $(2, -4)$ is not a solution to either inequality.

The point $(-3, 0)$ is a solution to the first inequality, but not to the second inequality.

The point $(5, -1)$ is a solution to the second inequality, but not to the first inequality.

The point $(1, 4)$ is a solution to both inequalities. It is a solution to the system.

In a system of more than two inequalities, the solution is the intersection of all the half-planes that are solutions to the individual inequalities.

The graph on the lower right shows the solutions to the following system of inequalities:

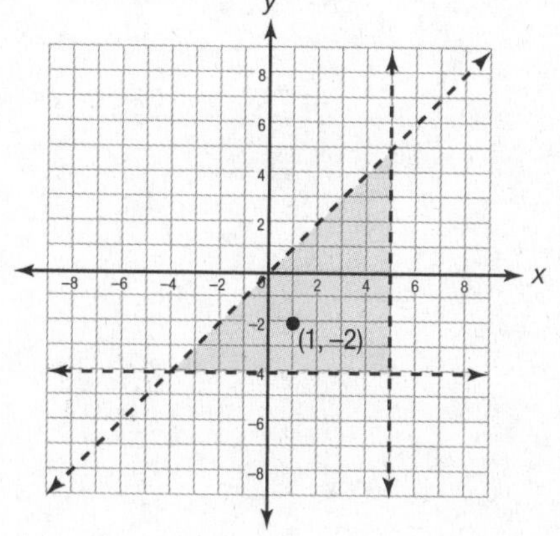

$$\begin{cases} y > -4 \\ x < 5 \\ y < x \end{cases}$$

The graph shows that the point $(1, -2)$ lies in the triangular region where all three half-planes intersect, so it is a solution to the system.

Connect

Graph the solution for the following system of inequalities.

$$\begin{cases} y < 3x - 3 \\ y < -\frac{1}{2}x + 1 \end{cases}$$

1

Graph the first inequality.

The related equation, $y = 3x - 3$, is represented by the line through $(0, -3)$ and $(1, 0)$.

Since the inequality symbol is $<$, use a dashed line and shade below the line.

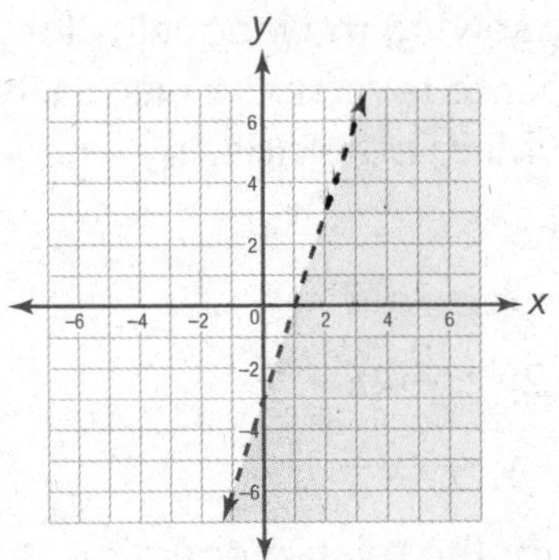

2

Graph the second inequality on the same coordinate plane.

The related equation, $y = -\frac{1}{2}x + 1$, is represented by the line through $(0, 1)$ and $(2, 0)$.

Since the inequality symbol is $<$, use a dashed line and shade below the line.

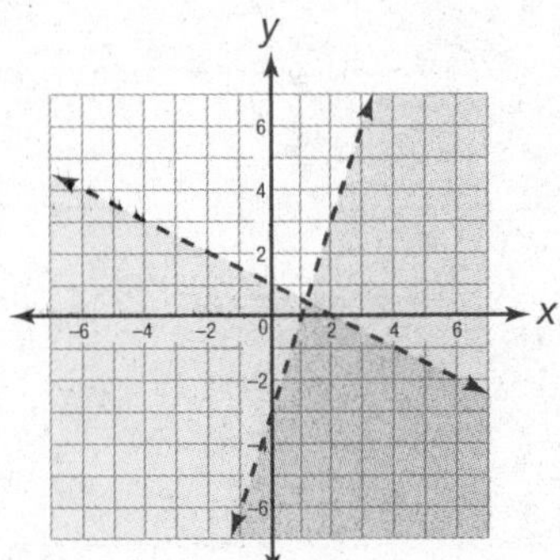

3

Identify the solution.

▶ The darker region below both lines represents the solution set for the system of inequalities.

Is the point $(4, -1)$ a solution to the system of inequalities $y < 3x - 3$ and $y < -\frac{1}{2}x + 1$?

EXAMPLE Graph the solution to the following system of inequalities.

$$\begin{cases} y \geq 2x + 3 \\ -2y - 2 \geq -4x \end{cases}$$

1 Graph the first inequality.

The related equation, $y = 2x + 3$, is represented by the line through (0, 3) and (−1, 1).

Since the inequality symbol is $\geq$, use a solid line and shade above the line.

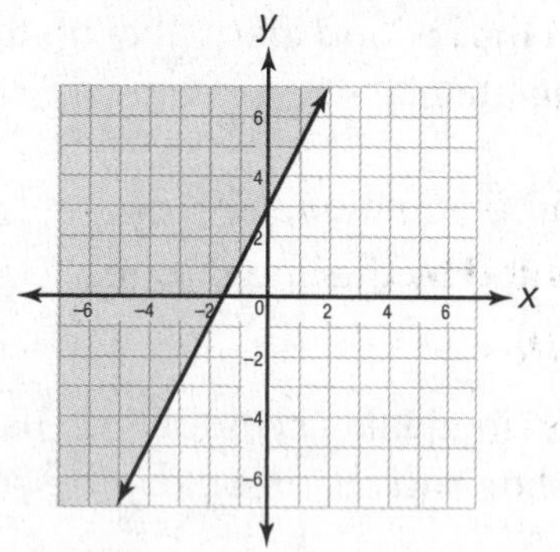

2 Graph the second inequality on the same coordinate plane.

Begin by solving the inequality for *y*. Remember to reverse the inequality sign when dividing both sides by a negative number.

$$-2y - 2 \geq -4x$$

$$-2y \geq -4x + 2$$

$$y \leq 2x - 1$$

The line for the related equation, $y = 2x - 1$, passes through (0, −1) and (1, 1). Since the inequality symbol is $\leq$, use a solid line and shade below.

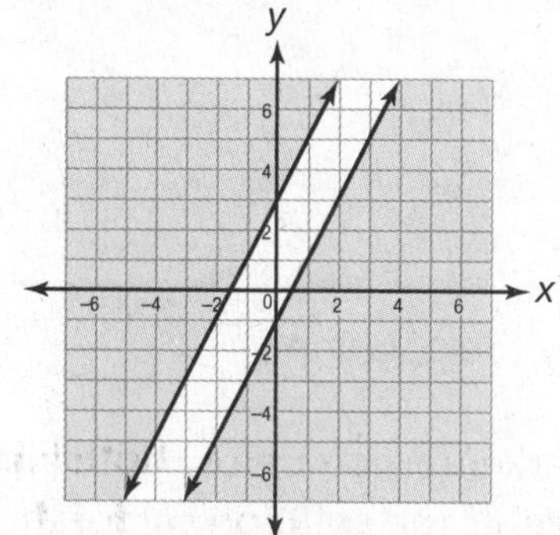

3 Identify the solution.

The two lines are parallel, which means that they will never intersect.

▶ The two regions have no points in common. Thus, the system of inequalities has no solution.

MODEL

Can a system of inequalities whose graph consists of parallel boundaries have a solution? If so, draw a graph to support your answer.

Problem Solving

READ

A jewelry maker is creating a line of bracelets and necklaces with a new type of chain. The bracelets are 8 inches long, and the necklaces are 14 inches long. She has 280 inches of chain. It takes her 4 hours to make a bracelet and 3 hours to make a necklace. She can work no more than 120 hours this month.

Write a system of inequalities to model the number of bracelets and the number of necklaces that the jewelry maker can create this month. Then determine how many necklaces and bracelets she can produce.

PLAN

Write a system of inequalities to describe the situation.

Let x be the number of bracelets and y be the number of necklaces she can make.

Since these are numbers of real objects, they cannot be negative numbers.

So, $x \geq$ ______ and $y \geq$ ______.

It takes 8 inches of chain to make a bracelet and 14 inches to make a necklace. The total amount of chain used must be less than or equal to the total amount available, 280 inches.

So, ____x + ____$y \leq 280$.

It takes 4 hours to make a bracelet and 3 hours to make a necklace. The total amount of time spent making the jewelry this month must be no more than 120 hours.

So, $4x + 3y$ ____ 120.

SOLVE

The boundary lines for this system of inequalities are graphed on the coordinate plane to the right. Shade the region that represents the solution.

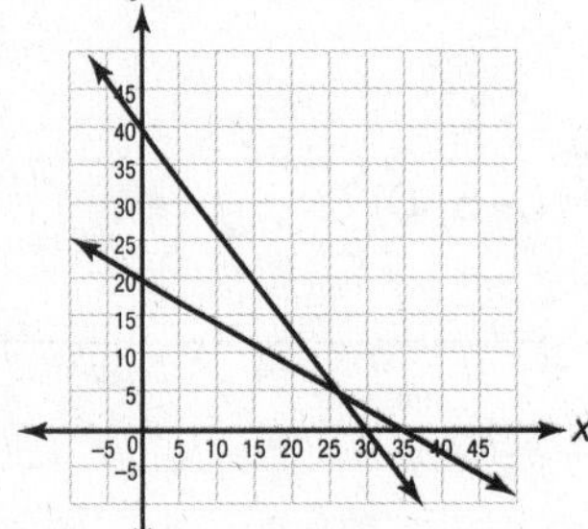

CHECK

The point (15, ____) lies within the solution region. Show that it satisfies all 4 inequalities.

$15 \geq 0$ ✓

____ ≥ 0

$8(15) + 14($____$) \leq 280$ → ______ ≤ 280

$4(15) + 3($____$)$ ____ 120 → ________________

Practice

Determine whether each point is a solution to the inequality graphed below.

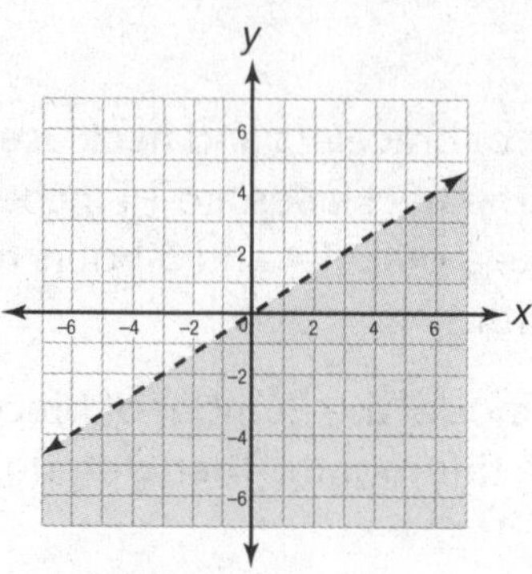

1. (−3, −1)

____

2. (2, 0)

____

3. (6, 4)

____

Points on a dashed boundary line are not included in a solution set. Points on a solid boundary line are included in a solution set.

Determine whether each point is a solution to the system of inequalities graphed below.

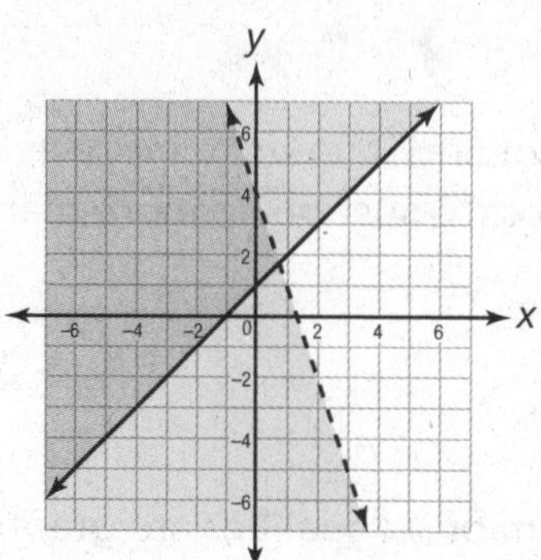

4. (−5, 0)

____

5. (1, −4)

____

6. (−2, −1)

____

7. (0, 4)

____

REMEMBER A solution to a system of inequalities must be a solution for each inequality in the system.

Use the graph below to answer questions 8 and 9. Choose the best answer.

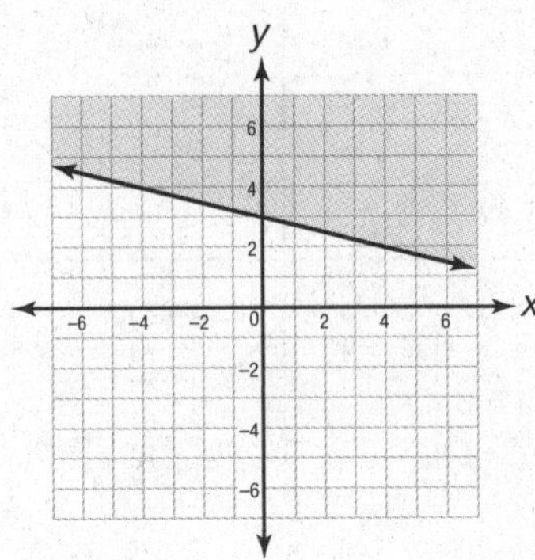

8. Which point is **not** part of the solution set for this inequality?

A. (0, 3)

B. (3, 3)

C. (4, 0)

D. (−4, 6)

9. Which inequality is represented by the graph?

A. $y > -\frac{1}{4}x + 3$

B. $y < -\frac{1}{4}x + 3$

C. $y \leq -\frac{1}{4}x + 3$

D. $y \geq -\frac{1}{4}x + 3$

Use the graph below to answer questions 10 and 11. Choose the best answer.

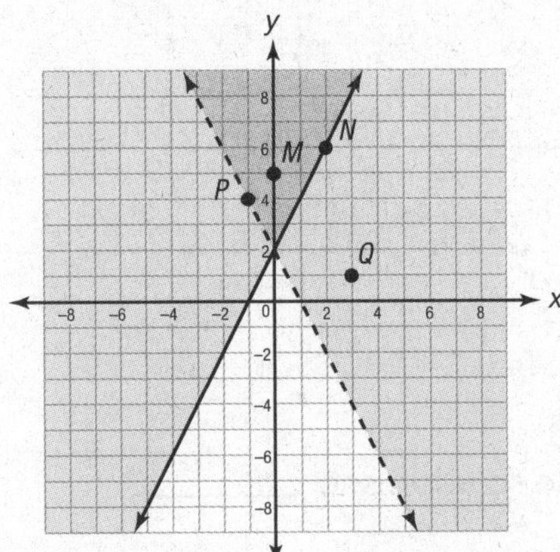

10. Which points are included in the solution set for this system of inequalities?

A. *M* only

B. *M* and *N*

C. *M*, *N*, and *P*

D. *M* and *Q*

11. Which system of inequalities is represented by this graph?

A. $\begin{cases} y \geq 2x + 2 \\ y < -2x + 2 \end{cases}$

B. $\begin{cases} y \geq 2x + 2 \\ y > -2x + 2 \end{cases}$

C. $\begin{cases} y > 2x + 2 \\ y > -2x + 2 \end{cases}$

D. $\begin{cases} y \leq 2x + 2 \\ y < -2x + 2 \end{cases}$

Use the graph below to answer questions 12–14.

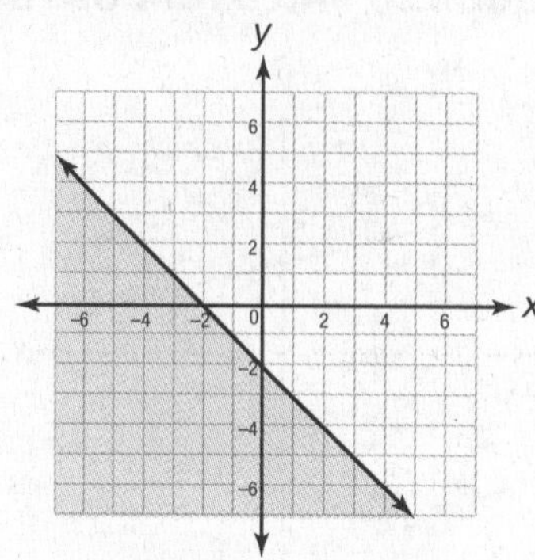

12. Name a point that is part of the solution set. ________

13. Name a point that is **not** part of the solution set. ________

14. Write the inequality represented by the graph.

____

Use the graph below to answer questions 15–17.

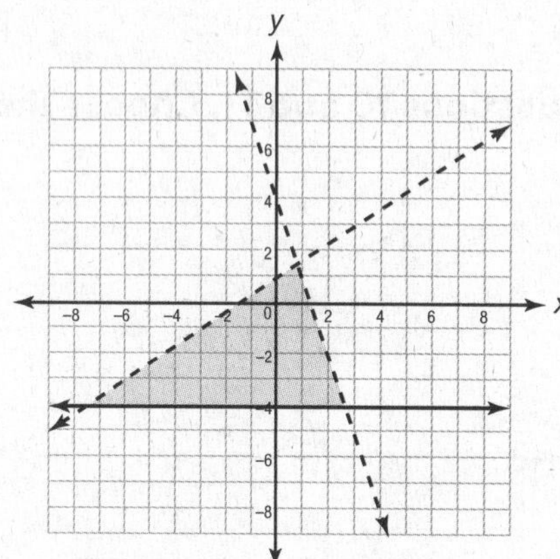

15. Name a point that is part of the solution set. ________

16. Name a point that is **not** part of the solution set. ________

17. Write the system of inequalities represented by the graph.

____

____

____

Graph each inequality.

18. $y \leq \frac{4}{5}x - 1$

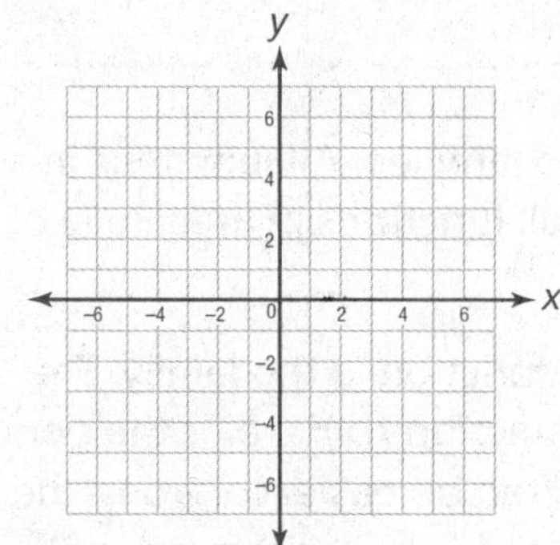

19. $6x - 2y < 8$

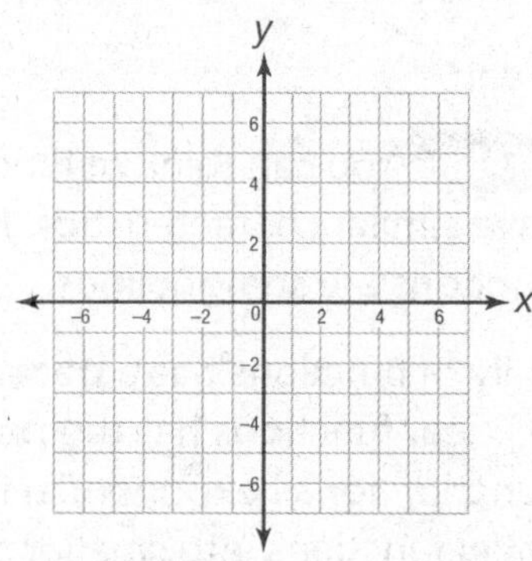

20. SHOW A farmer will plant corn and soy on his farm this year. He has a total of 25 acres available for planting. Each acre of corn costs \$350 to plant, and each acre of soy costs \$150 to plant. His costs must be no more than \$5,250.

Let x be the number of acres of corn to be planted and let y be the number of acres of soy to be planted. Write a system of four inequalities to describe the situation. Then graph the system.

____

____

____

____

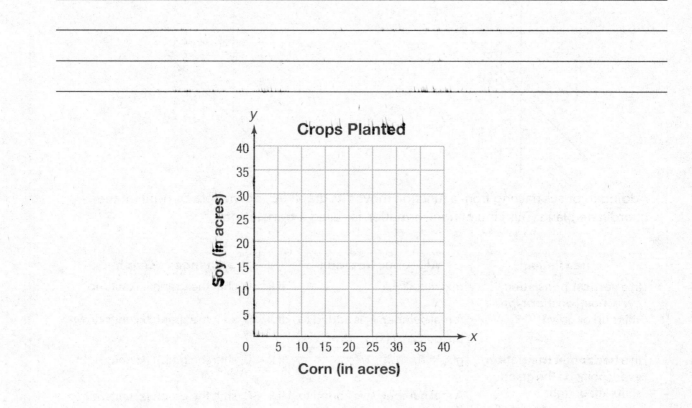

Crops Planted

y

40
35
30
25
20
15
10
5
0

5 10 15 20 25 30 35 40 x

Soy (in acres)

Corn (in acres)

LESSON 18

Translating Functions

UNDERSTAND You can think of functions as being grouped into families. All functions in a family have similar characteristics. For example, the graphs of all functions in the family of linear functions are straight lines.

Each family of functions has a **parent function**, the most basic function in the family. The family of linear functions has the parent function $f(x) = x$. The function $f(x) = e^x$ is the general parent function for all exponential functions. However, it can often be easier to group the exponential functions into smaller subfamilies that have the same base, such as $f(x) = 2^x$ and $f(x) = 23.5^x$.

If you change the parent function by adding, subtracting, multiplying, or dividing by a constant, you transform the function and make a new function from the same family. For example, the function $g(x) = x - 3$ is different from the parent function $f(x)= x$, but it is still in the linear function family. Changing the equation of the function also changes the graph of the function. This change to the graph is called a **transformation**.

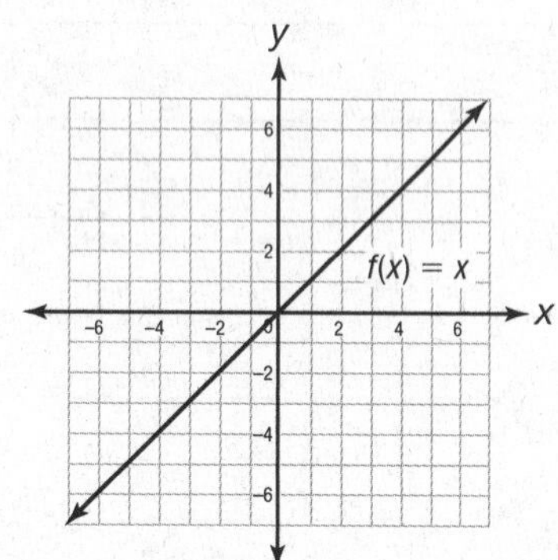

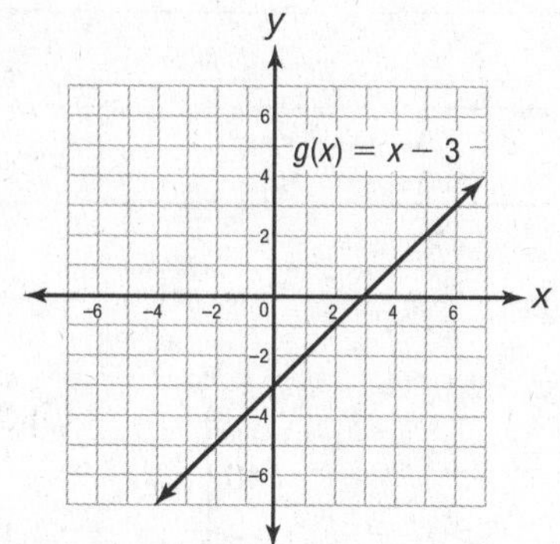

Adding to or subtracting from a function moves its graph up, down, left, or right on the coordinate plane. This kind of transformation is called a **translation**.

Translation	Algebraic Notation	Change to Graph
In a **vertical translation**, every point on the graph shifts up or down.	$g(x) = f(x) + k$ A real number, k, is added to the output, $f(x)$.	If $k > 0$, shift the graph $\|k\|$ units up. If $k < 0$, shift the graph $\|k\|$ units down.
In a **horizontal translation,** every point on the graph shifts left or right.	$g(x) = f(x + k)$ A real number, k, is added to the input, x.	If $k < 0$, shift the graph $\|k\|$ units right. If $k > 0$, shift the graph $\|k\|$ units left.

Connect

The exponential function $f(x) = 3^x$ is graphed on the coordinate plane below. Make a table of values for the function $g(x) = 3^x + 2$. Then graph function g on the same coordinate plane. Describe how function f could be translated to form function g and how translating a function affects its size and shape.

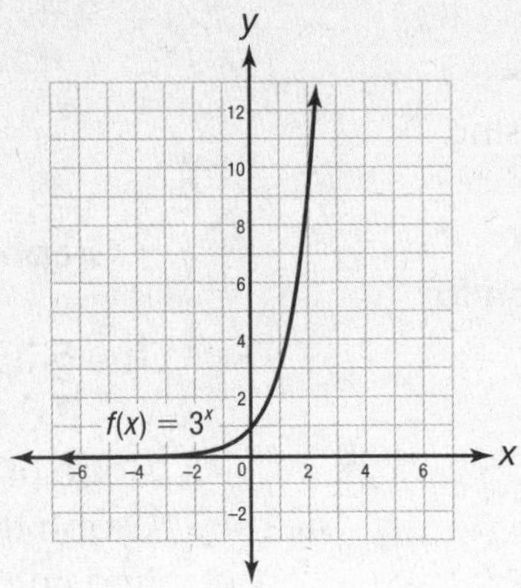

1 Create a table of values for $g(x) = 3^x + 2$.

x	$g(x) = 3^x + 2$	g(x)
−2	$g(-2) = 3^{-2} + 2 = \frac{1}{9} + 2 = \frac{19}{9}$	$\frac{19}{9}$
−1	$g(-1) = 3^{-1} + 2 = \frac{1}{3} + 2 = \frac{7}{3}$	$\frac{7}{3}$
0	$g(0) = 3^0 + 2 = 1 + 2 = 3$	3
1	$g(1) = 3^1 + 2 = 3 + 2 = 5$	5
2	$g(2) = 3^2 + 2 = 9 + 2 = 11$	11

2 Plot the ordered pairs for function g and connect them with a curve.

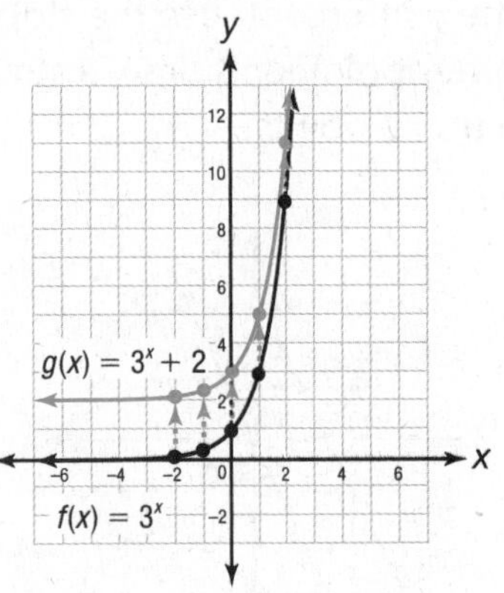

3 Compare the graphs.

- Each point on the graph of function g is 2 units above its corresponding point on function f. So, function g is the result of a vertical translation of function f 2 units up.

Since all we are doing is sliding the graph in the coordinate plane, the size and shape of the graph have not changed.

DISCUSS

Since you were given the graph of $f(x) = 3^x$, could you have graphed $g(x) = 3^x + 2$ without creating a table of values first? Explain.

EXAMPLE A Let $f(x) = 2x$ and define a function g such that $g(x) = f(x + 3)$. Graph both functions, f and g, on the same coordinate plane. Compare the two graphs and identify how function f could be translated to form function g.

1 Write function g in terms of x by using functional notation.

For the function g, use the expression for $f(x)$ and replace x with $(x + 3)$.

$g(x) = f(x + 3)$

$g(x) = 2(x + 3)$

$g(x) = 2x + 6$

2 Graph function f.

The graph of f is the graph of the equation $y = f(x)$ or $y = 2x$. This equation has a slope of 2 and a y-intercept at (0, 0). Graph the y-intercept, use the slope to find another point, and draw a straight line through those points.

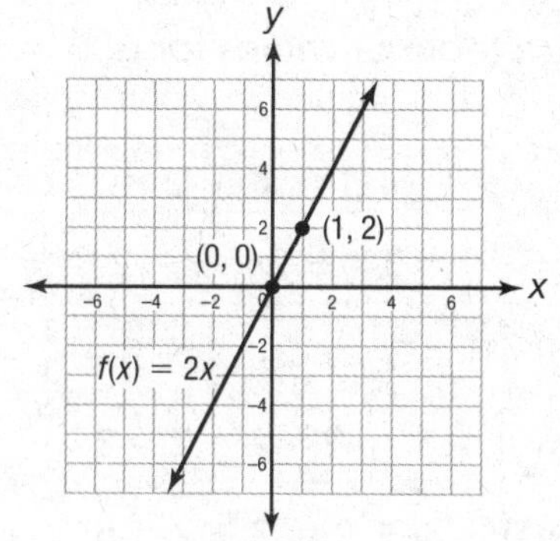

3 Graph function g.

The graph of g is the graph of the equation $y = g(x)$ or $y = 2x + 6$. This equation has a slope of 2 and a y-intercept at (0, 6). Graph the y-intercept, use the slope to find another point, and draw a straight line through those points.

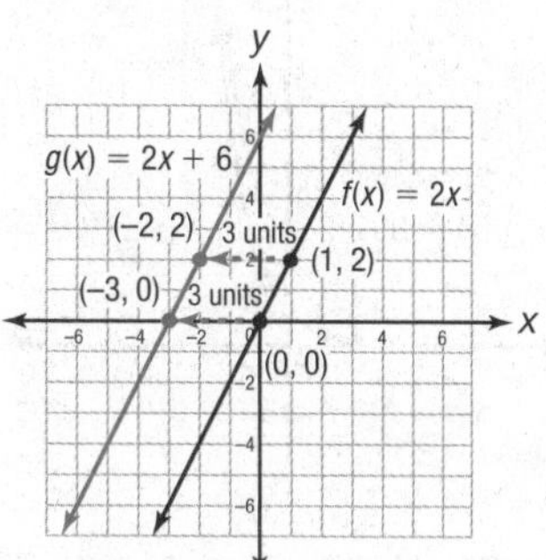

4 Compare the graphs.

- Each point on function g is 3 units to the left of the corresponding point on function f.

This makes sense. When 3 is added to the input, as it was in $g(x) = f(x + 3)$, the result is a translation of 3 units to the left.

Notice that both lines have the same slope, 2. So, translating a line horizontally does not change its slope.

TRY

On the grid shown in Step 3 above, graph $h(x) = f(x - 3)$. Describe how function f could be translated to form function h.

EXAMPLE B A linear function f is graphed below. On the same coordinate plane, graph the function $g(x) = f(x) - 5$. Identify the transformation.

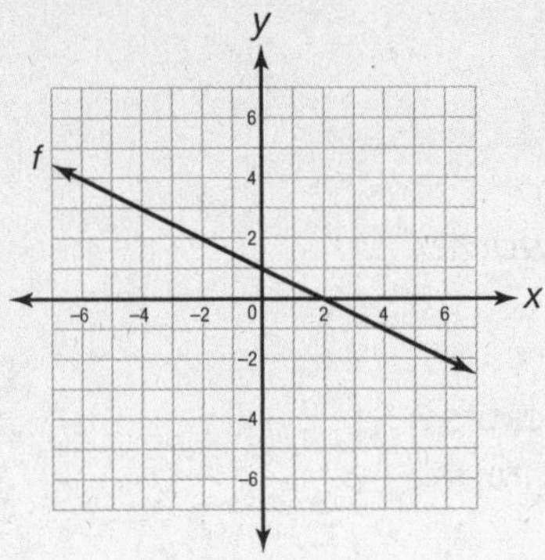

1 Describe the translation.

$g(x) = f(x) - 5$ is in the form $g(x) = f(x) + k$, where $k = -5$.

When a numerical value, k, is added to an output, $f(x)$, the result is a vertical shift.

Since k is the negative number -5, shift the graph 5 units down.

2 Graph the function g.

Shift two points on the graph of function f down 5 units. Then draw a line through them.

(0, 1) is translated 5 units down to (0, −4).

(2, 0) is translated 5 units down to (2, −5).

▶

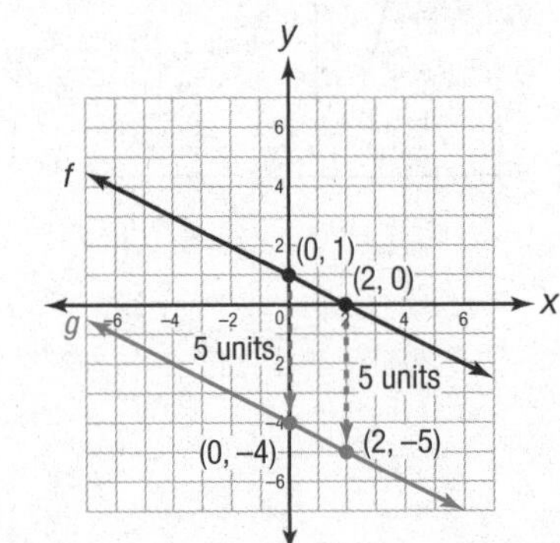

The transformation is a vertical translation 5 units down.

DISCUSS

The equations for functions f and g are not given. Can you determine if their slopes are the same? Explain how.

EXAMPLE C The graph of $f(x) = \left(\frac{1}{2}\right)^x$ is shown. Translate function f to form the function $h(x) = f(x - 4) + 2$. Graph h and write its explicit equation.

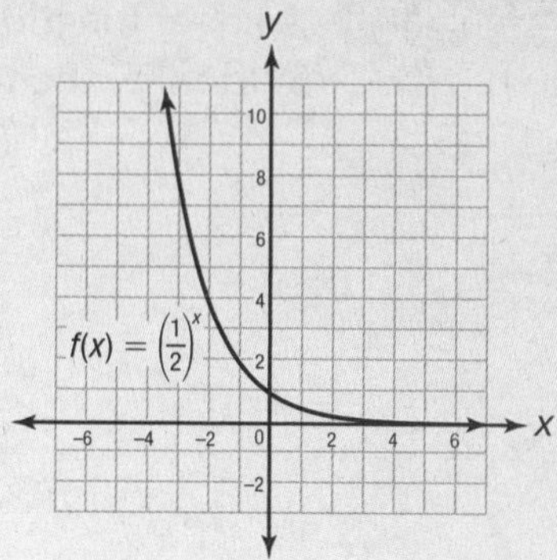

1 Describe the translation by using words and symbols.

Subtracting 4 from the input, x, indicates a horizontal translation. Translate the graph 4 units to the right.

Adding 2 to the output, $f(x - 4)$, indicates a vertical translation. Translate the graph 2 units up.

2 Graph h.

Choose several points on the graph of f and translate each point 4 units to the right and 2 units up.

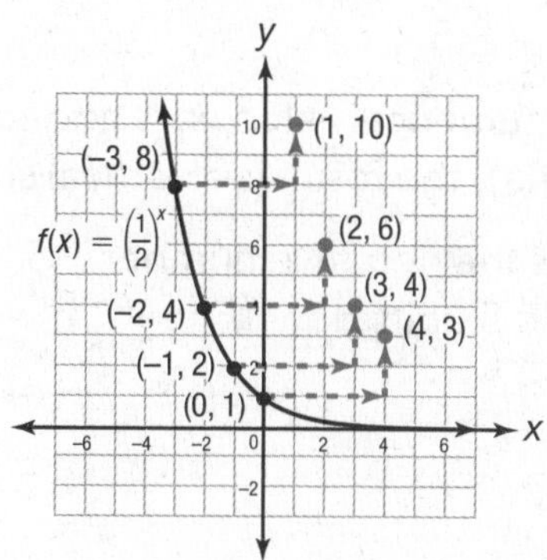

3 Connect the points with a smooth curve.

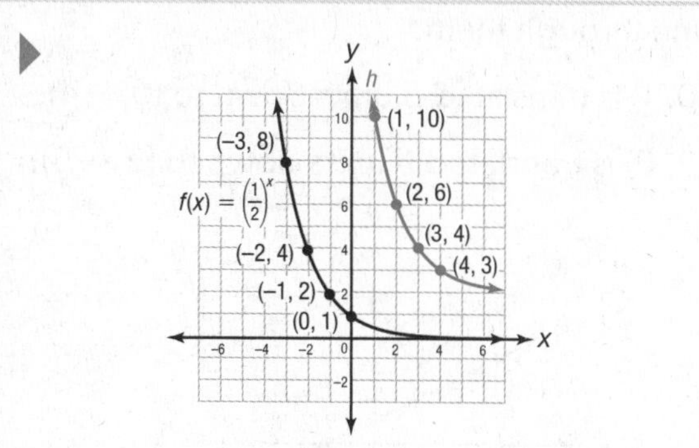

4 Write an equation for h.

The translation involved subtracting 4 from the input and adding 2 to that output. So, subtract 4 from x, which is the exponent in $\left(\frac{1}{2}\right)^x$, and then add 2 to the resulting expression.

▶ $h(x) = \left(\frac{1}{2}\right)^{x-4} + 2$.

CHECK

Use a graphing calculator to check your work. Press Y=.

For Y_1, enter (1/2)^X. For Y_2, enter (1/2)^(X – 4) + 2. Press 2nd GRAPH to bring up a table of values. Press GRAPH to view the graph.

EXAMPLE D Functions f and g are graphed on the right. Using function notation, write an equation describing $g(x)$ in terms of $f(x)$. Then use the equation given for $f(x)$ to write an equation for $g(x)$ in terms of x.

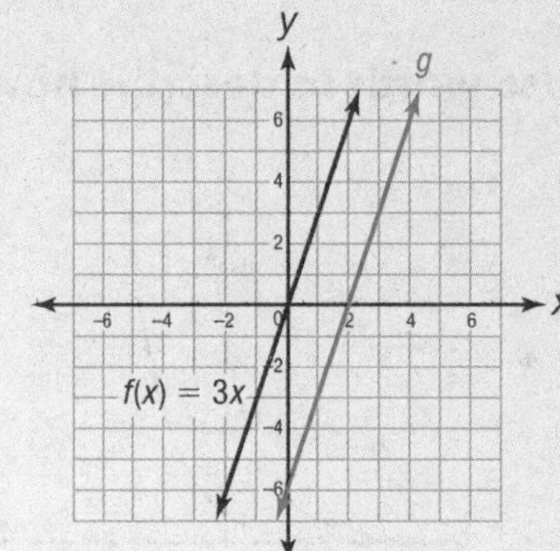

1 Identify how f could be translated to form g.

Choose a point on f, such as (0, 0).

If this point is translated 2 units to the right, it would cover point (2, 0), which is on the graph of g.

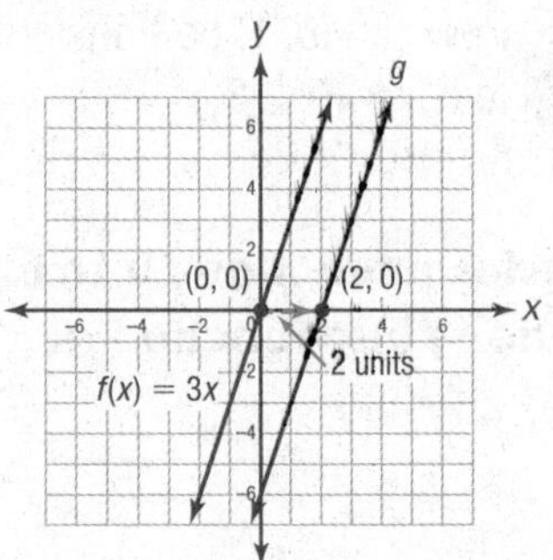

Verify that any point on f, if translated 2 units to the right, has a corresponding point on g.

2 Write the function $g(x)$ in terms of $f(x)$.

To represent a horizontal translation of 2 units to the right, add -2 to the input, x.

So $g(x) = f(x - 2)$.

3 Write the function $g(x)$ in terms of x.

To find an explicit expression for $g(x)$, substitute $(x - 2)$ for x in the expression for $f(x)$.

$g(x) = f(x - 2)$

$g(x) = 3(x - 2)$

▶ $g(x) = 3x - 6$

CHECK

Use a graphing calculator to check that $g(x) = 3x - 6$ is the correct equation for function g.

Practice

Use words to describe how function *f* could be translated to form function *g* in one step.

1.

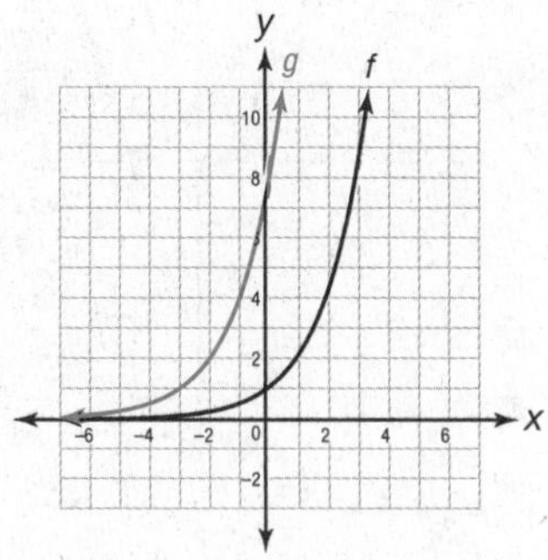

2.

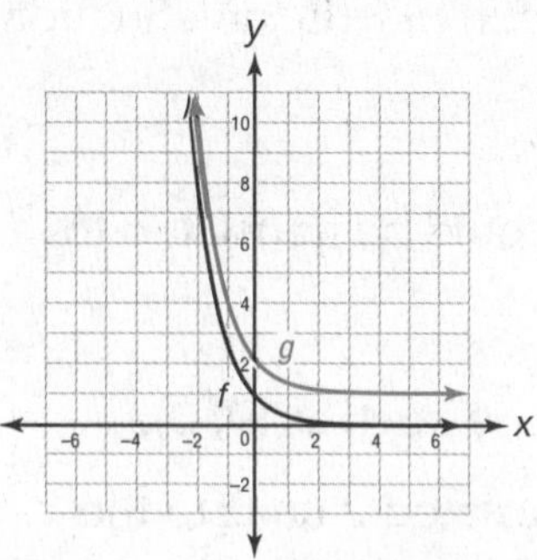

HINT How can (0, 1) be translated to cover (0, 2)?

Use words to describe a horizontal translation that would transform function *f* into function *g*. Then describe a vertical translation that would transform function *f* into function *g*.

3.

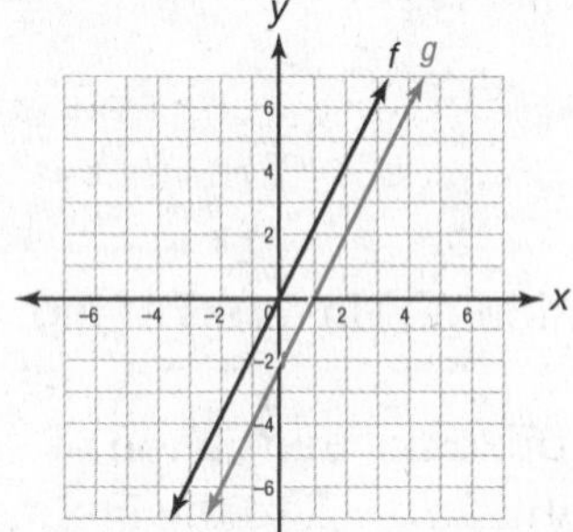

horizontal translation: ____________________

vertical translation: ____________________

REMEMBER Horizontal means left and right. Vertical means up and down.

4.

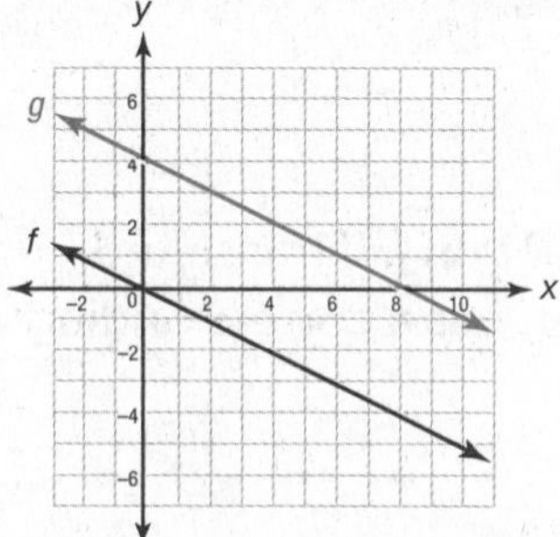

horizontal translation: ____________________

vertical translation: ____________________

Write *true* or *false* for each statement. If false, rewrite the statement to make it true.

5. A translation is a slide of a graph to a new location on the coordinate plane.

6. If $g(x) = f(x) - k$, then the graph of f is translated k units down to form the graph of g.

7. If $g(x) = f(x - k)$, then the graph of f is translated k units left to form the graph of g.

Translate the graph of f according to the verbal description to form g and draw the graph for g on the same coordinate plane. Then write an equation for $g(x)$ in terms of x.

8. Translate the graph of f 5 units up to form g.

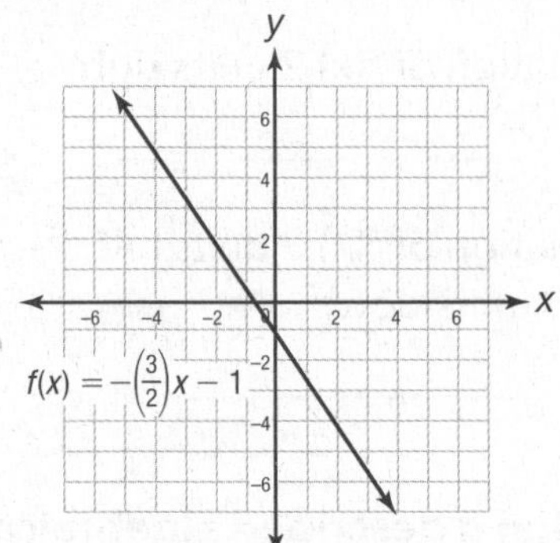

$g(x) =$ ____________

9. Translate the graph of f 3 units to the right to form g.

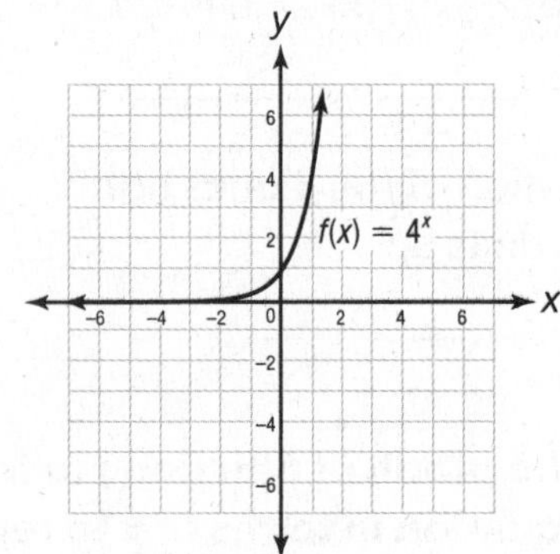

$g(x) =$ ____________

Choose the best answer. Use your graphing calculator to check your answer.

10. The graphing calculator screen below shows the graph of $f(x) = 1.5x$ and the graph of g.

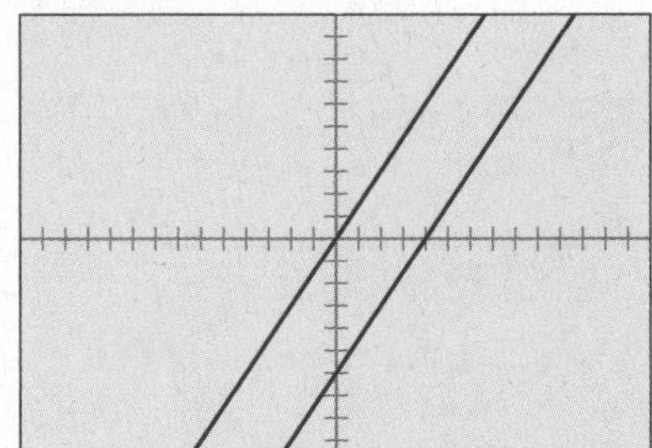

Which equation could represent $g(x)$ in terms of $f(x)$?

A. $g(x) = f(x) + 6$

B. $g(x) = f(x) - 6$

C. $g(x) = f(x + 6)$

D. $g(x) = 6f(x)$

11. The graphing calculator screen below shows the graph of $f(x) = 2^x$ and the graph of g.

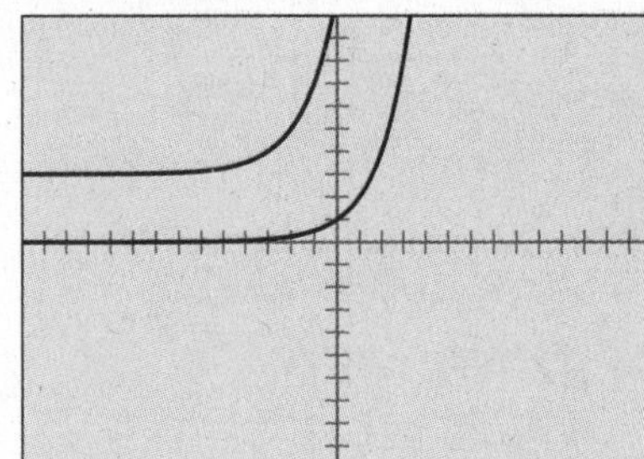

Which equation could represent $g(x)$ in terms of $f(x)$?

A. $g(x) = f(x + 3) + 3$

B. $g(x) = f(x - 3) + 3$

C. $g(x) = f(x + 3) - 3$

D. $g(x) = f(x - 3) - 3$

Write an explicit expression in terms of x for each function $g(x)$ described below. For questions 12–17, $f(x) = 5^x$.

12. translation of $f(x)$ 2 units up

$g(x) =$ ________________

13. translation of $f(x)$ 2 units down

$g(x) =$ ________________

14. translation of $f(x)$ 2 units left

$g(x) =$ ________________

15. translation of $f(x)$ 2 units right

$g(x) =$ ________________

16. translation of $f(x)$ 3 units right and 3 units up

$g(x) =$ ________________

17. translation of $f(x)$ 3 units left and 3 units down

$g(x) =$ ________________

Translate the graph of function f to form the translated function g described algebraically. Write an equation in terms of x to represent the translated image.

18. $g(x) = f(x) + 5$

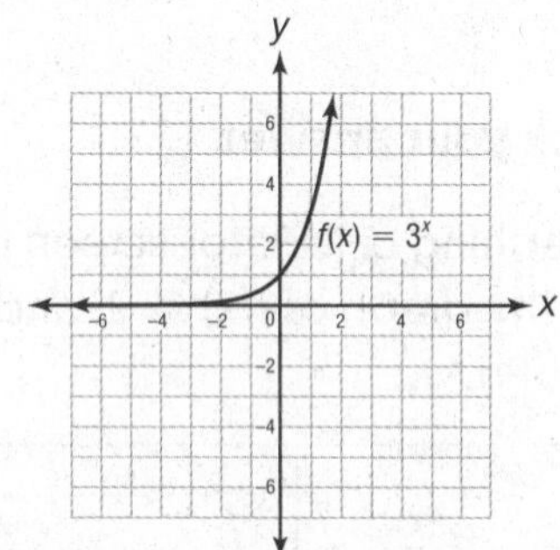

$g(x) =$ ________________

19. $g(x) = f(x + 5)$

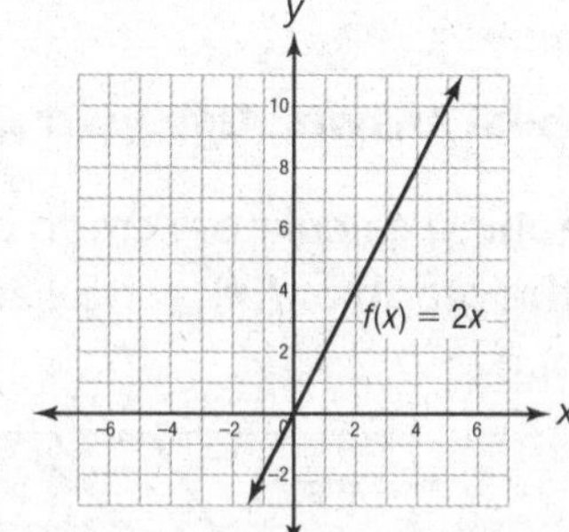

$g(x) =$ ________________

20. $g(x) = f(x - 6) - 4$

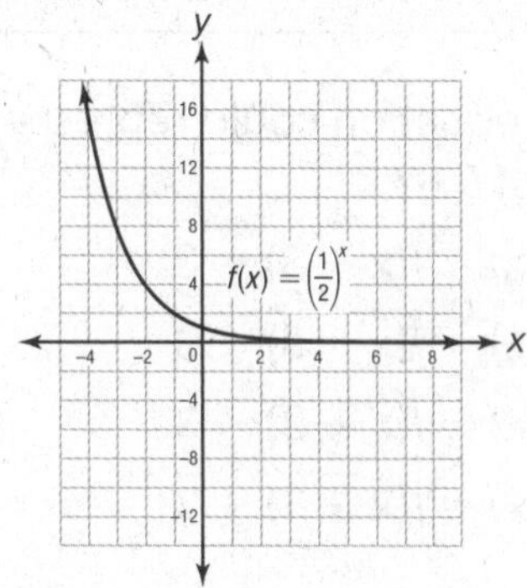

$g(x) =$ ________________

21. $g(x) = f(x - 4) - 3$

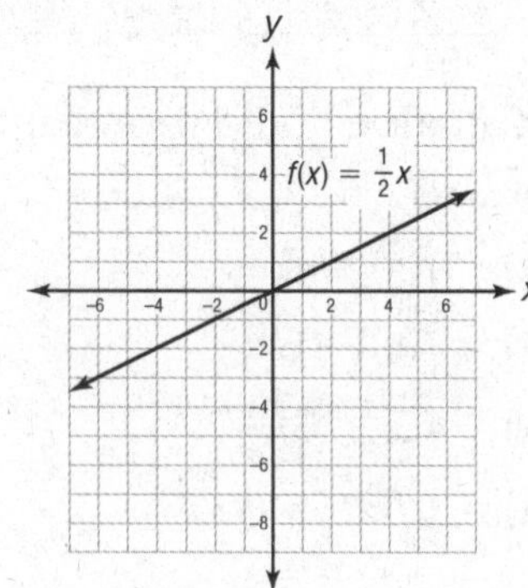

$g(x) =$ ________________

Function f was translated to form function g according to the rule given. For each rule, identify the value of k. Include the sign. Briefly explain how you know.

22.

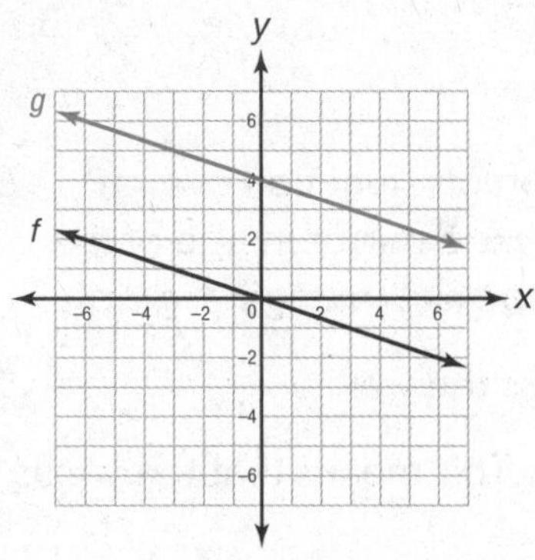

$g(x) = f(x) + k$; $k =$ _____

____

____

23.

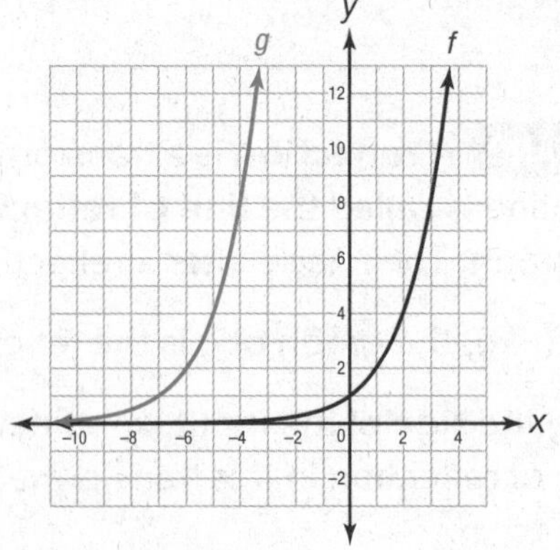

$g(x) = f(x + k)$; $k =$ _____

____

____

Examine the following situations and respond in complete sentences.

24. EXPLAIN Macy graphed $f(x) = -4x$ and parallel line g. She believes that since the rule for the translation is $g(x) = f(x + 1)$, the equation for g must be $g(x) = -4x + 1$. Explain why Macy's reasoning is flawed. Then identify the correct equation for g.

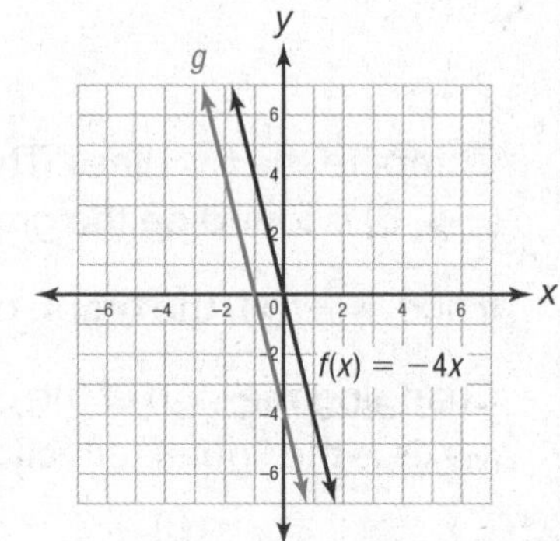

____

____

____

25. DESCRIBE Zack used to charge only an hourly rate to mow lawns, as shown by the graph of function p. Because of rising costs, he now charges a set fee for each job in addition to his hourly rate, as shown by the graph of function n. Use algebraic notation to describe how p could be translated to form n. Use what you know about translations to explain how the new costs differ from the old costs.

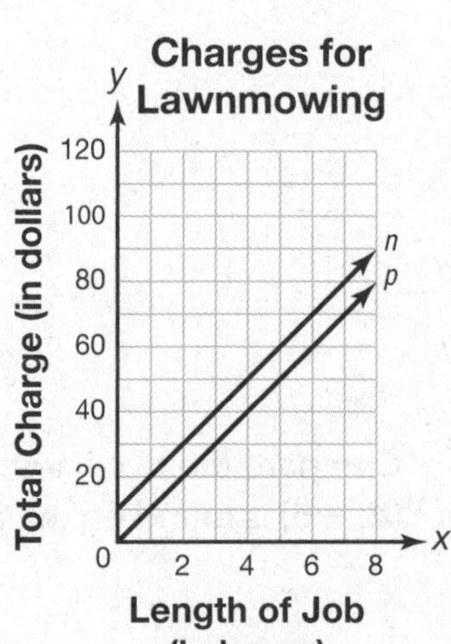

____

____

____

LESSON 19

Reflecting Functions

UNDERSTAND A **reflection** is a transformation that can flip the graph of a function over a line. That line is called the **line of reflection**. The new graph looks like a mirror image of the original graph. The image after a reflection is the same size and shape as the original graph.

If $g(x) = f(-x)$, the graph of g is the reflection of the graph of f across the y-axis.

Changing the sign of the input, x, reflects the graph over the y-axis. This means that the y-axis is the line of reflection in this transformation.

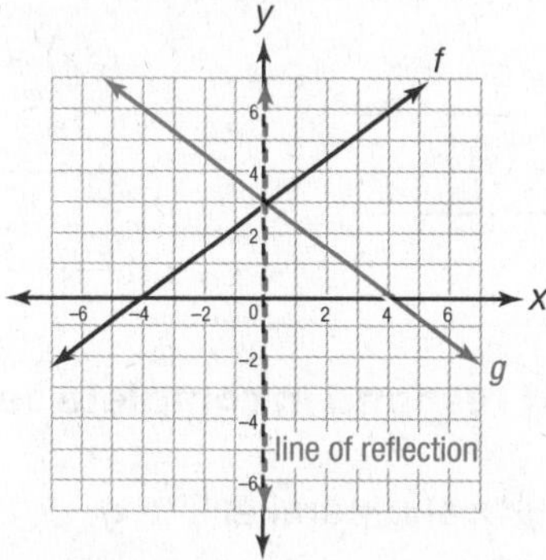

Compare the two lines. The point (4, 6) is found on the graph of f. The corresponding point (−4, 6) is found on the graph of g. The point (−4, 6) is the reflection of (4, 6) across the y-axis.

If $h(x) = -f(x)$, the graph of h is the reflection of the graph of f across the x-axis.

Changing the sign of the output, $f(x)$, reflects the graph over the x-axis. This means that the x-axis is the line of reflection in this transformation.

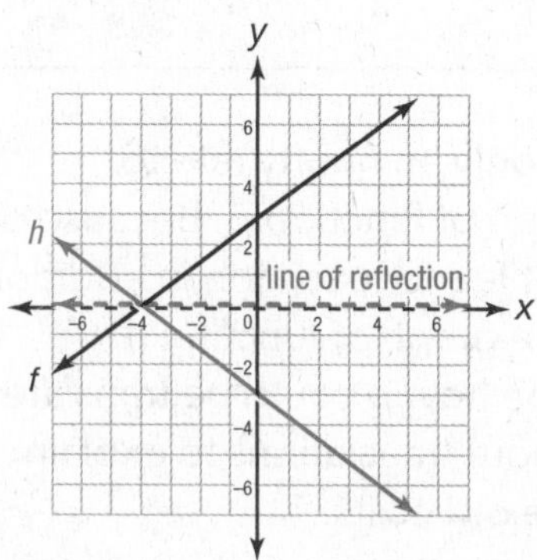

Compare the two lines. The point (4, 6) is found on the graph of f. The corresponding point (4, −6) is found on the graph of h. The point (4, −6) is the reflection of (4, 6) across the x-axis.

Connect

The graph of the exponential function $f(x) = 3^x$ is shown. On the same coordinate plane, graph function $g(x) = -f(x)$.

Compare the graphs and describe the reflection.

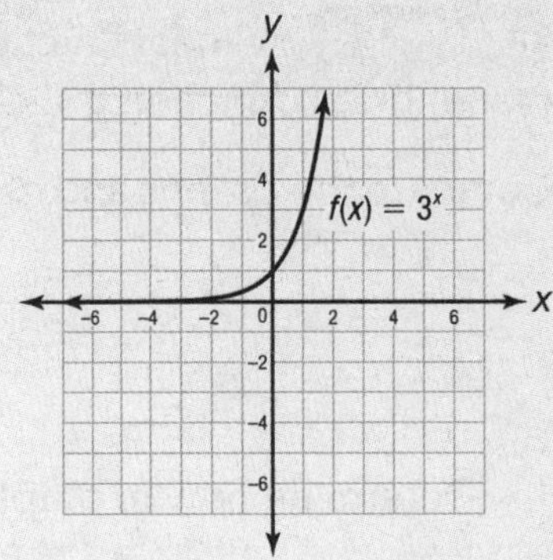

1 Write the equation for g.

We know that $f(x) = 3^x$ and that the reflected image is equal to $g(x) = -f(x)$.

Substitute the expression for $f(x)$ to find an expression for $g(x)$.

$$g(x) = -f(x) = -(3^x)$$

2 Create a table of values for function g.

x	$g(x) = -(3^x)$	$g(x)$
-2	$g(-2) = -(3^{-2}) = -\left(\frac{1}{3^2}\right) = -\frac{1}{9}$	$-\frac{1}{9}$
-1	$g(-1) = -(3^{-1}) = -\left(\frac{1}{3^1}\right) = -\frac{1}{3}$	$-\frac{1}{3}$
0	$g(0) = -(3^0) = -(1) = -1$	-1
1	$g(1) = -(3^1) = -(3) = -3$	-3
2	$g(2) = -(3^2) = -(9) = -9$	-9

3 Graph $g(x)$ and compare it to $f(x)$.

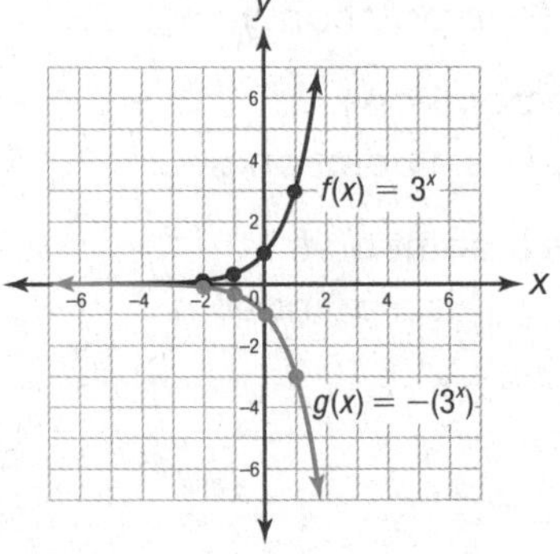

Consider (1, 3) and (1, −3). Each has the same input, x, but the outputs have opposite signs.

Also, notice that (1, 3) and (1, −3) are the same distance from the x-axis but lie on different sides of it.

This is true for every pair of corresponding points on the two functions.

▶ The graph of g is the result of a reflection of the graph of f across the x-axis.

CHECK

Use a graphing calculator to check your work.

Press Y=. Enter $Y_1 = 3^X$.

Enter $Y_2 = -3^X$.

Press 2nd GRAPH to bring up a table of values, and compare them.

Press GRAPH. Compare the graphs to the ones shown on the left.

EXAMPLE A A linear function f is graphed. On the same coordinate plane, graph function g such that $g(x) = f(-x)$.

Compare the graphs and describe the reflection.

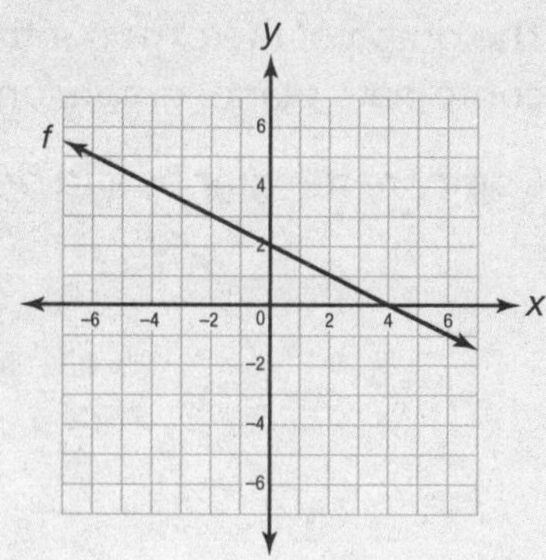

1 Determine how to graph g.

No explicit function was given for f, but the graph of g can be found by using the graph of f.

The algebraic notation $g(x) = f(-x)$ means that the opposite value of each input, x, will be used.

So, find points on the graph of f, change the sign of each x-value, and graph the resulting points.

2 Find several points on the graph of g.

$(-2, 3)$ is a point on f.

Find the opposite of the input (x-value) and keep the same output (y-value).

$(-2, 3) \rightarrow (2, 3)$
So, $(2, 3)$ is a point on g.

$(2, 1)$ is a point on f.
So, $(-2, 1)$ is a point on g.

$(6, -1)$ is a point on f.
So, $(-6, -1)$ is a point on g.

3 Graph g and describe the reflection.

Plot the points that you found and draw a straight line through them to graph g.

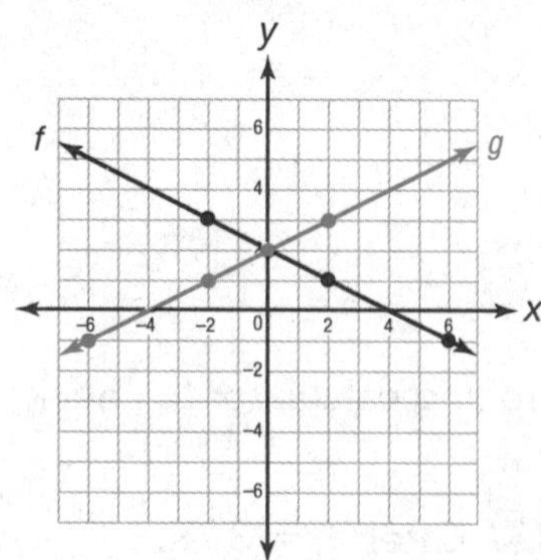

Each point on f and its corresponding point on g are the same distance from the y-axis, but they lie on different sides of it.

▶ The graph of g is the result of a reflection of f across the y-axis.

DISCUSS

Identify key features, such as the intercepts and slopes, of functions f and g. How are the key features of f and its reflected image similar? How are they different?

EXAMPLE B Exponential functions f and g are graphed. Use function notation to define $g(x)$ in terms of $f(x)$.

If the equation for function f is $f(x) = 2^x - 2$, write an equation for g.

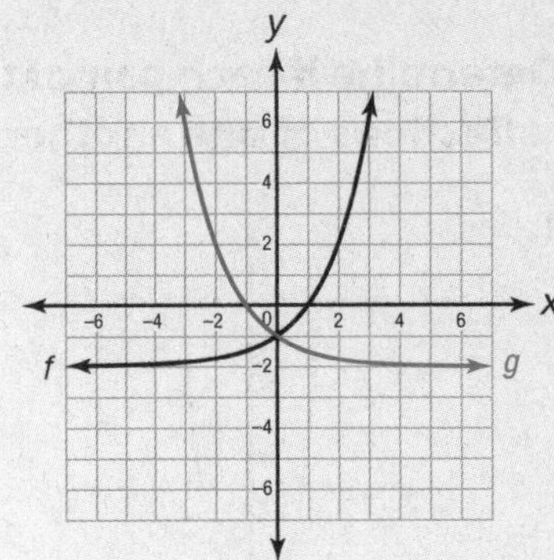

1 Describe the transformation.

The graphs are mirror images of one another. So, this is a reflection.

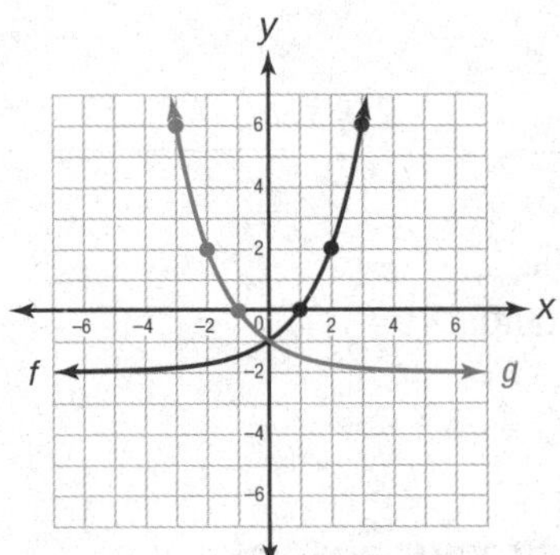

Points $(-2, 2)$ and $(2, 2)$ lie on the same horizontal line, but they are on different sides of the y-axis. Each is the same distance from the y-axis.

Other pairs of points from f and g share this characteristic. So, f can be reflected across the y-axis to form g.

2 Use function notation to describe the reflection.

For each pair of corresponding points, the inputs, x, are opposites and the outputs are the same.

▶ Each point (x, y) on f has a corresponding point $(-x, y)$ on g, so this reflection can be described as $g(x) = f(-x)$.

3 Write an explicit equation for $g(x)$.

To write $g(x)$, write the expression for $f(x)$ and replace x with $-x$.

If $f(x) = 2^x - 2$, then $g(x) = 2^{-x} - 2$.

▶ $g(x) = 2^{-x} - 2$

TRY

Use what you know about negative exponents to express $g(x) = 2^{-x} - 2$ in a different way. (Hint: The number raised to the exponent x will be less than 1.)

Practice

Determine if each pair of functions *f* and *g* are reflections of one another *across the x-axis*, reflections of one another *across the y-axis*, or *neither*.

1.

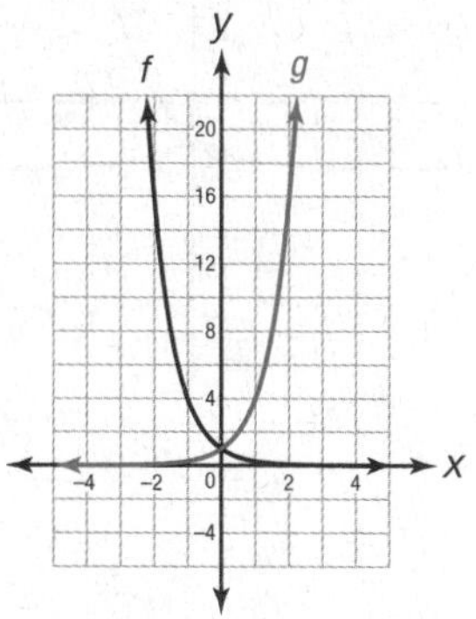

____

2.

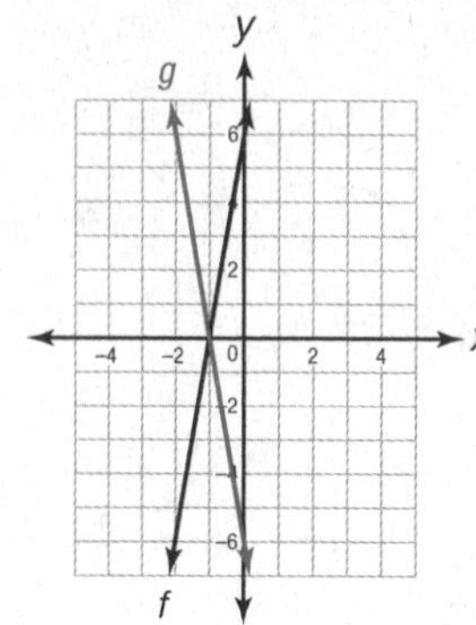

____

3.

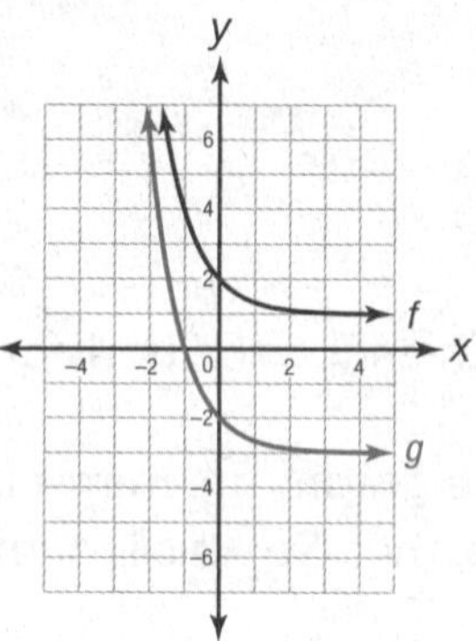

____

HINT: Find pairs of corresponding points. Which changed: the input or the output?

Choose the best answer. Use your graphing calculator to check your answer.

4. The graphing calculator screen below shows $f(x) = 2^x$ and its reflection g. Which could represent $g(x)$?

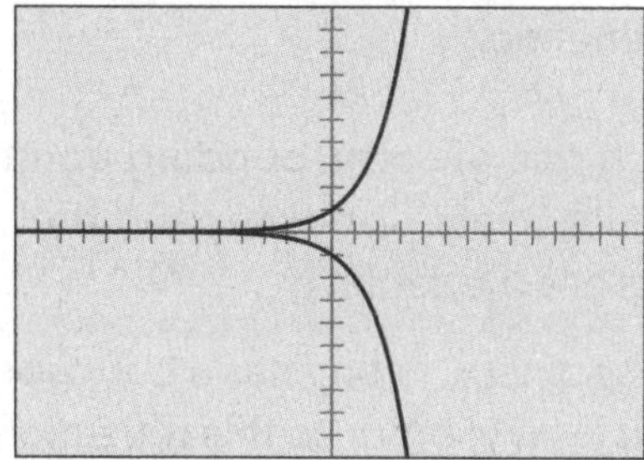

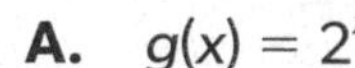

A. $g(x) = 2^x$

B. $g(x) = 2^{-x}$

C. $g(x) = -(2^x)$

D. $g(x) = -(2^{-x})$

5. The graphing calculator screen below shows $f(x) = -3x - 4$ and its reflection g. Which is **not** true of the functions?

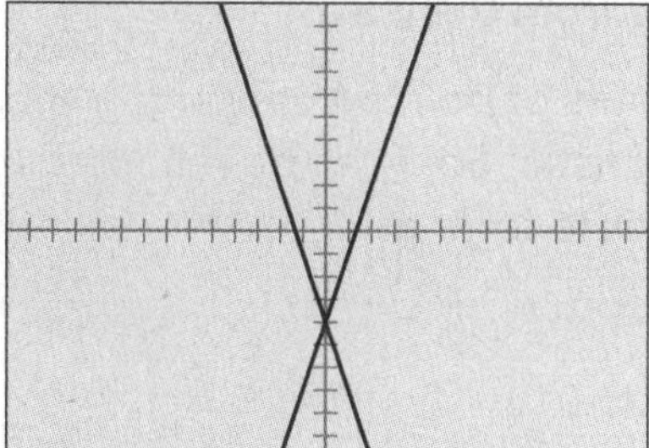

A. $g(x) = f(-x)$

B. Function f was reflected across the y-axis to form g.

C. Both f and g have the same y-intercept.

D. Both f and g have the same slope.

Graph g. Then write an equation for $g(x)$ in terms of x.

6. $g(x) = f(-x)$

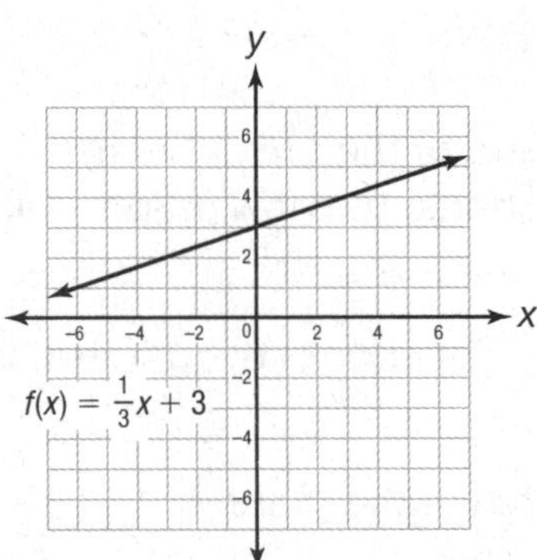

$g(x) =$ ______________

7. $g(x) = -f(x)$

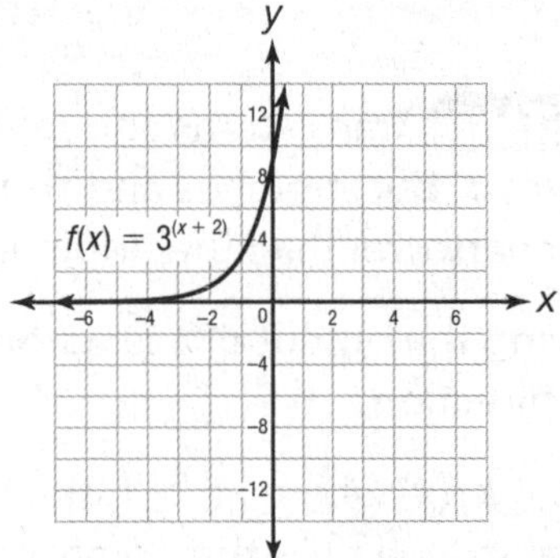

$g(x) =$ ______________

Answer the following questions.

8. **JUSTIFY** Maggie graphed functions f and g as shown. Maggie says that g is the result of a reflection of f across the x-axis. Jay says that g is actually the result of a reflection of f across the y-axis. Who is correct? Justify your answer.

$g(x) = -x$ $f(x) = x$

____

____

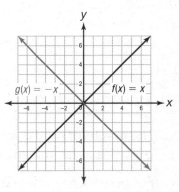

9. **SEPARATE** A graph can be reflected across a point, such as the origin. If $j(x) = -f(-x)$, then j is the reflection of f across the origin. How could you use two different reflections to produce the same graph of j?

____

____

LESSON 20

Stretching and Shrinking Functions

Vertical Stretches and Shrinks

UNDERSTAND Translations and reflections do not change the size of the graph being transformed, but stretches and shrinks do. After a stretch or a shrink, the new graph looks wider or narrower than the original graph.

Multiplying the output of a function, $f(x)$, by a constant stretches or shrinks the graph in the vertical direction.

For $g(x) = k\,f(x)$ where $|k| > 1$, the graph of g is a **vertical stretch** of the graph of f. A vertical stretch pulls the points on the graph away from the x-axis.

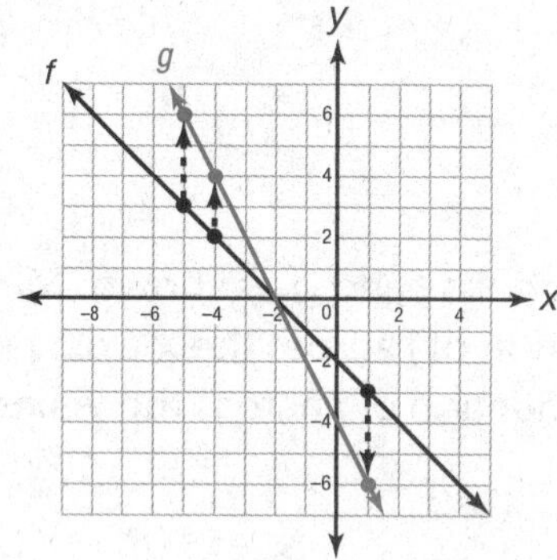

The graphs of f and g above illustrate the vertical stretch $g(x) = 2f(x)$. Notice how each point on g is twice as far from the x-axis as its corresponding point on f.

For $g(x) = k\,f(x)$ where $0 < |k| < 1$, the graph of g is a **vertical shrink** of the graph of f. A vertical shrink pushes the points of a graph toward the x-axis.

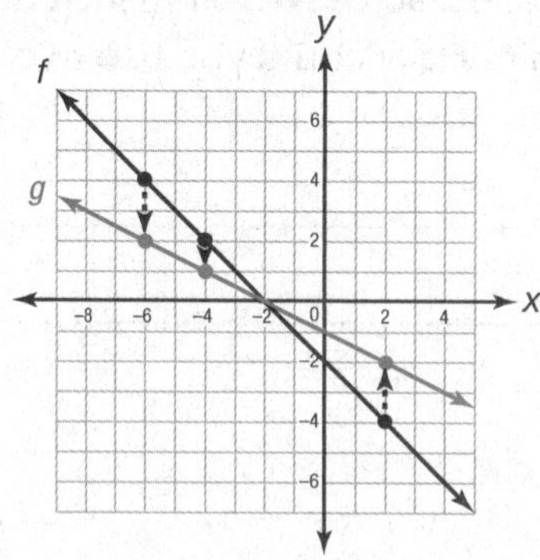

The graphs of f and g above illustrate the vertical shrink $g(x) = \frac{1}{2}f(x)$. Notice how each point on g is half as far from the x-axis as its corresponding point on f.

Notice that, after a vertical stretch or shrink, the new function always has the same x-intercept as the original function. This point cannot be shrunk toward or stretched away from the x-axis because it is on the x-axis.

Connect

The exponential function $f(x) = 2^x$ is graphed on the right. Graph $g(x) = 4(2^x)$ on the same coordinate plane. Is g the result of a vertical stretch or a vertical shrink of f? by what factor?

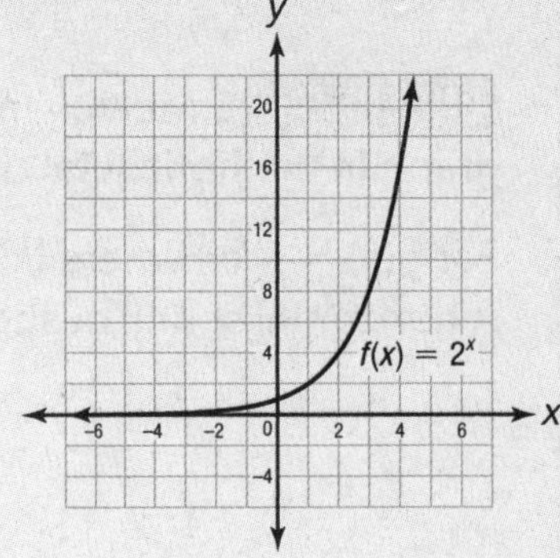

1

Create a table of values for g.

x	$g(x) = 4(2^x)$	$g(x)$
−2	$g(-2) = 4(2^{-2}) = 4\left(\frac{1}{4}\right) = 1$	1
−1	$g(-1) = 4(2^{-1}) = 4\left(\frac{1}{2}\right) = 2$	2
0	$g(0) = 4(2^0) = 4(1) = 4$	4
1	$g(1) = 4(2^1) = 4(2) = 8$	8
2	$g(2) = 4(2^2) = 4(4) = 16$	16

2

Graph g.

Plot those ordered pairs $(x, g(x))$ on the coordinate plane and connect them with a smooth curve.

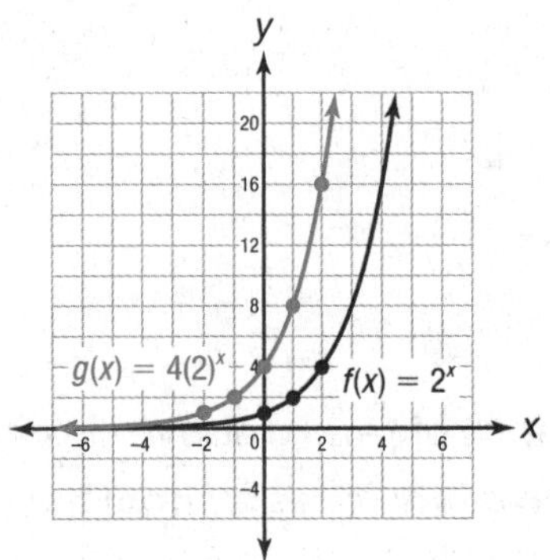

3

Compare the graphs and identify the transformation.

The point (0, 1) on the graph of f is transformed to (0, 4) on the graph of g.

The point (1, 2) is transformed to (1, 8).

The point (2, 4) is transformed to (2, 16).

Notice that for each pair of points, the input is the same, but the output is 4 times as great.

The equation of g also shows that the output, $f(x)$, was multiplied by 4.

▶ The graph of g is the result of a vertical stretch of f by a factor of 4.

TRY

On the coordinate plane above, graph $h(x) = \frac{1}{4}(2^x)$. Is this a vertical stretch or a vertical shrink? by what factor?

Horizontal Stretches and Shrinks

UNDERSTAND Multiplying the input of a function, x, by a constant stretches or shrinks the graph in the horizontal direction.

For $g(x) = f(kx)$ where $|k| > 1$, the graph of g is a **horizontal shrink** of the graph of f. A horizontal shrink pushes the points of a graph toward the y-axis.

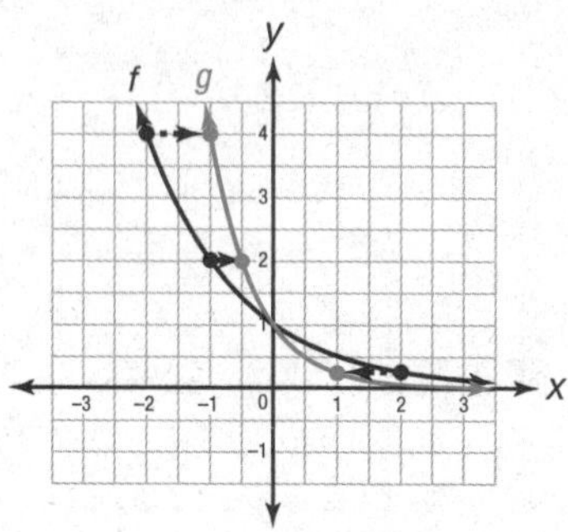

The graphs of f and g above illustrate the horizontal shrink $g(x) = f(2x)$. Notice how each point on g is half as far from the y-axis as its corresponding point on f.

For $g(x) = f(kx)$ where $0 < |k| < 1$, the graph of g is a **horizontal stretch** of the graph of f. A horizontal stretch pulls the points of a graph away from the y-axis.

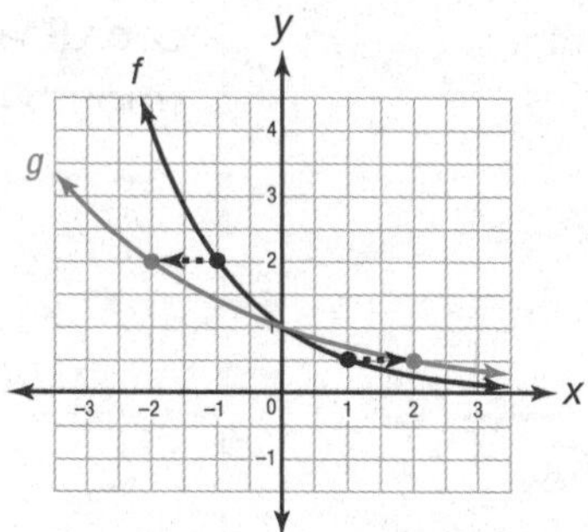

The graphs of f and g above illustrate the horizontal stretch $g(x) = f\left(\frac{1}{2}x\right)$. Notice how each point on g is twice as far from the y-axis as its corresponding point on f.

Notice that the factor of the stretch or shrink is the reciprocal of the constant. In the case of a horizontal stretch or shrink, k is not the factor by which a graph is stretched or shrunk; $\frac{1}{k}$ is.

Notice that, after a horizontal stretch or shrink, the new function always has the same y-intercept as the original function. This point cannot be shrunk toward or stretched away from the y-axis because it is on the y-axis.

Connect

Graph the linear function $f(x) = \frac{1}{2}x + 2$. Then graph its image, g, resulting from the transformation described below.

$g(x) = f(3x)$

Is this an example of a horizontal stretch or shrink? by what factor?

1 Create a table of values for f.

x	$f(x) = \frac{1}{2}x + 2$	$f(x)$
−6	$f(-6) = \frac{1}{2}(-6) + 2$ $= -3 + 2 = -1$	−1
0	$f(0) = \frac{1}{2}(0) + 2 = 0 + 2 = 2$	2
6	$f(6) = \frac{1}{2}(6) + 2 = 3 + 2 = 5$	5

2 Write an equation and create a table of values for g.

Since $g(x) = f(3x)$, replace x with $3x$ to find the equation for g.

$g(x) = f(3x) = \frac{1}{2}(3x) + 2 = \frac{3}{2}x + 2.$

x	$g(x) = \frac{3}{2}x + 2$	$g(x)$
−2	$g(-2) = \frac{3}{2}(-2) + 2$ $= -3 + 2 = -1$	−1
0	$g(0) = \frac{3}{2}(0) + 2 = 0 + 2 = 2$	2
2	$g(2) = \frac{3}{2}(2) + 2 = 3 + 2 = 5$	5

3 Use those points to graph the functions.

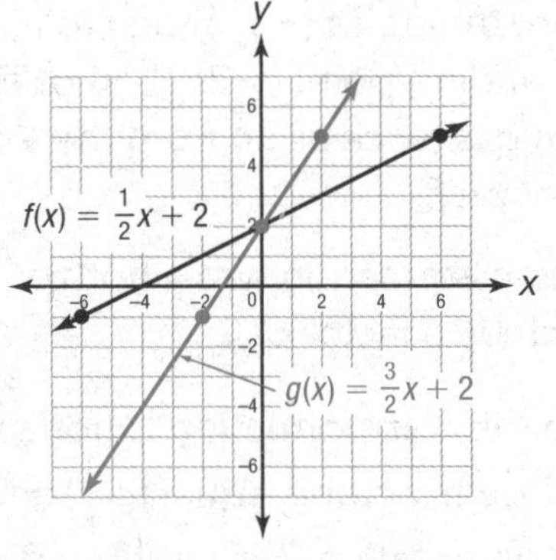

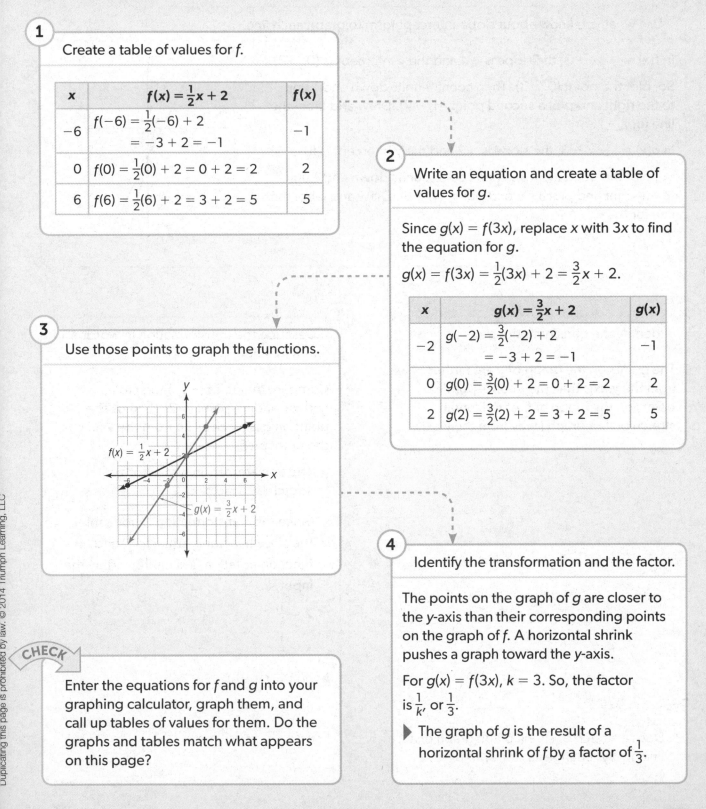

4 Identify the transformation and the factor.

The points on the graph of g are closer to the y-axis than their corresponding points on the graph of f. A horizontal shrink pushes a graph toward the y-axis.

For $g(x) = f(3x)$, $k = 3$. So, the factor is $\frac{1}{k}$, or $\frac{1}{3}$.

▶ The graph of g is the result of a horizontal shrink of f by a factor of $\frac{1}{3}$.

CHECK

Enter the equations for f and g into your graphing calculator, graph them, and call up tables of values for them. Do the graphs and tables match what appears on this page?

EXAMPLE A Graph the linear functions $f(x) = -4x - 3$ and $g(x) = -2x - 3$.

Use words to describe the transformation, including if it is a horizontal stretch or a horizontal shrink, and by what factor. Then write an equation for $g(x)$ in terms of $f(x)$.

1 Use what you know about slope-intercept form to graph each line.

In $f(x) = -4x - 3$, the slope is -4 and the y-intercept is $(0, -3)$.

So, plot the point $(0, -3)$. Then count 4 units down and 1 unit to the right and plot a second point, $(1, -7)$. Draw and label the line for f.

In $g(x) = -2x - 3$, the slope is -2 and the y-intercept is $(0, -3)$.

So, plot the point $(0, -3)$. Then count 2 units down and 1 unit to the right and plot a second point, $(1, -5)$. Draw and label the line for g.

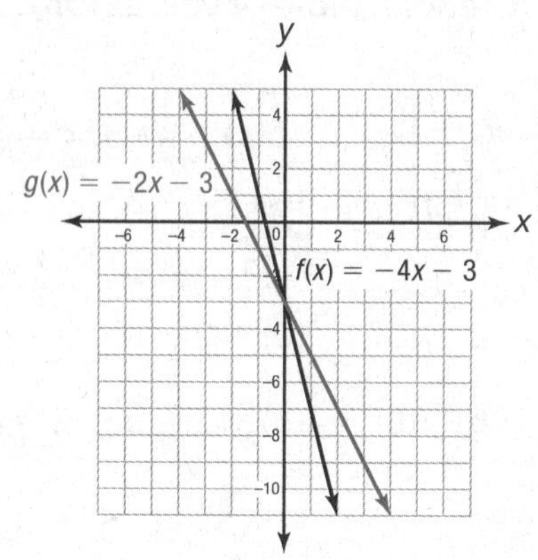

2 Identify the transformation.

The points on the graph of g are farther from the y-axis than their corresponding points on the graph of f. A horizontal stretch pulls a graph away from the y-axis.

3 Describe the transformation in words and as a function.

Compare the point $(-1, 1)$ on f to its corresponding point $(-2, 1)$ on g. The point on g is twice as far from the y-axis as the point on f.

▶ The transformation was a horizontal stretch by a factor of 2.

Since this transformation is horizontal, the stretch factor is equal to $\frac{1}{k}$, and, in function notation, k is multiplied by the input, x.

$$2 = \frac{1}{k}$$

$$k = \frac{1}{2}$$

▶ $g(x) = f\left(\frac{1}{2}x\right)$

DISCUSS

Does a stretch or shrink of the graph of a line always change its slope? Explain.

EXAMPLE B The graph of function f was transformed to create the graph of function g, as shown. Was f stretched or shrunk, horizontally or vertically, and by what factor? If $f(x) = 4^x + 8$, what is the equation of $g(x)$?

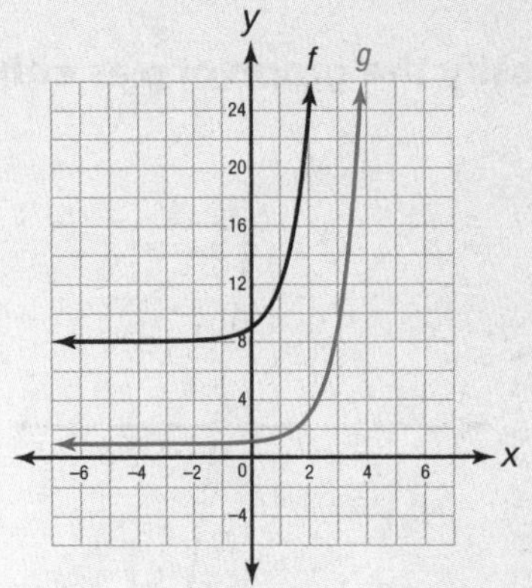

1 Examine the key features to determine how f was transformed.

As you move left on the graph of f, the values of $f(x)$ get very close to 8. So, f appears to have an asymptote at $y = 8$.

Many points on the graph of g lie below that asymptote, so points from the graph of f must have been moved much closer to the x-axis. Thus, g appears to be a vertical shrink of f.

2 Identify the factor of the shrink.

In a vertical shrink, the output is multiplied by a factor, k. So, compare points.

A vertical shrink has the form $g(x) = kf(x)$.

So, $k = \frac{g(x)}{f(x)}$ for all x.

The point (2, 24) on the graph of f was shrunk to (2, 3) on the graph of g.

$k = \frac{g(2)}{f(2)} = \frac{3}{24} = \frac{1}{8}$

3 Find the equation for $g(x)$.

$g(x) = \frac{1}{8} f(x) = \frac{1}{8}(4^x + 8) = \frac{1}{8} \cdot 4^x + 1$

DISCUSS

Suppose $f(x) = 4^x + 8$ is shrunk horizontally by a factor of $\frac{1}{8}$ to form function h. Will the equation of h be $h(x) = 4^{\frac{1}{8}x} + 8$ or $h(x) = 4^{8x} + 8$? Explain.

Practice

Classify the graph of *g* as either a *vertical stretch* or a *vertical shrink* of the graph of *f*.

1.

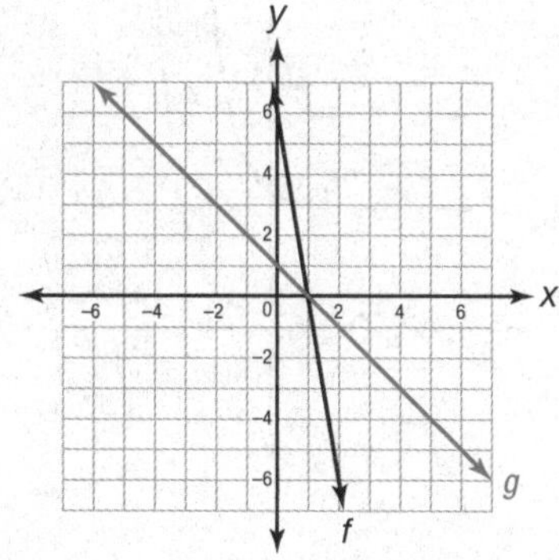

____

2.

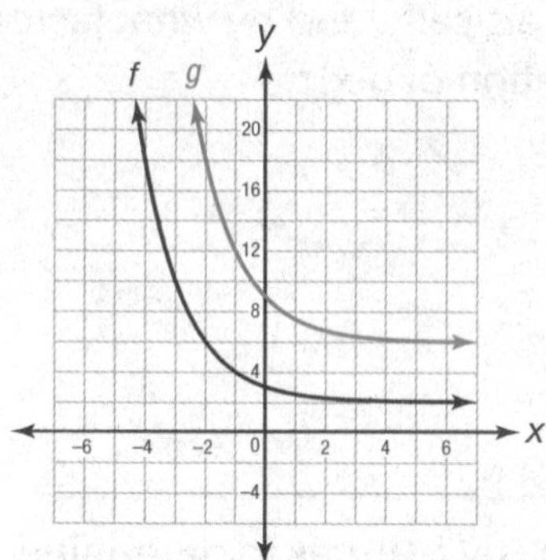

____

A vertical shrink draws points closer to the *x*-axis.

Classify the graph of *g* as either a *horizontal stretch* or a *horizontal shrink* of the graph of *f*.

3.

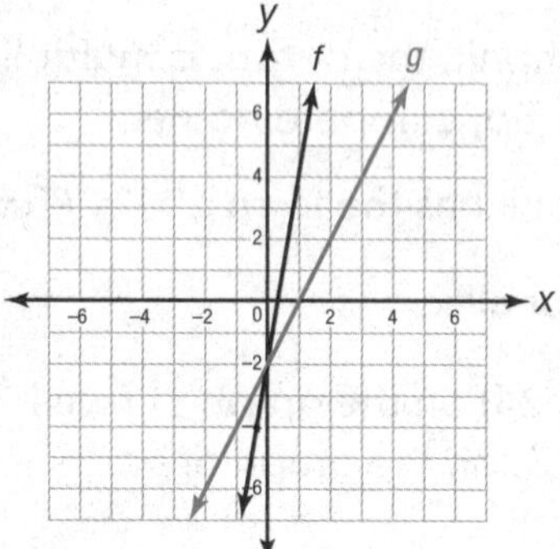

____

4.

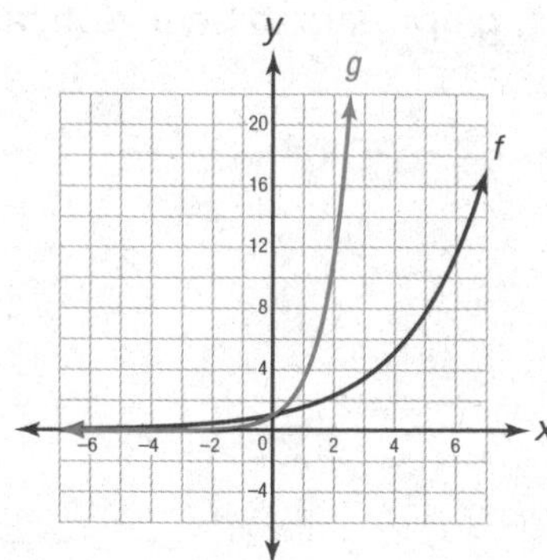

____

Is *g* closer to or farther away from the *y*-axis?

Fill in each blank with an appropriate word, phrase, or expression.

5. A horizontal ____________ pushes the points of a graph toward the *y*-axis.

6. A horizontal ____________ pulls the points of a graph away from the *y*-axis.

7. If $g(x) = kf(x)$ and $|k| > 1$, then *g* is the result of a vertical stretch of *g* by a factor of ____________.

8. If $g(x) = f(kx)$ and $|k| > 1$, then *g* is the result of a horizontal shrink of *g* by a factor of ____________.

Graph each function g on the coordinate plane below it. Classify each graph of g as either a vertical stretch or a vertical shrink of the graph of f. Then identify the factor.

9. $g(x) = 2x - 6$

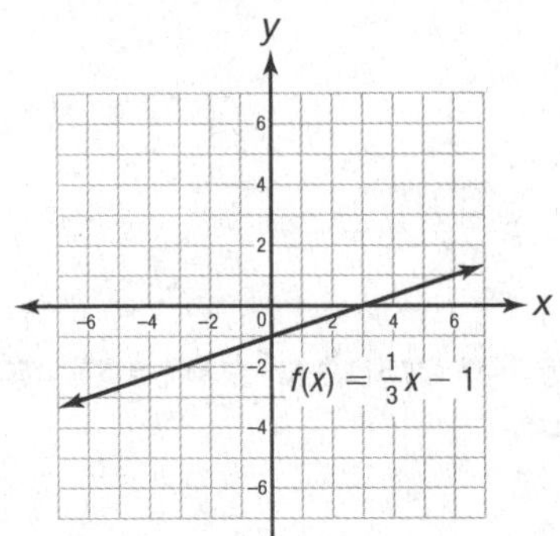

transformation: vertical __________

factor: __________

10. $g(x) = \frac{1}{2}(2^x)$

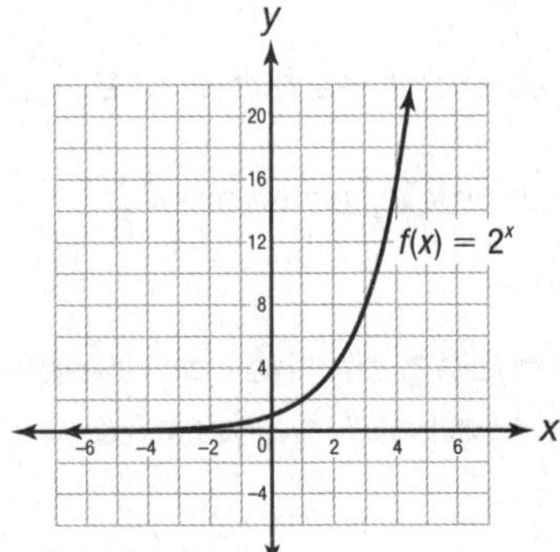

transformation: vertical __________

factor: __________

Graph each function g on the coordinate plane below it. Classify each graph of g as either a horizontal stretch or a horizontal shrink of the graph of f. Then identify the factor.

11. $g(x) = -5x + 1$

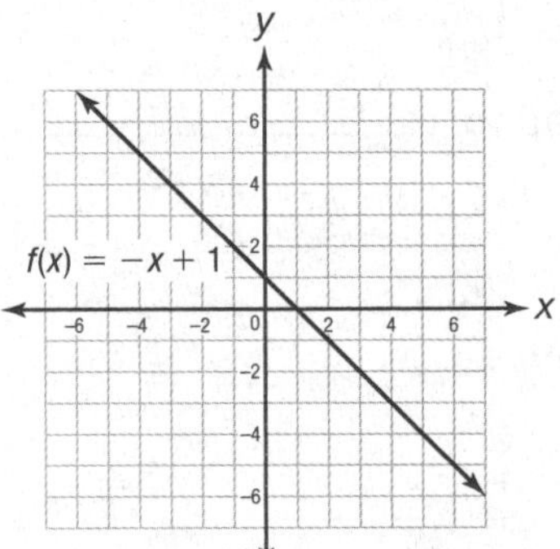

transformation: horizontal __________

factor: __________

12. 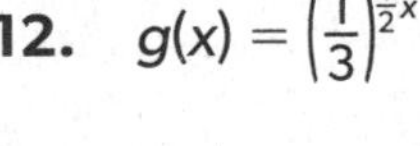 $g(x) = \left(\frac{1}{3}\right)^{\frac{1}{2}x}$

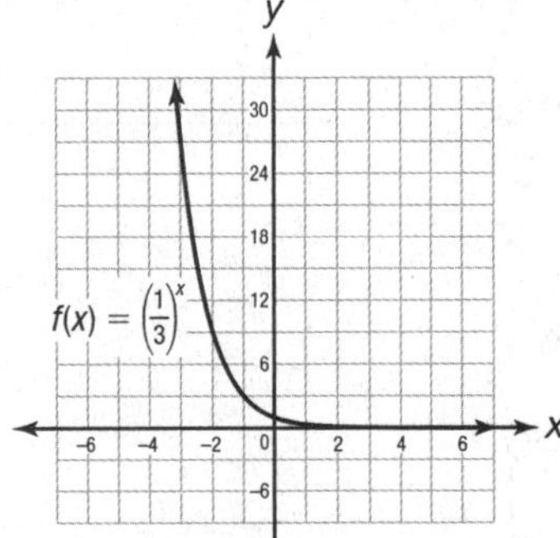

transformation: horizontal __________

factor: __________

Match each verbal description of a translation of $f(x) = 6^x$ with the equation of its transformed image by writing the correct letter next to each description.

13. vertical stretch by a factor of 8	______	**A.**	$g(x) = 6^{8x}$
14. vertical shrink by a factor of $\frac{1}{8}$	______	**B.**	$g(x) = 8(6^x)$
15. horizontal stretch by a factor of 8	______	**C.**	$g(x) = 6^{\frac{1}{8}x}$
16. horizontal shrink by a factor of $\frac{1}{8}$	______	**D.**	$g(x) = \frac{1}{8}(6^x)$

Graph each function g on the coordinate plane below it. Classify each graph of g as a stretch or a shrink of the graph of f, horizontal or vertical, and by what factor.

17. $g(x) = \frac{3}{2}f(x)$

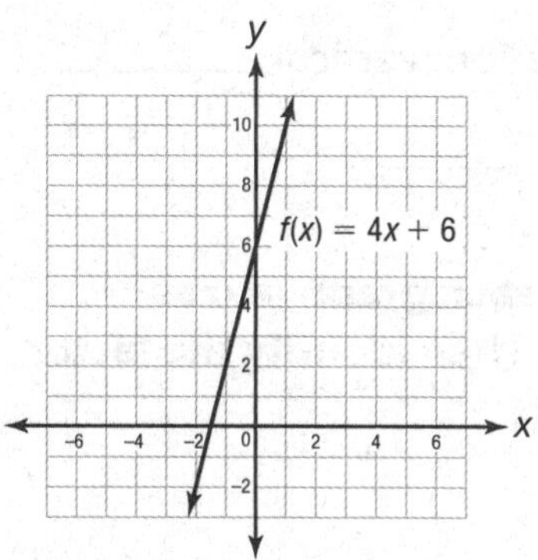

transformation: ______________________

factor: ____________

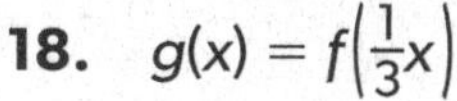

18. $g(x) = f\left(\frac{1}{3}x\right)$

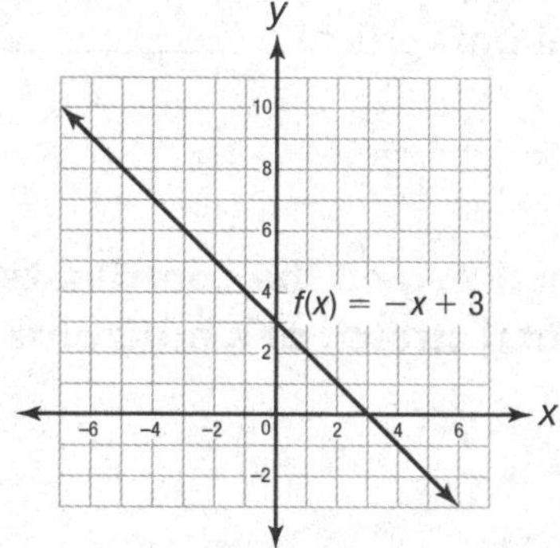

transformation: ______________________

factor: ____________

19. $g(x) = \frac{1}{2}f(x)$

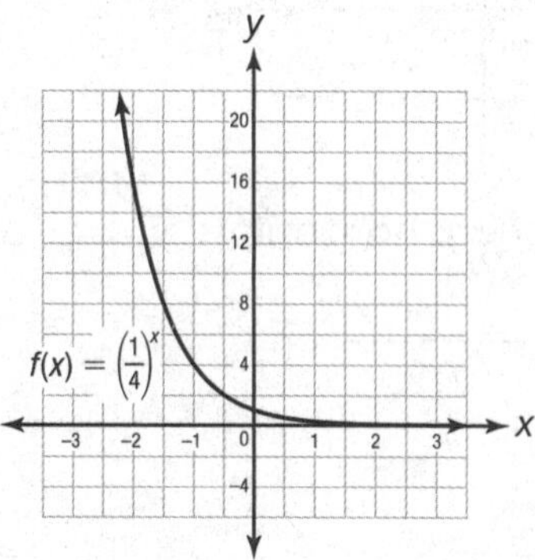

transformation: ______________________

factor: ____________

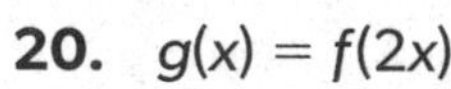

20. $g(x) = f(2x)$

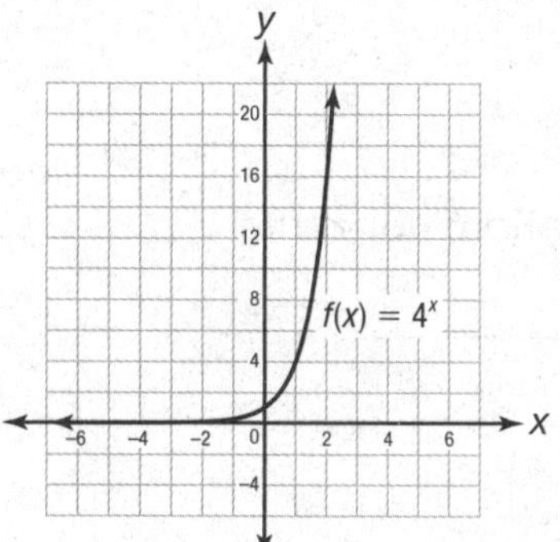

transformation: ______________________

factor: ____________

Graph the functions described and provide the desired information about them.

21. RESTATE Graph $f(x) = 2x - 2$ and its image, g, after a horizontal stretch by a factor of 4. Write equations for $g(x)$ in terms of $f(x)$ and in terms of x.

$g(x) =$ ______ $f($______$x)$

$g(x) =$ ______ $x -$ ______

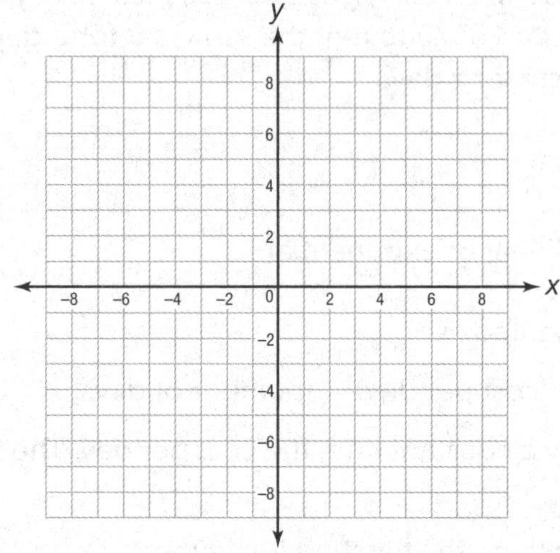

22. DISTINGUISH The graph of $f(x) = 3^x$ is shown. Graph $g(x) = -\frac{1}{3}f(x)$. Then describe the two transformations needed to create the image, g, from the graph of f.

____

____

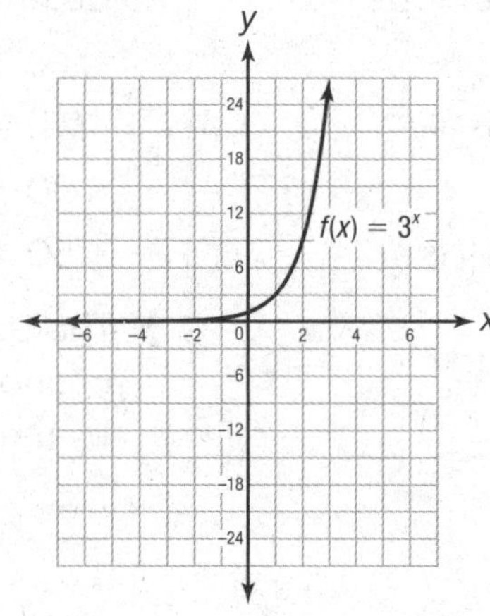

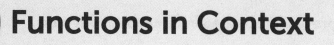

LESSON 21 Functions in Context

People often use functions to model real-world relationships. These functions tell how one quantity changes in relation to another quantity. Representations of these functions, such as tables, graphs, or equations, can be used to answer questions about the relationships or to make predictions.

EXAMPLE A The EZ Car Rental Company charges a set fee plus a daily rate to rent a car. It costs $90 to rent an economy car for 1 day and $170 to rent the same car for 3 days. Write a function to model the cost of renting an economy car for x days.

1 Decide if this relationship is linear or exponential.

The relationship can be represented as:

(total charge) = (set fee) + (cost per day) × (number of days, x)

The variable, x, is multiplied by a constant rate, the cost per day. The set fee is then added to that product.

Since the rate of change is constant, the function is linear.

2 Find the cost per day.

The cost per day is the slope of the linear function. Find two points and use the slope formula to find the cost per day.

A 1-day rental costs $90. So, (1, 90) is a solution for this function.

A 3-day rental costs $170. So, (3, 170) is also a solution.

$$\text{cost per day} = \frac{170 - 90}{3 - 1} = \frac{80}{2} = 40$$

3 Find the set fee and write the function.

We can use an ordered pair, such as (1, 90), to determine the complete equation.

$$f(x) = (\text{set fee}) + 40x$$
$$f(1) = (\text{set fee}) + 40(1)$$
$$90 = (\text{set fee}) + 40$$
$$50 = (\text{set fee})$$

▶ The cost, $f(x)$, in dollars of renting an economy car for x days can be modeled by the equation $f(x) = 50 + 40x$.

Substitute 1 day and 3 days into your model function to check that it outputs $90 and $170, respectively.

EXAMPLE B Mr. Vega bought a new car for \$20,000. He used a function to estimate how its value will depreciate, or decrease over time.

Age in Years, t	0	1	2	3	4
Value in Thousands of Dollars, $v(t)$	20	16	12.8	10.24	8.192

What type of function did Mr. Vega use to model this relationship? Describe the rate at which the car depreciates. Write an equation for the function.

1 Test to see if the function is linear.

Examine the decrease in value from year to year.

1 year after purchase: $v(0) - v(1) = 20 - 16 = 4$, or \$4,000

Between years 1 and 2: $v(1) - v(2) = 16 - 12.8 = 3.2$, or \$3,200

Between years 2 and 3: $v(2) - v(3) = 12.8 - 10.24 = 2.56$, or \$2,560

The rate of depreciation is not constant, so this model is not a linear function.

2 Test to see if the function is exponential.

Compare the value of the car in successive years.

1 year after purchase: $\frac{v(1)}{v(0)} = \frac{16}{20} = 0.8$

Between years 1 and 2: $\frac{v(2)}{v(1)} = \frac{12.8}{16} = 0.8$

Between years 2 and 3: $\frac{v(3)}{v(2)} = \frac{10.24}{12.8} = 0.8$

Each year, the value of the car is 0.8, or 80%, of its value the previous year. This means the car's value is decreasing at a constant percent rate. Functions that decrease at a constant percent rate are exponential functions.

3 Determine an equation for the function.

The constant percent rate is 80%, or 0.8. This is the factor by which the previous year is multiplied to get the next year.

$v(1) = v(0) \cdot 0.8$

$v(2) = v(1) \cdot 0.8 = (v(0) \cdot 0.8) \cdot 0.8$
$= v(0) \cdot (0.8)^2$

$v(3) = v(2) \cdot 0.8 = (v(0) \cdot (0.8)^2) \cdot 0.8$
$= v(0) \cdot (0.8)^3$

You can see a pattern forming. For any year x after purchase, the car's value is given by $v(x) = v(0) \cdot (0.8)^x$.

Substitute $v(0)$, the initial value, 20.

▶ $v(x) = 20 \cdot (0.8)^x$

MODEL

Make a graph to illustrate the depreciation of the car over time.

EXAMPLE C Leah opened a checking account and bought a certificate of deposit (CD) on the same day. She deposits money into her checking account each month. The amount in her checking account, C, can be modeled by $C(t) = 50(12)t$, or $C(t) = 600t$, where t is the time in years since the account was opened.

Leah's CD has a set annual interest rate, and the interest is compounded monthly. The amount in her CD can be modeled by the function $A(t) = 800\left(1 + \frac{0.03}{12}\right)^{12t}$, where t is the time in years since she deposited the money.

Interpret the parameters of functions C and A in this situation.

1 Interpret the parameters of $C(t)$.

The problem explains that t represents time in years, and there are 12 months in 1 year. The quantity $\frac{12 \text{ months}}{\text{year}} \times t \text{ years}$ gives a number of months.

Thus, the 50 likely represents the amount deposited each month.

$\frac{\$50}{\cancel{\text{month}}} \times \frac{12 \cancel{\text{ months}}}{\cancel{\text{year}}} \times t \cancel{\text{ years}} =$ the money in the checking account at time t

2 Interpret the parameters of $A(t)$.

The equation for A, an exponential growth function, shows an amount earning compound interest. The formula for calculating this amount, A, is $A = P\left(1 + \frac{r}{n}\right)^{nt}$, where P is the principal, r is the annual interest rate, and n is the number of times the interest is compounded per year.

So, in $A(t) = 800\left(1 + \frac{0.03}{12}\right)^{12t}$, 800 is P, the principal; 0.03 is r, the interest rate; and 12 is n, the number of times the interest is compounded per year. This means that Leah deposited \$800 in a CD at 3% annual interest, compounded monthly.

EXAMPLE D Combine functions C and A above to build a function that shows the total amount of money Leah has in both accounts at any time, t.

Combine both functions by adding them to form a new function, L.

$$L(t) = C(t) + A(t)$$
$$= 50(12)t + 800\left(1 + \frac{0.03}{12}\right)^{12t}$$
$$= 600t + 800(1.0025)^{12t}$$

▶ The total amount in both accounts after t months is: $L(t) = 600t + 800(1.0025)^{12t}$.

TRY

Leah always keeps \$200 hidden at home, which she calls her "emergency fund." Write a function for the total amount of money Leah has in her checking account, CD, and emergency fund at any time t.

Problem Solving

READ

Abdul buys a bus card with a value of \$30. Each time he takes a bus ride, \$1.50 is deducted from his card. Write a function that can be used to model this situation. Then use the function to determine the value of the bus card after Abdul takes 4 rides.

PLAN

Since the value decreases at a constant rate per ride, model this with a(n) __________ function.

Write an equation and then use the equation to solve the problem.

SOLVE

The initial value of his card is \$30. So, when he has taken 0 rides, there is \$30 left on his card. The point (0, _____) is an ordered pair for this function. It is also the _____-intercept.

Each time Abdul takes a bus ride, \$1.50 is deducted from his card.

So, the rate of change, or slope, is _______. This rate should be negative because

____.

Substituting _______ for *m*, the slope, and _______ for *b*, the *y*-intercept, gives the equation:

$c(x) =$ _____ $x +$ _____

If Abdul takes 4 rides, the value of his card, in dollars, will be:

$c(4) = ($_______$)(4) +$ _______ $=$ _______

CHECK

The initial value of the card is \$30: $c(0) = 30$.

The value decreases by \$1.50 each time he rides the bus.

After 1 ride, the value will be: $c(1) = 30.00 - 1.50 = 28.50$

After 2 rides, the value will be: $c(2) = 28.50 - 1.50 =$ _______

After 3 rides, the value will be: $c(3) =$ ______________________________

After 4 rides, the value will be: $c(4) =$ ______________________________

Is this the same value you found for $c(4)$ when you used the equation? _______

▶ This situation can be modeled by the equation $c(x) =$ _______________.

After taking 4 rides, the value of Abdul's card will be \$__________.

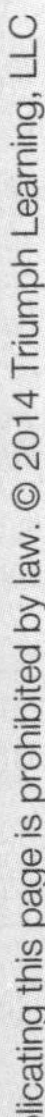

Practice

For each situation, identify the type of function (*linear* or *exponential*) that could model it. Then write a function to model the relationship.

1. The highest possible grade for a report is 100 points. Each day the report is late, the teacher deducts 10 points.

Days Late, x	0	1	2	3	4
Starting Grade, $g(x)$	100	90	80	70	60

function type: ____________________

$g(x) =$ ____________________

REMEMBER If the rate of change is constant, the function is linear.

2. Sixteen teams are participating in a tournament. Only the winning teams in each round advance to the next round.

Number of Rounds Completed, x	0	1	2	3	4
Teams Remaining, $f(x)$	16	8	4	2	1

function type: ____________________

$f(x) =$ ____________________

3. As soon as a Web site went up, it received 1 hit. After one minute, it had received 4 hits. The number of hits continued to quadruple each minute after that.

Time Since Launch, in minutes, x	0	1	2	3	4
Number of Hits, $h(x)$	1	4	16	64	256

function type: ____________________

$h(x) =$ ____________________

4. A cake decorator charges a \$30 set fee for each cake plus \$20 for each color of icing required.

Colors of Icing Required, x	1	2	3	4	5
Cost of Cake in dollars, $c(x)$	50	70	90	110	130

function type: ____________________

$c(x) =$ ____________________

Choose the best answer.

5. A salesperson earns a weekly salary plus a commission on each appliance he sells. The function $p(x) = 200 + 0.05x$ shows his weekly earnings if x represents his weekly sales, in dollars. Which is also true?

A. His weekly salary is \$205.

B. He earns \$200 for each appliance he sells.

C. He earns \$0.05 for each appliance he sells.

D. He earns a 5% commission for each appliance he sells.

6. The equation $A(t) = 900(0.85)^t$ represents the value of a motor scooter t years after it was purchased. Which statement is also true of this situation?

A. When new, the scooter cost \$765.

B. When new, the scooter cost \$900.

C. The scooter's value is decreasing at a rate of 85% each year.

D. The scooter's value is decreasing at a rate of 0.15% each year.

Use the following information for questions 7–10.

Trini bought a car by using a combination of a private loan from her parents and an auto loan from a bank. For both loans, the amount Trini will have to pay depends on the number of years before she pays it back.

7. The private loan is a simple interest loan. The amount Trini must pay to her parents can be modeled by the function $p(t) = 5{,}000 + 5{,}000(0.03)(t)$, where t is the number of years before she repays the loan. What do the values 5,000 and 0.03 represent in this model?

____

____

8. The bank charges an annual interest rate that is compounded monthly. The amount Trini must pay to the bank can be modeled by the function $c(t) = 10{,}000\left(1 + \frac{0.06}{12}\right)^{12t}$, where t is the number of years before she repays the loan. What do the values 10,000; 0.06; and 12 represent in this model?

____

____

9. Combine functions p and c to build a new function, a, which will show the total amount Trini must repay in car loans if she repays them after t years.

$a(t) =$ ______________________________

10. Use function a to determine the total amount of money she will have to repay if she repays the loan after 5 years.

____

Solve.

11. SHOW Marcus is buying a plane ticket. If he purchases his ticket on the day of his departure, it will cost \$239. The ticket costs less if he buys it earlier. If he purchases it 20 days before his departure, it will cost \$189. Model this situation by using a linear function. Then determine the cost of the ticket if Marcus buys it 3 days before his departure.

____

____

12. CREATE A ball is dropped from a height of 50 centimeters onto a hard floor and bounces back up to $\frac{2}{5}$ of its original height. On each successive bounce, it rebounds to $\frac{2}{5}$ of its previous height. Model this situation with a function. List the height to which the ball bounces on its first, second, third, and fourth bounces.

____

____

____

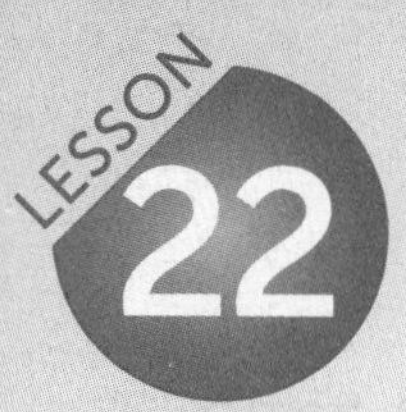

Arithmetic Sequences

UNDERSTAND A **sequence** is an arrangement of numbers or objects that follows a rule or a pattern. Take a look at the Fibonacci sequence:

1, 1, 2, 3, 5, 8, 13, 21, 34, ...

Each number in the sequence is called a **term**. The pattern of the Fibonacci sequence is that each term is equal to the sum of the two previous terms. This rule is an example of using a **recursive process**, because finding a term depends on knowing previous terms. When defining a recursive process, you must define at least one previous term.

The variable a is often used to stand for the terms in a sequence. The first term is a_1, the second is a_2, and so on. The nth term of the sequence is written a_n, where n can be any positive integer. This notation is useful for writing the sequence's rule mathematically. The equations below represent the rule for the Fibonacci sequence.

$a_1 = 1$ $\qquad a_2 = 1$ $\qquad a_n = a_{n-1} + a_{n-2}$

UNDERSTAND In an **arithmetic sequence**, each term is found by adding a fixed number, called the **common difference (*d*)**, to the previous term. The arithmetic sequence 3, 5, 7, 9, 11, 13, ... has a common difference of 2.

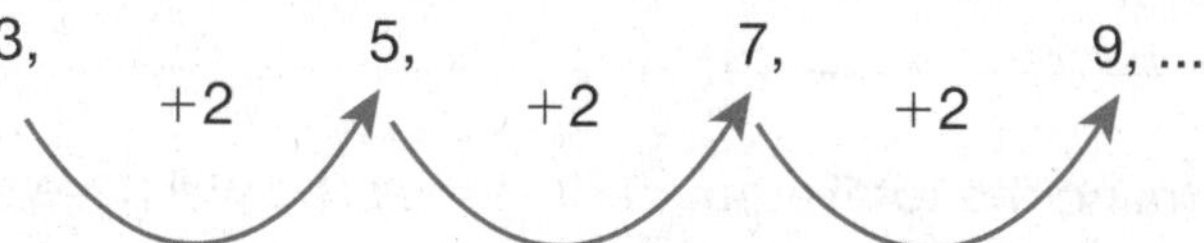

If you know any term in an arithmetic sequence, you can add the common difference to it to find the next term. The following equation is a recursive definition of an arithmetic sequence.

$a_n = a_{n-1} + d$

You can derive an explicit equation to find any term in an arithmetic sequence, as long as you know the first term.

$a_1 = a_1$

$a_2 = a_1 + d$

$a_3 = a_2 + d = a_1 + d + d = a_1 + 2d$

$a_4 = a_3 + d = a_1 + 2d + d = a_1 + 3d$

Notice the pattern. To find a desired term, add the first term, a_1, to a multiple of the common difference, d. The coefficient of d is 1 less than the number of the desired term.

$a_n = a_1 + (n - 1)d$

Connect

Below are the first four terms in an arithmetic sequence.

25, 22, 19, 16

Use a recursive process to find the next 3 terms in the sequence. Plot the first seven terms on a coordinate plane.

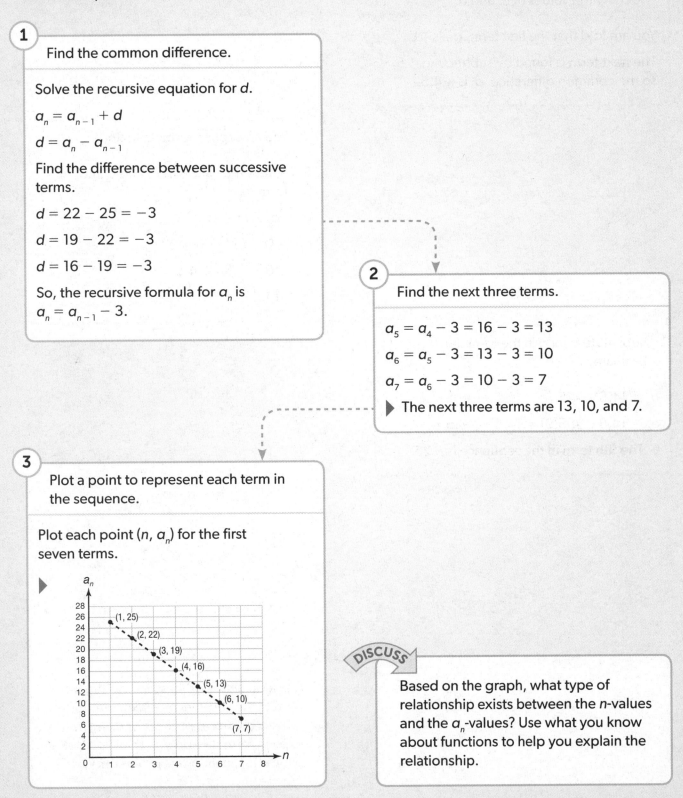

1 Find the common difference.

Solve the recursive equation for d.

$a_n = a_{n-1} + d$

$d = a_n - a_{n-1}$

Find the difference between successive terms.

$d = 22 - 25 = -3$

$d = 19 - 22 = -3$

$d = 16 - 19 = -3$

So, the recursive formula for a_n is $a_n = a_{n-1} - 3$.

2 Find the next three terms.

$a_5 = a_4 - 3 = 16 - 3 = 13$

$a_6 = a_5 - 3 = 13 - 3 = 10$

$a_7 = a_6 - 3 = 10 - 3 = 7$

▶ The next three terms are 13, 10, and 7.

3 Plot a point to represent each term in the sequence.

Plot each point (n, a_n) for the first seven terms.

▶

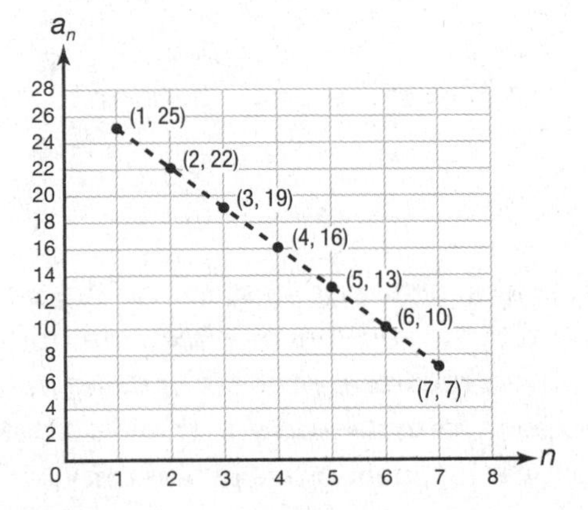

DISCUSS

Based on the graph, what type of relationship exists between the n-values and the a_n-values? Use what you know about functions to help you explain the relationship.

EXAMPLE In a certain arithmetic sequence, each term is found by subtracting 4.5 from the previous term. If the first term in the sequence is 10, what is the 9th term in the sequence?

1 Identify the values of a_1 and d.

You are told that the first term, a_1, is 10.

The next term is found by subtracting 4.5, so the common difference, d, is -4.5.

2 Write an explicit formula to find a_n.

Substitute the values of a_1 and d into the formula.

$a_n = a_1 + (n - 1)d$

$a_n = 10 + (n - 1)(-4.5)$

$a_n = 10 - 4.5n + 4.5$

$a_n = 14.5 - 4.5n$

3 Substitute 9 for n in the formula. Evaluate.

$a_n = 14.5 - 4.5n$

$a_9 = 14.5 - 4.5(9) = 14.5 - 40.5 = -26$

▶ The 9th term in the sequence is -26.

CHECK

Use a recursive process to find the 9th term in the sequence. Which method—using a recursive process or using an explicit formula—do you think is a better choice for solving this problem? Why?

Problem Solving

READ

Ami is training for a long-distance race. She ran for 30 minutes per day on three days this week. Each week she will increase her daily running time by 5 minutes. By the 6th week, for how many minutes will she run each day that she trains?

PLAN

She increases her running time by the same number of minutes each week. So, this is an arithmetic sequence.

Write an explicit formula to represent the situation. Then find the ______ term in the sequence.

SOLVE

Her daily running time during the 1st week is 30 minutes, so a_1 = ______.

She will increase her daily running time by 5 minutes each week, so d = ______.

Find a_6, the number of minutes she will run each day during the 6th week.

$a_n = a_1 + (n - 1)d$

$a_6 = 30 + ($______ $- 1)($______$) =$ ______________________

CHECK

Use a recursive process to check the answer.

$a_2 = 30 +$ ______ $=$ ______

$a_3 =$ ______ $+$ ______ $=$ ______

$a_4 =$ ______ $+$ ______ $=$ ______

$a_5 =$ ______ $+$ ______ $=$ ______

$a_6 =$ ______ $+$ ______ $=$ ______

Do you get the same value for a_6? ______

▶ By the sixth week, Ami will be running ______ minutes each day that she trains.

Practice

Determine if each sequence is an arithmetic sequence. If it is, identify the common difference.

1. 5, 3, 1, −1, −3, ...

____

2. 2, 2, 4, 6, 10, ...

____

3. $\frac{3}{2}, \frac{5}{2}, \frac{7}{2}, \frac{9}{2}, \frac{11}{2}, \ldots$

____

Is the same number added to each term to get the next term?

Write a recursive process for each arithmetic sequence. Then use it to find the specified term.

4. 5, 9, 13, 17, 21, ...

a_1 = ______________

a_n = ______________

a_7 = ______________

5. 3, $2\frac{3}{4}$, $2\frac{1}{2}$, $2\frac{1}{4}$, 2, ...

a_1 = ______________

a_n = ______________

a_7 = ______________

6. 10, 3, −4, −11, −18, ...

a_1 = ______________

a_n = ______________

a_8 = ______________

REMEMBER In a recursive process, a_n is defined by using previous terms.

Write an explicit formula for the *n*th term and use it to find the specified term.

7. 11, 15, 19, 23, ...

a_n = ______________

a_8 = ______________

8. 100, 88, 76, 64, ...

a_n = ______________

a_{10} = ______________

9. 1.2, 1.8, 2.4, 3,...

a_n = ______________

a_{12} = ______________

Use the given information to find the specified term in each arithmetic sequence.

10. $a_1 = 14, d = 6$

a_4 = ______________

11. $a_1 = 52, d = -5$

a_6 = ______________

12. $a_1 = 0, d = \frac{1}{3}$

a_{15} = ______________

Choose the best answer.

13. The formula $a_n = 10 - 4n$ describes an arithmetic sequence. What are the first four terms in the sequence?

A. 6, 2, −2, −6

B. 6, 2, 0, −2

C. 10, 6, 2, −2

D. 14, 18, 22, 26

14. For an arithmetic sequence, $a_1 = 21$. Its recursive formula is $a_n = a_{n-1} + 11$. Which explicit formula can be used to find the *n*th term in the sequence?

A. $a_n = 10 - 11n$

B. $a_n = 10 + 11n$

C. $a_n = 21 - 11n$

D. $a_n = 21 + 11n$

Use the arithmetic sequence below for questions 15–17.

2, 5, 8, 11, ...

15. Write an explicit formula in terms of n to show how to find the nth term in this sequence.

____

16. Plot points (n, a_n) on the grid to represent the first six terms in the sequence.

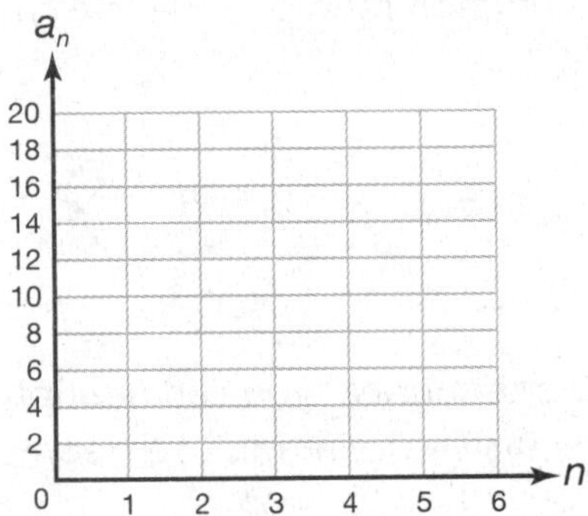

What does the slope of the graph represent?

____

17. Think of this sequence as a function. What type of function is it? What are its domain and its range? Explain your thinking.

____

____

____

Use sequences to describe the situation.

18. COMPOSE Steve is buying a new tablet computer on layaway. He makes an initial payment of $50 and will increase the payment each month as shown by the table. Write a recursive formula and an explicit formula to describe this sequence. Explain how you determined the formulas.

Month (n)	Payment in $ (a_n)
1	50
2	60
3	70
4	80
5	90

____

____

____

____

LESSON

23 Geometric Sequences

UNDERSTAND In a **geometric sequence**, each pair of consecutive terms is related by a **common ratio**, *r*.

To find a term in the sequence, multiply the previous term by the common ratio. The geometric sequence 1, 3, 9, 27, 81, ... has a common ratio of 3. Each term is multiplied by 3 in order to yield the next term.

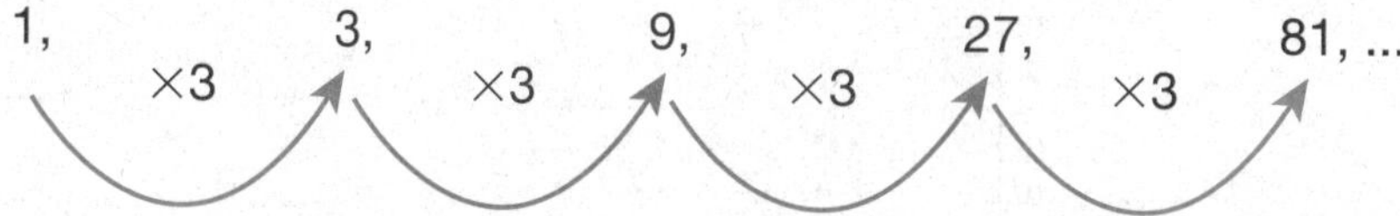

If you know any term in a geometric sequence, you can multiply it by the common ratio to find the next term. The following is a recursive definition of a geometric sequence:

$$a_n = a_{n-1} \cdot r$$

Suppose you wanted to find the 100th term in this sequence. As with arithmetic sequences, using the recursive definition would require a lot of steps. Fortunately, you can derive an explicit equation to find any term in a geometric sequence, as long as you know the first term. Examine the formulas for the first few terms.

$$a_1 = a_1$$

$$a_2 = a_1 \cdot r$$

$$a_3 = a_2 \cdot r = a_1 \cdot r \cdot r = a_1 \cdot r^2$$

$$a_4 = a_3 \cdot r = a_1 \cdot r^2 \cdot r = a_1 \cdot r^3$$

$$a_5 = a_4 \cdot r = a_1 \cdot r^3 \cdot r = a_1 \cdot r^4$$

Notice the pattern. To find a desired term, multiply the first term, a_1, by a power of the common ratio, *r*. The exponent of *r* is 1 less than the number of the desired term. Written mathematically, this is:

$$a_n = a_1 \cdot r^{n-1}$$

Connect

Below are the first four terms in a geometric sequence.

1, 2, 4, 8

Use a recursive process to find the next 3 terms in the sequence. Plot the first seven terms on a coordinate plane.

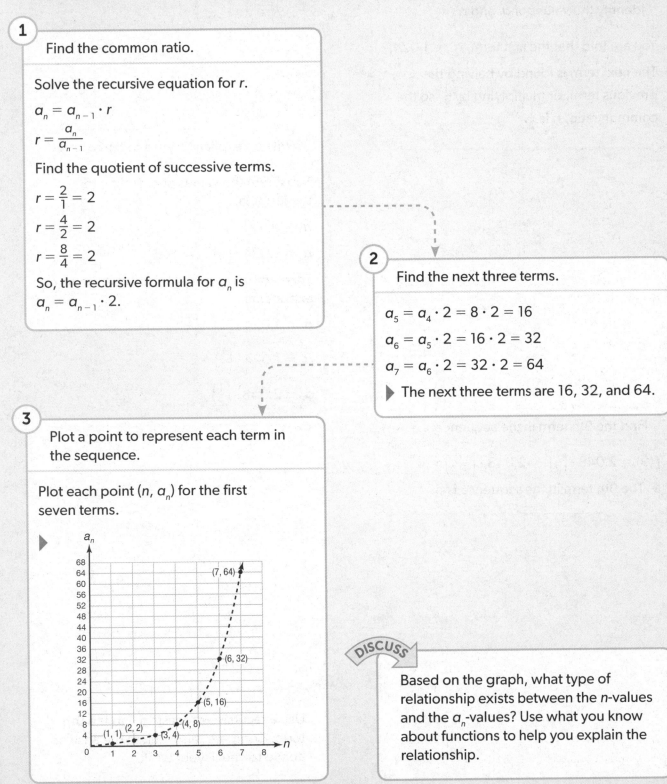

1 Find the common ratio.

Solve the recursive equation for *r*.

$a_n = a_{n-1} \cdot r$

$r = \frac{a_n}{a_{n-1}}$

Find the quotient of successive terms.

$r = \frac{2}{1} = 2$

$r = \frac{4}{2} = 2$

$r = \frac{8}{4} = 2$

So, the recursive formula for a_n is $a_n = a_{n-1} \cdot 2$.

2 Find the next three terms.

$a_5 = a_4 \cdot 2 = 8 \cdot 2 = 16$

$a_6 = a_5 \cdot 2 = 16 \cdot 2 = 32$

$a_7 = a_6 \cdot 2 = 32 \cdot 2 = 64$

▶ The next three terms are 16, 32, and 64.

3 Plot a point to represent each term in the sequence.

Plot each point (n, a_n) for the first seven terms.

▶

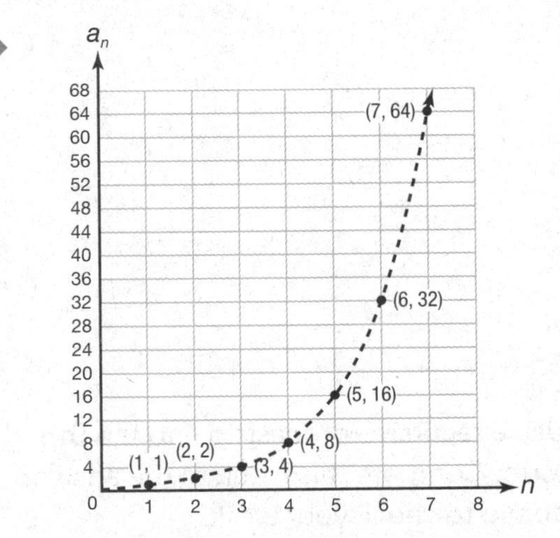

DISCUSS

Based on the graph, what type of relationship exists between the *n*-values and the a_n-values? Use what you know about functions to help you explain the relationship.

EXAMPLE A geometric sequence has an initial value of 1,024, and each term in the sequence is half of the previous term. Write an explicit formula to find any term in the sequence. Then use that formula to find the 9th term in the sequence.

1 Identify the values of a_1 and r.

You are told that the first term, a_1, is 1,024.

The next term is found by halving the previous term, or multiplying by $\frac{1}{2}$, so the common ratio, r, is $\frac{1}{2}$.

2 Write an explicit formula to find a_n.

Substitute the values of a_1 and r into the formula.

$a_n = a_1 \cdot r^{n-1}$,

$a_n = 1{,}024 \cdot \left(\frac{1}{2}\right)^{n-1}$

This can be simplified by using the laws of exponents.

$a_n = 1{,}024 \cdot \left(\frac{1}{2}\right)^{n} \cdot \left(\frac{1}{2}\right)^{-1}$

$a_n = 1{,}024 \cdot \left(\frac{1}{2}\right)^{n} \cdot 2$

$a_n = 2{,}048 \cdot \left(\frac{1}{2}\right)^{n}$

3 Find the 9th term in the sequence.

$f(9) = 2{,}048 \cdot \left(\frac{1}{2}\right)^{9} = 2{,}048 \cdot \left(\frac{1}{512}\right) = 4$

▶ The 9th term in the sequence is 4.

CHECK

Use a recursive process to find the 9th term. Compare this result to the answer above to check your work.

Problem Solving

READ

Jenny started a chain letter by e-mail. She sent it to five of her friends and asked them to each send it to five of their friends. Assume that no one breaks the chain and that no person receives the e-mail twice. How many e-mails will be sent during the 6th generation? (Treat Jenny's e-mails as the 1st generation of the letter.)

PLAN

Each person who receives the e-mail sends it to five friends.

Each of those people also sends it to five friends. So, the total number of e-mails sent in each generation is ______ times the number of e-mails sent in the previous generation.

So, a recursive process can be used to find the answer.

SOLVE

In the 1st generation, 5 e-mails were sent. So, $a_1 = 5$.

In the 2nd generation, 5 times as many e-mails will be sent, and so on.

2nd generation: $a_2 = 5 \cdot 5 =$ ______

3rd generation: $a_3 =$ ______ $\cdot 5 =$ ______

4th generation: $a_4 =$ ______ $\cdot 5 =$ ______

5th generation: $a_5 =$ ______ $\cdot 5 =$ ______

6th generation: $a_6 =$ ______ $\cdot 5 =$ ______

CHECK

The numbers of e-mails sent in each generation are the terms of a geometric sequence. So, check the answer by writing an explicit formula.

We know that $a_1 =$ ______ and the common ratio, r, is 5.

$a_n = a_1 \cdot r^{n-1}$

$a_n =$ ______ $\cdot$ (______)$^{n-1}$

Use the formula to find a_6.

$a_6 =$ ______ $\cdot$ (______)$^{6-1} =$ ____________________

Did you get the same value for a_6? ______

▶ If the chain is not broken, then exactly ____________ e-mails will be sent in the sixth generation.

Practice

Determine if each sequence is a geometric sequence. If it is, identify the common ratio.

1. 5, 10, 15, 20, 25, ... ______

2. 7, −14, 28, −56, 112, ... ______

3. 16, 24, 36, 54, 81, ... ______

REMEMBER A common ratio can be positive or negative.

Write a recursive process for each geometric sequence. Then use it to find the specified term.

4. 1, 6, 36, 216, ...

$a_1 =$ ______

$a_n =$ ______

$a_6 =$ ______

5. $\frac{1}{4}, \frac{1}{16}, \frac{1}{64}, \frac{1}{256}, \ldots$

$a_1 =$ ______

$a_n =$ ______

$a_6 =$ ______

6. 0.05, 0.5, 5, 50, ...

$a_1 =$ ______

$a_n =$ ______

$a_7 =$ ______

What number is multiplied by each term to get the next term?

Write an explicit formula for the *n*th term and use it to find the specified term.

7. $3, 2, \frac{4}{3}, \frac{8}{9}, \ldots$

$a_n =$ ______

$a_6 =$ ______

8. 3, −9, 27, −81, ...

$a_n =$ ______

$a_8 =$ ______

9. 12, 24, 48, 96, ...

$a_n =$ ______

$a_{10} =$ ______

Use the given information to find the specified term in each geometric sequence.

10. $a_1 = 3, r = 20$

$a_4 =$ ______

11. $a_1 = 5{,}000; r = 0.2$

$a_6 =$ ______

12. $a_1 = 2, r = -4$

$a_7 =$ ______

Choose the best answer.

13. The formula $a_n = -10 \cdot (3)^{n-1}$ describes a geometric sequence. Which recursive formula also describes this sequence?

A. $a_1 = 1; a_n = a_{n-1} \cdot -30$

B. $a_1 = 3; a_n = a_{n-1} \cdot -10$

C. $a_1 = -10; a_n = a_{n-1} \cdot 3$

D. $a_1 = -1; a_n = a_{n-1} \cdot 30$

14. Which formula can be used to find the *n*th term in the sequence below?

128, 96, 72, 54, ...

A. $a_n = 128 \cdot \left(\frac{3}{4}\right)^{n-1}$

B. $a_n = 128 \cdot \left(\frac{4}{3}\right)^{n-1}$

C. $a_n = 128 \cdot \left(\frac{3}{4}\right)^{n}$

D. $a_n = 128 \cdot \left(\frac{4}{3}\right)^{n}$

Use the geometric sequence below for questions 15–17.

80, 40, 20, 10, ...

15. Write an explicit formula in terms of n to show how to find the nth term in this sequence.

____

16. Plot points (n, a_n) on the grid on the right to represent the first six terms in the sequence.

Find the average rate of change between each adjacent pair of points.

____

____

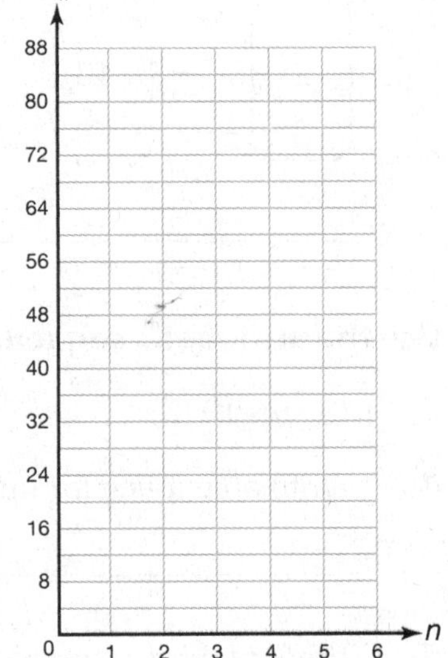

17. Think of this sequence as a function. What type of function is it? What are its domain and its range? Explain your thinking.

____

____

____

18. SHOW A petri dish contains 4 viruses. Each hour, the number of viruses increases, as shown in the table. The population change can be modeled by a geometric sequence. Write a recursive formula and an explicit formula that can model this sequence. Use the formulas to predict how many viruses will be in the dish by the 7th hour.

Hour (n)	Population (a_n)
1	4
2	12
3	36
4	108
5	324

recursive formula: _______________

explicit formula: _______________

$a_7 =$ _______________

UNIT

2 Review

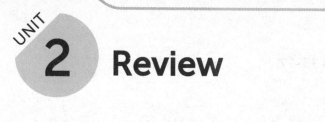

Determine whether each relation represented is a function or not. Write *yes* or *no*.

1.

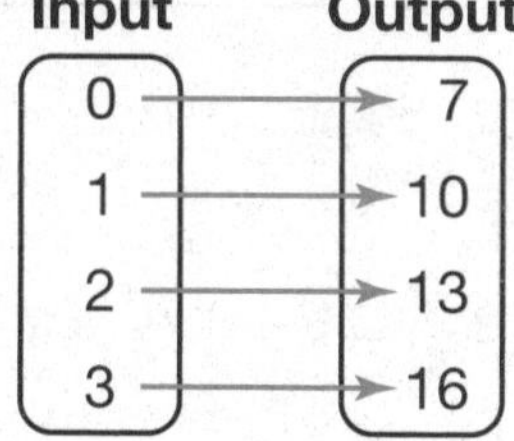

____

2.

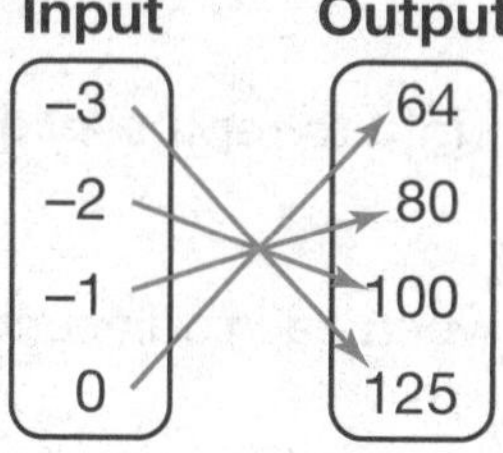

____

3.

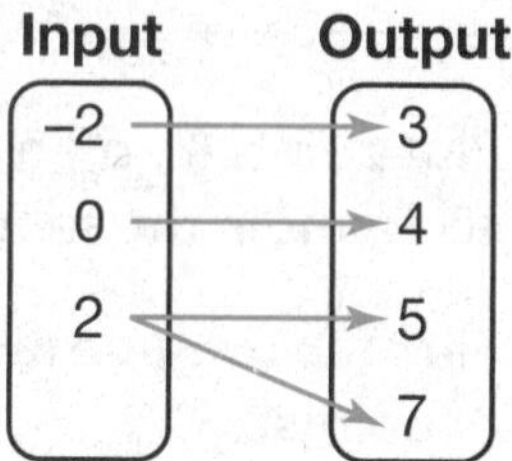

____

Use the arithmetic sequence below for questions 4–6.

18, 14, 10, 6, ...

4. Write an explicit formula for the *n*th term.

____

5. What is the tenth term in this sequence?

____

6. Think of this sequence as a function. What type of function is it? What are its domain and its range?

____

Graph each function. Then identify the *x*- and *y*-intercepts of each graph.

7. $f(x) = -2x + 6$

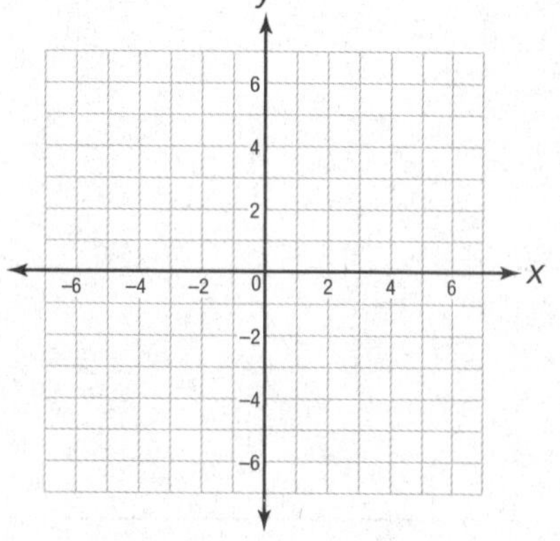

x-intercept: ______________

y-intercept: ______________

8. $f(x) = 2\left(\frac{1}{2}\right)^x$

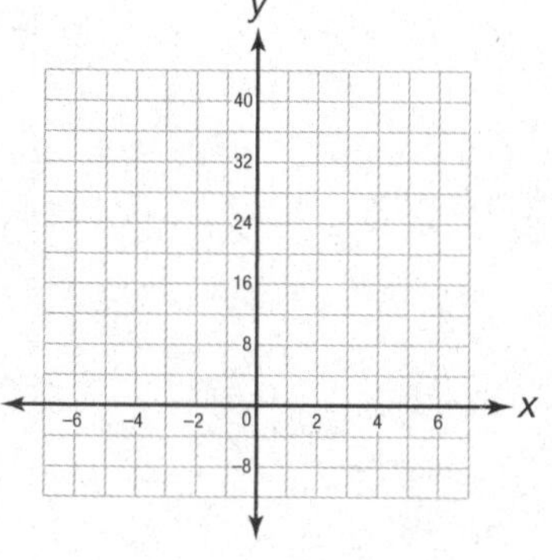

x-intercept: ______________

y-intercept: ______________

Fill in the blanks by writing an operation sign and a number to show how the *y*-values are changing over each interval. Then classify the function as *linear* or *exponential*.

9.

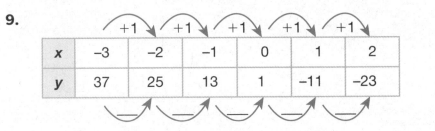

x	–3	–2	–1	0	1	2
y	37	25	13	1	–11	–23

Above the table (changes in x): +1, +1, +1, +1, +1

Below the table (changes in y): ___, ___, ___, ___, ___

Function type: ________________

Write each expression in the requested form.

10. $\sqrt[5]{x^2}$ in exponential form __________

11. $(16a)^{\frac{3}{2}}$ in radical form __________

Use the graph and table below for questions 12 and 13. The graph represents an exponential function *f*. The table lists several ordered pairs for a linear function *g*.

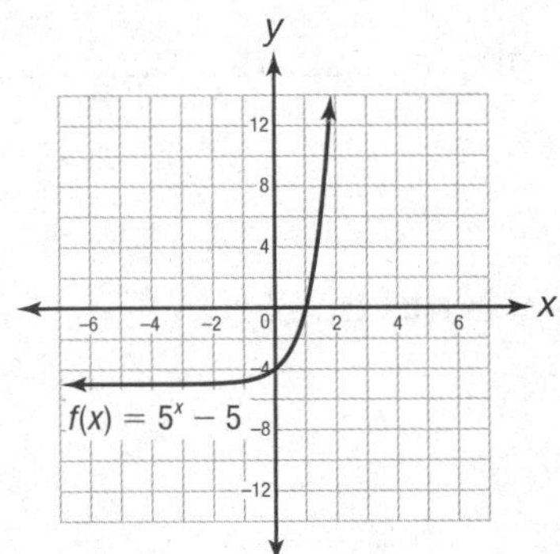

$g(x) = 5x - 5$	
x	$g(x)$
–1	–10
0	–5
1	0
2	5
3	10

12. Compare the intervals for which the functions are positive and negative.

____

____

13. Compare and contrast the end behavior of the functions.

____

____

Solve each system of equations algebraically.

14. $\begin{cases} x - 2y = 11 \\ 2x + 5y = 4 \end{cases}$

____

15. $\begin{cases} 2x - 5y = 40 \\ -4x + 3y = -10 \end{cases}$

____

Graph g. Then write an explicit equation for $g(x)$ in terms of x.

16. $g(x) = f(x + 2)$

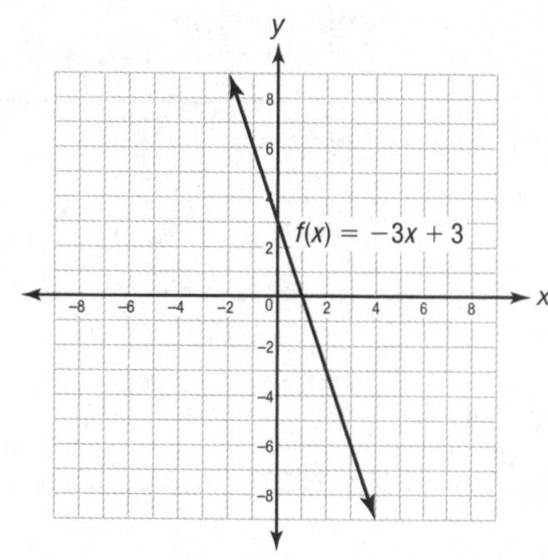

$g(x) =$ ____________________

17. $g(x) = -f(x)$

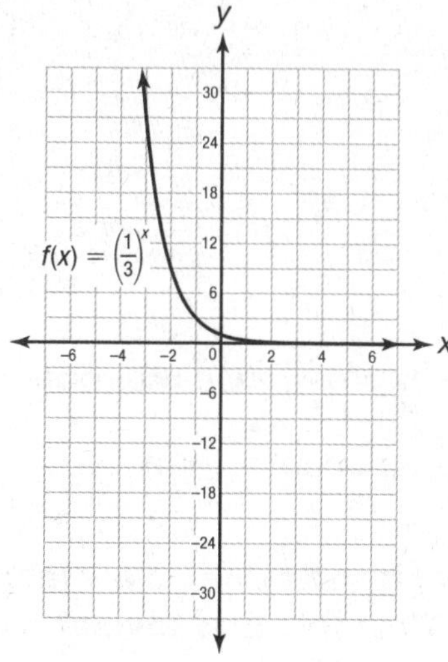

$g(x) =$ ____________________

Choose the best answer.

18. Based on the graph on the right, which statement is **not** true?

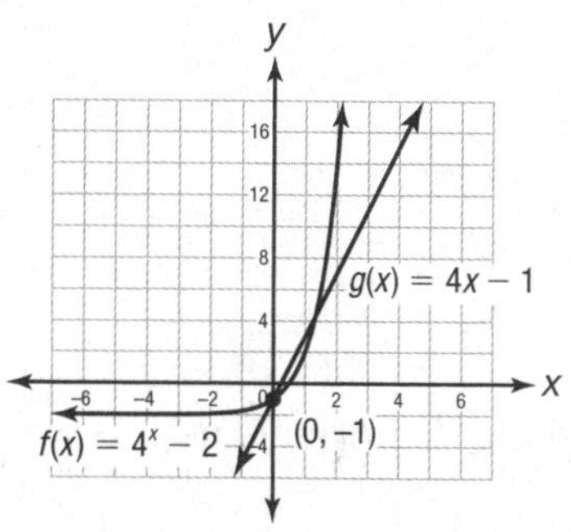

A. Functions f and g have the same x-intercept.

B. The ordered pair (2, 14) is a solution for $f(x)$.

C. The ordered pair (2, 7) is a solution for $g(x)$.

D. The value of $f(x)$ begins to exceed $g(x)$ during the interval between $x = 1$ and $x = 2$.

Graph each inequality or system of inequalities. Shade the portion of the graph that represents the solution set.

19. $2y - 3x > 4$

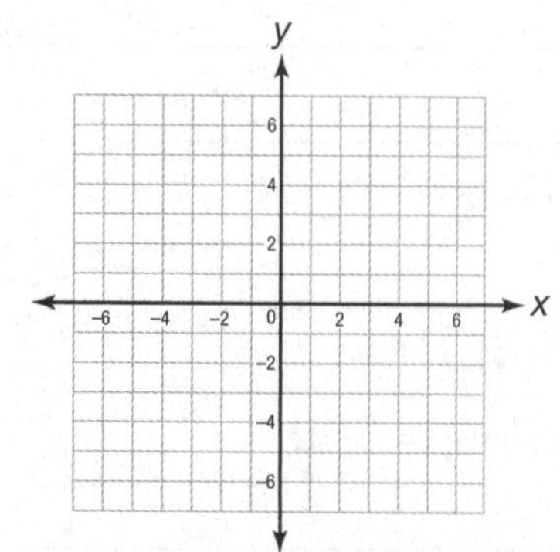

20. $\begin{cases} y < \frac{2}{3}x - 2 \\ y \geq -x \end{cases}$

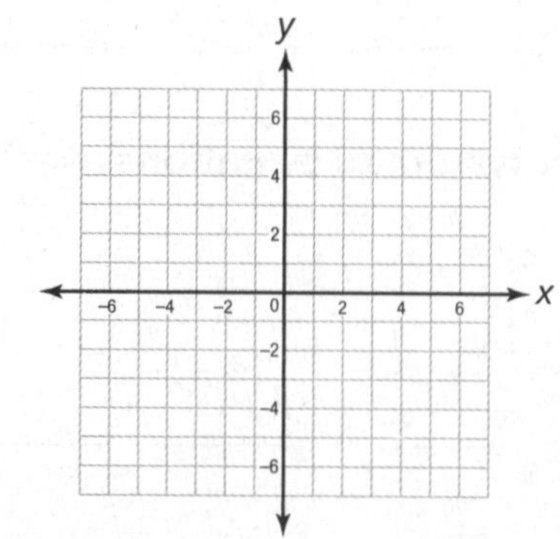

Rewrite each side of the equation as a function. Then graph the functions to solve for x.

21. $2x + 6 = -\frac{1}{2}x - 4$

$f(x) =$ ____________________

$g(x) =$ ____________________

$x =$ ______

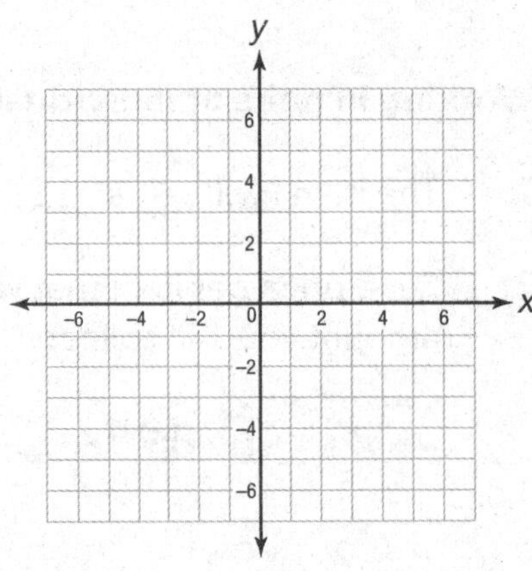

Examine the following situations and respond in complete sentences.

22. CLASSIFY With each swing of a pendulum, the length of its swing becomes less, as shown in the table below. Write an explicit formula to model the length of the arc in terms of the number of the swing. Classify the list of arc lengths as either an arithmetic or geometric sequence and explain how you know.

Number of Swing (n)	Arc Length (a_n)
1	30
2	27
3	24.3
4	21.87
5	19.683

____

____

____

23. CREATE The cost of using the Internet at an Internet café equals a set fee plus a certain rate per minute. Four minutes of Internet use cost $3, and eight minutes of Internet use cost $4. On the grid, make a graph to represent this situation and write an equation to model the situation. Find the slope of the graph and interpret its meaning in this situation.

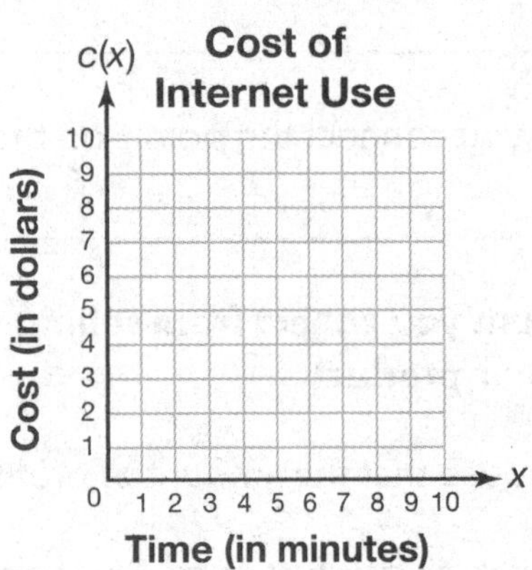

____

____

Performance Task

TAKING CARE OF Business

Working in pairs or individually, pretend you are starting your own business.

1. The item I will sell is ________________. The name of my new business is ________________.

2. Set a price per item that you will charge. Create a table, a graph, and an equation to show f, the amount you will collect if you sell up to 10 items. Represent the number of items as x.

x	$f(x) =$ ______________
1	
2	
3	
4	
5	
6	
7	
8	
9	
10	

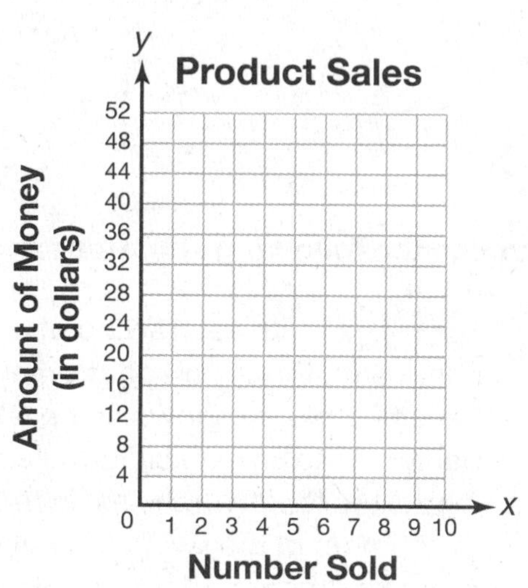

3. Explain how you determined the equation for f.

____

4. Did you connect the points on the graph with a solid line? a dashed line? no line? Explain why.

____

The amount you collect from selling your product is not the same as the profit you earn from selling your product.

5. Suppose that the amount of profit you earn is equal to $\frac{3}{5}$ of what you collect.

   So, if each product costs \$5, then your profit for selling 1 product is: $\$5 \cdot \frac{3}{5} =$ ____________.

   Using algebraic notation, represent this as a transformation: $p(x) =$ ____________ $f(x)$.

   What type of transformation of f does it represent? ______________________

6. Write an equation for p. Then graph it on the coordinate plane above, using a different colored pen or pencil than you used to draw the graph of f. Does this show the transformation you expected?

____

Profits are important to you, but your customers are only concerned with how much your product will cost them. They want to pay as little as possible.

The graph below shows how much one of your competitors, Company G, charges for the same product, including shipping.

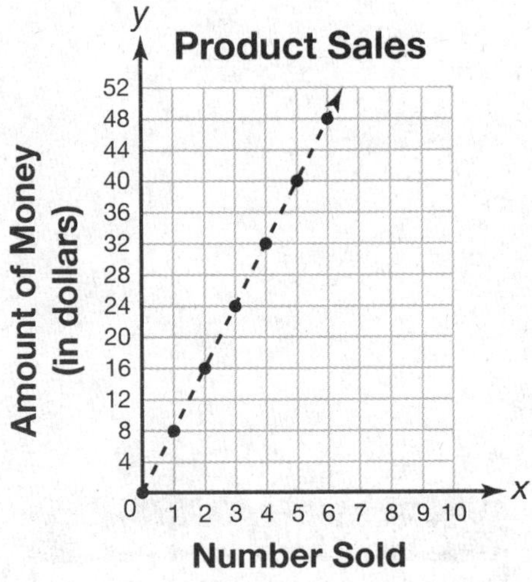

7. Based on the graph, how much does Company G charge per product? Explain how you know.

____

8. Copy your original graph of function *f* from the previous page onto the graph above. Use a different color and label it *f*. After checking with your local shipper, you find that you will need to charge customers 15 dollars to ship any items. Transform the graph of *f* using this equation:

$h(x) = f(x) + 15$

Identify the transformation: _______________

Then write an explicit equation for *h*: $h(x) =$ _______________

9. Based on your graph, when would it be cheaper for Mr. Smith to order from Company G? When would it be cheaper to order from you? Would the price ever be the same from both companies?

____

____

Grade 8	Algebra I	Geometry & Algebra II

Expressions & Equations
Understand connections between proportional relationships, lines, and linear equations.

Functions
Use functions to model relationships between quantities.

Statistics and Probability
Investigate patterns of associations in bivariate data.

Statistics and Probability
Interpreting Categorical and Quantitative Data
Summarize, represent, and intepret data on a single count or measurement variable.
Summarize, represent, and intepret data on two categorical and quantitative variables.
Interpret linear models.

Functions
Interpreting Functions
Interpret functions that arise in applications in terms of the context.

Statistics and Probability
Interpreting Categorical and Quantitative Data
Summarize, represent, and intepret data on a single count or measurement variable.
Making Inferences and Justifying Conclusions
Make inferences and justify conclusions from sample surveys, experiments, and observational studies.
Conditional Probability and the Rules of Probability
Understand independence and conditional probability and use them to interpret data.

Unit 3
Descriptive Statistics

Lesson 24 Displaying and Analyzing Data 186

Lesson 25 Investigating Measures of Center 194

Lesson 26 Investigating Spread............................ 202

Lesson 27 Constructing and Analyzing Box Plots 208

Lesson 28 Constructing and Analyzing Two-Way Frequency Tables 216

Lesson 29 Constructing and Analyzing Scatter Plots......... 224

Lesson 30 Best Fit and Correlation 230

Unit 3 Review... 238

Unit 3 Performance Task...................................... 242

LESSON

24 Displaying and Analyzing Data

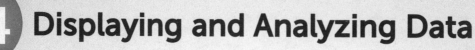

Collecting and Displaying Data

UNDERSTAND Often, one of the first steps to answering a question is collecting data. For example, suppose you wanted to know how tall bean plants grow in sunny conditions. To answer this question, you could find some bean plants on a farm or growing in the wild or anywhere that gets plenty of sunlight and record their heights. This is an example of an **observational study**.

However, another option is to grow bean plants of your own. You could grow some bean plants on your windowsill and some others in a dark closet. After a time, record their heights. This is an example of an **experimental study**. In this study, you directly controlled the conditions that affect the plants, such as temperature, water, and soil, so that the results depended only on the amount of light that the plants received.

UNDERSTAND No matter what type of study you choose, it helps to organize your data in a data display. If the data are numerical and you have relatively few data points, a **dot plot** may be a good way to display them. The base of a dot plot is a number line that lists the possible values of the data. Each data point is represented by a dot placed over its value on the number line. A sample dot plot is shown below.

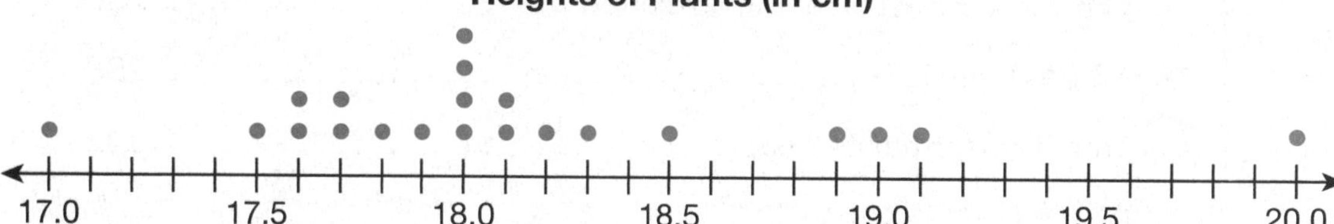

A **histogram**, another kind of data display, groups data points into ranges and shows how many of the data points fall in each range. All ranges or intervals in a histogram are of equal size, and they do not overlap. The sample histogram below shows the same data as in the dot plot above.

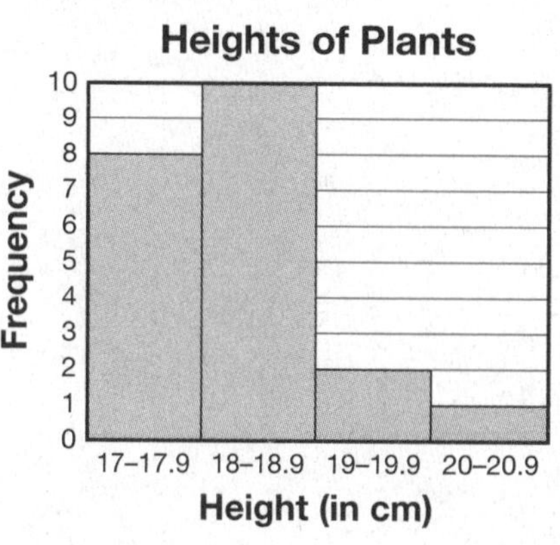

Connect

The chairman of a company asked his chief financial officer to track the closing price of the company's stock over 20 trading days. The stock prices, in dollars, are listed below.

26.70, 26.50, 26.90, 26.70, 26.60, 25.50, 25.10, 25.30, 25.10, 26.50,

27.40, 26.60, 26.80, 26.70, 26.70, 27.60, 27.40, 27.80, 27.60, 27.90

Create a histogram for the stock price data.

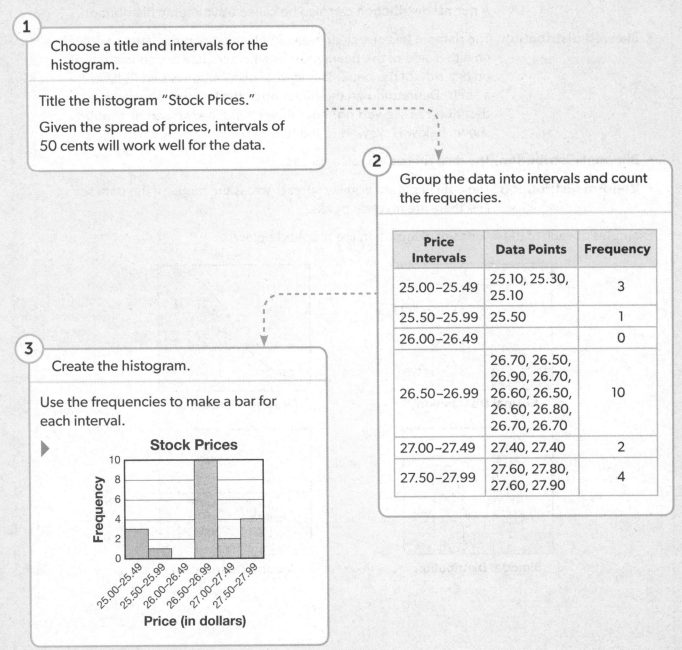

1 Choose a title and intervals for the histogram.

Title the histogram "Stock Prices."

Given the spread of prices, intervals of 50 cents will work well for the data.

2 Group the data into intervals and count the frequencies.

Price Intervals	Data Points	Frequency
25.00–25.49	25.10, 25.30, 25.10	3
25.50–25.99	25.50	1
26.00–26.49		0
26.50–26.99	26.70, 26.50, 26.90, 26.70, 26.60, 26.50, 26.60, 26.80, 26.70, 26.70	10
27.00–27.49	27.40, 27.40	2
27.50–27.99	27.60, 27.80, 27.60, 27.90	4

3 Create the histogram.

Use the frequencies to make a bar for each interval.

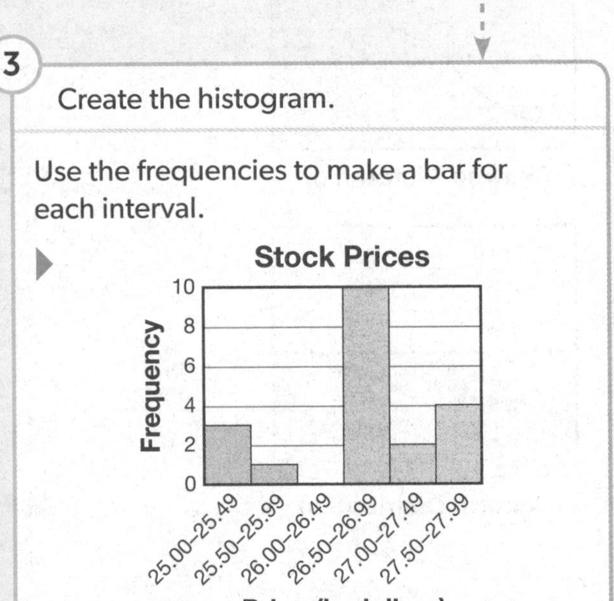

DISCUSS

What are some advantages of using a dot plot instead of a histogram?

Data Distributions

UNDERSTAND You can use the distribution of a data set, or its shape, to interpret it and to compare it to other data sets. Four kinds of distributions are described below.

- **Normal distribution**: The data set has one clear peak in the center with other data points spread equally on both sides of the peak. Because of its appearance, this kind of distribution is sometimes referred to as a bell curve. A normal distribution can also be called a symmetric distribution.
- **Skewed distribution**: The data set has one clear peak. But instead of being spread equally on either side of the peak, most or all of the data are concentrated on one side of the peak. This kind of distribution is said to have a "tail." Depending on the direction of the tail, the data can be described as skewed right or skewed left. The skewed distribution shown below is skewed to the left.
- **Bimodal distribution**: The data set has two clear peaks.
- **Uniform distribution**: The data items are equally spread across the range of the data set, and there are no clear peaks.

Examples of each of these kinds of distribution are graphed below.

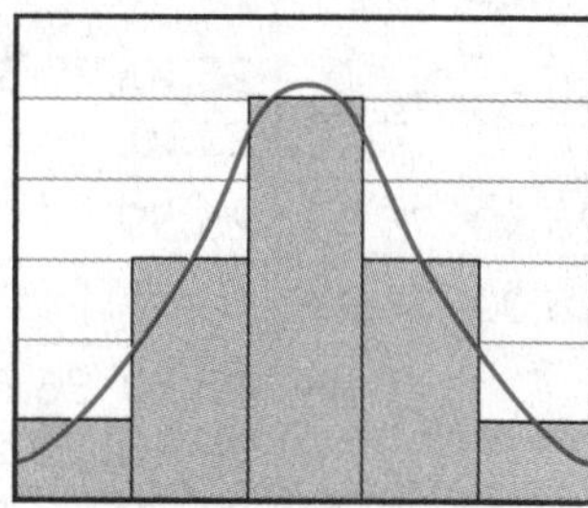

Normal Distribution

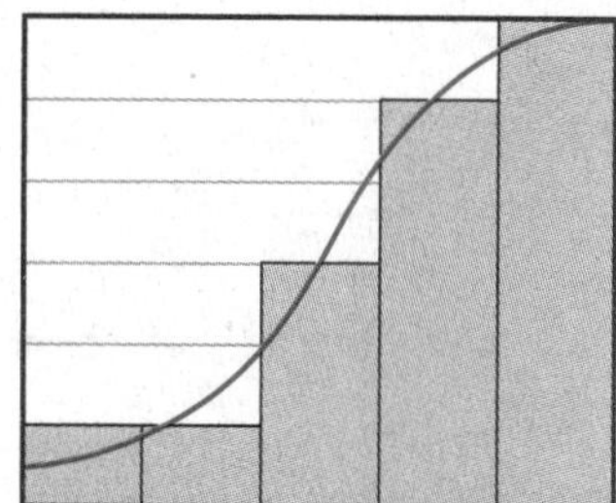

Skewed Distribution

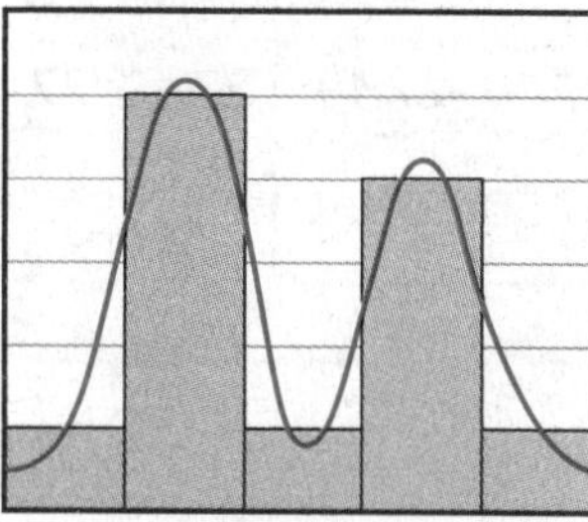

Bimodal Distribution

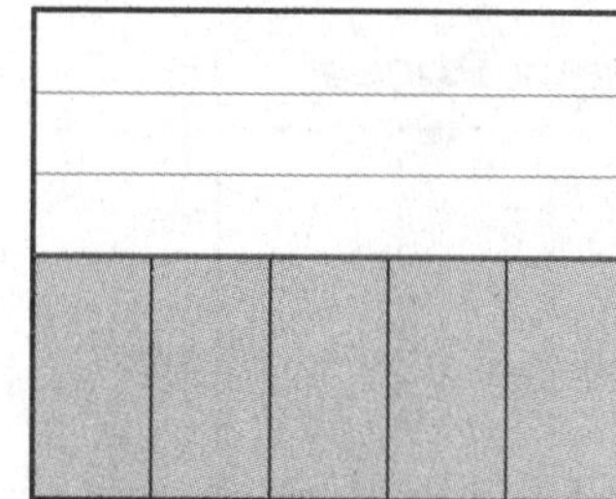

Uniform Distribution

Connect

The weights, in pounds, of a group of cats entered in a cat show are given below.

$1\frac{1}{2}$, 2, 2, 3, 3, 4, 4, 4, $4\frac{1}{2}$, 5, 5, 5, $5\frac{1}{2}$, $5\frac{3}{4}$,
6, 6, 6, 6, $6\frac{1}{4}$, $6\frac{1}{2}$, 7, 7, 7, 7, $7\frac{1}{2}$, $7\frac{3}{4}$, 8,
8, $8\frac{1}{2}$, $8\frac{1}{2}$, 9, 9, $9\frac{1}{4}$, $9\frac{3}{4}$, 10, 10, $10\frac{1}{2}$, 11, 13

Use the data to construct a histogram. Then describe the distribution of the data.

1 Choose intervals for your histogram.

The weights range from $1\frac{1}{2}$ to 13 pounds. Intervals of 2 pounds would be a good choice.

2 Divide the data into intervals and count frequencies.

Weight (w) Intervals	Data Points (in lb)	Frequency
$0 \le w < 2$	$1\frac{1}{2}$	1
$2 \le w < 4$	2, 2, 3, 3	4
$4 \le w < 6$	4, 4, 4, $4\frac{1}{2}$, 5, 5, 5, $5\frac{1}{2}$, $5\frac{3}{4}$	9
$6 \le w < 8$	6, 6, 6, 6, $6\frac{1}{4}$, $6\frac{1}{2}$, 7, 7, 7, 7, $7\frac{1}{2}$, $7\frac{3}{4}$	12
$8 \le w < 10$	8, 8, $8\frac{1}{2}$, $8\frac{1}{2}$, 9, 9, $9\frac{1}{4}$, $9\frac{3}{4}$	8
$10 \le w < 12$	10, 10, $10\frac{1}{2}$, 11	4
$12 \le w < 14$	13	1

Notice that each interval includes its lower boundary value, but not the upper boundary. So, on the histogram, the bar located between 2 and 4 will include data points of 2 lb, but not 4 lb.

3 Construct the histogram. Then describe the distribution.

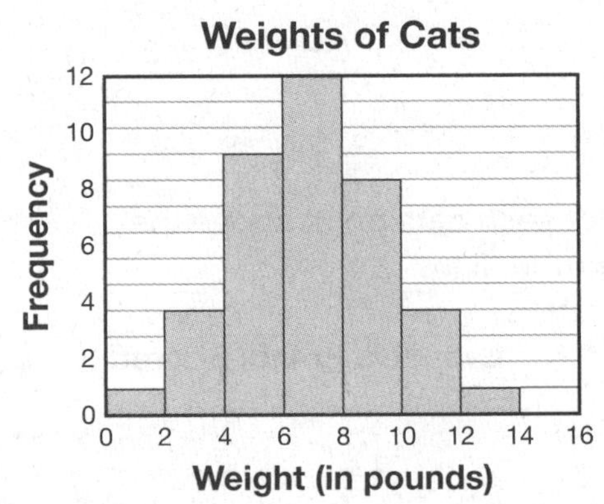

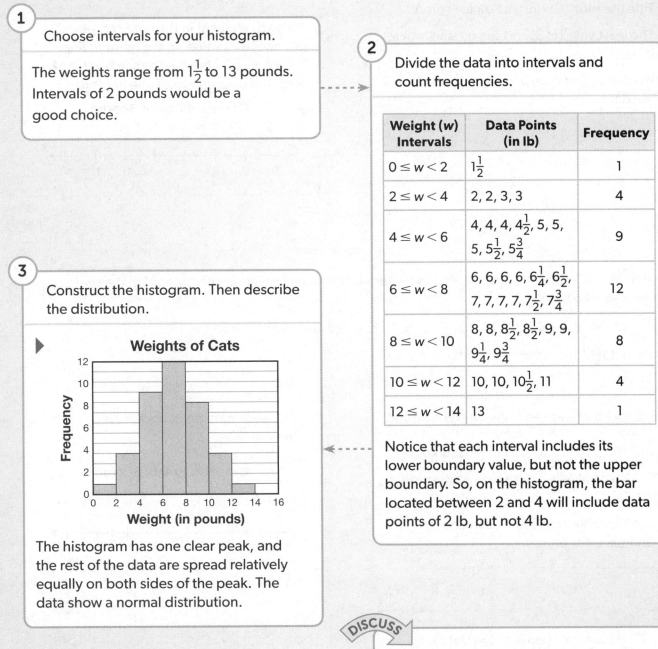

The histogram has one clear peak, and the rest of the data are spread relatively equally on both sides of the peak. The data show a normal distribution.

DISCUSS

How would the data have to change to show a skewed distribution? A bimodal distribution?

EXAMPLE A The list below shows how many points Corinna scored in each of 16 basketball games:

8, 3, 3, 9, 4, 7, 10, 4, 5, 9, 5, 7, 6, 8, 10, 6

Make a dot plot of Corinna's points.

1 Choose a range and title for the dot plot.

Title the plot "Corinna's Points Scored."

The least value is 3, and the greatest value is 10.

A number line from 0 to 14 will include all the data.

2 Plot each data point above a number line.

For each element in the data set, place a dot above its value on the number line. If multiple points have the same value, stack the dots on top of one another.

Corinna's Points Scored

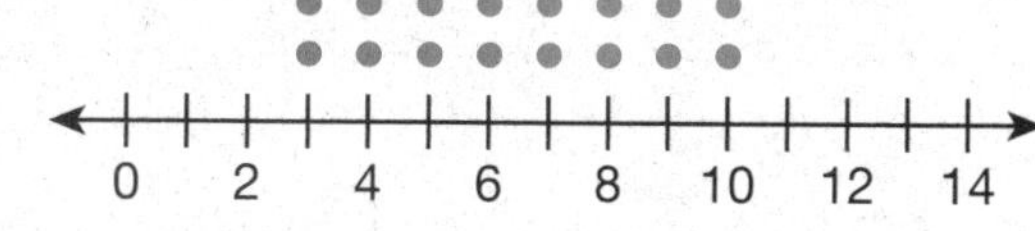

Leanne is on Corinna's team. The list below shows how many points Leanne scored in the same 16 basketball games:

13, 14, 9, 12, 13, 13, 14, 10, 9, 12, 6, 5, 7, 11, 10, 8

Make a dot plot of Leanne's points.

1 Choose a range and title for the dot plot.

Title the plot "Leanne's Points Scored."

The least value is 5, and the greatest value is 14.

Use the same range that you used for Corinna's dot plot.

2 Plot each data point above the number line.

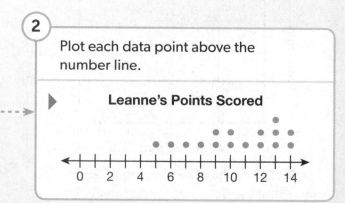

Leanne's Points Scored

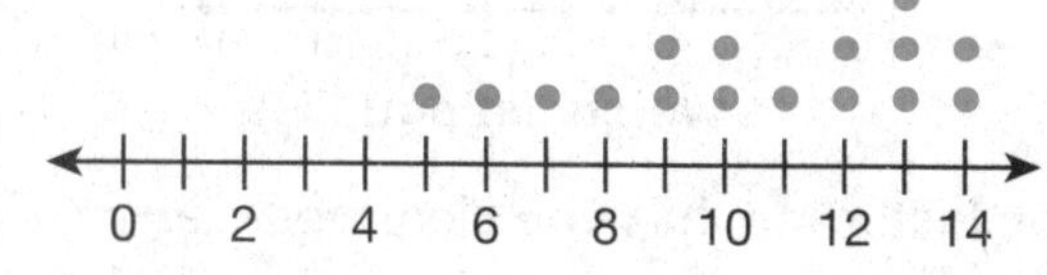

DISCUSS

Compare the shapes of the dot plots. What do their shapes tell you about the distributions of Corinna's and Leanne's scores?

EXAMPLE B The two histograms below show the ages of wait staff at two restaurants.

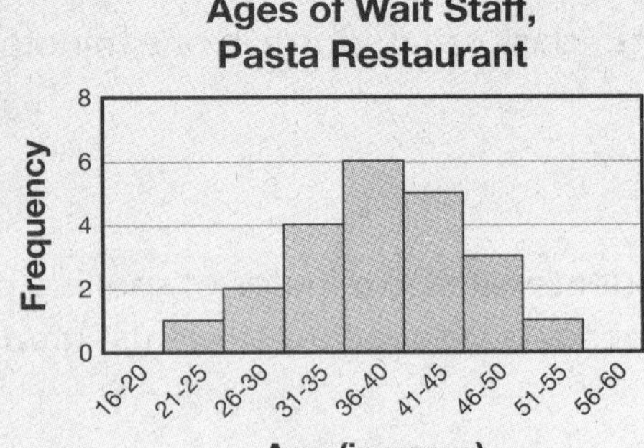

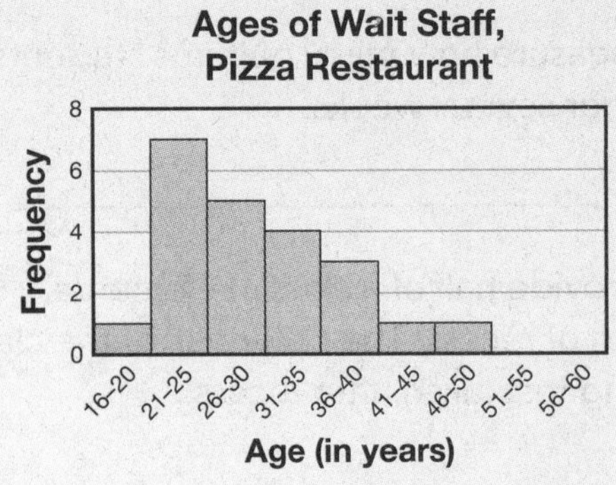

Identify the kind of distribution shown by each histogram. Use the shapes of the data sets to compare them.

1 Describe the shape of the histogram for the pasta restaurant.

The histogram is nearly symmetrical and has a central peak at ages 36–40.

Its shape most closely matches a bell curve.

The ages of the wait staff at the pasta restaurant show a normal distribution.

2 Describe the shape of the histogram for the pizza restaurant.

The histogram has one peak. The majority of the data are in a "tail" that extends to the right of the peak.

The ages of the wait staff at the pizza restaurant show a distribution skewed to the right.

3 Use the shapes of the histograms to interpret each data set.

The normal distribution of the data from the pasta restaurant shows that the ages of its wait staff are relatively evenly distributed around the 36–40 age range.

The data from the pizza restaurant is skewed to the right, and most of the data fall below the 36–40 age range. So, in general, the wait staff of the pizza restaurant is younger than that of the pasta restaurant.

TRY

The ages of the wait staff at a seafood restaurant are listed below.

18, 21, 23, 26, 26, 27, 28, 29, 30, 31, 35, 39, 42, 46, 48, 49, 49, 50, 51, 53, 54, 57

On a separate sheet of paper, create a histogram for the data. Compare its shape to the two histograms on this page.

Practice

For questions 1 and 2, classify each study as *observational* or *experimental*.

1. You measure how many pull-ups students in your P.E. class can perform in one minute each week for several weeks.

____

2. You provide half of a class of elementary school students with 20 minutes of spelling practice instead of recess. The other half of the class goes to recess. You record students' grades on a spelling test taken after recess.

____

For questions 3–5, use the given information. Create a histogram for each data set. Describe the distribution of each data set.

Students in the 1st and 2nd period biology classes took the same test. Their test scores are listed below.

3. 1st period test scores:

100, 91, 86, 73, 81, 100, 93, 94, 86, 86, 99, 93, 98, 84, 80, 97, 93, 87, 70, 97, 94, 88, 85, 96, 90

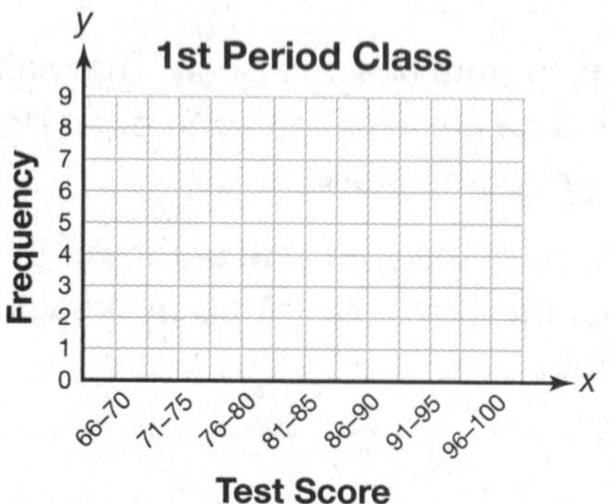

Distribution: _______________

4. 2nd period test scores:

81, 87, 95, 85, 83, 82, 76, 68, 86, 83, 93, 87, 76, 87, 71, 100, 76, 91, 73, 80, 80, 84, 87, 88, 73

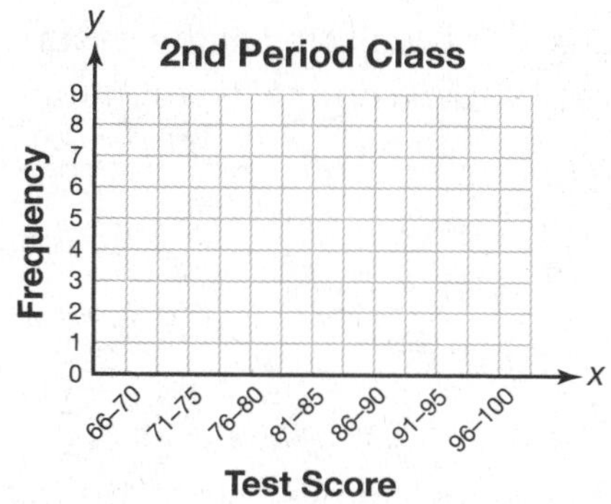

Distribution: _______________

5. Compare and contrast the histograms for the biology classes in questions 4 and 5.

____

____

Create a dot plot for the given data. Describe the shape of the data.

6. Nathaniel opened 20 peanut shells and recorded the number of peanuts he found in each shell.

   3, 2, 0, 1, 5, 2, 1, 2, 3, 1, 2, 2, 1, 2, 2, 3, 2, 3, 1, 2

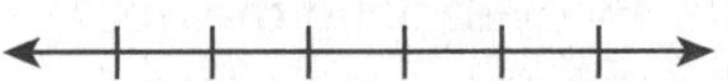

____

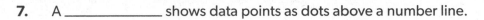

Fill in each blank with an appropriate word or phrase.

7. A ______________ shows data points as dots above a number line.

8. A ______________ shows how frequently data occur within certain ranges or intervals.

9. ______________ used in a histogram must be equal.

10. A ______________ distribution is symmetric and resembles a bell curve.

11. A ______________ distribution has two distinct peaks.

12. A ______________ distribution has a "tail" that extends more to one side of the graph than the other.

13. COMPARE Antoine surveyed 200 high school students to find out how many hours they slept this past Saturday night and how many hours they slept this past Monday night. The histograms show the data he collected.

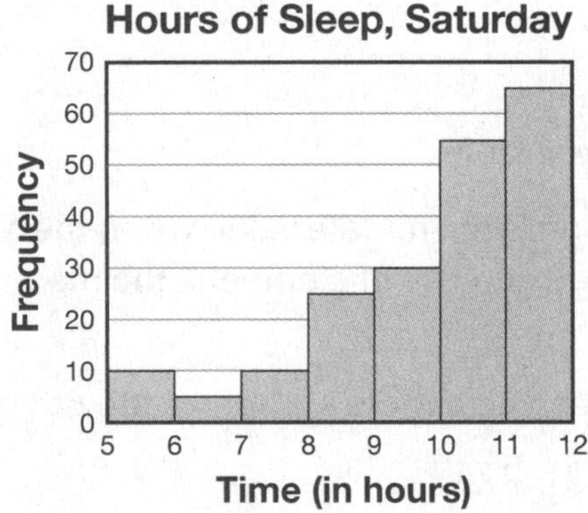

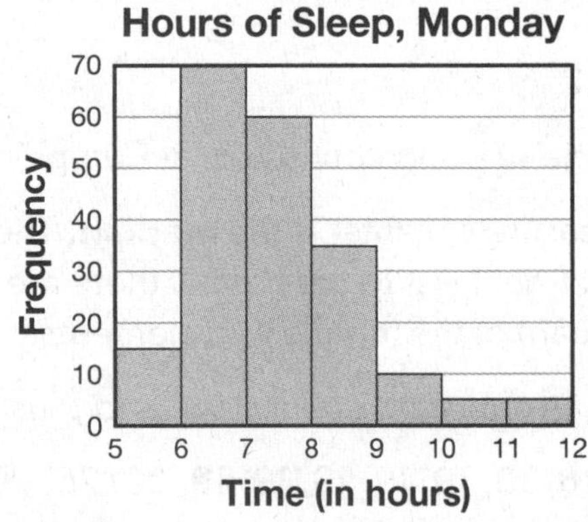

Compare the distributions of data on the two graphs. How do they differ? For what reason could they be so different? Explain.

____

____

____

LESSON 25

Investigating Measures of Center

UNDERSTAND One way to describe a data set is by using a **measure of center**. A measure of center, such as the mean, represents the average of a set of data and can be used to describe the set.

The dot plot below shows the ages of all Camp Sparrow counselors. By eyeballing the dot plot, you can see that the data are centered around the value 19. If someone asked you how old the camp counselors are, you would probably say around 19.

Ages of Camp Counselors

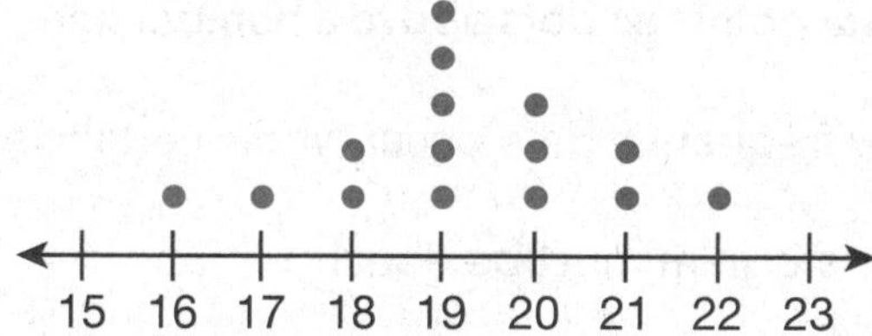

Each dot in the dot plot represents an element in the data set. All 15 elements from the data set are listed below.

16, 17, 18, 18, 19, 19, 19, 19, 19, 20, 20, 20, 21, 21, 22

A data set can have several kinds of measures of center. One measure of center is the **mean**, which is the average of the values in a data set. To calculate the mean, divide the sum of the elements by the total number of elements.

$$\text{mean} = \frac{16 + 17 + 18 + 18 + 19 + 19 + 19 + 19 + 19 + 20 + 20 + 20 + 21 + 21 + 22}{15}$$

$$= \frac{288}{15}$$

$$= 19.2$$

The mean age of camp counselors at Camp Sparrow is 19.2.

Another measure of center is the **median**. The median is the middle value when the elements are ordered from least to greatest. If there are an even number of elements, the median is the average (mean) of the middle two elements.

Since there are 15 camp counselors, and thus 15 ages, the middle number is the 8th value.

16, 17, 18, 18, 19, 19, 19, $\underline{19}$, 19, 20, 20, 20, 21, 21, 22

The median age of the camp counselors is 19.

Some data sets contain **outliers**. An outlier is a data point that is either much greater or far less than the rest of the data points. It lies far outside the group that contains the rest of the data. For example, a camp counselor who was 41 would be an outlier. An outlier can affect which measure of center best describes the data set. In general, when a data set contains an outlier, the median is a better measure of center than the mean.

Connect

Below are the scores that Justin earned on his last 8 homework assignments.

80, 95, 0, 90, 95, 80, 85, 90

What are his mean homework score and median homework score?

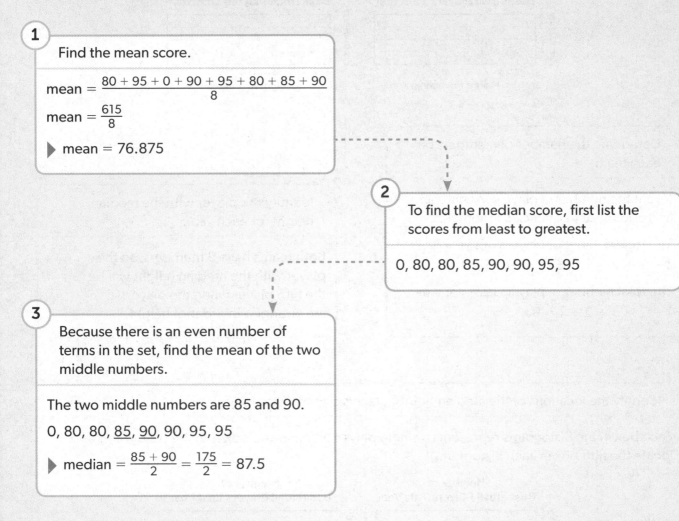

1

Find the mean score.

$$\text{mean} = \frac{80 + 95 + 0 + 90 + 95 + 80 + 85 + 90}{8}$$

$$\text{mean} = \frac{615}{8}$$

▶ mean = 76.875

2

To find the median score, first list the scores from least to greatest.

0, 80, 80, 85, 90, 90, 95, 95

3

Because there is an even number of terms in the set, find the mean of the two middle numbers.

The two middle numbers are 85 and 90.

0, 80, 80, <u>85</u>, <u>90</u>, 90, 95, 95

▶ $\text{median} = \frac{85 + 90}{2} = \frac{175}{2} = 87.5$

DISCUSS

Compare the mean and median of Justin's homework grades. Which measure better describes the center of the data? Explain.

EXAMPLE A The histograms shown relate the heights of the members of the girls' basketball teams this year and last year. Compare the median heights for the two teams.

Heights of Basketball Players This Year

Frequency: 1, 2, 3, 4

Height (in inches): 63, 64, 65, 66, 67, 68, 69, 70, 71, 72

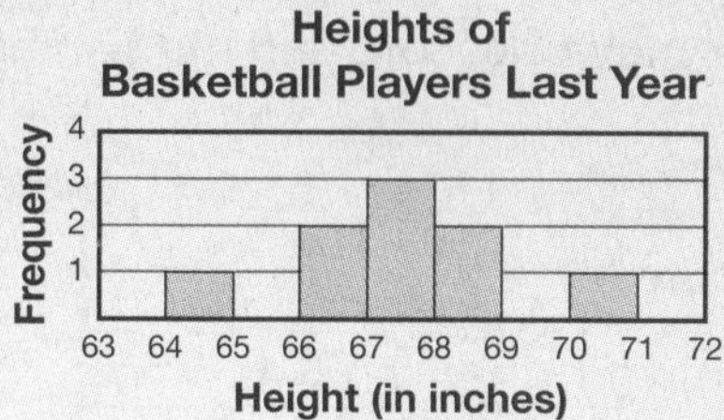

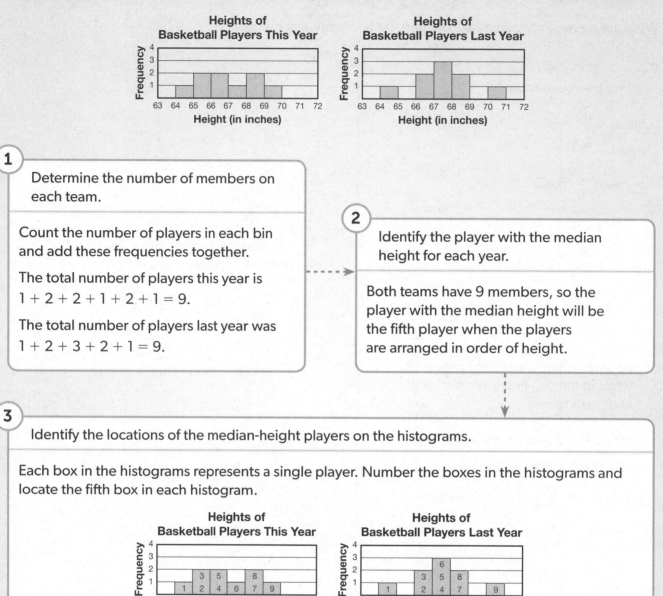

1 Determine the number of members on each team.

Count the number of players in each bin and add these frequencies together.

The total number of players this year is $1 + 2 + 2 + 1 + 2 + 1 = 9$.

The total number of players last year was $1 + 2 + 3 + 2 + 1 = 9$.

2 Identify the player with the median height for each year.

Both teams have 9 members, so the player with the median height will be the fifth player when the players are arranged in order of height.

3 Identify the locations of the median-height players on the histograms.

Each box in the histograms represents a single player. Number the boxes in the histograms and locate the fifth box in each histogram.

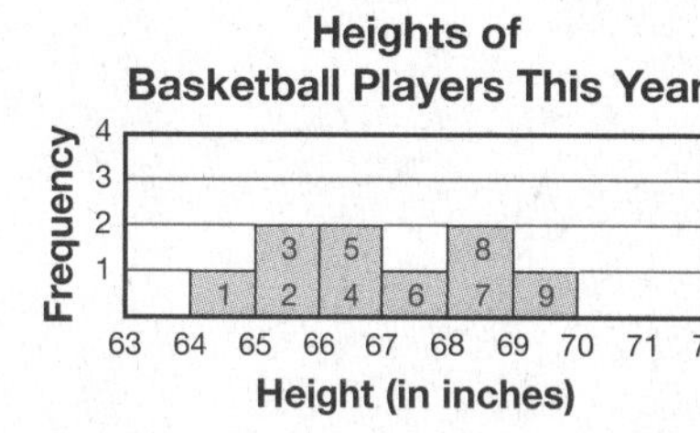

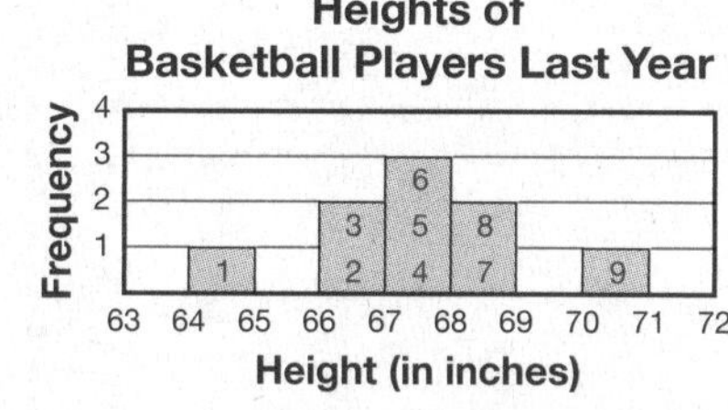

4 Compare the medians.

▶ Since the median this year falls between 66 and 67 inches, and the median height last year fell between 67 and 68 inches, the median height was greater last year.

Why is it not possible to use these histograms to find exact medians and means?

EXAMPLE B Two classes held contests to see which could memorize the greatest number of digits of the number π. Eight students from each class competed. The dot plots show the total number of digits recalled by each of the competitors. Compare the number of digits recalled by competitors in the two classes.

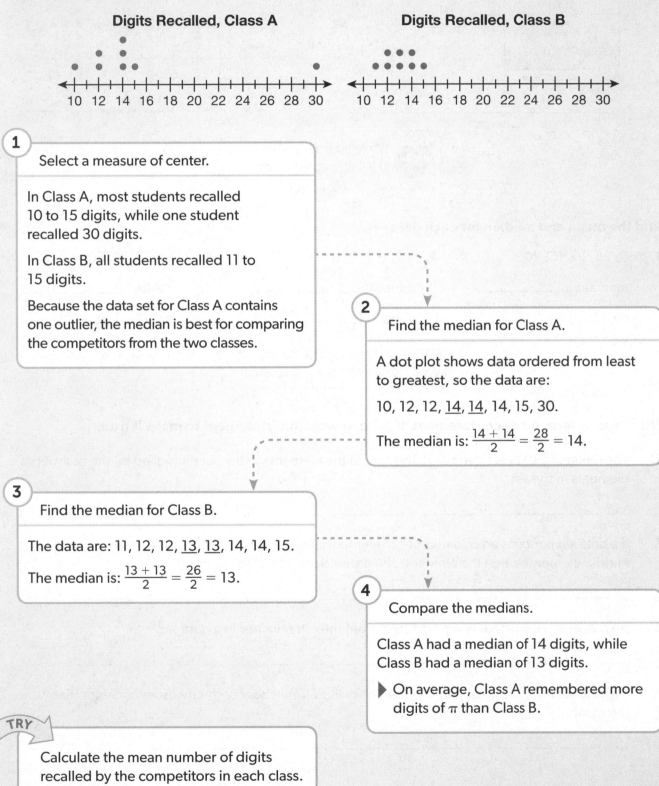

Digits Recalled, Class A

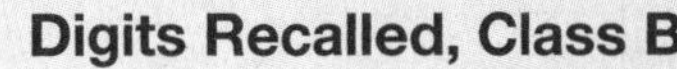

Digits Recalled, Class B

1 Select a measure of center.

In Class A, most students recalled 10 to 15 digits, while one student recalled 30 digits.

In Class B, all students recalled 11 to 15 digits.

Because the data set for Class A contains one outlier, the median is best for comparing the competitors from the two classes.

2 Find the median for Class A.

A dot plot shows data ordered from least to greatest, so the data are:

10, 12, 12, <u>14</u>, <u>14</u>, 14, 15, 30.

The median is: $\frac{14 + 14}{2} = \frac{28}{2} = 14$.

3 Find the median for Class B.

The data are: 11, 12, 12, <u>13</u>, <u>13</u>, 14, 14, 15.

The median is: $\frac{13 + 13}{2} = \frac{26}{2} = 13$.

4 Compare the medians.

Class A had a median of 14 digits, while Class B had a median of 13 digits.

▶ On average, Class A remembered more digits of π than Class B.

TRY

Calculate the mean number of digits recalled by the competitors in each class.

Practice

Locate the specific interval that contains the median for each data set that is displayed. When possible, determine the exact median.

1.

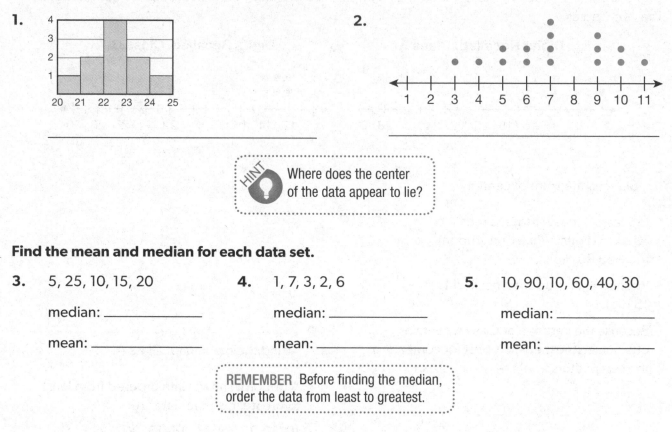

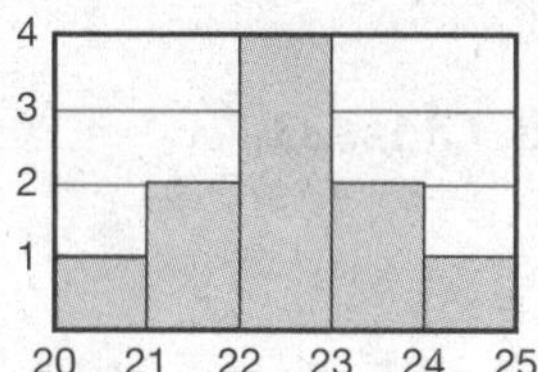

2.

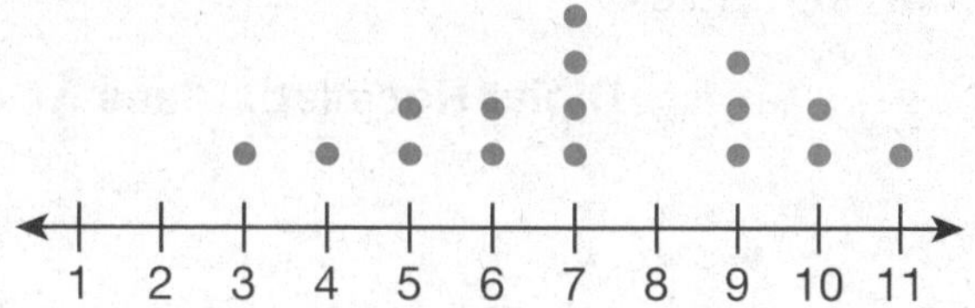

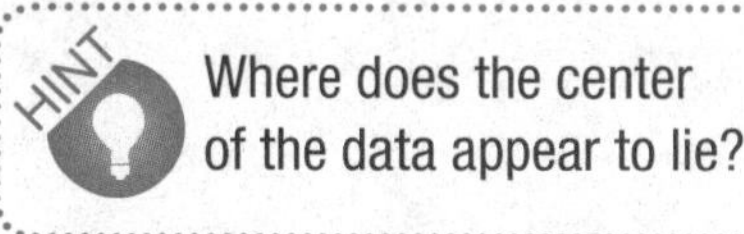

HINT
Where does the center of the data appear to lie?

Find the mean and median for each data set.

3. 5, 25, 10, 15, 20

median: ____________

mean: ____________

4. 1, 7, 3, 2, 6

median: ____________

mean: ____________

5. 10, 90, 10, 60, 40, 30

median: ____________

mean: ____________

REMEMBER Before finding the median, order the data from least to greatest.

Write *true* or *false* for each statement. If false, rewrite the statement to make it true.

6. The mean of a data set is equal to the sum of the elements in the set multiplied by the number of elements in the set.

____

7. If a data set contains an odd number of elements, the median is equal to the mean of the two middle elements when the elements are ordered from least to greatest.

____

8. An outlier is a value that is very different from the other values in a data set.

____

9. If a data set includes an outlier, the median will probably be a better measure of center than the mean.

____

Find the median for each data set or determine the interval in which the median must fall. Then compare the medians.

10. The dot plots show Kyla's Spanish quiz scores during the 1st and 2nd semesters.

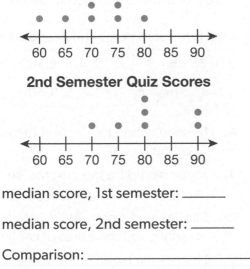

1st Semester Quiz Scores

60 65 70 75 80 85 90

2nd Semester Quiz Scores

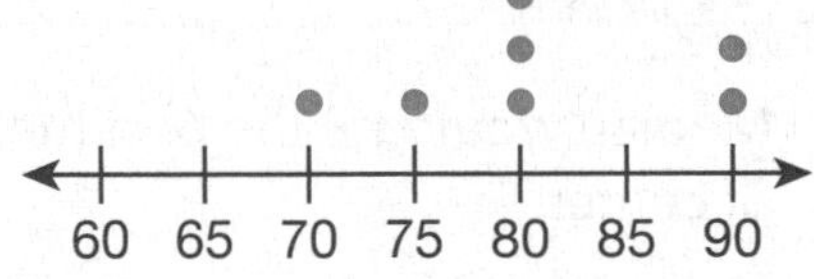

median score, 1st semester: ______

median score, 2nd semester: ______

Comparison: ______________________

11. The histograms show the daily high temperatures in two cities.

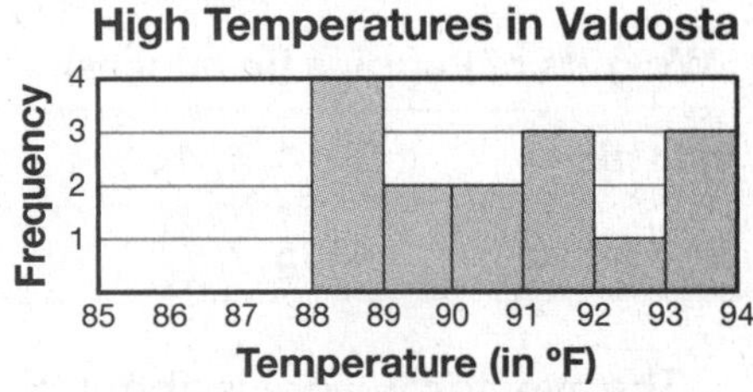

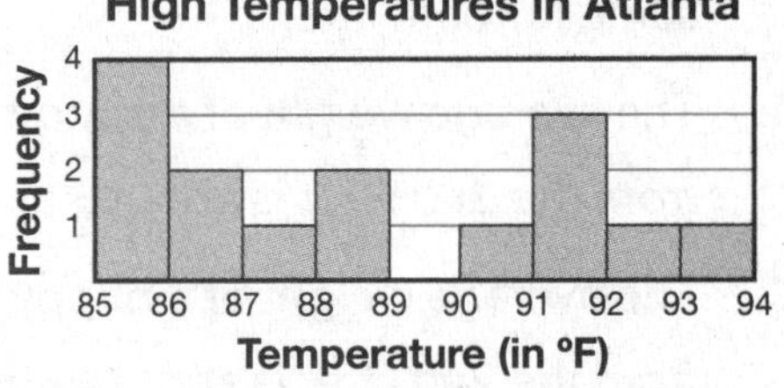

median high temperature, Valdosta: ______

median high temperature, Atlanta: ______

Comparison: ______________________

Find the mean for each data set. Then compare the means.

12. The tables show the number of ads that were sold by the actors and stage-crew members working on a school play.

Actor	Rajiv	Amy	Penny	Leonard	Adriel
Ads Sold	4	4	5	6	7

Crew Member	Tina	Ben	Ronny	Irene	Cris
Ads Sold	6	7	8	9	9

mean number sold, actors: ______

mean number sold, crew members: ______

Comparison: ______________________

13. The dot plots show the number of hours of television watched yesterday by students from two homerooms.

Hours of Television Watched, Room 101

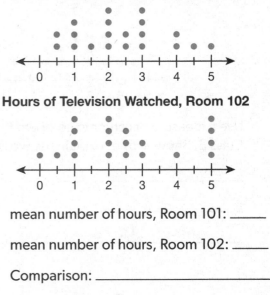

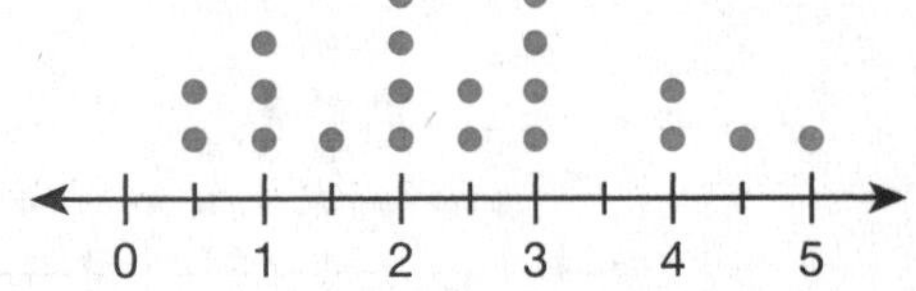

Hours of Television Watched, Room 102

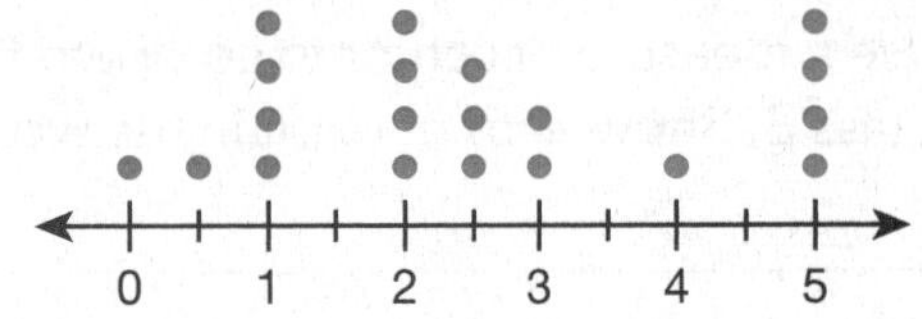

mean number of hours, Room 101: ______

mean number of hours, Room 102: ______

Comparison: ______________________

Choose the best answer.

14. Which statement accurately compares the average weight of a puppy from the 2nd litter to the average weight of a puppy from the 1st litter?

Weights of Puppies (in ounces)

1st Litter	$3\frac{1}{2}$, 4, 4, $4\frac{1}{2}$
2nd Litter	$4\frac{1}{2}$, 5, 7, $7\frac{1}{2}$

A. The average weight is about the same for both litters.

B. The average weight of a puppy from the 2nd litter is about $\frac{1}{2}$ as great.

C. The average weight of a puppy from the 2nd litter is about $1\frac{1}{2}$ times as great.

D. The average weight of a puppy from the 2nd litter is about $2\frac{1}{2}$ times as great.

15. To compare two shipments, five packages from each shipment were chosen at random and weighed. Which measure or measures of center would be best to use if you wanted to compare the weight of a typical package from each shipment?

Weights of Packages (in pounds)

1st Shipment	2, 4, 6, 8, 10
2nd Shipment	3, 3, 5, 8, 50

A. Median would be the best measure of center.

B. Mean would be the best measure of center.

C. Median and mean would both be equally good measures of center.

D. Neither the mean nor the median would be a good measure of center.

Compare measures of center.

16. Students in two biology classes began growing mung bean plants on the same day. The dot plots show the heights of the plants one week after being planted.

Plant Heights (in cm), Class A

4 6 8 10 12 14

Plant Heights (in cm), Class B

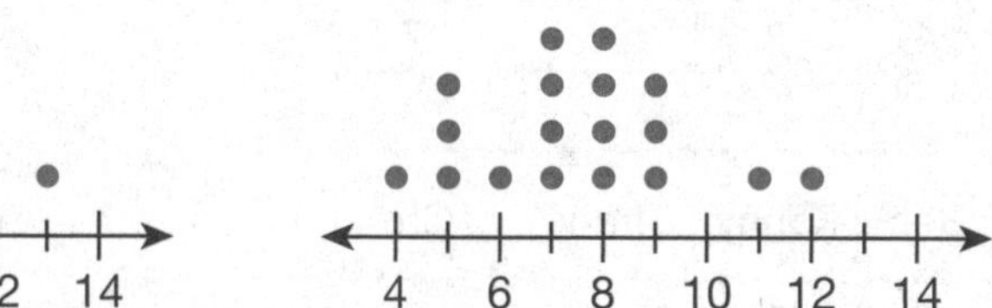

Use a measure of center to compare the heights of plants in Class A to the heights of plants in Class B. Show and/or explain the work you did to determine your answer.

17. The dot plots show the hourly wages of supermarket cashiers at two stores.

Hourly Wages (in dollars), Thrifty Shop

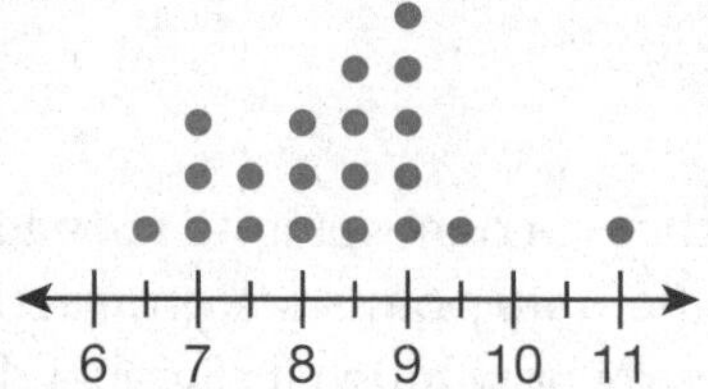

Hourly Wages (in dollars), Wayne Foods

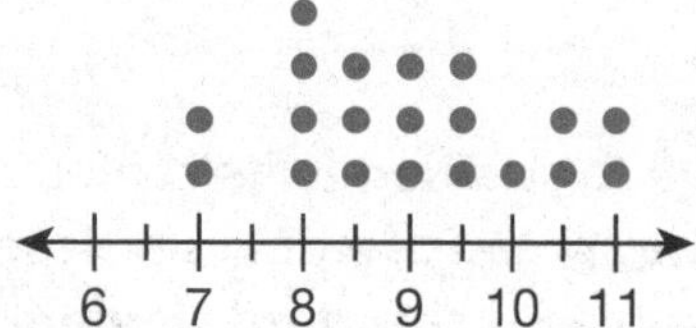

Use a measure of center to compare the wages of cashiers at Thrifty Shop and at Wayne Foods. Explain the work you did to make your comparison.

____

____

____

18. COMPARE The histograms show the number of health bars sold by 9th-grade and 10th-grade students.

Health Bar Sales, Grade 9

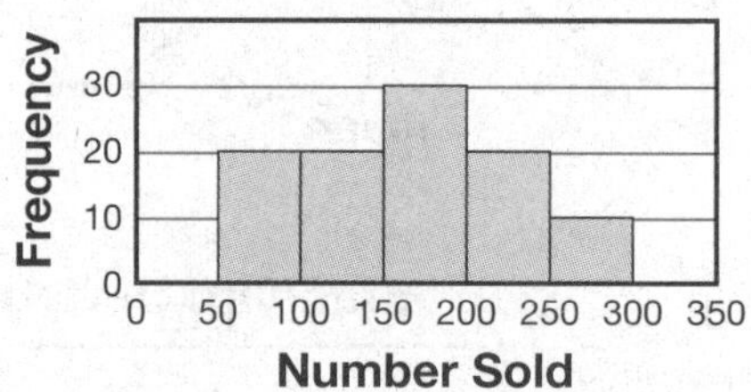

Health Bar Sales, Grade 10

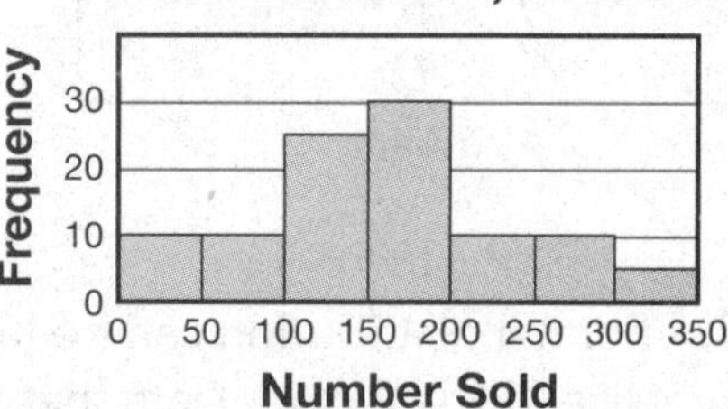

Locate the specific interval that contains the median for each data set, and use those medians to compare the number of health bars sold by 9th-grade students to the number sold by 10th-grade students. Could you use these data to do a detailed comparison of the two grades' sales? Explain your answer.

____

____

____

19. CHOOSE The table on the right lists the scores for students in two P.E. classes who went bowling on Friday.

Which measure of center—mean or median—is best for comparing the data sets? Explain why. Use that measure to compare Classes 1 and 2.

Bowling Scores

Class 1	Class 2
78, 80, 82, 95, 98, 102, 105, 110, 120, 290	75, 80, 88, 90, 103, 105, 110, 112, 115, 120

____

____

____

LESSON

26 Investigating Spread

UNDERSTAND In addition to its center, another characteristic of a data set is its **spread**, or variability. The spread of a data set describes how closely the data points are grouped. One measure of spread is **standard deviation**, which describes by how much individual data points vary from the mean. A data set with a small standard deviation has more data points that are closer to the mean; the data in such a set are less variable. A data set with a large standard deviation has more data points that are farther from the mean; the data in such a set are more variable.

Less Variable

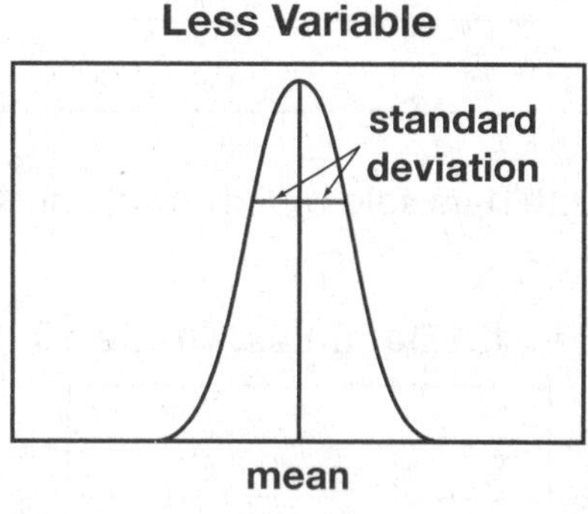

More Variable

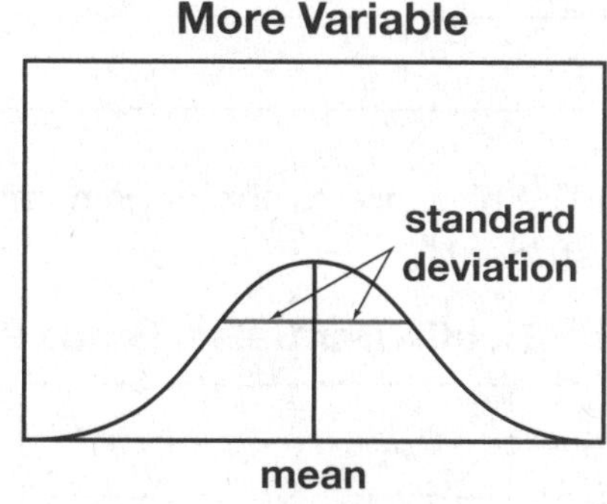

UNDERSTAND A normal distribution can be modeled with a bell curve, like those shown. Data that are normally distributed conform to the following rules:

- 68% of the data are within 1 standard deviation of the mean.
- 95% of the data are within 2 standard deviations of the mean.
- 99.7% of the data are within 3 standard deviations of the mean.

Standard Deviations

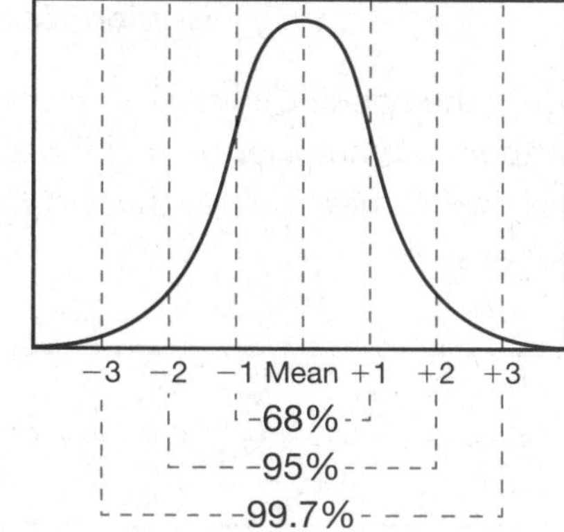

Consider a normally distributed set of data with a mean of 30 and a standard deviation of 5. 68% of the data in that set will fall between 25 and 35, 95% of the data will fall between 20 and 40, and 99.7% will fall between 15 and 45.

In a normal distribution, the data are spread evenly around the mean. Just as outliers can affect measures of center, they can also have a great effect on a data set's standard deviation.

Connect

The number of ads sold by each of the 10 students on the yearbook staff is listed below.

2, 3, 3, 5, 5, 5, 5, 6, 8, 8

The ad sales data is shown in the histogram to the right. Calculate the standard deviation for this data set.

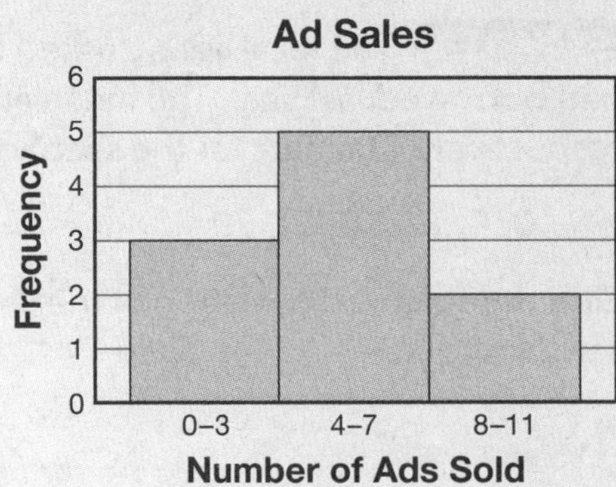

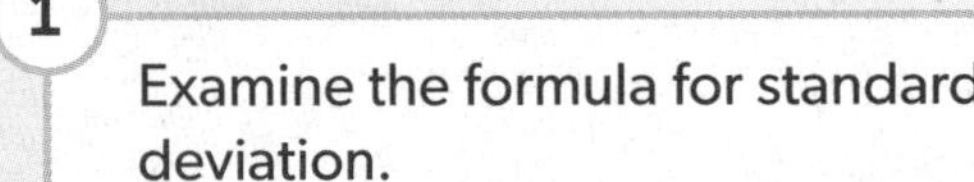

1 Examine the formula for standard deviation.

The standard deviation, s, is given by the formula below, where Σ represents "the sum of," x_i is ith element in the data set, $\bar{x}$ is the mean of the data, and n is the number of elements in the data set.

$$s = \sqrt{\frac{\Sigma(x_i - \bar{x})^2}{n - 1}}$$

2 Calculate the mean, $\bar{x}$.

To find the mean, add the values and then divide by the number of values.

$$\bar{x} = \frac{2 + 3 + 3 + 5 + 5 + 5 + 5 + 6 + 8 + 8}{10}$$

$$\bar{x} = \frac{50}{10} = 5$$

3 Find the differences between the values and the mean. Then square them.

Data Point x_i	Deviation from Mean $x_i - \bar{x}$	Square of Deviation $(x_i - \bar{x})^2$
2	$2 - 5 = -3$	$(-3)^2 = 9$
3	$3 - 5 = -2$	$(-2)^2 = 4$
3	$3 - 5 = -2$	$(-2)^2 = 4$
5	$5 - 5 = 0$	$0^2 = 0$
5	$5 - 5 = 0$	$0^2 = 0$
5	$5 - 5 = 0$	$0^2 = 0$
5	$5 - 5 = 0$	$0^2 = 0$
6	$6 - 5 = 1$	$1^2 = 1$
8	$8 - 5 = 3$	$3^2 = 9$
8	$8 - 5 = 3$	$3^2 = 9$

4 Calculate the standard deviation.

Remember that Σ means "the sum of." Find the sum of the squared deviations.

$$9 + 4 + 4 + 0 + 0 + 0 + 0 + 1 + 9 + 9 = 36$$

Divide the sum by one less than the number of elements, $n - 1$.

$$\frac{36}{10 - 1} = \frac{36}{9} = 4$$

Finally, take the square root to find the standard deviation.

$$s = \sqrt{4} = 2$$

▶ The standard deviation is 2.

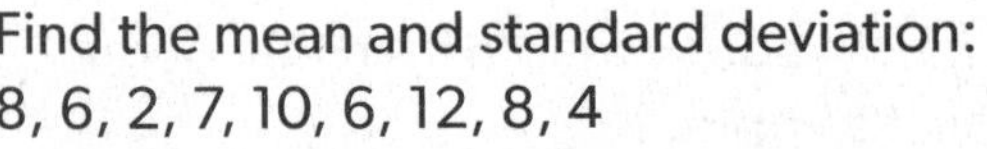

Find the mean and standard deviation: 8, 6, 2, 7, 10, 6, 12, 8, 4

EXAMPLE A The local library asked two random samples of 6 patrons how many books each person had borrowed last year. The mean and standard deviation for the first sample were 29 and 11, respectively. The data for the second sample are shown below.

0, 5, 12, 36, 51, 70

Find the standard deviation of the second sample's data. Then compare the variability of the two samples' data.

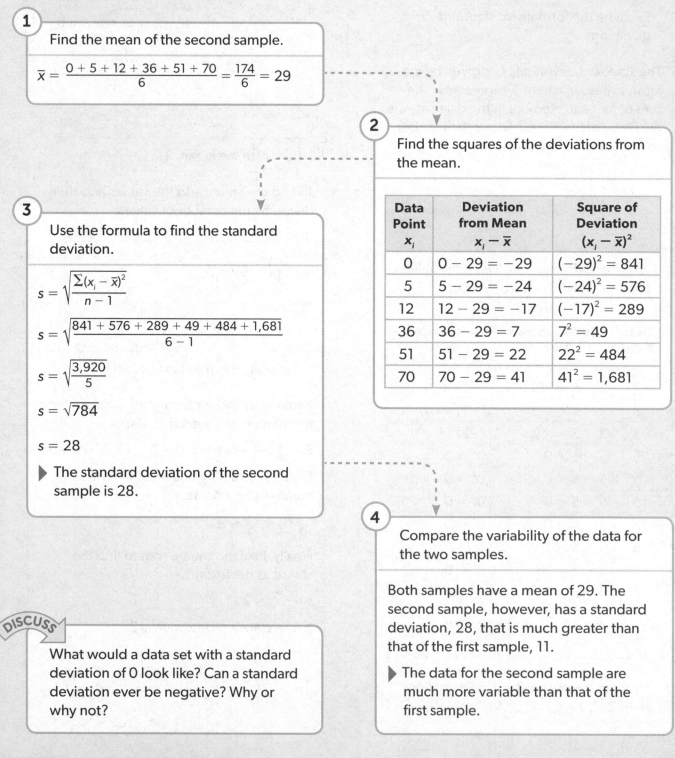

1 Find the mean of the second sample.

$$\bar{x} = \frac{0 + 5 + 12 + 36 + 51 + 70}{6} = \frac{174}{6} = 29$$

2 Find the squares of the deviations from the mean.

Data Point x_i	Deviation from Mean $x_i - \bar{x}$	Square of Deviation $(x_i - \bar{x})^2$
0	$0 - 29 = -29$	$(-29)^2 = 841$
5	$5 - 29 = -24$	$(-24)^2 = 576$
12	$12 - 29 = -17$	$(-17)^2 = 289$
36	$36 - 29 = 7$	$7^2 = 49$
51	$51 - 29 = 22$	$22^2 = 484$
70	$70 - 29 = 41$	$41^2 = 1{,}681$

3 Use the formula to find the standard deviation.

$$s = \sqrt{\frac{\sum(x_i - \bar{x})^2}{n - 1}}$$

$$s = \sqrt{\frac{841 + 576 + 289 + 49 + 484 + 1{,}681}{6 - 1}}$$

$$s = \sqrt{\frac{3{,}920}{5}}$$

$$s = \sqrt{784}$$

$$s = 28$$

▶ The standard deviation of the second sample is 28.

4 Compare the variability of the data for the two samples.

Both samples have a mean of 29. The second sample, however, has a standard deviation, 28, that is much greater than that of the first sample, 11.

▶ The data for the second sample are much more variable than that of the first sample.

DISCUSS

What would a data set with a standard deviation of 0 look like? Can a standard deviation ever be negative? Why or why not?

EXAMPLE B Julie recorded her grades for her first six French assignments.

88, 92, 94, 94, 96, 100

The mean is 94 and the standard deviation is 4. But Julie forgot that, because she turned in the first assignment three days late, her grade was marked down from 88 to 58. Calculate the standard deviation of Julie's actual grades. Then compare the standard deviations of the two data sets.

1 Calculate the mean of Julie's actual grades.

The new data set replaces 88 with 58: 58, 92, 94, 94, 96, 100

The lower grade will pull down the mean.

$$\bar{x} = \frac{58 + 92 + 94 + 94 + 96 + 100}{6} = 89$$

2 Find the squares of the deviations from the mean.

Data Point x_i	Deviation from Mean $x_i - \bar{x}$	Square of Deviation $(x_i - \bar{x})^2$
58	$58 - 89 = -31$	$(-31)^2 = 961$
92	$92 - 89 = 3$	$3^2 = 9$
94	$94 - 89 = 5$	$5^2 = 25$
94	$94 - 89 = 5$	$5^2 = 25$
96	$96 - 89 = 7$	$7^2 = 49$
100	$100 - 89 = 11$	$11^2 = 121$

3 Use the formula to find the standard deviation of Julie's actual grades.

$$s = \sqrt{\frac{\Sigma(x_i - \bar{x})^2}{n - 1}}$$

$$s = \sqrt{\frac{961 + 9 + 25 + 25 + 49 + 121}{6 - 1}}$$

$$s = \sqrt{\frac{1{,}190}{5}}$$

$$s = \sqrt{238}$$

$$s \approx 15.4$$

▶ The standard deviation is about 15.4.

4 Compare the standard deviations.

The outlier, 58, had a huge effect on the standard deviation, changing it from 4 to about 15.4. The greater standard deviation of 15.4 makes Julie's actual grades appear very variable. The majority of her grades, however, are clustered from 92 to 100.

▶ The introduction of an outlier makes Julie's actual grades seem much more variable than her recorded grades, all of which are clustered closely together.

DISCUSS

For data set *A*, $\bar{x} = 12$ and $s = 5$. For data set *B*, $\bar{x} = 12$ and $s = 1.2$. Which data set do you think has more variability? Which is more likely to contain at least one outlier?

Practice

For questions 1 and 2, compare the variability of the data sets shown by each pair of graphs.

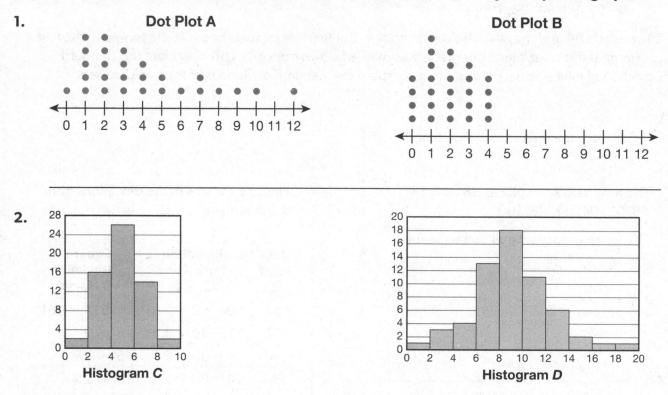

1.

Dot Plot A

Dot Plot B

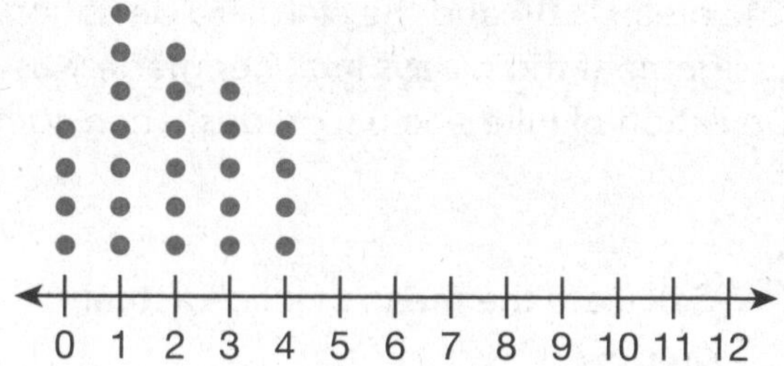

____

2.

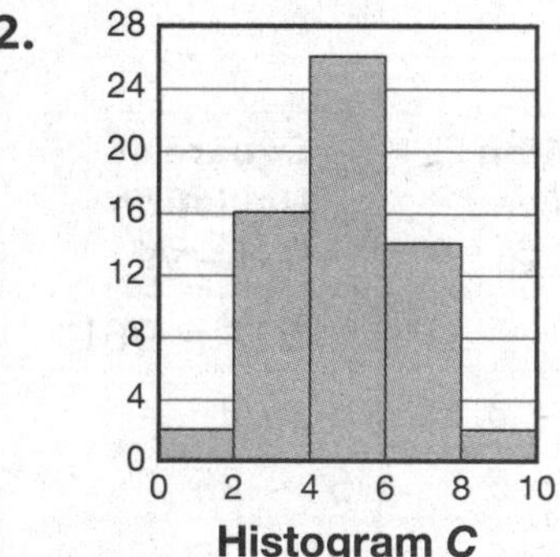

Histogram *C*

Histogram *D*

____

Find the standard deviation for each data set, using the given mean. Round to the nearest tenth, if necessary.

3. 1, 2, 2, 4, 6

$\bar{x} = 3$

____

4. 39, 42, 45, 47, 52

$\bar{x} = 45$

____

5. −15, 5, 20, 50

$\bar{x} = 15$

____

Write *true* or *false* for each statement. If false, rewrite the statement so it is true.

6. Standard deviation is a measure of center.

____

7. For data that show a normal distribution, 95% of the data are within 2 standard deviations of the mean.

____

8. The larger the standard deviation is for a data set, the more variable the data in the set are.

____

Use your knowledge of standard deviation to answer the following.

9. The cholesterol levels of a large population were taken and analyzed. The data were normally distributed about the mean, 183, and the standard deviation of the data was 23. Fill in the sentences below with the correct numbers.

68% of the population had cholesterol levels between 160 and ________.

________% of the population had cholesterol levels between 137 and 229.

99.7% of the population had cholesterol levels between ________ and ________.

10. Below are the weights, in pounds, of a group of packages to be shipped.

11, 17, 19, 23

Given that $\overline{x} = 17.5$, find the standard deviation. If a fifth package that weighs 45 pounds were added to the data, how would you expect that to affect the standard deviation? Explain.

____

____

____

Use the information below for questions 11 and 12.

Keitaro competes in the long jump. The distances, in meters, that he jumped during his most recent meet are shown below.

4.8, 4.8, 4.9, 5.0, 5.1, 5.4

11. SHOW Keitaro wants to know how variable his jumps were during the recent meet. Calculate the mean and standard deviation, both to the nearest tenth, for Keitaro's jumps. Show your work.

____

____

12. COMPARE Keitaro's final jump of 5.4 meters is declared to be a foul at the last minute. The length is not recorded, and he does not get another attempt. Keitaro records this distance as 0.0. Calculate the mean and the standard deviation, both to the nearest tenth, for the revised set of data. Compare the mean and standard deviation of the new data set to that of the original data set.

____

____

____

____

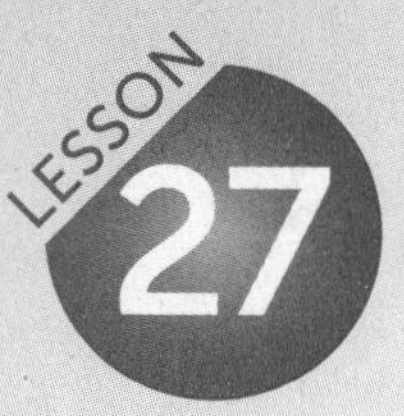

Constructing and Analyzing Box Plots

UNDERSTAND Besides standard deviation, another measure of spread is the **interquartile range (IQR)**. The interquartile range measures the variability of the middle 50% of the data, which is bounded by the **first quartile (Q_1)** and the **third quartile (Q_3)**. Recall that the median, *M*, divides a set of data into two halves. The first quartile is the median of the lower half of the data set. The third quartile is the median of the upper half of the data set.

The diagram below shows the **lower extreme, upper extreme,** quartiles, and median of a data set, as well as the interquartile range. It also helps illustrate how the median and quartiles divide a data set into four discrete sets of data.

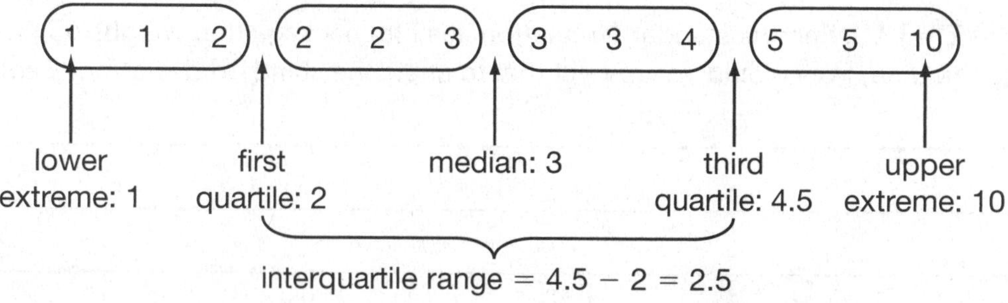

A **box plot** (sometimes called a box-and-whisker plot) is an excellent way to display the extremes, quartiles, and median of a data set.

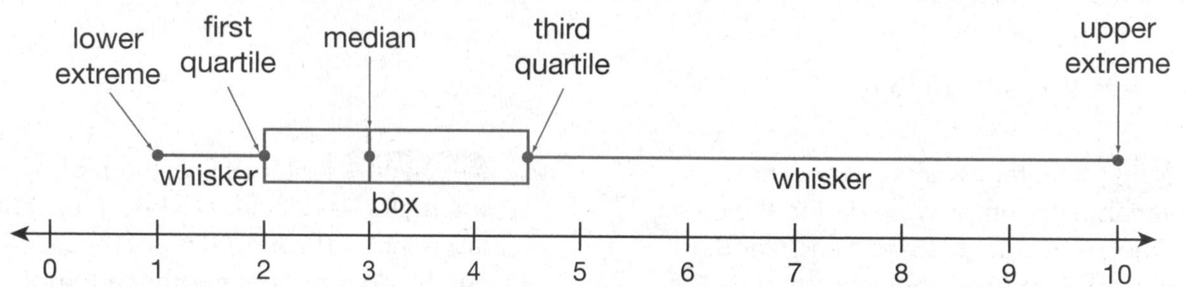

The box contains the middle 50% of the data, bounded by the first and third quartiles. The whiskers are on either end of the box. The left whisker contains the lower 25% of the data, and the right whisker contains the upper 25% of the data.

Outliers have much less effect on median and IQR than they do on mean and standard deviation. Consider the example above and imagine that the upper extreme is 110, instead of 10. The first quartile, median, third quartile, and IQR would remain the same. The mean and standard deviation, however, would be much greater.

In general, standard deviation is a better measure of spread for data with a symmetric distribution and without outliers. For data with a skewed, or nonsymmetric, distribution and with outliers, IQR is usually a better measure of variability.

Connect

The following data set contains an outlier.

12, 37, 16, 19, 12, 17, 14, 20, 15, 18

Would the interquartile range (IQR) or the standard deviation of the set be a better measure of spread? Explain. Then, calculate that measure.

1 Determine which measure of spread is more likely to describe the data better.

The data set appears to have an outlier, 37, which will have a greater effect on the standard deviation than on the IQR.

▶ Data that contain outliers are described better by IQR than by standard deviation.

2 Find the median.

Order the data from least to greatest.

12, 12, 14, 15, 16, 17, 18, 19, 20, 37

The data set contains ten values, so the median is the mean of the fifth and sixth values.

12, 12, 14, 15, <u>16</u>, <u>17</u>, 18, 19, 20, 37

$M = \frac{16 + 17}{2} = \frac{33}{2} = 16.5$

3 Identify the first quartile and the third quartile.

The lower half of the data set is 12, 12, <u>14</u>, 15, 16.

The median of the lower half is 14. $Q_1 = 14$.

The upper half of the data is 17, 18, <u>19</u>, 20, 37.

The median of the upper half is 19. $Q_3 = 19$.

4 Calculate the interquartile range.

The interquartile range is the difference of the third and first quartiles.

$IQR = Q_3 - Q_1 = 19 - 14$

▶ $IQR = 5$

DISCUSS

If the outlier value were changed from 37 to 57, would it affect the IQR? What if it were changed from 37 to 1?

EXAMPLE A The data below show the number of miles that members of a running club ran last week.

4, 6, 8, 9, 10, 12, 16, 16, 30

Create a box plot to display the data. Then find the interquartile range of the data.

1 Identify the median, first quartile, and third quartile.

The data are already in order. Find the middle data value.

4, 6, 8, 9, <u>10</u>, 12, 16, 16, 30

$M = 10$

2 Identify the first and third quartiles.

The lower half of the data set is 4, 6, 8, 9.

$Q_1 = \frac{6 + 8}{2} = \frac{14}{2} = 7$

The upper half of the data set is 12, 16, 16, 30.

$Q_3 = \frac{16 + 16}{2} = \frac{32}{2} = 16$

3 Create a box plot.

Draw a number line from 0 to 30. Plot points above 7 and 16 to represent Q_1 and Q_3. Draw a box connecting them. Plot a point above 10 for the median, and draw a vertical line segment through that point. Plot points above 4 and 30 to show the extremes. Draw a whisker from each extreme to the edge of the box.

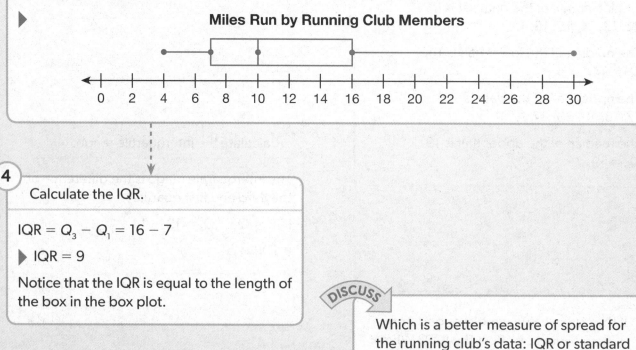

Miles Run by Running Club Members

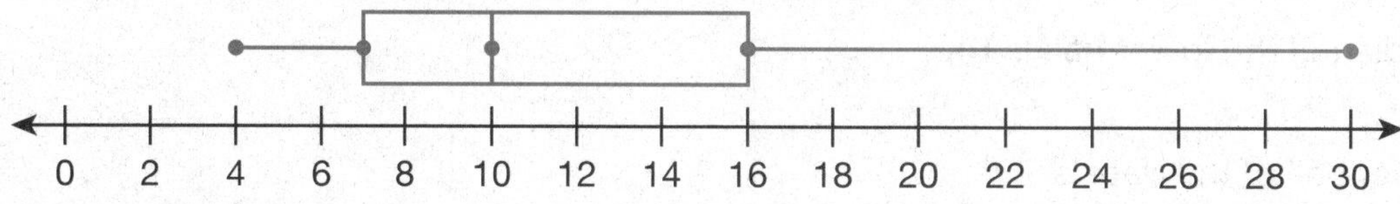

4 Calculate the IQR.

$IQR = Q_3 - Q_1 = 16 - 7$

 $IQR = 9$

Notice that the IQR is equal to the length of the box in the box plot.

Which is a better measure of spread for the running club's data: IQR or standard deviation? Why?

EXAMPLE B The box plots below represent the numbers of cookbooks sold by 20 male athletes and 20 female athletes as part of a fund-raiser for school sports. Compare the medians and interquartile ranges for the two samples.

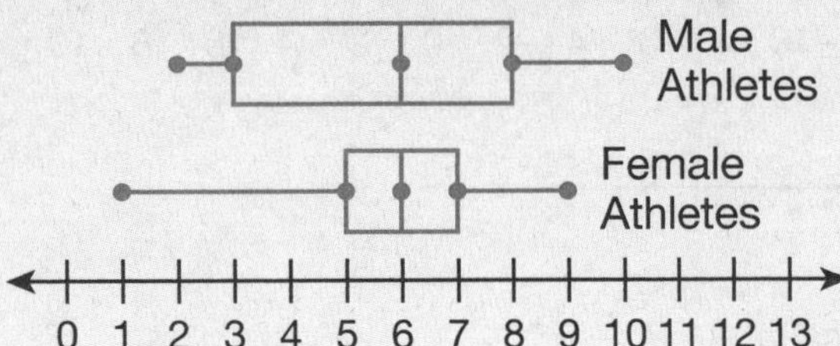

1 Identify and compare the medians.

On a box plot, the median is identified by the line (or point) within the box.

The median for male athletes is 6.

The median for female athletes is also 6.

▶ On average, male and female athletes sold the same number of cookbooks, 6.

2 Identify and compare the interquartile ranges.

Remember that the IQR is the difference of the third and first quartiles.

For male athletes, $Q_3 = 8$ and $Q_1 = 3$, so the IQR $= 8 - 3 = 5$.

For female athletes, $Q_3 = 7$ and $Q_1 = 5$, so the IQR $= 7 - 5 = 2$.

▶ The IQR of the data for the male athletes is greater than the IQR for the female athletes, so the data for male athletes has greater variability than the data for the female athletes.

DISCUSS

For which data set is standard deviation more likely to be a better measure of spread than IQR?

Practice

Use the box plot for questions 1–5.

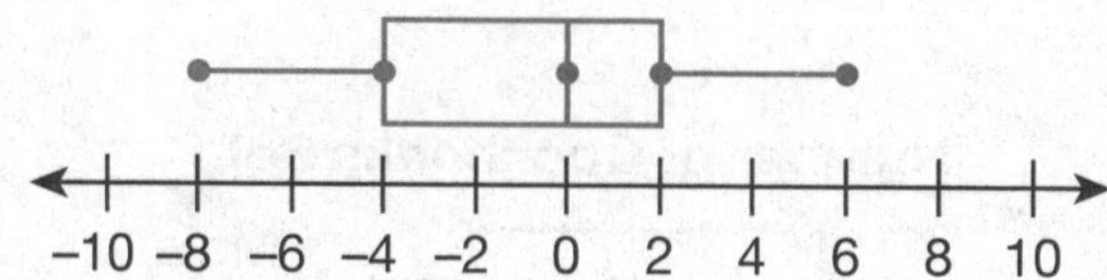

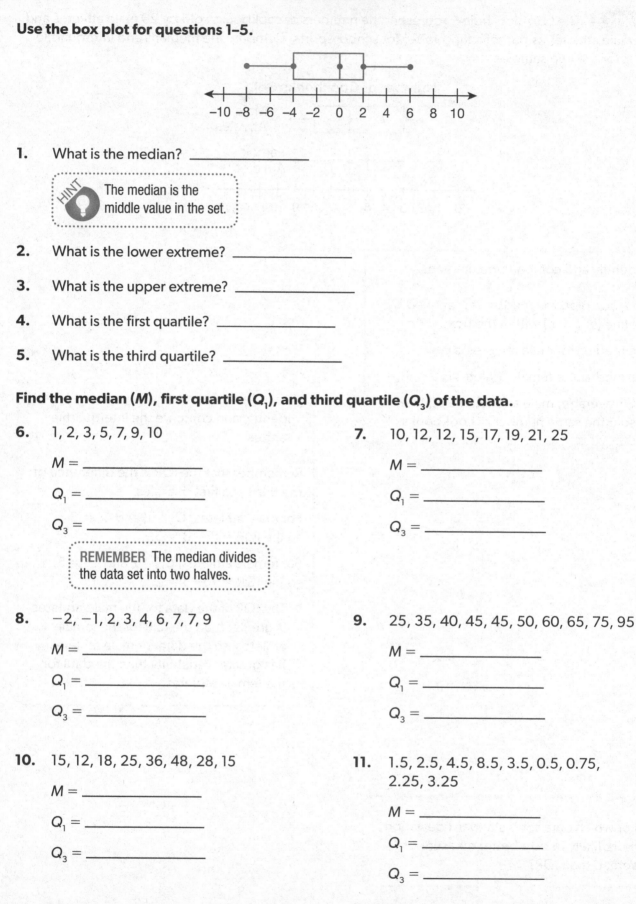

1. What is the median? ____________

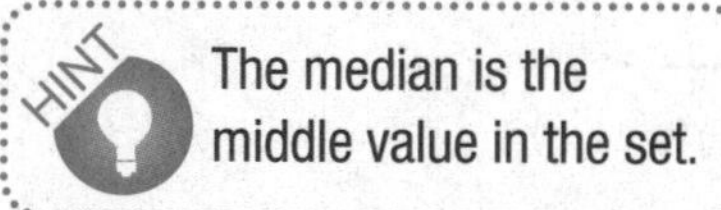

HINT
The median is the middle value in the set.

2. What is the lower extreme? ____________
3. What is the upper extreme? ____________
4. What is the first quartile? ____________
5. What is the third quartile? ____________

Find the median (*M*), first quartile (Q_1), and third quartile (Q_3) of the data.

6. 1, 2, 3, 5, 7, 9, 10

   $M =$ ____________

   $Q_1 =$ ____________

   $Q_3 =$ ____________

   REMEMBER The median divides the data set into two halves.

7. 10, 12, 12, 15, 17, 19, 21, 25

   $M =$ ____________

   $Q_1 =$ ____________

   $Q_3 =$ ____________

8. −2, −1, 2, 3, 4, 6, 7, 7, 9

   $M =$ ____________

   $Q_1 =$ ____________

   $Q_3 =$ ____________

9. 25, 35, 40, 45, 45, 50, 60, 65, 75, 95

   $M =$ ____________

   $Q_1 =$ ____________

   $Q_3 =$ ____________

10. 15, 12, 18, 25, 36, 48, 28, 15

    $M =$ ____________

    $Q_1 =$ ____________

    $Q_3 =$ ____________

11. 1.5, 2.5, 4.5, 8.5, 3.5, 0.5, 0.75, 2.25, 3.25

    $M =$ ____________

    $Q_1 =$ ____________

    $Q_3 =$ ____________

Write *true* or *false* for each statement. If false, rewrite each statement so it is true.

12. In a box plot, the box represents the upper 25% of the data.

____

13. The quartiles and the median divide a data set into four smaller sets of data.

____

14. For a data set with an outlier, standard deviation is generally a better measure of spread than interquartile range.

____

15. The interquartile range is the difference of the upper extreme and the lower extreme.

____

Calculate the interquartile range of the data.

16.

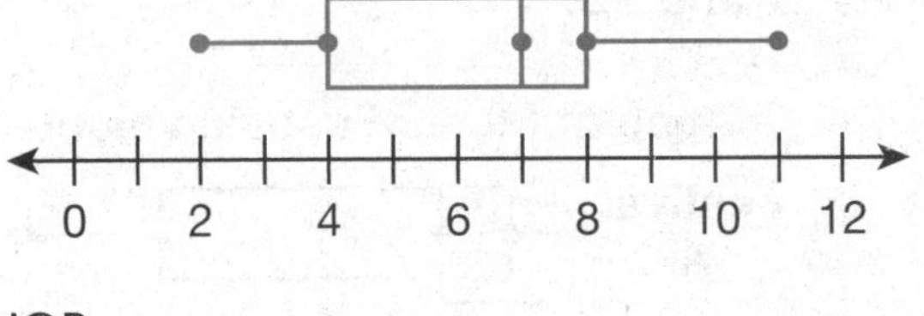

IQR = ____________

17.

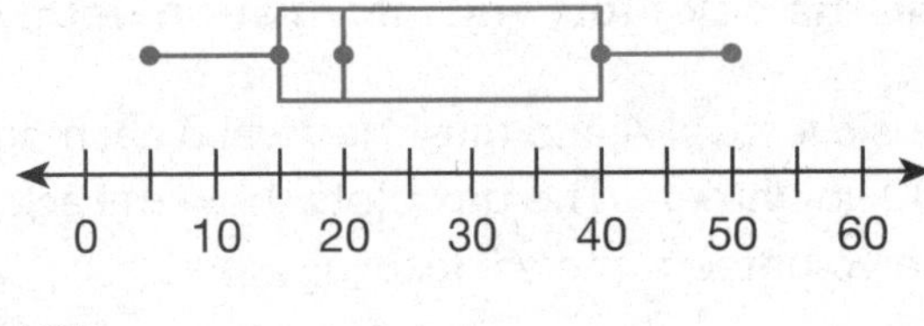

IQR = ____________

18.

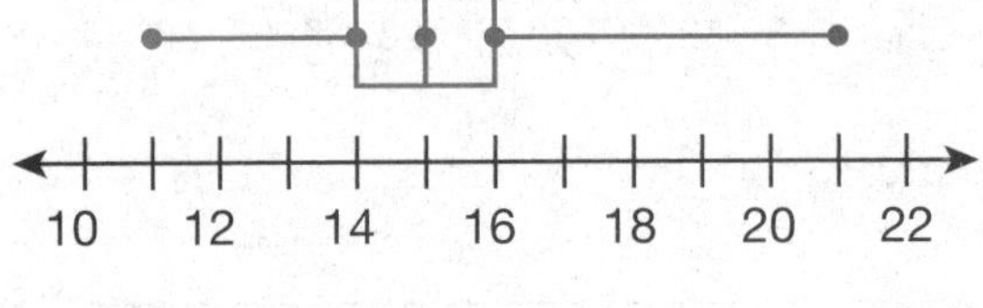

IQR = ____________

19.

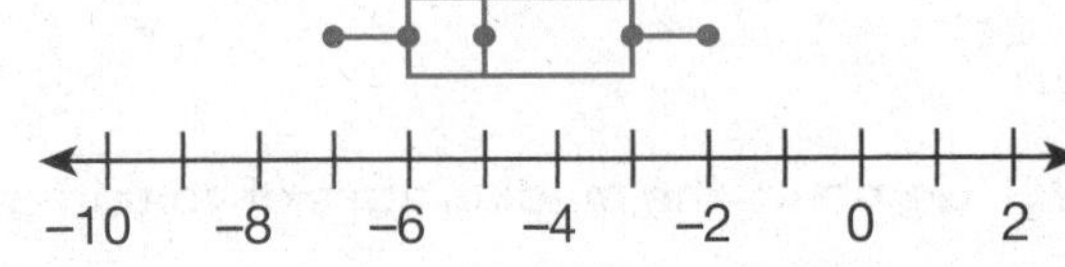

IQR = ____________

Choose the best answer.

20. The box plot shows the test scores earned by students in a biology class. Which statement about the test scores is **not** true?

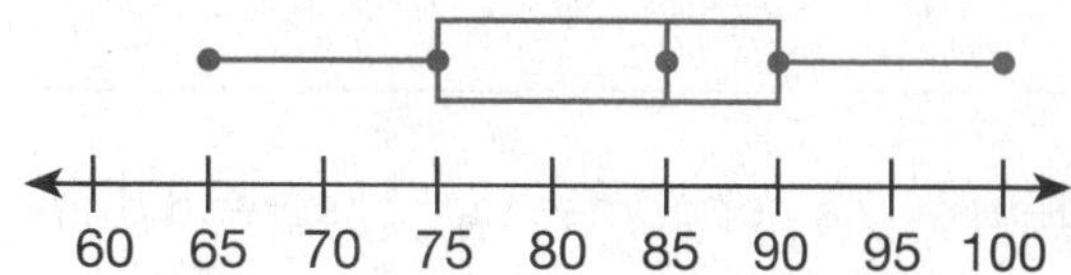

A. The scores ranged from 65 to 100.

B. The median score earned was an 85.

C. 25% of students scored less than 75 points on the test.

D. 50% of students had scores that ranged from 75 to 85 points.

21. The box plot shows the prices of 20 skirts for sale at a boutique. Which statement about the prices is true?

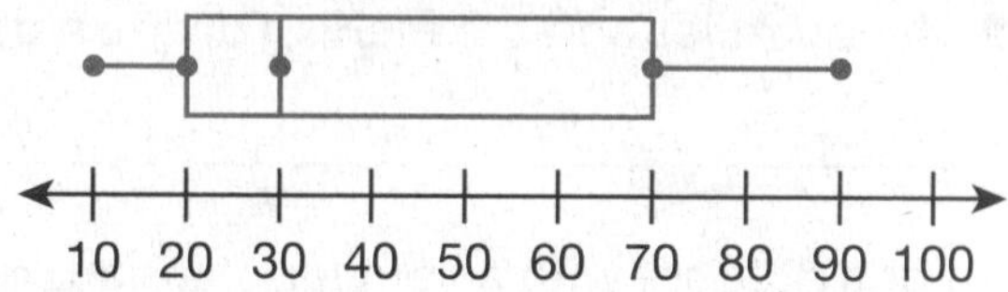

A. The highest-priced skirt costs $100.

B. The median price of a skirt is $70.

C. Half the skirts have prices that range from $20 to $70.

D. The prices of the skirts are close to the median and not very variable.

Use the box plots and information below for questions 22 and 23.

Music festival *A* and music festival *B* each had 100 volunteers. The box plots show the ages of the volunteers at each festival.

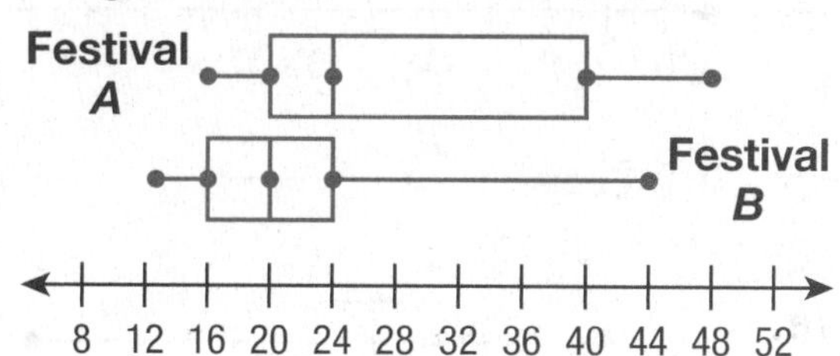

22. Compare the median ages of volunteers at each festival.

____

23. Which festival has more variability in the ages of its volunteers? Explain your answer.

____

____

Choose a measure of variability for the data.

24. A zoologist recently gathered data on birth weights for African elephants in various nature preserves. The data show a symmetric distribution. Which measure of variability would better describe the zoologist's data: standard deviation or interquartile range? Explain your answer.

____

____

Use the box plots for questions 25–28.

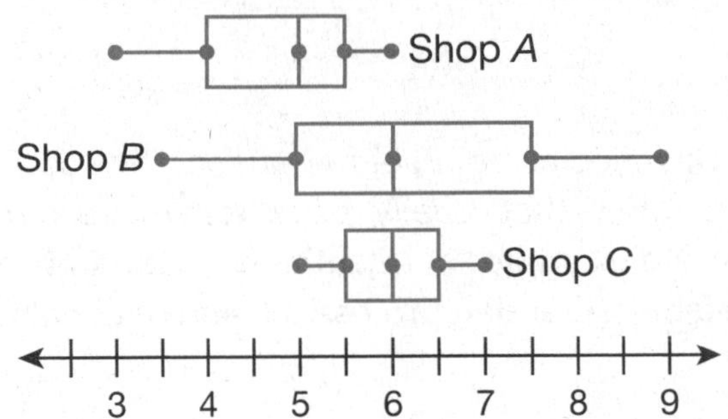

25. Identify the median price of a sandwich at each shop.

Shop *A*: *M* = ______________

Shop *B*: *M* = ______________

Shop *C*: *M* = ______________

26. Calculate the IQR of sandwich prices at each shop.

Shop *A*: IQR = ______________

Shop *B*: IQR = ______________

Shop *C*: IQR = ______________

27. If you wanted to buy a sandwich but not spend much money, which shop would you try first? Why?

____

____

28. Compare the variability of the sandwich prices at the three shops.

____

____

____

Use the information below for questions 29 and 30.

Mrs. Heath visited her aunt in Nome, Alaska, for the first ten days of January 2012. She recorded the daily low temperature, in degrees Fahrenheit (°F), each day:

−27, −27, −31, −33, −34, −33, −34, −25, −29, −26

29. ORGANIZE Organize these data by displaying them in a box plot. Use the number line provided below.

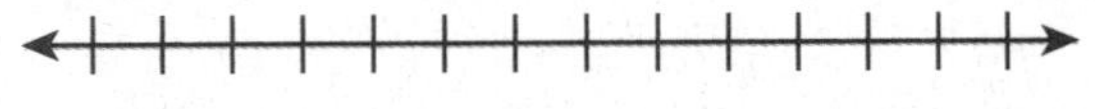

30. JUSTIFY Mrs. Heath said, "The weather was very, very cold and did not vary much during the trip." Is her statement accurate? Use one or more measures of variability to justify your answer.

____

____

____

____

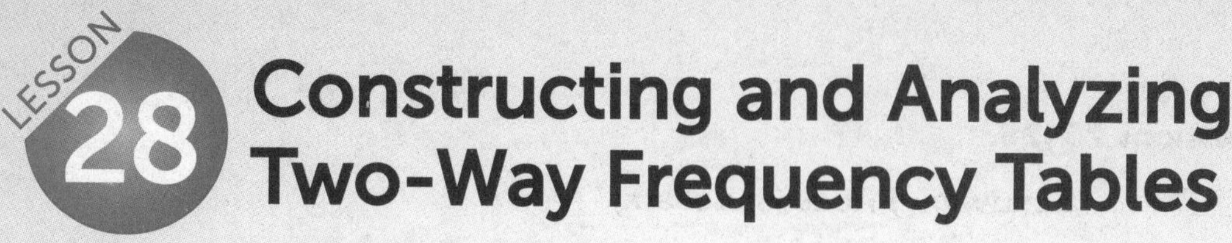

LESSON 28 Constructing and Analyzing Two-Way Frequency Tables

UNDERSTAND Data can be classified as being either quantitative data or categorical data. **Quantitative data** involve numbers that usually result from measurement. Temperature, height, cost, and population are examples of quantitative data. **Categorical data** take on values that are names or labels. Gender, profession, and nationality are examples of categorical data.

When researchers collect data, they often ask more than one question. Comparing the results of those questions can reveal relationships among the data. To compare two categorical variables, you can enter the frequencies for each category into a **two-way frequency table**.

The two-way frequency table below displays the results of a survey that examined the relationship between gender and video game play. The table shows **joint frequencies** and **marginal frequencies**.

	Play Daily	Play Occasionally	Total
Boys	16	8	24
Girls	4	12	16
Total	20	20	40

Joint frequencies are in the body of the table.

Marginal frequencies are in the "Total" row and "Total" column.

Sometimes you are less interested in the actual frequency count than in the percentage of data values that fall into each category. These percentages are the **relative frequencies**. When displayed in a table, they form a **two-way relative frequency table**. The percentages in the middle of a relative frequency table are called **conditional frequencies**.

	Play Daily	Play Occasionally	Total
Boys	40%	20%	60%
Girls	10%	30%	40%
Total	50%	50%	100%

Conditional frequencies are in the body of the table.

Marginal frequencies are in the "Total" row and "Total" column.

Two-way tables help us see associations between two variables. For example, the above table shows that 40% of the students surveyed are boys who play video games daily and that 10% of the students surveyed are girls who play video games daily, so 50%, or half, of the students surveyed play video games daily. Based on this survey, it seems that boys are more likely to play video games daily than girls.

Connect

Kyra asked students and parents of students at her high school whether they are in favor of or against a proposal to remove the juice machine from the school cafeteria. The two-way frequency table on the right displays the results of the survey.

	For	Against	Total
Students	5	37	42
Parents	20	18	38
Total	25	55	80

Identify and interpret the marginal and joint frequencies in the table.

1 Identify and interpret the marginal frequencies.

Marginal frequencies are in the "Total" column and in the "Total" row.

The marginal frequencies in the "Total" column show that 42 students and 38 parents were surveyed. Roughly equal numbers of parents and students were surveyed.

The marginal frequencies in the "Total" row show that 25 people surveyed supported the proposal and 55 were against it. More than twice as many people surveyed were against the proposal as were in favor of it.

Both sets of marginal frequencies show that Kyra surveyed a total of 80 people.

2 Identify and interpret the joint frequencies by row.

Joint frequencies are in the body of the table, not the "Total" column or row.

The first row shows that 5 students support the proposal, while 37 oppose it.

A large majority of students do not support removing the juice machine.

The second row shows that 20 parents support the proposal, while 18 oppose it.

Parents are about evenly split on the proposal.

3 Identify and interpret the joint frequencies by column.

The first column shows that 5 students and 20 parents are for the proposal.

Many more parents than students support removing the juice machine.

The second column shows that 37 students and 18 parents are against the proposal.

Many more students than parents are against the proposal.

Would your understanding of the situation be different if you only had the marginal frequencies? What do you learn from the joint frequencies that is not shown in the marginal frequencies?

EXAMPLE A The P.E. teachers at a high school are organizing an intramural league. They asked ninth-grade students which sport they would most like to play. The results are shown in the frequency table below.

	Basketball	Kickball	Volleyball	Total
Boys	50	30	12	92
Girls	18	32	58	108
Total	68	62	70	200

Create a two-way relative frequency table for the entire table. Based on the data, should the P.E. teachers create a basketball league? Explain.

1 Calculate each relative frequency.

Find the relative frequencies for the entire table. Each relative frequency will be the quotient of the corresponding frequency divided by the total frequencies

	Basketball	Kickball	Volleyball	Total
Boys	$\frac{50}{200} = 0.25$	$\frac{30}{200} = 0.15$	$\frac{12}{200} = 0.06$	$\frac{92}{200} = 0.46$
Girls	$\frac{18}{200} = 0.09$	$\frac{32}{200} = 0.16$	$\frac{58}{200} = 0.29$	$\frac{108}{200} = 0.54$
Total	$\frac{68}{200} = 0.34$	$\frac{62}{200} = 0.31$	$\frac{70}{200} = 0.35$	$\frac{200}{200} = 1.00$

2 Determine whether basketball is the most popular choice.

The two-way relative frequency table shows 34% of students surveyed prefer basketball. That is not significantly more than the percent who prefer kickball and is less than the percent who prefer volleyball.

▶ The data show that there is some support, but not overwhelming support, for a basketball league.

DISCUSS

Based on the data, is there an obvious choice for which sport the teachers should select? Explain your thinking.

EXAMPLE B Carter surveyed 20 ninth-grade students and 30 twelfth-grade students at random. He asked the students whether they were involved in school clubs. After creating a two-way frequency table of his results, he calculated the relative frequencies for each row of his table. The relative frequencies are shown on the right.

	One or More Clubs	No Clubs	Total
9th Grade	30%	70%	100%
12th Grade	80%	20%	100%
Total	60%	40%	100%

Create a frequency table for Carter's data. Then create a two-way relative frequency table for the columns in the frequency table.

1 Use the relative frequencies and the given information to create a frequency table.

You know that Carter surveyed 20 ninth-graders and 30 twelfth-graders. Use those numbers to fill in the Total column. Then use the relative frequencies to calculate the frequencies.

▶

	One or More Clubs	No Clubs	Total
9th Grade	$0.3 \cdot 20 = 6$	$0.7 \cdot 20 = 14$	20
12th Grade	$0.8 \cdot 30 = 24$	$0.2 \cdot 30 = 6$	30
Total	$0.6 \cdot 50 = 30$	$0.4 \cdot 50 = 20$	50

2 Use the frequencies in the table you created to find the relative frequencies by column.

To create a two-way relative frequency table based on columns, divide each value in a column by the total frequency for that column.

▶

	One or More Clubs	No Clubs	Total
9th Grade	$\frac{6}{30} = 20\%$	$\frac{14}{20} = 70\%$	$\frac{20}{50} = 40\%$
12th Grade	$\frac{24}{30} = 80\%$	$\frac{6}{20} = 30\%$	$\frac{30}{50} = 60\%$
Total	$\frac{30}{30} = 100\%$	$\frac{20}{20} = 100\%$	$\frac{50}{50} = 100\%$

DISCUSS

What associations do you find in the data in the relative frequency table? Do you see different associations in the data when you look at the relative frequency table by rows compared to the relative frequency table by columns?

Practice

Circle and label marginal frequencies and either joint frequencies or conditional frequencies.

1.

	Smart Phone	No Smart Phone	Total
Boys	15	10	25
Girls	19	6	25
Total	34	16	50

HINT A two-way frequency table has joint frequencies and marginal frequencies.

2.

	Smart Phone	No Smart Phone	Total
Boys	30%	20%	50%
Girls	38%	12%	50%
Total	68%	32%	100%

Fill in each blank with an appropriate word or phrase.

3. A two-way frequency table allows you to organize __________ data.

4. __________ frequencies are entries in the "Total" row and "Total" column of a frequency table.

5. __________ frequencies are entries in the body of a two-way relative frequency table.

6. Given a two-way frequency table, you can find relative frequencies for each ________, for each __________, or for the entire table.

Use the information and the two-way frequency table for questions 7 and 8.

A group of U.S. history teachers asked students where they would most like to go for an overnight field trip. The table shows the results.

	Washington, D.C.	Williamsburg, VA	Total
Boys	77	28	105
Girls	20	75	95
Total	97	103	200

7. Interpret the marginal frequencies.

____

____

8. Interpret the joint frequencies.

____

____

Use the information and the two-way relative frequency table for questions 9 and 10.

Byron asked fellow high school students and their parents if they support a proposal to replace the current school food vendor with a new food vendor.

	New Vendor	Current Vendor	Total
Parents	0.36	0.14	0.50
Students	0.24	0.26	0.50
Total	0.60	0.40	1.00

9. Interpret the marginal frequencies.

____

____

10. Interpret the conditional frequencies.

____

____

Use this information for question 11.

Twenty students were asked which type of music they like best. Three boys said hip-hop, four boys said jazz, and two boys said rock. Six girls said hip-hop, one girl said jazz, and four girls said rock.

11. Use the grid below to create a two-way frequency table for the data.

Use the information below for questions 12–15.

Erika asked ten high school seniors if they owned a car and if they had an afterschool job. Her results are shown in the table.

Car	yes	yes	no	no	yes	no	no	yes	no	yes
Job	yes	no	yes	yes	yes	no	no	yes	no	yes

12. Use Erika's results to complete the two-way frequency table below.

	Car	**No Car**	**Total**
Job			
No Job			
Total			

13. Complete the table below to show relative frequencies for each column in the table you created for question 12. Express the frequencies as percentages.

	Car	**No Car**	**Total**
Job			
No Job			
Total			

14. Does the two-way relative frequency table show a possible association between owning a car and having an afterschool job? Explain.

____

____

____

15. Does the two-way relative frequency table show a possible association between **not** owning a car and having an afterschool job? Explain.

____

____

____

Use the information and table for questions 16–20.

The two-way frequency table shows the results of a survey in which ninth-grade students were asked which world language elective they most wanted to take next semester.

	Spanish	French	German	Total
Boys	80	30	10	120
Girls	30	20	30	80
Total	110	50	40	200

Use the grids below to create three different two-way relative frequency tables for the data. Express frequencies as decimals. Round to the nearest thousandth.

16. Show relative frequencies for the entire table.

	Spanish	French	German	Total
Boys				
Girls				
Total				

17. Show relative frequencies for each row.

	Spanish	French	German	Total
Boys				
Girls				
Total				

18. Show relative frequencies for each column.

	Spanish	French	German	Total
Boys				
Girls				
Total				

19. EXAMINE Examine the two-way relative frequency tables you created above. Describe two or more associations you see in the data.

____

____

____

20. CONCLUDE The school will offer a total of 8 sections of world language classes for ninth-grade students next semester. How many sections should be Spanish? French? German? Explain your answers.

____

____

____

LESSON 29

Constructing and Analyzing Scatter Plots

UNDERSTAND When you study the relationship between two variables—such as the heights and shoe sizes of a group of students—you are working with **bivariate data**. Bivariate data can be written as a set of (x, y) ordered pairs and graphed on a coordinate plane. This kind of graph is called a **scatter plot**. A scatter plot can help you interpret bivariate data. The scatter plot below shows a set of ordered pairs in which the x-values represent heights and the y-values represent shoe sizes.

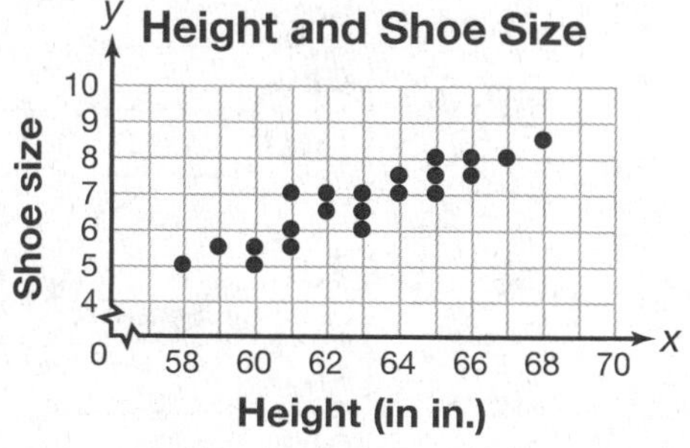

Look at the shape formed by the plotted points. The shape resembles a straight line. This suggests a linear relationship between the variables. You can draw a line to fit, or model, the data. The line you draw represents a linear function. If the line is a good fit, you can use the graph and the equation of the line to interpret and make predictions about the data.

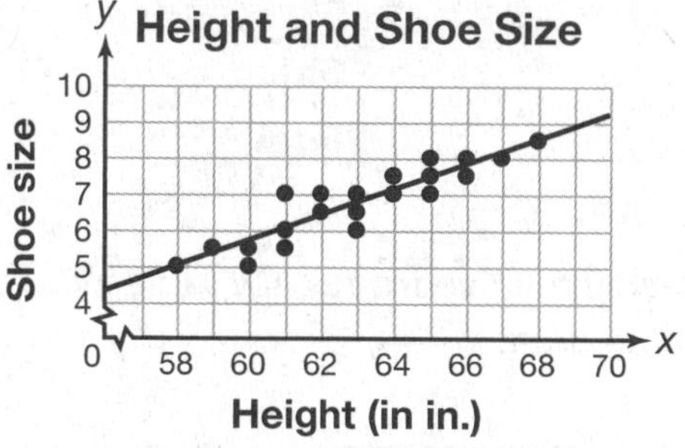

The line appears to be a good fit. The data points slant up from left to right, indicating a positive linear relationship. The line has a positive slope and is close to most data points.

You could also show that the line is a good fit for the data by calculating **residuals**. For each point (x, y) on the scatter plot, there is a corresponding point $(x, \hat{y})$ on the line of fit. A residual is equal to the difference $y - \hat{y}$. Residuals measure the difference of each actual y-value and the expected y-value ($\hat{y}$), which is based on the equation of the line of fit.

Residuals help you determine how accurately the linear function could predict actual points on the scatter plot. That is, if the values of the residuals are relatively small, the linear function is a good fit for the data. So, for any value of x, you could use the equation of the line to make a good prediction about what the value of y would be, and vice versa.

Connect

Draw a line of fit for each of the scatter plots. Determine how well each fits the data.

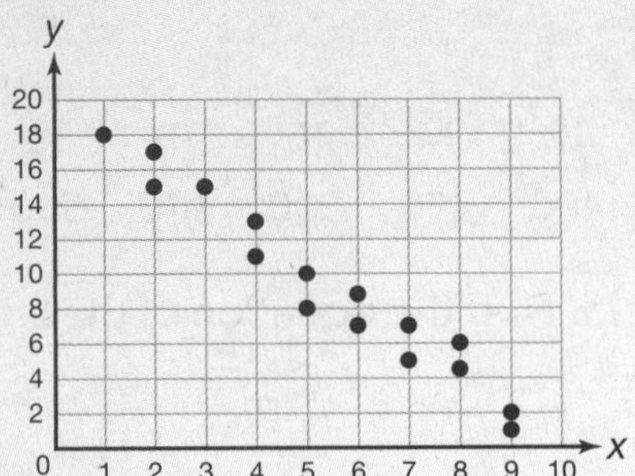

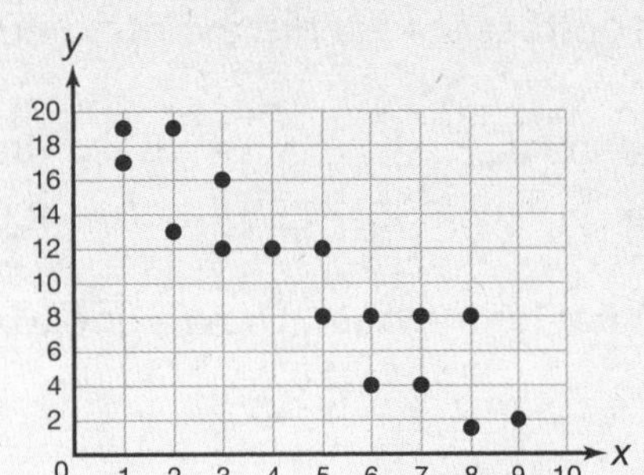

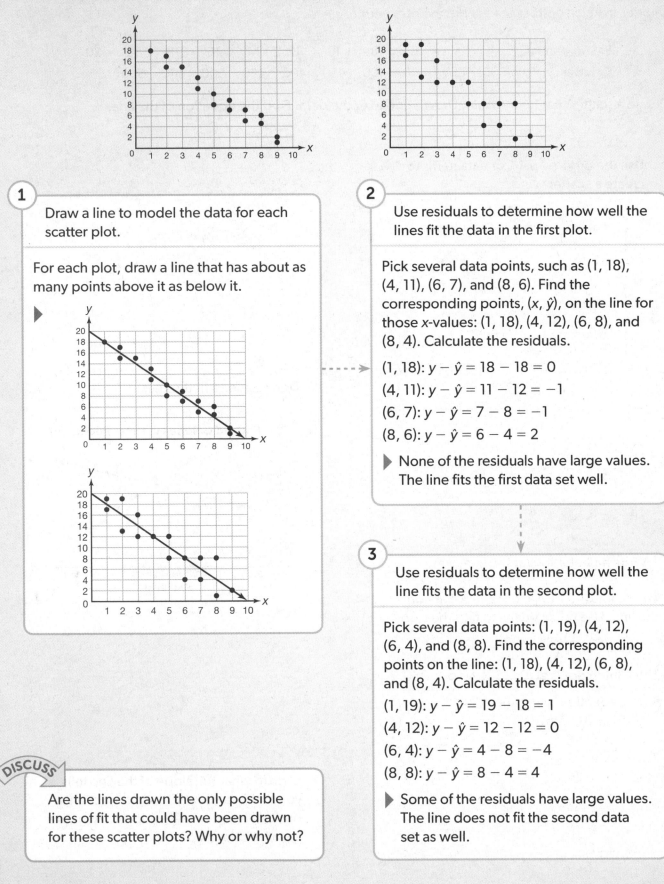

1 Draw a line to model the data for each scatter plot.

For each plot, draw a line that has about as many points above it as below it.

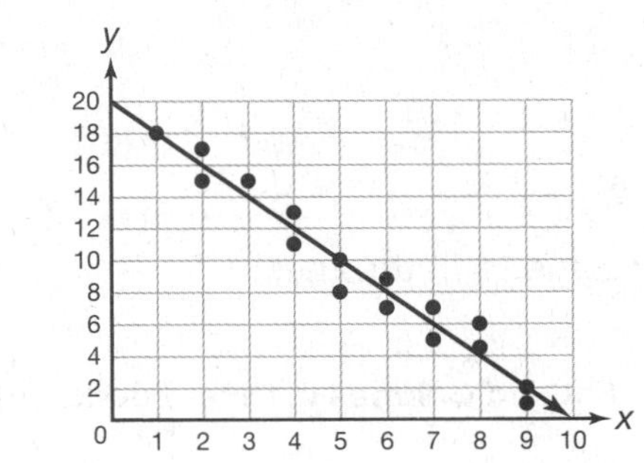

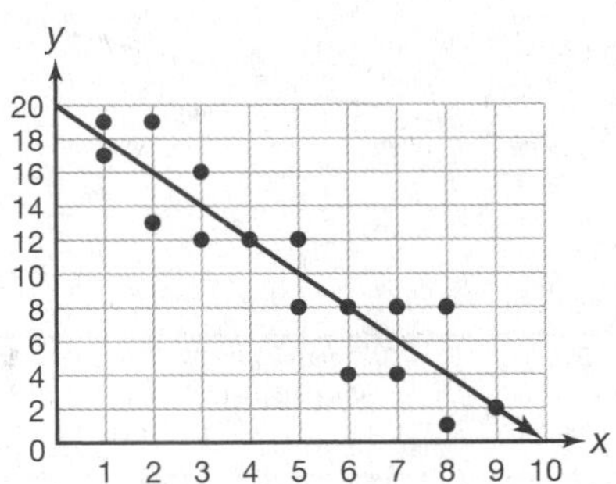

2 Use residuals to determine how well the lines fit the data in the first plot.

Pick several data points, such as (1, 18), (4, 11), (6, 7), and (8, 6). Find the corresponding points, $(x, \hat{y})$, on the line for those x-values: (1, 18), (4, 12), (6, 8), and (8, 4). Calculate the residuals.

(1, 18): $y - \hat{y} = 18 - 18 = 0$

(4, 11): $y - \hat{y} = 11 - 12 = -1$

(6, 7): $y - \hat{y} = 7 - 8 = -1$

(8, 6): $y - \hat{y} = 6 - 4 = 2$

▶ None of the residuals have large values. The line fits the first data set well.

3 Use residuals to determine how well the line fits the data in the second plot.

Pick several data points: (1, 19), (4, 12), (6, 4), and (8, 8). Find the corresponding points on the line: (1, 18), (4, 12), (6, 8), and (8, 4). Calculate the residuals.

(1, 19): $y - \hat{y} = 19 - 18 = 1$

(4, 12): $y - \hat{y} = 12 - 12 = 0$

(6, 4): $y - \hat{y} = 4 - 8 = -4$

(8, 8): $y - \hat{y} = 8 - 4 = 4$

▶ Some of the residuals have large values. The line does not fit the second data set as well.

DISCUSS

Are the lines drawn the only possible lines of fit that could have been drawn for these scatter plots? Why or why not?

EXAMPLE For a health project, Dylan recorded the number of grams of fat and the number of calories in lunch entrees sold at his favorite diner.

Fat (in grams)	4	6	8	8	10	12	14	16	18	18	20
Calories	300	250	300	400	450	400	350	500	400	500	500

Create a scatter plot for the data. Draw a line to fit the data. Find the equation of the line.

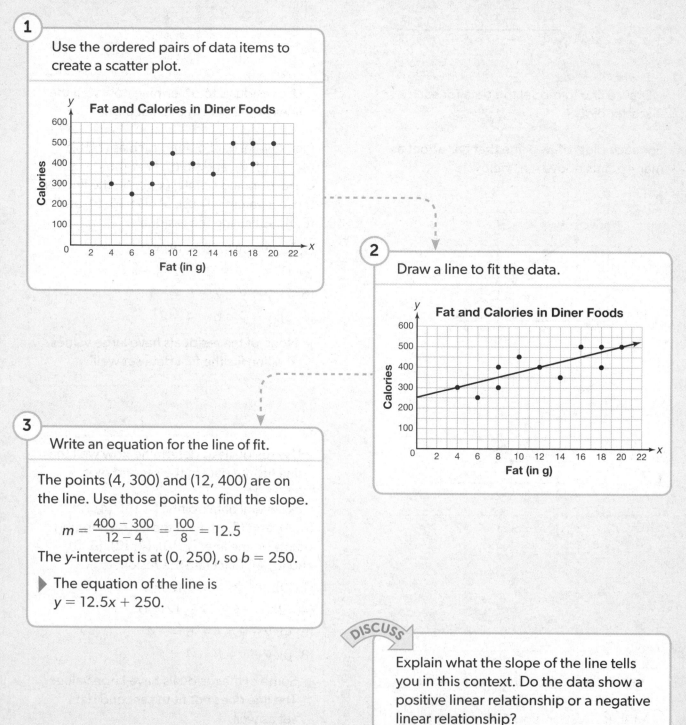

1 Use the ordered pairs of data items to create a scatter plot.

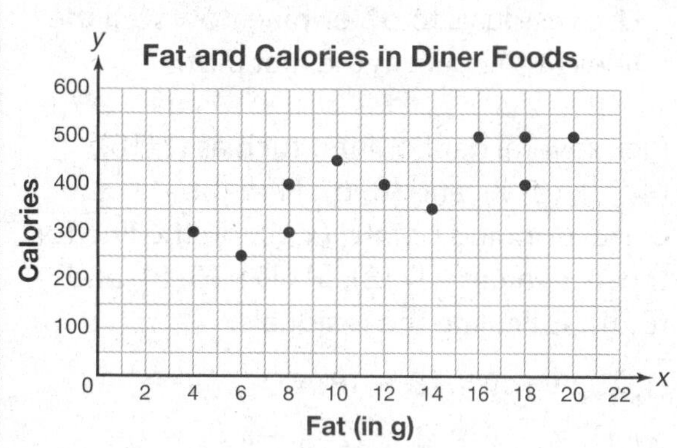

2 Draw a line to fit the data.

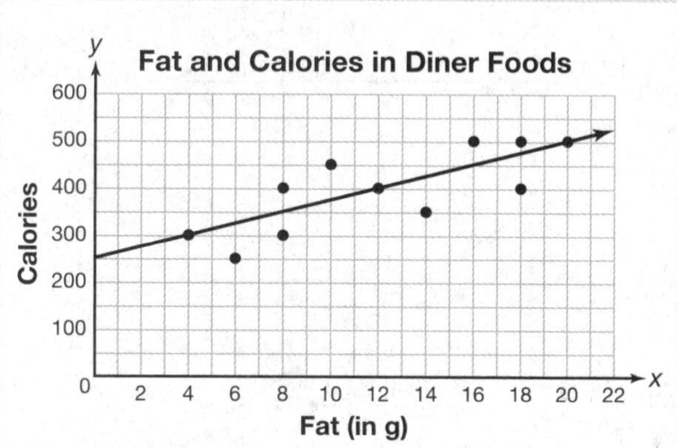

3 Write an equation for the line of fit.

The points (4, 300) and (12, 400) are on the line. Use those points to find the slope.

$$m = \frac{400 - 300}{12 - 4} = \frac{100}{8} = 12.5$$

The y-intercept is at (0, 250), so $b = 250$.

▶ The equation of the line is $y = 12.5x + 250$.

DISCUSS

Explain what the slope of the line tells you in this context. Do the data show a positive linear relationship or a negative linear relationship?

Problem Solving

READ

The scatter plot shows the ages of various Model Z smartphones, in months, and the prices for which they sold. Predict how much Trent will pay if he buys a Model Z smartphone that is 5 years old.

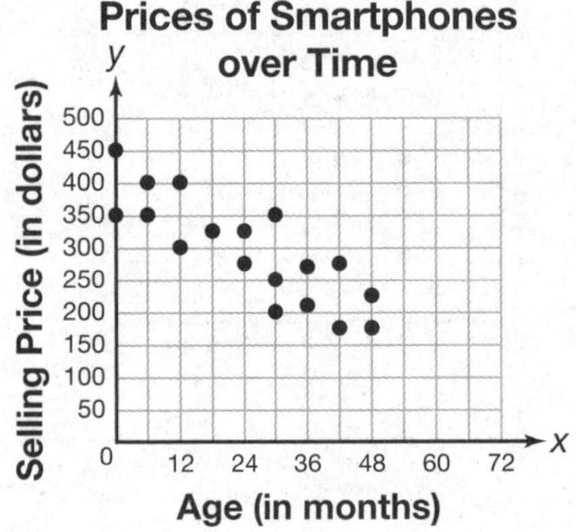

PLAN

Draw a _____ to fit the data. Write the equation of the _____, and use it to predict the price for a phone that is 5 years, or _____ months, old.

SOLVE

On the scatter plot, draw a line that fits the data.

Choose two points on the line, (_____, _____) and (_____, _____).

Use the points to find the slope of the line. $m =$ _____

In this context, the slope represents _____________________________________.

Find the *y*-intercept of the line. Extend the line to the *y*-axis if necessary. $b =$ _____

The equation for the line is $y =$ _______________.

In this context, the *y*-intercept represents _____________________________________.

To predict the cost of a 5-year-old smartphone, substitute 60 for *x* in the equation. $_____

CHECK

Pick three data points from the scatter plot: (_____, _____), (_____, _____), (_____, _____).

Find the points with corresponding *x*-values on the line of fit:

(_____, _____), (_____, _____), (_____, _____).

Calculate the residual for each point. Each residual is relatively _________.

Does the line fit the data well? _____ Is your answer a reasonable prediction? _____

▶ A good prediction is that Trent will pay about _____ for a Model Z smartphone that is 5 years old.

Practice

Describe the relationship shown in each scatter plot as either *positive* or *negative*.

1.

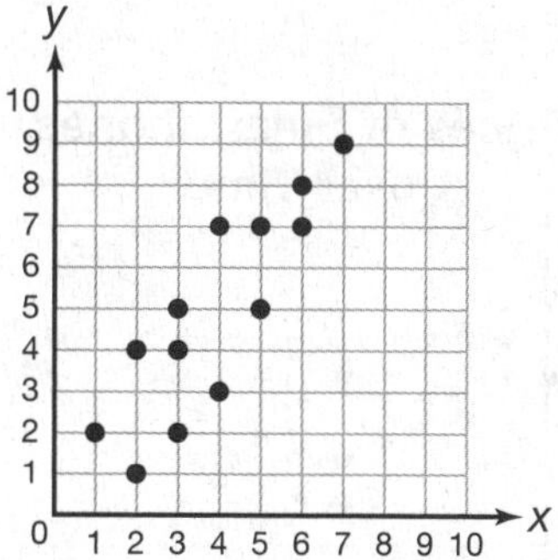

____

2.

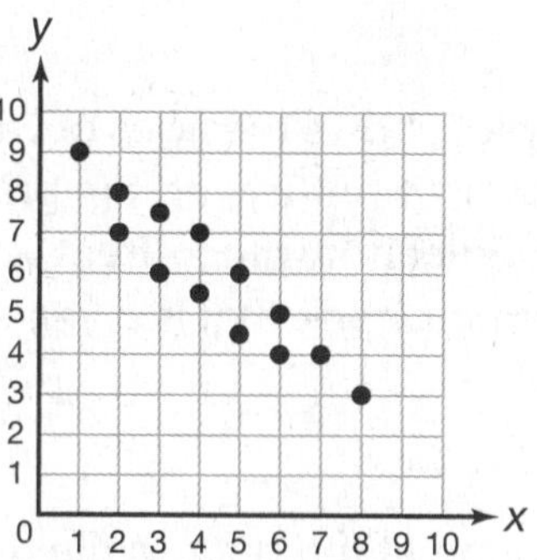

____

A line that slants from lower left to upper right has a positive slope.

Use the information and table below for questions 3 and 4.

The table below shows T-shirt sales data for a store one weekend.

Price, *x* (in dollars)	4	8	8	12	12	16	20	20	24	24
Number Sold, *y*	32	26	30	22	26	20	12	20	14	10

3. Create a scatter plot for the data. Then draw a line of fit for the data.

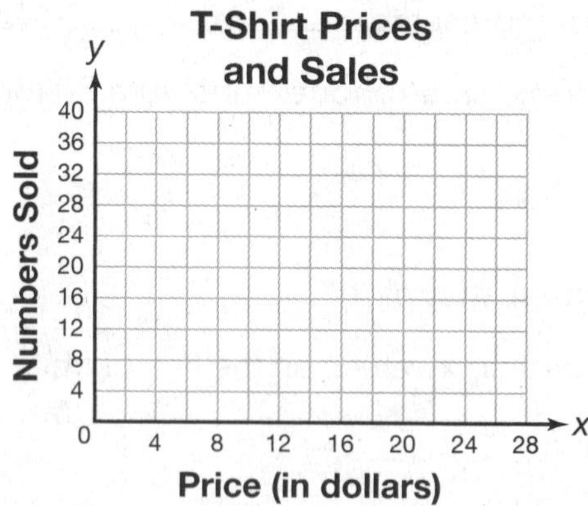

4. Find the slope of the line of fit. What does it represent in the context of this problem?

____

____

Assess the fit of the lines to the data.

5. The lines of fit in the scatter plots below are identical.

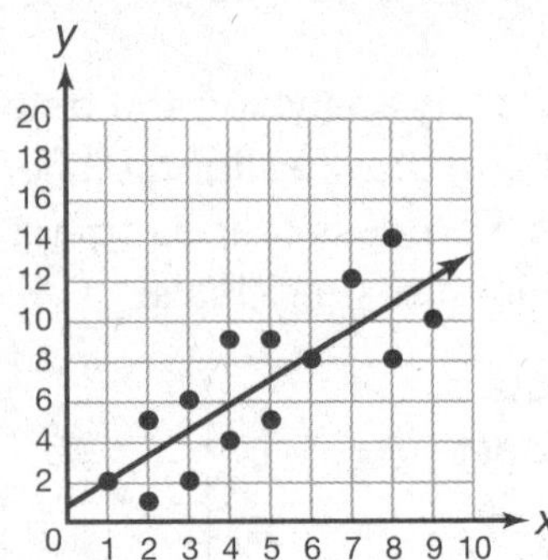

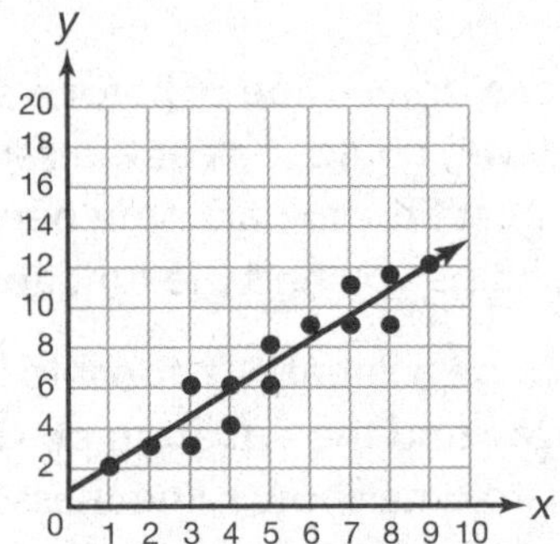

Which line better fits the data in its scatter plot? How did you determine your answer?

____

____

Use the information and scatter plot to the right for questions 6 and 7.

The scatter plot shows the number of hours of sleep that students got the night before a test and their scores on the test.

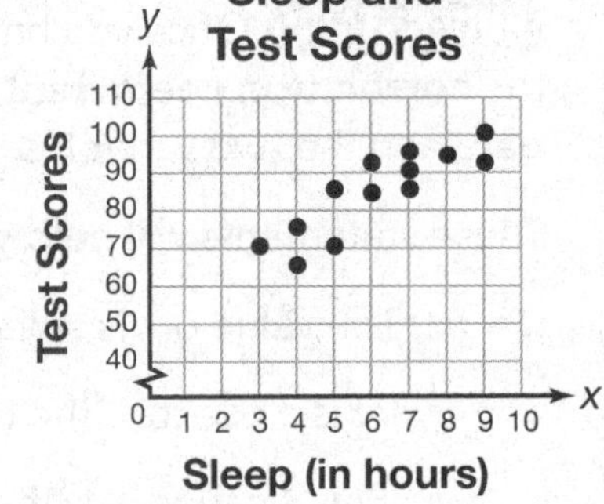

6. INTERPRET Draw a line of fit for the scatter plot. Identify the slope and y-intercept of the line. What does each represent in the context of this problem?

____

____

____

7. PREDICT Write the equation of the line. Then use the equation to predict a student's test score if she gets only 2 hours of sleep before the next test.

____

____

____

Best Fit and Correlation

UNDERSTAND You can draw a line of fit for a scatter plot by analyzing the data visually. Someone else, however, could look at the same data and draw a slightly different line. To find the line that best fits the data, you need to use a process called regression analysis. Regression analysis helps you find the function that minimizes residuals.

When there seems to be a linear relationship in the data, regression analysis can find the equation of a **line of best fit**. But not all bivariate data show a linear association. In some cases, the relationship between the variables is better modeled by a curve, as in the scatter plot shown. For data that do not have a linear association, you will need to find a **curve of best fit**. To find the equation of either a line of best fit or a curve of best fit, you can use a graphing calculator to perform a regression analysis.

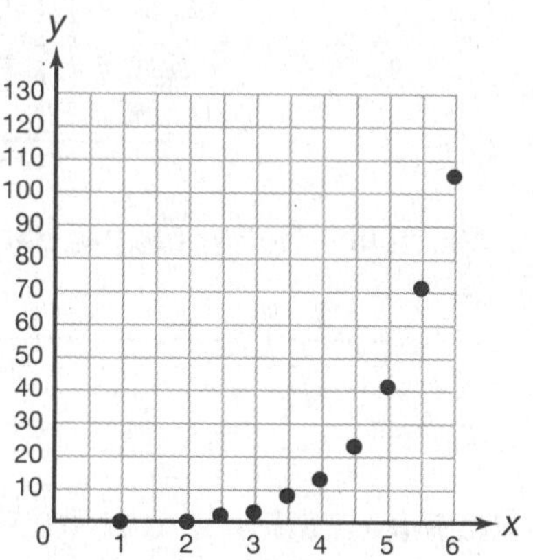

UNDERSTAND Once you have determined the line of best fit for bivariate data, you can use the **correlation coefficient**, r, to describe the strength and direction of the relationship between the two variables.

These statements will help you interpret a correlation coefficient.

- The value of r is always in the range $-1 \leq r \leq 1$.
- If r is close to 1, the data show a strong positive correlation
- If r is close to -1, the data show a strong negative correlation.
- If $r = 0$, the data do not show a linear correlation.

When bivariate data have a strong correlation, the predictions you make by using the line of best fit are likely to be very accurate. When there is a weak correlation, these predictions will tend to be less accurate. A positive correlation means that as one variable increases, the other variable tends to increase also. A negative correlation means that as one variable increases, the other tends to decrease.

The correlation coefficient, r, is calculated using a rather complex formula involving residuals. Fortunately, you can use a calculator to do that work for you!

Keep in mind that there is a crucial difference between correlation and causation. A strong correlation does not tell you that x is the cause of y. For example, buying lemonade and going to the beach might be strongly correlated, but one does not cause the other.

Connect

On a graphing calculator, create a scatter plot and draw a curve of best fit for the data in the table below.

Time, x (in minutes)	0	2	4	6	8	10
Number of Bacteria, y	5	11	25	57	130	290

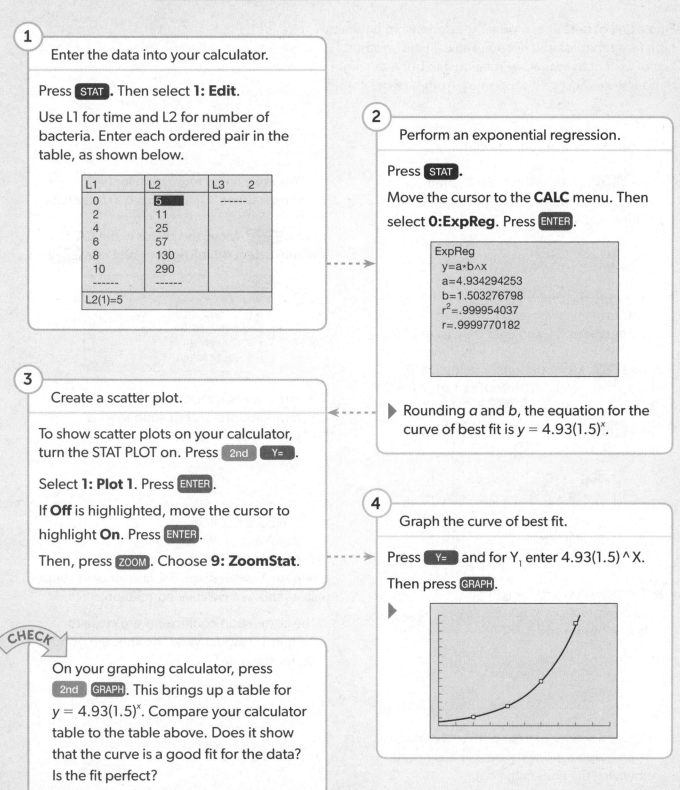

1 Enter the data into your calculator.

Press STAT. Then select **1: Edit**.

Use L1 for time and L2 for number of bacteria. Enter each ordered pair in the table, as shown below.

L1	L2	L3 2
0	5	------
2	11	
4	25	
6	57	
8	130	
10	290	
------	------	

L2(1)=5

2 Perform an exponential regression.

Press STAT.

Move the cursor to the **CALC** menu. Then select **0:ExpReg**. Press ENTER.

```
ExpReg
 y=a*b^x
 a=4.934294253
 b=1.503276798
 r²=.999954037
 r=.9999770182
```

▶ Rounding a and b, the equation for the curve of best fit is $y = 4.93(1.5)^x$.

3 Create a scatter plot.

To show scatter plots on your calculator, turn the STAT PLOT on. Press 2nd Y=.

Select **1: Plot 1**. Press ENTER.

If **Off** is highlighted, move the cursor to highlight **On**. Press ENTER.

Then, press ZOOM. Choose **9: ZoomStat**.

4 Graph the curve of best fit.

Press Y= and for Y_1 enter 4.93(1.5) ^ X.

Then press GRAPH.

▶

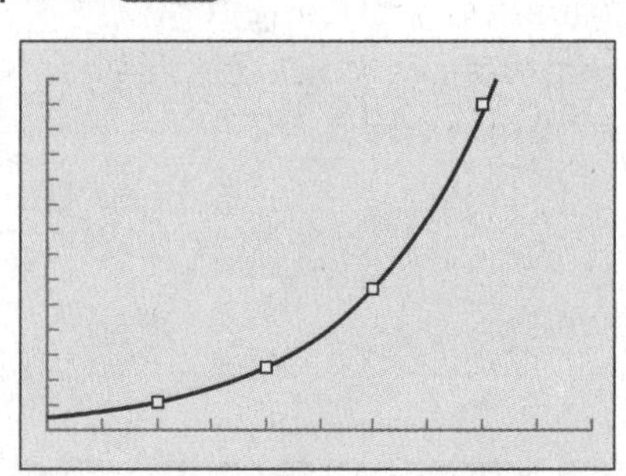

CHECK

On your graphing calculator, press 2nd GRAPH. This brings up a table for $y = 4.93(1.5)^x$. Compare your calculator table to the table above. Does it show that the curve is a good fit for the data? Is the fit perfect?

EXAMPLE The table on the right shows the daily high temperatures on six days and the number of cups of hot soup and of cold soup that were sold at a soup stand on each day.

Find a line of best fit to model the relationship between high temperatures and hot soup sales. Find another line of best fit to model the relationship between high temperatures and cold soup sales. Compare the lines.

Daily High Temperature	Cups of Hot Soup Sold	Cups of Cold Soup Sold
30	85	1
40	70	16
50	45	35
60	22	52
70	12	60
80	2	86

1 Enter the data in your calculator.

Press STAT. Then select **1: Edit**. Enter daily high temperatures in L1, hot soup sales in L2, and cold soup sales in L3.

2 Perform a linear regression for high temperatures (L1) and hot soup sales (L2).

Press STAT. Move the cursor to the **CALC** menu. Select **4:LinReg(ax+b)**. Press ENTER.

```
LinReg
 y=ax+b
 a=-1.748571429
 b=135.5047619
 r²=.972959429
 r=-.9863870908
```

▶ The equation modeling high temperatures vs. hot soup sales is $y = -1.75x + 135.5$.

3 Perform a linear regression for high temperatures (L1) and cold soup sales (L3).

Press STAT. Move the cursor to the **CALC** menu. Then select **4:LinReg(ax+b)**. Press ENTER. Now press 2nd STAT. Select **1:L1**. Press ,. Then press 2nd STAT again. Select **3:L3**. Press ENTER.

```
LinReg
 y=ax+b
 a=1.64
 b=-48.53333333
 r²=.9877168439
 r=-.9938394457
```

▶ The equation modeling high temperatures vs. cold soup sales is $y = 1.64x - 48.5$.

4 Compare the lines.

The line for hot soup sales shows a negative correlation. The line for cold soup sales shows a positive correlation.

The correlation coefficients are close to −1 and 1, respectively. The lines are good fits for the data.

MODEL

Create a scatter plot for both sets of data. Then graph the lines of best fit. Compare how well the lines fit the data.

Problem Solving

READ

The table shows data for a cup of hot water that is cooling.

Find an equation for an exponential function that models the data. Then predict how many degrees Fahrenheit above room temperature the water will be if left to cool for 20 minutes.

Time (in minutes)	Degrees Fahrenheit above Room Temperature
0	134
2	113
4	95
6	80
8	67
10	56

PLAN

Use a graphing calculator to perform a(n)

_____________ regression.

Then use a calculator table to solve the problem.

SOLVE

Enter the data in your calculator as L1 and L2.

Perform the exponential regression but with a few extra steps.

Press STAT.

Move the cursor to the **CALC** menu. Then select **0:ExpReg**.

Now press VARS. Move the cursor to **Y-VARS.** Select **1:Function**. Then select **1:Y_1**.

Press ENTER twice.

The screen shows that the equation is _________________________.

Press Y=. Because of those extra steps, the equation is already entered as Y_1.

Press 2nd GRAPH to bring up the table of values.

Scroll down. The table shows that when $x = 20$, $y \approx$ __________.

CHECK

Substitute 20 for x in the equation for the curve of best fit and solve.

$y =$ ____

Do you get the same answer? Why or why not? ___________________________________

____

▶ After 20 minutes, the hot water will probably be about ______ °F above room temperature.

Practice

Use *line* or *curve* to tell which kind of model best fits each data set.

1.

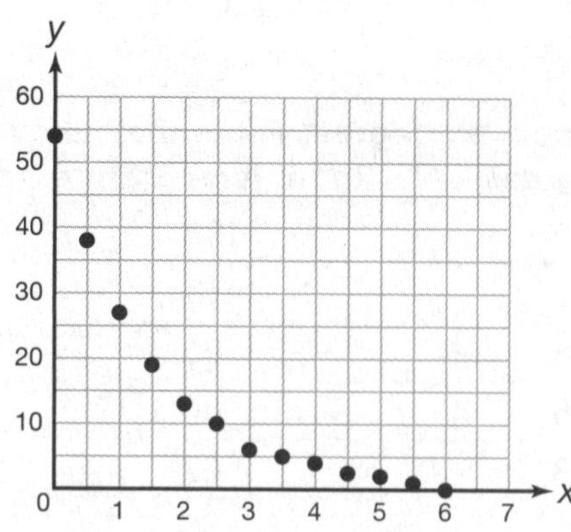

____

2.

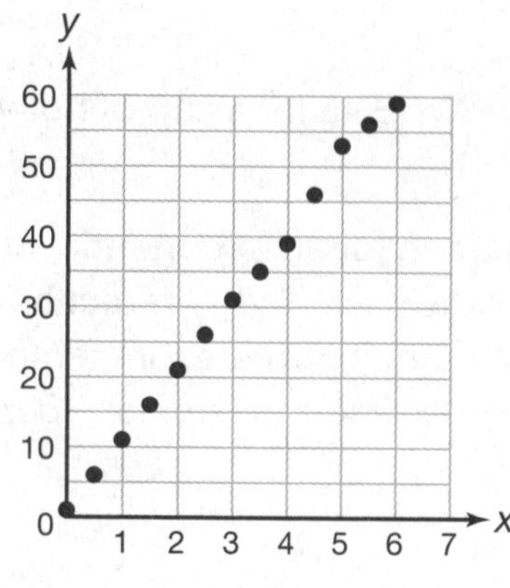

____

Use *strong, weak, positive, negative,* or *no linear correlation* to describe what each correlation coefficient, *r*, tells you about a bivariate data set.

3. $r = 0$

____

4. $r = 0.250$

____

5. $r = -0.895$

____

REMEMBER The closer r is to 1 or -1, the stronger the correlation.

Write *true* or *false* for each statement. If false, rewrite the statement so it is true.

6. A line of best fit will help you predict values for variables with complete accuracy.

____

____

7. Not all bivariate data show a linear correlation, so sometimes data are better modeled by a curve than a line.

____

____

8. If regression analysis shows that there is a strong correlation between two variables, x and y, then x must cause y.

____

____

Choose the best answer.

Use a calculator for questions 9 and 10.

9. Which equation is the best model for the table of values shown below?

x	y
1	3
2	6.5
3	10
4	14
5	17

A. $y = -0.55x + 3.55$
B. $y = 0.55x + 3.55$
C. $y = 3.55x - 0.55$
D. $y = -3.55x - 0.55$

10. Which equation is the best model for the table of values shown below?

x	y
1	12
2	48
3	190
4	770
5	3,070

A. $y = 4(2.99^{-x})$
B. $y = 4(2.99^{x})$
C. $y = 2.99(4^{-x})$
D. $y = 2.99(4^{x})$

Use the information and table for questions 11–13.

The table to the right shows the daily high temperatures on six days and the number of air conditioners and space heaters a store sold on those days.

Daily High Temperature (in °F)	Air Conditioners Sold	Space Heaters Sold
30	0	20
40	4	14
50	8	12
60	11	6
70	16	2
80	23	1

11. Find the equation of the line of best fit that models the relationship between high temperatures and air conditioner sales. Then, find the correlation coefficient.

____

12. Find the equation of the line of best fit that models the relationship between high temperatures and space heater sales. Then, find the correlation coefficient.

____

13. Compare and contrast the two lines of best fit and the correlation coefficients. How do the two lines differ? Which is a better fit for its data set? Explain your answers.

____

____

____

Use the information, table, and scatter plot below for question 14.

Mrs. Chen started a business 20 years ago. The table and scatter plot show the number of employees her growing business has had over a period of 20 years.

Years in Business	Number of Employees
0	3
5	7
10	19
15	46
20	115

14. Use your calculator to perform an exponential regression for the data. What is the equation of the curve of best fit? Graph that curve on the scatter plot above.

____

Use the information, table, and scatter plot below for questions 15 and 16.

The table and scatter plot both show the heights and weights of a randomly selected sample of football players from an all-star team.

Height (in inches)	Weight (in pounds)
67	150
68	180
69	175
70	180
71	190
72	185
72	200
73	210
74	200
75	220

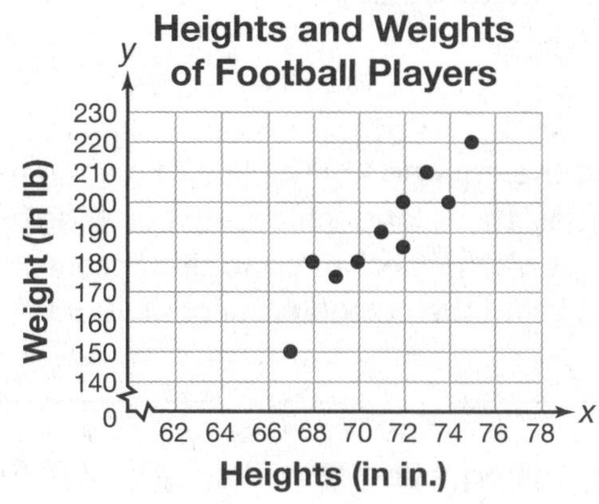

15. Use your calculator to perform a linear regression of the data. What is the equation of the line of best fit? What is the correlation coefficient?

____

16. Graph that line on the scatter plot above. How good a fit is the line?

____

Choose the best answer.

17. What does the screenshot on the right show about the data being considered?

    A. A line with a positive slope is a good fit for the data.

    B. A line with a negative slope is a good fit for the data.

    C. A linear function is not a good model for the data.

    D. An exponential function is the only good model for the data.

```
LinReg
  y=ax+b
  a=-26.18521429
  b=58.89810714
  r²=.5700873883
  r=-.7550413156
```

Solve.

18. PREDICT A scientist is studying how the population of ducks in a pond has been changing over a 40-year period. The table on the right shows her data.

    Use exponential regression to predict the population of ducks in 2020. Show or explain your work.

Year	Population
1970 (Enter: 0)	900
1980 (10)	450
1990 (20)	225
2000 (30)	150
2010 (40)	100

___

___

19. CONCLUDE The scatter plot below shows data for the number of ice cream cones sold and the number of bee stings treated at a lake resort. Based on the data, can you conclude that eating ice cream causes bee stings? If not, what can you conclude?

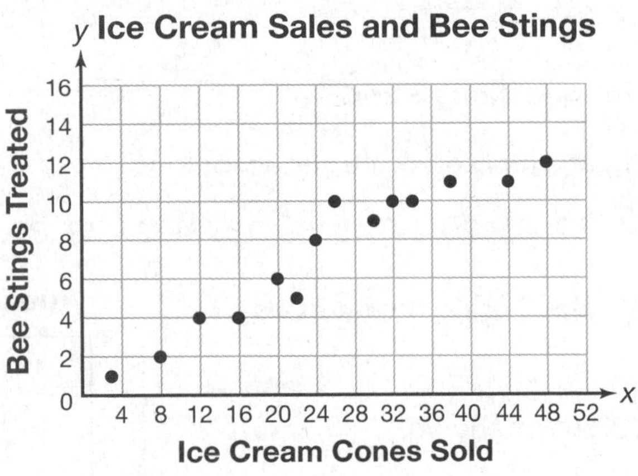

___

___

UNIT 3

Review

Calculate the specified measure of center for each pair of data sets. Then write a statement comparing those measures in the context of the question.

1. The dot plots show the scores for the members of two quiz bowl teams.

Quiz Bowl Scores, Team *A*

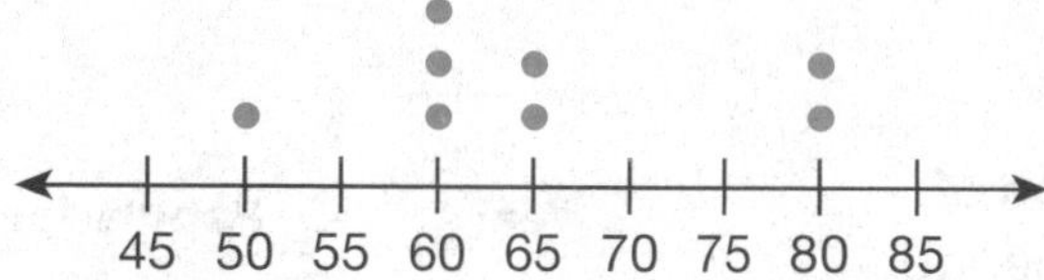

Quiz Bowl Scores, Team *B*

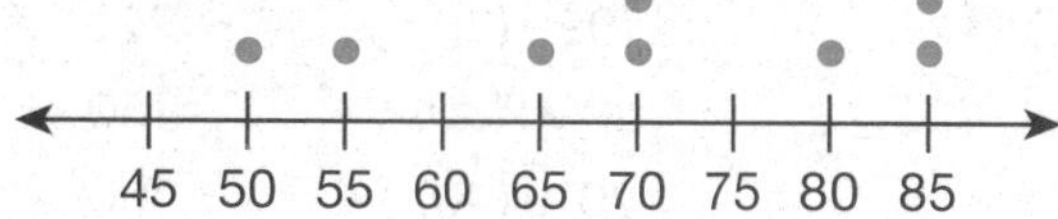

mean score, Team *A*: ______

mean score, Team *B*: ______

Comparison: ____________________

____

2. The dot plots show the ages of members of two glee clubs.

Ages of School Glee Club Members

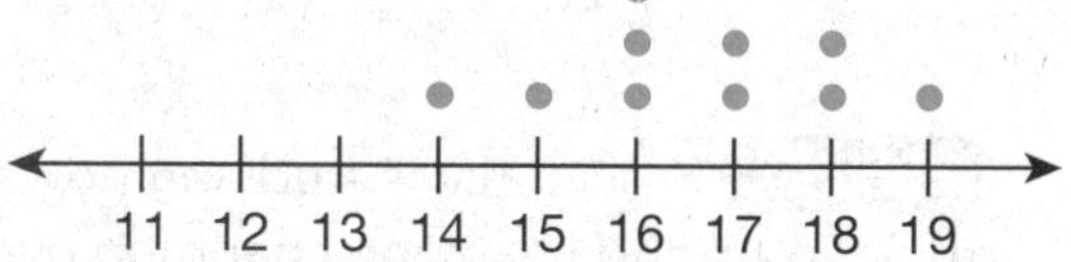

Ages of All-County Glee Club Members

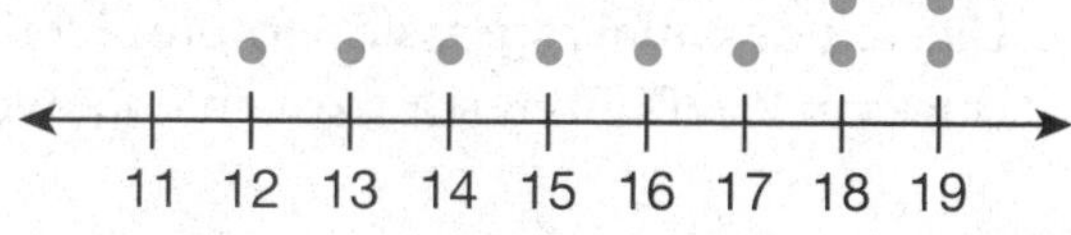

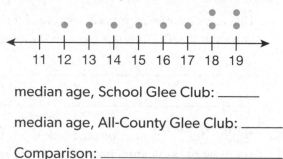

median age, School Glee Club: ______

median age, All-County Glee Club: ______

Comparison: ____________________

____

Use the information below for questions 3 and 4.

The ages of volunteers working at a food bank are shown below.

12, 70, 25, 27, 13, 31, 20, 62, 33, 20, 15, 48, 35, 16, 21, 24, 19, 39, 45, 19, 53, 19

3. Create a histogram for the data, using the intervals shown on the graph.

4. Describe the type of distribution shown.

____

Ages of Food Bank Volunteers

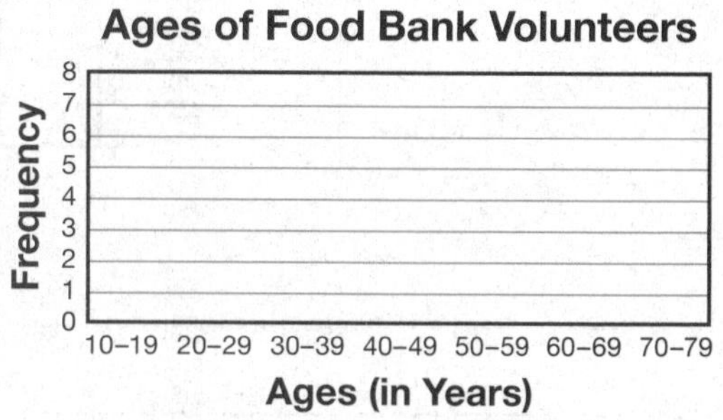

Calculate the standard deviation for each data set. Round your answers to the nearest tenth.

5. 4, 10, 15, 19
$\overline{x} = 12$

______

6. 21, 29, 33, 64, 73
$\overline{x} = 44$

______

7. 2, 4, 5, 5, 6
$\overline{x} = 4.4$

______

Use the information below and the two-way frequency table on the right for questions 8–10.

At Sam's high school, students are required to take social studies for three years. Sam asked fellow high school students and their parents if they supported a proposal to require students to take social studies every year of high school.

	Every Year	Not Every Year	Total
Parents	70	34	104
Students	28	68	96
Total	98	102	200

8. Use the table to create a two-way relative frequency table based on the total number of people surveyed.

	Every Year	Not Every Year	Total
Parents			
Students			
Total			

9. Identify and interpret the marginal frequencies for the table you created.

____

____

10. Identify and interpret the conditional frequencies for the table you created.

____

____

For questions 11–13, according to the given correlation coefficient, describe the linear association of two variables as *positive* or *negative* and as *strong* or *weak*.

11. $r = -0.992$ ______________

12. $r = 0.289$ ______________

13. $r = 0.865$ ______________

Use the information and graphs below for question 14.

Sarah and Gabe each conducted the same psychology experiment involving memory. They recorded their data in these scatter plots. Their lines of fit are identical.

a.

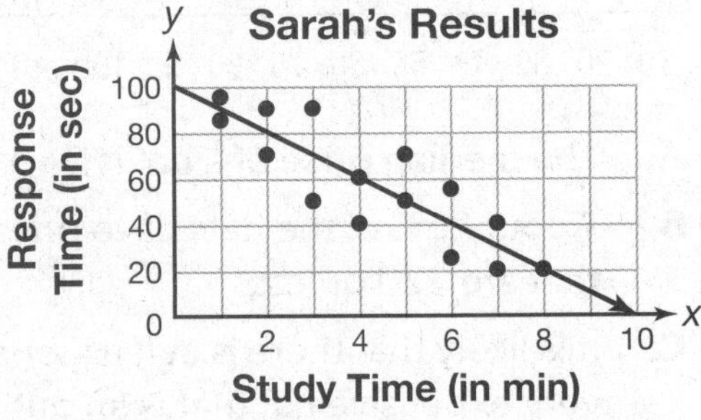

b.

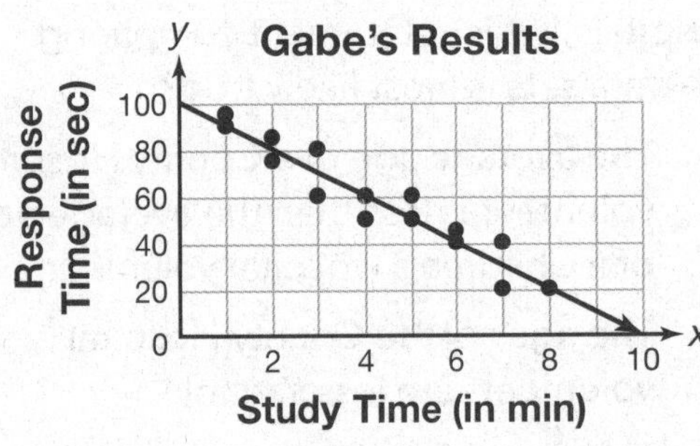

14. Which line is a better fit for the data it models? How did you determine your answer?

____

Choose the best answer.

15. The scatter plot compares the number of bags of popcorn sold and the number of beverages sold at a movie theater each day over two weeks. Which conclusion can be drawn from the scatter plot?

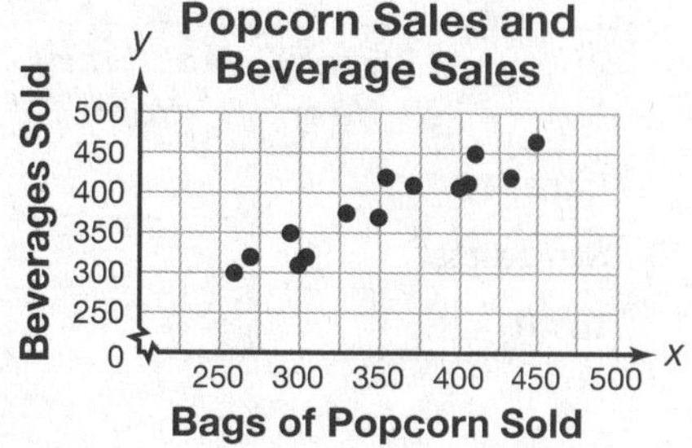

A. There is a negative correlation between popcorn sales and beverage sales.

B. There is a positive correlation between popcorn sales and beverage sales.

C. There is no correlation between popcorn sales and beverage sales.

D. Buying popcorn causes people to buy beverages.

16. Which measure or measures of center would be best to use if you wanted to compare the average amount of time that Johanna and Latifah exercise in a typical week?

Daily Exercise over One Week (in minutes)

Johanna	20, 20, 30, 35, 40
Latifah	20, 20, 25, 25, 100

A. Median would be the best measure of center.

B. Mean would be the best measure of center.

C. Median and mean would be equally good measures of center.

D. Neither the mean nor the median would be a good measure of center.

17. The mean age of all volunteers at Children's Hospital is 25, and the standard deviation for the ages is 2. The mean age of all volunteers at County Hospital is also 25, but the standard deviation is 5.6. If there are about the same number of volunteers at both hospitals, which statement comparing the data sets is most likely true?

A. The average age of a County Hospital volunteer is less than the average age of a Children's Hospital volunteer.

B. The ages of the County Hospital volunteers are less variable.

C. The ages of the County Hospital volunteers are more variable.

D. The ages of volunteers at both hospitals are equally variable.

18. The box plot below shows the prices of the hats for sale. Which statement about the prices is **not** true?

Hat Prices (in dollars)

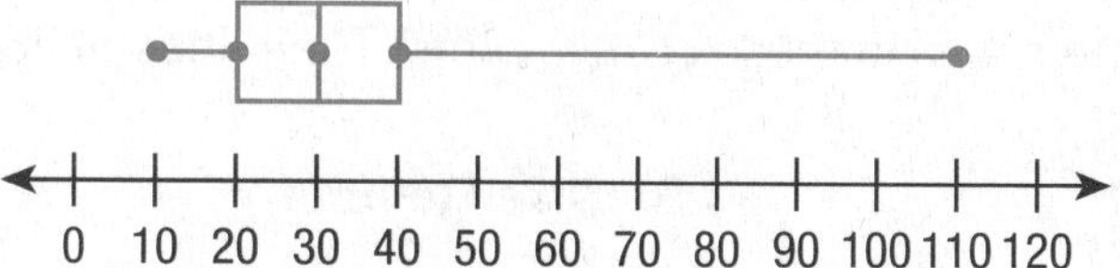

A. The median price of a hat is \$40.

B. About 25% of the hats have prices that are \$20 or less.

C. It is likely that there is at least one very expensive hat that is an outlier.

D. The prices of most hats are close to the median and not very variable.

Use the information and table below for questions 19 and 20.

The owner of several bookstores wanted to know what happened to book sales over time after an anticipated book's release date. She collected data from her stores. Her data are shown below.

Weeks Since Release	1	2	2	2	3	3	4	4	5
Copies Sold	56	60	52	48	52	40	48	40	40

19. Use the grid on the right to create a scatter plot for the data. Eyeball the scatter plot and draw a line to fit the data. Describe the relationship shown by the scatter plot.

____

20. Identify the slope and the *y*-intercept of the line you drew. What do they represent in this situation?

____

____

Solve.

21. PREDICT A hotel added several large banquet halls 6 years ago. The table shows the number of events hosted at the hotel since the banquet halls opened.

Years Since Opening	Number of Events
1	10
2	19
3	32
4	52
5	80
6	130

Use your calculator to perform an exponential regression for these data. Use your model to predict the number of events that will be held in 2 years (8 years since the halls opened).

____

22. ASSESS Students in Mr. Jackson's 3rd and 4th period world history classes took the same test. Their scores are listed in the table below from least to greatest.

3rd period	81, 87, 87, 88, 90, 91, 92, 92, 93, 94, 97, 100
4th period	57, 82, 83, 85, 86, 86, 88, 89, 91, 91, 91, 94, 98

For which class is standard deviation a more accurate measure of spread? For which class is IQR a more accurate measure? Explain.

____

____

____

____

Performance Task

Make It BIG

Materials: graphing calculator

Working in small groups or individually, pretend that you and some friends have started up a band and are trying to make it big. However, making money while making music is harder than you might think.

1. What is the name of your band? What style of music does your band play?

2. One of your bandmates says she got a very good deal on a new guitar. She spent \$199. Below are the prices of similar new guitars at a local store. Identify the first quartile, median, and third quartile of the data. Then create a box plot of these data.

\$200, \$220, \$150, \$300, \$250, \$280, \$350, \$180, \$200, \$300

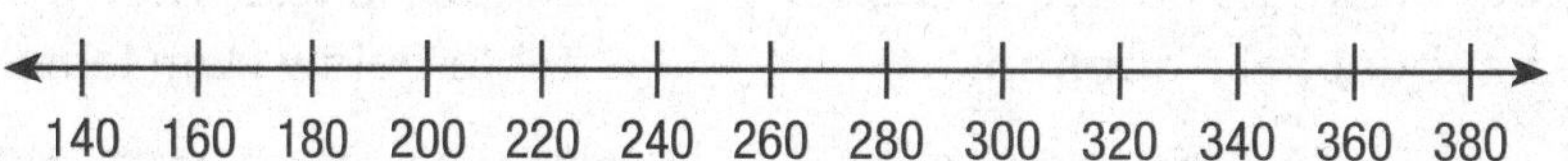

3. Compare the amount your bandmate paid for the guitar to the box plot above. Did she get a very good deal, an average deal, or a not very good deal? Explain.

Another way to earn money is by selling CDs at your shows, but how much should you charge for a CD? You decide to experiment and vary the price at each show. You then record how many CDs are sold at each show.

Price, in dollars (x)	5	8	10	12	15	20
CDs Sold (y)	20	16	15	11	5	1

4. What type of correlation do you think these data show and why?

5. Create a scatter plot of the data in the table.

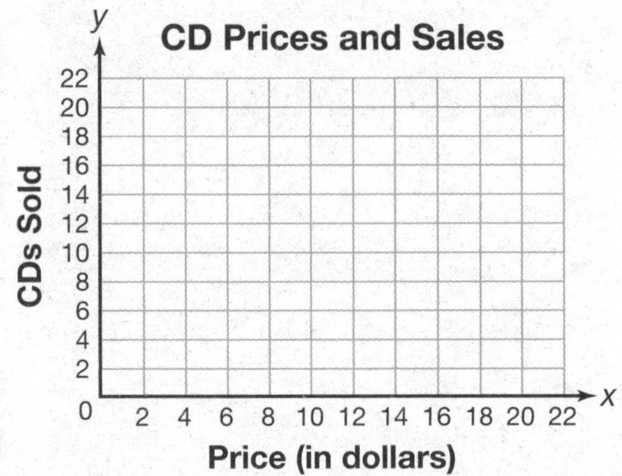

6. Use a calculator to find the equation of a line of best fit to model the data. Then graph the line of best fit on the scatter plot above. How good a fit is the line?

7. Based on your equation and your line of best fit, how many CDs do you predict you would sell if you set the price at $14? Explain or show your work.

8. Do you think a higher price causes fewer people to buy CDs? What other factors might affect how many CDs you sell?

Grade 8

Expressions & Equations

Understand connections between proportional relationships, lines, and linear equations.

Analyze and solve linear equations and pairs of simultaneous linear equations.

Functions

Define, evaluate, and compare functions.

Algebra I

Algebra

Seeing Structure in Expressions

Interpret the structure of expressions.

Write expressions in equivalent forms to solve problems.

Arithmetic with Polynomials and Rational Expressions

Perform arithmetic operations on polynomials.

Creating Equations

Create equations that describe numbers or relationships.

Reasoning with Equations and Inequalities

Solve equations and inequalities in one variable.

Solve systems of equations.

Geometry & Algebra II

Number and Quantity

The Complex Number System

Perform arithmetic operations with complex numbers.

Use complex numbers in polynomial identities and equations.

Algebra

Seeing Structure in Expressions

Interpret the structure of expressions.

Arithmetic with Polynomials and Rational Expressions

Perform arithmetic operations on polynomials.

Understand the relationship between zeros and factors of polynomials.

Use polynomial identities to solve problems.

Rewrite rational expressions.

Reasoning with Equations and Inequalities

Understand solving equations as a process of reasoning and explain the reasoning.

Functions

Interpreting Functions

Analyze functions using different representations.

Geometry

Expressing Geometric Properties with Equations

Translate between the geometric description and the equation for a conic section.

Unit 4
Expressions and Equations

Lesson 31 Polynomials 246

Lesson 32 Interpreting Complex Expressions 252

Lesson 33 Writing Equivalent Polynomial and Exponential Equations 258

Lesson 34 Writing and Graphing Quadratic Equations and Inequalities 268

Lesson 35 Solving Quadratic Equations 278

Lesson 36 Solving Linear-Quadratic Systems 286

Unit 4 Review 292

Unit 4 Performance Task 296

LESSON 31 Polynomials

UNDERSTAND A **polynomial** consists of constants and variables joined together by addition, subtraction, and/or multiplication. The constants and variables are grouped into one or more terms, each of which can be an individual number, a single variable, or a product of numbers and/or variables with exponents that are non-negative integers.

The polynomial $6ab + 9 - 14c^{10}$ has three terms. The first term, $6ab$, is joined to the second term, 9, through addition. The third term, $14c^{10}$, is joined to the other terms through subtraction. Or you could say that the term $-14c^{10}$ is added to the other terms.

The expression $200 \cdot 7^t - 1$ is not a polynomial because the first term contains a variable, t, in the exponent. This is an exponential expression. The expression $7fg^{-1}$ is not a polynomial because it has a negative exponent. This is equal to $\frac{7f}{g}$, which is a rational expression.

UNDERSTAND Polynomials with 1, 2, or 3 terms can be grouped into categories.

- A **monomial** is a polynomial having only 1 term, such as $12xy^3$.
- A **binomial** is a polynomial having exactly 2 terms, such as $y^2 + 4$.
- A **trinomial** is a polynomial having exactly 3 terms, such as $4x^4 - \frac{1}{6}x + 11$.

Polynomials can also be categorized according to their **degree**. The degree of a monomial with one variable is equal to the value of the variable's exponent. The monomial $5t^3$ has degree 3. The degree of a polynomial is equal to the highest degree of its terms. The three terms of the polynomial $x^5 - 3x^2 + 4$ have degrees 5, 2, and 0, respectively, so this polynomial is of degree 5.

UNDERSTAND The standard form of a polynomial contains no like terms. For example, the expression $2x^2 + 3x - x - 7$ simplifies to $2x^2 + 2x - 7$. The like terms, $3x$ and $-x$, can be combined by using the distributive property.

If a polynomial has more than one degree, express it in standard form by writing its terms in descending order of degree. In other words, the exponents should go from greatest to least. For example, the polynomial $4 + 5a^3 - 2a^6 - 3a$ written in standard form is $-2a^6 + 5a^3 - 3a + 4$.

UNDERSTAND The set of integers is a collection of every integer number. You know that whenever you add or subtract two integers, the result is also an integer. The product of any two integers is also an integer. The set of integers is said to be closed under addition, subtraction, and multiplication.

The set of polynomials includes every possible polynomial. When any two polynomials are added or subtracted, the result is always a polynomial. Multiplying two polynomials together also always produces a polynomial. Like the set of integers, the set of polynomials is closed under addition, subtraction, and multiplication.

Connect

Add the polynomials and write the sum in standard form: $(9x - 2x^2 + 13) + (7x^2 + 1 - 3x)$.

1 Use properties of addition to group like terms together.

$(9x - 2x^2 + 13) + (7x^2 + 1 - 3x)$	Use the associative property to remove parentheses.
$9x - 2x^2 + 13 + 7x^2 + 1 - 3x$	Use the commutative property to reorder the terms.
$9x - 3x - 2x^2 + 7x^2 + 13 + 1$	Use the associative property to insert parentheses.
$(9x - 3x) + (-2x^2 + 7x^2) + (13 + 1)$	

2 Combine like terms.

Use the distributive property to combine like terms.

$(9x - 3x) + (-2x^2 + 7x^2) + (13 + 1)$

$(9 - 3)x + (-2 + 7)x^2 + (13 + 1)$

$6x + 5x^2 + 14$

3 Rewrite the result in standard form.

The term with the highest degree is $5x^2$. The term with the next-highest degree is $6x$. The constant term will be last.

▶ The sum is the polynomial $5x^2 + 6x + 14$.

Find the difference of the polynomials and write your answer in standard form: $(4a^2 - 6a + 2) - (a^2 - 5)$.

1 Group like terms together.

Since the second polynomial is being subtracted, be sure to distribute the negative sign to both terms in the binomial.

$(4a^2 - 6a + 2) - (a^2 - 5)$

$4a^2 - 6a + 2 - a^2 + 5$

$4a^2 - a^2 - 6a + 2 + 5$

$(4a^2 - a^2) - 6a + (2 + 5)$

2 Combine like terms.

$(4a^2 - a^2) - 6a + (2 + 5)$
$3a^2 - 6a + 7$

Note that this is already in standard form.

▶ The difference is the polynomial $3a^2 - 6a + 7$.

Find the difference.
$(6b^3 + b^2 + 14) - (-3b^3 - 9b)$

EXAMPLE A Find the product: $(2z + 3)(8z^4 + 3z + 7)$.

1 Apply the distributive property.

You can distribute the trinomial to each term in the binomial.

$(2z + 3)(8z^4 + 3z + 7)$

$2z(8z^4 + 3z + 7) + 3(8z^4 + 3z + 7)$

2 Multiply the first term in the binomial by each term in the trinomial.

Distribute 2z to each term in the trinomial. Remember: When multiplying exponential terms with the same base, add the exponents.

$2z(8z^4 + 3z + 7) + 3(8z^4 + 3z + 7)$

$2z(8z^4) + 2z(3z) + 2z(7) + 3(8z^4 + 3z + 7)$

$16z^5 + 6z^2 + 14z + 3(8z^4 + 3z + 7)$

3 Multiply the second term in the binomial by each term in the trinomial.

Distribute 3 to each term in the trinomial.

$16z^5 + 6z^2 + 14z + 3(8z^4 + 3z + 7)$

$16z^5 + 6z^2 + 14z + 3(8z^4) + 3(3z) + 3(7)$

$16z^5 + 6z^2 + 14z + 24z^4 + 9z + 21$

4 Combine like terms.

Reorder the terms so that they are in descending order of degree. Place like terms together.

$16z^5 + 6z^2 + 14z + 24z^4 + 9z + 21$

$16z^5 + 24z^4 + 6z^2 + (14z + 9z) + 21$

$16z^5 + 24z^4 + 6z^2 + 23z - 21$

▶ The product is the polynomial $16z^5 + 24z^4 + 6z^2 + 23z - 21$.

DISCUSS

The set of polynomials is closed under addition, subtraction, and multiplication. This means that the sum, difference, and product of polynomials is always a polynomial. Is the set closed under division? Consider the example $(3x^2 + 1) \div x$.

EXAMPLE B The rectangle shown below has length $3x + 1$ and width $2x$. Find expressions for its perimeter and area, and confirm that each is a polynomial.

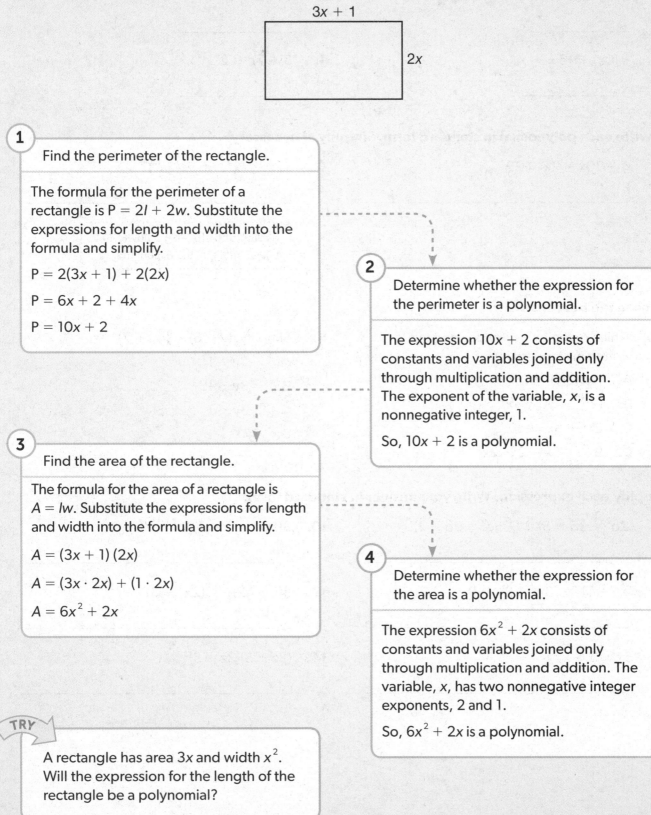

$3x + 1$

$2x$

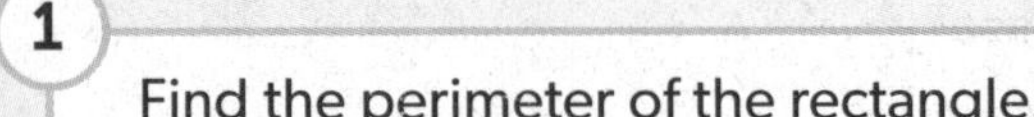

1 Find the perimeter of the rectangle.

The formula for the perimeter of a rectangle is $P = 2l + 2w$. Substitute the expressions for length and width into the formula and simplify.

$P = 2(3x + 1) + 2(2x)$

$P = 6x + 2 + 4x$

$P = 10x + 2$

2 Determine whether the expression for the perimeter is a polynomial.

The expression $10x + 2$ consists of constants and variables joined only through multiplication and addition. The exponent of the variable, x, is a nonnegative integer, 1.

So, $10x + 2$ is a polynomial.

3 Find the area of the rectangle.

The formula for the area of a rectangle is $A = lw$. Substitute the expressions for length and width into the formula and simplify.

$A = (3x + 1)(2x)$

$A = (3x \cdot 2x) + (1 \cdot 2x)$

$A = 6x^2 + 2x$

4 Determine whether the expression for the area is a polynomial.

The expression $6x^2 + 2x$ consists of constants and variables joined only through multiplication and addition. The variable, x, has two nonnegative integer exponents, 2 and 1.

So, $6x^2 + 2x$ is a polynomial.

TRY

A rectangle has area $3x$ and width x^2. Will the expression for the length of the rectangle be a polynomial?

Practice

Write *yes* if the expression is a polynomial and *no* if it is not.

1. $3x^2 + 2x - 7^{-2x}$

____

2. $13a^2b + 9c$

____

3. $-10z^7 + 16\frac{1}{2}$

____

4. $5 + 7p - 2^p$

____

Rewrite each polynomial in standard form. Simplify, if necessary.

5. $x^3 + 10x - 2x^6 + 12$

____

6. $12x + 7x^2 - 6 + (2x^2)^4$

____

REMEMBER To raise a power to a power, multiply the exponents.

Choose the best answer.

7. Which of the following polynomials is written in standard form?

A. $8x + 11x^2$

B. $(x^2)^3 - 90x + x^5$

C. $2x^4 + 8x^3 + 10$

D. $9x^2 + 5x - 2 - 2x^2$

8. Simplify: $(y - 6) - (4y + 7)$

A. $-3y - 1$

B. $-3y - 13$

C. $-3y + 1$

D. $3y + 1$

Simplify each expression. Write your answer in standard form.

9. $(2a^2 - 3a + 5) + (-5a^2 + 9a - 2)$

____

10. $3(5b^2 - 1) + 2(2b^2 - 7b + 10)$

____

11. $(2y + 11) - (3y^2 + 2y - 1)$

____

12. $8(x^2 - 2) - 3(2x^2 + 3)$

____

13. $6x^2y(3 - xy^4)$

____

14. $(3z + 5)(3z - 5)$

____

Simplify each expression and determine whether the result is a polynomial. Write *yes* if the expression is a polynomial and *no* if it is not. If it is not a polynomial, explain why not.

15. $(3ab^2 + 1)(a - 2)$

____

____

16. $\frac{1}{2}(4xy - 12y) - (3^y + 1)$

____

____

Solve.

17. The diagram below shows an unshaded square inside a shaded square.

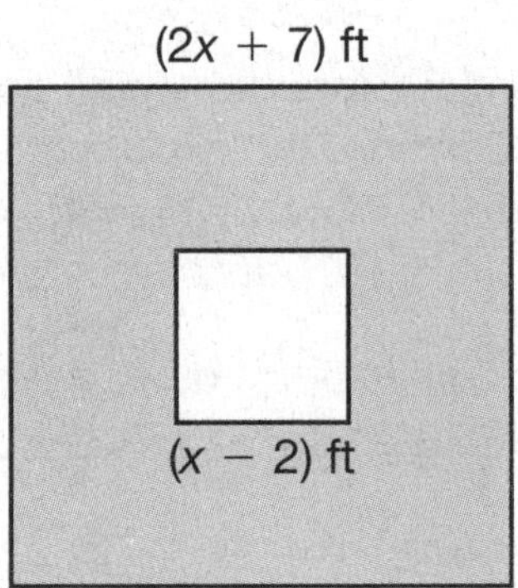

What is the area of the large square (including the unshaded region)? ______________

What is the area of the smaller unshaded square? ______________

What is the area of the shaded region inside the larger square? ______________

18. PREDICT Will the product of $7p^3r + 2r$ and $16s^2 - 3st$ be a polynomial? How do you know?

____

____

19. CREATE Create a polynomial using the variable q. Write it in standard form.

____

Interpreting Complex Expressions

UNDERSTAND A **quadratic expression** is a polynomial expression in which the highest degree of the variable is 2. The standard form for a quadratic expression is $ax^2 + bx + c$, where $a \neq 0$.

In real-world situations, quadratic expressions may represent situations in which the rate of change itself is changing in a predictable way. Consider the quadratic expression $\frac{1}{2}at^2 + vt + d$. The constant term d is some initial value, such as the distance that a sprinter is from a finish line at time $t = 0$. The constant coefficient v is the initial value of the rate of change, such as the sprinter's speed at time $t = 0$. The constant coefficient $\frac{1}{2}a$ describes how that rate of change changes. For example, a might be the constant acceleration of the sprinter as he or she runs toward the finish line.

UNDERSTAND Recall that an exponential expression has a constant base raised either to a variable or to a variable expression. Consider the exponential expression $a \cdot b^{dx} + c$. The parameter in the exponent, d, alters the factor by which the quantity changes. The factor, or percent rate of change, is no longer simply b, but b^d.

If t is a variable for time, an expression of the form $a(3)^{2t}$ describes a quantity that triples every half hour. You can see this by substituting $\frac{1}{2}$ into the expression.

$$a(3)^{2\left(\frac{1}{2}\right)} = a(3)^1 = a(3)$$

Using the power of a power property, you can see that this situation is equivalent to a quantity being multiplied by 9 every hour.

$$a(3)^{2t} = a(3^2)^t = a(9)^t$$

An expression of the form $a(3)^{\frac{t}{2}}$ describes a quantity that triples every two hours. You can see this by substituting 2 into the expression.

$$a(3)^{\frac{2}{2}} = a(3)^1 = a(3)$$

Recall that expressions containing fractional exponents can be translated into radical expressions. Using the power of a power property, you can see that this situation is equivalent to a quantity being multiplied by $\sqrt{3}$ every hour.

$$a(3)^{\frac{t}{2}} = a(3^{\frac{1}{2}})^t = a(\sqrt{3})^t$$

Connect

Interpret the constant, linear, and quadratic terms in each equation below given the context.

a. A ball is thrown with an upward initial velocity of 12 feet per second from a cliff 40 feet high. The ball's height t seconds after it is thrown is described by the equation $-16t^2 + 12t + 40$.

b. A ball is dropped from a platform that is 25 feet tall. At time t seconds after it is dropped, the height of the ball in feet is described by the equation $-16t^2 + 25$.

c. A ball is launched upward at a speed of 35 feet per second from a machine on the ground. The ball's height after t seconds is described by the equation $-16t^2 + 35t$.

1

Examine the constant terms.

In scenario a, the constant term, 40, corresponds to the initial height of the ball above the ground, 40 feet. In scenario b, the constant term is 25. The building is 25 feet tall, so this is also the initial height of the ball. In scenario c, no constant term is shown, so the constant term is 0. The ball is launched from the ground, so its initial height is 0 feet off the ground.

▶ The constant term gives the initial height of the object.

2

Examine the linear terms.

In scenario a, the coefficient of the linear term corresponds to the initial velocity of the ball, 12 feet per second upward. In scenario b, no linear term is shown, so the linear term is $0t$. The ball is dropped, so its initial velocity is 0 feet per second. In scenario c, the coefficient of the linear term is the ball's initial velocity when launched, 35 feet per second upward.

▶ The coefficient of t gives the initial velocity of the object, or the velocity at time $t = 0$.

3

Examine the quadratic terms.

All of the expressions begin with the term $-16t^2$. The coefficient, -16, is related to each ball's acceleration, or change in velocity. Gravity is pulling each ball downward, causing it to accelerate. In situation b, for example, the ball begins to fall very slowly. By the time it hits the ground, it is falling at a much faster speed, because gravity has caused it to accelerate. The coefficient is negative because down is considered the negative direction, while up is the positive direction.

▶ The coefficient of t^2 relates to the object's acceleration, in this case due to gravity.

TRY

After a rock is thrown, its height above the ground, in feet, is given by the expression $-16t^2 + 48t + 50$. Interpret the constants in the expression.

EXAMPLE A A rectangular quilt has a length of 5 feet and a width of 3 feet. Squares will be added to the quilt, so that both its width and its length will increase by x feet. The are of the enlarged quilt is given by the product $(5 + x)(3 + x)$. Find a polynomial expression for the area of the enlarged quilt and interpret the expression's terms.

1 Interpret the factors of the product.

The factor $(5 + x)$ is the new length of the quilt, which results from adding x feet to the original 5-foot length.

The factor $(3 + x)$ is the new width of the quilt, which results from adding x feet to the original 3-foot width.

2 Calculate a polynomial for the new area.

To find the area, multiply the length by the width.

$(5 + x)(3 + x)$

$15 + 5x + 3x + x^2$

$x^2 + 8x + 15$

▶ The area of the enlarged quilt will be $x^2 + 8x + 15$ square feet.

3 Interpret the terms of the area expression.

Draw a picture of the enlarged quilt.

The constant term, 15, represents the area of the original quilt, which is included in the enlarged quilt.

The linear term $8x$ is the sum of $5x$ and $3x$, which represent rectangular sections of the enlarged quilt that are adjacent to the original quilt.

The quadratic term, x^2, represents the square section in the far corner of the enlarged quilt.

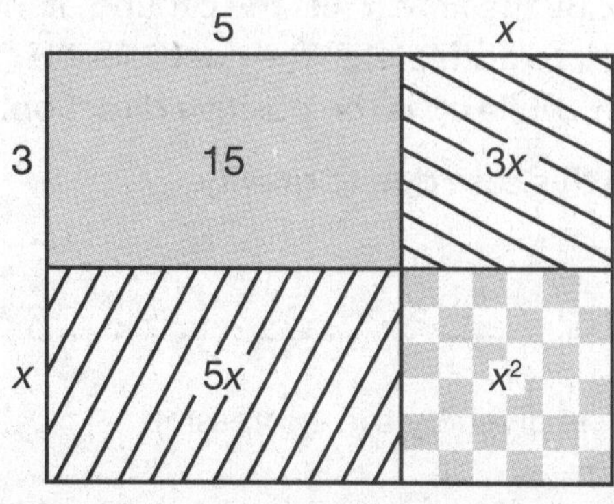

TRY

A square poster has side length b. The poster will be enlarged so that its dimensions are tripled. Find an expression for the area of the enlarged poster and interpret the parameters of the expression.

EXAMPLE B Recall that the half-life of a substance is the time it takes for half of that substance to break down or decay. The formula for the amount of a decaying substance that remains at time t is $N_0\left(\frac{1}{2}\right)^{\frac{t}{t_{\frac{1}{2}}}}$ where N_0 is the initial amount of an element, $t_{\frac{1}{2}}$ is the half-life of the element, and t is the variable for time. The half-life for argon–41 is 2 hours. Write and simplify an expression for the amount of argon–41 remaining from an initial sample at time t. How much will remain of a 100-gram argon-41 sample after 1 hour?

1 Substitute the given information into the formula and simplify.

Since the half-life of argon–41 is 2 hours, the variable t should be given in hours as well. So, let $t_{\frac{1}{2}} = 2$.

$N_0\left(\frac{1}{2}\right)^{\frac{t}{t_{\frac{1}{2}}}}$ Substitute the value of $t_{\frac{1}{2}}$.

$N_0\left(\frac{1}{2}\right)^{\frac{t}{2}}$ Apply the power of a power property to separate the exponent.

$N_0\left(\left(\frac{1}{2}\right)^{\frac{1}{2}}\right)^t$ Convert the expression to a radical.

$N_0\left(\sqrt{\frac{1}{2}}\right)^t$

2 Interpret the expression.

The amount of argon–41 remaining at time t is equal to $N_0\left(\sqrt{\frac{1}{2}}\right)^t$.

This means that, for each hour that passes, the amount in the sample is multiplied by $\sqrt{\frac{1}{2}}$.

3 Determine how much of a 100-gram argon–41 sample will remain after 1 hour.

Substitute 100 for N_0 and 1 for t in the above expression.

$100 \cdot \left(\sqrt{\frac{1}{2}}\right)^1 \approx 70.7$

▶ There will be approximately 70.7 grams of argon-41 remaining after 1 hour.

On your calculator, enter $100 \div \sqrt{2}$ to find the amount of argon-41 that remains after 1 hour. Then, without pushing any other buttons, divide the answer on your calculator by $\sqrt{2}$ again. What result do you get? How does this relate to argon–41's half-life?

Practice

Determine an expression to represent each situation.

1. A cannonball was launched with an initial upward velocity of 55 feet per second from a tower 28 feet off the ground. The height of the ball above the ground, in feet, can be modeled by an expression having the form $-16t^2 + bt + c$, where t is the number of seconds since the cannonball was launched.

What is the value of b, the coefficient of t? __________

What is the value of c, the constant term? __________

Therefore, the expression for the height of the ball at time t is ______________________.

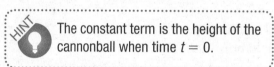

HINT: The constant term is the height of the cannonball when time $t = 0$.

2. The half-life of acetaminophen in a person's body is about 3 hours. Suppose someone takes a dose of 650 mg at 3 P.M. The amount of the drug left in his or her system h hours after taking it can be expressed by $N_0\left(\frac{1}{2}\right)^{\frac{h}{h_{\frac{1}{2}}}}$.

What is the value of N_0? ________ What is the value of $h_{\frac{1}{2}}$? ________

Therefore, the expression is ____________________.

Interpret the parts of the expressions.

3. A penny was dropped off the top of a building. Its height, in feet, t seconds after being dropped is given by the expression $-16t^2 + 70$. What was the height of the building? ________

4. To make a sign, a student cut off a small square piece from a posterboard. She cut x inches from the width of the posterboard and $2x$ inches from its length. The area of the original posterboard, in square inches, can be represented by the quadratic expression $2x^2 + 24x + 64$.

What was the area, in square inches, of the sign? __________

5. The enrollment at a new school increases at a constant percent rate. After y years, the number of students enrolled is given by the expression $52 \cdot 3^{\frac{y}{5}}$.

How many students did the school have when it opened? __________

After how many years does the number of students triple? __________

By what factor does enrollment increase from one year to the next? Express your answer as a real number in radical form. __________

Choose the best answer.

6. A population of deer doubles every three years. In 2010, there were 35 deer. Which of the following gives the number of deer y years after 2010?

   A. $35 \cdot 2^{\frac{y}{3}}$ B. $35 \cdot \left(\frac{1}{2}\right)^{\frac{y}{3}}$

   C. $35 \cdot 2^{3y}$ D. $35 \cdot 3^{\frac{y}{2}}$

7. The half life of radon-219 is approximately 4 seconds. Which best represents the amount of a 50-gram sample of radon-219 that would remain after t seconds?

   A. $50 \cdot \left(\frac{1}{2}\right)^t$ B. $50 \cdot \left(\sqrt[4]{\frac{1}{2}}\right)^t$

   C. $\sqrt[4]{50} \cdot \left(\frac{1}{2}\right)^t$ D. $50 \cdot \left(\frac{1}{8}\right)^t$

Solve.

8. The ring shown on the right has an inner radius of 2 centimeters and a thickness of a centimeters. Find an expression for the area of the ring (the shaded portion). ______________

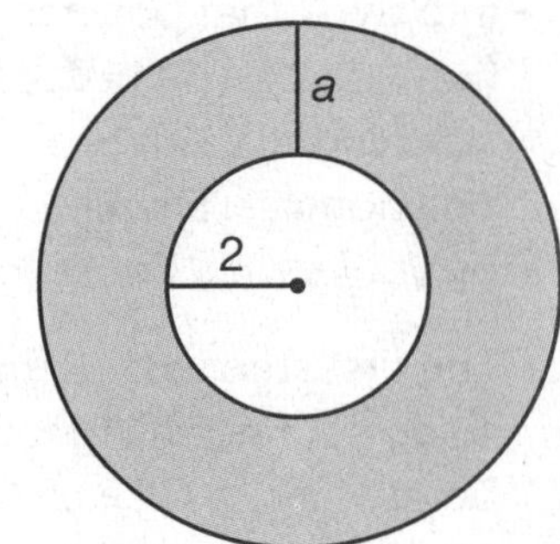

9. COMPARE Two arrows were shot by two archers. The red arrow's height, in feet, t seconds after being shot is described by the expression $-16t^2 + 260t + 5$. The blue arrow's height, in feet, t seconds after being shot is described by the expression $-16t^2 + 300t + 4$.

   Which arrow was fired from a greater height? ______________

   What was that height? ______________

   Which arrow was fired with a greater initial upward velocity? ______________

   What was that upward velocity? ______________

10. IDENTIFY The number of cows on a ranch can be described by the expression $14 \cdot 2^{\frac{y}{5}}$, and the number of sheep on the ranch can be described by the expression $21 \cdot 2^{2y}$. In both equations, y is the number of years since the ranch purchased the initial herds. Identify each herd's doubling time, or the amount of time it takes for the herd to double in size.

    ____

    ____

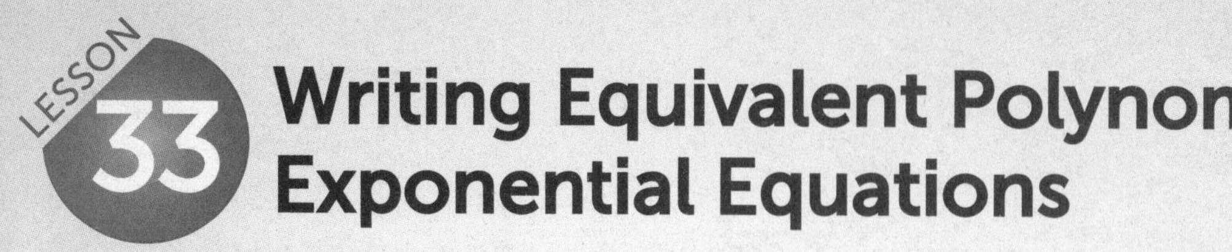

LESSON 33 Writing Equivalent Polynomial and Exponential Equations

Factoring Quadratic Expressions

UNDERSTAND Multiplying two linear binomial expressions results in a quadratic expression.

$$(2x + 1)(3x - 5) = 6x^2 - 7x - 5$$

Notice that the product of these two binomials simplified to a trinomial.

UNDERSTAND Multiplying two numbers yields a product. The reverse of this process is separating a number into factors. For example, the number 20 can be separated into $4 \cdot 5$. The **prime factorization** of a number is the string of **prime numbers** which, when multiplied, yield that number. The prime factorization of 20 is $2^2 \cdot 5$.

Polynomials also have prime factorizations. A polynomial is prime if it cannot be factored into two other polynomials. The polynomial $6x^2 - 7x - 5$ has the prime factorization $(2x + 1)(3x - 5)$ because both of these binomial factors cannot be factored further. The factors of a polynomial can be numbers, variables, or expressions. There are several methods of factoring polynomials. Examples in this lesson will demonstrate some of these methods. When factoring on your own, choose the method with which you are most comfortable.

The first step in factoring is always to factor out any numbers or variables common to all terms. To do so, find the greatest common factor (GCF) of all of the terms. The terms in the expression below have a GCF of $2x$.

$$12x^3 - 14x^2 - 10x = 2x(6x^2 - 7x - 5)$$

From the multiplication performed at the top of this page, you know that $(2x + 1)$ and $(3x - 5)$ are the factors of $6x^2 - 7x - 5$.

$$2(6x^2 - 7x - 5) = 2(2x + 1)(3x - 5)$$

Neither of these binomials can be factored further, so this is the prime factorization of the polynomial. Not all trinomials can be factored. For example, $x^2 + x + 1$ is a prime polynomial.

UNDERSTAND If you memorize the forms of some special polynomials, you can write their factorizations without going through the steps above.

	Polynomial	Factorization
Square of a sum	$a^2 + 2ab + b^2$	$(a + b)^2$
Square of a difference	$a^2 - 2ab + b^2$	$(a - b)^2$
Difference of squares	$a^2 - b^2$	$(a + b)(a - b)$
Sum of cubes	$a^3 + b^3$	$(a + b)(a^2 - ab + b^2)$
Difference of cubes	$a^3 - b^3$	$(a - b)(a^2 + ab + b^2)$

Connect

Factor the quadratic expression $8x^2 - 20x - 12$ into its prime factors.

1

Factor out any constant and/or variable factors common to all of the terms.

Each term is evenly divisible by 4.

$$8x^2 - 20x - 12 = 4(2x^2 - 5x - 3)$$

The trinomial $2x^2 - 5x - 3$ has the form $ax^2 + bx + c$ with $a = 2$, $b = -5$, and $c = -3$. Factor this trinomial, if possible.

2

Find the factors of a and of c.

The prime factorization of $2x^2 - 5x - 3$ will have the form $(mx + p)(nx + q)$.

$(mx + p)(nx + q)$

$mnx^2 + mqx + npx + pq$

$mnx^2 + (mq + np)x + pq$

The constants m and n are factors of a. The constants p and q are factors of c.

The quadratic term has the coefficient 2. Find the factor pairs of 2. The possible values of m, n are 1, 2 and 2, 1.

The constant term is -3. The possible values of p, q are $-1, 3$; $1, -3$; $3, -1$ and $-3, 1$.

3

Determine which factor pairs combine to yield b.

The coefficient of the linear term, b, is equivalent to $mq + np$. For this polynomial, $b = -5$. So, find the factor pairs for which $mq + np = -5$. Be careful that you substitute the correct values for p and q.

m, n	p, q	$mq + np$
1, 2	$-1, 3$	$(1)(3) + (2)(-1) = 1$
	$1, -3$	$(1)(-3) + (2)(1) = -1$
	$3, -1$	$(1)(-1) + (2)(3) = 5$
	$-3, 1$	$(1)(1) + (2)(-3) = -5$ ✓

4

Substitute the values for m, n, p, and q.

Based on the table, $m = 1$, $n = 2$, $p = -3$, and $q = 1$. Substitute these into $4(mx + p)(nx + q)$.

$$4(1x - 3)(2x + 1)$$

These binomials cannot be factored any further.

▶ The factored form of $8x^2 - 20x - 12$ is $4(x - 3)(2x + 1)$.

TRY

Fully factor the polynomial $3x^2 - 27x + 60$.

Rearranging Equations and Exponents

UNDERSTAND When rearranging quadratic equations, it can be necessary to take the square root of both sides of the equation. Consider solving the quadratic equation $x^2 = 4$ for x.

$x^2 = 4$ — Take the square root of both sides.

$x = \pm\sqrt{4} = \pm 2$

Notice that a $\pm$ (plus-or-minus) sign was added when the square root was taken. Consider that both 2 and -2 are square roots of 4 because $2^2 = 4$ and $(-2)^2 = 4$. When working with numbers, we generally express the square root as the positive value, which is called the **principal square root**. However, the negative value is also a solution.

Examine how to solve the quadratic equation $y = x^2 + 2x + 1$ for x.

$y = x^2 + 2x + 1$	Factor $x^2 + 2x + 1$. Notice that it is a perfect square trinomial.
$y = (x + 1)^2$	Take the square root of both sides.
$\pm\sqrt{y} = x + 1$	Subtract 1 from both sides.
$x = \pm\sqrt{y} - 1$	

This is actually two separate equations: $x = \sqrt{y} - 1$ and $x = -\sqrt{y} - 1$. Taken together, they are equivalent to the original equation, $y = x^2 + 2x + 1$.

Not all trinomials are perfect squares; in fact, some cannot be factored at all. However, equations containing such quadratic trinomials can still be solved for x by using the method of **completing the square**. For an equation $y = ax^2 + bx + c$, this process involves adding $\left(\frac{b}{2a}\right)^2$ to both sides. Consider solving the quadratic equation $y = x^2 + 4x + 1$ for x.

$y = x^2 + 4x + 1$	Subtract 1 from both sides.
$y - 1 = x^2 + 4x$	Add $\left(\frac{4}{2 \cdot 1}\right)^2$, or 4, to both sides.
$y + 3 = x^2 + 4x + 4$	Factor the right side, which is now a perfect square trinomial.
$y + 3 = (x + 2)^2$	Take the square root of both sides.
$\pm\sqrt{y + 3} = x + 2$	Subtract 2 from both sides.
$x = \pm\sqrt{y + 3} - 2$	

UNDERSTAND Exponential expressions and equations can be rewritten by using the properties of exponents, including rational exponents. For example, the power of a power property allows $\left(2^{\frac{1}{3}}\right)^x$ to be rewritten as $2^{\left(\frac{1}{3}\right)x}$, or as $(2^x)^{\frac{1}{3}}$. This allows you to simplify exponential expressions such as $(9^x)^{\frac{1}{2}}$.

$$(9^x)^{\frac{1}{2}} = \left(9^{\frac{1}{2}}\right)^x = (\sqrt{9})^x = 3^x$$

In fact, any expression of the form d^{px} can be rewritten in the form b^x, and vice versa.

$$5^{\frac{1}{3}x} = (\sqrt[3]{5})^x \quad \text{and} \quad 3^x = \left(3^{\frac{1}{2}}\right)^{2x} = (\sqrt{3})^{2x}$$

Connect

A car has an initial speed of 24 m/s and is accelerating at a constant rate of 4 m/s^2. The distance, D, covered by this car is described by the equation $D = \frac{1}{2}(4)t^2 + 24t$, where t is the time in seconds. How long will it take the car to travel 90 meters?

1 Determine the quantity for which to solve.

The equation is given in terms of D, the distance, but the question asks for the time. So, rearrange the equation to isolate the variable t.

2 Begin to isolate t by completing the square.

$D = \frac{1}{2}(4)t^2 + 24t$

$D = 2t^2 + 24t$

In order the complete the square, the coefficient of the squared term must be 1. So, begin by dividing both sides of the equation by 2.

$\frac{1}{2}D = t^2 + 12t$

Now, add a constant to make a perfect square trinomial. The coefficient of t is 12, and half of 12 is 6. So, add 6^2, or 36, to both sides. Then factor the trinomial.

$\frac{1}{2}D + 36 = t^2 + 12t + 36$

$\frac{1}{2}D + 36 = (t + 6)^2$

3 Solve the equation for t.

$\frac{1}{2}D + 36 = (t + 6)^2$ Take the square root of both sides.

$t + 6 = \pm\sqrt{\frac{1}{2}D + 36}$ Subtract 6 from both sides.

$t = \pm\sqrt{\frac{1}{2}D + 36} - 6$

4 Substitute the value of D to determine t.

$D = 90$ meters

$t = \pm\sqrt{\frac{1}{2}(90) + 36} - 6$

$t = \pm\sqrt{45 + 36} - 6$

$t = \pm\sqrt{81} - 6$

$t = \pm 9 - 6$

$t = 3$ or $t = -15$

▶ The car will take 3 seconds to travel 90 meters.

DISCUSS

Why was the second answer, $t = -15$, not a solution?

EXAMPLE A Factor the polynomial $2x^7 - 2x$ completely.

1 Factor out any factors that are common to both terms.

The GCF of the coefficients is 2.

$$2x^7 - 2x = 2(x^7 - x)$$

In the remaining expression, the terms have a common factor of x.

$$2(x^7 - x) = 2x(x^6 - 1)$$

2 Look for special case formulas.

We can rewrite the term x^6 as $(x^3)^2$ using the power of a power property of exponents. Notice that $(x^3)^2$ and 1 are both perfect squares. Therefore, the polynomial $x^6 - 1$ is a difference of squares.

Recall: $a^2 - b^2 = (a + b)(a - b)$. In this case, $a = x^3$ and $b = 1$. Therefore:

$$2x(x^6 - 1) = 2x((x^3)^2 - 1)$$
$$= 2x(x^3 + 1)(x^3 - 1)$$

3 Look for ways to factor the expression further.

Notice that the expression $(x^3 + 1)$ is a sum of cubes and the expression $(x^3 - 1)$ is a difference of cubes. Use the formulas in the table on the first page of this lesson to factor these expressions.

$$2x(x^3 + 1)(x^3 - 1) = 2x(x + 1)(x^2 - x + 1)(x^3 - 1)$$
$$= 2x(x + 1)(x^2 - x + 1)(x - 1)(x^2 + x + 1)$$

None of these expressions can be factored further.

▶ The prime factorization of $2x^7 - 2x$ is $2x(x + 1)(x^2 - x + 1)(x - 1)(x^2 + x + 1)$.

TRY

We factored the binomial $(x^6 - 1)$ by rewriting it as $((x^3)^2 - 1)$, but it could also be rewritten as $((x^2)^3 - 1)$. Factor this binomial as a difference of cubes and compare your answer to the one found above.

EXAMPLE B The general formula to calculate compound interest, A, is $A = P(1 + r)^t$, where P is the principal, r is the interest rate per time period, and t is the number of time periods. A credit card company charges interest of 2% every month on any unpaid balance. The equivalent yearly interest rate is the amount that would be charged on the unpaid balance if it were carried, or remained unpaid, for a year. Find the yearly interest rate that would be equivalent to a monthly interest rate of 2%.

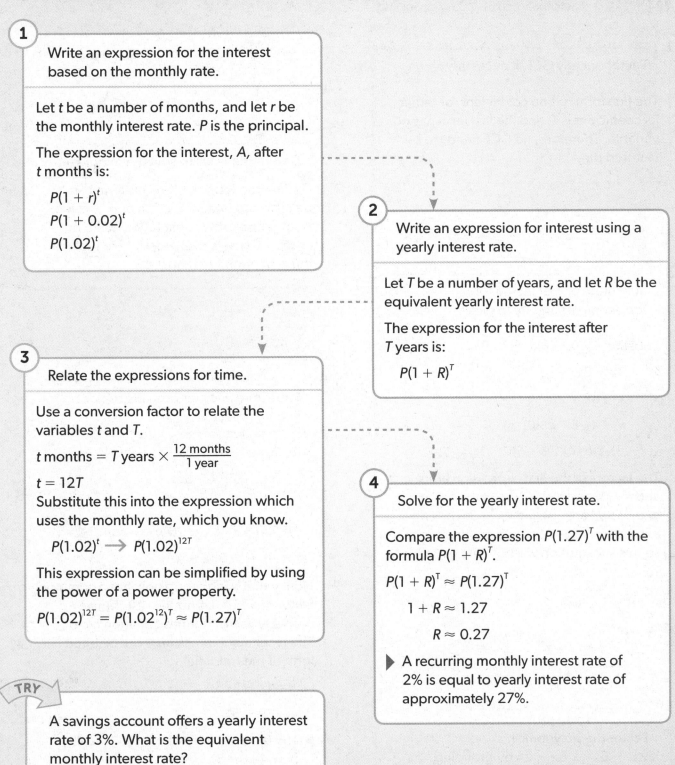

1 Write an expression for the interest based on the monthly rate.

Let t be a number of months, and let r be the monthly interest rate. P is the principal.

The expression for the interest, A, after t months is:

$P(1 + r)^t$

$P(1 + 0.02)^t$

$P(1.02)^t$

2 Write an expression for interest using a yearly interest rate.

Let T be a number of years, and let R be the equivalent yearly interest rate.

The expression for the interest after T years is:

$P(1 + R)^T$

3 Relate the expressions for time.

Use a conversion factor to relate the variables t and T.

$t \text{ months} = T \text{ years} \times \frac{12 \text{ months}}{1 \text{ year}}$

$t = 12T$

Substitute this into the expression which uses the monthly rate, which you know.

$P(1.02)^t \rightarrow P(1.02)^{12T}$

This expression can be simplified by using the power of a power property.

$P(1.02)^{12T} = P(1.02^{12})^T \approx P(1.27)^T$

4 Solve for the yearly interest rate.

Compare the expression $P(1.27)^T$ with the formula $P(1 + R)^T$.

$P(1 + R)^T \approx P(1.27)^T$

$1 + R \approx 1.27$

$R \approx 0.27$

▶ A recurring monthly interest rate of 2% is equal to yearly interest rate of approximately 27%.

TRY

A savings account offers a yearly interest rate of 3%. What is the equivalent monthly interest rate?

One special method for factoring is called grouping. Grouping involves separating a polynomial into groups of terms and using the distributive property to factor out the same binomial or other polynomial from each group. Often during grouping, one of the terms—often the middle one—is separated into two terms. Not every separation will lead to successful factoring.

EXAMPLE C Factor $x^2 - 9x + 20$ by grouping.

1 Factor out any GCF, if necessary.

The first term has no coefficient, or rather its coefficient is 1, and the last term has no variable. Therefore, no GCF needs to be factored out.

2 Determine ways to split the middle term.

The middle term is $-9x$. This term can be replaced with $(-8x - x)$ or $(-x - 8x)$. Another possible substitution could be $(-4x - 5x)$. It is even possible to replace this term with $(-11x + 2x)$.

3 Substitute one of the possible replacements and try to factor.

Substitute $(-x - 8x)$ for $-9x$.

$x^2 - 9x + 20$

$x^2 - x - 8x + 20$

$(x^2 - x) + (-8x + 20)$

$x(x - 1) + (-4)(2x + 5)$

The factors of the first expression are x and $x - 1$, and the factors of the second expression are -4 and $2x + 5$. The two expressions do not have a common factor, so this substitution will not help us factor.

4 Substitute another possible replacement and try to factor.

Substitute $(-4x - 5x)$ for $-9x$.

$x^2 - 9x + 20$

$x^2 - 4x - 5x + 20$

$(x^2 - 4x) + (-5x + 20)$

$x(x - 4) + (-5)(x - 4)$

Notice that each group now has a common factor of $x - 4$. Using the distributive property, factor out this common factor. The resulting expression is the factored form of the trinomial.

$(x - 4)(x + (-5))$

$(x - 4)(x - 5)$

▶ The factored form of $x^2 - 9x + 20$ is $(x - 4)(x - 5)$.

TRY

Factor the polynomial $2x^3 - 6x^2 - 8x + 24$ by grouping.

The method of completing the square can help you factor a polynomial.

EXAMPLE D Factor the polynomial $4x^2 - 8x - 5$ by completing the square.

1 Set the polynomial equal to y and isolate the variable terms.

Turning the expression into an equation can help you keep track of the terms more easily.

Let $y = 4x^2 - 8x - 5$.

Move the constant term to the left side of the equation.

$$y + 5 = 4x^2 - 8x$$

2 Factor out any constant GCF, if possible, and complete the square.

The terms $4x^2$ and $-8x$ have a common factor of 4.

$$y + 5 = 4x^2 - 8x$$

$$y + 5 = 4(x^2 - 2x)$$

Complete the square within the parentheses by adding $\left(-\frac{2}{2}\right)^2$, or 1.

Remember to multiply by 4 when adding to the left side.

$$y + 5 + 4(1) = 4(x^2 - 2x + 1)$$

$$y + 9 = 4(x - 1)^2$$

$$y = 4(x - 1)^2 - 9$$

3 Look for a pattern in the new expression.

Notice that $4(x - 1)^2$ and 9 are perfect squares, so treat the expression $4(x - 1)^2 - 9$ as the difference of two squares.

$$4(x - 1)^2 - 9$$

$$[2(x - 1) + 3][2(x - 1) - 3]$$

$$(2x - 2 + 3)(2x - 2 - 3)$$

$$(2x + 1)(2x - 5)$$

▶ The factored form of $4x^2 - 8x - 5$ is $(2x + 1)(2x - 5)$.

CHECK

Choose a value for x and substitute it into both the original and factored forms of the polynomial. Do both simplify to the same number?

Practice

Fully factor each expression.

1. $8a^3 - 4a^2$ ______

2. $b^2 + 8b + 16$ ______

3. $c^2 - 121$ ______

Factor out the GCF of the coefficients and of any common variables.

4. $5d^2 - 50d + 125$ ______

5. $x^2 + 7x - 8$ ______

6. $2y^2z + 16yz + 30z$ ______

7. $10x^3 - 70x^2 + 120x$ ______

8. $s^3 + 64$ ______

9. $9t^2 - 49$ ______

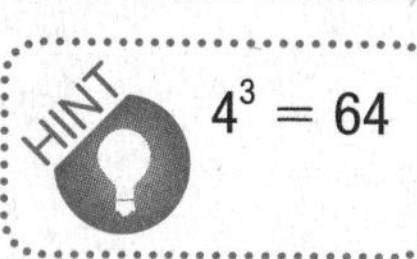

Simplify each exponential expression by using the properties of exponents.

10. $(16 \cdot 3^x)^{\frac{1}{4}}$ ______

11. $\left(5^{\frac{2}{3}}\right)^{3y}$ ______

12. $\left(2^{\frac{y}{2}}\right)^{2x}$ ______

Complete the square to write an equivalent equation containing a squared binomial.

13. $y^2 - 6y = 0$ ______

14. $x^2 + 8x + 3 = y$ ______

15. $2x^2 + 36x = y$ ______

Solve for *x*.

16. $y = 4x^2$ ______

17. $y = x^2 - 12x + 36$ ______

18. $y = x^2 + 20x$ ______

Choose the best answer.

19. A savings account offers an annual interest rate of 5%, compounded annually. Which is closest to the equivalent monthly interest rate for the account?

A. 0.33%

B. 0.41%

C. 3.3%

D. 4.1%

20. Which of the following equations is equivalent to $a^3b^3 - 216$?

A. $(ab - 6)(a^2b^2 - 6ab + 6)$

B. $(ab - 6)(a^2b^2 - 6ab + 36)$

C. $(ab - 6)(ab + 6ab + 36)$

D. $(ab - 6)(a^2b^2 + 6ab + 36)$

Solve.

21. A biologist put some living cells into a petri dish. After 3 hours, she noticed that the number of cells had increased by a factor of 8. After 6 hours, the number of cells had increased by a factor of 64. The number of cells after h hours is described by the expression $c \cdot 8^{\frac{h}{3}}$, where c is the original number of cells in the petri dish.

By what factor does the sample grow in a 1-hour period? __________

22. A cannonball is fired straight up into the air at a speed of 64 feet per second. Its height, h, after t seconds is described by the equation $h = -16t^2 + 64t$.

Solve this equation for t. ______________________________

After how many seconds will the cannonball land on the ground ($h = 0$)? __________

23. **INVESTIGATE** Recall the half-life equation $y = N_0\left(\frac{1}{2}\right)^{\frac{t}{t_{\frac{1}{2}}}}$ where N_0 is the initial amount of an element, $t_{\frac{1}{2}}$ is the half-life of the element, t is the variable for time, and y is the amount of the original substance remaining. The radioactive element polonium 218 (Po-218) has a half-life of 3 minutes.

Write an equation that gives the amount remaining from a 150-gram sample of Po-218 after t minutes. ____________________

Use the power of a power property to find the percentage of a Po-218 sample that will remain after 1 minute. Round your answer to the nearest percent. ____________________

How much of the 150-gram sample will remain after 1 minute? ____________________

24. **EXPLAIN** A rectangle has an area equal to $x^2 + 2x - 48$. If its length is equal to $x + 8$, what binomial represents its width? Explain how you determined your answer.

____

____

Writing and Graphing Quadratic Equations and Inequalities

Writing Quadratic Equations

UNDERSTAND You know that the motion of an object moving at a constant speed or velocity can be modeled by a linear equation. But what if that velocity is changing? If it changes in a uniform way, or in other words, if the velocity's rate of change is constant, then the object's motion can be modeled by a quadratic equation.

A quadratic equation has the form $y = ax^2 + bx + c$, where a, b, and c are constants. When modeling a moving object, x is usually the time that the object has been moving and y is the distance it has traveled in some direction. In that case, a is related to the object's acceleration, or the rate of change of its velocity. The constant b is the object's initial velocity, or its velocity at time $x = 0$, and the constant c is the object's initial distance from some measuring point, such as its height above the ground.

A vehicle accelerates when the driver steps on the gas pedal. It decelerates when the driver steps on the brake pedal. Deceleration is just a form of acceleration in which the speed decreases. The pull of gravity causes objects to accelerate as they rise or fall, and this pull is generally equivalent everywhere on Earth. Objects that are thrown or launched into the air are sometimes called projectiles. When writing an equation dealing with gravity, a is usually equal to -16 ft/s^2 (feet per second squared) or -4.9 m/s^2 (meters per second squared). Paying attention to the units can help you assure that you have set up the equation correctly.

UNDERSTAND A quadratic equation is sometimes built by multiplying linear factors. For example, the product of two unknown numbers can be written as a quadratic equation. If an integer is represented by x, the next consecutive integer is $x + 1$. The product of these two numbers is $x(x + 1)$ or $x^2 + x$.

Equations representing the area of a figure are often quadratic. Notice that area is measured in square units. For example, a square with side length x inches has an area of x inches $\times$ x inches or x^2 square inches.

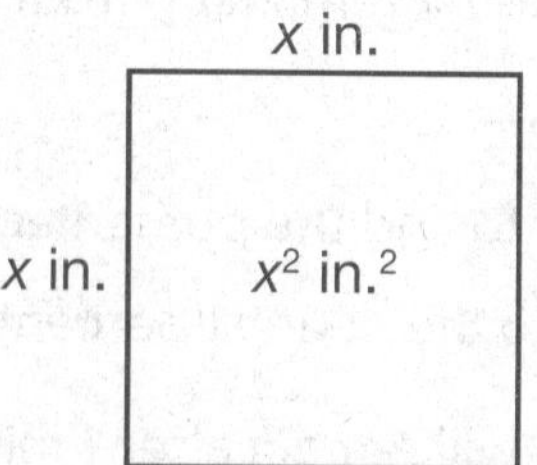

Quadratic equations are also useful for modeling the selling of products in business. Generally, as the price of something goes up, fewer people want to buy it, so sellers set the price so they can sell as many of their goods as possible. A simple model for this situation uses quadratic equations to model how much money the seller will make.

Connect

A company manufactures and sells bongo drums. If it sells the drums for \$50, it sells about 100 of them each day. If it lowers the price to \$40, it sells about 300 of them daily. Suppose the relationship between the price of a set of drums and the number of drums sold is linear. Write an equation for the revenue that the company makes, based on the number of drum sets it sells.

1 Examine the relationship between price per unit and number of units sold.

Let p be the price of a set of bongo drums. Let n be the number of drum sets that the company sells in a day.

If the number of sets that the company sells depends on the price and if the relationship between these variables is linear, then this situation can be modeled by an equation of the form $n = mp + b$.

2 Write an equation comparing price to number sold.

Since the problem gives you two points on the line, you can write the equation for that line. First, find the slope.

$$m = \frac{n_1 - n_2}{p_1 - p_2} = \frac{100 - 300}{50 - 40} = \frac{-200}{10} = -20$$

This gives the equation $n = -20p + b$. Substitute the point (50, 100) to find b.

$(100) = -20(50) + b$

$100 = -1{,}000 + b$

$1{,}100 = b$

The equation $n = -20p + 1{,}100$ compares price per drum set to the number sold.

3 Solve the equation for the price.

This equation can be rearranged to give the value of p in terms of n.

$n = -20p + 1{,}100$

$n - 1{,}100 = -20p$

$p = -\frac{1}{20}n + 55$

4 Write an equation for revenue.

The revenue, r, that the company makes is equal to the price per set times the number of sets, $r = p \cdot n$.

Substituting our expression for the price, $p = -\frac{1}{20}n + 55$, gives a quadratic equation in terms of n, the number of sets of drums sold.

$r = \left(-\frac{1}{20}n + 55\right) \cdot n$

▶ $r = -\frac{1}{20}n^2 + 55n$

TRY

The cost, c, to manufacture n drum sets is $c = 6n + 850$. The company's profit is equal to its revenue minus its costs. Write an equation for m, the daily profit for making and selling n sets of bongo drums.

Graphing Quadratic Equations and Inequalities

UNDERSTAND The graph of a quadratic equation in **standard form** $y = ax^2 + bx + c$ is a U-shaped curve called a **parabola**. If the **leading coefficient**, a, is positive, the parabola will open upward. If the leading coefficient is negative, the parabola will open downward.

To graph a quadratic equation, it helps to write it in **vertex form**, $y = a(x - h)^2 + k$. The standard form can be changed into the vertex form by using the method of completing the square. The point (h, k) is the **vertex** of the parabola, its highest or lowest point. When graphing a parabola, it often helps to graph the vertex first. Later, you will see how the constant a can help you find other points on the parabola. Notice that the left half of the parabola is the mirror image of the right half.

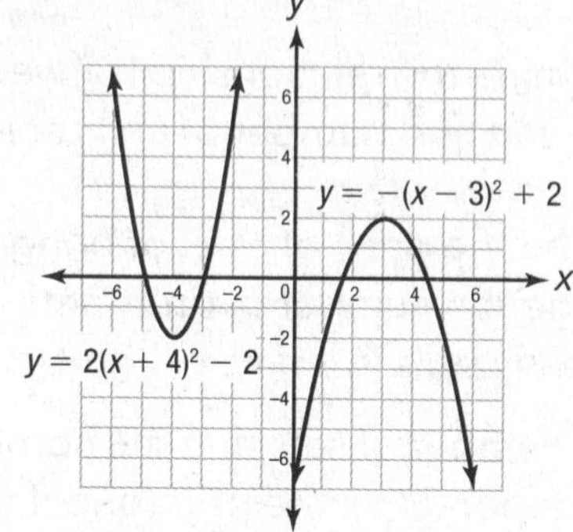

UNDERSTAND Quadratic expressions can be used in inequalities as well as in equations. Recall that the solution to a linear inequality in two variables is a half-plane that represents a set of many coordinate pairs. Similarly, the solution set to a quadratic inequality is also a portion of the plane. Instead of the boundary being a line, though, it is a parabola.

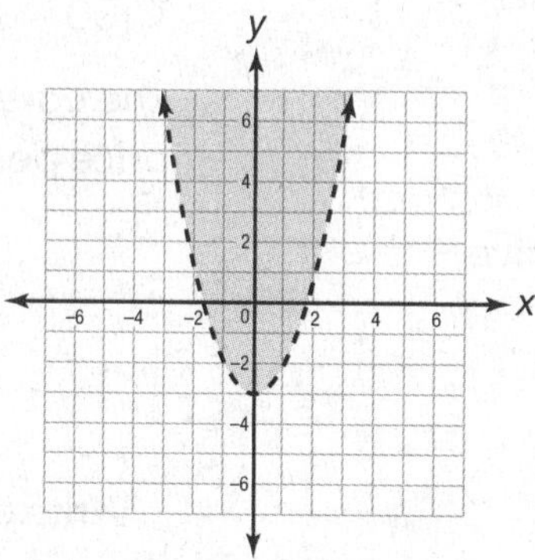

Many of the rules for graphing linear inequalities also apply to graphing quadratic inequalities. Write quadratic inequalities in standard form or vertex form, and follow the rules below.

- For quadratic inequalities with a $<$ or $>$ sign, use a dashed boundary to show that the parabola is not a part of the solution.
- For quadratic inequalities with a $\leq$ or $\geq$ sign, use a solid boundary to show that the parabola is a part of the solution.
- For quadratic inequalities with a $<$ or $\leq$ sign, shade below the parabola. Shade outside a parabola that opens upward or inside a parabola that opens downward.
- For quadratic inequalities with a $>$ or $\geq$ sign, shade above the parabola. Shade inside a parabola that opens upward or outside a parabola that opens downward.

As with any inequality, it is always a good idea to pick a test point to verify that you have shaded the correct region of the graph.

Connect

An arrow that is fired straight up will fly to a greater height than an arrow that is fired at an angle. Robin fires an arrow from the ground at an unknown angle and with an initial velocity of 75 meters per second. Write and graph an inequality for H, the height of the arrow in meters, t seconds after it was fired.

1 Write an inequality for the height.

The expression for the height of a projectile is $\frac{1}{2}at^2 + vt + d$.

The arrow is fired from the ground, so its initial height, d, is 0 meters.

The arrow will reach the greatest possible height if fired straight up, so its initial upward velocity, v, would be the full 75 m/s.

Because gravity is acting on the arrow, its acceleration is -9.8 m/s^2.

So, the maximum height that the arrow can reach at time t is $-4.9t^2 + 75t$.

The height, H, can be no greater than the maximum height. So, $H \leq -4.9t^2 + 75t$.

2 Make a table for the boundary $H = -4.9t^2 + 75t$.

t	$-4.9t^2 + 75t$	H
0	$-4.9(0)^2 + 75(0)$ $0 + 0$	0
5	$-4.9(5)^2 + 75(5)$ $-122.5 + 375$	252.5
7	$-4.9(7)^2 + 75(7)$ $-240.1 + 525$	284.9
8	$-4.9(8)^2 + 75(8)$ $-313.6 + 600$	286.4
10	$-4.9(10)^2 + 75(10)$ $-490 + 750$	260
15	$-4.9(15)^2 + 75(15)$ $-1102.5 + 1125$	22.5

3 Graph the inequality.

Plot the points from your table and connect them with a smooth curve. Since the inequality symbol is $\leq$, use a solid line and shade below the parabola. Graph the inequality on a coordinate plane.

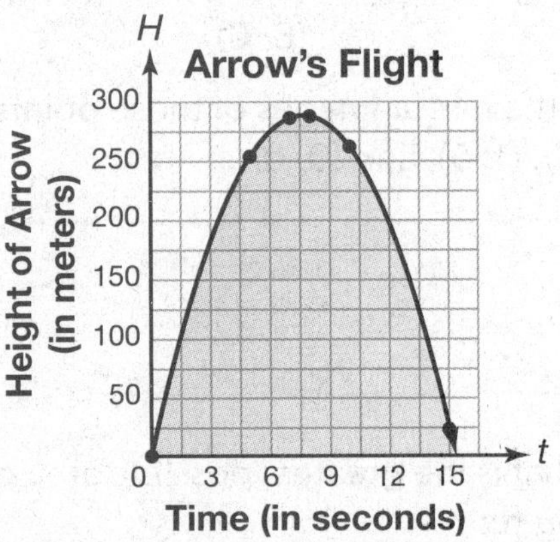

DISCUSS

Could the arrow ever reach a height of 350 meters?

EXAMPLE A Elizabeth wants to build a rectangular dog run for her pet corgi, Duke. She will use 12 meters of fencing to build the dog run. Write an equation for the area of the dog run, y, with a length of x meters. Then make a graph to show the possible area values.

1 Find the width in terms of x.

Let d be the width of the dog run. Elizabeth has 12 meters of fencing, so the perimeter of the dog run will be 12 meters.

$$2x + 2d = 12$$
$$2d = 12 - 2x$$
$$d = 6 - x$$

2 Write an equation for the area within the fence.

To find the area, y, multiply the length by the width.

$$y = xd$$
$$y = (x)(6 - x)$$
$$y = 6x - x^2$$
$$y = -x^2 + 6x$$

3 Put the equation in vertex form by completing the square.

$$y = -x^2 + 6x$$
$$y = -(x^2 - 6x)$$
$$y + (-1)(9) = -(x^2 - 6x + 9)$$
$$y - 9 = -(x - 3)^2$$
$$y = -(x - 3)^2 + 9$$

4 Find points on the parabola.

The vertex, (h, k), is at $(3, 9)$ and $a = -1$. Add multiples of a to find other points.

$$(3 + 1, 9 + 1^2a) = (3 + 1, 9 + 1(-1)) = (4, 8)$$

$$(3 + 2, 9 + 2^2a) = (3 + 2, 9 + 4(-1)) = (5, 5)$$

$$(3 + 3, 9 + 3^2a) = (3 + 3, 9 + 9(-1)) = (6, 0)$$

Plot the mirror images of these points at $(2, 8)$, $(1, 5)$, and $(0, 0)$.

5 Graph the parabola.

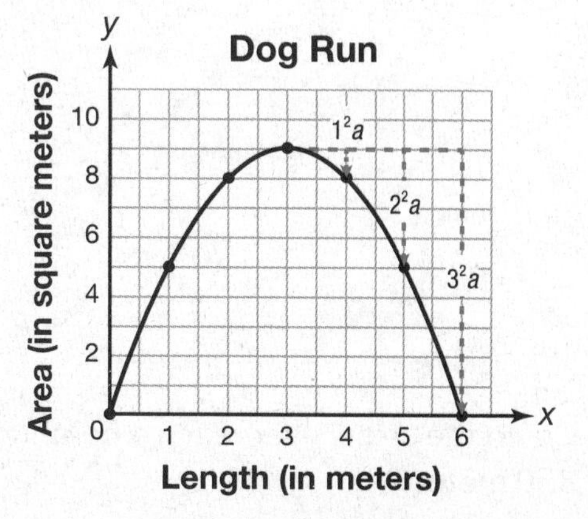

DISCUSS

What is the greatest possible area of the dog run?

An equation can be quadratic in more than one variable. For example, the equation $x^2 + y^2 = 3$ is a quadratic equation. Its graph is a circle, not a parabola. The graph of $(x - h)^2 + (y - k)^2 = r^2$ is a circle centered at (h, k) with a radius r units long.

EXAMPLE B Graph the quadratic equation $(x + 2)^2 + y^2 = 9$.

1 Interpret the parameters of the circle.

Compare the equation to the standard form equation of a circle, $(x - h)^2 + (y - k)^2 = r^2$.

For the equation $(x + 2)^2 + y^2 = 9$, the x-coordinate of the center, h, is -2 since $(x + 2)$ is equivalent to $(x - (-2))$.

The y-coordinate of the center, k, is 0 since y^2 is equivalent to $(y - 0)^2$.

The square of the radius is 9.

$$r^2 = 9$$

$$\sqrt{r^2} = \sqrt{9}$$

$$r = \pm 3$$

Since a radius is a physical length, $r = -3$ does not make sense. The radius must be 3, the principle square root of 9.

2 Locate the center of the circle.

The center of the circle, (h, k), for the equation $(x + 2)^2 + y^2 = 9$ is $(-2, 0)$.

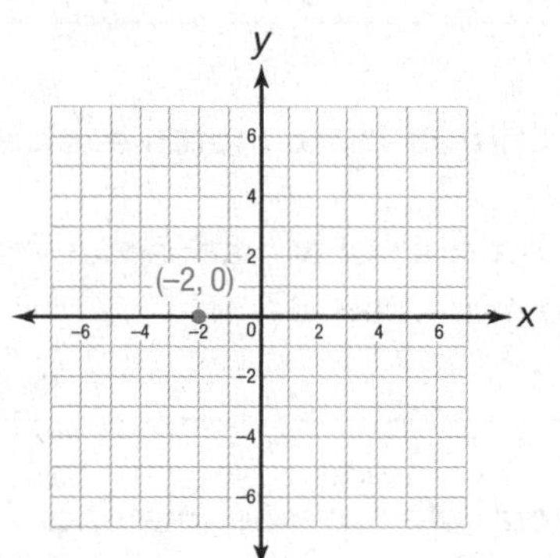

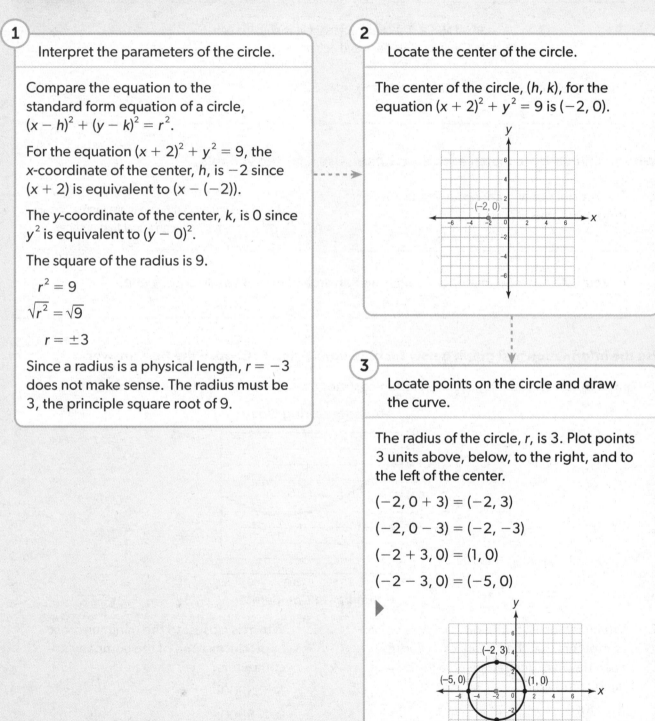

3 Locate points on the circle and draw the curve.

The radius of the circle, r, is 3. Plot points 3 units above, below, to the right, and to the left of the center.

$(-2, 0 + 3) = (-2, 3)$

$(-2, 0 - 3) = (-2, -3)$

$(-2 + 3, 0) = (1, 0)$

$(-2 - 3, 0) = (-5, 0)$

TRY

Graph the equation $(x - 1)^2 + (y + 3)^2 = 1$.

Practice

Write a quadratic equation to match each description. Use *x* for the variable.

1. A triangle is four times as tall as the length of its base. The triangle's area is 24 square units.

____

REMEMBER The area of a triangle is equal to half the product of its base and height.

2. The product of two consecutive odd numbers is 323.

____

Write an inequality to match each description. Use *n* for the variable.

3. The product of two consecutive numbers is no more than 37.

____

If a quantity can be no more than a certain number, then it can equal that number.

4. A rectangle has a perimeter of 26 units and an area of more than 30 square units.

____

Use the information and graph below for questions 5 and 6. Choose the best answer.

The graph below shows the daily production costs for a factory that manufactures computers.

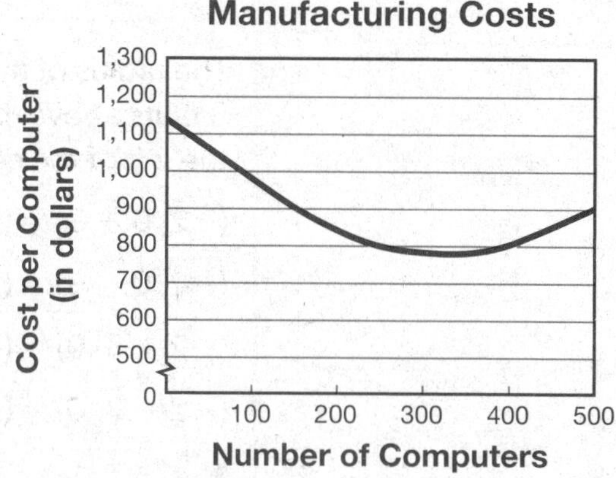

5. Which is closest to the optimal number of computers that the factory can produce each day in order to minimize the cost of each computer?

A. 100

B. 200

C. 300

D. 400

6. Which is closest to the minimum cost of producing one of the company's computers?

A. \$300

B. \$800

C. \$900

D. \$1,200

Identify the vertex of the parabola that represents each equation.

7. $y = x^2 + 4x + 4$

8. $y = 3x^2 - 12x + 13$

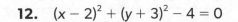

9. $y = x^2 - 6x + 9$

10. $y = -x^2 - 2x$

Graph each equation.

11. $y = x^2 - 2x - 2$

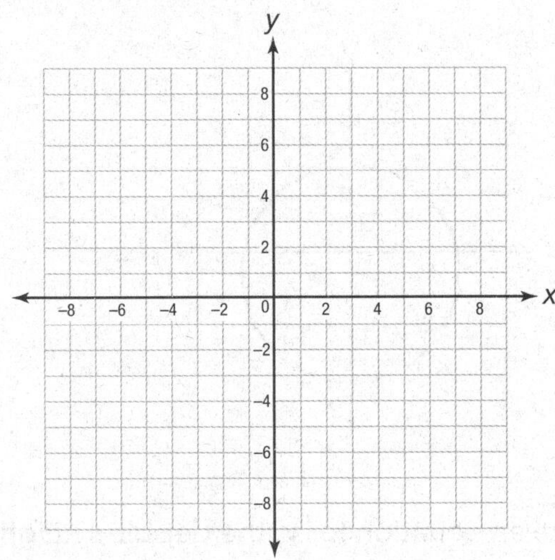

12. $(x - 2)^2 + (y + 3)^2 - 4 = 0$

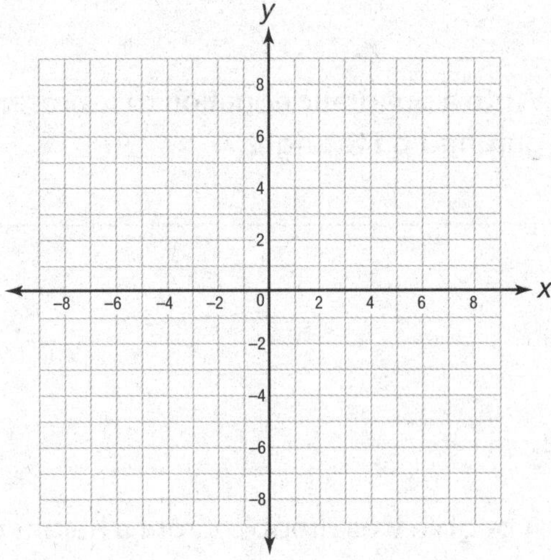

Graph each inequality.

13. $y \geq 2x^2 + 4x - 1$

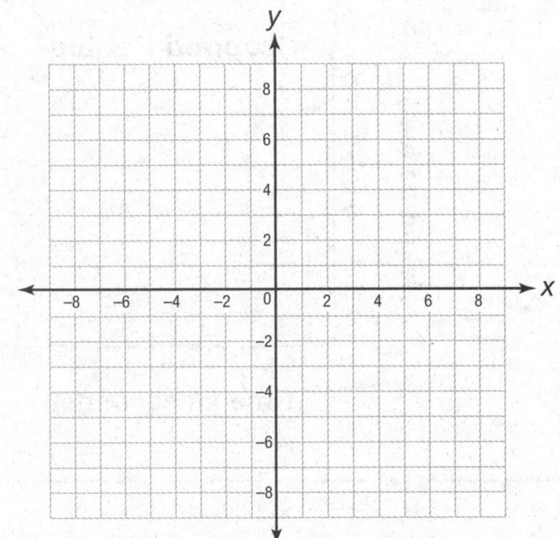

14. $y > -x^2 + 6x - 7$

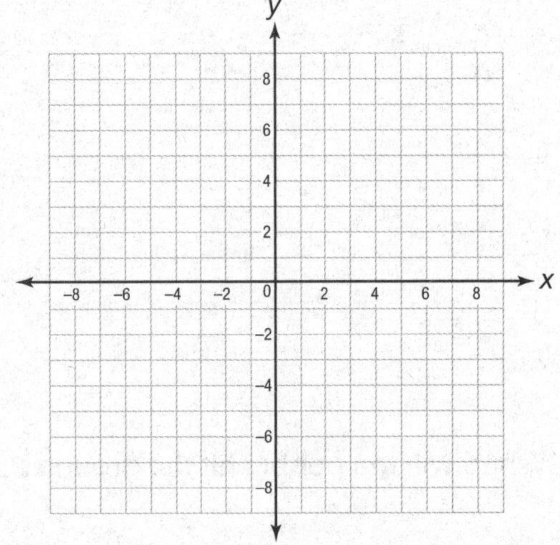

Write a quadratic equation to represent each situation.

15. A ball was thrown with an initial upward velocity of 80 feet per second from an initial height of 4 feet. Write an equation for h, the height of the ball in feet, t seconds after it was thrown.

____

16. The rectangle to the right has an unshaded square inside it. The area of the shaded region is 31 square units. Write an equation that could be used to find x.

____

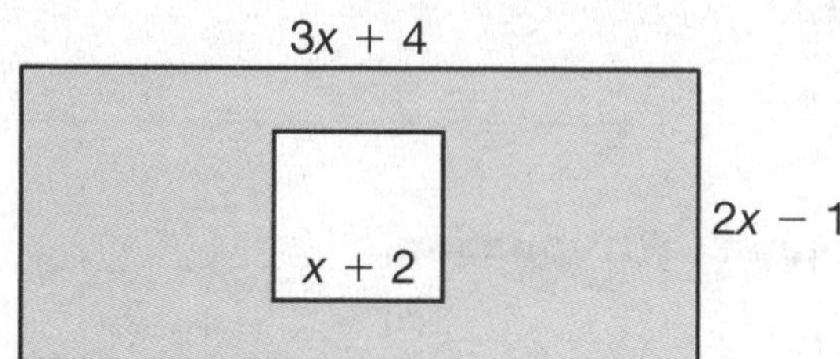

17. Write a quadratic equation to represent the circle graphed on the right.

____

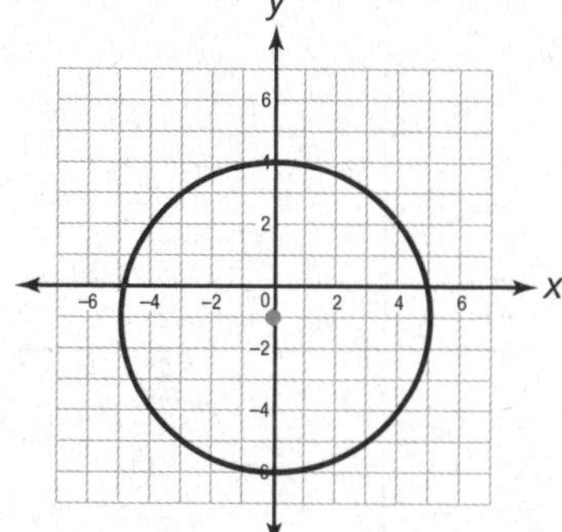

Solve.

18. A pebble was dropped from a height of 100 feet. Write an equation for y, the pebble's height in feet, x seconds after being dropped.

____

Fill in the table and graph your equation on the coordinate grid below.

x	$y =$	y
0		
0.5		
1		
1.5		
2		
2.5		

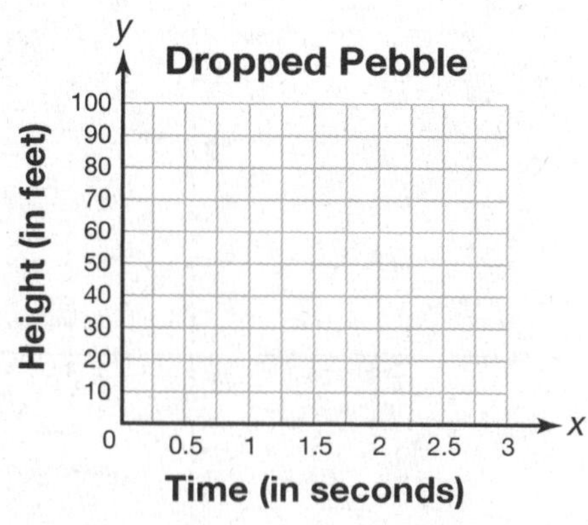

When will the pebble hit the ground? ______________________________

19. GRAPH The Western High soccer team is washing cars to raise money for a trip to a tournament. During one previous car wash, the team charged $5 and washed 44 cars. At another car wash, they charged $10 and washed 24 cars. Assume there is a linear relationship between the amount they charge and the number of cars they wash.

Write an equation for the number of cars they wash, x, in terms of the price they charge, p.

____

Solve that equation for p. ______________________________

Write an equation for the total amount of money, r, that they take in if they wash x cars.

____

Graph your equation for r on the coordinate plane.

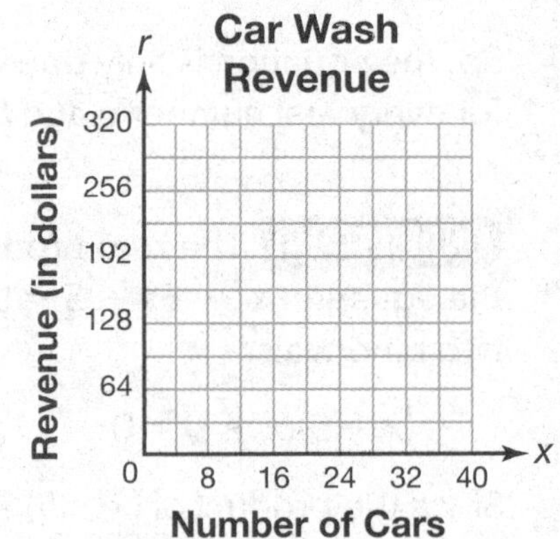

What is the greatest amount of money that the team could raise?

____

How many cars must they wash to raise that much money?

____

At what price will they raise that money? ______________________________

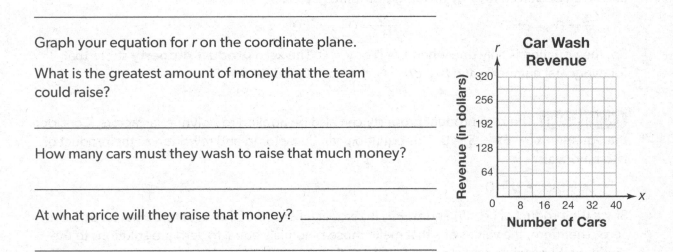

20. APPLY Huma is making a wooden frame for a picture that is 10 inches by 12 inches. The entire picture will be visible inside the frame. The frame's width will be the same all the way around.

Write an expression for the length of the frame, including the photo. ______________

Write an expression for the height of the frame, including the photo. ______________

Huma plans to paint the frame blue (not including the picture inside.) Write an equation for the area of the front of the picture frame that she must paint. ______________

Solving Quadratic Equations

Solving Quadratic Equations through Factoring

UNDERSTAND A quadratic equation in one variable has the standard form $ax^2 + bx + c = 0$. The solutions to such an equation are the values of x that make the equation true. When you substitute a solution value for x into the expression $ax^2 + bx + c$ and evaluate, the result is 0. A quadratic equation can have one or two real solutions, or it can have no real solution.

Consider the equation $xy = 0$. This equation can be solved for x by dividing both sides by y, and it can be solved for y by dividing both sides by x.

$$\frac{xy}{y} = 0 \rightarrow x = 0 \qquad\qquad \frac{xy}{x} = 0 \rightarrow y = 0$$

So, the equation is only true when $x = 0$ or $y = 0$. The **zero product property** states that, for every real number a and b, if $ab = 0$, then $a = 0$ and/or $b = 0$.

UNDERSTAND The zero product property can also be applied to polynomial factors. Consider the equation $x^2 + 6x + 5 = 0$. This equation can be factored and rewritten as the product of two binomials.

$$(x + 5)(x + 1) = 0$$

Since the product of $(x + 5)$ and $(x + 1)$ is zero, at least one of those factors must be equal to zero. Therefore, the values of x that make those binomials equal to zero are solutions to the equation. Set each binomial equal to zero and solve for x.

$$x + 5 = 0 \quad \text{or} \quad x + 1 = 0$$

$$x = -5 \qquad\qquad x = -1$$

Therefore, the quadratic equation $x^2 + 6x + 5 = 0$ has two real solutions: $x = -5$ and $x = -1$, or the set $\{-5, -1\}$. This same process can be used to solve any quadratic equation in one variable if its quadratic expression can be factored.

When solving a quadratic equation, make sure your solutions make sense. For example, the height of a ball, h, thrown from a building at time t might be represented by the equation $h = -16t^2 + 16t + 320$. To find the time when the ball hits the ground, let $h = 0$ and solve the equation $0 = -16t^2 + 16t + 320$. The solutions to this equation are $t = 5$ seconds and $t = -4$ seconds. Since negative time does not make sense in this situation, -4 is an **extraneous solution**. The ball will hit the ground after 5 seconds.

Connect

Solve the quadratic equation $12x^2 = 4 - 2x$.

1 Rewrite the equation in standard form.

Use the addition and subtraction properties of equality to move all of the non-zero terms to one side of the equation.

$$12x^2 = 4 - 2x$$
$$12x^2 + 2x = 4$$
$$12x^2 + 2x - 4 = 0$$

2 Begin factoring the quadratic expression.

First, factor out the GCF of the terms. Each term is divisible by 2.

$$12x^2 + 2x - 4 = 0$$
$$2(6x^2 + x - 2) = 0$$

According to the zero product property, this means that either:

$2 = 0$ or $6x^2 + x - 2 = 0$

Since 2 cannot equal 0, the trinomial must be equal to 0.

3 Factor the new quadratic expression.

When a quadratic trinomial has a leading coefficient other than 1 or −1, it is often easiest to factor by grouping. Find the product of the leading coefficient and the constant term, $a \cdot c$. In this case, $6 \cdot -2 = -12$.

List the factor pairs of −12: −1 and 12, −2, and 6, −3 and 4, 3 and −4, 2 and −6, and 1 and −12. The only factors that add up to 1, the value of b, are −3 and 4. So substitute $-3x + 4x$ for x.

$$6x^2 + x - 2 = 0$$
$$6x^2 - 3x + 4x - 2 = 0$$
$$3x(2x - 1) + 2(2x - 1) = 0$$
$$(3x + 2)(2x - 1) = 0$$

4 Solve for x.

Apply the zero product property again. Set each binomial factor equal to 0 and solve for x.

$$(3x + 2)(2x - 1) = 0$$

$3x + 2 = 0$ or $2x - 1 = 0$

$3x = -2$ $\qquad$ $2x = 1$

$x = -\frac{2}{3}$ $\qquad$ $x = \frac{1}{2}$

▶ The solutions of the equation are $x = -\frac{2}{3}$ and $x = \frac{1}{2}$.

CHECK

Substitute $x = -\frac{2}{3}$ and $x = \frac{1}{2}$ into the original equation, and show that true statements result for both values of x.

Other Methods of Solving Quadratic Equations

UNDERSTAND Some simple quadratic equations can be solved by simply taking the square root of both sides.

$x^2 = 144$	Take the square root of both sides.
$x = \pm 12$	Remember to include the $\pm$ sign.

What would happen if the radicand were negative? Consider the equation $x^2 = -100$. There is no real number that, when multiplied by itself, is equal to -100. In this case, the equation has no real solution. Quadratic equations that have no real solution instead have imaginary solutions. The imaginary number i is equal to $\sqrt{-1}$.

$x^2 = 100 \cdot -1$	Take the square root of both sides.
$x = \pm\sqrt{100} \cdot \sqrt{-1}$	Substitute i for $\sqrt{-1}$ and simplify.
$x = \pm 10i$	

So, the equation $x^2 + 100 = 0$ has two imaginary solutions, $10i$ and $-10i$.

UNDERSTAND Taking the square root can also be used to solve equations in which the coefficient of the x-term is not zero, such as $x^2 - 6x = 7$. By using the method of completing the square, you can put this equation in a form that can be solved by taking the square root.

$x^2 - 6x = 7$	Add $\left(\frac{6}{2}\right)^2$, or 9, to both sides.
$x^2 - 6x + 9 = 16$	Rewrite the left side as a perfect square trinomial.
$(x - 3)^2 = 16$	Take the square root of both sides.
$x - 3 = \pm 4$	Add 3 to both sides.
$x = 3 \pm 4$	

The solution set is $\{-1, 7\}$.

UNDERSTAND When a quadratic is not easily factorable and completing the square is inconvenient, you can solve it by using the **quadratic formula**, which is shown below.

$$x = -b \pm \sqrt{\frac{b^2 - 4ac}{2a}}$$

Plug in the values of a, b, and c from the standard form $ax^2 + bx + c = 0$ and evaluate to find the solutions. The portion of the formula underneath the radical sign is called the **discriminant**. The discriminant determines the number of real solutions to the equation.

- When $b^2 - 4ac > 0$, the equation has two real solutions.
- When $b^2 - 4ac = 0$, the equation has one real solution.
- When $b^2 - 4ac < 0$, the equation has no real solutions.

Connect

Derive the quadratic formula by applying the method of completing the square to $ax^2 + bx + c = 0$.

1 Isolate the variable terms and divide out the coefficient of x^2.

$ax^2 + bx + c = 0$ Subtract c from both sides.

$ax^2 + bx = -c$ Divide both sides by a.

$x^2 + \frac{b}{a}x = -\frac{c}{a}$

2 Complete the square.

The coefficient of x is now $\frac{b}{a}$. To complete the square, first divide this term by 2 and then square the result. Add the resulting expression, $\frac{b^2}{4a^2}$, to both sides of the equation.

$x^2 + \frac{b}{a}x = -\frac{c}{a}$

$x^2 + \frac{b}{a}x + \frac{b^2}{4a^2} = -\frac{c}{a} + \frac{b^2}{4a^2}$

Write the left side as a perfect trinomial.

$\left(x + \frac{b}{2a}\right)^2 = -\frac{c}{a} + \frac{b^2}{4a^2}$

3 Combine the terms on the right and take the square root of both sides.

Rewrite the fractions on the right side so that they have a common denominator, and then add them.

$\left(x + \frac{b}{2a}\right)^2 = -\frac{c}{a} + \frac{b^2}{4a^2}$

$\left(x + \frac{b}{2a}\right)^2 = -\frac{4ac}{4a^2} + \frac{b^2}{4a^2}$

$\left(x + \frac{b}{2a}\right)^2 = \frac{b^2 - 4ac}{4a^2}$

Take the square root of both sides.

$x + \frac{b}{2a} = \pm\sqrt{\frac{b^2 - 4ac}{4a^2}}$

4 Solve for x.

The square root of a fraction is equal to the square root of the numerator over the square root of the denominator. Use this to simplify the radical.

$x + \frac{b}{2a} = \pm\frac{\sqrt{b^2 - 4ac}}{\sqrt{4a^2}}$

$x + \frac{b}{2a} = \pm\frac{\sqrt{b^2 - 4ac}}{2a}$

Subtract $-\frac{b}{2a}$ from both sides and combine the terms on the right side.

$x = -\frac{b}{2a} \pm \frac{\sqrt{b^2 - 4ac}}{2a}$

$x = \frac{-b \pm \sqrt{b^2 - 4ac}}{2a}$

CHECK

Solve the equation $x^2 - 2x - 48 = 0$ first by completing the square and then by using the quadratic formula. Do you get the same solutions using both methods?

EXAMPLE A Solve for x: $x^2 - 10x + 30 = 5$

1

Move all constant terms to one side of the equation.

Subtract 30 from both sides.

$$x^2 - 10x + 30 = 5$$
$$x^2 - 10x = -25$$

2

Use the method of completing the square.

In this equation, $b = -10$. Find $\left(\frac{b}{2}\right)^2$.

$$\left(-\frac{10}{2}\right)^2 = (-5)^2 = 25$$

Add 25 to both sides.

$$x^2 - 10x + 25 = -25 + 25$$
$$x^2 - 10x + 25 = 0$$

3

Solve for x.

Rewrite the quadratic as a squared binomial. Then take the square root of both sides.

$$x^2 - 10x + 25 = 0$$
$$(x - 5)^2 = 0$$
$$\sqrt{(x - 5)^2} = \sqrt{0}$$
$$x - 5 = 0$$
$$x = 5$$

This equation has only one solution.

▶ The solution of the equation is 5.

DISCUSS

What would you expect the discriminant to be for this equation? Find the discriminant and see if your prediction is correct. Remember to write the equation in standard form first.

EXAMPLE B Heidi rolls a ball down a ramp that is 12.5 feet long. As the ball rolls, it speeds up. The distance that the ball has traveled down the ramp in feet, d, is given by the equation $d = 2.5t^2 + 10t$, where t is the time that the ball has been rolling, in seconds. When will the ball reach the bottom of the ramp?

1 Write an equation in standard form.

The ball will reach the end of the ramp when it has rolled 12.5 feet. Substitute 12.5 for d in the equation.

$$d = 2.5t^2 + 10t$$
$$12.5 = 2.5t^2 + 10t$$
$$0 = 2.5t^2 + 10t - 12.5$$

This equation does not appear easily factorable. Use the quadratic formula.

2 Use the quadratic formula to solve for t.

In the equation $0 = 2.5t^2 + 10t - 12.5$, $a = 2.5$, $b = 10$, and $c = -12.5$.

$$t = \frac{-b \pm \sqrt{b^2 - 4ac}}{2a}$$
$$t = \frac{-10 \pm \sqrt{(10)^2 - 4(2.5)(-12.5)}}{2(2.5)}$$
$$t = \frac{-10 \pm \sqrt{100 + 125}}{5}$$
$$t = \frac{-10 \pm \sqrt{225}}{5}$$
$$t = \frac{-10 \pm 15}{5}$$
$$t = \frac{-10 + 15}{5} \quad \text{or} \quad t = \frac{-10 - 15}{5}$$
$$t = \frac{5}{5} \qquad t = -\frac{25}{5}$$
$$t = 1 \qquad t = -5$$

Time cannot be negative. Therefore, -5 is an extraneous solution and can be discarded.

▶ It takes the ball 1 second to roll 12.5 feet down the ramp.

3 Check your answer.

Substitute 1 for t in the equation $d = 2.5t^2 + 10t$.

$$d = 2.5t^2 + 10t$$
$$d = 2.5(1)^2 + 10(1)$$
$$d = 2.5 + 10$$
$$d = 12.5$$

This is the length of the ramp, so the solution is correct.

MODEL

Graph the equation $d = 2.5t^2 + 10t$. At about what value or values of t does d equal 12.5? Does this agree with the solution above?

Practice

Write each equation in standard form. Then write the factored form of the quadratic expression. Then give the solution(s) to the equation.

1. $x^2 + 8x = 9$

____________ $= 0$

______ ______ $= 0$

solution set: ______

2. $x^2 = 49$

____________ $= 0$

______ ______ $= 0$

solution set: ______

3. $2x^2 - 14x + 29 = 9$

____________ $= 0$

______ (______) (______) $= 0$

solution set: ______

4. $3x^2 + 3 = x^2 - 3x + 2$

____________ $= 0$

______ (______) (______) $= 0$

solution set: ______

REMEMBER Factor out the GCF of the coefficients.

Solve by taking the square root of both sides.

5. $2x^2 = 162$

solution set: ______

6. $x^2 - 4x + 4 = 100$

solution set: ______

7. $x^2 = -9$

solution set: ______

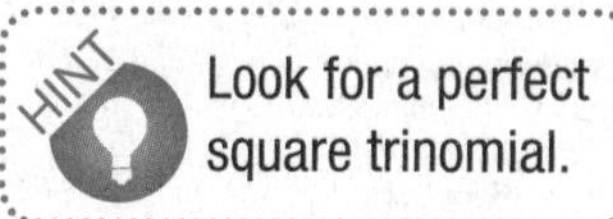
HINT
Look for a perfect square trinomial.

Choose the best answer.

8. What is the discriminant of the equation $0 = 4x^2 - 9x - 1$?

A. -13

B. 0

C. 65

D. 97

9. How many real solutions does the equation $3x^2 + 10x + 11 = 99$ have?

A. 0

B. 1

C. 2

D. cannot be determined

Complete the square and write the resulting equation. Then solve.

10. $x^2 + 2x = 63$

$(\_\_\_\_\_\_)^2 = \_\_\_\_\_\_$

solution set: ______

11. $x^2 - 4x - 21 = 0$

$(\_\_\_\_\_\_)^2 = \_\_\_\_\_\_$

solution set: ______

Solve by using the quadratic formula.

12. $-3x^2 + x + 10 = 0$

solution set: ______

13. $12x^2 + 11x = 3x + 15$

solution set: ______

Solve.

14. The product of two consecutive odd numbers is 143. What are the two numbers?

____

15. In a hockey league, every team plays every other team exactly once. For *n* teams, the number of hockey games that must be scheduled is given by the expression $\frac{n^2 - n}{2}$. Ray's hockey league schedules 36 games. How many teams are in Ray's league? __________

16. The length of a rectangle is 9 times its width. Its area is 81 square meters. What are the dimensions of the rectangle? __________

17. **INTERPRET** The height of a cannonball, in feet, is described by the equation $h = -16t^2 + 64t$, where *t* is the time in seconds since it was fired into the air. At what times is the height of the cannonball 0 feet? At what time will the cannonball fall to the ground?

____

____

18. **ANALYZE** The price, *p*, of a necklace at a jewelry store varies according to the equation $p = -\frac{1}{5}x + 40$, where *x* is the number of necklaces sold per month. The amount of money collected from selling necklaces, *r*, is $r = -5p^2 + 200p$. At what prices will the store collect no revenue from selling necklaces? Why will it not collect any revenue at these prices?

____

____

____

LESSON 36

Solving Linear-Quadratic Systems

UNDERSTAND A system of two or more equations can include linear and nonlinear equations. In a linear-quadratic system, there is one linear equation and one quadratic equation, each in two variables, usually x and y.

Recall that the solution to a system of linear equations is the ordered pair that satisfies every equation in the system. The same is true for the solution or solutions to a linear-quadratic system. Any (x, y) pair that satisfies both equations in the system is a solution to that system.

A linear-quadratic system can have zero, one, or two real solutions. Any point where the graphs of the equations intersect is a solution to the system. If the line representing the linear equation crosses the graph of the quadratic equation in two places, the system has two real solutions. If the line is **tangent** to the graph of the quadratic equation, the system has only one solution. If the line does not intersect the graph of the quadratic equation at all, the system has no real solution.

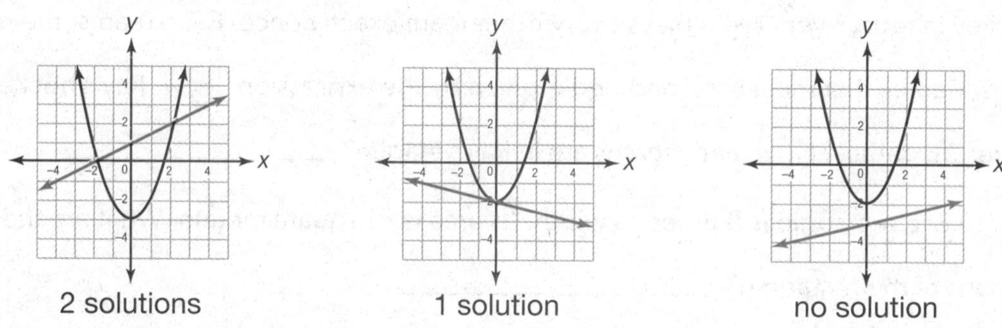

2 solutions   1 solution   no solution

Though only parabolas are shown, the statements above apply to a system consisting of a linear equation and any quadratic equation, including equations whose graphs are circles.

To solve a linear-quadratic system using algebra, use the substitution method. Rewrite the linear equation to isolate one of the variables. Then substitute the equivalent expression for that variable into the quadratic equation. The result will be a quadratic equation in one variable. From that point, you can use any of the methods you have learned to solve for the value(s) of that variable. These include factoring, taking the square root of both sides, completing the square, and using the quadratic formula. Once you know the value or values of that variable, you can substitute each of them back into one of the original equations in order to find the corresponding value of the other variable.

Connect

Solve the system using algebra: $\begin{cases} 3x = y + 4 \\ y = x^2 + 18x + 40 \end{cases}$

1 Solve the linear equation for y.

$$3x = y + 4$$
$$3x - 4 = y$$
$$y = 3x - 4$$

2 Use substitution to produce an equation in one variable.

Since $y = 3x - 4$, substitute this expression for y in the quadratic equation.

$$y = x^2 + 18x + 40$$
$$3x - 4 = x^2 + 18x + 40$$

The result is a quadratic equation with only one variable, x.

3 Solve for the remaining variable.

Rewrite the equation in standard form.

$$3x - 4 = x^2 + 18x + 40$$
$$-4 = x^2 + 15x + 40$$
$$0 = x^2 + 15x + 44$$

Factor the equation and use the zero product property.

$$0 = x^2 + 15x + 44$$
$$0 = (x + 4)(x + 11)$$
$$x + 4 = 0 \quad \text{or} \quad x + 11 = 0$$
$$x = -4 \qquad\qquad x = -11$$

4 Find the values of the other variable.

Substitute the values of x into the linear equation to find the corresponding values of y.

For $x = -4$:

$$3(-4) = y + 4$$
$$-12 = y + 4$$
$$-16 = y$$

For $x = -11$:

$$3(-11) = y + 4$$
$$-33 = y + 4$$
$$-37 = y$$

▶ The solutions to the system are $(-4, -16)$ and $(-11, -37)$.

CHECK

Use your graphing calculator to graph the equations. Then, check the solution by using the TABLE feature or the intersect function in the CALCULATE menu.

EXAMPLE Use algebra to find the points of intersection of the line represented by the equation $y = 4x + 6$ and the circle represented by the equation $(x - 3)^2 + (y - 1)^2 = 17$.

1 Substitute to form a quadratic equation in one variable.

The points of intersection of the two graphs are the solutions to the system containing both equations. The linear equation is already solved for y, so substitute the equivalent expression, $4x + 6$, for y into the quadratic equation.

$(x - 3)^2 + (y - 1)^2 = 17$

$(x - 3)^2 + (4x + 6 - 1)^2 = 17$

$(x - 3)^2 + (4x + 5)^2 = 17$

2 Put the quadratic equation in standard form.

Expand both of the squared binomials. Then combine them.

$(x - 3)^2 + (4x + 5)^2 = 17$

$(x^2 - 6x + 9) + (16x^2 + 40x + 25) = 17$

$(x^2 + 16x^2) + (-6x + 40x) + (9 + 25) = 17$

$17x^2 + 34x + 34 = 17$

Subtract 17 from both sides to put the equation in standard form.

$17x^2 + 34x + 17 = 0$

3 Find the solutions.

The terms have a GCF of 17, so divide both sides of the equation by 17.

$\frac{17x^2}{17} + \frac{34x}{17} + \frac{17}{17} = \frac{0}{17}$

$x^2 + 2x + 1 = 0$

This is a perfect square trinomial. Write it as a squared binomial and solve for x.

$(x + 1)^2 = 0$

$\sqrt{(x + 1)^2} = \pm\sqrt{0}$

$x + 1 = 0$

$x = -1$

Substitute -1 for x to find y.

$y = 4x + 6$

$y = 4(-1) + 6 = 2$

▶ The system has one solution, $(-1, 2)$.

TRY

Solve the system below by graphing both equations.

$$\begin{cases} y = \frac{1}{3}x + 1 \\ (x - 2)^2 + (y + 2)^2 = 9 \end{cases}$$

Problem Solving

READ

A model rocket is launched straight up with an initial velocity of 80 ft/s. At the same time, a bird is flying overhead at an altitude of 89.6 ft. The bird is descending 1.6 feet every second as it flies. At what times will the rocket and the bird have the same elevation?

PLAN

Write one equation for the height, h, of the bird at time t. Write another equation for the height, h, of the rocket at time t. Solve the system containing these two equations.

SOLVE

The bird's change in height is -1.6 ft/s, and its height at time $t = 0$ is 89.6 ft. So, the equation for the bird's elevation is $h =$ ______$t + 89.6$.

The model rocket has an initial velocity of 80 ft/s and an initial height of 0 ft since it is on the ground. So, the equation for the rocket's elevation is $h = -16t^2 +$ ______t.

Substitute ________________ for h. Then put the equation in standard form.

______$t + 89.6 = -16t^2 +$ ______t

$0 = -16t^2 +$ ______$t - 89.6$

Use the ________________ formula to solve for t.

$$t = \frac{-(\_\_\_\_) \pm \sqrt{(81.6)^2 - 4(-16)(\_\_\_\_)}}{2(\_\_\_\_)}$$

$t =$ ______________ or $t =$ ______________

CHECK

Substitute each value of t into both equations to confirm that it yields the same value of h.

For $t =$ ________:

$h =$ ______(______) $+ 89.6$ $h = -16($______$)^2 +$ ______(______)

$h =$ ______ $h =$ ______

For $t =$ ________:

$h =$ ______(______) $+ 89.6$ $h = -16($______$)^2 +$ ______(______)

$h =$ ______ $h =$ ______

▶ The bird and rocket will the same height after _____ seconds and _____ seconds.

Practice

Solve the systems of equations by graphing. Give your answers as ordered pairs.

1. $\begin{cases} (x-2)^2 + (y-1)^2 = 9 \\ y = x + 2 \end{cases}$

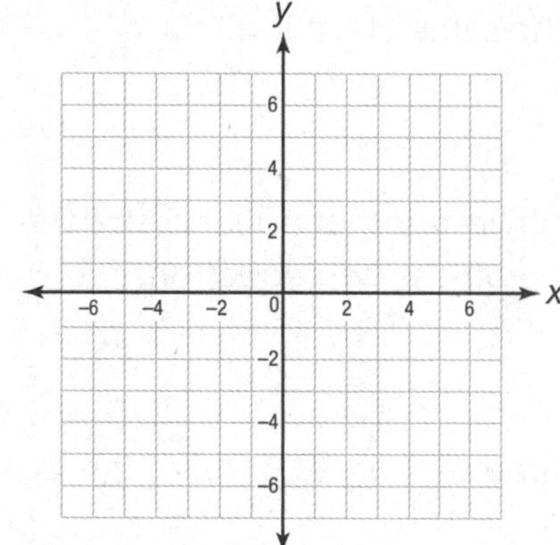

____

2. $\begin{cases} y = x^2 + 8x + 11 \\ y = 2x + 2 \end{cases}$

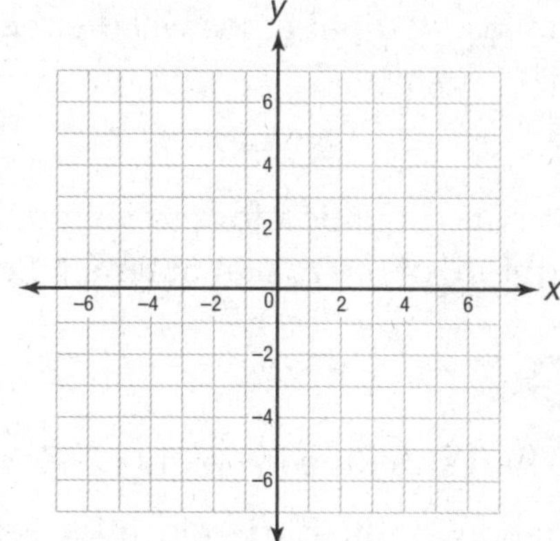

____

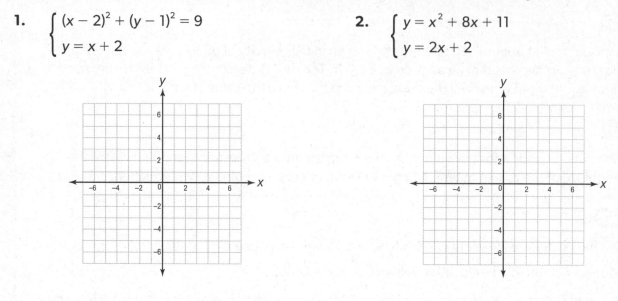

REMEMBER Find the points of intersection.

Choose the best answer.

3. Which is/are the solution(s) to the following system?

$\begin{cases} y = x^2 - 6x + 8 \\ y = 2x - 4 \end{cases}$

A. (2, 0)

B. (2, 0), (6, 8)

C. (8, 6)

D. (0, 2), (8, 6)

Substitute the coordinate pairs into both equations.

4. Gina correctly graphed this system on her graphing calculator:

$\begin{cases} y = x - 6 \\ y = x^2 + 2x + 3 \end{cases}$

A picture of her calculator screen is shown below.

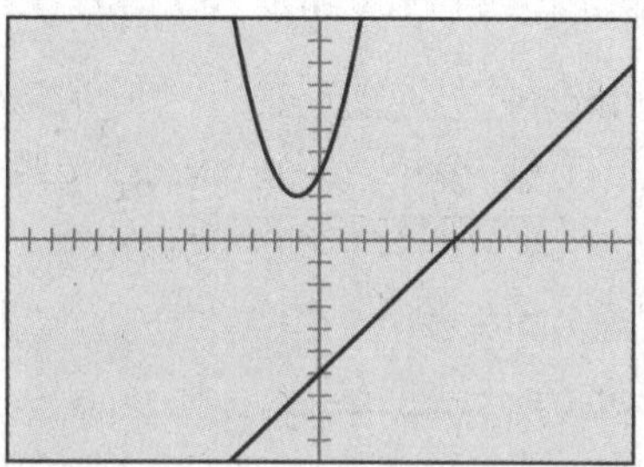

How many solutions does this system have?

A. 0 **C.** 2

B. 1 **D.** 3

Solve the systems of equations algebraically. Give your answers as ordered pairs.

5. $\begin{cases} y = x^2 + 9x + 1 \\ 4y + 12x = 4 \end{cases}$

____

6. $\begin{cases} y = 2x^2 - x - 15 \\ -y = 6x + 3 \end{cases}$

____

7. $\begin{cases} y = 3x^2 + 3x + 9 \\ y = 5x + 2 \end{cases}$

____

Solve.

8. The height of a ball t seconds after it was thrown is modeled by the equation $h = -16t^2 + 67t$, where h is its height in feet above the ground. At the same time, a bird flying through the air had a height of $h = 3t + 48$. Solve the system of two equations to find the time(s) when the ball and the bird were at the same elevation, and find that elevation.

____

____

9. DRAW A fenced-in, square park is 30 feet on each side. The entrance to the park is in the center of the south edge of the park. At the center of the park is a fountain with a diameter of 10 feet. Luis is meeting Samantha in the park. Samantha is 25 feet north and 5 feet west of the entrance. Can Luis walk a straight-line path from the entrance to where Samantha is sitting? Explain your answer.

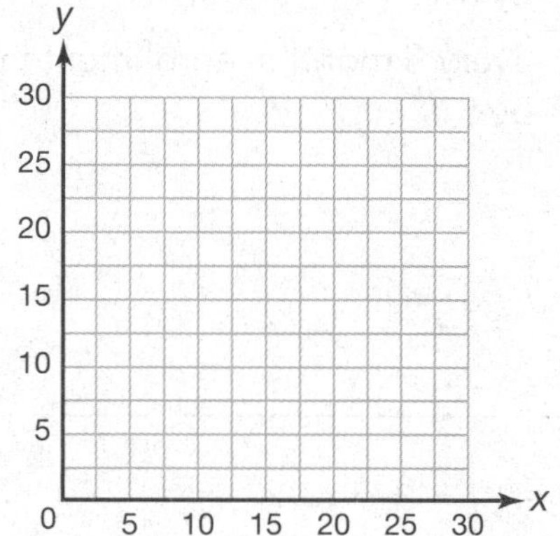

____

____

____

10. INTERPRET The Jump Shot company sells basketballs. The amount of money, M, that the company takes in from selling b basketballs per day is modeled by the equation $M = -2b^2 + 40b$. The amount of money, M, that it costs the company to make b basketballs per day is modeled by the equation $M = 10b + 100$. Solve the system:

$$\begin{cases} M = -2b^2 + 40b \\ M = 10b + 100 \end{cases}$$

____

If profit is equal to the amount of money made minus the cost, does the company make a profit at these solution point(s)? Why or why not?

____

____

If the company sells 7 basketballs per day, is it making a profit? How do you know?

____

____

UNIT

4 Review

Write each quadratic expression in factored form.

1. $x^2 - 2x - 15$

2. $x^2 - 18x + 81$

3. $4x^2 - 25$

Write each equation in vertex form.

4. $y = x^2 + 14x$

5. $y = x^2 - 6x + 1$

6. $y = 2x^2 + 4x$

Choose the best answer.

7. Which of the following equivalences can be used to factor $x^8 - y^8$?

A. difference of squares, $a^2 - b^2 = (a + b)(a - b)$

B. difference of cubes, $a^3 - b^3 = (a - b)(a^2 + ab + b^2)$

C. sum of cubes, $a^3 + b^3 = (a + b)(a^2 - ab + b^2)$

D. square of a difference, $(a - b)^2 = a^2 - 2ab + b^2$

8. The number of students, s, enrolled at a school t years after it opened is modeled by the equation $s = 425(1.05)^{\frac{t}{2}}$. Which of the following is true?

A. When the school opened, there were 105 students.

B. When the school opened, there were 5 students.

C. Every 2 years, enrollment increases by 5%.

D. Every 6 months, enrollment increases by 5%.

Solve each quadratic equation.

9. $3a^2 - 4 = 188$

10. $d^2 = -25$

11. $b^2 - 10b + 2 = 98$

12. $5f^2 - 3f = 8$

13. $4c^2 + 28c = 120$

14. $g^2 - 4g = 7$

Solve each system by substitution.

15. $\begin{cases} x^2 + y^2 = 25 \\ 3x - y = -5 \end{cases}$

____

16. $\begin{cases} y = x^2 + 30x + 100 \\ 6x = y + 44 \end{cases}$

____

Choose the best answer.

17. A baseball was launched from a pitching machine that was placed on a platform. The height of the ball in feet, h, is given by the equation $h = -16t^2 + 85t + 9$, where t is the time in seconds since the ball was launched. What is the meaning of the term $85t$?

    A. The platform was 85 feet high.

    B. The ball was launched with an initial upward velocity of 85 feet per second.

    C. The ball was launched with an initial upward velocity of 85 miles per hour.

    D. The upward velocity is changing at a rate of 85 miles per hour per second.

18. Which of the following statements is **not** true?

    A. The sum of two polynomials is always a polynomial.

    B. The difference of two polynomials is always a polynomial.

    C. The product of two polynomials is always a polynomial.

    D. The quotient of two polynomials is always a polynomial.

Write an equation in one variable to describe each situation. Then solve the problem.

19. A cannonball was shot from the ground into the air with an initial velocity of 160 feet per second. At what time is the cannonball's elevation 400 feet?

    Equation: ____________________ Solution: ____________________

20. The product of two consecutive odd numbers is 1,295. What are the numbers?

    Equation: ____________________ Solution: ____________________

21. A rectangle's length is four more than twice its width. Its area is 160 square inches. What is its length?

    Equation: ____________________ Solution: ____________________

Write an equation in two variables to model each situation. Then graph the equation.

22. A penny was dropped from the window of a building, 64 feet above the ground. Write an equation for the height of the penny, h, at time t seconds after it was dropped. Graph the height of the penny over time.

____

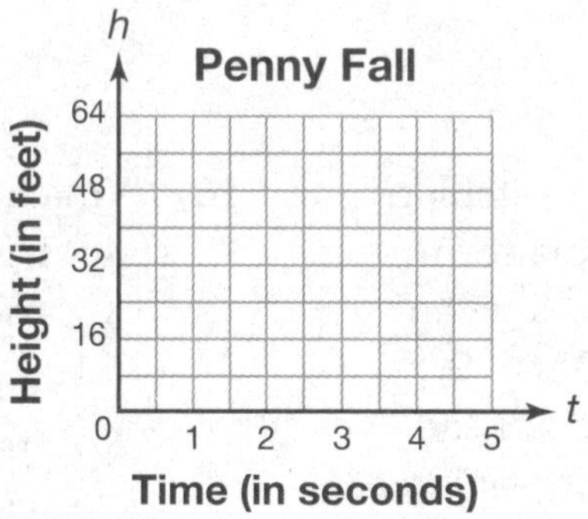

23. An electronics store discovers that it can sell 5 televisions per day by pricing them at \$150. When the televisions are on sale for \$100, the store sells 10 of them every day. Write a linear equation to compare the price of a television, p, to the number sold, x. Then, write a quadratic equation to compare the revenue, m, from selling televisions to the number sold, x. Graph this quadratic equation.

____

____

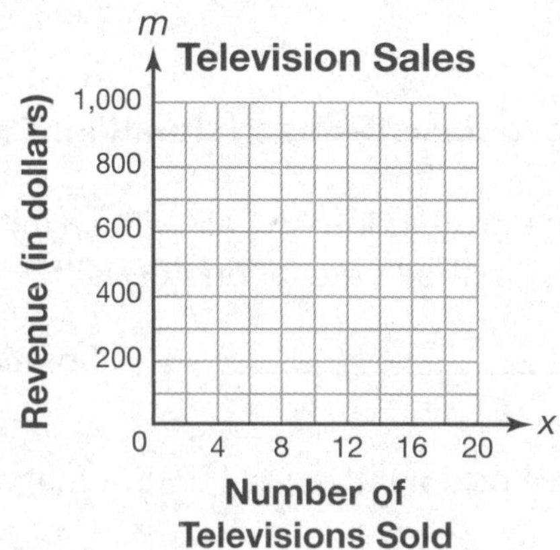

Write an equivalent equation.

24. The centripetal force of an object traveling on a circular path is given by the formula $F = \frac{mv^2}{r}$, where F is the force, m is the object's mass, v is the object's velocity, and r is the radius of the circle. Rewrite the formula to solve for v. ____________________

Write each expression in the form $a \cdot b^x$.

25. $2 \cdot 3^{3x}$ ____________

26. $8 \cdot 2^{\frac{x}{2}}$ ____________

27. $10^{\frac{2x}{5}}$ ____________

Solve.

28. The elevation of a rock dropped from the top of a building that is 300 meters tall is modeled by $h = 300 - 4.9t^2$, where t is the time in seconds after the rock was dropped and h is its elevation in meters. At the same time, a bird in front of the building is rising into the air with an elevation described by $h = 2.7t + 41$. Solve the system of equations, and interpret the solution(s). Is/are the solution(s) valid? Why or why not?

____

____

____

29. ANALYZE The size of a population of hummingbirds over time can be modeled by the equation $p = 55(2)^{\frac{t}{3}}$. How can the constant 55 be interpreted? If t is time in months, how long does it take for the hummingbird population to double?

____

____

____

30. MODEL The diagram below shows a triangle with base $(x + 5)$ and height $2x$ inside a shaded rectangle with length $(3x + 1)$ and width $(3x - 5)$.

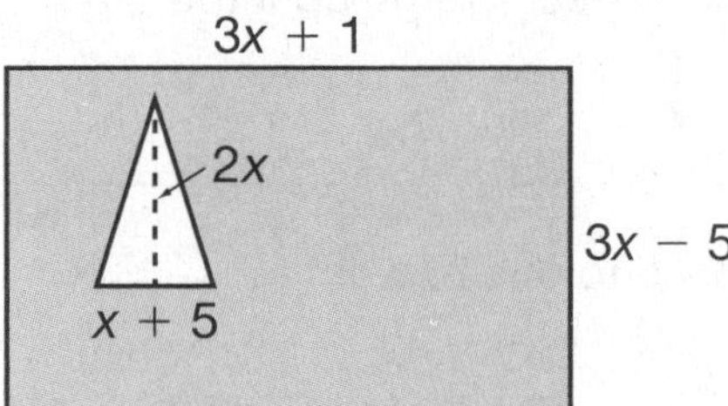

Find the following, in terms of x:

The area of the rectangle: ____________

The area of the triangle: ____________

The area of the shaded region: ____________

Performance Task

The *MORE* You Know

Work individually or in a group to answer the questions below.

You have been doing so well in your math courses that you decide to begin tutoring other students. You're not sure how much to charge for a tutoring session, so you ask around to see how many students would sign up, based on different rates. The table below gives the results of your survey.

Cost of a Tutoring Session, *p*	Students Willing to Sign Up, *x*
\$21	4
\$14	8
\$7	12

1. Write an equation that yields the number of students, x, that will sign up for a tutoring session that costs p dollars.

____

2. Write an equivalent equation that gives the price of a tutoring session based on the number of people willing to pay that price.

____

3. On the coordinate grid, graph the equation for the price that you created in question 2.

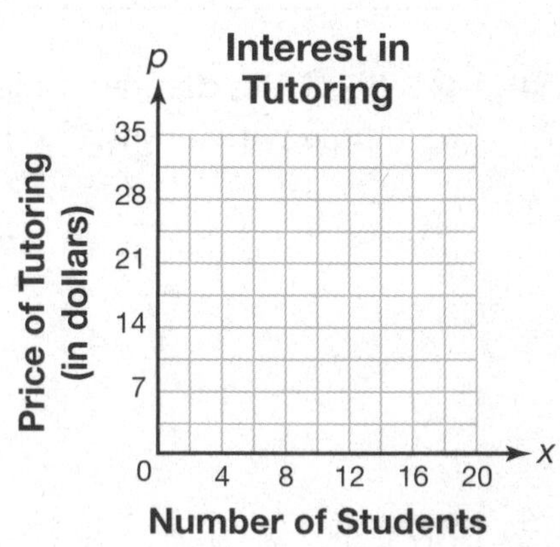

How many students would you expect to sign up if the lessons were free?

____

At what prices would you expect no one to want a tutoring session?

____

4. If you tutor x students each week and charge p dollars per tutoring session, write an equation for m, the amount of money you would expect to make each week from tutoring, in terms of x and p.

____

5. Write an equation for m in terms of x only. (Substitute an expression in terms of x for the variable p in your revenue equation.)

____

6. Complete the square to find the vertex of the equation that you created in question 5.

____

Graph this equation.

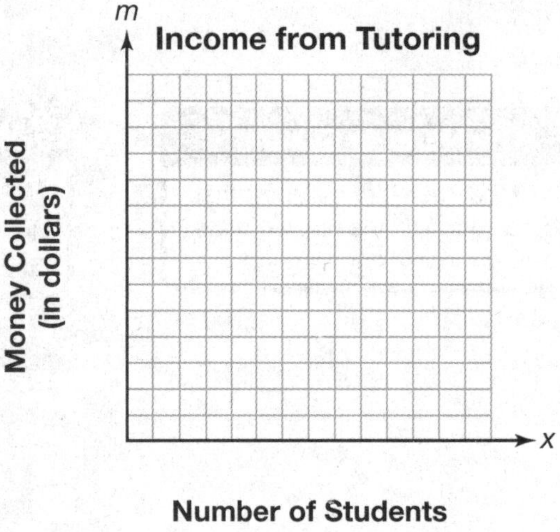

7. For what number of students would you expect to make the most money from tutoring?

____

How much money would you expect to make each week if you tutored this many students?

____

8. Set $m = 0$ and solve the resulting equation. What do the resulting values of x mean?

____

____

9. Now, write an equation for m in terms of p only.

____

10. Complete the square to find the vertex of the equation that you created in question 9.

____

Graph this equation.

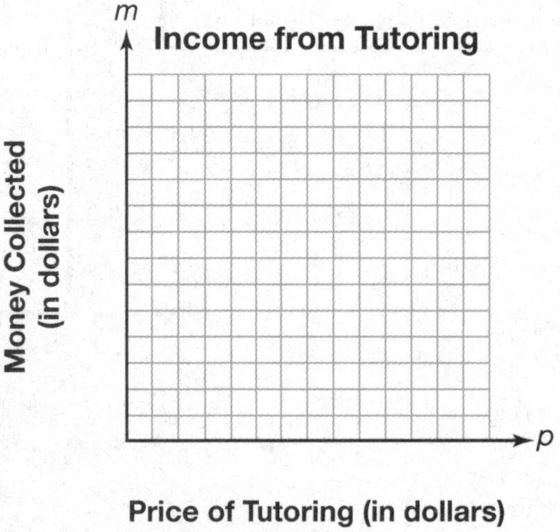

11. At what price would you expect to make the most money from tutoring?

____

12. Set $m = 0$ and solve the resulting equation. What do the resulting values of p mean?

____

____

Grade 8

The Number System

Know that there are numbers that are not rational, and approximate them by rational numbers.

Functions

Define, evaluate, and compare functions.

Use functions to model relationships between quantities.

Algebra I

Number and Quantity

The Real Number System

Use properties of rational and irrational numbers.

Functions

Interpreting Functions

Interpret functions that arise in applications in terms of the context.

Analyze functions using different representations.

Building Functions

Build a function that models the relationship between two quantities.

Build new functions from existing functions.

Linear, Quadratic, and Exponential Models

Construct and compare linear, quadratic, and exponential models and solve problems.

Geometry & Algebra II

Algebra

Creating Equations

Create equations that describe numbers or relationships.

Functions

Interpreting Functions

Interpret functions that arise in applications in terms of the context.

Building Functions

Build a function that models the relationship between two quantities.

Build new functions from existing functions.

Linear, Quadratic, and Exponential Models

Construct and compare linear, quadratic, and exponential models and solve problems.

Trigonometric Functions

Extend the domain of trigonometric functions using the unit circle.

Model periodic phenomena with trigonometric functions.

Prove and apply trigonometric identities.

Unit 5
Quadratic Functions and Modeling

Lesson 37 Rational and Irrational Numbers 300

Lesson 38 Key Features of Quadratic Functions 306

Lesson 39 Transforming Quadratic Functions 316

Lesson 40 Absolute Value, Step, and Piecewise Functions 326

Lesson 41 Inverse Functions 332

Lesson 42 Comparing Functions 338

Lesson 43 Modeling with Functions 346

Unit 5 Review 352

Unit 5 Performance Task 356

Rational and Irrational Numbers

UNDERSTAND The real numbers can be divided into two sets: the **rational numbers** and the **irrational numbers**. A rational number is any number that can be written as the quotient of two integers, $\frac{a}{b}$. All fractions and integers are rational numbers. Irrational numbers cannot be written as fractions. The set of irrational numbers consists of non-terminating, non-repeating decimals including π, e, and square roots such as $\sqrt{3}$.

UNDERSTAND You know that the sum of any two integers, $a + b$, is also an integer and that the product of any two integers, ab, is also an integer. Because of this, it is said that the set of integers is closed under addition and multiplication. The set of rational numbers is also closed under addition and multiplication.

The sum of rational numbers is always a rational number. Let $\frac{a}{b}$ and $\frac{c}{d}$ be rational numbers, such that a, b, c, and d are integers and b and d are not 0.

$$\frac{a}{b} + \frac{c}{d} = \frac{ad}{bd} + \frac{bc}{bd} = \frac{ad + bc}{bd}$$

Since a, b, c, and d are integers, the products ad, bc, and bd must also be integers. Since ad and bc are integers, their sum, $ad + bc$, must be an integer. So the final expression is the quotient of two integers, which is a rational number.

The product of rational numbers is also a rational number. Again, let $\frac{a}{b}$ and $\frac{c}{d}$ be rational numbers, such that a, b, c, and d are integers and b and d are not 0.

$$\frac{a}{b} \cdot \frac{c}{d} = \frac{ac}{bd}$$

Just as above, ac and bd must be integers, so the expression is a quotient of two integers.

Subtracting one rational number from another yields a rational number, and dividing any rational number by a rational number other than zero also yields a rational number.

The sum of a rational number and an irrational number is always irrational. The product of a rational number and an irrational number is also irrational, as long as the rational number is not 0. You will explore why this is true on the next page.

UNDERSTAND When dealing with square roots, you can factor out perfect square factors.

$$\sqrt{18} = \sqrt{9 \cdot 2} = \sqrt{9} \cdot \sqrt{2} = 3\sqrt{2}$$

You can also use the distributive property to combine like terms involving irrational numbers.

$$4\pi + \pi = 5\pi$$

$$3\sqrt{5} + 7\sqrt{5} = 10\sqrt{5}$$

Connect

Prove that the sum and product of the irrational number $\sqrt{2}$ and the rational number $\frac{1}{2}$ are irrational.

1 Prove that the sum is irrational.

One way to prove something is to begin by assuming that the opposite is true and then finding a contradiction.

Represent the sum by $s = \sqrt{2} + \frac{1}{2}$, and assume that s is a rational number.

Add $-\frac{1}{2}$ to both sides.

$$s = \sqrt{2} + \frac{1}{2}$$

$$s + \left(-\frac{1}{2}\right) = \sqrt{2}$$

If s is a rational number, then the expression $s + \left(-\frac{1}{2}\right)$ is the sum of two rational numbers, which you know must be a rational number. However, the sum is $\sqrt{2}$, which is not rational.

This is a contradiction, so the assumption that s is a rational number must be incorrect.

▶ Therefore, the sum $\sqrt{2} + \frac{1}{2}$ must be an irrational number.

2 Prove that the product is irrational.

Represent the product by $p = \sqrt{2} \cdot \frac{1}{2}$, and assume that p is a rational number.

Multiply both sides by 2.

$$p = \sqrt{2} \cdot \frac{1}{2}$$

$$p \cdot 2 = \sqrt{2}$$

If p is a rational number, then the expression $p \cdot 2$ is the product of two rational numbers, which you know must be a rational number. However, $\sqrt{2}$ is not rational.

This is a contradiction, so the assumption that p is a rational number must be incorrect. Therefore, the product $\sqrt{2} \cdot \frac{1}{2}$ must be an irrational number.

DISCUSS

The product of two irrational numbers can be rational or irrational. Can you think of an example of two irrational numbers whose product is rational?

EXAMPLE A Simplify the expression: $2\sqrt{3} + 10 + \sqrt{27} - 2\sqrt{49}$

1 Factor out any perfect square factors from the radicals.

Examine each radicand and determine if it contains a factor that is a perfect square.

The radicand of $2\sqrt{3}$ is 3, which is a prime number. It has no factors.

The radicand of $\sqrt{27}$ is 27, which has a factor of 9.

The radicand of $2\sqrt{49}$ is 49, which is a perfect square.

$2\sqrt{3} + 10 + \sqrt{27} - 2\sqrt{49}$

$2\sqrt{3} + 10 + \sqrt{9 \cdot 3} - 2\sqrt{7^2}$

$2\sqrt{3} + 10 + \sqrt{3^2 \cdot 3} - 2(7)$

$2\sqrt{3} + 10 + 3\sqrt{3} - 14$

2 Combine like terms and simplify.

Use the commutative, associative, and distributive properties to combine square root terms which have the same radicand.

$2\sqrt{3} + 10 + 3\sqrt{3} - 14$

$2\sqrt{3} + 3\sqrt{3} + 10 - 14$

$(2\sqrt{3} + 3\sqrt{3}) + (10 - 14)$

$(2 + 3)\sqrt{3} + (10 - 14)$

$5\sqrt{3} - 4$

▶ The expression simplifies to $5\sqrt{3} - 4$.

EXAMPLE B Simplify the expression: $\sqrt[3]{16} + \sqrt[3]{24} - 4\sqrt[3]{54}$

1 Factor out any perfect cube factors from the radicals.

The steps used to simplify square roots can be applied to radicals of any index.

Factor out the perfect cubes from these cube roots.

$\sqrt[3]{16} + \sqrt[3]{24} - 4\sqrt[3]{54}$

$\sqrt[3]{8 \cdot 2} + \sqrt[3]{8 \cdot 3} - 4\sqrt[3]{27 \cdot 2}$

$\sqrt[3]{2^3 \cdot 2} + \sqrt[3]{2^3 \cdot 3} - 4\sqrt[3]{3^3 \cdot 2}$

$2\sqrt[3]{2} + 2\sqrt[3]{3} - 4 \cdot 3\sqrt[3]{2}$

$2\sqrt[3]{2} + 2\sqrt[3]{3} - 12\sqrt[3]{2}$

2 Combine like terms.

The terms $2\sqrt[3]{2}$ and $-12\sqrt[3]{2}$ have the same index, 3, and the same radicand, 2.

$2\sqrt[3]{2} + 2\sqrt[3]{3} - 12\sqrt[3]{2}$

$2\sqrt[3]{3} - 10\sqrt[3]{2}$

The expression cannot be simplified further.

▶ The expression simplifies to $2\sqrt[3]{3} - 10\sqrt[3]{2}$.

TRY

Simplify the expression: $10\sqrt{20} + 2\sqrt{45} + 5$

EXAMPLE C A square has sides of length 32 inches. Find the length of its diagonal. Is this length a rational or irrational number?

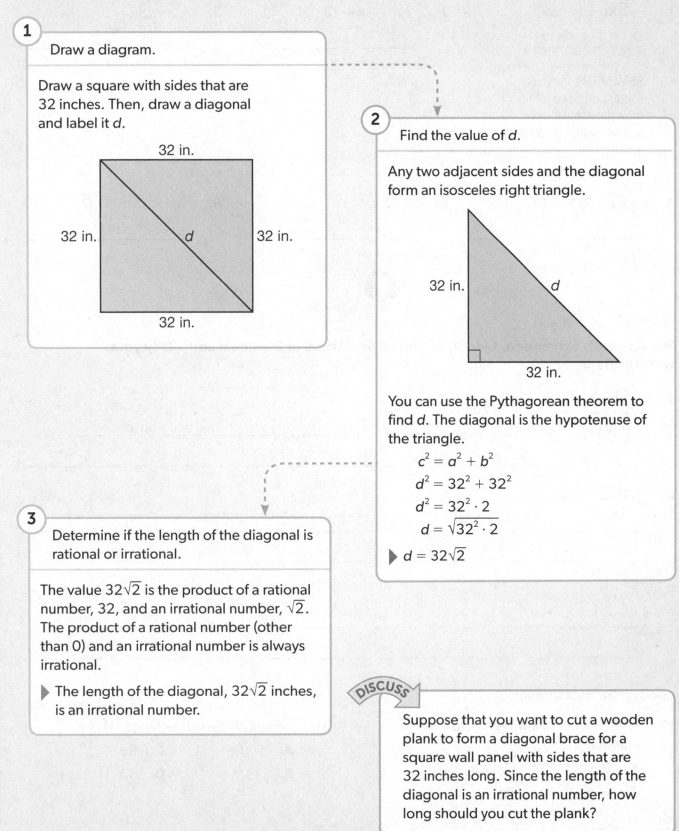

1 Draw a diagram.

Draw a square with sides that are 32 inches. Then, draw a diagonal and label it *d*.

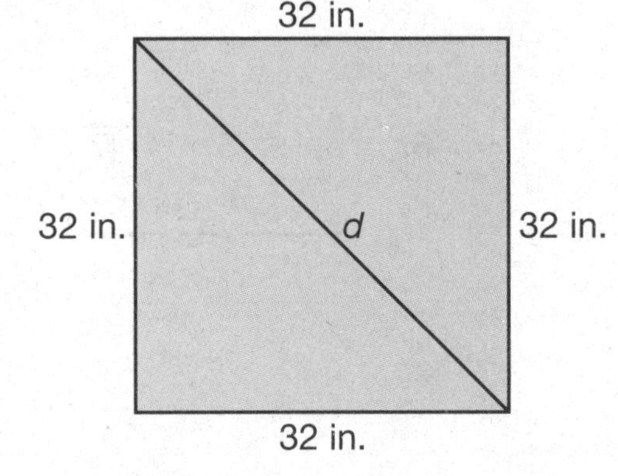

2 Find the value of *d*.

Any two adjacent sides and the diagonal form an isosceles right triangle.

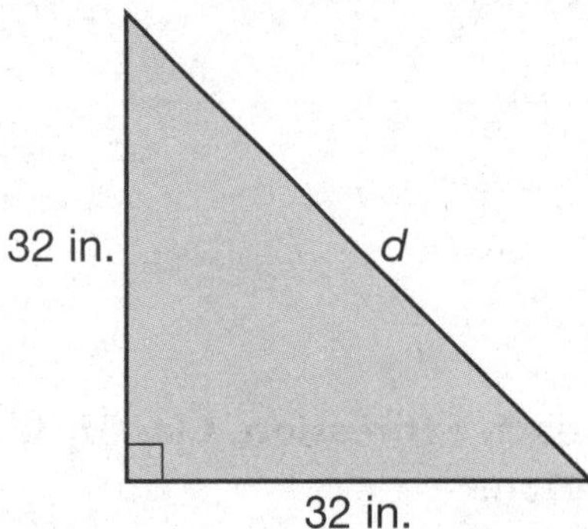

You can use the Pythagorean theorem to find *d*. The diagonal is the hypotenuse of the triangle.

$$c^2 = a^2 + b^2$$
$$d^2 = 32^2 + 32^2$$
$$d^2 = 32^2 \cdot 2$$
$$d = \sqrt{32^2 \cdot 2}$$

▶ $d = 32\sqrt{2}$

3 Determine if the length of the diagonal is rational or irrational.

The value $32\sqrt{2}$ is the product of a rational number, 32, and an irrational number, $\sqrt{2}$. The product of a rational number (other than 0) and an irrational number is always irrational.

▶ The length of the diagonal, $32\sqrt{2}$ inches, is an irrational number.

DISCUSS

Suppose that you want to cut a wooden plank to form a diagonal brace for a square wall panel with sides that are 32 inches long. Since the length of the diagonal is an irrational number, how long should you cut the plank?

Practice

Simplify each expression.

1. $\sqrt{200} - 1 - 5\sqrt{2}$

$5\sqrt{2} - 1$

2. $7\pi - 2\pi + 13$

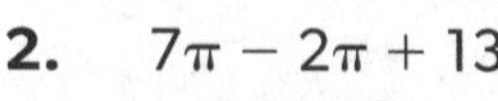

3. $\sqrt{2} \cdot \sqrt{32}$

8

REMEMBER In radical expressions, like terms have the same index and the same radicand.

4. $\sqrt[3]{40} + 2(9 - 2\sqrt[3]{5})$

5. $4\sqrt[3]{250}$

6. $6 - \sqrt{75} + \sqrt{147}$

$6 + 2\sqrt{3}$

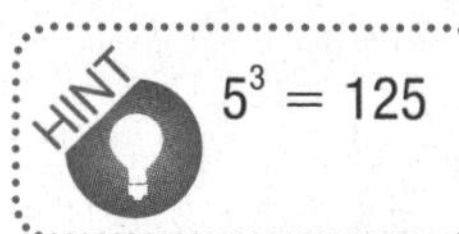

$5^3 = 125$

Simplify each expression. Classify the result as rational or irrational and justify your classification.

7. $\sqrt{24} + \sqrt{96}$

$6\sqrt{6}$. it is irrational because it cannot be writen as a fraction.

8. $10\sqrt[3]{16} - \sqrt[3]{54} + 17$

3/2 it is rational because the original answer, is, can be writon as 3/2 an improper fraction.

9. $3 \cdot \sqrt{\frac{1}{4}}$

Choose the best answer.

10. Which of the following is a rational number?

A. 3π **C.** $\sqrt{3} + 3$

B. $6\sqrt{8}$ **D.** $4\sqrt{16}$ (circled)

11. Simplify the expression: $(3\sqrt{11})^2$

A. $9\sqrt{11}$ **C.** 99 (circled)

B. 33 **D.** $33\sqrt{11}$

Solve.

12. A rectangle has dimensions of 3 feet by 1 foot. What is the length of the diagonal of the rectangle? Is the length a rational or irrational number?

---

13. A square has an area of 50 square meters. What is the length of one side of the square? Is the length a rational or an irrational number?

---

14. The period of a pendulum is the time, in seconds, that it takes the pendulum to go through a complete swing. The period of a pendulum with length L meters can be described by the equation $T = 2\pi\sqrt{\frac{L}{g}}$, where g is a gravitational constant and T is the period in seconds. Find the period of a pendulum that is 24 meters long if $g = 6$. Is this a rational or irrational number? Explain.

---

15. APPLY A rock was dropped from a platform 80 feet above the ground. The rock's height, h, is given by $h = -16t^2 + 80$, where t is the time, in seconds, since the rock was dropped.

Write an equation in one variable to find the time at which the rock hit the ground.

Solve the equation and interpret the answer. Is the answer a rational or irrational number?

---

16. DISPROVE Give examples to prove that the following statements are not true.

The product of two irrational numbers is always irrational.

The product of a rational number and an irrational number is always irrational.

Key Features of Quadratic Functions

Domain and Intercepts

UNDERSTAND A **quadratic function** is a function where the highest degree of the input variable is 2. The **standard form** of a quadratic function is $f(x) = ax^2 + bx + c$. The graph of a quadratic function is a parabola that opens upward or downward. The domain of an unrestricted quadratic function is all real numbers. This means that the input variable, usually x, can have any value.

It also means that the function's graph stretches across the entire coordinate plane, from $-\infty$ to ∞. Because of this, the graph must cross the y-axis, so every unrestricted quadratic function has a y-intercept. Just as with linear and exponential functions, the y-intercept of a quadratic function can be found by substituting 0 for x. For a function of the form $f(x) = ax^2 + bx + c$, the y-intercept is located at $(0, c)$.

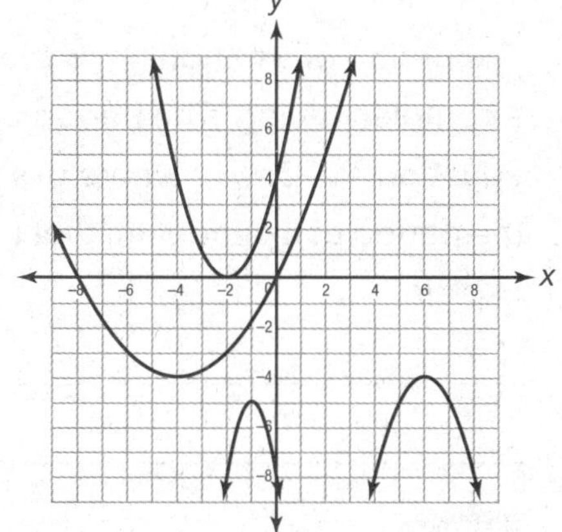

UNDERSTAND A quadratic function can have 0, 1, or 2 x-intercepts. The x-intercepts of a quadratic function are the points at which $f(x) = 0$. The x-coordinates of the x-intercepts of a function are the **zeros** of the function. For example, if function f has an x-intercept of $(9, 0)$, then 9 is a zero of f because $f(9) = 0$.

To find the x-intercepts of a quadratic function, solve the equation $f(x) = 0$. This can be done by factoring, by completing the square and taking the square root, or by using the quadratic formula. Factoring the equation can make the zeros of the function obvious. Examine the factored function below.

$$f(x) = (x - m)(x - n)$$

If $x = m$, the first factor becomes 0; and if $x = n$, the second factor becomes 0. Any number multiplied by 0 equals 0, so m and n are the zeros of the function. When the zeros, m and n, are irrational numbers, it is often easiest to find them by using the quadratic formula.

UNDERSTAND If a function has two zeros, the zeros divide it into positive and negative intervals.

Consider the graph of $f(x) = -x^2 + 4$ to the right.The zeros of the function are -2 and 2. The value of $f(x)$ is positive on the interval $-2 < x < 2$ because the graph is above the x-axis there. The value of $f(x)$ is negative on the intervals $-\infty < x < -2$ and $2 < x < \infty$.

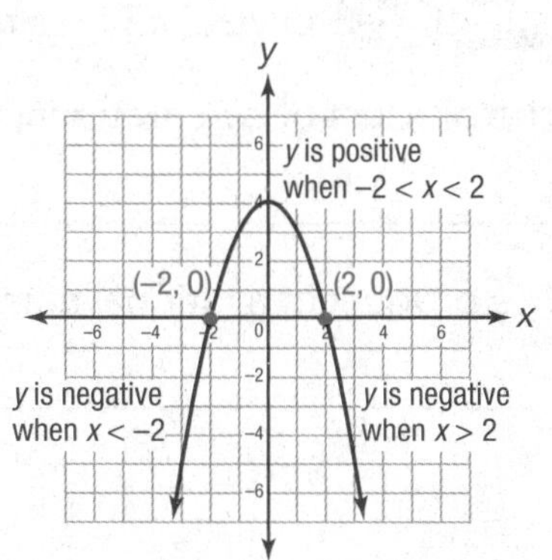

Connect

Find the x- and y-intercepts of the quadratic function: $f(x) = -x^2 + x + 6$

1 Find the y-intercept.

To find the y-intercept, evaluate $f(0)$ by substituting 0 for x.

$f(0) = -(0)^2 + 0 + 6$

$f(0) = 0 + 0 + 6$

$f(0) = 6$

The y-intercept is (0, 6).

2 Find any x-intercepts.

Substitute 0 for $f(x)$ and solve the resulting equation. Begin by dividing both sides by the leading coefficient, −1. Then factor.

$$-x^2 + x + 6 = 0$$

$$\frac{-x^2 + x + 6}{-1} = \frac{0}{-1}$$

$$x^2 - x - 6 = 0$$

$$(x - 3)(x + 2) = 0$$

$$x - 3 = 0 \quad \text{or} \quad x + 2 = 0$$

$$x = 3 \qquad\qquad x = -2$$

The zeros of the function are 3 and −2, so the x-intercepts are (3, 0) and (−2, 0).

Find the x- and y-intercepts of the quadratic function: $f(x) = 2x^2 + 8$

1 Find the y-intercept.

Find $f(0)$.

$f(0) = 2(0)^2 + 8$

$f(0) = 2 \cdot 0 + 8$

$f(0) = 0 + 8$

$f(0) = 8$

The y-intercept is (0, 8).

2 Find any x-intercepts.

Set $f(x)$ equal to 0 and solve for x.

$$2x^2 + 8 = 0$$

$$\frac{2x^2 + 8}{2} = \frac{0}{2}$$

$$x^2 + 4 = 0$$

$$x^2 = -4$$

There are no real values of x that are solutions to the equation $x^2 = -4$. The function has no real zeros, so its graph has no x-intercept.

TRY

Write a quadratic function that has x-intercepts at (9, 0) and (−1, 0) and a y-intercept at (0, 27).

Range, Symmetry, and End Behavior

UNDERSTAND The domain of an unrestricted quadratic function is all real numbers, but its range always has either an upper boundary or a lower boundary. An upper boundary of a function is called a **maximum**. A lower boundary is called a **minimum**. The maximum or minimum of a quadratic function is the y-coordinate of the **vertex** of its graph.

To find the maximum or minimum of a function, put its equation in vertex form. A quadratic function in vertex form is written $f(x) = a(x - h)^2 + k$. The vertex of that function is at (h, k). Notice that in vertex form h is subtracted from x, but k is added to the expression $a(x - h)^2$. So, for the function $f(x) = (x + 3)^2 + 7$, the vertex is at $(-3, 7)$, not $(3, 7)$ or $(-3, -7)$. For the function $g(x) = (x - 3)^2 - 7$, the vertex is at $(3, -7)$.

Recall that a quadratic expression can be transformed into vertex form by completing the square. For a quadratic function in standard form $f(x) = ax^2 + bx + c$, the vertex is located at $\left(-\frac{b}{2a}, f\left(-\frac{b}{2a}\right)\right)$. The parabola graphed to the right has its vertex at $(1, 2)$, so the function f has a maximum of 2. The range of the function is $f(x) \leq 2$.

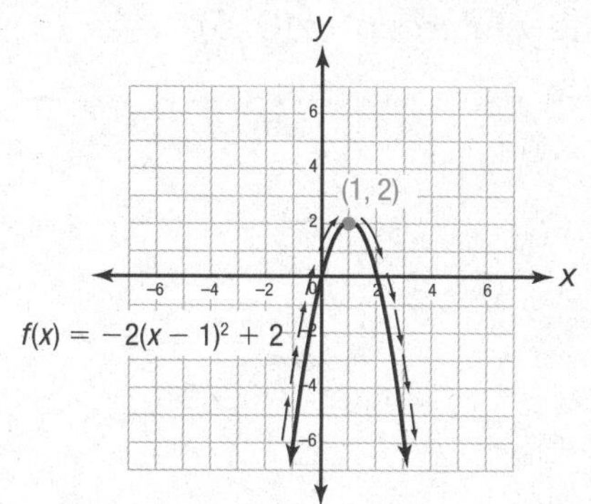

The vertex is the turning point of a parabola. The x-coordinate of the vertex divides the domain into two intervals, one on which the function is increasing and another on which the function is decreasing. On the graph above, the function f is increasing on the interval $x < 1$ and decreasing on the interval $x > 1$.

UNDERSTAND A vertical line drawn through the vertex of the graph of a quadratic function divides it into two halves. These two halves are mirror images of each other. This line is called the **axis of symmetry**, and the two halves of the parabola are called branches. For a parabola with vertex (h, k), the axis of symmetry is $x = h$.

UNDERSTAND To assess the end behavior of a quadratic function, look at the ends of the branches. For every quadratic function, the branches point in the same direction: either both upward or both downward.

In both standard form and vertex form, the value of a tells a great deal about the graph of the function. If $a > 0$, the parabola opens upward. This means that the function has a minimum value and that both branches point upward and approach positive infinity. If $a < 0$, the parabola opens downward. This means that the function has a maximum value and that both branches point downward and approach negative infinity.

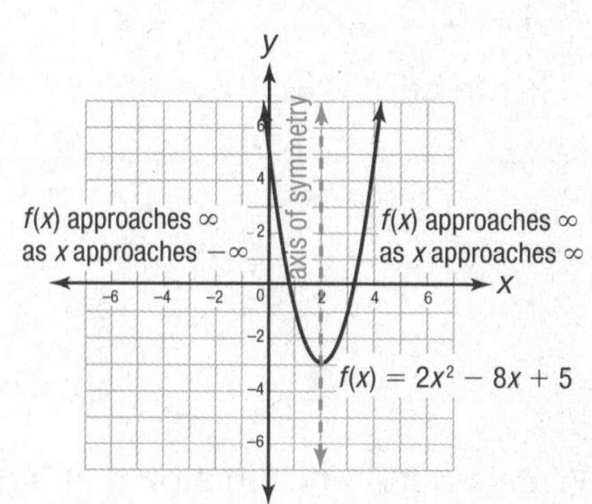

Connect

Identify the end behavior, vertex, maximum, minimum, range, and axis of symmetry of the function $f(x) = 3x^2 - 24x + 50$.

1 Examine the parameter a.

Comparing the function to standard form $f(x) = ax^2 + bx + c$, the value of a is 3. This means that the parabola opens upward, so as x approaches $-\infty$, $f(x)$ approaches ∞, and, as x approaches ∞, $f(x)$ approaches ∞. It also means that the function has some minimum value of $f(x)$ but no maximum.

2 Write the function in vertex form.

To identify the other key features, find the vertex. To do this, put the function in vertex form by completing the square.

$$f(x) = 3x^2 - 24x + 50$$
$$f(x) - 50 = 3x^2 - 24x$$
$$f(x) - 50 = 3(x^2 - 8x)$$
$$f(x) - 50 + 3(16) = 3(x^2 - 8x + 16)$$
$$f(x) - 2 = 3(x - 4)^2$$
$$f(x) = 3(x - 4)^2 + 2$$

3 Use the vertex to find minimum and range.

Compare the function to the vertex form $f(x) = a(x - h)^2 + k$, where the vertex is (h, k). In the function $f(x) = 3(x - 4)^2 + 2$, $h = 4$ and $k = 2$, so the vertex is (4, 2).

The maximum or minimum of a quadratic function is the y-coordinate, k, of the vertex of its graph. We have already determined that the function has no maximum, so 2 must be the minimum.

The range of a quadratic function is either all values less than or equal to the maximum or all values greater than or equal to the minimum. So the range of the function is $f(x) \geq 2$.

4 Use the vertex to find the axis of symmetry.

The axis of symmetry of the graph of a quadratic function is the line $x = h$. For this function, the vertex's x-coordinate, h, is 4, so the axis of symmetry is the vertical line $x = 4$.

CHECK

For $f(x) = 3x^2 - 24x + 50$, evaluate $\left(-\frac{b}{2a}, f\left(-\frac{b}{2a}\right)\right)$ and confirm that this formula gives the vertex found above. Then graph $y = 3x^2 - 24x + 50$ to confirm the other key features.

EXAMPLE A For the function $f(x) = (x - 2)^2 - 5$, find the vertex, axis of symmetry, end behavior, maximum or minimum, and intercepts. Then, use these key features to draw a graph of the function.

1

Identify the vertex, axis of symmetry, end behavior, and maximum or minimum.

The function is already written in vertex form, $f(x) = a(x - h)^2 + k$.

The vertex, (h, k), is found at $(2, -5)$.

The axis of symmetry, $x = h$, is $x = 2$.

The value of a is 1, which is positive, so the graph of the function opens upward, both branches point upward, and the function has a minimum of -5.

2

Find the y-intercept.

To find the y-intercept, find $f(0)$.

$$f(x) = (x - 2)^2 - 5$$

$$f(0) = (0 - 2)^2 - 5$$

$$f(0) = (-2)^2 - 5$$

$$f(0) = 4 - 5$$

$$f(0) = -1$$

The y-intercept is at $(0, -1)$.

3

Find any x-intercepts.

Substitute 0 for $f(x)$ and solve.

$$f(x) = (x - 2)^2 - 5$$

$$0 = (x - 2)^2 - 5$$

$$5 = (x - 2)^2$$

$$\pm\sqrt{5} = x - 2$$

$$2 \pm \sqrt{5} = x$$

The x-intercepts are $(2 + \sqrt{5}, 0)$ and $(2 - \sqrt{5}, 0)$.

4

Graph the function.

Plot the vertex and the intercepts.

Because parabolas are symmetric, the y-intercept, $(0, -1)$, has a corresponding point on the other side of $x = 2$ at $(4, -1)$. Draw a smooth parabolic curve through these points.

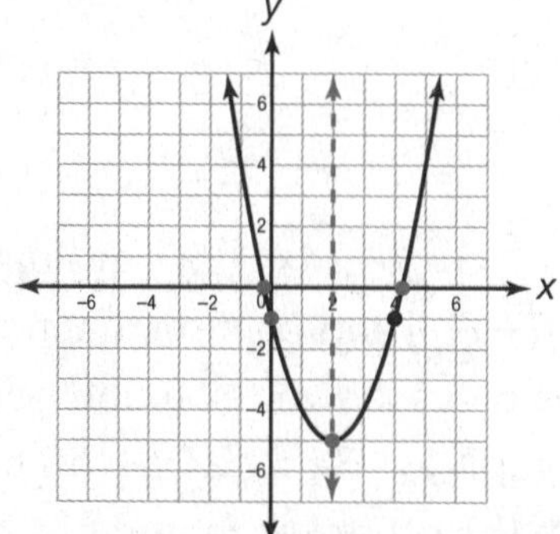

DISCUSS

What methods could you use to improve your graph?

EXAMPLE B A cannonball was fired from a cannon on a ship and landed in the water. Its height in feet above the water is described by the function $h(t) = -16t^2 + 76t + 20$, where t is the time, in seconds, since the cannon was fired. Find the span of time when the cannonball was in the air, the span of time when it was rising, and the span of time when it was falling. Also, find the greatest height that the cannonball reached.

1 Examine the situation.

The cannonball was in the air from time $t = 0$ until it landed in the water. When it landed in the water, its height was 0 feet. Find time t when the cannonball landed in the water by setting $h(t) = 0$.

The greatest height of the cannonball is the maximum value of $h(t)$. The cannonball rose on the interval where its height was increasing, and it fell on the interval where its height was decreasing.

2 Find the span of time when the cannonball was in the air.

In the function $h(t) = -16t^2 + 76t + 20$, $a = -16$, $b = 76$, and $c = 20$.

$$t = \frac{-b \pm \sqrt{b^2 - 4ac}}{2a}$$

$$t = \frac{-76 \pm \sqrt{(76)^2 - 4(-16)(20)}}{2(-16)}$$

$$t = \frac{-76 \pm \sqrt{7{,}056}}{-32}$$

$$t = \frac{-76 + 84}{-32} \quad \text{or} \quad t = \frac{-76 - 84}{-32}$$

$$t = -0.25 \qquad t = 5$$

Since time cannot be negative, $t = -0.25$ is an extraneous solution. The cannonball landed in the water after 5 seconds.

3 Find the greatest height that the cannonball reached, the span of time when it was rising, and the span of time when it was falling.

For a quadratic function of the form $f(x) = ax^2 + bx + c$, the vertex is $\left(-\frac{b}{2a}, f\left(-\frac{b}{2a}\right)\right)$.

Find $-\frac{b}{2a}$.

$-\frac{76}{2(-16)}$

$-\frac{76}{-32}$

2.375

Find $f(-\frac{b}{2a})$.

$f(2.375) = -16(2.375)^2 + 76(2.375) + 20$

$f(2.375) = -90.25 + 180.5 + 20$

$f(2.375) = 110.25$

The vertex is found at (2.375, 110.25). The cannonball reached a maximum height of 110.25 feet. It was rising on the interval $0 < t < 2.375$ and was falling on the interval $2.375 < t < 5$.

Graph the function on a graphing calculator to check your answers.

Practice

Write each function in vertex form. Then identify the vertex.

1. $f(x) = x^2 - 20x + 91$

vertex form: ____________________

vertex: ____________________

2. $f(x) = -x^2 + 12x - 29$

vertex form: ____________________

vertex: ____________________

3. $f(x) = 2x^2 + 20x + 58$

vertex form: ____________________

vertex: ____________________

REMEMBER Factor out any leading coefficient before completing the square.

Identify whether the function has a maximum or minimum by circling the appropriate word, and then write the maximum or minimum of the function.

4. $f(x) = -3(x - 11)^2 - 12$

maximum/minimum: ________

5. $f(x) = x^2 + 8x + 66$

maximum/minimum: ________

For each function, give its intervals of increase and decrease.

6. $f(x) = 4(x + 13)^2 - 20$

interval of increase: __________

interval of decrease: __________

7. $f(x) = -x^2 + 18x - 73$

interval of increase: __________

interval of decrease: __________

REMEMBER The vertex is the turning point of a parabola, where it changes between increasing and decreasing.

Determine the intercepts of each function.

8. $f(x) = x^2 - 8x + 7$

x-intercept(s): __________

y-intercept(s): __________

9. $f(x) = -2x^2 - 24x - 72$

x-intercept(s): __________

y-intercept(s): __________

10. $f(x) = (x - 2)^2 + 3$

x-intercept(s): __________

y-intercept(s): __________

Choose the best answer.

11. Which function is graphed to the right?

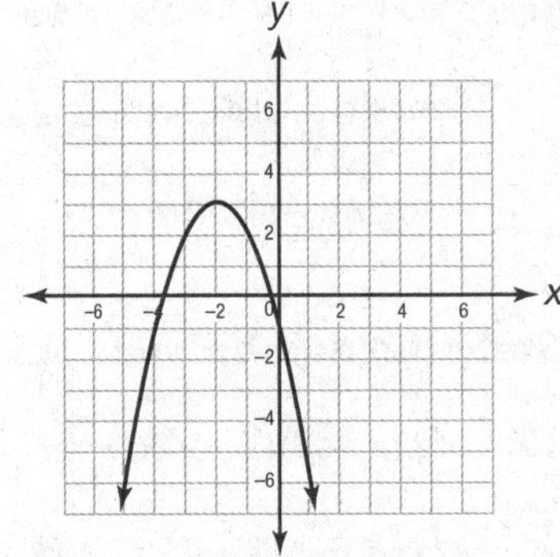

A. $f(x) = (x + 2)^2 + 3$

B. $f(x) = -(x + 2)^2 + 3$

C. $f(x) = -(x - 2)^2 - 3$

D. $f(x) = -(x + 3)^2 + 2$

12. What is the axis of symmetry for the function graphed to the right?

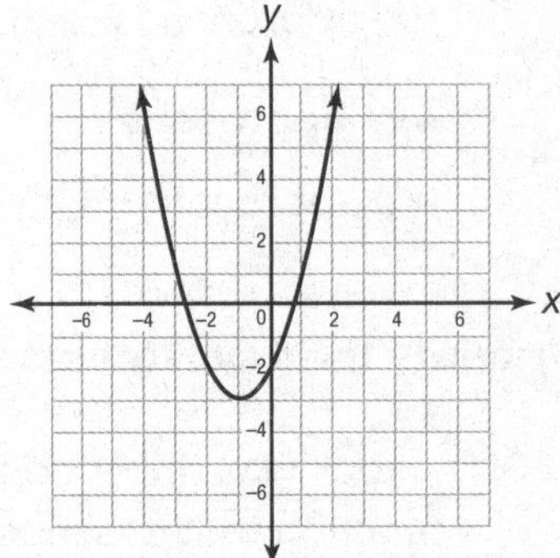

A. $x = -3$

B. $y = -3$

C. $x = 0$

D. $x = -1$

13. Which of the following is true of the function graphed to the right?

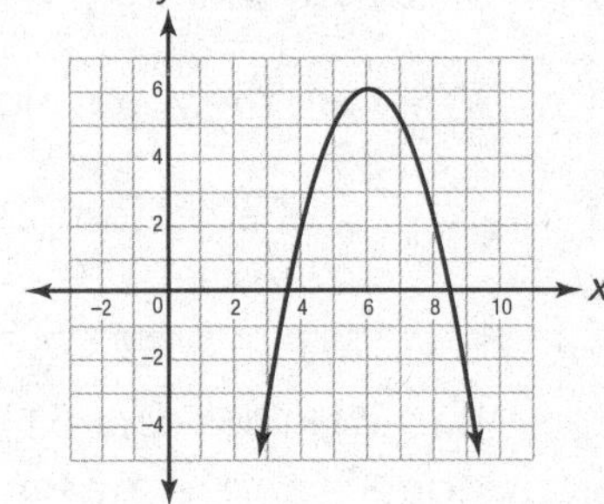

A. It has a positive leading coefficient, a.

B. It is increasing on the interval $(-\infty, 6)$.

C. Its vertex is (7, 5).

D. Its minimum value is 6.

14. What are the zeros of the function graphed to the right?

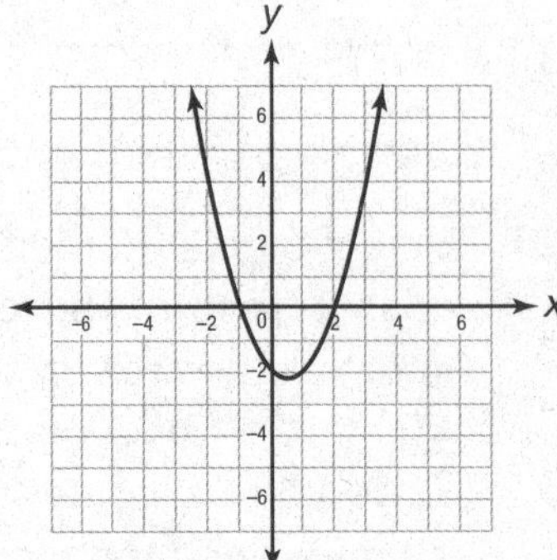

A. −1 only

B. −2 only

C. 1 and −2

D. −1 and 2

For each function, give the interval(s) in which the function's value is positive and the interval(s) in which its value is negative.

15. $f(x) = -x^2 - 8x - 15$

positive interval(s): __________

negative interval(s): __________

16. $f(x) = x^2 + 4$

positive interval(s): __________

negative interval(s): __________

State the end behavior of each function.

17. $f(x) = 3x^2 + 4x + 5$

As x approaches $-\infty$,

$f(x)$ approaches ______.

As x approaches ∞,

$f(x)$ approaches ______.

18. $f(x) = (x + 99)^2 - 100$

As x approaches $-\infty$,

$f(x)$ approaches ______.

As x approaches ∞,

$f(x)$ approaches ______.

19. $f(x) = -5(x - 2)^2 + 2$

As x approaches $-\infty$,

$f(x)$ approaches ______.

As x approaches ∞,

$f(x)$ approaches ______.

Identify the key features.

20. A rock was dropped from the top of a building. The function that describes its height in feet x seconds after it was dropped is $f(x) = 64 - 16x^2$. A graph of the function is shown to the right.

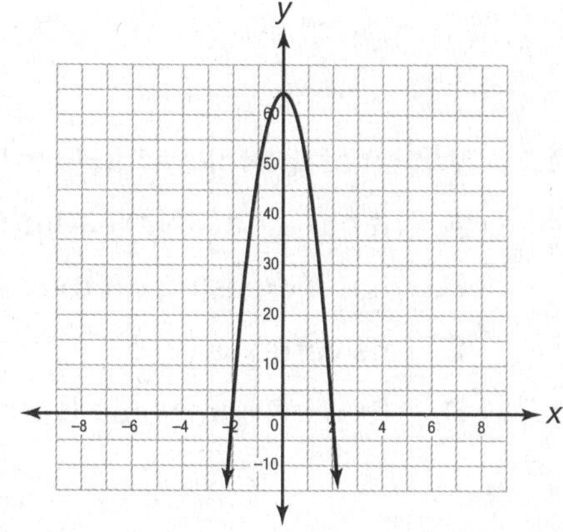

What are the zeros of the function, and what do they mean?

____

____

Based on the context of the situation, what are a reasonable domain and range for the function? Explain.

____

____

21. A rectangular garden bed will have a width that is 3 meters less than its length. The total area must be no more than 10 square meters. The area, in square meters, is given by the function $f(x) = x^2 - 3x$. A graph of the function is shown to the right. Based on the context of the situation, what are a reasonable domain and range for the function? Explain.

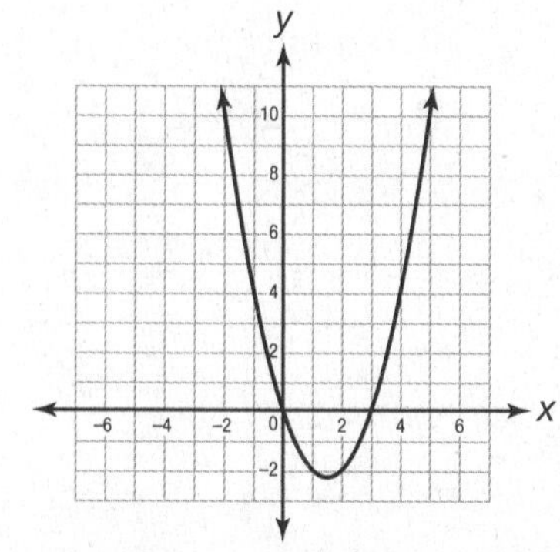

____

____

____

22. Give each of the following for the function $f(x) = -(x + 3)^2 + 4$.

vertex: ____________

maximum or minimum (circle one):

____

axis of symmetry: ____________

end behavior: ____________

____

____

____

interval of increase: ____________

interval of decrease: ____________

y-intercept: ________

zero(s): ________

positive interval(s): ____________

negative interval(s): ____________

Graph the function on the coordinate plane.

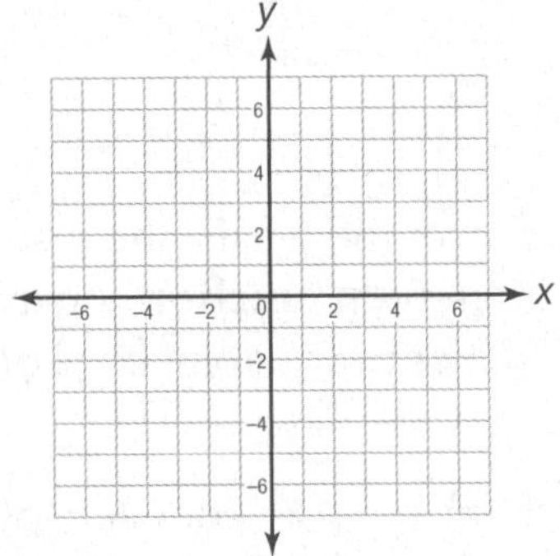

23. Give each of the following for the function $f(x) = x^2 - 4x + 3$.

vertex: ____________

maximum or minimum (circle one):

____

axis of symmetry: ____________

end behavior: ____________

____

____

____

interval of increase: ____________

interval of decrease: ____________

y-intercept: ________

zero(s): ________

positive interval(s): ____________

negative interval(s): ____________

Graph the function on the coordinate plane.

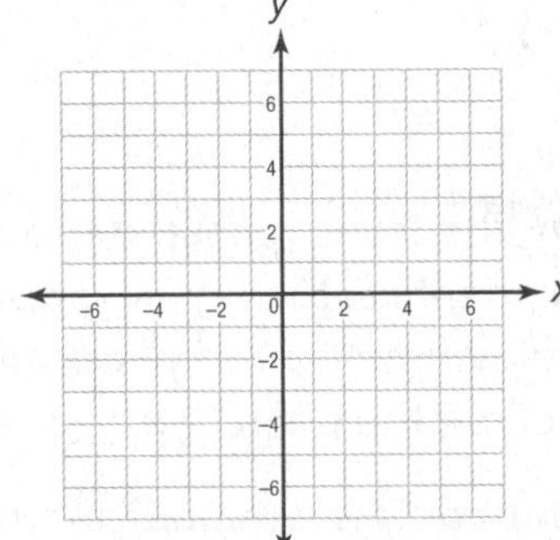

24. **EXAMINE** How many zeros does a function in the form $f(x) = x^2 - 2ax + a^2$ have? Explain.

____

____

25. **FIND AN EQUATION** Write the equation of a quadratic function that is negative on the interval $(-\infty, \infty)$.

____

Transforming Quadratic Functions

Translations and Reflections

UNDERSTAND The **parent function**, or most basic function, for the family of quadratic functions is $f(x) = x^2$. All quadratic functions can be thought of as transformations of this parent function. For example, adding a constant to the output or the input value translates the graph of the function vertically or horizontally.

Adding a constant to the output results in a vertical translation. The graph of $g(x) = f(x) + k$ moves the parent function k units up, if k is positive, or $|k|$ units down, if k is negative.

Adding a constant to the input results in a horizontal translation. The graph of $g(x) = f(x + k)$ moves the parent function k units left, if k is positive, and $|k|$ units right, if k is negative.

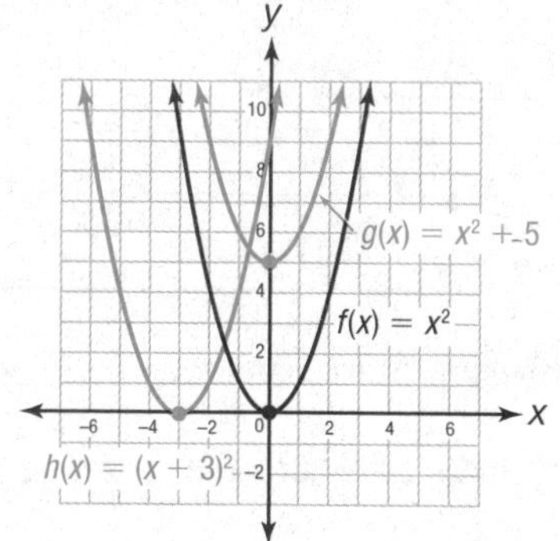

UNDERSTAND Another way to transform a quadratic function is by reflection. Changing the sign of the output, as in $g(x) = -f(x)$, reflects its graph over the x-axis. Changing the sign of the input, as in $g(x) = f(-x)$, reflects the graph over the y-axis.

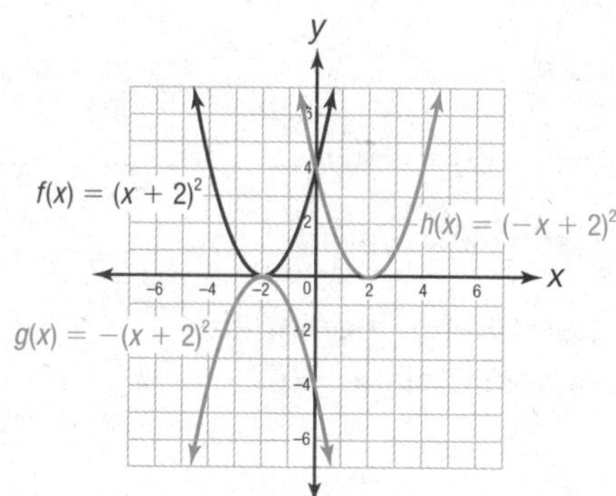

UNDERSTAND If you reflected the graph of the function $f(x) = x^2$ over the y-axis, the result would be identical to original graph. This means that $f(x) = x^2$ is an **even function**. An even function is symmetrical with respect to the y-axis, so $f(-x) = f(x)$. For every point (x, y) of an even function, the point $(-x, y)$ is also a point on the function.

An **odd function** is symmetrical with respect to the origin, so $f(-x) = -f(x)$. For every point (x, y) on an odd function, the point $(-x, -y)$ is also a point on the function. The functions $f(x) = x$ and $f(x) = x^3$ are odd functions.

Connect

The graph of a function $f(x)$ is shown below. Graph the function $g(x)$, which is the result of translating $f(x)$ 5 units up and then reflecting the translated graph across the y-axis.

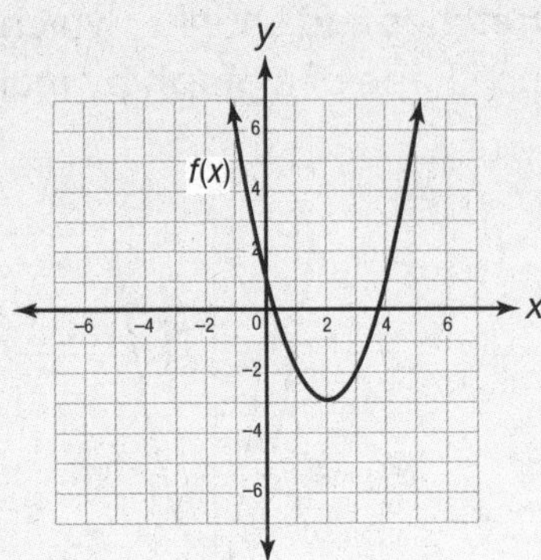

1 Translate the function.

The function is translated 5 units up, so slide each point on the graph up 5 units. This is equivalent to adding 5 to each point's y-coordinate.

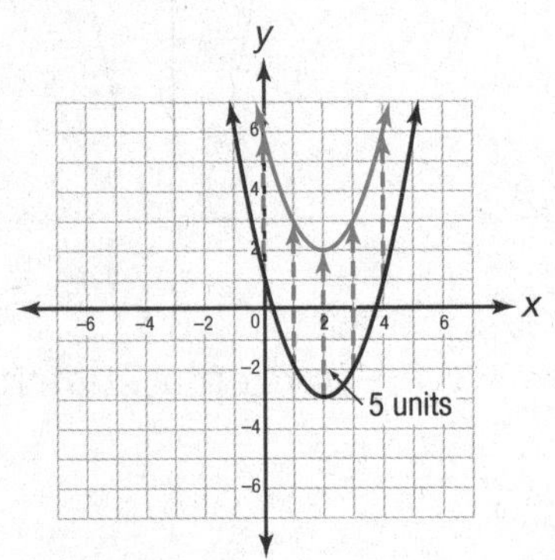

2 Reflect the function.

To reflect a graph across the y-axis, move each point from one side of the y-axis to the opposite side. Be sure that the reflected point is the same distance from the y-axis as the original point. This is equivalent to changing the sign of each x-coordinate.

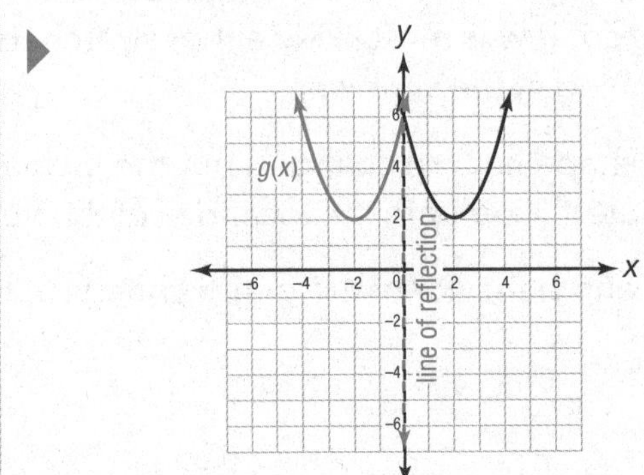

DISCUSS

Is $g(x)$ an even function? Is it an odd function?

Stretches and Shrinks

UNDERSTAND Translations and reflections produce graphs that are the same size and shape as the original graph. Stretches and shrinks, which are other types of transformations, change the size and shape of a graph by making it narrower or wider.

When you multiply the output of a function by a constant, the graph of the function becomes stretched or shrunk vertically. This means that the points of the graph are pulled away from or pushed towards the x-axis. The graph of $g(x) = kf(x)$ represents a vertical stretch of the graph of f if $k > 1$. The graph of $g(x) = kf(x)$ represents a vertical shrink of the graph of f if $0 < k < 1$.

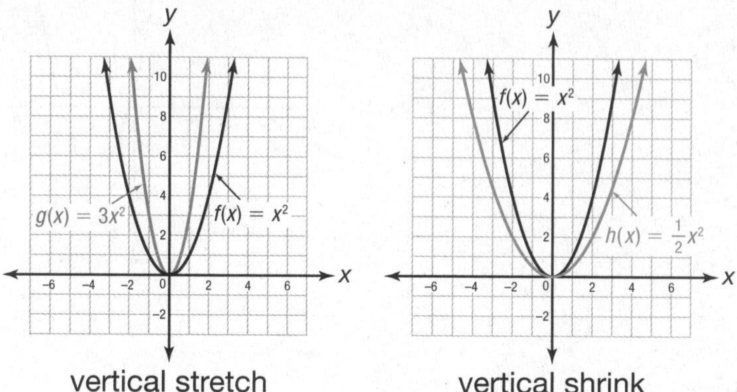

vertical stretch

vertical shrink

When you multiply the input of a function by a constant, the graph of the function becomes stretched or shrunk horizontally, meaning that the points of the graph are pulled away from or pushed towards the y-axis. The graph of $g(x) = f(kx)$ represents a horizontal shrink of the graph of f if $k > 1$. The graph of $g(x) = f(kx)$ represents a horizontal stretch of the graph of f if $0 < k < 1$.

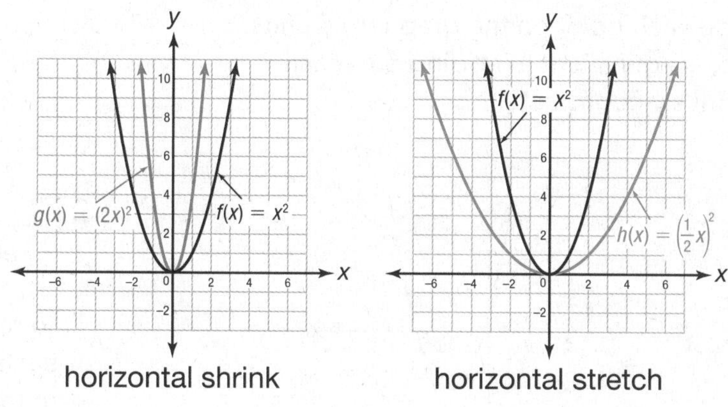

horizontal shrink

horizontal stretch

UNDERSTAND You can determine the equation of a transformed quadratic function by comparing its graph to the graph of the original function. If the shape of the graph was changed, it was most likely either stretched or shrunk. Be sure to compare the shapes beginning at the vertexes.

If the shape has not changed but the location of the vertex has, the function has likely been translated. Compare the locations of the vertexes in order to determine the translation.

If the end behavior of the graph changed, the function was likely reflected across the x-axis.

Connect

The function $f(x) = (x - 1)^2 - 1$ is shown on the coordinate grid to the right. Graph the functions $g(x) = 4f(x)$ and $h(x) = f(2x)$. Then identify the transformations which produced functions g and h from f.

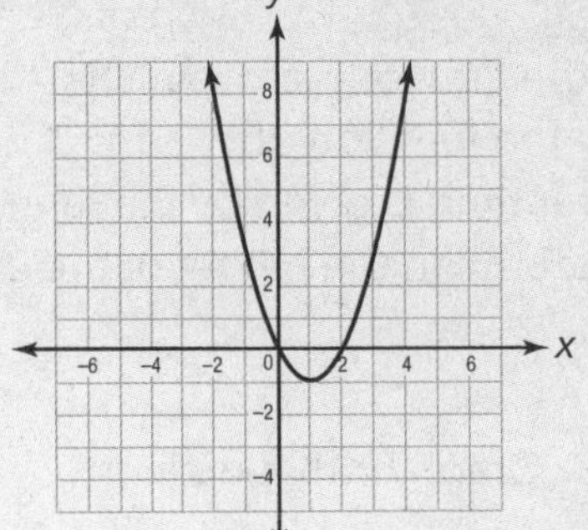

1 Find the equation for $g(x)$.

Since $g(x) = 4f(x)$, multiply $f(x)$ by 4.

$g(x) = 4[(x - 1)^2 - 1]$

$g(x) = 4(x^2 - 2x)$

$g(x) = 4x^2 - 8x$

Make a table of values for the function.

x	$g(x) = 4x^2 - 8x$	$g(x)$
−1	$4(-1)^2 - 8(-1) = 12$	12
0	$4(0)^2 - 8(0) = 0$	0
1	$4(1)^2 - 8(1) = -4$	−4
2	$4(2)^2 - 8(2) = 0$	0
3	$4(3)^2 - 8(3) = 12$	12

2 Find the equation for $h(x)$.

Since $h(x) = f(2x)$, substitute $2x$ for x in the equation and simplify.

$h(x) = (2x - 1)^2 - 1$

$h(x) = (4x^2 - 4x + 1) - 1$

$h(x) = 4x^2 - 4x$

Make a table of values for the function.

x	$h(x) = 4x^2 - 4x$	$h(x)$
−1	$4(-1)^2 - 4(-1) = 8$	8
0	$4(0)^2 - 4(0) = 0$	0
1	$4(1)^2 - 4(1) = 0$	0
2	$4(2)^2 - 4(2) = 8$	8
3	$4(3)^2 - 4(3) = 24$	24

3 Graph all three functions on the same coordinate grid.

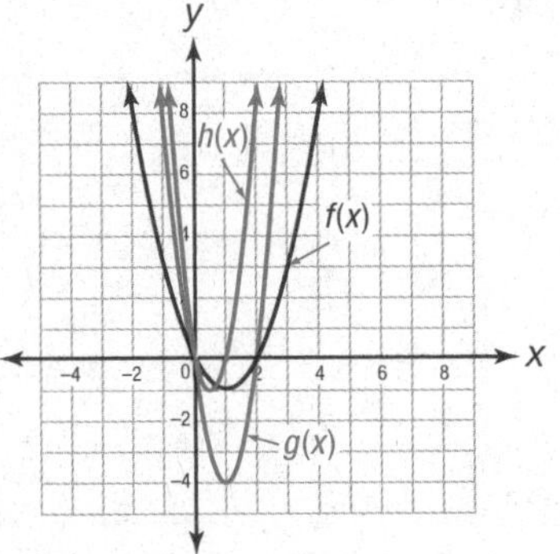

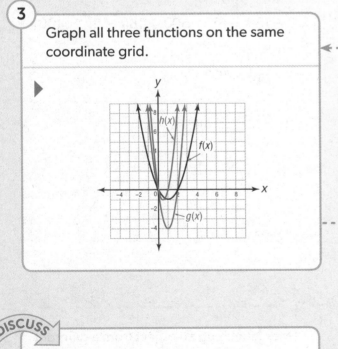

4 Compare the graphs to identify the transformations.

▶ The graph of $g(x)$ is longer than the graph of $f(x)$. The points of the graph have been pulled away from the x-axis in both directions, so it is a vertical stretch. The graph of $h(x)$ is narrower than $f(x)$. The points have been pushed towards the y-axis, so it is a horizontal shrink.

DISCUSS

Do the graphs of $g(x)$ and $h(x)$ have the same vertex as $f(x)$? the same axis of symmetry?

EXAMPLE A The town of Oceanside is planning a fireworks show to celebrate the town's founding. If the fireworks are launched from a barge on the ocean, the height of the fireworks over time is given by the function $b(t) = -16(t - 5)^2 + 400$. If they are launched from a cliff on the coast, their height over time is given by the function $c(t) = -16(t - 5)^2 + 500$. Graph both functions and compare them. Determine the height of the cliff.

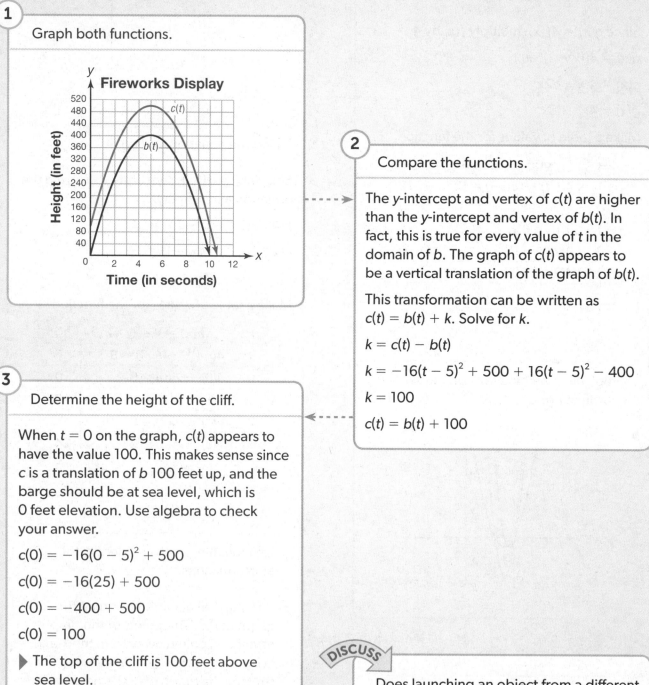

1

Graph both functions.

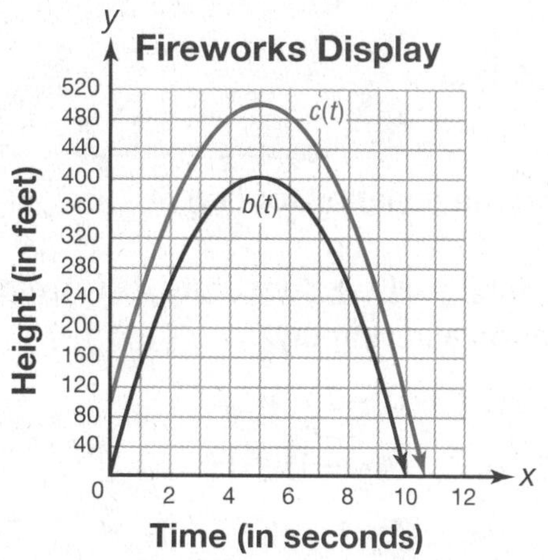

2

Compare the functions.

The y-intercept and vertex of $c(t)$ are higher than the y-intercept and vertex of $b(t)$. In fact, this is true for every value of t in the domain of b. The graph of $c(t)$ appears to be a vertical translation of the graph of $b(t)$.

This transformation can be written as $c(t) = b(t) + k$. Solve for k.

$k = c(t) - b(t)$

$k = -16(t - 5)^2 + 500 + 16(t - 5)^2 - 400$

$k = 100$

$c(t) = b(t) + 100$

3

Determine the height of the cliff.

When $t = 0$ on the graph, $c(t)$ appears to have the value 100. This makes sense since c is a translation of b 100 feet up, and the barge should be at sea level, which is 0 feet elevation. Use algebra to check your answer.

$c(0) = -16(0 - 5)^2 + 500$

$c(0) = -16(25) + 500$

$c(0) = -400 + 500$

$c(0) = 100$

▶ The top of the cliff is 100 feet above sea level.

DISCUSS

Does launching an object from a different height affect the maximum height it reaches? Does it affect the time that the object remains in the air?

EXAMPLE B The graph of $f(x) = x^2 + 6x + 6$ is shown to the right, along with the graph of $g(x)$. The function $g(x)$ is a transformation of $f(x)$. Find the equation for $g(x)$ in terms of $f(x)$ and in terms of x.

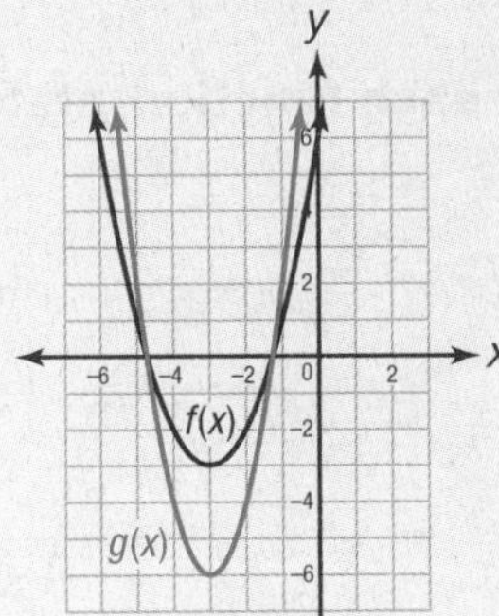

1 Compare the graphs.

The graphs have slightly different shapes. They have the same x-intercepts but different vertexes and y-intercepts. The graph of g appears to be a vertical stretch of the graph of f.

Since the graph of g was transformed vertically, compare points with the same x-coordinates.

x	$f(x)$	$g(x)$
−5	1	2
−4	−2	−4
−3	−3	−6
−2	−2	−4
−1	1	2

2 Write an equation for $g(x)$ in terms of $f(x)$.

A vertical stretch can be written in the form $g(x) = kf(x)$. Solving for k, $k = \frac{g(x)}{f(x)}$. Use your table to find k for multiple values of x.

$$\frac{g(-5)}{f(-5)} = \frac{2}{1} = 2$$

$$\frac{g(-4)}{f(-4)} = \frac{-4}{-2} = 2$$

$$\frac{g(-3)}{f(-3)} = \frac{-6}{-3} = 2$$

$$\frac{g(-2)}{f(-2)} = \frac{-4}{-2} = 2$$

$$\frac{g(-1)}{f(-1)} = \frac{2}{1} = 2$$

The value of k is the same for every pair of points in the table, so g is indeed a vertical stretch.

▶ $g(x) = 2f(x)$

3 Write an equation for $g(x)$ in terms of x.

Substitute the expression for $f(x)$ into $g(x) = 2f(x)$.

$g(x) = 2f(x)$

$g(x) = 2(x^2 + 6x + 6)$

▶ $g(x) = 2x^2 + 12x + 12$

CHECK

Using your graphing calculator, graph $f(x) = x^2 + 6x + 6$ and $g(x) = 2x^2 + 12x + 12$. Do the graphs match the ones shown above?

Practice

For each function, state whether it is *even*, *odd*, or *neither*.

1.

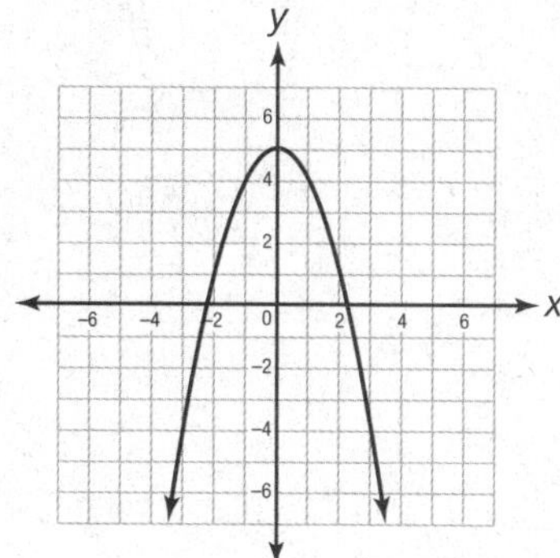

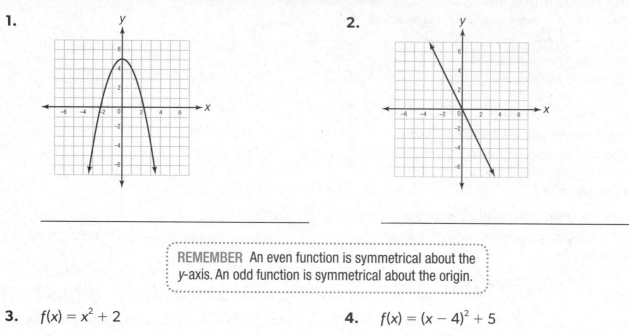

2.

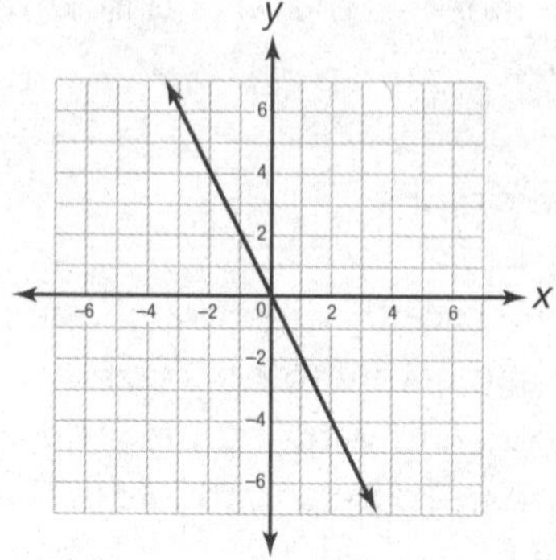

______________________________ ______________________________

REMEMBER An even function is symmetrical about the y-axis. An odd function is symmetrical about the origin.

3. $f(x) = x^2 + 2$

____

4. $f(x) = (x - 4)^2 + 5$

____

State the effect of each transformation on the graph of the parent function, $f(x) = x^2$.

5. $g(x) = (x - 7)^2$

____

____

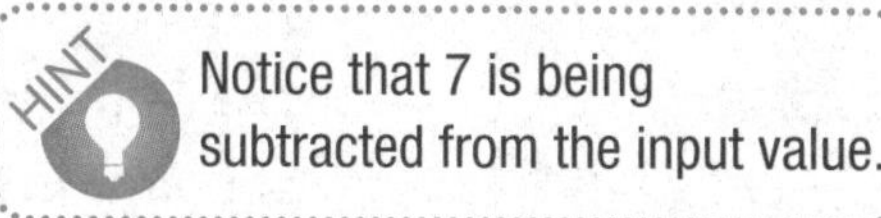

Notice that 7 is being subtracted from the input value.

6. $h(x) = \left(\frac{1}{4}x\right)^2$

____

____

Choose the best answer.

7. The graph shows $f(x) = -x^2$ and $g(x)$, a transformation of $f(x)$. Which gives an expression for $g(x)$?

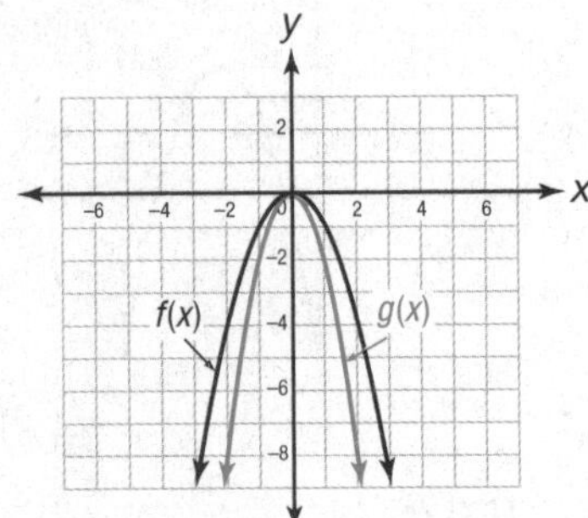

A. $g(x) = -\frac{1}{2}x^2$

B. $g(x) = -2x^2$

C. $g(x) = -x^2 - 1$

D. $g(x) = (2x)^2$

8. Which describes the transformation of $f(x)$ to $g(x)$?

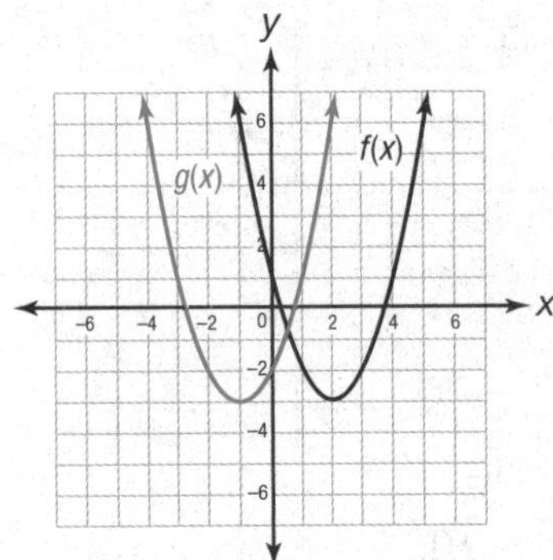

A. $g(x) = f(x) + 3$

B. $g(x) = f(x) - 3$

C. $g(x) = f(x + 3)$

D. $g(x) = f(x - 3)$

9. Which describes the transformation of $h(x)$ to $j(x)$?

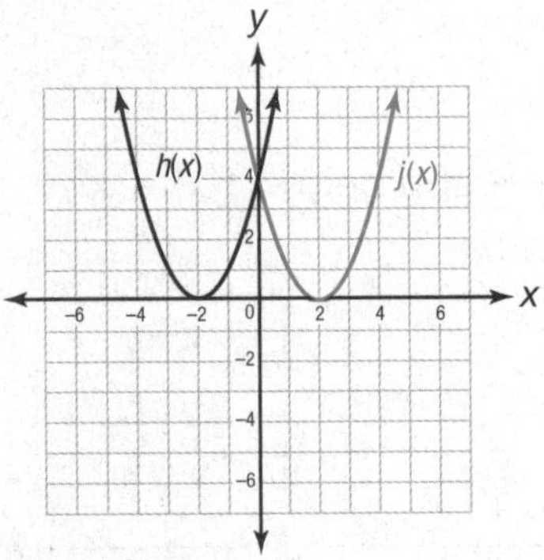

A. $j(x) = h(-x)$

B. $j(x) = -h(x)$

C. $j(x) = h(x) + 4$

D. $j(x) = h(x) - 4$

10. Which of the following is true of the function shown below?

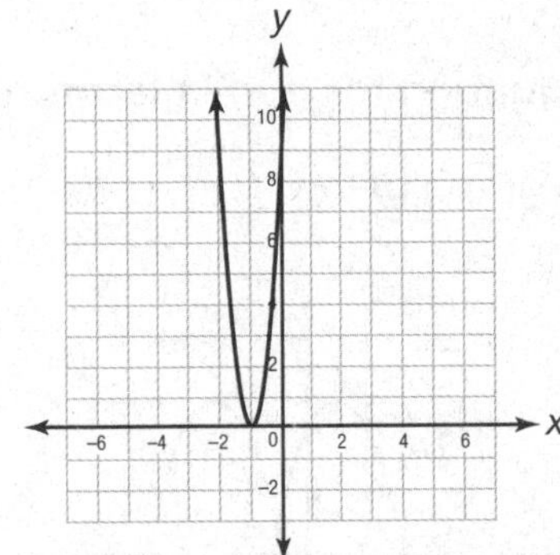

A. It is an even function.

B. It is an odd function.

C. It is both even and odd.

D. It is neither even nor odd.

The graph of $f(x)$ is given. Graph $g(x)$ on the same coordinate grid.

11. $g(x) = 3f(x)$

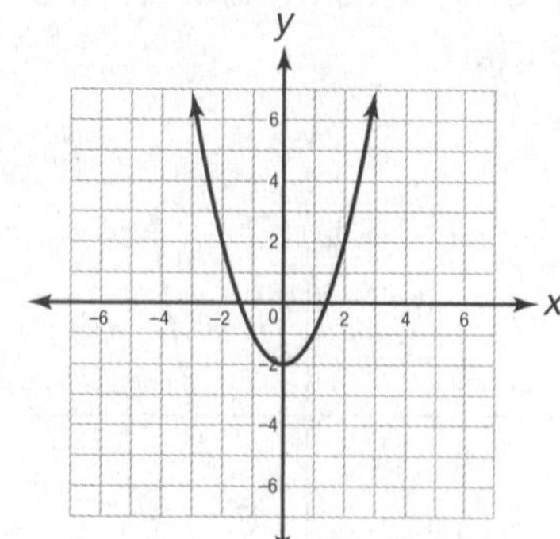

12. $g(x) = f(x) - 4$

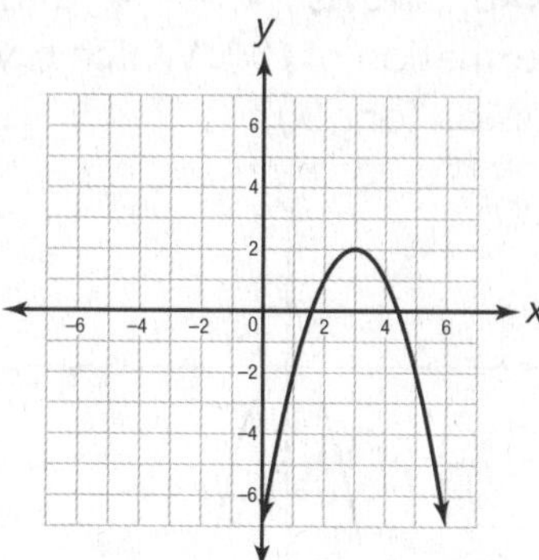

13. $g(x) = -f(x)$

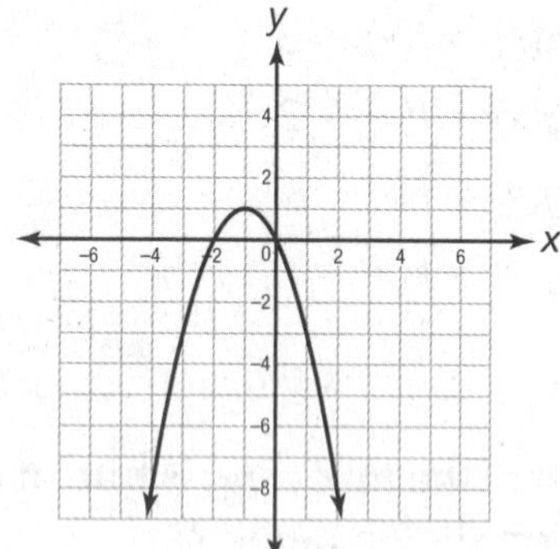

14. $g(x) = -f(x) + 2$

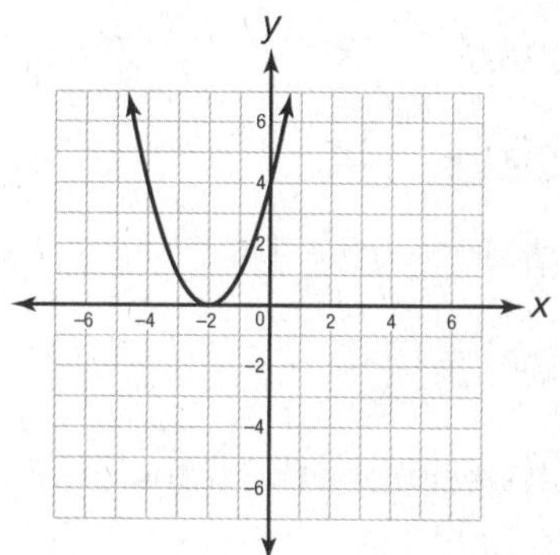

Find the equation for $g(x)$ in terms of $f(x)$ and in terms of x.

15. In the graph below, $f(x) = -(x - 3)^2 + 5$.

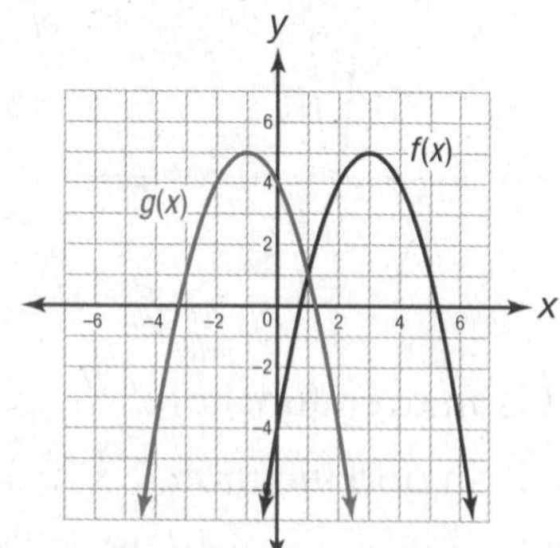

$g(x) =$ ________________

$g(x) =$ ________________

16. In the graph below, $f(x) = x^2 - 4x + 1$.

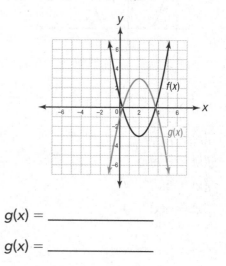

$g(x) =$ ________________

$g(x) =$ ________________

Answer in complete sentences.

17. COMPARE The graphs of $a(x)$ and $b(x)$ are shown below.

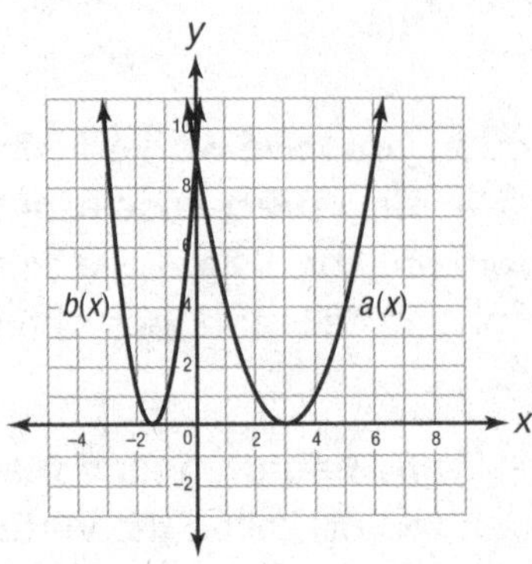

Compare the widths of the graphs. One of the graphs was reflected across the y-axis, and then its input was multiplied by 2 in order to produce the other graph. Which is the original graph before the transformation? How do you know?

18. THINK CRITICALLY Can a quadratic function ever be an odd function? Explain.

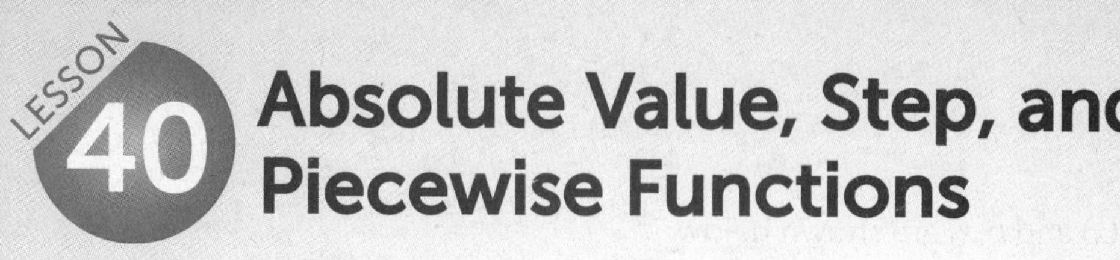

LESSON 40 Absolute Value, Step, and Piecewise Functions

UNDERSTAND Until now, every function you have worked with had the same rule, or equation, over its entire domain. However, a **piecewise function** is defined by more than one rule for distinct intervals in its domain. For example, a cell phone carrier might charge one rate for the first 500 minutes of phone calls and then charge a higher rate after that.

UNDERSTAND The function $f(x) = |x|$ is an **absolute value function**. Its V-shaped graph is formed by two rays with a common endpoint, called the vertex. As in a parabola, the vertex is a minimum or a maximum, and the branches of the function are mirror images of each other. An absolute value function can be written as a piecewise function.

$$f(x) = \begin{cases} -x, & \text{if } x < 0 \\ x, & \text{if } x \geq 0 \end{cases}$$

Like linear, exponential, and quadratic functions, absolute value functions are **continuous**, meaning that you can draw the entire graph without picking up your pencil. An absolute value function could be used to describe your distance from a particular spot as you walk past it.

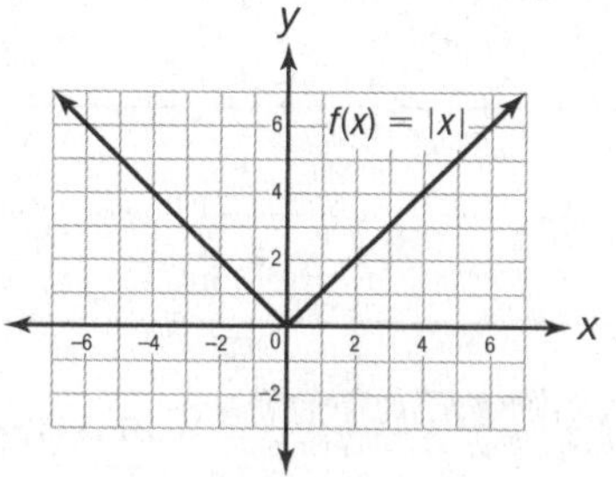

UNDERSTAND **Step functions** are piecewise functions made up of horizontal line segments. One type of step function is the **floor function**, which is also called the **greatest integer function**, $f(x) = \lfloor x \rfloor$. It outputs the greatest integer that is less than or equal to the input. In other words, it rounds down to the nearest integer.

Another step function, the **ceiling function**, which is also called the **least integer function**, outputs the least integer greater than or equal to the input. It rounds up to the nearest integer. This function is written symbolically as $f(x) = \lceil x \rceil$.

Step functions are not continuous. Each open circle represents an endpoint that is not part of the function. The closed circle having the same x-coordinate is part of the function. The functions are discontinuous at each of these x-coordinates.

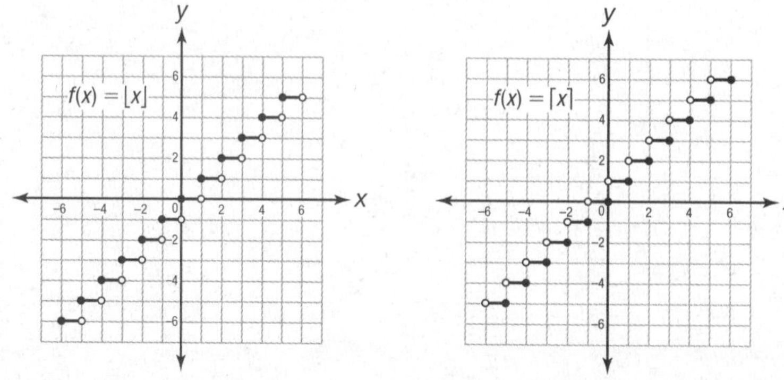

Connect

Compare the absolute value function below to the linear and quadratic functions shown.

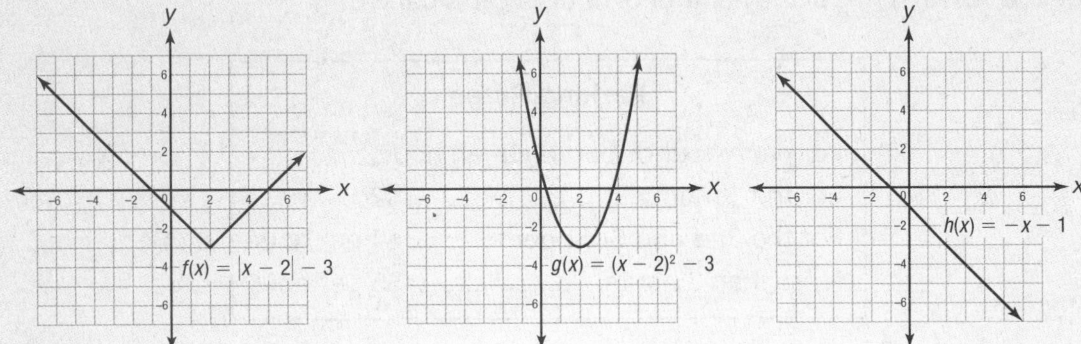

1 Compare the graphs of the absolute value function and the quadratic function.

Each graph has its vertex at $(2, -3)$ and thus its axis of symmetry at $x = 2$. Each vertex is also the point at which the function changes from decreasing to increasing. The graphs have different x- and y-intercepts but similar end behavior.

2 Compare the equations of the absolute value function and the quadratic function.

The absolute value symbols group the terms in the same way that parentheses do in the vertex form of a quadratic function. In both $f(x)$ and $g(x)$, 2 is subtracted from the input and then 3 is subtracted from the expression within the grouping symbols (parentheses or absolute value bars).

3 Compare the graphs of the absolute value function and the linear function.

The portions of the graphs on the interval $x < 2$ are identical rays. They have the same slope, y-intercept, and x-intercept.

4 Compare the equations of the absolute value function and the linear function.

The expression $x - 2$ has a negative value whenever $x < 2$. Therefore, on this interval, $|x - 2| = -(x - 2)$.

If $x < 2$: $f(x) = -(x - 2) - 3$

$f(x) = -x + 2 - 3$

$f(x) = -x - 1$

This is identical to the expression for $h(x)$.

TRY

Find the equation of the linear function that coincides with the increasing portion of $f(x)$.

EXAMPLE A The sign below shows weekend parking rates for a garage. Graph a piecewise function to describe the cost in terms of the number of hours a car is parked.

Parking Rates	
For each hour or portion of an hour:	
For the 1st hour	\$2
For the 2nd and 3rd hours	\$4 per hour
More than 3 hours	\$5 per hour

1 Determine intervals based on the information.

The sign contains three hourly rates: one for the first hour, another for the second and third hours, and another for any hours after that. These rates correspond to the intervals $0 < t \leq 1$, $1 < t \leq 3$, and $t > 3$.

Because customers are charged for a portion of an hour as though it were a full hour, these intervals are also divided into 1-hour intervals. These are ceiling functions.

2 Calculate the charge for each interval.

The cost is \$2 for up to 1 hour.

The second and third hours cost \$4 each. So, more than 1 hour and up to 2 hours costs \$2 + \$4 = \$6, and more than 2 hours and up to 3 hours costs \$6 + \$4 = \$10.

Every subsequent hour costs \$5. So, more than 3 hours and up to 4 hours costs \$10 + \$5 = \$15, more than 4 hours and up to 5 hours costs \$15 + \$5 = \$20, and so on.

This piecewise function can be written as

$$f(t) = \begin{cases} 2, & \text{if } 0 < t \leq 1 \\ 2 + 4\lceil t - 1 \rceil, & \text{if } 1 < t \leq 3 \\ 10 + 5\lceil t - 3 \rceil, & \text{if } t > 3 \end{cases}$$

3 Graph the function.

Graph these constant values for each interval.

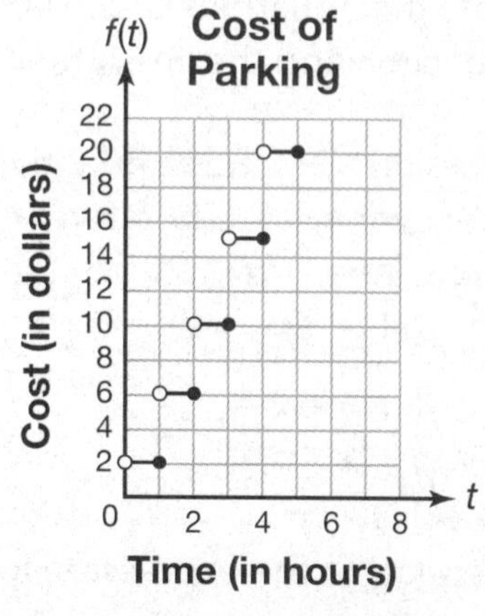

On weekdays, the cost to park in the garage is given by the function $f(t) = \lceil 2t \rceil$ for $t > 0$. Graph this function and describe the charge for parking in words.

EXAMPLE B Graph the function described below.

$$f(x) = \begin{cases} \left(\frac{1}{2}\right)^x - 2, & \text{if } x \leq -1 \\ 2x + 2, & \text{if } -1 < x \leq 2 \\ x^2 - 6x + 5, & \text{if } x > 2 \end{cases}$$

1 Graph the first interval.

The expression in the first interval represents an exponential function with an asymptote at $y = -2$, a y-intercept of $(0, -1)$, and an x-intercept of $(-1, 0)$.

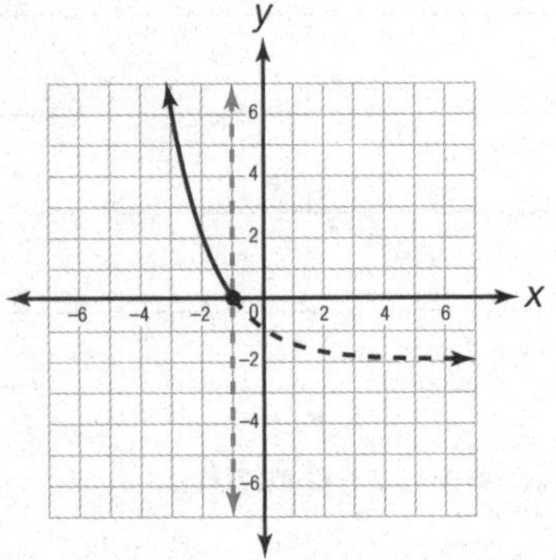

2 Graph the second interval.

The expression in the second interval represents a linear function with a y-intercept of $(0, 2)$, an x-intercept of $(-1, 0)$, and a slope of 2.

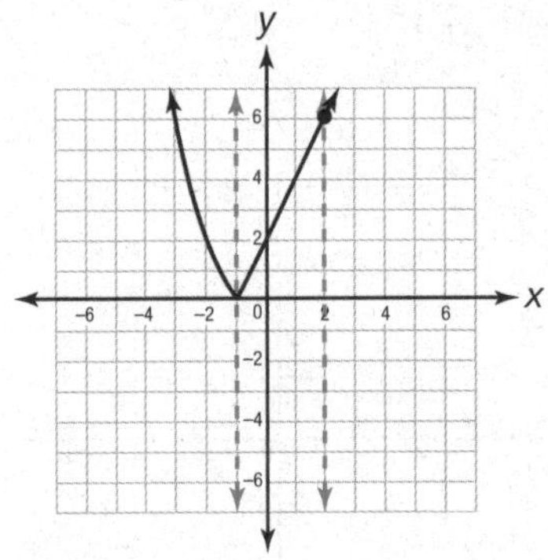

3 Graph the final interval.

The expression in the third interval represents a quadratic function with a y-intercept of $(0, 5)$, x-intercepts of $(1, 0)$ and $(5, 0)$, and a vertex of $(3, -4)$.

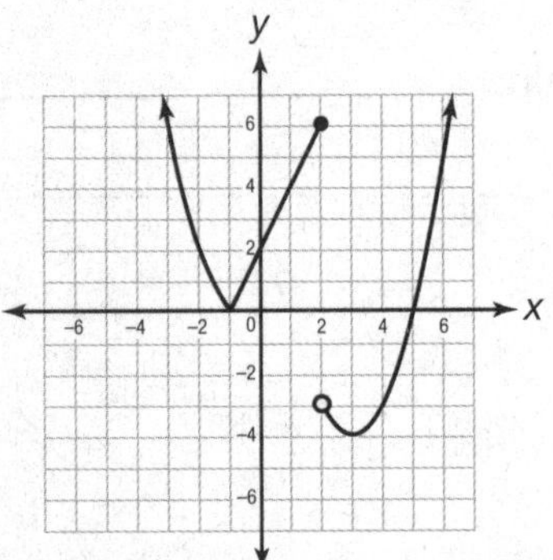

TRY

What are the domain and range of this function? Is it a continuous function?

Practice

Compare the domain, end behavior, range, and intercepts of the functions.

1. $f(x) = |x + 4| - 2$ and $g(x) = 2^x - 2$

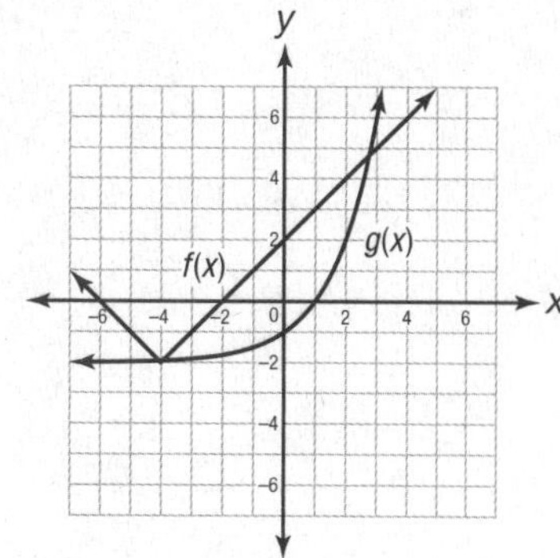

____

____

____

____

2. $h(x) = \left\lceil \frac{1}{2}x \right\rceil$ and $j(x) = \frac{1}{2}x$

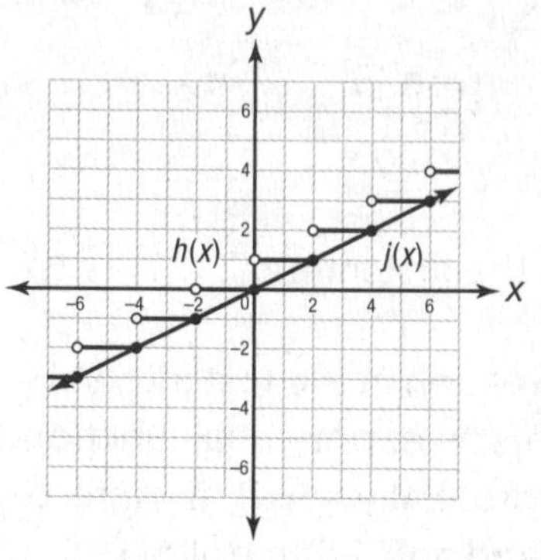

____

____

____

____

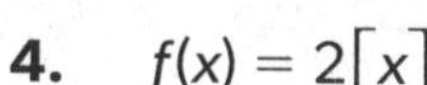

For questions 3–6, graph each function. Then determine its domain and range.

3. $f(x) = \lfloor x \rfloor + 1$

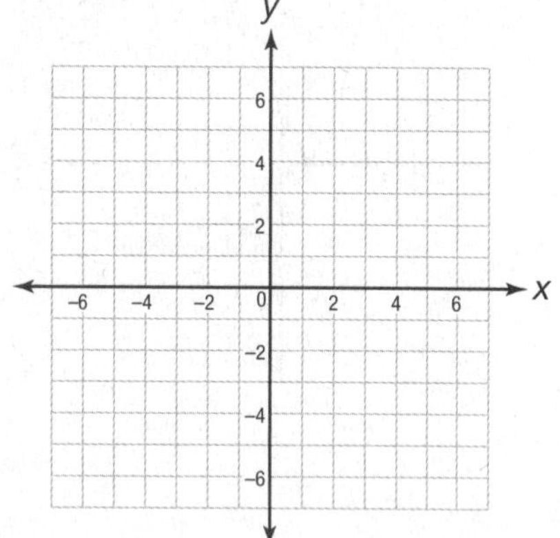

domain: ______________________________

range: ______________________________

4. $f(x) = 2\lceil x \rceil$

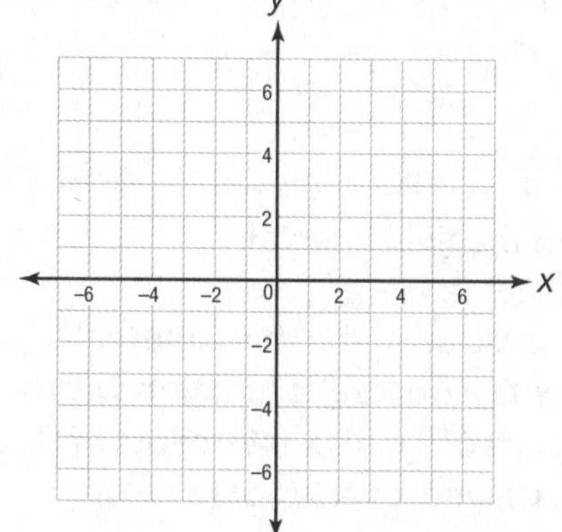

domain: ______________________________

range: ______________________________

5. $f(x) = |x + 1| - 4$

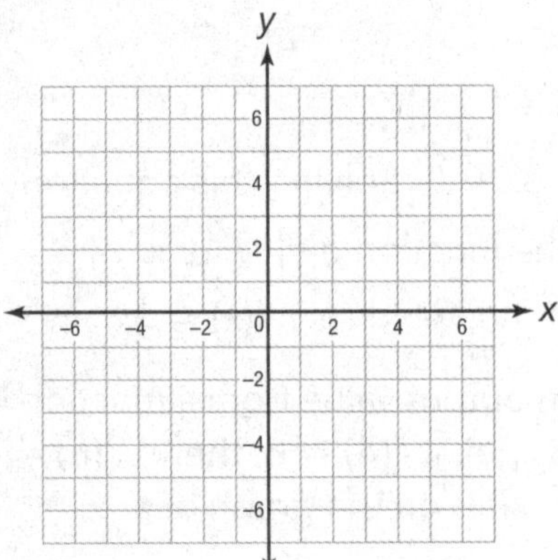

domain: ______________________

range: ______________________

6. $f(x) = \begin{cases} x^2, & \text{if } -2 \le x < 1 \\ x, & \text{if } 1 \le x \le 4 \end{cases}$

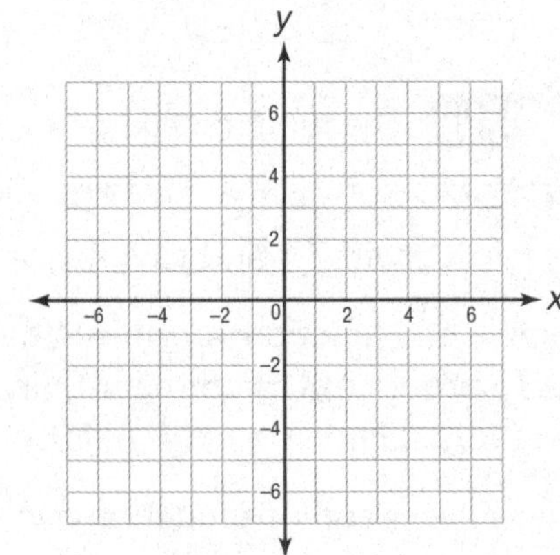

domain: ______________________

range: ______________________

Create a graph to model each situation.

7. GRAPH A mobile phone provider charges $0.10 per text message for the first 100 messages and $0.25 per text message after that.

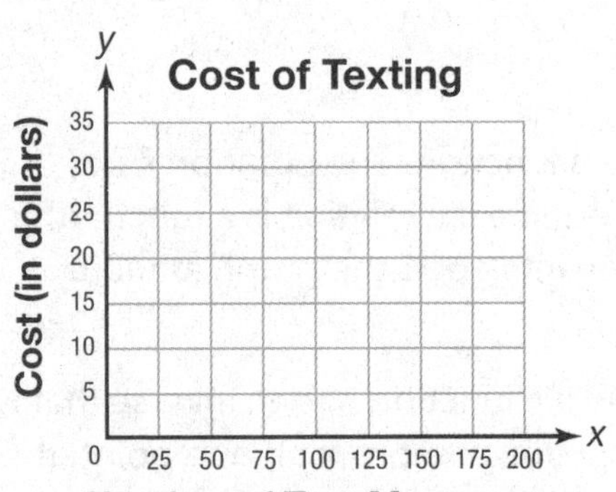

8. APPLY Cameron kicks a rubber ball straight at a concrete wall. It bounces against the wall and rolls back to her. The distance between Cameron and the ball is given by $d(t) = -2|t - 5| + 10$, where t is the time, in seconds.

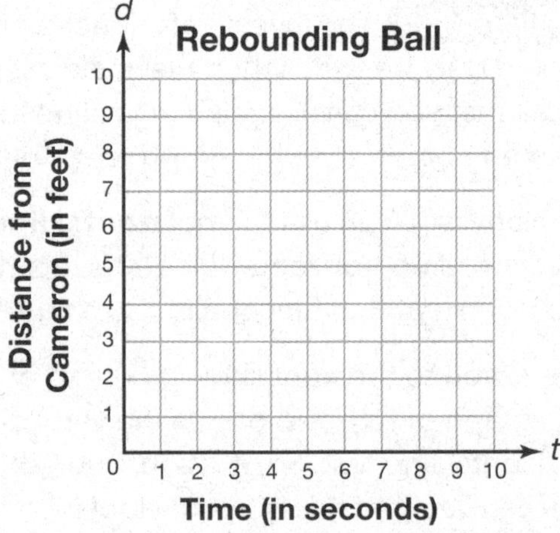

How far is Cameron from the wall?

____

When will the ball return to Cameron?

____

LESSON

41 Inverse Functions

UNDERSTAND The function $f(x) = 3x - 6$ has the graph $y = 3x - 6$. Solving this equation for x produces $x = \frac{1}{3}y + 2$. This equation can be written as the function $g(y) = \frac{1}{3}y + 2$. By replacing g with f^{-1} and y with x, you have the **inverse** of $f(x)$, which is $f^{-1}(x) = \frac{1}{3}x + 2$.

The inverse of a function "undoes" the function. Plugging an output value from a function into its inverse produces the corresponding input value. For example, if $f(4) = 6$, then $f^{-1}(6) = 4$. In other words, if the point (4, 6) is on the graph of f, then (6, 4) is on the graph of f^{-1}.

Reflecting the graph of a function over the line $y = x$ produces the graph of the function's inverse. The coordinate grid below shows $f(x) = 2x$ and its inverse $f^{-1}(x) = \frac{x}{2}$. The dashed line shows $y = x$.

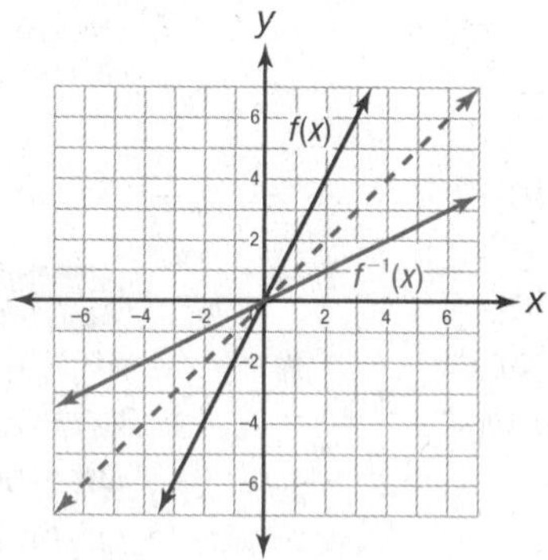

UNDERSTAND The inverse of a function may or may not be a function. The notation $f^{-1}(x)$ should only be used when the inverse is a function. To determine if a relation is a function, recall that you can use the vertical line test. If no vertical line intersects the graph at more than one point, then the graph represents a function.

Similarly, you can use the **horizontal line test** to determine if a function has an inverse that is a function. If no horizontal lines intersect the graph of the function at more than one point, then the inverse of that function is also a function.

The graph to the right shows $f(x) = x^2$ and its inverse, $y = \pm\sqrt{x}$. The graph of $f(x) = x^2$ passes the vertical line test but not the horizontal line test. So, it is a function, but its inverse is not. You can see that this is true by looking at the graph of $y = \pm\sqrt{x}$, which does not pass the vertical line test.

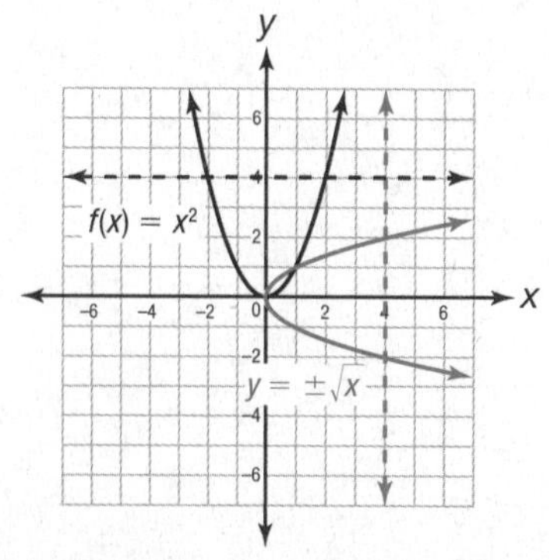

It is important to examine the domain of a function when determining its inverse. A function with a restricted domain will have an inverse with a restricted range.

Connect

Find and graph the inverse of the function $f(x) = \frac{1}{4}x + 2$. Is the inverse a function?

1 Find the inverse equation.

Change $f(x)$ to y. Then switch x and y and solve for y.

$$f(x) = \frac{1}{4}x + 2$$
$$y = \frac{1}{4}x + 2$$
$$x = \frac{1}{4}y + 2$$
$$x - 2 = \frac{1}{4}y$$
$$4x - 8 = y$$
$$y = 4x - 8$$

2 Graph the inverse.

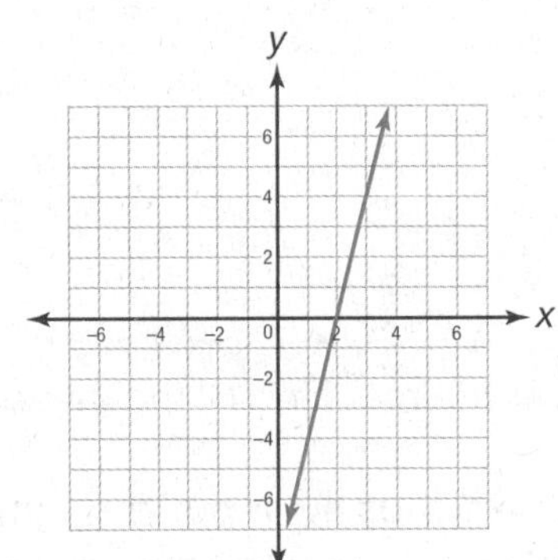

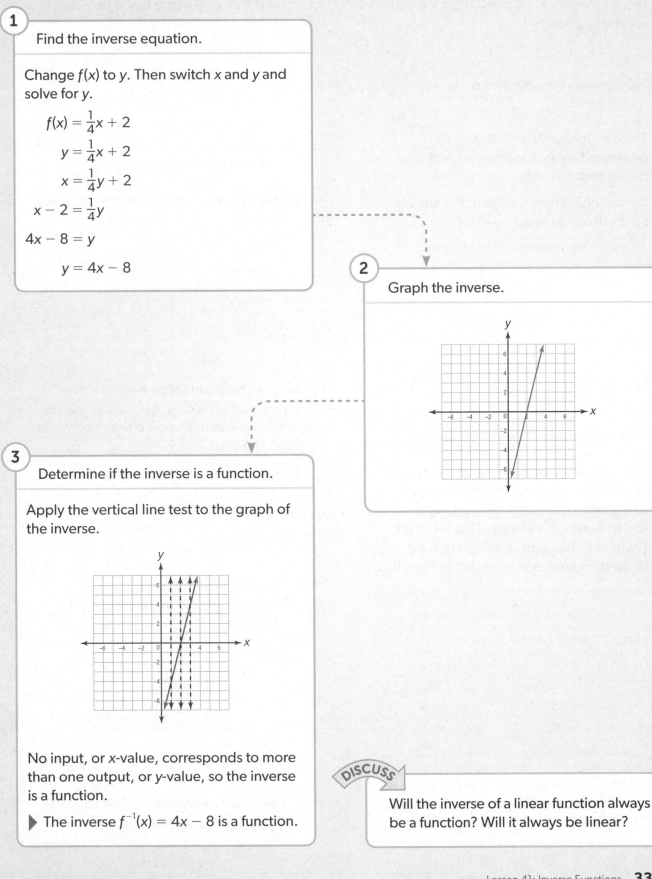

3 Determine if the inverse is a function.

Apply the vertical line test to the graph of the inverse.

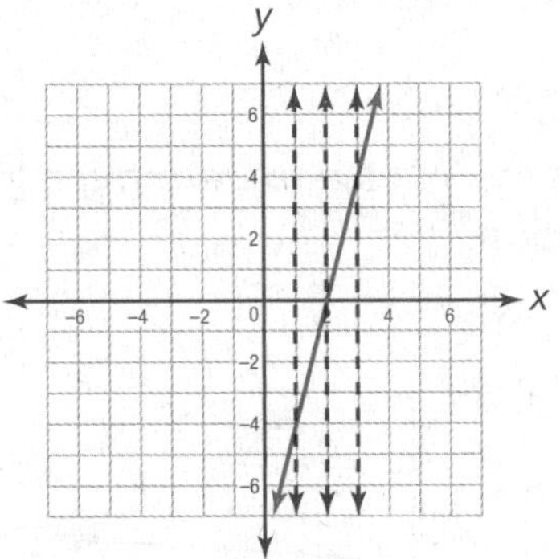

No input, or x-value, corresponds to more than one output, or y-value, so the inverse is a function.

▶ The inverse $f^{-1}(x) = 4x - 8$ is a function.

DISCUSS

Will the inverse of a linear function always be a function? Will it always be linear?

EXAMPLE A The area of a rectangle whose length is nine times its width is given by the function $f(x) = 9x^2$, where x is the rectangle's width. Find and interpret the inverse of the function. Is the inverse a function?

1 Determine the restrictions on the function.

Since x represents a width and $f(x)$ represents an area, neither variable can have a negative value.

So, the domain and range of the function are both represented by $(0, \infty)$.

2 Find the inverse equation.

Change $f(x)$ to y. Then switch x and y and solve for y.

$$f(x) = 9x^2$$

$$y = 9x^2$$

$$x = 9y^2$$

$$\frac{1}{9}x = y^2$$

$$\pm\frac{1}{3}\sqrt{x} = y$$

Since x and y cannot be negative, the inverse contains only the positive values of y. So, we can disregard the negative in front of the radical.

The inverse equation is $y = \frac{1}{3}\sqrt{x}$.

3 Interpret the meaning of the inverse.

The inverse swaps the input and output of a function. The input of the quadratic function is the width of the rectangle, and its output is the area of the rectangle. Therefore, the input of its inverse is the rectangle's area, and its output is its width.

4 Graph the inverse to determine if it is a function.

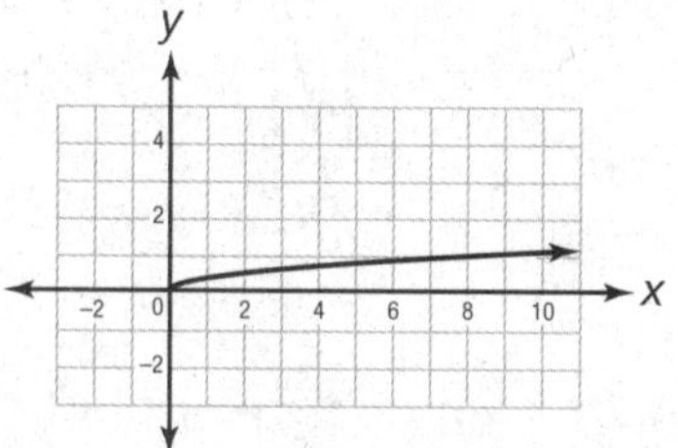

▶ The graph passes the vertical line test, so the inverse is a function.

TRY

If the function $g(x) = x^2$ is restricted to its left branch, the domain $(-\infty, 0)$, what is its inverse? Is the inverse a function?

EXAMPLE B Find and graph the inverse of the function $g(x) = \frac{1}{8}x^3 + 1$. Use the inverse to solve the equation $\frac{1}{8}t^3 + 1 = 9$.

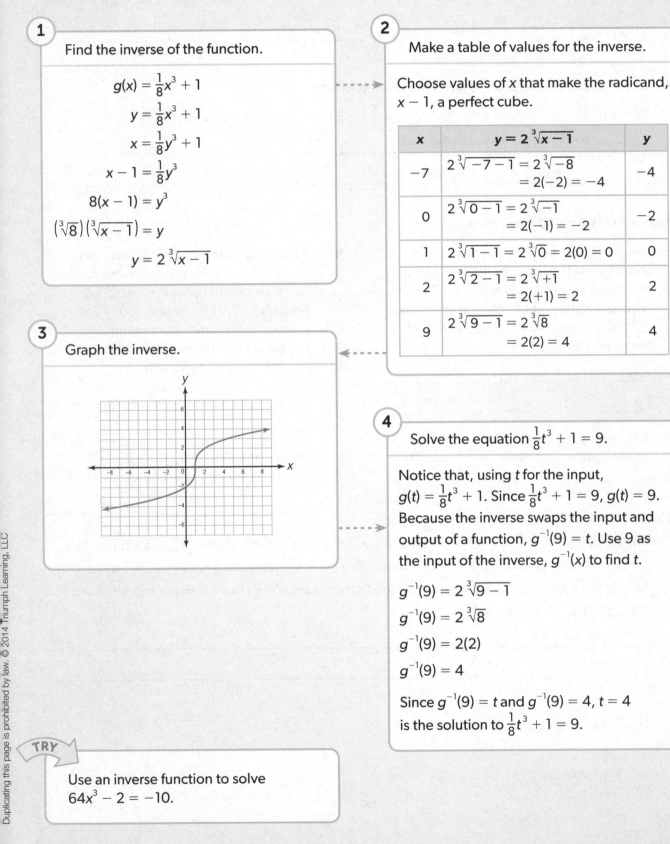

1 Find the inverse of the function.

$$g(x) = \frac{1}{8}x^3 + 1$$
$$y = \frac{1}{8}x^3 + 1$$
$$x = \frac{1}{8}y^3 + 1$$
$$x - 1 = \frac{1}{8}y^3$$
$$8(x - 1) = y^3$$
$$\left(\sqrt[3]{8}\right)\left(\sqrt[3]{x - 1}\right) = y$$
$$y = 2\sqrt[3]{x - 1}$$

2 Make a table of values for the inverse.

Choose values of x that make the radicand, $x - 1$, a perfect cube.

x	$y = 2\sqrt[3]{x - 1}$	y
−7	$2\sqrt[3]{-7-1} = 2\sqrt[3]{-8} = 2(-2) = -4$	−4
0	$2\sqrt[3]{0-1} = 2\sqrt[3]{-1} = 2(-1) = -2$	−2
1	$2\sqrt[3]{1-1} = 2\sqrt[3]{0} = 2(0) = 0$	0
2	$2\sqrt[3]{2-1} = 2\sqrt[3]{+1} = 2(+1) = 2$	2
9	$2\sqrt[3]{9-1} = 2\sqrt[3]{8} = 2(2) = 4$	4

3 Graph the inverse.

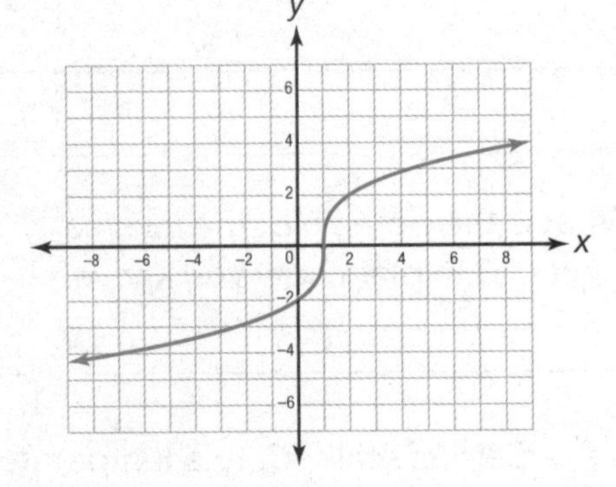

4 Solve the equation $\frac{1}{8}t^3 + 1 = 9$.

Notice that, using t for the input, $g(t) = \frac{1}{8}t^3 + 1$. Since $\frac{1}{8}t^3 + 1 = 9$, $g(t) = 9$. Because the inverse swaps the input and output of a function, $g^{-1}(9) = t$. Use 9 as the input of the inverse, $g^{-1}(x)$ to find t.

$$g^{-1}(9) = 2\sqrt[3]{9 - 1}$$
$$g^{-1}(9) = 2\sqrt[3]{8}$$
$$g^{-1}(9) = 2(2)$$
$$g^{-1}(9) = 4$$

Since $g^{-1}(9) = t$ and $g^{-1}(9) = 4$, $t = 4$ is the solution to $\frac{1}{8}t^3 + 1 = 9$.

TRY

Use an inverse function to solve $64x^3 - 2 = -10$.

Practice

For each function, find its inverse function.

1. $f(x) = \frac{3}{4}x$

$f^{-1}(x) =$ ________

2. $g(x) = 7x - 21$

$g^{-1}(x) =$ ________

3. $h(x) = \frac{2}{3}x + 2$

$h^{-1}(x) =$ ________

Find the inverse and determine whether it is a function.

4. $f(x) = \frac{1}{25}x^2$

____

____

5. $g(x) = \frac{1}{2}x - 5$

____

____

6. $h(x) = \frac{x^3}{64}$

____

____

Answer the following questions.

7. Gianni is paid $45 per day plus $15 per hour for each shift he works. His pay is modeled by the function $f(x) = 15x + 45$, where x is the number of hours worked. Find the inverse function and interpret its input and output.

____

____

How many hours must he work in order to make $135 in one day?

____

8. Aisha rides her bicycle at an average speed of 250 meters per minute. The distance of her morning ride can be described by the function $g(x) = 250x$, where x is the time spent riding, in minutes. Find the inverse function and interpret its input and output.

____

____

What is the domain of the inverse function? Explain how you know.

____

9. The function $F(C) = \frac{9}{5}C + 32$ converts a temperature on the Celsius scale, C, to a temperature on the Fahrenheit scale, $F(C)$. The function $C(F) = \frac{5}{9}F - \frac{160}{9}$ converts a temperature on the Fahrenheit scale, F, to a temperature on the Celsius scale, $C(F)$. How are these two functions related? How do you know?

____

____

10. The function f is defined as $f(x) = \sqrt[4]{x^3 + 3x + 15}$. If $f^{-1}(1) = -2$, for what value of a does $\sqrt[4]{a^3 + 3a + 15} = 1$?

---

11. THINK CRITICALLY The function $A(x) = \pi x^2$ models the area of a circle with radius x.

What is the domain of the function?

Find the inverse and interpret its input and output.

What is the domain of the inverse? Explain how you know.

---

12. GRAPH The volume of a cube with edge length e is modeled by the function $v(e) = e^3$. Find a function for the edge of a cube, given its volume. Then, fill in the tables and graph both functions on the coordinate grid below. Round answers to the nearest tenth, when needed.

---

edge (e)	volume (v)
−2	
−1	
0	
1	
2	

volume	edge

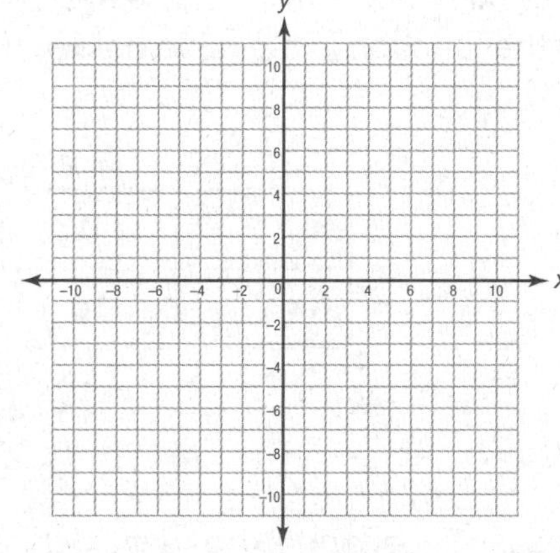

Based on the situation, are domains or ranges of your graphs restricted? Why?

LESSON 42

Comparing Functions

UNDERSTAND Functions can be useful as models for real-world situations. They allow you to explore and understand the relationship between two quantities and to make predictions about how they change. Analyzing and comparing the key features of such models is often an important step in solving real-world problems.

UNDERSTAND One aspect of functions that we can compare is rate of change. Recall that the average rate of change between two points on a function is the difference of y-values divided by the difference of the x-values.

The rate of change for a linear function is constant. The change in $f(x)$ is the same over equal intervals. Consider the linear function $f(x) = 4x - 3$. Every time x increases by 1, the value of $f(x)$ increases by 4, which is the slope, m, of the function.

The rates of change for an exponential function grow or shrink by a common factor over equal intervals. Consider the exponential function $f(x) = 3^x$. For intervals of length 1, the values grow by a factor of 3, which is the base, b, of the function. In other words, the values triple.

Like exponential functions, quadratic functions do not have constant rates of change. The rates of change of quadratic functions change in a different way than those of exponential functions.

Recall that quadratic functions are often written in standard form $f(x) = ax^2 + bx + c$ or vertex form $f(x) = a(x - h)^2 + k$. The average rates of change increase by $2a$ over intervals of length 1. For the function in the table below, $f(x) = 2x^2 - 8x + 10$, $a = 2$, so $2a = 2(2) = 4$.

+1 +1 +1 +1

x	0	1	2	3	4
$f(x)$	10	4	2	4	10

−6 −2 +2 +6

+4 +4 +4

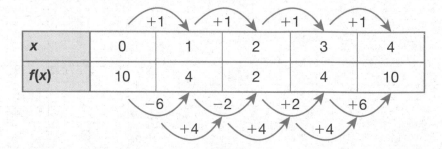

Because linear and exponential functions are either always increasing or always decreasing, their rates of change are either all positive or all negative. Quadratic functions have positive rates of change on some intervals and negative rates of change on others. The vertex of a parabola marks the point where the rates of change switch between positive and negative. The rate of change at the vertex is 0.

Connect

Explore the average rates of change on unit intervals for the quadratic function $f(x) = x^2$.

1

Find the average rate of change on the interval $0 \leq x \leq 1$.

Find the points at the ends of this interval.

$f(0) = (0)^2 = 0$

$f(1) = (1)^2 = 1$

So, find the rate of change from (0, 0) to (1, 1).

$\frac{1-0}{1-0} = \frac{1}{1} = 1$

2

Find average rates of change for subsequent unit intervals.

The next unit interval is $1 \leq x \leq 2$.

$f(2) = (2)^2 = 4$

Find the rate of change from (1, 1) to (2, 4).

$\frac{4-1}{2-1} = \frac{3}{1} = 3$

Then, the next unit interval is $2 \leq x \leq 3$.

$f(3) = (3)^2 = 9$

Find the rate of change from (2, 4) to (3, 9).

$\frac{9-4}{3-2} = \frac{5}{1} = 5$

3

Find average rates of change for previous unit intervals.

Moving to the left, the previous interval is $-1 \leq x \leq 0$.

$f(-1) = (-1)^2 = 1$

$\frac{0-1}{0-(-1)} = \frac{-1}{1} = -1$

After that, the previous intervals are $-2 \leq x \leq -1$ and $-3 \leq x \leq -2$.

$f(-2) = (-2)^2 = 4$

$\frac{1-4}{-1-(-2)} = \frac{-3}{1} = -3$

$f(-3) = (-3)^2 = 9$

$\frac{4-9}{-2-(-3)} = \frac{-5}{1} = -5$

4

Analyze these rates of change on the graph of the function.

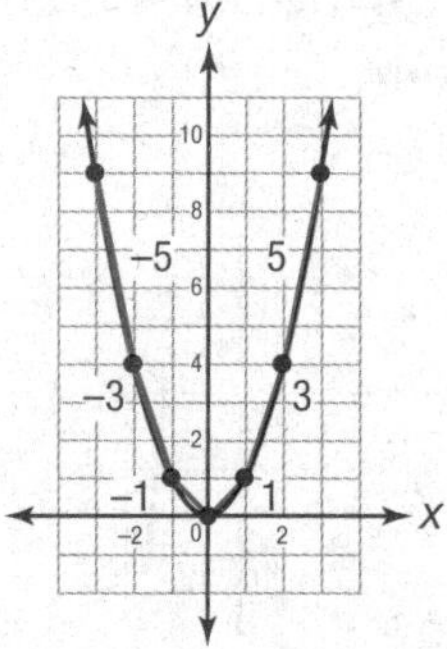

On opposite sides of the vertex, the rates of change are opposites (negatives) of each other. The rates of change form the sequence of odd numbers …-5, -3, -1, 1, 3, 5,…

DISCUSS

Explore the average rates of change on unit intervals for $f(x) = 3x^2$ and $g(x) = \frac{1}{2}x^2$. How do the rates of change relate to the coefficients of x^2?

EXAMPLE A Use what you know about rates of change to graph the function $f(x) = 2(x - 5)^2 - 9$.

1 Plot the vertex and use rate of change to find another point.

The equation is already in vertex form, $f(x) = a(x - h)^2 + k$. For this function, $a = 2$ and the vertex, (h, k), is at $(5, -9)$.

The rate of change between the vertex and a point one unit to its right will be a, or $\frac{a}{1}$.

Since $a = 2$, count 2 units up and 1 unit to the right. Plot a point there.

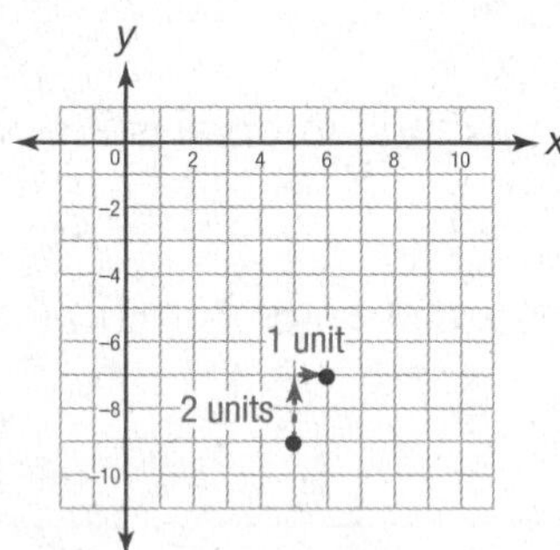

2 Plot more points on this branch.

The rate of change between this point and the point one unit to its right will be $3a$.

$3a = 3(2) = 6$

Count 6 units up and 1 unit to the right. Plot a point there.

From that point, count up $5a$, or 10 units, and 1 unit over to plot another point.

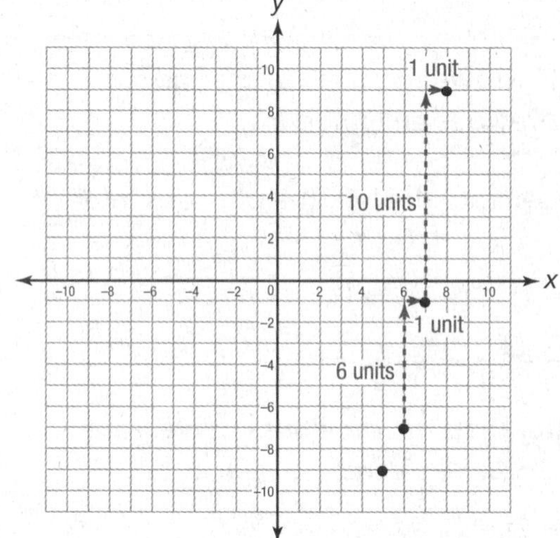

You can use this same technique to plot points on the left branch. You can also use the fact that parabolas are symmetric over the axis of symmetry to plot them.

3 Plot points on the other branch and connect them.

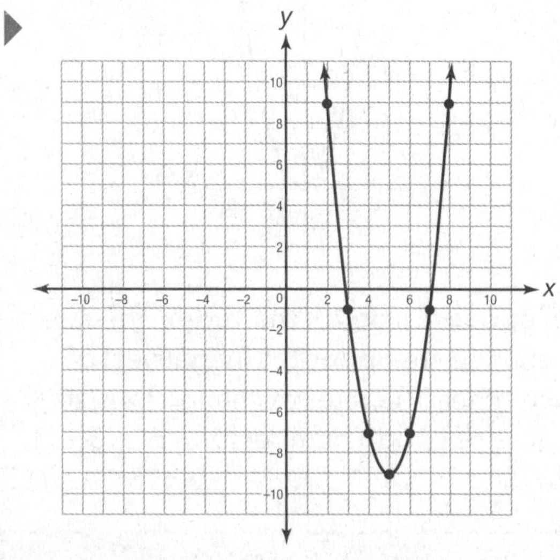

TRY

Use what you know about rates of change to graph $g(x) = -2x^2 + 8$.

EXAMPLE B Compare the following functions for $x \geq 0$.

$f(x) = 2x$ $\quad$ $g(x) = 2x^2$ $\quad$ $h(x) = 2^x$

1

Make a table of values for the three functions.

x	f(x)	g(x)	h(x)
0	0	0	1
1	2	2	2
2	4	8	4
3	6	18	8
4	8	32	16
5	10	50	32
6	12	72	64
7	14	98	128
8	16	128	256
9	18	162	512

2

Analyze the table.

For the first few values of x, the values of all three functions are fairly close together. Starting around $x = 4$, the quadratic and exponential functions have much higher values than the linear function. The y-values for $g(x)$ and $h(x)$ are fairly close together until $x = 8$, and then the function values increase much faster for the exponential function.

3

Graph the functions on the same coordinate grid.

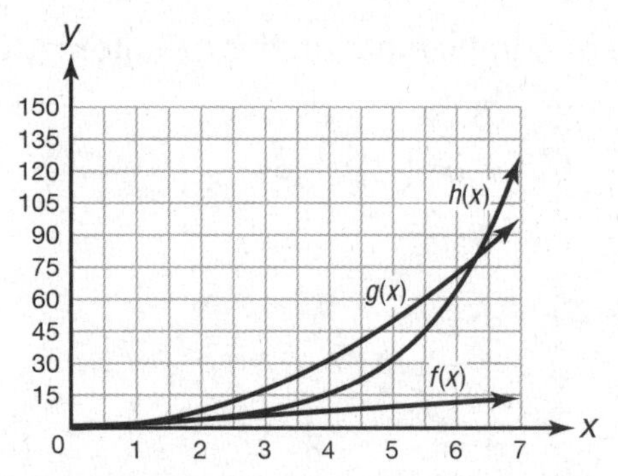

4

Analyze the graph and draw conclusions.

- The linear function increases at a constant rate. Both the quadratic and exponential functions increase at variable rates. As compared to the quadratic function, the exponential function increases more slowly at first and then much more quickly as the value of x increases. After these two functions intersect, at about (6.3, 80), the value of the exponential function will always be greater than the value of the quadratic function.

DISCUSS

Compare how the rates of change for each function vary as x increases. Which type of function will always have the highest values for very large values of x?

EXAMPLE C Compare the key features of the quadratic function $f(x) = -(x + 1)^2 + 4$ to the exponential function $g(x)$ shown on the coordinate plane to the right. Include the domain and range, end behavior, and intercepts.

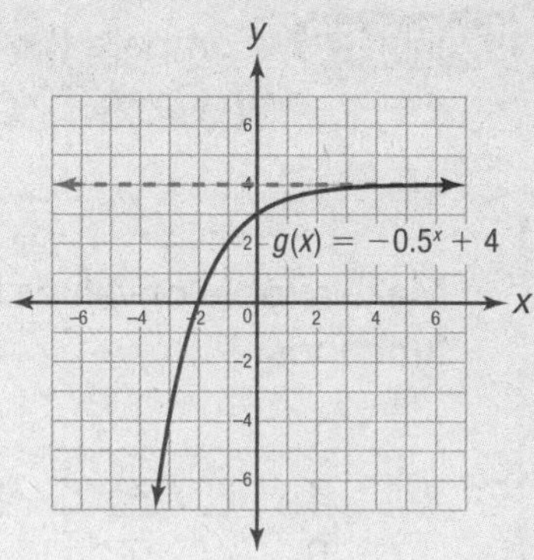

1 Compare the domains and ranges.

The domain of both functions is the set of all real numbers.

The quadratic function is in vertex form. It has a negative leading coefficient and a vertex at $(-1, 4)$. This means that 4 is the maximum value of the function and that the range is $(-\infty, 4]$.

The exponential function approaches the asymptote $y = 4$ from below. The value 4 is its upper boundary, but unlike f, 4 is not in the range of g. The function g has a range of $(-\infty, 4)$.

2 Compare the end behaviors.

Since the quadratic function has a negative leading coefficient, both arms point downward. So, as x approaches positive and negative infinity, $f(x)$ approaches $-\infty$.

Now, look at the graph of the exponential function. As x approaches $-\infty$, $g(x)$ approaches $-\infty$. As x approaches ∞, $g(x)$ approaches 4.

3 Compare the intercepts.

Find the intercepts of the quadratic function.

$f(0) = -(0 + 1)^2 + 4 = -(1) + 4 = 3$

The quadratic function has a y-intercept at $(0, 3)$.

$$0 = -(x + 1)^2 + 4$$

$$(x + 1)^2 = 4$$

$$x + 1 = \pm 2$$

$$x = -1 \pm 2$$

$$x = 1 \text{ or } x = -3$$

The function $f(x)$ has two x-intercepts, at $(1, 0)$ and $(-3, 0)$.

According to the graph, the function $g(x)$ has only one x-intercept, at $(-2, 0)$. It has the same y-intercept as f, at $(0, 3)$.

CHECK

Graph both functions on your calculator and check the comparisons made above, using the GRAPH and the TABLE features.

EXAMPLE D Deborah has $1,000 that she plans to invest either in a Treasury bill or in a savings account. The value of the Treasury bill is given by the function $A(T) = 1{,}000(1.0018)^T$, where T is the time, in years, since the money was invested. The value of the savings account over 3 months is given in the table to the right. Which option will give her a higher return on her investment?

Time (in months)	Value (in dollars)
0	1,000.00
1	1,000.80
2	1,001.60
3	1,002.40

1 Find the monthly percent increase for the savings account.

To find the percent increase per month, use the formula $\frac{\text{change in value}}{\text{original value}}$. Test a few months to make sure this rate is consistent.

$$\frac{1{,}000.80 - 1{,}000}{1000} = \frac{0.80}{1{,}000} = 0.0008$$

$$\frac{1{,}001.60 - 1{,}000.80}{1000.80} = \frac{0.80}{1{,}000.80} \approx 0.0008$$

$$\frac{1{,}002.40 - 1{,}001.60}{1001.60} = \frac{0.80}{1{,}001.60} \approx 0.0008$$

The monthly interest rate for the savings account is 0.08%.

2 Find the equivalent monthly interest rate for the Treasury bill.

In the equation $A(T) = 1{,}000(1.0018)^T$, T is given in years. Use dimensional analysis to change years into months.

$$T \text{ years} = t \text{ months} \times \frac{1 \text{ year}}{12 \text{ months}}$$

So, replace T with $\frac{t}{12}$.

$$A(t) = 1{,}000(1.0018)^{\frac{t}{12}}$$

Use the power of a power property to convert the equation into the form $A = P(1 + r)^t$.

$$A(t) = 1{,}000\left(1.0018^{\frac{1}{12}}\right)^t$$

$$A(t) \approx 1{,}000(1.00015)^t$$

$$1 + r \approx 1.00015$$

$$r \approx 0.00015$$

The monthly interest rate for the Treasury bill is about 0.015%.

▶ Deborah should invest her money in the savings account.

Find the equivalent annual interest rate for the savings account.

Practice

Compare the functions.

1. Compare the functions $f(x) = x$ and $g(x) = \lfloor x \rfloor$ in terms of domain and range, intercepts, and end behavior.

2. Compare the functions *h* and *j*, as shown below, in terms of intercepts, maximums and minimums, and rate of change.

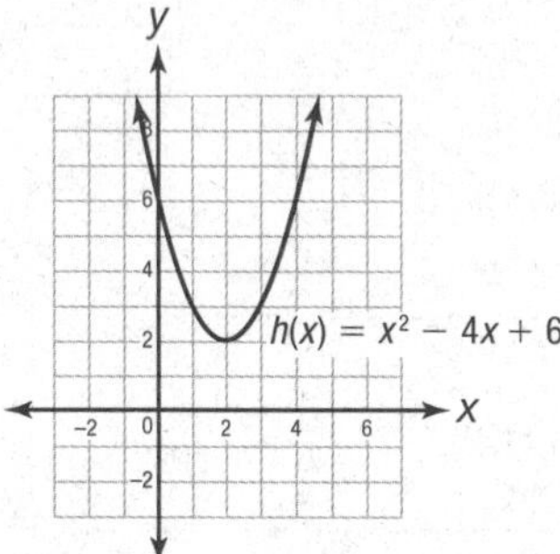

x	$j(x) = 2^x$
−2	0.25
−1	0.5
0	1
1	2
2	4
3	8
4	16

Answer the following questions.

3. The table below shows a quadratic function. What is the average rate of change for the function on the interval [2, 3]?

x	0	1	2	3	4	5
f(x)	3	−2	−5	−6	−5	−2

4. The enrollment at a high school can be modeled by the function $e(x) = 1{,}784(1.02)^x$, where *x* is the time in years. What does the base of the expression, 1.02, tell you about the rate of change of the school's enrollment over time? Is enrollment increasing or decreasing?

5. The inventors of a new technology want to track how quickly people begin using their new product. On the day of its release, there were 120 units in circulation. The table to the right shows circulation data for the 5 months since the release. One inventor predicted a growth rate modeled by the formula $y = 120(1.09)^t$, where t is the time, in months, since the release. Was his prediction accurate? Compare the rates of change in the data and the formula.

Month	Units in Circulation
0	120
1	129
2	139
3	149
4	160
5	172

____

____

6. **ANALYZE** The state legislature is debating two tax plans. Plan A charges an income tax of 4% for people who make up to $50,000 per year and 6% for people who make more than that. Plan B charges a tax of 5% on all incomes. Write a piecewise function for Plan A and a linear function for Plan B to describe the amount of tax on x dollars of earned income. Graph the function.

Plan A: $a(x) =$

Plan B: $b(x) =$

Would anyone pay the same rate under both plans?

____

____

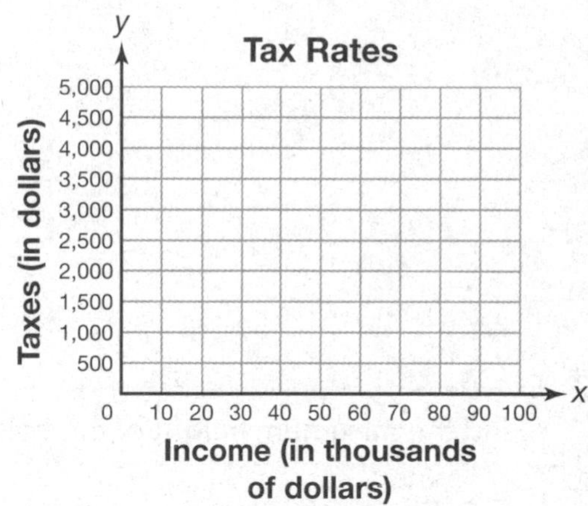

7. **COMPARE** The functions $f(x) = (x - 4)^2 - 5$ and $g(x) = |x - 4| - 5$ both have their vertex at $(4, -5)$ and have the same end behavior. Compare the rates of change of the functions.

____

____

LESSON

43 Modeling with Functions

EXAMPLE A A ball was kicked from the ground into the air with an initial upward velocity of 32 feet per second. Write an equation to model the height of the ball and find the maximum height that it reached.

1 Determine what type of function to use.

The ball follows a path that goes up into the air and falls back to the ground. Its rate of change in height will be positive but decreasing for a time, then 0, and then negative and increasing. This describes a quadratic function.

2 Write a function.

Recall that the height of a projectile, in feet, can be modeled using a function in the form $f(t) = -16t^2 + vt + c$, where t is the time in seconds, v is the initial upward velocity in feet per second, and c is the initial height in feet.

In this situation, the initial upward velocity is 32 feet per second. The ball was kicked from the ground, so the initial height is 0 feet. Substitute these values into the function.

$$f(t) = -16t^2 + vt + c$$

$$f(t) = -16t^2 + 32t + 0$$

▶ $f(t) = -16t^2 + 32t$

3 Find the maximum height of the ball.

The leading coefficient of the function, -16, is negative, so this function has a maximum. The maximum value of $f(x)$ is the y-coordinate of the vertex of its graph. Find the vertex by completing the square.

$$f(t) = -16t^2 + 32t$$

$$f(t) = -16(t^2 - 2t)$$

$$f(t) - 16(1) = -16(t^2 - 2t + 1)$$

$$f(t) - 16 = -16(t - 1)^2$$

$$f(t) = -16(t - 1)^2 + 16$$

The vertex of the graph of f is at (1, 16).

▶ The maximum height of the ball is 16 feet above the ground.

TRY

When will the ball land on the ground?

EXAMPLE B A rolling ball bounces off a wall and rolls back toward the kicker. The wall is 15 feet from the kicker, and the ball is traveling at 10 feet per second. Write a function to model the distance of the ball from the wall since it was kicked. When will the ball return to the kicker?

1 Determine what type of function to use.

As the ball rolls toward the wall, its distance from the wall will be decreasing at a constant rate. It then hits the wall and travels away at a constant rate. During this time, its distance from the wall is increasing.

An absolute value function has two constant rates of change over its domain, one negative and one positive. Use an absolute value function to model the ball's distance from the wall over time.

2 Sketch the shape of the function's graph.

Think about the shape of the graph. The ball begins 15 feet away from the wall, so (0, 15) is its y-intercept. From here, the graph will slope down, meaning the ball is getting closer to the wall. When the ball is 0 feet from the wall, it hits the wall and bounces back. This is the turning point, or vertex, of the graph.

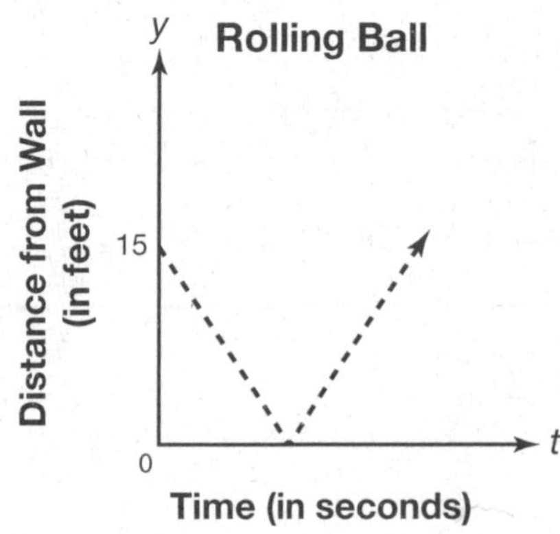

3 Write the equation of the graph.

Since the vertex of the graph is on the x-axis, the function will have the form $y = |mx + b|$.

The y-intercept is (0, 15), so $b = 15$.

The speed of the ball is 10 feet per second. The graph slopes down from the y-intercept, so the slope must be negative. $m = -10$.

▶ The ball's distance from the wall is modeled by $f(t) = |15 - 10t|$.

4 Find the time when the ball will return to the kicker.

The kicker is 15 feet from the wall, so find the times when $f(t) = 15$.

$15 = |15 - 10t|$

$\pm 15 = 15 - 10t$

$15 = 15 - 10t$ or $-15 = 15 - 10t$

$0 = -10t$ $\quad$ $-30 = -10t$

$0 = t$ $\quad$ $3 = t$

Time 0 is when the ball is kicked.

▶ The ball will return to the kicker 3 seconds after it was kicked.

CHECK

Substitute $t = 3$ into your absolute value equation and verify that the result is 15. Then graph the function on your graphing calculator to see if it matches the sketch above.

EXAMPLE C A factory manufactures amateur sports uniforms, which include a shirt and a hat. The daily cost to produce x shirts is modeled by the function $f(x) = 0.5x^2 - 15x + 150$. The daily cost to produce x hats is modeled by the function $g(x) = 0.5x^2 - 5x + 50$. Find a function to model the total daily cost to produce x uniforms. Then, find and interpret the vertex and zeros of the function.

1 Find the function to describe the cost of making x shirts and x hats.

The cost of producing the uniforms is the sum of the cost of producing the shirts and the cost of producing the hats. Add the functions together.

$h(x) = f(x) + g(x)$

$h(x) = (0.5x^2 - 15x + 150) + (0.5x^2 - 5x + 50)$

Combine like terms to simplify the function.

▶ $h(x) = x^2 - 20x + 200$

2 Find and interpret the vertex of the function.

Recall that the vertex of a parabola of the form $y = ax^2 + bx + c$ is found at $\left(\frac{-b}{2a}\right), h\left(\frac{-b}{2a}\right)$. In the function in Step 1, $a = 1$ and $b = -20$. First, find the x-coordinate.

$x = \frac{-b}{2a}$

$x = \frac{-(-20)}{2(1)}$

$x = 10$

The y-coordinate is $h\left(\frac{-b}{2a}\right)$, or $h(10)$.

$h(10) = (10)^2 - 20(10) + 200$

$h(10) = 100 - 200 + 200$

$h(10) = 100$

The vertex of the parabola is (10, 100). Since the function has a positive leading coefficient, this represents a minimum for the function. It means that the minimum cost for producing uniforms is \$100, and it occurs when it produces 10 hats and 10 shirts.

3 Find and interpret the zeros of the function, if any.

In the previous step, we found the minimum of the function is 100. Since the minimum value is greater than zero, $h(x)$ will never equal 0. Thus, the function has no zeros. Since the solution has no zeroes, there is no number of uniforms for which the costs will be \$0.

▶ Manufacturing any number of uniforms will cost some amount of money.

Find $f(10)$ and $g(10)$ and add them together. Is the result 100?

EXAMPLE D A ball is dropped from a height of 144 feet. Three seconds after being dropped, the ball strikes the ground. It rebounds up to a height of 16 feet, staying in the air for 2 more seconds. Write a function to describe the ball's motion during the first 5 seconds after it was dropped.

1 Examine the information given in the problem.

The ball's initial height, 144 feet, corresponds to the point (0, 144). At time $x = 3$, the ball hit the ground. This corresponds to the point (3, 0).

Over the next 2 seconds, the ball bounced up to a height of 16 feet and then hit the ground again. So the ball hit the ground for the second time 5 seconds after it was dropped. This corresponds to (5, 0).

2 Write one part of a piecewise function to model the graph.

The heights of falling objects are modeled with quadratic functions. Since the graph is made up of pieces of two different parabolas, the situation can be modeled with a piecewise function.

The first piece of the function has vertex (0, 144). Substitute the vertex values into the vertex form for a parabola.

$f(x) = a(x - 0)^2 + 144$

Now substitute another point on the parabola, (3, 0), to find the value of a.

$$0 = a(3 - 0)^2 + 144$$
$$-144 = 9a$$
$$-16 = a$$

So, $f(x) = -16(x - 0)^2 + 144$, which simplifies to $f(x) = 144 - 16x^2$.

For $0 \le x \le 3$, the function is modeled by $f(x) = 144 - 16x^2$.

3 Write the second piece of the function.

The zeros of the second parabola are $x = 3$ and $x = 5$. A function with those zeros can be modeled as follows.

$f(x) = a(x - 3)(x - 5)$

$f(x) = a(x^2 - 8x + 15)$

Since gravity is still acting on the ball, a is still -16.

For $3 \le x \le 5$, the function is modeled by $f(x) = -16(x^2 - 8x + 15)$.

4 Write a function to model the ball's motion.

The motion of the ball is modeled by the following function:

$$f(x) = \begin{cases} 144 - 16x^2, & \text{if } 0 \le x \le 3 \\ -16x^2 + 128x - 240, & \text{if } 3 < x \le 5 \end{cases}$$

DISCUSS

How could you have used symmetry to find the equation for the second parabola?

Practice

Determine which type of function would best model each equation. Write *linear, quadratic, exponential, absolute value,* or *piecewise*.

1. The number of people in line to vote doubled every half hour. What type of function would model the number of people in line over time? ____________________

HINT: Doubling is equivalent to increasing at the constant percent rate of 100%.

2. A gas tank is leaking 0.15 gallon of gas every day. What type of function would model the amount of gas in the tank over time? ____________________

3. A clothing manufacturer sells shirts wholesale for \$8 each. If a customer orders more than 100 shirts, the price drops to \$6 each. What type of function gives the cost of the order based on the number of shirts? ____________________

4. While birdwatching, Amy sees a bird flying toward her and then over her head. The bird then continues to fly in a straight line away from her. What type of function would model Amy's distance from the bird over time? ____________________

Write a function to model each situation. Use *x* as the variable.

5. A lacrosse player threw a ball from a height of 6 feet with an initial upward velocity of 45 feet per second. Write a function for the height of the ball over time.

____

6. A city charges 6% sales tax for items that cost up to \$100, and 7.5% sales tax for items that cost more than \$100. Write a function that gives the sales tax of an item based on its price.

____

7. At the local fair, Oscar set up a booth for drawing caricatures. The amount of money he was paid for drawing *x* caricatures is given by $m(x) = -\frac{1}{6}x^2 + 26x$. He paid \$50 to rent the booth, and the materials to make each drawing cost about \$1.50. So, his costs are given by the function $c(x) = 1.5x + 50$. If his profits are equal to the difference of the money he is paid and his expenses, write a function for his profits, based on the number of caricatures he draws.

____

Solve.

8. A toy rocket that was launched from a platform 17 feet off the ground reached a maximum height of 81 feet 2 seconds after it was launched. Write a function to model the rocket's height over time.

____

When did the rocket hit the ground? ______________________________

Suppose that instead of being launched from the platform, the rocket was launched from the ground. Write a function to model the rocket's height over time in this scenario.

____

When would the rocket hit the ground in this scenario? ______________________________

9. WRITE MATH A car began traveling at an initial speed of 90 feet per second. When the driver applied the brakes, the car's speed decreased at a constant rate of 30 feet per second per second.

Write a function, $s(t)$, for the speed of the car after t seconds have passed. (Hint: The rate of change will be -30.) ______________________________

After how many seconds will the car's speed be 0 feet per second? ______________________________

Write a function for the distance, $d(t)$, that the car will travel in t seconds while it is slowing down. Recall that the distance traveled by an accelerating object over time t is given by the equation $d(t) = \frac{1}{2}at^2 + vt$, where a is the object's acceleration and v is its initial velocity.

____

After braking begins, how far will the car travel before it comes to a complete stop? ______________________________

10. COMPARE A rectangle has width x and length $x + 8$.

Write a function for the perimeter of the rectangle. ______________________________

Write a function for the area of the rectangle. ______________________________

Graph both functions on the coordinate grid to the right. Then compare their rates of change.

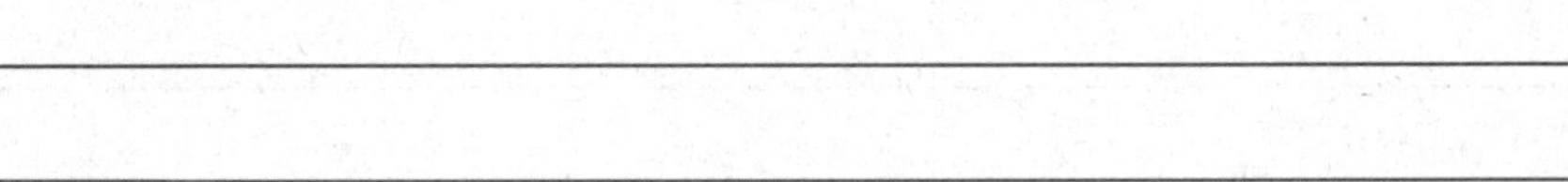

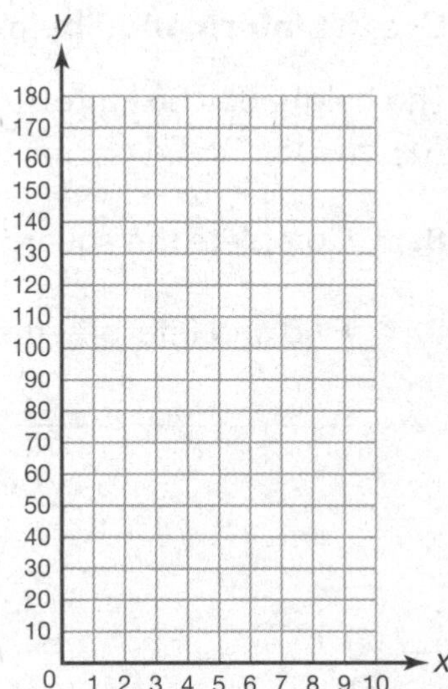

UNIT

5 Review

Write *rational* or *irrational* to describe the sum or product.

1. $3 \cdot \pi$ ______________ 2. $\frac{1}{15} + \frac{6}{21}$ ______________ 3. $5(100 + \sqrt{2})$ ______________

Write the inverse of each function. State whether the inverse is or is not also a function.

4. $f(x) = 3x + 7$ 5. $g(x) = 100x^2$

______________________ ______________________

______________________ ______________________

Use the graph to the right to answer questions 6 and 7.

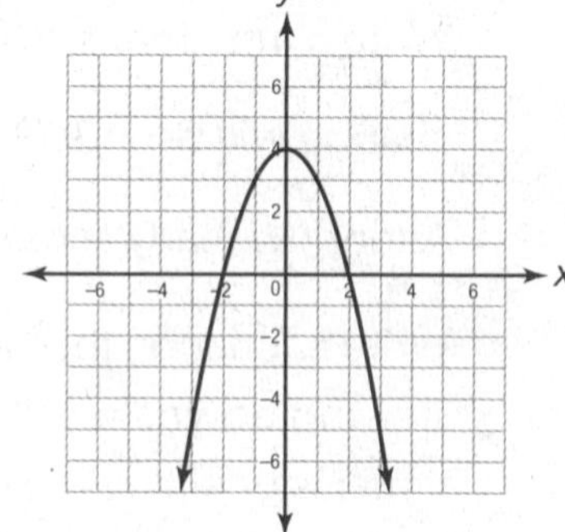

6. Is the function even, odd, or neither? Explain.

____

7. Describe the function, including its axis of symmetry, intercepts, maximum or minimum, intervals of increase and decrease, positive and negative intervals, and end behavior.

____

____

____

____

Use the information below to answer questions 8 and 9.

The height of a ball thrown from the top of a platform can be modeled by the equation $f(x) = -16x^2 + 64x - 34$, where $f(x)$ is the height, in feet, x seconds after the ball was thrown.

8. Complete the square to write the function in vertex form. ______________________

9. Find and interpret the coordinates of the vertex and the maximum of the function.

____

____

Choose the best answer.

10. Which transformation describes how $f(x)$ was transformed to create $g(x)$ on the coordinate grid below?

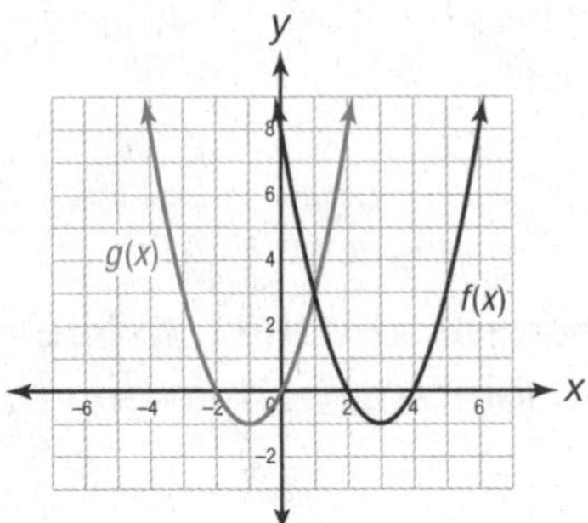

A. $g(x) = f(x - 4)$

B. $g(x) = f(x + 4)$

C. $g(x) = f(x) + 4$

D. $g(x) = f(x) - 4$

11. The number of cookies in a cookie jar is decreasing over time. Which of the following functions could model $c(x)$, the number of cookies left after x days?

A. $c(x) = 88^x$

B. $c(x) = 88(1.12)^x$

C. $c(x) = 88(2)^x$

D. $c(x) = 88(0.87)^x$

Use the function below to answer questions 12 and 13.

$f(x) = 2x^2 - 2x - 144$

12. Write the function in fully factored form. ____________________

13. What are the zeros of the function? ____________________

14. The table below represents a quadratic function.

x	0	1	2	3	4	5
f(x)	8	11	20	35	56	83

What is the average rate of change for the function on the interval [0, 1]? ____________

What is the average rate of change for the function on the interval [3, 4]? ____________

What is the average rate of change for the function on the interval [0, 4]? ____________

Write a function for the context below.

15. A baker sells cupcakes for \$3 each. Her revenue, in dollars, is modeled by the function $R(x) = 3x$, where x is the number of cupcakes sold. Her costs can be modeled by the function $C(x) = 0.02x^2 + 0.5x + 50$, where x is the number of cupcakes she produces. The function to model her profit in dollars, $P(x)$, is equal to her revenue minus her costs. Find an explicit equation for $P(x)$ in terms of x, the number of cupcakes she sells.

____

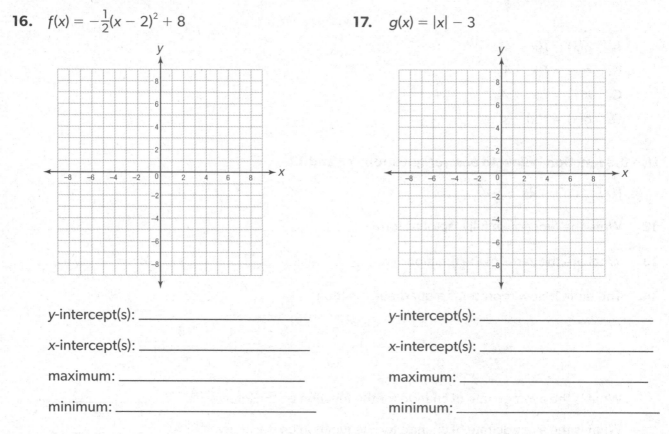

Graph each function on the coordinate grid. Identify the intercepts and the maximum or minimum for each function. If the function has no *x*-intercept, *y*-intercept, maximum, or minimum, write *none*.

16. $f(x) = -\frac{1}{2}(x - 2)^2 + 8$

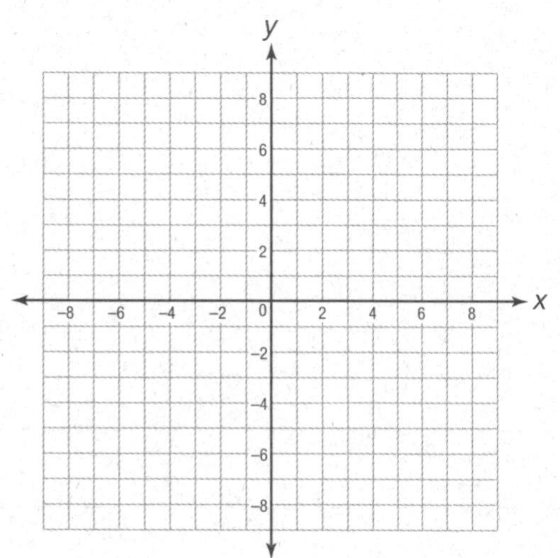

y-intercept(s): ______________

x-intercept(s): ______________

maximum: ______________

minimum: ______________

17. $g(x) = |x| - 3$

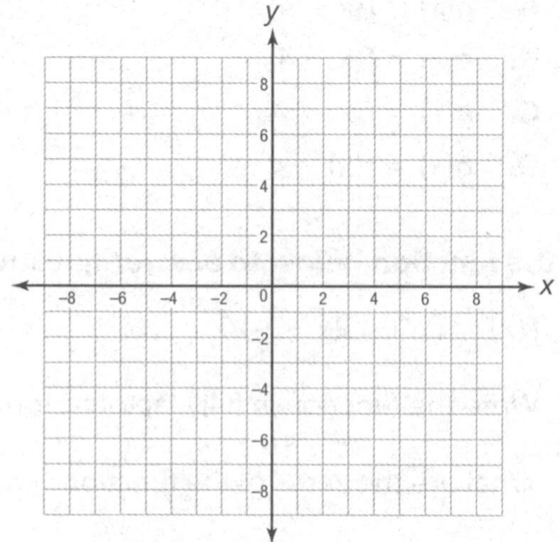

y-intercept(s): ______________

x-intercept(s): ______________

maximum: ______________

minimum: ______________

18. Find the inverse $f^{-1}(x)$ of the function $f(x) = \frac{2}{3}x + 12$. Then find the value of x that makes $f(x) = 10$ true.

____

If the ordered pair $(x, 10)$ lies on the function, what point must lie on the inverse function?

____

Use the table of values for the quadratic function *f* and the graph of the exponential function *g* below to answer question 19.

x	$f(x) = 20(x + 5)^2$
−10	500
−5	0
0	500
5	2,000
10	4500
15	8,000
20	12,500
25	18,000

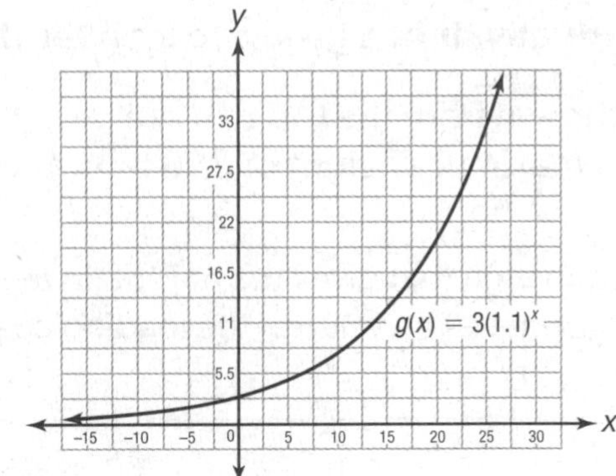

19. For most of the *x*-values shown on the table and in the graph, the values for the quadratic function are much higher than the values of the exponential function. Will this be the case over the rest of the domain? Explain.

____

____

____

Write and graph a function to model the situation.

20. MODEL A city charges a sales tax of 5% on purchases less than \$50 and a sales tax of 6% on purchases of \$50 or more.

Write a function to model the amount of sales tax on a purchase of *x* dollars.

____

Graph your function on the coordinate grid.

Performance Task

HEADS UP!

Work individually or in a group to answer the questions below.

A rock was thrown from the top of a building that is 192 feet tall. It reached its maximum height of 256 feet 2 seconds after it was thrown.

1. For any function that gives the height, in feet, of a thrown object as a function of time, in seconds, what is the value of the leading coefficient, *a*?

____

2. Write a function that models the height of the rock, *h*(*t*), in feet, *t* seconds after it was thrown.

____

3. After how many seconds will the rock hit the ground? ____________

4. Draw a graph on the coordinate grid to show the height of the rock from when it was thrown until it hit the ground.

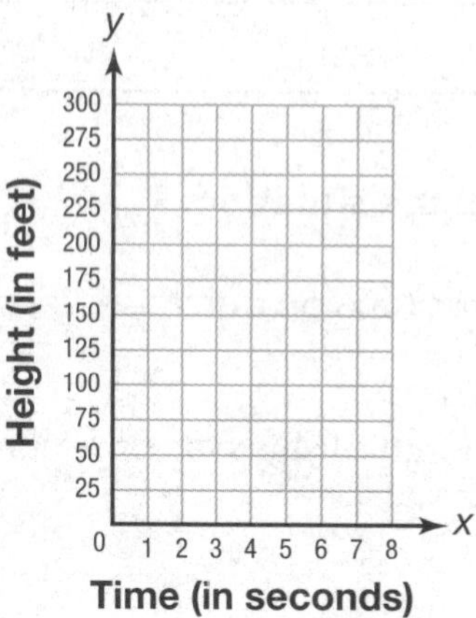

5. Identify the following for the function and its graph, and explain what each means in context:

y-intercept: ______________________________

vertex: ______________________________

zero: ______________________________

6. Fill in the table below for the height of the rock at various times.

t	0	1	2	3	4	5	6
h(t)							

7. Find the average rate of change over the following intervals:

$0 \le t \le 1$: ____________ $3 \le t \le 4$: ____________

$1 \le t \le 2$: ____________ $4 \le t \le 5$: ____________

$2 \le t \le 3$: ____________ $5 \le t \le 6$: ____________

8. Find the inverse of the function. ____________

Is the inverse of *h* also a function? ________

9. A person inside the building sees the rock falling past his window. He is on a floor 156 feet above the street. How long has the rock been in the air when this person sees it?

____

10. The rock was thrown with an initial upward velocity of 64 feet per second. Because of the pull of gravity, its velocity changes at a constant rate of −32 feet per second per second. Write a linear function that gives the velocity, $v(t)$, of the rock at time *t*.

____

11. Find the velocity of the rock at the following times:

0.5 second: ____________ 3.5 seconds: ____________

1.5 seconds: ____________ 4.5 seconds: ____________

2.5 seconds: ____________ 5.5 seconds: ____________

12. A negative vertical velocity means that the rock is moving downward, instead of upward. Unlike velocity, speed can never be negative. Speed, like distance or time, is always considered to be a positive quantity. When the falling rock has a velocity of –5 feet per second, it has a speed of 5 feet per second. Write a function that gives the speed, $s(t)$, of the rock at time *t*.

____

13. Suppose that the rock was actually thrown from a 32-foot-tall platform sitting on top of the building. Write a function for the height of the rock, $j(t)$, in this situation:

in terms of $h(t)$ ____________

in terms of *t* ____________

What type of transformation is this? ____________

14. If the rock were thrown from this 32-foot-tall platform on top of the building, after how long would it hit the ground? Give both the exact answer and the answer rounded to the nearest tenth.

____

Glossary

absolute value function a function in which the input is contained within absolute value symbols (Lesson 40)

accuracy how close a measurement or calculation is to its actual value (Lesson 2)

additive identity the number that, when added to a number *a*, gives the sum *a*; for real numbers, the additive identity is 0: $a + 0 = a$ (Lesson 4)

additive inverse for any real number *a*, the number $-a$, such that their sum is the additive identity: $a + (-a) = (-a) + a = 0$ (Lesson 4)

approximation a value used to represent a true measurement when an exact answer is not possible (Lesson 2)

arithmetic sequence a sequence in which successive terms have a common difference (Lesson 22)

asymptote a line that the graph of a function continuously approaches but never touches (Lesson 12)

axis of symmetry (of a parabola) a vertical line of symmetry passing through the vertex of a parabola (Lesson 38)

base the number or variable that is raised to a power in an exponential expression (Lessons 5, 9, 10)

bimodal distribution a distribution of data that, when graphed, shows two clear peaks (Lesson 24)

binomial a polynomial containing exactly two unlike terms (Lesson 31)

bivariate data statistical data in which two variables are being studied (Lesson 29)

box plot a graph above a number line that shows the lower and upper extremes, first and third quartiles, and median of a data set; also called a box-and-whisker plot (Lesson 27)

categorical data data that cannot be measured and are generally in the form of names or labels (Lesson 28)

ceiling function See **least integer function.** (Lesson 40)

coefficient a number that is multiplied by a variable in an expression or equation (Lesson 3)

common difference the number added to find the next term in an arithmetic sequence (Lesson 22)

common ratio the number by which each term in a geometric sequence is multiplied to obtain the next term (Lesson 23)

completing the square a method of converting a quadratic expression of the form $ax^2 + bx + c$ to the form $a(x - h)^2 + k$ (Lesson 33)

compound inequality an inequality that has two or more boundaries (Lesson 6)

conditional frequency a relative frequency in the body of a two-way relative frequency table (Lesson 28)

constant a number with a known value that does not change in a mathematical expression (Lesson 3)

continuous not having any jumps or breaks in shape; able to be drawn in one motion without interruption (Lesson 40)

conversion factor a number used to convert from one unit to another through multiplication or division (Lesson 1)

correlation coefficient a number r, where $-1 \le r \le 1$, that describes the strength of the association between two variables (Lesson 30)

curve of best fit the curve that most closely represents the relationship between variables that do not have a linear association (Lesson 30)

degree (of a polynomial) a characteristic of a polynomial determined by the highest exponent or sum of exponents of any term (Lesson 31)

dependent variable a variable, often y or $f(x)$, that provides the output value of an equation or function (Lesson 3)

dimensional analysis a method of determining or checking a mathematical expression for a given context by examining units (Lesson 1)

discriminant the radicand expression, $b^2 - 4ac$, from the quadratic formula, which can be used to determine how many real roots a quadratic equation has (Lesson 35)

domain the set of all the first elements (inputs) of a relation (Lesson 11)

dot plot a data display that represents data values as dots over a number line (Lesson 24)

element an individual value from a set (Lesson 11)

elimination method a method for solving systems of equations where equations are multiplied by constants and added and/or subtracted so as to eliminate all but one variable (Lesson 15)

end behavior the behavior of a graph as it is followed farther and farther in either direction (Lesson 12)

estimate a value made inexact on purpose in order to make calculations easier or to generalize about a population (Lesson 2)

even function a function that is symmetrical with respect to the y-axis (Lesson 39)

experimental study a study in which the researcher controls variables in order to determine their effect (Lesson 24)

exponent the number in an exponential expression that indicates how many times a base is multiplied by itself (Lesson 10)

exponential decay a relationship modeled by a function of the form $f(x) = a \cdot b^x$ in which $a > 0$ and $0 < b < 1$ (Lesson 9)

exponential equation an equation in which the variable is in the exponent (Lessons 5, 9)

exponential function a function of the form $f(x) = a \cdot b^x + c$, in which the input, x, is the exponent of a constant, b (Lesson 11)

exponential growth a relationship modeled by a function of the form $f(x) = a \cdot b^x$ in which $a > 0$ and $b > 1$ (Lesson 9)

extraneous solution a value of a variable that is obtained by solving an equation but that is not a solution to the equation or to the situation that the equation models (Lesson 35)

first quartile (Q_1) the median of the lower half of a data set (Lesson 27)

floor function See **greatest integer function.** (Lesson 40)

function a relation in which every input is assigned to exactly one output (Lesson 11)

geometric sequence a sequence in which consecutive terms have a common ratio (Lesson 23)

greatest integer function a step function that outputs the greatest integer that is less than or equal to the input; also called a floor function (Lesson 40)

half-plane the portion of the coordinate plane that lies on one side of a line (Lesson 17)

histogram a data display that uses bars to show how frequently data occur within certain ranges or intervals (Lesson 24)

horizontal line test a test in which if any horizontal line crosses a graph of a relation at two or more points, then the inverse of that relation is not itself a function (Lesson 41)

horizontal shrink a transformation that pushes the points of a figure or graph toward the y-axis (Lesson 20)

horizontal stretch a transformation that pulls the points of a figure or graph away from the y-axis (Lesson 20)

horizontal translation a slide of a graph or figure in the right or the left direction on the coordinate plane (Lesson 18)

independent variable a variable, often x, that serves as the input value of an equation or function (Lesson 3)

index a small number indicating what root is being taken in a radical expression (Lesson 10)

input the first value, often an x-coordinate, in an ordered pair for a function; the value that is entered into a function in order to produce the related output (Lesson 11)

interquartile range (IQR) a measure of the spread of the middle 50% of a data set; equal to the difference of the first and third quartiles of the set (Lesson 27)

inverse (of a function) the relation that swaps the input and output of a given function (Lesson 41)

irrational number a number that cannot be written as a quotient of integers (Lesson 37)

joint frequency a frequency in the body of a two-way frequency table (Lesson 28)

leading coefficient (of a quadratic equation) the coefficient a of a quadratic equation in standard form, $y = ax^2 + bx + c$ (Lesson 34)

least integer function a step function that outputs the least integer that is greater than or equal to the input; also called a ceiling function (Lesson 40)

linear equation an equation in which every variable is raised to the first power (Lessons 5, 8)

linear function a function of the form $f(x) = mx + b$, in which the input, x, is raised to the first power and whose graph is a straight line (Lesson 11)

line of best fit the line that most closely represents the relationship between variables that have a linear association; also called a trend line (Lesson 30)

line of reflection the line over which a figure or graph is flipped to produce a mirror image (Lessons 19)

lower extreme the least value in a data set (Lesson 27)

marginal frequency an entry in the "Total" row or "Total" column of a two-way frequency table or a two-way relative frequency table (Lesson 28)

maximum the point on a graph that has the greatest y- or $f(x)$-value (Lessons 12, 38)

mean the sum of all the terms in a data set divided by the total number of terms (Lesson 25)

measure of center a value that represents the middle or average of a data set (Lesson 25)

median the middle value in a data set that is ordered from least to greatest (Lesson 25)

minimum the point on a graph that has the least y- or $f(x)$-value (Lessons 12, 38)

monomial a polynomial containing only one term (Lesson 31)

multiplicative identity the number which, when multiplied by a number a, gives the product a; for real numbers, the multiplicative identity is 1: $a \times 1 = a$ (Lesson 4)

multiplicative inverse for any real number a other than 0, the number $\frac{1}{a}$ such that their product is the multiplicative identity: $a \times \frac{1}{a} = \frac{1}{a} \times a = 1$ (Lesson 4)

normal distribution a distribution of data which, when graphed, is symmetrical and resembles a bell curve (Lesson 24)

observational study a study in which variables are observed or outcomes are measured, but no attempt is made to control variables or affect outcomes (Lesson 24)

odd function a function that is symmetrical with respect to the origin (Lesson 39)

outlier an element that is very different from the other elements in the same data set (Lesson 25)

output the second value, often a y-coordinate, in an ordered pair for a function; the value that is produced when a function is evaluated for a given input (Lesson 11)

parabola the U-shaped graph of a quadratic function (Lesson 34)

parent function the most basic function in a family, or group, of related functions (Lessons 18, 39)

piecewise function a function in which the output is calculated according to two or more rules, depending on the input (Lesson 40)

polynomial a collection of constants and variables joined through addition, subtraction, and multiplication (Lesson 31)

power the exponent in an exponential expression; the number that indicates how many times a base is used as a factor (Lesson 10)

prime factorization a string of prime factors whose product is a given number or polynomial (Lesson 33)

prime number a positive integer that cannot be divided without remainder by any positive integer other than itself and 1 (Lesson 33)

principal square root the positive square root of a number (Lesson 33)

quadratic expression a polynomial expression of degree 2 (Lesson 32)

quadratic formula the formula $x = \frac{-b \pm \sqrt{b^2 - 4ac}}{2a}$ used to find the solutions to a quadratic equation of the form $ax^2 + bx + c = 0$ (Lesson 35)

quadratic function a function in which the highest power of the variable is 2 (Lesson 38)

quantitative data data that can be measured and are in numerical form (Lesson 28)

radical an expression of the form $\sqrt{r}$ or $\sqrt[n]{r}$, where *r* is a number or expression (Lesson 10)

radicand the number or expression inside a radical ($\sqrt{\ }$) sign (Lesson 10)

range (of a function) the set of all the second elements (outputs) in a relation (Lesson 11)

rate of change the value by which one quantity changes when another related quantity increases by a unit amount (Lesson 13)

rational exponent in an exponential expression, an exponent that is a rational number (Lesson 10)

rational number a number that can be written as a quotient of integers, $\frac{a}{b}$ (Lesson 37)

reciprocal the multiplicative inverse of a number (Lesson 4)

recursive process a process that requires knowing or computing previous terms in order to find the value of a desired term (Lesson 22)

reflection a transformation that flips a figure or graph over a point or line (Lesson 19)

relation a set of ordered pairs (Lesson 11)

relative frequency the ratio of a frequency for a category to the total frequencies in a row, a column, or an entire table (Lesson 28)

residual the difference of an observed *y*-value on a scatter plot and a predicted *y*-value, based on a line of fit (Lesson 29)

root a factor of a number that, when multiplied by itself a given number of times, equals the number (Lesson 10)

scatter plot a graph that shows the relationship between two variables; a graph on which data are plotted as points (x, y) on a coordinate plane (Lesson 29)

sequence a predictable arrangement of numbers, expressions, pictures, or other objects that follows a pattern or rule (Lesson 22)

skewed distribution a distribution of data which, when graphed, shows a "tail" that extends much more to one side of the graph than to the other (Lesson 24)

slope the ratio of the vertical change to the horizontal change for the graph of a linear equation (Lessons 8, 13)

slope-intercept form a form of a linear equation, $y = mx + b$, where *m* is the slope and *b* is the *y*-intercept of the graph (Lessons 8, 14)

spread (of a data set) describes how data in a given data set are distributed or grouped (Lesson 26)

standard deviation a measure of spread for a set of data that indicates how much a data set varies from the mean (Lesson 26)

standard form (of a quadratic equation) the form $y = ax^2 + bx + c$ of a quadratic equation in which *a*, *b*, and *c* are constants (Lesson 34)

standard form (of a quadratic function) the form $f(x) = ax^2 + bx + c$ of a quadratic function (Lesson 38)

step function a piecewise function in which each interval has a constant value and which forms a graph made up of "steps" (Lesson 40)

substitution method a method for solving systems of equations where one variable is replaced by an equivalent expression in the other variable (Lesson 15)

system of linear equations a grouping of two or more linear equations written using the same variables (Lesson 15)

tangent intersecting a curve at only one point (Lesson 36)

term (of an expression) a combination of constants and/or variables joined together through multiplication or division (Lesson 3)

term (of a sequence) a number, expression, picture, or other object that is part of a sequence (Lesson 22)

third quartile (Q_3) the median of the upper half of a data set (Lesson 27)

transformation an operation that changes a figure or graph according to a rule (Lesson 18)

translation a transformation that moves all of the points on a figure the same distance in the same direction (Lesson 18)

trinomial a polynomial containing exactly three unlike terms (Lesson 31)

two-way frequency table a data display used to display and interpret frequencies for categorical variables (Lesson 28)

two-way relative frequency table a data display used to display and interpret relative frequencies for categorical variables (Lesson 28)

uniform distribution a distribution of data in which all values have the same frequency (Lesson 24)

upper extreme the greatest value in a data set (Lesson 27)

variable a letter or symbol that represents an unknown or changing number in a mathematical expression (Lesson 3)

vertex the turning point for the graph of a quadratic or absolute value function (Lessons 34, 38)

vertex form (of a quadratic equation) the form $y = a(x - h)^2 + k$ of a quadratic equation in which (h, k) is the vertex (Lesson 34)

vertical line test test in which if any vertical line crosses a graph at two or more points, then the graph does not represent a function (Lesson 11)

vertical shrink a transformation that pushes the points of a figure or graph toward the x-axis (Lesson 20)

vertical stretch a transformation that pulls the points of a figure or graph away from the x-axis (Lesson 20)

vertical translation a slide of a graph or figure up or down on the coordinate plane (Lesson 18)

x-intercept a point $(a, 0)$ at which a graph crosses the x-axis (Lesson 12)

***y*-intercept** a point (0, *b*) at which a graph crosses the *y*-axis (Lessons 8, 12)

zero (of a function) an input value for a function that produces 0 as the output; equal to the *x*-coordinate of an *x*-intercept of the function (Lesson 38)

zero product property property stating that if the product of two numbers or expressions is equal to 0, then one of those numbers or expressions must be equal to 0 (Lesson 35)

Formula Sheet

Linear Equations	
Standard Form:	$Ax + By = C$
Slope-Intercept Form:	$y = mx + b$
Point-Slope Form:	$y - y_1 = m(x - x_1)$

Exponential Equations	
Exponential Growth:	$y = a \cdot b^x + c, b > 1$
Exponential Decay:	$y = a \cdot b^x + c, 0 < b < 1$
Compound Interest:	$A = P\left(1 + \frac{r}{n}\right)^{nt}$

Quadratic Equations	
Standard Form:	$y = ax^2 + bx + c$
Vertex Form:	$y = a(x - h)^2 + k$

Polynomial Identities	
Square of a Sum:	$a^2 + 2ab + b^2 = (a + b)^2$
Square of a Difference:	$a^2 - 2ab + b^2 = (a - b)^2$
Difference of Squares:	$a^2 - b^2 = (a + b)(a - b)$
Sum of Cubes:	$a^3 + b^3 = (a + b)(a^2 - ab + b^2)$
Difference of Cubes:	$a^3 - b^3 = (a - b)(a^2 + ab + b^2)$

Arithmetic Sequence	
Recursive Process:	$a_n = a_{n-1} + d$
Explicit Formula:	$a_n = a_1 + (n - 1)d$

Geometric Sequence	
Recursive Process:	$a_n = a_{n-1} \cdot r$
Explicit Formula:	$a_n = a_1 \cdot r^{n-1}$

Transformations of Functions	
Horizontal Translation:	$g(x) = f(x + k)$
Vertical Translation:	$g(x) = f(x) + k$
Reflection across x-axis:	$g(x) = -f(x)$
Reflection across y-axis:	$g(x) = f(-x)$
Vertical Stretch:	$g(x) = kf(x), \lvert k \rvert > 1$
Vertical Shrink:	$g(x) = kf(x), 0 < \lvert k \rvert < 1$
Horizontal Stretch:	$g(x) = f(kx), 0 < \lvert k \rvert < 1$
Horizontal Shrink:	$g(x) = f(kx), \lvert k \rvert > 1$

Properties of Exponents	
Product of Powers:	$a^n \cdot a^m = a^{n+m}$
Power of a Product:	$(ab)^m = a^m b^m$
Power of a Power:	$(a^n)^m = a^{n \cdot m}$
Power of Zero:	$a^0 = 1$ for all $a \neq 0$
Quotient of Powers:	$\frac{a^m}{a^n} = a^{m-n}$ for all $a \neq 0$
Power of a Quotient:	$\left(\frac{a}{b}\right)^m = \frac{a^m}{b^m}$ for all $b \neq 0$
Negative Powers:	$a^{-n} = \frac{1}{a^n}$ and $\frac{1}{a^{-n}} = a^n$ for all $a \neq 0$
Rational Powers:	$a^{\frac{m}{n}} = \sqrt[n]{a^m} = (\sqrt[n]{a})^m$

Standard Deviation
$s = \sqrt{\frac{\sum(x_i - \bar{x})^2}{n-1}}$

Interquartile Range
the difference of the third quartile, Q_3, and the first quartile, Q_1, of a data set

Common Conversions	
12 inches = 1 foot	100 centimeters = 1 meter
3 feet = 1 yard	1000 meters = 1 km
5,280 feet = 1 mile	2.54 centimeters = 1 inch
8 ounces = 1 cup	2 pints = 1 quart
2 cups = 1 pint	4 quarts = 1 gallon
60 seconds = 1 minute	7 days = 1 week
60 minutes = 1 hour	52 weeks ≈ 1 year
24 hours = 1 day	365 days ≈ 1 year

Math Tool: Number Lines

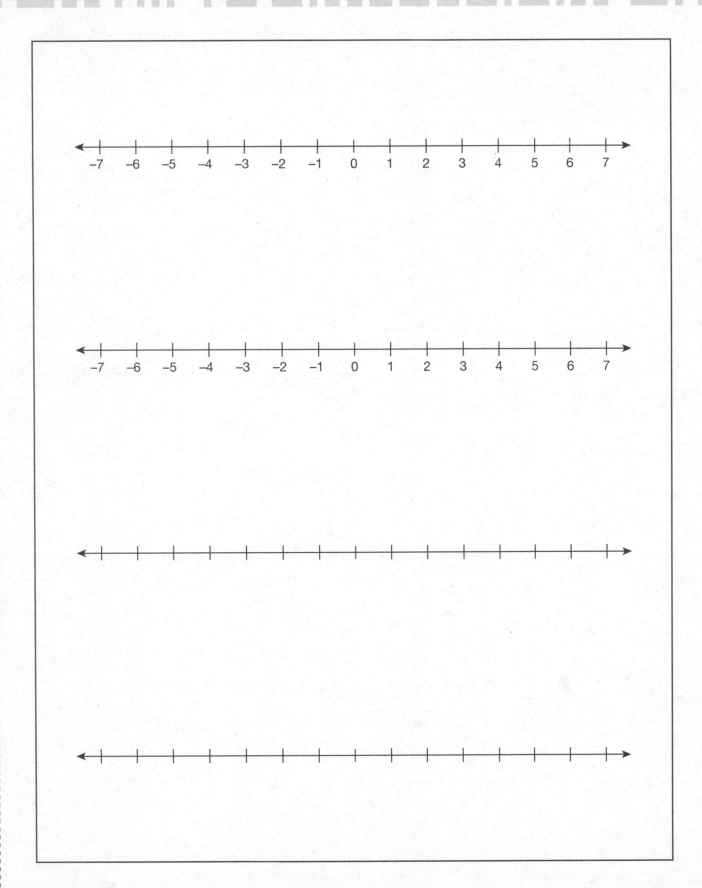

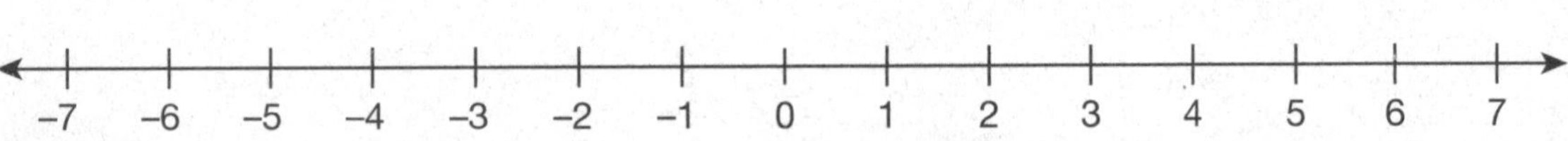

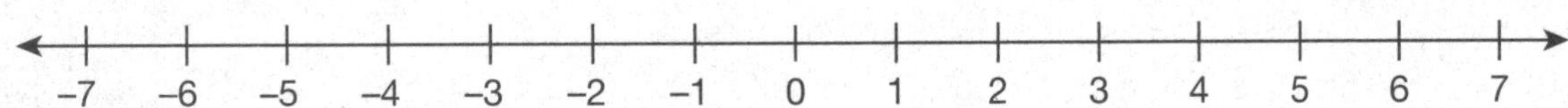

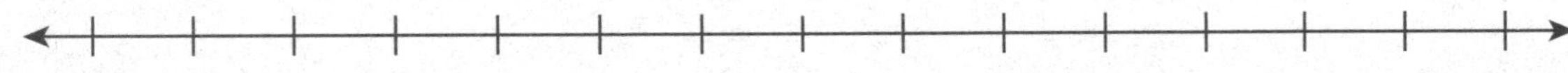

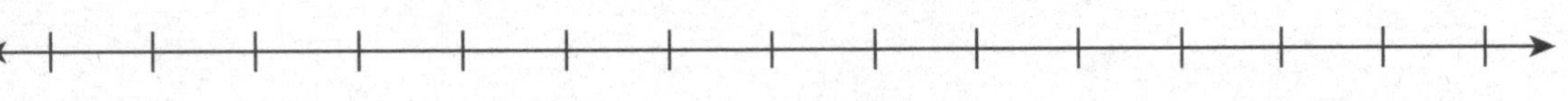

Math Tool: Coordinate Planes

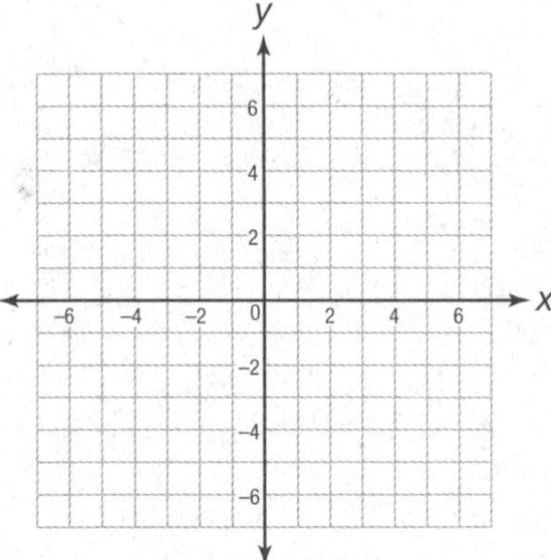

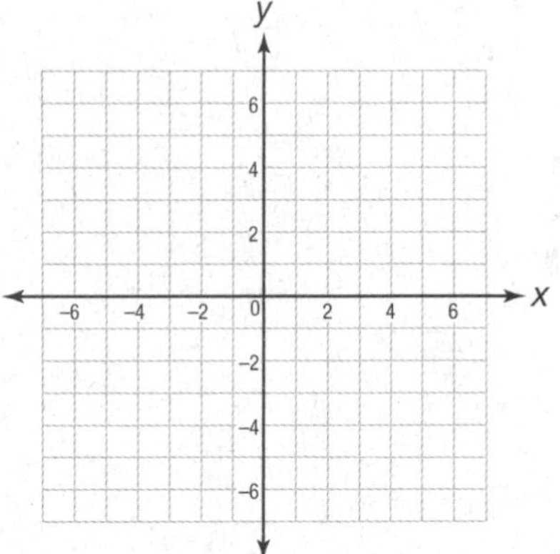

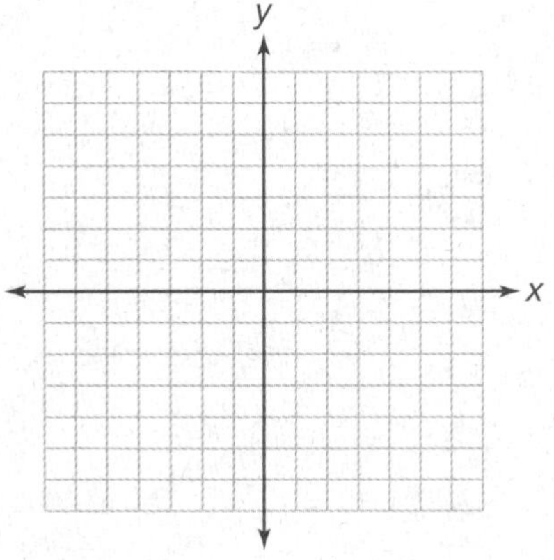

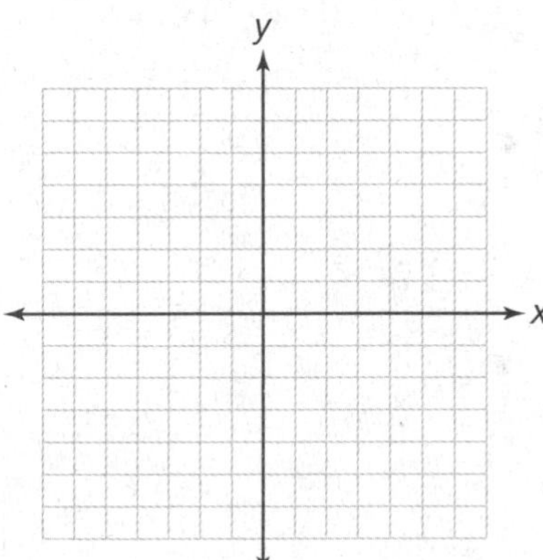

Math Tool: Coordinate Planes

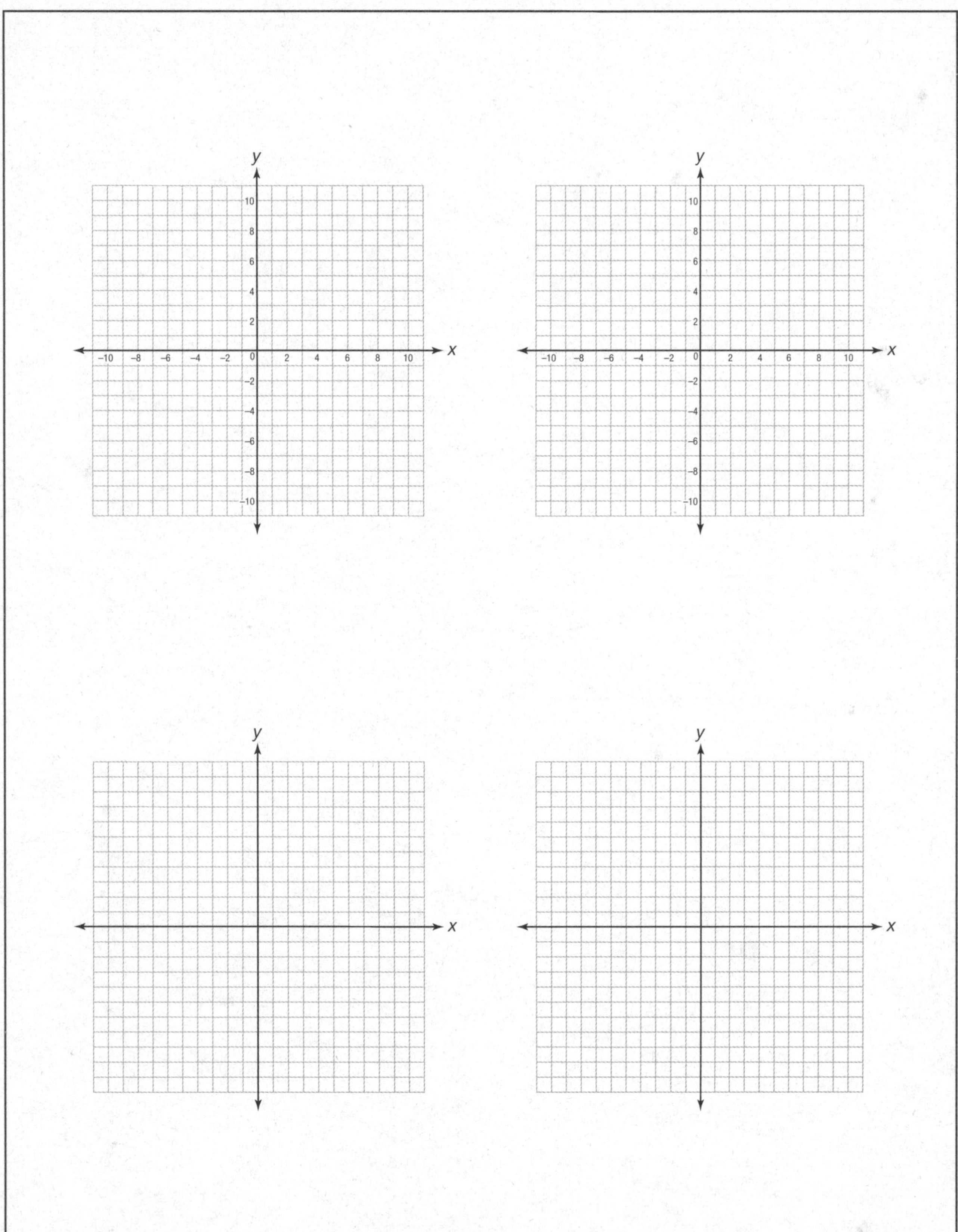

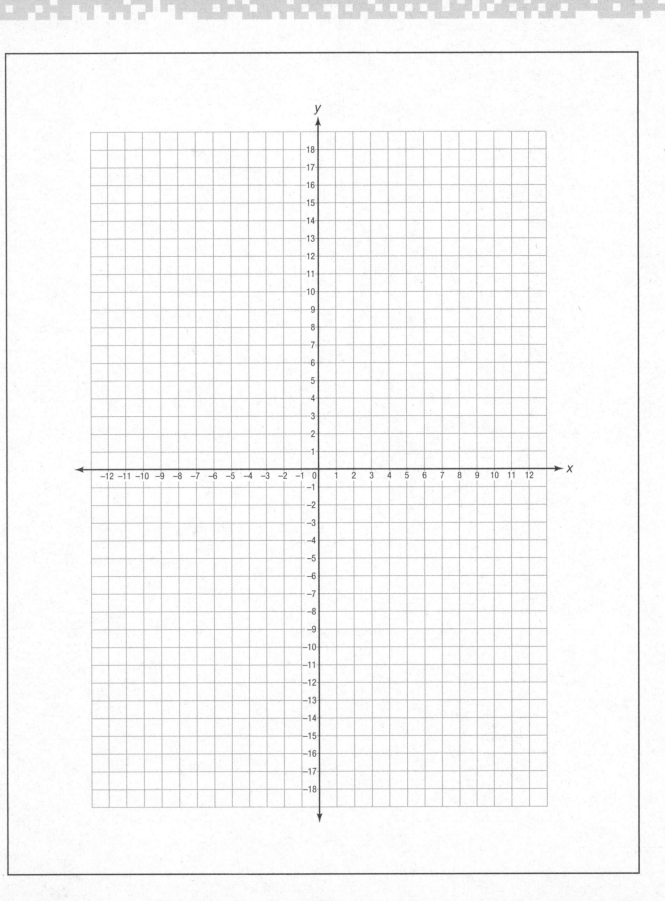

Math Tool: Coordinate Plane

Math Tool: Coordinate Plane

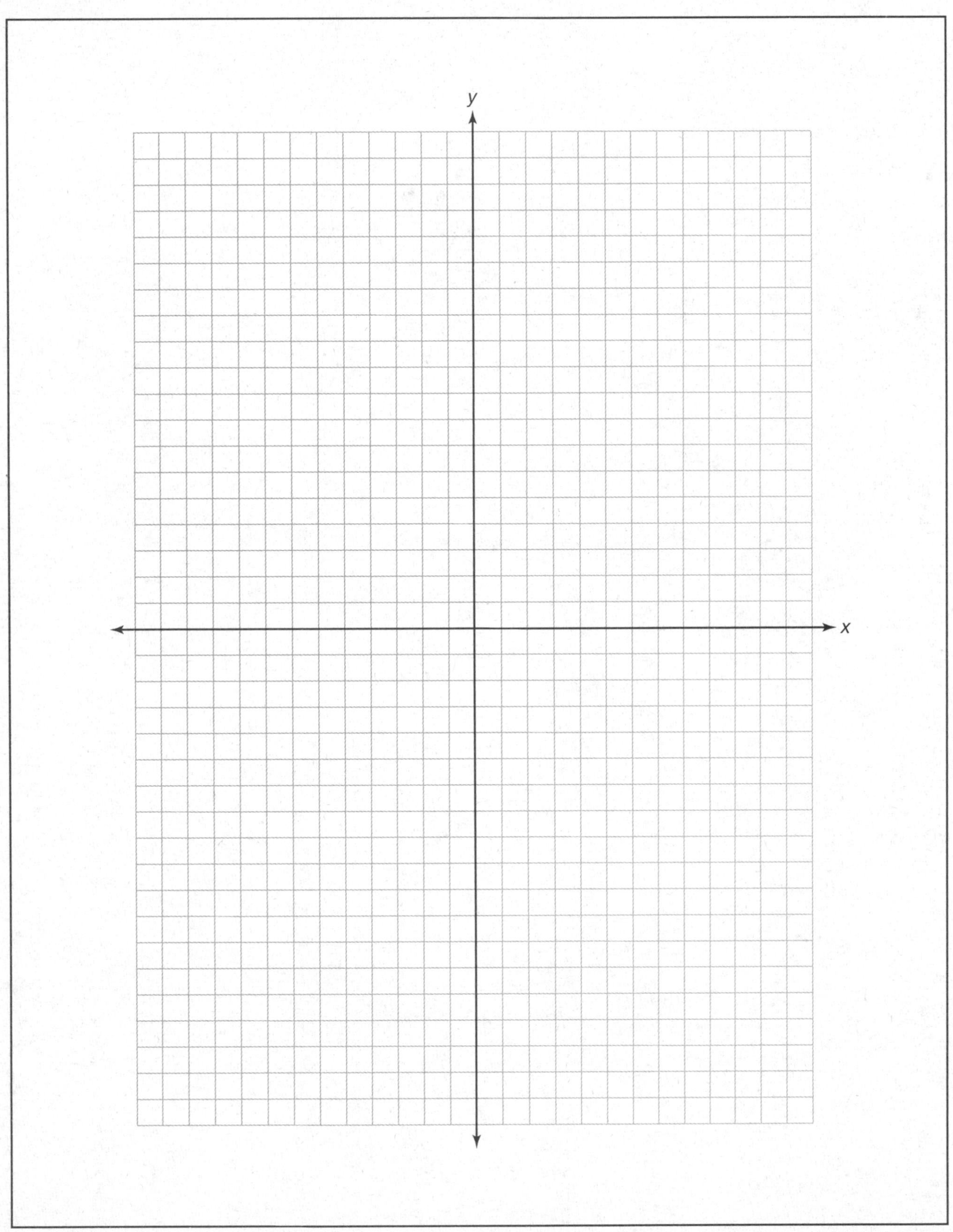

Math Tool: First Quadrant Coordinate Planes

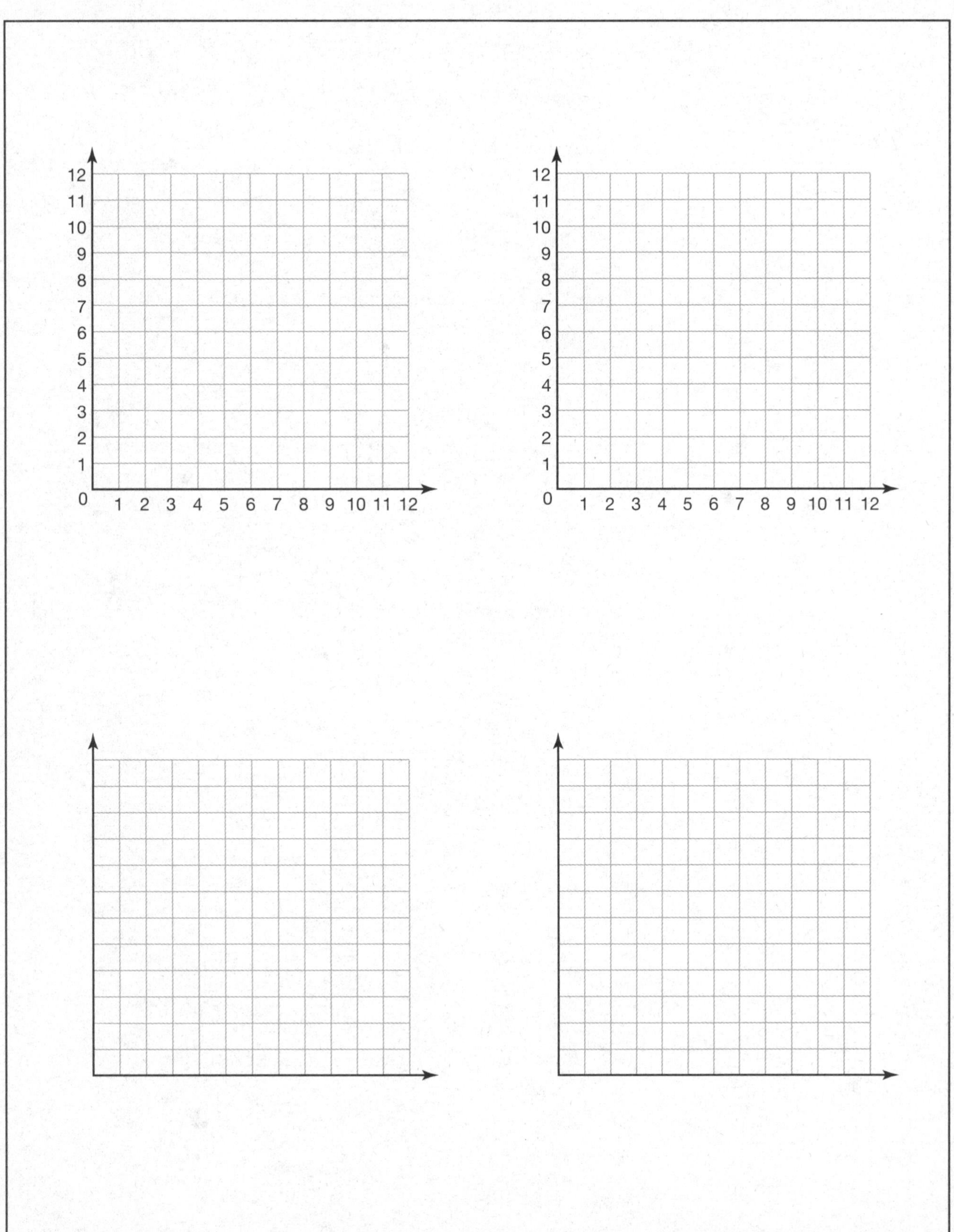

Math Tool: Grid Paper

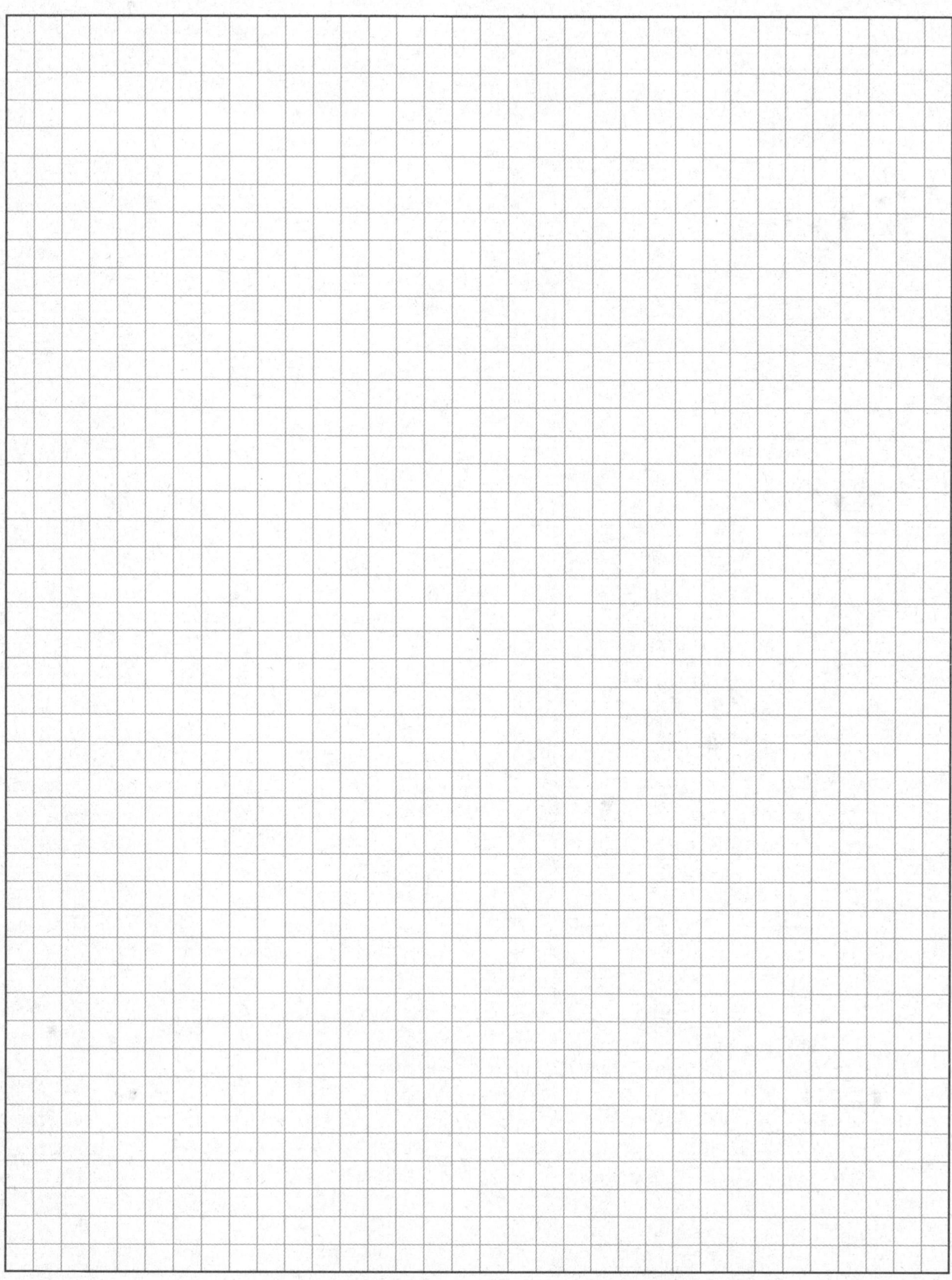

Notes

Notes